THE PAPERS OF
THOMAS JEFFERSON

THE PAPERS OF
Thomas Jefferson

Volume 3
18 June 1779 to 30 September 1780

JULIAN P. BOYD, EDITOR

LYMAN H. BUTTERFIELD AND MINA R. BRYAN,

ASSOCIATE EDITORS

PRINCETON, NEW JERSEY

PRINCETON UNIVERSITY PRESS

1951

Printed in the United States of America by
Princeton University Press, Princeton, New Jersey

DEDICATED TO THE MEMORY OF

ADOLPH S. OCHS

PUBLISHER OF THE NEW YORK TIMES

1896-1935

WHO BY THE EXAMPLE OF A RESPONSIBLE

PRESS ENLARGED AND FORTIFIED

THE JEFFERSONIAN CONCEPT

OF A FREE PRESS

GUIDE TO EDITORIAL
APPARATUS

1. TEXTUAL DEVICES

The following devices are employed throughout the work to clarify the presentation of the text.

[. . .], [. . . .] One or two words missing and not conjecturable.

[. . .]¹, [. . . .]¹ More than two words missing and not conjecturable; subjoined footnote estimates number of words missing.

[   ] Number or part of a number missing or illegible.

[roman] Conjectural reading for missing or illegible matter. A question mark follows when the reading is doubtful.

[*italic*] Editorial comment inserted in the text.

⟨*italic*⟩ Matter deleted in the MS but restored in our text.

2. DESCRIPTIVE SYMBOLS

The following symbols are employed throughout the work to describe the various kinds of manuscript originals. When a series of versions is recorded, *the first to be recorded is the version used for the printed text.*

Dft draft (usually a composition or rough draft; later drafts, when identifiable as such, are designated "2d Dft," &c.)

Dupl duplicate

MS manuscript (arbitrarily applied to most documents other than letters)

N note, notes (memoranda, fragments, &c.)

PoC polygraph copy

PrC press copy

RC recipient's copy

SC stylograph copy

Tripl triplicate

All manuscripts of the above types are assumed to be in the hand of the author of the document to which the descriptive symbol pertains. If not, that fact is stated. On the other hand, the following types of manuscripts are assumed *not* to be in the hand of the author, and exceptions will be noted:

FC   file copy (applied to all forms of retained copies, such as letter-book copies, clerks' copies, &c.)

Tr   transcript (applied to both contemporary and later copies; period of transcription, unless clear by implication, will be given when known)

3. LOCATION SYMBOLS

The locations of documents printed in this edition from originals in private hands, from originals held by institutions outside the United States, and from printed sources are recorded in self-explanatory form in the descriptive note following each document. The locations of documents printed from originals held by public institutions in the United States are recorded by means of the symbols used in the National Union Catalog in the Library of Congress; an explanation of how these symbols are formed is given above, Vol. 1: xl. The list of symbols appearing in each volume is limited to the institutions represented by documents printed or referred to in that volume.

CSmH	Henry E. Huntington Library, San Marino, California
CtY	Yale University Library
DLC	Library of Congress
DNA	The National Archives
DeHi	Historical Society of Delaware, Wilmington
InHi	Indiana Historical Society, Indianapolis
MA	Amherst College Library
MH	Harvard College Library
MHi	Massachusetts Historical Society, Boston
MdAA	Hall of Records, Annapolis
MdHi	Maryland Historical Society, Baltimore
MeHi	Maine Historical Society, Portland
MiU-C	William L. Clements Library, University of Michigan
MoSHi	Missouri Historical Society, St. Louis
NHi	New-York Historical Society, New York City
NN	New York Public Library
NcDAH	North Carolina Department of Archives and History, Raleigh

NhD   Dartmouth College Library
NjP   Princeton University Library
PHi   Historical Society of Pennsylvania, Philadelphia
PPAP   American Philosophical Society, Philadelphia
RPA   Rhode Island Department of State, Providence
TxU   University of Texas Library
Vi   Virginia State Library, Richmond
ViHi   Virginia Historical Society, Richmond
ViLxW Washington and Lee University Library
ViU   University of Virginia Library
ViW   College of William and Mary Library
ViWC   Colonial Williamsburg, Inc., Williamsburg, Virginia
WHi   State Historical Society of Wisconsin, Madison

4. OTHER ABBREVIATIONS

The following abbreviations are commonly employed in the annotation throughout the work.

TJ   Thomas Jefferson

TJ Editorial Files   Photoduplicates and other editorial materials in the office of *The Papers of Thomas Jefferson*, Princeton University Library

TJ Papers   Jefferson Papers (Applied to a collection of manuscripts when the precise location of a given document must be furnished, and always preceded by the symbol for the institutional repository; thus "DLC: TJ Papers, 4:628-9" represents a document in the Library of Congress, Jefferson Papers, volume 4, pages 628 and 629.)

PCC   Papers of the Continental Congress, in the Library of Congress

RG   Record Group (Used in designating the location of documents in the National Archives.)

5. SHORT TITLES

The following list includes only those short titles of works cited with great frequency, and therefore in very abbreviated form, throughout this edition. Their expanded forms are given here only in the degree of fullness needed for unmistakable identification. Since it is impossible to anticipate all the works to be cited in such very abbreviated form, the list is appropriately revised from volume to volume.

Biog. Dir. Cong. *Biographical Directory of Congress, 1774-1927*

Bland Papers *The Bland Papers: Being a Selection from the Manuscripts of Colonel Theodorick Bland, Jr.*

B.M. Cat. British Museum, *General Catalogue of Printed Books*, London, 1931—. Also, *The British Museum Catalogue of Printed Books, 1881-1900*, Ann Arbor, 1946.

B.N. Cat. *Catalogue général des livres imprimés de la Bibliothèque Nationale. Auteurs.*

Burk-Girardin, *Hist. of Va.* John Burk, *The History of Virginia . . . Continued by Skelton Jones and Louis Hue Girardin*

Burnett, *Letters of Members* Edmund C. Burnett, ed., *Letters of Members of the Continental Congress*

C & D See *Va. Gaz.*

Cal. Franklin Papers *Calendar of the Papers of Benjamin Franklin in the Library of the American Philosophical Society*, ed. I. Minis Hays

Cal. Wash. Corr. with Officers Library of Congress, *Calendar of the Correspondence of George Washington . . . with the Officers*

Clark Papers See *George Rogers Clark Papers*

CVSP *Calendar of Virginia State Papers . . . Preserved in the Capitol at Richmond*

Conv. Jour. See *Va. Conv. Jour.*

D & H See *Va. Gaz.*

D & N See *Va. Gaz.*

DAB *Dictionary of American Biography*

DAE *Dictionary of American English*

DAH *Dictionary of American History*

DNB *Dictionary of National Biography*

Epistolary Record Jefferson's MS Index to Letters Written and Received (in DLC: TJ Papers)

Evans Charles Evans, *American Bibliography*

Ford Paul Leicester Ford, ed., *The Writings of Thomas Jefferson*, "Letterpress Edition," N.Y., 1892-1899

Fry-Jefferson Map *The Fry & Jefferson Map of Virginia and Maryland: A Facsimile of the First Edition*, Princeton, 1950

George Rogers Clark Papers, 1771-1781; also 1781-1784 *George Rogers Clark Papers*, ed. James A. James, Illinois State Historical Library, *Collections*, VIII, XIX

HAW   Henry A. Washington, ed., *The Writings of Thomas Jefferson*, Washington, 1853-1854

Heitman   Francis B. Heitman, *Historical Register of Officers of the Continental Army*, new edn., Washington, 1914; also the same compiler's *Historical Register and Dictionary of the United States Army* [1789-1903], Washington, 1903

Hening   William W. Hening, *The Statutes at Large; Being a Collection of All the Laws of Virginia*

JCC   *Journals of the Continental Congress, 1774-1789*, ed. W. C. Ford and others, Washington, 1904-1937

JHB   *Journals of the House of Burgesses of Virginia, 1619-1776*, Richmond, 1905-1915

JHD   *Journal of the House of Delegates of the Commonwealth of Virginia* (cited by session and date of publication)

Johnston, "Jefferson Bibliography"   Richard H. Johnston, "A Contribution to a Bibliography of Thomas Jefferson," *Writings of Thomas Jefferson*, ed. Lipscomb and Bergh, xx, separately paged following the Index

L & B   Andrew A. Lipscomb and Albert E. Bergh, eds., *The Writings of Thomas Jefferson*, "Memorial Edition," Washington, 1903-1904

L.C. Cat.   *A Catalogue of Books Represented by Library of Congress Printed Cards*, Ann Arbor, 1942-1946; also *Supplement*, 1948

Library Catalogue, 1783   Jefferson's MS list of books owned and wanted in 1783 (original in Massachusetts Historical Society)

Library Catalogue, 1815   *Catalogue of the Library of the United States*, Washington, 1815

Library Catalogue, 1829   *Catalogue. President Jefferson's Library*, Washington, 1829

Marraro, *Mazzei*   Howard R. Marraro, *Philip Mazzei: Virginia's Agent in Europe*, New York, 1935

OED   *A New English Dictionary on Historical Principles*, Oxford, 1888-1933

Official Letters   *Official Letters of the Governors of the State of Virginia*, ed. H. R. McIlwaine

P & D   See *Va. Gaz.*

PMHB   *The Pennsylvania Magazine of History and Biography*

Randall, *Life*   Henry S. Randall, *The Life of Thomas Jefferson*

Randolph, *Domestic Life*   Sarah N. Randolph, *The Domestic Life of Thomas Jefferson*

Report   *Report of the Committee of Revisors Appointed by the General Assembly of Virginia in MDCCLXXVI*, Richmond, 1784

Sabin   Joseph Sabin and others, *Bibliotheca Americana. A Dictionary of Books Relating to America*

Swem, "Va. Bibliog."   Earl G. Swem, "A Bibliography of Virginia," Virginia State Library, *Bulletin*, VIII, X, XII (1915-1919)

Swem and Williams, "Register of the General Assembly of Va." Appended to: Virginia State Library, *Fourteenth Annual Report*, 1917

TJR   Thomas Jefferson Randolph, ed., *Memoir, Correspondence, and Miscellanies, from the Papers of Thomas Jefferson*, Charlottesville, 1829

Tucker, *Life*   George Tucker, *The Life of Thomas Jefferson*, Philadelphia, 1837

Tyler, *Va. Biog.*   Lyon G. Tyler, *Encyclopedia of Virginia Biography*

Va. Conv. Jour.   *Proceedings of the Convention of Delegates . . . in the Colony of Virginia* (cited by session and date of publication)

Va. Council Jour.   *Journals of the Council of the State of Virginia*, ed. H. R. McIlwaine

Va. Gaz.   *Virginia Gazette* (Williamsburg, 1751-1780, and Richmond, 1780-1781). Abbreviations for publishers of the several newspapers of this name, frequently published concurrently, include the following: C & D (Clarkson & Davis), D & H (Dixon & Hunter), D & N (Dixon & Nicolson), P & D (Purdie & Dixon). In all other cases the publisher's name is not abbreviated

VMHB   *Virginia Magazine of History and Biography*

WMQ   *William and Mary Quarterly*

CONTENTS

CONTENTS

CONTENTS

CONTENTS

CONTENTS

CONTENTS

CONTENTS

CONTENTS

1780

CONTENTS

CONTENTS

CONTENTS

CONTENTS

CONTENTS

CONTENTS

CONTENTS

CONTENTS

CONTENTS

CONTENTS

CONTENTS

CONTENTS

ILLUSTRATIONS

VOLUME 3

18 June 1779 to 30 September 1780

JEFFERSON CHRONOLOGY

VOLUME 3

1779 June 26. General Assembly adjourned.

1779 October 4 to December 24. General Assembly in session (Williamsburg).

1780 January 21. TJ elected a member of the American Philosophical Society.

1780 January-April. TJ prepared plans for building Fort Jefferson at the mouth of the Ohio River.

1780 April-July. Series of tory insurrections in western Virginia.

1780 April 10? TJ took up residence in Richmond, the new capital of Virginia.

1780 March-December. Brig. Gen. J. P. G. Muhlenberg in command of Continental troops in Virginia.

1780 May 1 to July 14. General Assembly in session (Richmond).

1780 May 12. Surrender of Charleston to the British; numerous Virginia officers and men made prisoners.

1780 May. TJ named one of the directors for locating the public buildings and enlarging the town of Richmond.

1780 June 2. TJ reelected governor of Virginia for one year.

1780 June 13. Maj. Gen. Horatio Gates appointed to command the southern army. He arrived in Virginia early in July and took command at Hillsborough, N.C., about the middle of July.

1780 June. TJ established a line of expresses from the armies in the Carolinas to Richmond and from Richmond to Alexandria.

1780 July 11. Arrival of the French fleet and army at Newport, R.I.

1780 August 16. Gates defeated by Cornwallis at Camden, S.C.; rout of the Virginia militia and loss of their arms and supplies.

1780 August. George Rogers Clark's successful expedition against the Shawnees and other Indian tribes on the Ohio.

1780 September 6. Resolution of Congress recommending surrender of western claims by the states as a means of obtaining ratification of the Articles of Confederation.

1780 September. TJ began forming plans for an expedition by George Rogers Clark against Detroit.

James Madison. Portrait by
Charles Willson Peale, 1783.

THE PAPERS OF
THOMAS JEFFERSON

From William Phillips

Colonel Carters House June 18th: 1779

I must lament the having lost, by your Succeeding Mr: Henry in the Government of Virginia, a very agreeable neighbour of whose Society I had promised myself a great share, and proposed with my friend Reidesel to have profited of your and Mrs: Jefferson's acquaintance during our residence in this Country. As it is I do assure you I wish you personally every possible good.

I request to put the Troops of Convention under your protection; I need not enter upon topics and particulars relating to them as you, Sir, are perfectly informed of our Situation.

Should a want of Provisions at any time cause our moving I will hope you may have the goodness to let me have a prior notice of it as far as may be consistent with your publick Station.

You may recollect, Sir, that General Reidesel's family and mine have proposed an excursion to the Berkley Springs. I beg to know if you have any objection to it.

Permit me to send my best Compliments to Mrs: Jefferson and the Young Lady.

I am, Sir, with much personal Respect Your most obedient and very humble Servant, W. PHILLIPS

RC (MoSHi). Salutation apparently obscured by discoloring of MS.

To David Shepherd

SIR Williamsburg, June 18, 1779.

You are desired to give notice to such recruits under the act of Assembly passed last winter as may not yet have marched from your county, to hold themselves in readiness to assemble at your courthouse at a moment's warning from you. An officer will be immediately appointed, from whom you will receive notice of the day on which he will attend at your courthouse to receive them; and the necessities of the service oblige me to conjure your attention to their punctual delivery at the time he shall appoint.

I am, Sir, Your very humble Servant,   TH: JEFFERSON

RC (WHi). Printed circular, signed by TJ; "To the County Lieutenant of Ohio" written in a clerk's hand at the lower left of the page.

DAVID SHEPHERD was appointed lieutenant of the newly formed county of Ohio in Jan. 1777, and held that office until his death in 1795 (Thwaites and Kellogg, *Revolution on the Upper Ohio, 1775-1777*, p. 196). The ACT OF ASSEMBLY for speedily recruiting the Virginia regiments on Continental establishment was passed in the Oct. 1778 session (Hening, IX, 588-92).

To Cyrus Griffin

SIR   Wmsburg June 19. 79

The within resolution will inform you of the honourable appointment to which you are elected by the voice of your Country, which I do myself the pleasure to notify to you. The present urgencies of the public business, require as early an attendance as you can possibly bestow, and will I hope be my excuse when I urge you to give us your most speedy aid. I am Sir Yr. very hble Servt,

TH: JEFFERSON

RC (TxU). In a clerk's hand; signed by TJ. Enclosure missing.

At foot of text the addressee's name, in the clerk's hand and apparently removed from the cover and mounted here, is given as Samuel Griffin; this is an error for Cyrus Griffin, who was elected to Congress on 18 June to serve for one year from Nov. 1779 (JHD, May 1779, 1827 edn., p. 55; Samuel Griffin was appointed a member of the Board of War the same day). A virtually identical signed letter of the same date to one of the other persons elected at this time is owned by Gilman Country School, Baltimore; TJ presumably wrote identical letters to all of the others elected on 18 June: Gabriel Jones, Edmund Randolph, James Mercer, William Fitzhugh, Patrick Henry, and Meriwether Smith.

To John Jay

SIR   Williamsburgh June 19. 1779.

Our delegates by the last post informed us that we might now obtain blank letters of marque for want of which our people have long and exceedingly suffered. I have taken the liberty therefore of desiring them to apply for fifty, and transmit them by a safe conveyance.

The inclosed order being in it's nature important and generally interesting, I thought it my duty to lay it before Congress as early as possible, with the reasons supporting it; nothing doubting but it will meet with their approbation; it's justice seems to have been confirmed by the general sense of the people here.

Before the receipt of your letter desiring a state to be made out of the ravages and enormities, unjustifiable by the usage of civilized nations, committed by the enemy on their late invasion near Portsmouth, I had taken measures for the same purpose meaning to transmit them to you. They are not yet returned to me. I have given the same orders with respect to their still later proceedings in the county of Northumberland.

Our trade has never been so distressed since the time of Lord Dunmore as it is at present by a parcel of trifling privateers under the countenance of two or three larger vessels who keep our little naval force from doing any thing. The uniform train of events which during the whole course of this war we are to suppose has rendered it improper that the American fleet or any part of it should ever come to relieve or countenance the trade of certain places, while the same train of events has as uniformly rendered it proper to confine them to the protection of certain other parts of the continent is a lamentable arrangement of fortune for us. The same ill luck has attended us as to the disposition of the prizes taken by our navy, which tho' sometimes taken just off our capes, it has always been expedient to carry elsewhere. A British prize would be a more rare phaenomenon here than a comet, because the one has been seen, but the other never was.

I have the pleasure to inclose you the particulars of Colo. Clarke's success against St. Vincenne, as stated in his letter but lately received, the messenger with his first letter having been killed. Also a letter from Colo. Shelby stating the effect of his success against the seceding Cherokees of Chuccamogga. The damage done them was the killing about half a dozen, burning 11 towns, 20,000 bushels of corn probably collected to forward the expeditions which were to have been planned at the council which was to meet Governor Hamilton at the mouth of Tenissee, and taking as many goods as sold for twenty five thousand pounds. I have the honour to be Sir Your most obedient & most humble servt.,

TH: JEFFERSON

RC (DLC: PCC, No. 71, 1). Endorsed by Charles Thomson: "Letter from T. Jefferson Govr. of Virginia June 19. 1779. Read 28. Referred to Mr Marchant Mr Armstrong Mr Smith & to commee. of intelligence & their report thereon brought in July 8. 1779." Enclosures: Virginia Council, Order of 16 June 1779, placing Henry Hamilton in irons (q.v., above); MS copies of G. R. Clark's letter to Gov. Henry, 29 Apr. 1779 (also printed above), and of Evan

Shelby to Gov. Henry, 4 June 1779, with its several enclosures (see under that date, above).

A report on this letter and its enclosures, brought in by Henry Marchant

and adopted by Congress on 8 July, conveyed the thanks of Congress to Cols. Clark and Shelby for their achievements (JCC, XIV, 809-10).

To George Washington

SIR   Williamsburg June 19th: 1779.

I have the pleasure to enclose you the particulars of Colo. Clarkes success against St. Vincenne as stated in his letter but lately received, the messenger with his first letter having been killed. I fear it will be impossible for Colo. Clarke to be so strengthened as to enable him to do what he desires. Indeed the express who brought this letter gives us reason to fear St. Vincenne is in danger from a large body of Indians collected to attack it and said when he came from Kuskuskies to be within 30 leagues of the place. I also enclose you a letter from Colo. Shelby stating the effect of his success against the seceding cherokees and chuccamogga. The damage done them was killing a dozen, burning 11 Towns, 20,000 bushels of Corn collected probably to forward the expeditions which were to have been planned at the Council which was to meet Governor Hamilton at the mouth of Tenissee, and taking as many goods as sold for £25,000. I hope these two blows coming together and the depriving them of their head will in some measure effect the quiet of our frontieres this summer. We have intelligence also that Colo. Bowman from Kentuckey is in the midst of the Shawnee country with 300 men and hope to hear a good account of him. The enclosed order being in its nature important and generally interesting, I think it proper to transmit it to you with the reasons supporting it. It will add much to our satisfaction to know it meets [your] approbation.

I have the honor to be with every sentiment of private respect & public gratitude, Sir Your most obedient & most hble. servant,

THOS. JEFFERSON

P.S. The distance of our north western counties from the scene of Southern service and the necessity of strengthening our Western quarter have induced the Council to direct the new levies from the Counties of Yohogania, Ohio, monongalia, Frederick, Hampshire, Barkly, Rockingham and greenbriar amounting to somewhat less than 300 men to enter into the 9th. Regiment at Pittsburgh. The aid they may give there will be so immediate and important and what they could do to the Southward would be so late as I hope will apologize for their interference.

Tr (DLC). Enclosures: G. R. Clark to Patrick Henry, 29 Apr. 1779, q.v.; Evan Shelby to Patrick Henry, 4 June 1779, q.v., with enclosures listed there, copies of which were likewise enclosed to Washington; Order of Virginia Council placing Henry Hamilton in irons, 16 June 1779, q.v.

To Charles Scott

Sir   Williamsburgh June 21. 1779.

Your letter by Colo. Buford is just put into my hand. I observe on that part which relates to the cloathing of your new levies that Colo. Parker has probably not communicated to you my answer of June 10. to his letter on that subject written during your absence. In that I stated fully what was done, doing, and likely to be accomplished in that business. I am now to add that the linen therein mentioned as coming from Petersburgh is come and making up. The issues of shoes to all other persons have been stopped from that time, so that these also are under preparation. Nevertheless, as after every effort it is probable we shall not be able to supply every thing we wish you could compromise with as many as possible at the following prices fixed by the assembly the 19th. inst. A coat £23-10—a waistcoat £10-15—a pr. of breeches £9-5—a Shirt £9-8—a hat £5—a pr. of Stockings 30/—a pr. of shoes £5. I desired also from Colo. Parker a return of what the men had received that we might know what to send them.

Colo. Buford will receive here £9000. for reenlisting the soldiers. I would have sent you money also for the compromise abovementioned but had no given principles to fix on any sum. As it is probable the whole of Buford's money will not be used instantly if he can accomodate you with such sums as you may want your draughts in his favour to replace it shall receive instant honour.

In pursuance of a resolution of assembly we have laid off the Commonwealth into the following districts for the purpose of collecting the new levies still remaining in their counties, and rendesvousing them at the places here named.

Loudoun, Fauquier, Pr. Wm., Fairfx, Stafford, K. George, Culpepper, Spotsylvania, & Orange at Fredericksburgh.

Richmond, Lancaster, Westmoreland & Northumbld. at New-Castle. The officer Capt. Vincent Redman of Richmond.

Essex, K & Queen, K. Wm., Caroline, & Hanover at New-Castle.

Middlesex, Gloster, Eliz. city, Warwick, York, James city and
Wmsburgh at Wmsburgh.

Henrico, Goochland, Louisa, Albemarle, Fluvanna at Richmond.

Amherst, Buckingham, Cumberland, Powhatan at Richmond. The
officer Lieutt. James Barnett of Amherst.

Princess Anne, Norfolk, Nansemond, Isle of Wight at Petersburgh.

New-Kent, Chas. City, Surry, Pr. George, Dinwiddie, Chestfd. and
Amelia at Petersburgh.

Southampton, Sussex, Brunswick at Brunswick Ct. house. The
officer Capt. Nathaniel Lucas of Brunswick.

Lunenburgh, Mecklenburgh, Pr. Edwd., Charlotte at Mecklenburgh Ct-house.

Halifx., Bedford, Pittsylva., Henry at Halifx Ct-house. The officer
Alexr. Cummings.

Augusta, Rockbridge, Botetourt, Washington, Montgomery at
Halifx Ct. h. The officer Lt. Robert Elliot.

We hope you will appoint Continental officers to receive the men
at the above places at such times as our officers shall be ready to
deliver them.

The levies from Rockingham, Frederick, Hampshire, Shenandoah, Green briar, Ohio, Monongalia, Yohogania, were so distant
from the scene of Southern service, were so convenient to the Northern where we are pushed, that we have ordered them to recruit our
9th. regiment at Pittsbgh., and I have written to Genl. Washington
on the subject hoping his approbation. A draught is to be ordered
against such districts as did not furnish their men. We shall instruct the same officers to make a second collection of them, and
hope you will take measures for receiving them by an officer or
officers if you should be gone.

I trouble you with our whole scheme because it will enable you
[to] judge what force you will receive, and when, and to cooperate
with us which I know your cordiality for the public service disposes
you to do: and I think it a happiness that we have to arrange this
matter with you.

It is with pleasure I learn from Colo. Finnie that you have
pleased yourself as to the horse directed to be purchased. The difference of sex is surely not to be regarded. The caparison is preparing, but I fear (when I take a view of our workmen) it will
hardly be worthy the givers or receiver. Pistols he think will be
difficult to get. We know not whether you received the £500 voted

you by the assembly. I shall advise Colo. Buford to enquire at the Treasury and carry it if you did not.

I am with great & sincere personal esteem founded as well on our earlier acquaintance as your more recent public merits Your friend & servt.,   TH: JEFFERSON

RC (PHi). Recipient identified from content; see note below.

YOUR LETTER: Not found. TJ's AN-SWER OF JUNE 10: Not found. The Assembly's resolution of THE 19TH INST. pertaining to prices of soldiers' outfits is in JHD, May 1779, 1827 edn., p. 58; that for COLLECTING THE NEW LEVIES (passed 4 June) is at p. 34. On 29 May the Assembly had voted £500 and a

horse to Brig. Gen. Scott for his prompt response to appeals by the state for defense against a threatened British invasion under Adm. Collier. Scott was in command of a force of Continental recruits intended for the relief of South Carolina, and soon continued on his way, for the British did not extend their aggressions beyond the Portsmouth area (same, p. 27; *Official Letters*, I, 366-8; *Va. Gaz.* [D & N], 15 May 1779).

To Richard Caswell

SIR   Wmsburg June 22d. 1779

The Washington and Caswell Gallies belonging to this Commonwealth originally built for the protection of Ocracock Inlet in conjunction with others proposed to be built by your State being so much out of repair as to render it necessary to incur a considerable expense to refit them for Service, their condition and future station were submitted to the consideration of our General Assembly. Our Trade through that inlet to and from South Quay has from experience been found inconvenient and therefore of itself has got mostly into a different channel, so that the little remaining there from this State will not justify the Expense of keeping those Gallies any longer at their present Station. We are uninformed whether you were diverted from your purpose of building the additional Gallies to act in conjunction with ours by a similar Want of importance in the trade, or of necessaries to build Gallies. If the latter, and you think the Washington and Caswell may be made to answer your purpose, we are authorized by the General Assembly to offer them to you at such fair estimation as may be agreed on between us, I apprehend without difficulty. I shall be obliged by your Answer to this; as early as convenient, as we are directed, if you should not want them, to dispose of them otherwise for the Service of this State.

I have the honor to be your Excellency's most obedt & mo: hble Servt,   TH: JEFFERSON

RC (NcDAH); in a clerk's hand, signed by TJ. Addressed: "His Excel-lency, Richard Caswell Esqr. Governor of North Carolina." Endorsed: "Govr.

Jeferson 22d. June 1779." Enclosed in TJ to Richard Caswell, 30 June 1779, q.v.

On 19 June the General Assembly resolved: "That the Governor be desired immediately to make an offer to the State of North Carolina of the Washington and Caswell gallies now in that State, at a fair valuation; and that if the said offer should not be accepted, that he order them to be dismantled, and the materials, guns, ammunition, &c. brought over to this State for the use of the navy, and the hulls to be disposed of for the best price that can be had" (JHD, May 1779, 1827 edn., p. 58).

From William Fleming

DEAR SIR   Philadelphia; 22d. June 1779.

Your obliging letter, without a signature, came safe to hand. As letters frequently miscarry between this and Virginia it was a good caution, which I shall take the liberty to follow.

That peace and the independance of the thirteen states are within our power is a point not well established; but thus much I think myself at liberty to say, that Congress, long before my arrival here, were called on to declare on what terms they would consent to a peace?—and to fix their ultimatum. They have been debating the matter ever since, and have not yet come to a point, tho' I think there is now a prospect of that necessary business being shortly finished. The difficulties have mostly arisen in the East, but have been supported from the south side of Powtomack; tho' much of that support is now withdrawn. The extreme delay in this business necessarily gives great uneasiness to the French minister, but that he was about to return to his own country in disgust is not true. This climate is very unfavourable to his constitution, and he had it much at heart to leave it before the hot season came on, and now only waits the determination of Congress on this important business. He thinks there have been combinations to break the alliance, and to throw America into the arms of G. Britain, on her acknowledging our independency, in which opinion many have joined him; the ratification of the treaty, therefore, by the Virginia assembly was highly pleasing to him, as I doubt not you will see by his letter acknowledging the receipt of it. A few members of Congress who got intimation of the ratification, expressed their dislike to the proceeding, as being against the spirit of the confederation, tho' nothing was publicly said on the subject. However, I am of opinion that the occasion warranted the measure; and I think it high time for Virginia to look to her own importance and to provide for her own security, in case of disunion.

I am pleased to hear the measures taking for putting our finances on a better footing, that being the most tender ground on which we stand. Congress are wasting much time on the subject and I am clearly of your opinion, that it is nonsensical quackery. Their resolution of the 2d. of January last, calling in the two emissions, is a proof of it.

General Sullivan has about 4000 men on his Indian expedition, of the success of which few, I believe, have very sanguine hopes, especially since the commissary of provisions laid before Congress the generals requisition for extra provisions, signed with his own hand, a copy of which I inclose for your amusement.

We are informed that John Dodge is on his way to Virginia.

I will not congratulate you, but my country on their choice of a chief magistrate. It will break in on your domestic plan and you'll find it a troublesome office during the war.

Please to present me very respectfully to Mrs. Jefferson. Farewell.

It has just occurred that I must liberate this letter to save the postage.

RC (DLC). Unsigned. Enclosure missing; see below.

For the ratification of the treaty with France by Virginia, and the French minister's reply, see TJ to Gérard, 8 June, and Gérard to TJ, 22 June 1779. General Sullivan's REQUISITION, a copy of which Fleming enclosed to TJ, was laid before Congress on 4 June (JCC, XIV, 685).

From Conrad Alexandre Gérard

Mr.   à Philadelphie le 23 [i.e., 22] Juin 1779.

J'ai reçu la lettre dont V. E. m'a honoré au nom de l'assemblée generale de Virginie ainsi que l'expedition autentique de l'acte que cette assemblée a passé pour ratifier les traités conclus entre le Roi mon maitre et les 13. Etats unis de l'Amerique Septentrionale.

Je M'estime heureux d'avoir à transmettre à S. Mté. un temoignage aussi autentique de la facon de penser et des procedés d'un Etat aussi puissant; Il lui sera d'autant plus agréable que le tems et l'experience ayant constatés la convenance et l'utilité de ces traités une approbation aussi reflechie ne peut qu'être une preuve éclatante d'une conviction entiere et d'un sentiment permanent profondement gravé dans les coeurs; D'ailleurs cette démarche étant faite dans un moment de crise dont les ennemis interieurs et exterieurs de l'Amérique s'efforcent de profiter pour semer la division entre les alliés, cette demarche détruira jusques dans sa racine le faux espoir qu'ils se sont plu jusqu'ici à nourrir et les mêmes sentimens paroissant etre communs aux autres Etats, leurs ennemis qui Sont en même tems ceux de l'alliance Seront enfin également convaincus de deux verités importantes 1°. Qu'ils ne peuvent pas conquerir l'Amerique par les armes. 2°. Que l'union entre la France et les Etats est inacessible à leurs traits, et que la confiance mutuelle rendra toujours infructueuses leurs attaques clandestines.

Je crois donc, Monsieur, pouvoir assurer V. E. que le Roi mon maitre recevra cette communication avec la sensibilité et la Satisfaction la plus vive et la plus sincere, S. Mté., n'ayant point d'autre objet dans la guerre actuelle ainsi que dans son alliance que l'independance et le bonheur de l'Amerique. Elle desire uniquement de voir regner l'union entre les Etats et la confiance mutuelle entre les Alliés, parceque c'est le moyen le plus efficace et le plus promt d'arriver au but salutaire de la paix que les deux parties se proposent.

Je suis personnellement très sensible, Mr., aux sentiments et aux dispositions que l'assemblée de Virginie a bien voulu manifester à mon égard. Devoir, conviction, attachement, tout me lie au service de la cause commune. Il y a deja longtems que je mets ma gloire et mon bonheur à tâcher de lui etre utile et j'ose assurer V. E. que si quelques faits étoient capables de m'allarmer, ils ne pourroient qu'être de nature à allarmer également tout fidel citoyen de L'Amerique.

Je suplie V. E. de vouloir bien faire agréer à l'assemblée de la Republique de la Virginie les sentimens que je viens d'exprimer ainsi que ceux du respect et de la reconnoissance dont je serai flatté de trouver les occasions de lui donner des preuves. Recevés en même tems l'assurance du profond respect avec lequel j'ay l'honneur d'etre &tc.   M.   De V. E.   L. t. h. et T. O. S.

FC (Arch. Aff. Etr., Paris, Corr. Pol., E-U, Suppl., vol. 1); captioned: "Copie de la réponse de M. Gérard à S. E. le Governeur de la Virginie. . . ." Another copy (Arch. Aff. Etr., E-U, vol. 8), dated 22 June, docketed: "Joint au No. 101. du 22. Juin 1779" (i.e., Gérard to Vergennes, 22 June, printed in Gérard's *Despatches and Instructions*, p. 740-1, q.v.). The missing recipient's copy was transmitted to TJ in Meriwether Smith's letter of 25 June 1779, q.v.

See TJ to Gérard, 8 June 1779, and enclosure.

To St. George Tucker

Dr Sir   Williamsburgh June 22. 1779.

As to an undoubted zeal for the cause of the American states you have always added a proper disposition to aid the island of Bermudas in her distresses, we have cast our eyes on you as a proper person to communicate to them what we are authorized to do by a recommendation from Congress and resolution of our assembly. For this purpose I take the liberty of inclosing to you three copies of a resolution of council to be forwarded if you please to such person in Bermuda as you think best, and by such different opportunities as may ensure the safe passage of one. It is true the relief is small, but if you can intimate under the rose that they bring Brobdinag bushels of salt, I imagine the same measure might be meted to them. I am Dr. Sir Your very humble servt.,

TH: JEFFERSON

RC (O. O. Fisher, Detroit, 1950). Addressed by TJ: "St. George Tucker esq. Petersburgh." On a blank page of the letter appear: (1) A copy of an advice of the Virginia Council of State, dated 21 June 1779, reading as follows: "In Council, June 21st: 1779.

"The Governor is advised to inform Mr. St. G. Tucker that he is authorised to permit 1000 Bushels of Corn to be exported to the Island of Bermuda, in such vessels as shall be sent from the Island to recieve the same, with Salt in exchange, Bushel for Bushel. The Corn shall be ready stored at the Town of Petg. [Petersburg] where the salt will be expected to be delivered. A Copy.

A:B: C:C:"

(2) A certificate by Benjamin Powell, justice of the peace in Williamsburg, dated 6 Sep. 1780, declaring that St. George Tucker appeared before him and took oath on that day that he (Tucker) "did recieve the Letter hereto annexed from his Excy. Thomas Jefferson Esqr. Governor of this Commonwealth, inclosing a Resolve of the privy Council attested by Archibald Blair Clerk of that Council, of which the preceeding is a true Copy, the Original of which was by this Deponent transmitted to Henry Tucker Esqr. of the Island of Bermuda."

A RECOMMENDATION FROM CONGRESS: On 18 May 1779 Congress, after protracted debate and much about-facing by some of the members, agreed to recommend to the executives of Pennsylvania, Delaware, Maryland, and Virginia that each of these states export 1,000 bushels of Indian corn "for the relief of the distressed inhabitants" of Bermuda (JCC, XIII, 471-2; XIV, 501-2, 553, 555-6, 595-6, 608-10). The RESOLUTION OF OUR ASSEMBLY, taking off the general embargo on exports for this particular purpose, was adopted on 19 June 1779 (JHD, May 1779, 1827 edn., p. 58).

From John Jay

Philadelphia, 24 June 1779. Circular to the state executives enclosing resolve of Congress, 22 June 1779, to prevent plundering of the inhabitants of places in the enemy's possession.

FC (DLC: PCC, No. 14); 1 p. Enclosure (Vi), signed by Charles Thomson and endorsed by TJ; printed in JCC, XIV, 758-9.

Appointment of a Boundary Commissioner

[24 June 1779]

Daniel Smith esqr. is appointed a Commissioner for extending the Boundary Line between Virginia and North Carolina, in the room of the Revd. James Madison who declines acting. Certified under my hand and the Seal of the Commonwealth this 24th Day of June in the Third year of the Commonwealth Annoque Domini 1779.   TH: JEFFERSON

MS (DLC: Rives Papers). In a clerk's hand, signed by TJ.

On the proposal to extend THE BOUNDARY LINE BETWEEN VIRGINIA AND NORTH CAROLINA, see a resolution of the House of Delegates, 15 June 1779 (JHD, May 1779, 1827 edn., p. 48-9).

From Meriwether Smith

DEAR SIR   Philadelphia June 24h. 1779

The enclosed Letter to Genl. Nelson is from Mr. de Francy and contains a Copy of a Memorial transmitted to the Genl. Assembly last Winter, upon the Subject of a Dispute which Mr. de Francy had with the Governor and Council concerning the Quality of some Tobo. tendered to him in payment for Goods purchased on account of the state by their order.

I have told him that I am confident your Attachment to the French Nation and the true Interests of your Country, will dispose you chearfully to give him every Satisfaction consistent with your Duty and the Honour of the State. I have only to add that Mr. de *Beaumarchais*, for whom he is Agent in these states, as well as Mr. de Francy himself, has been peculiarly unfortunate in being considered and treated as a mere Adventurer, in all his Transactions with these States. If Genl. Nelson should not be in Williamsburg on the Recceipt of this Letter, you are requested to peruse that directed to him as it relates only to the Subject of the Memorial. I am, with real Regard, Dr. Sir Your most obedt. & hble Servt.,

MERIWETHER SMITH

RC (DLC).

J. B. L. T. DE FRANCY, agent for Caron DE BEAUMARCHAIS, arrived in America on 1 Dec. 1777 to begin his prolonged negotiations for the shipment of tobacco in return for the advances of arms and ammunition sent to America.

For De Francy's account of his difficulties in his mission, see Elizabeth S. Kite, *Beaumarchais and the War of American Independence*, Boston, 1918, II, ch. XXI. The LETTER TO GENL. NELSON and the MEMORIAL have not been located.

To William Phillips

SIR   Williamsburgh June 25. 1779

Your favors of the 18th. instant came to hand yesterday. I had written that very day to Col. Bland to allow Lt. Campbell and Capt.

Bertling to come to the flag as was desired but no opportunity of sending my letter had occurred. Immediately on receiving your letters and knowing that Lt. Campbell was as far as Richmond on his way a permit was dispatched to him to come to the place where the flag lies and perform the several duties you desired, an officer of the commonwealth being directed to attend also. The interview was fixed to be on the 3d of July which was said to be as early as the superfluous clothing could be got down.

The appointment which has withdrawn me from the society of my late neighbors, in which character I with pleasure considered yourself, General and Madme. de Riedesel for that cause as much as any other is not likely to add to my happiness. The hour of private retirement to which I am drawn by my nature with a propensity almost irresistible, and which would again join me to the same agreeable circle, will be the most welcome of my life.

Should any event take place which should render your removal necessary, tho' I foresee no probability of such an one, you may be assured of receiving the earliest intelligence which I may be permitted to give according to your desire: and that I shall in every circumstance which shall depend on me endeavor to make the situation of the officers and soldiers of the Convention troops as comfortable as possible, warranted as I have no doubt I shall be, by a continuance of proper conduct within them. This has authorized me particularly to assure you that no impediment can arise on my part to the excursion proposed by your family and Genl. Reidesell's to the Berkeley springs for your amusement: tho' I foresee that it will lessen the satisfaction of the short recess from business which I have a hope of being able to take within a few weeks.

Dft (DLC). Endorsed: "Philips Majr. Genl." Alterations made during composition not noted here.

YOUR FAVORS OF THE 18TH: One of these is printed under its date, above; but the other, which TJ discusses in his first paragraph, is missing.

From Meriwether Smith

SIR   Philadelphia, June 25h. 1779.

Permit me to recommend to your particular Notice and Civilities Monsr: *de Francy*, who is the Agent of Monsr: de *Beaumarchais*, and honoured with his particular Esteem and Friendship. I shall be extremely deceived if you will not find him a Man of strict Honour and liberal Sentiments; disposed to render every Service to the State consistent with the Interest of his Patron and Employer; who, to facilitate the Views of some of our Countrymen, has met with unmerited Abuse and very injurious Treatment; disgraceful indeed, to the great Council of America. The Services rendered by Mr. de Beaumarchais to these United States, will for ever entitle him to their warmest Acknowledgments and most grateful Returns; and I rest assured that you will never be backward in your Endeavours to restore them to the good Opinion and Friendship of an able and most zealous Advocate for their Prosperity and Happiness.

I am requested by my Colleagues to transmit to you the Answer of the Minister Plenipotentiary of France to your Letter inclosing the Resolves of the Genl. Assembly of Virginia, ratifying the Treaties of Alliance and Commerce, entered into with that Court, which you will accordingly receive in the enclosed Letter. I shall consider these Resolves of the General Assembly as a Testimony of their Approbation of my Conduct, in opposing all those Measures which I conceived were calculated to destroy the Alliance; and altho' they are made very seasonably, and, I doubt not, will have a very good Effect, I cannot avoid telling you that I think it is necessary to be attentive to the Dispositions of the *People* and to observe whether their Conduct be conformable to the Spirit of those Resolutions: For, be assured, the M——r of F——e fears much more the Consequences of Seduction, than the Success of B——h Arms in America. The Establishing *Committees* through these States is by no Means considered in a favourable Point of View. It carries along with it the Appearance of a Design to place the Government again in the Hands of the People the better to conduct them to some favourable Object. I shall only remark, upon this Occasion, that *Committees* were formed for bringing about the Independence of these States, and may be very instrumental in establishing an *Alliance* with Britain. If I may be permitted to reason from the *Effect* of their Measures *here*, I will not hesitate to declare that the Object they have in View is not that which is assigned for the *Cause*.

I am not informed whether I am continued in the Delegation for the ensuing Year. If I am, there are some Matters of Importance which I wish to see finally settled in Congress, before I return to Virginia; when they are concluded, the Situation of my Family and private Affairs will demand my particular Attention. Yet I would not wish to withdraw myself intirely from the Service of my Country in these Times, as I flatter myself I can in some other Respects render it essential Services. With this Persuasion I am induced both by Duty and Inclination, to acquaint you that I will chearfully undertake any Negociations which the Exigency of the States may make it necessary for you to attempt in Europe. I am, Sir, with much Esteem, Your most obedient, & hble Servant,

MERIWETHER SMITH

P.S. Pray will you be so obliging to give me your Sentiments respecting the Currency of these States, and your Opinion of the proper Methods of redemption? Whether you approve of Such Plans as are founded upon the Principle contain'd in the inclosed publication, or whether Taxation alone is the simple or honest and radical cure for the Depreciation, and the best Means of Redemption?

RC (DLC). Endorsed: "Smith, Meriwether." Enclosure missing and not identified.

Smith must have learned that DE FRANCY intended going to Virginia after he had sent his letter of the previous day, q.v. The ANSWER OF THE MINISTER . . . OF FRANCE, enclosed in this letter: Gérard to TJ, 22 June 1779. Smith had been reelected to the Virginia DELEGATION to CONGRESS for another year on 18 June (JHD, May 1779, 1827 edn., p. 55).

From the Board of Trade

[*Williamsburg*] *26 June 1779*. Approval requested for the purchase of cloth for the army and navy. Signed by Thomas Whiting and Jacquelin Ambler. Countersigned: "In council July 2. 1779. Approved Th: Jefferson."

RC (CSmH); 1 p. Endorsed: "Representations to the Executive with Answers 26. June 1779."

On 18 June 1779 the Assembly by joint ballot elected Jacquelin Ambler, Duncan Rose, and Thomas Whiting members of the newly established Board of Trade (JHD, May 1779, 1827 edn., p. 55).

Appointment of Commissioners for Kentucky

[*Williamsburg*] *26 June 1779*. Appointment of William Fleming, James Steptoe, Edward Lyne, and James Barbour, commissioners for Kentucky District for settling the titles of claimers to unpatented land.

MS (ViLxW); in a clerk's hand, signed by TJ; 1 p.

WILLIAM FLEMING (1729-1795), state senator representing Botetourt, Washington, Montgomery, and Kentucky cos. in the session of May and June 1779, and a prominent participant in the affairs of the western counties (DAB; Grigsby, *Va. Federal Convention*, II, 40-54), is often confused with Judge William Fleming of Cumberland co., TJ's intimate friend and college classmate, who at this time was a delegate in Congress. The Bill for Settling Titles to Unpatented Lands (q.v., under 8-14 Jan. 1778) was not passed until June 1779.

To —— ——

A friend of mine (Mr. Henry Skipwith) is very desirous [of] locating 5000 acres of land in the country through which you will pass while running the line, and has desired me to engage some person to do it, to whom he will make a handsome compensation. I therefore take the liberty of recommending the business to you as I know you are as well able to do it as any body, and hope it will be made worth your trouble. He would have it in one body and on a watercourse. The earliest notice to him will be requisite. Perhaps Dr. Walker can assist in conveying that. I am Sir Your very humble servt., TH: JEFFERSON

RC (MdHi).

There is no indication of the name of the addressee of this letter. It was quite possibly addressed to Rev. James Madison, who on 24 June had been appointed (with Thomas Lewis and Robert Andrews) one of the commissioners to run the boundary line between Virginia and Pennsylvania (JHD, May 1779, 1827 edn., p. 64).

To Thomas Whiting

SIR   In Council June 26th. 1779

At the request of the directors of the public Buildings in Richmond, I am to desire that you will provide for them locks of different kinds fit for house doors, hinges for do., window glass, putty, lathing nails and shells. For the quantities I must refer you to the Directors themselves. I am Sir Your humble Servant,

TH: JEFFERSON

E N C L O S U R E

Memod. for the Board of Trade.

800 feet of Glass—10 by 12.
300 ℔ Putty
500 ℔ of white lead in Kegs ground.
50 Gallons Linseed oil
250000 4d. Nails for lathing
25000 Floaring 20d. brads:
25,000 20d. Nails.
50,000 6d. do.
20,000 10d. do.
Six large strong locks—12 pr. strong H. hinges
12 good locks for inside doors
Iron plates.
These the board of Trade is to Send for, on Acct. of the Directors for removeing Seat of Goverment
June 26th. 1779.   Archd Cary

RC (CSmH). In a clerk's hand, signed by TJ. Addressed: "Thomas Whiting Esquire" (a member of the Board of Trade). Enclosure (CSmH), printed herewith.

The Act for the removal of the seat of government was passed on 12 June 1779 (JHD, May 1779, 1827 edn., p. 44); and on 24 June, Turner Southall, ARCHIBALD CARY, Robert Goode, James Buchanan, and Robert Carter Nicholas were appointed directors for the public buildings at Richmond (same, p. 64). The materials here ordered were for the temporary buildings provided for in an amendment to the Act; see the bill as summarized under date of 29 May 1779, above. The offices of the government were moved to Richmond in Apr. 1780 (see Notice of Removal of Executive Office, printed below under 25 Mch. 1780).

From the Board of Trade

[*Williamsburg*] *29 June 1779*. There are no more than 1,450 hhds. of tobacco on hand belonging to the public and unengaged by contract. Instructions requested for procuring such quantities as may be necessary before an anticipated rise in price occurs. Signed by Whiting, Ambler, and Rose.

RC (CSmH); 1 p. Attached: TJ to Board of Trade, 1 July 1779; Board of Trade to TJ, 2 July 1779.

From John Jay

Philadelphia, 29 June 1779. Circular letter to the state executives enclosing an extract of a letter from Gen. Washington of 11 June and a resolve of Congress of 28 June, resulting from the general's letter, calling on the states speedily to fill up their battalions. Washington's letter is to be kept as secret as possible.

FC (DLC: PCC, No. 14); 1 p. Enclosures missing. Washington's letter is printed in his *Writings*, ed. Fitzpatrick, XV, 261-2; Congress' resolve in JCC, XIV, 780.

From the Board of Trade

[*Williamsburg*] *30 June and 1 July 1779*. Instructions desired concerning purchase of sundry articles from Thomas Pierce, John Carter, and Richard Burnly. Signed by Whiting, Ambler, and Rose.

RC (CSmH); 1 p. Both notes appear on the same page. Below them, in TJ's hand, is this instruction: "In council. July 1st. 1779. The board refers the determination on the above propositions totally and absolutely to the Board of Trade. Th: Jefferson."
These brief communications indicate that the newly constituted Board of Trade was uncertain of its authority to act and that TJ wished to assign to the Board responsibility for the determination of details. Upon receipt of TJ's instructions, the Board "Ordered that the State Agent purchase the goods offered by Mr. Pierce and Mr. Carter" (MS Minutes of Board of Trade in CSmH).

To Richard Caswell

SIR   Williamsburg June 30th. 1779.

Since writing the within, I learn that the Caswell Galley is sunk
at her station, that her bottom is eaten out, and her original form
such that she could not be hove down to be refitted. The within
proposition therefore, your Excellency will be pleased to understand
as confined to the Washington only.

By direction of the Assembly of this State, I do myself the honor
of enclosing their resolution containing a proposition for quieting
the minds and possessions of those settlers near our unextended
boundary as may have unwarily entered in the one State for lands
lying in the other. I hope it will be recommended to your patronage
as well by its justice as its tendency to promote that friendly harmony so necessary for our general good, and so agreeable to the
dispositions of the Citizens of our particular states towards each
other. The within letters to the Speakers of the two Houses of your
Assembly contain copies of the same resolution, which I take the
liberty of transmitting through your hands to them.

I am Sir with the greatest esteem & respect Your mo. ob. & mo.
huml Servt.,   TH: JEFFERSON

Tr (NcDAH); in Governor Richard
Caswell's Letter Book. RC listed as item
128 in an undated catalogue of Raphael
King, Ltd., London [ca. Dec. 1946].

TJ's letter to Caswell of 22 June was
evidently transmitted with this letter.

The RESOLUTION of the ASSEMBLY, passed
15 June 1779, concerning the extension
of the boundary line between Virginia
and North Carolina is printed in *State
Records of North Carolina*, XIV, 314, and
also in JHD, May 1779, 1827 edn., 48-9.

To Thomas Johnson

SIR   Williamsburgh June 30. 1779.

I beg you will be pleased to ascribe to the change in our administration and to my not becoming immediately possessed of all the
business which lay before the executive, your letter of the 7th. of
the last month remaining so long unanswered. It has happened
very unluckily that this was among the latest of the several matters
which have come to my hand.

I am to return you thanks for your obliging offer of a preference
in the purchase of two of your gallies. But it happens that we cannot become purchasers, having already full as many as we can
either man or maintain. We think the defence of our bay an object
so important that we would spare nothing to effect it within the

compass of our abilities. We trust that the same opinion prevails with you, so great a part of your state lying adjacent to the bay and it's waters; and of course that strong motives of expediency must have induced you to propose to lessen your force there. The late depredations on our coast and captures in the bay have put us on the greatest exertions we can make to put our little fleet into order for action. The force however must be small to which that is competent.

I have the honour to be with great respect Your Excellency's most obedient and most humble servt.,   TH: JEFFERSON

RC (MdHi). Addressed: "His Excellency Governor Johnson of Maryland." Endorsed: "30th. June 1779 Govr. Jefferson."

Gov. Johnson's letter of 7 May to TJ's predecessor, Patrick Henry, is printed in *Archives of Maryland*, XXI, p. 381.

Form of Commission to Deputy Attorney Generals

[June 1779?]

THE COMMONWEALTH OF VIRGINIA

To   Esquire, greeting:

Know you, that from the special Trust and Confidence which is reposed in your Patriotism, Abilities and good Conduct, you are, by these Presents, constituted and appointed Deputy Attorney for the County of   You are therefore to advise and prosecute on Behalf of the said Commonwealth within the said County, and to execute the said Office in all other Matters and Things thereunto relating; and also you are empowered to hold and enjoy all Profits and Emoluments which unto the same may of Right belong. Witness PATRICK HENRY, Esq; Governour or Chief Magistrate of the Commonwealth aforesaid, this   Day of   in the   Year of the Commonwealth, *Annoque Domini* 177

Printed form (DLC). The blanks have not been filled in. On verso appears a memorandum in TJ's hand, partly illegible, as follows: "query [. . . .] no law has authorised the governour to grant such a commission. if any person may do it, it must be the Attorney general whose deputy he is, & who therefore must give him letters of deputation." Accompanying this blank commission in the TJ Papers, 236: 42331ff. are other printed forms of commissions for sheriffs, county tobacco inspectors, assistant county tobacco inspectors, justices of the peace, and justices of the courts of oyer and terminer; all these are blank forms but include Patrick Henry's name as governor. They are omitted here.

Proclamation Expelling British Subjects

[1 July 1779]

By his Excellency Thomas Jefferson, esquire, Governor or Chief Magistrate of the Commonwealth of Virginia.

A PROCLAMATION.

WHEREAS the General Assembly, by their Act passed at their last session, entitled "An Act concerning Escheats and forfeitures from British Subjects," did declare "that (1.) all persons Subjects of his Britannick majesty, who on the nineteenth day of April in the year 1775, when hostilities were commenced at *Lexington*, between the United States of America, and the other parts of the British empire, were resident, or following their vocations in any part of the world other than the said United States, and have not since either entered into public employment of the said States or joined the same, and by Overt Act adhered to them; and (2) all such Subjects, inhabitants of any of the said United States, as were out of the said States on the same day, and have since by Overt Act adhered to the enemies of the said States; and (3) all inhabitants of the said States, who after the same day, and before the commencement of the Act of General Assembly intituled "An Act declaring what shall be treason," departed from the said States, and joined the Subjects of his Britannick Majesty of their own free will; or (4.) who by any County Court within this Commonwealth were declared to be British Subjects within the meaning and operation of the resolution of the General Assembly, of the 19th. day of December 1776, for enforcing the Statute Staple, should be deemed British subjects, And by their resolution of the twenty sixth day of the last month, they "required that all the persons so described, and now resident within this Commonwealth, should be banished from the same, and that proper measures should be taken to prevent their return, as also to exclude thereout all others so described; and not now resident within this Commonwealth," I have therefore thought fit, by and with the advice of the Council of State, to issue this my proclamation, hereby strictly charging and commanding all persons Coming under any one of the descriptions in the said Act, and now being within this Commonwealth to be, and appear before me in Council at Williamsburg, on or before the seventeenth day of August in this present year, in readiness to depart the Commonwealth in such manner as shall there be prescribed to them, as they will answer the contrary at their utmost peril: And I do moreover charge and enjoin all officers civil and military, and all other the good citizens of this Commonwealth, to apprehend and carry securely to the commanding officer of the militia of some County within this Commonwealth, all such persons, whom after the said day, they shall find lurking or being therein; And the commanding officers of the several Counties are in like manner charged and required to receive the said persons, and all others so described, whom by the strictest diligence they shall be able to discover and take, to convey them in safe custody to the public jail in the city of Williamsburg, and to make report of such their proceedings to me. And I do further prohibit all persons so described from entering into this Commonwealth during the continuance of the present war with their prince, under colour of any commission, passport, licence, or other pretence whatsoever; and do publish and make known to such of them as shall presume to violate this prohibition, that they shall be deemed and dealt with as spies, wheresoever they be taken.

Given at Williamsburg, on the first day of July, in the Year of our Lord, One thousand seven hundred and seventy nine.

☞ The County Lieutenants are desired to give personal notice of this proclamation to all those within their Counties, who are hereby required to attend on the Governor and Council.

A copy of a printed copy in the office of the Executive.
Attest.

SAM: COLEMAN, A.C.C.

Tr (DLC); probably from the printed text in *Va. Gaz.* (D & H), 3 July 1779.
On 26 June, the House of Delegates resolved that the governor, with advice of council, be required to banish all tory refugees (JHD, May 1779, 1827 edn., p. 68), in accordance with the terms of the Bill concerning Escheats and Forfeitures from British Subjects, printed under 4 June 1779, above.

To the Board of Trade

In council July 1. 1779.

If the board of trade will be pleased to resolve on the quantity of tobacco they think necessary to be purchased I will submit their resolution to the council, and make no doubt they will approve of it, as it seems to be their disposition to leave the board of trade very much to their own discretion. TH: JEFFERSON

RC (CSmH); written on leaf attached to Board of Trade to TJ, 29 June 1779; Tr in Minutes of Board of Trade (CSmH).

From the Board of Trade

[*Williamsburg*] *2 July 1779*. Making up the quantity of tobacco to 3,000 hhds. is probably all the state can afford at this time, although this quantity may not be sufficient. Signed by Whiting and Ambler. Countersigned: "In council 2. July 1779. Approved   Th: Jefferson."

RC (CSmH). Appears on the same page as TJ's letter to Board of Trade, 1 July 1779.

To Riedesel

Sir   Forest. July 4. 1779.

Your kind letter of June 19. I received on the 2d instt. It is now some time since Colo. Bland wrote for leave to grant Permits to Capt. Bartling and Lt. Campbell to come to the Argyle flag. Leave was immediately given by letter to Col. Bland. Sometime after I received another letter from him, accompanied with one from General Philips informing me that Lt. Campbell was come as far as Richmond and waited for a permit to proceed. A permit was instantly made out and dispatched. Capt. Bartling was not mentioned on that occasion and therefore no permit made out for him. The 3d. instt. was fixed on for Lt. Campbell to be at the flag to do his business. And it was only on the day before that your letter came by post; I shall instantly write to Capt. Bartling giving him license to proceed, if his business remains still to be done, by a conveyance which occurs tomorrow. I thought it necessary to give you this detail of circumstances, that any delays which may happen might be ascribed to those accidents which may have truly caused them.

I thank you for your kind congratulations; tho' condolances would be better suited to the occasion; not only on account of the labours of the office to which I am called, and it's withdrawing me from retirement, but also the loss of the agreeable society I have left, of which Madme. de Riedesel and yourself were an important part. Mrs. Jefferson in this particular sympathizes with me, and especially on her separation from Madme. de Riedesel. We are told you set out for the Berkeley springs about the middle of this month. We fear that this excursion, necessary for your amusement to diversify the scenes of discomfort, may deprive us of the pleasure of seeing you when we come to Monticello the last of this month. We shall stay there about a month. Mrs. Jefferson joins me in compliments to yourself and Madme. de Riedesel. I shall be able to execute her commission as to the spoons and bring them up with me.

I have the honor to be with much esteem Your most obedient & most humble servt.,   TH: JEFFERSON

RC (NN). The MS bears no evidence that the letter was addressed to Riedesel, but it is so catalogued and the content confirms this ascription.

Riedesel's LETTER OF JUNE 19 is missing. On the PERMITS for Baertling and Campbell, see TJ to Bland, 18 June, and Phillips to TJ, 25 June 1779.

From William Phillips

SIR   Colonel Carters House July 5th. 1779.

I have received from Colonel Bland a Copy of the Letter you were pleased to write him in answer to my request for Lieutenant Governour Hamilton a british prisoner of war being allowed to make me a visit at this place. I have also read in a public print the resolution of a Council held at Williamsburg on the 16th of June 1779 with your orders in Consequence; this publick paper seems of such great consequence that I will take leave to adjoin it to this Letter as it is upon the subject matter of part of those resolutions that I have thought proper to address you.

I shall not take upon me to animadvert upon the variety of accusations advanced against Lieutenant Governour Hamilton, whether they may be founded upon positive facts, be matter of hearsay, or taken from the reports of interested men. I have read Lt. Governour Hamiltons proclamation or address to the inhabitants of the Ilinois as published in a Virginia Gazette of June 26th 1779. which I apprehend to be alluded to in the Council beforementioned, and I profess to not see any denunciation of vengeance against the Americans, no call for blood, nor any threats of general massacres of men, women and children.

I might enlarge a great deal were I to enter upon the subject of a particular State taking up a determination of retaliation for supposed injuries which, if true, must necessarily belong to the Continent of America at large, and possibly the American Congress might be the proper Body to give force to any opinions upon so interesting and so great a matter.

But Sir having premised that I esteemed these subjects as of so high nature as to render me an improper person to enter into a discussion of them I shall cease writing upon any other matter than what merely relates to Lieutenant Governour Hamilton's being put into the dungeon of a Jail, and loaded with irons, by your orders as Governour of Virginia.

Lieutenant Governour Hamilton surrendered himself and the post he had defended upon an express capitulation with Colo. Clark the American Commanding Officer of the troops which attacked Mr. Hamilton's post; this capitulation, by which Lieutenant Govr. Hamilton and the troops under his command became prisoners of war, took place after a discussion of articles and some meetings between the Lieutenant Governour and Colo. Clark, and passed through all the usual forms, practised in war among civilized nations, and I need not to you sir who are a man of knowledge and discernment, remark upon the sacredness of capitulations, or point out the horrors of a war carried on upon other principles. It rests therefore that Lt. Governour Hamilton, in seeming violation of a capitulation entered into by him with Colonel Clark, is loaded with irons and confined in the dungeon of a common jail by your orders as Governour of Virginia.

Sir I will suppose what I should be miserable to think true for believe me my sentiments of justice, humanity and honour are in direct opposition to those charges of blood and cruelty exhibited against Lieutenant Governour Hamilton, I will suppose sir that Gentleman to have acted under every description given of him in the adjoined paper, it might assuredly have been a reason for Colo. Clark's refusing any terms, and upon taking the fort of St. Vincents to have put the Lieut. Governour and every other person to the sword, but, sir, it pleased Colo. Clarke to receive and grant terms of Capitulation, upon the faith and honour of which Lieutenant Governour Hamilton surrendered the post St. Vincennes to the American Arms; and it matters not how barbarous the disposition of the Lieutenant Governour might have been previous to the surrender, the capitulation was assuredly sacred, and should remain so, unless Lieut. Governour Hamilton has infringed upon it posterior to its being made, and signed by both parties.

Had Lt. Governour Hamilton been taken by surprize, or surrenderd at discretion, he would have been certainly left to the mercy of his enemies and it would have depended upon them to have acted by him with humanity or the contrary as they thought proper, and whatever term might have been given to their conduct towards him no supposition of breach of treaty would have arisen.

Under this description of the matter, Sir, which upon mature consideration, I will believe to be perfectly true, I will venture, who am no prisoner, but a resident in this country, under the solemn faith of a publick treaty and the sacred pledge of a private parole, I will venture sir to entreat of you to reconsider the circumstances of Lt. Governour Hamilton's situation, and to take into your consideration, whether under the positive articles of a capitulation as I have before observed, that Gentleman ought not to be at Liberty in the same manner with every other prisoner of war.

My motives for thus earnestly addressing you, spring from feelings of the purest humanity and strictest probity, and wishing with an honest sincerity of heart that the unhappy war, which is so likely to continue between Great Britain and America, might be carried on with mercy, not cruelty, with every attention to public and private faith and with liberality and honour.

From my residence in Virginia I have conceived the most favourable sentiments of the Gentlemen of the Country, and from my personal Knowledge of you, Sir, I am led to imagine it must have been very dissonant to the feelings of your mind to have inflicted so severe a weight of misery and stigma of dishonour upon the unfortunate Gentleman in question, but sir I am sure when you reflect upon the possible consequences of this act it will give an alarm to those lively sentiments and those liberal principles which I really believe you possess.

I will therefore, Sir, request to put a claim for this british Officer Lieutenant Governour Hamilton being set at liberty and considered as a prisoner of war, who has become such under every positive and sacred article of a capitulation made with the American Officer Colo. Clark.

I desire to assure you sir that I do not wish or intend to enter into any literary altercation upon this subject, the civil matter relating to it I leave to those higher in authority and more at liberty to discuss it, but as a british General Officer it is natural for me to endeavour at relieving the distress of a british Officer, who in his present situation at this inclement season of the year, and under every aggravating circumstance of ill health, chains, and confinement in the dungeon of a common jail must inevitably perish and die unless immediately released.

I have not mentioned any thing relating to the two other persons, who are confined with Mr. Hamilton as their situation will naturally depend on that of the Lieutenant Governour.

I am to return you my sincere thanks for your obliging declarations in favour of the troops of Convention; I dare say they will continue their good Conduct and make no doubt of their receiving every humane treatment from you sir, and the executive power of Virginia. Your polite attention to me claims my acknowledgments, and I shall be sorry that my going to the warm springs may prevent my making them personally to you at Monti Cello.

I am Sir with much personal respect Your most obedient and most humble servant,   W Phillips

Tr (DLC: Washington Papers), enclosed originally in Phillips to Theodorick Bland, same date (DLC: PCC, No. 57), which intimated that Phillips might be obliged to appeal Hamilton's case to Gen. Washington. Accompanying it was a letter from Phillips to Hamilton, same date and location, assuring him that strong representations had been made to TJ, and that the case might be carried to the American commander in chief. A later transcript is in DLC; being a letterpress copy, ill-punctuated, it is a less satisfactory text than the transcript in the Washington Papers. Still another transcript is in DLC: PCC, No. 57.

On the Hamilton case generally, see TJ to Bland, 8 June, and the Virginia Council's Order, 16 June 1779, with references in notes there.

From Meriwether Smith

Sir   Philadelphia, July 6h. 1779

I wrote to you on the 24h. of June by Mr. de Francy; since which I have received Advice that I am continued in the Delegation to Congress; But the Terms are such as are very injurious to my personal Interest and Honor; and I am not certain that I shall accept of the Appointment on such Terms.

It is notorious that I have been concerned in Trade, for upwards of ten Years; and I could easily demonstrate that very few Men in a Public Character in Virga. have made so great a Sacrifice of Interest as I have done since the Commencement of the present Troubles. I have not however been engaged in the Business of *Speculation*, as it is called. My Managers in Virginia have received Consignments from foreign Merchants and thence my profits arose. I have not even written a Letter to them on the Subject of Trade or given them any Advice since I left Virga.

I wish that *direct* Measures only had been taken to remove me from Congress, and that no Option had been left to me. It would then have been necessary for me only to evince to my Country the Rectitude of my Conduct whilst in the Service of it. But my Enemies, not content with attempting to displace me by a direct Vote, have availed themselves of a circumstance to procure a Law which either removes me from Office or deprives me of a considerable Means of Subsistence. If I refuse to accept of my Appointment, I know the Use they will make of my Refusal to render me unpopular; and if I do accept of it, I shall add an Injury to those already done to my Children, which may be irreparable. Under these Circumstances, I must return to Virginia before the End of my Present Delegation, that I may consult with my Friends and take my Measures accordingly. I hope to be able to give the Genl. Assembly a clear and satisfactory Account of my Conduct, at their next Meeting. They will then perhaps be able to judge, whether my Views have been directed to other Objects than the Prosperity and Happiness of my Country, and whether I have merited the Treatment I have received.

The Man who looks into his Heart and finds himself free from Guilt, gains Strength from Opposition, and by a firm and persevering Conduct will sooner or later prevail against it. In my Absence, My Enemies may attack my Character and Conduct; but the Time will come when I shall meet them face to face, and it will be well for them if I do not make them ashamed. I am with Esteem & Regards Your most obedt. & most hbl Servt.,

MERIWETHER SMITH

RC (DLC). The TERMS . . . INJURIOUS TO MY PERSONAL INTEREST AND HONOR are undoubtedly explained by an Act, introduced and passed in great haste by the House between 15 and 17 June just prior to the election of a new delegation to Congress on 18 June, requiring all delegates to take oath that they were not engaged and would not engage in domestic or foreign trade (JHD, May 1779, 1827 edn., p. 49-52; Hening, X, 113). The Act was prompted by "the Lee Party" and was aimed at Smith and Griffin; see Cyrus Griffin to Burges Ball, n.d., quoted in Burnett, *Letters of Members*, IV, No. 466, note 2; R. H. Lee, *Letters*, II, 103, 106; and William Whipple to Lee, 23 Aug. 1779, Burnett, *Letters of Members*, IV, No. 488 and note 7.

From John Jay

Philadelphia, 8 July 1779. Circular letter to the state executives enclosing a resolve of Congress of 29 June announcing that $20,000,000 is to be raised by a new loan and giving the terms on which this sum is to be borrowed.

FC (DLC: PCC, No. 14); 1 p. Enclosure not located; printed in JCC, XIV, 783-5.

From Richard Henry Lee

Chantilly, 8 July 1779. Acknowledges TJ's letter of 17 June. "Every good Whig will wish success to a governor whose principles of action are not the incentives of whim, or the suggestions of partiality; but who is influenced by motives of sound whiggism, which I take to be those of genuine philanthropy. . . . In Virginia we have properly two frontiers, one bordered by a wilderness, the other by a Sea. Into both of these issue savages, and into the latter the most savage." Sketches a comprehensive plan for defending the coasts of Virginia against piratical raiders, not by fixed forts and batteries, which may easily be taken, but by movable ones, that is, naval vessels. Asks how recruiting officers are to be supplied with money for bounties promised to recruits. Approves the placing of Hamilton in irons and the reasons given therefor. Believes the provinces of Holland will soon actively resent British insults to their commerce.

RC (DLC); 5 p. Printed: R. H. Lee, *Letters*, II, 82-6.

From George Washington

SIR   Head Qrs. New Windsor July the 10. 1779

On the 4th Instant I had the Honor to receive Your Letter of the 19th. of June. Your Excellency will permit me to offer you my sincere congratulations upon your appointment to the Government of Virginia.

I thank you much for the accounts Your Excellency has been pleased to transmit me of the successes of Cols. Clarke and Shelby. They are important and interesting and do great honor to the Officers and Men engaged in the Enterprizes. I hope these successes will be followed by very happy consequences. If Colo. Clarke could by any means gain possession of Detroit, it would in all probability effectually secure the friendship or at least the neutrality of most of the Western Indians.

I have no doubt of the propriety of the proceedings against Governor Hamilton, Dejean and Lamothe. Their cruelties to our unhappy people who have fallen into their hands and the measures they have pursued to excite the savages to acts of the most wanton barbarity discriminate them from common prisoners, and most fully authorise the treatment decreed in their case.

Your Excellency will have heard of the Enemy's movements up Hudson's river. It was generally supposed from the force in which they came and from a variety of Other circumstances that our posts in the Highlands were their Object; however they did not attempt them. They took post themselves on Verplanks and Stoney points on the opposite sides of the River where they have established very strong Garrisons, and from their peninsular and indeed almost insular forms it will be very difficult if practicable to dislodge them. The taking of these positions was, among other considerations, to distress and cut off our best communication between the States East and West of the River. Since they have done this Genl. Clinton with the main body of his Army has fallen down the River to Philipsbourg and the Country above Kings bridge. They seem determined to prosecute the system of War threatned by the Commissioners and afterwards sanctioned by Parliament on a discussion of the point. And a Detachment sent up the Sound last week disembarked, plundered New Haven, burnt some Houses there and at East Haven, reimbarked and on the 7th relanded and burnt almost the Town of Fairfield, except a few Houses. The Militia upon these occasions, considering their number and the sudden manner in which they assembled, behaved with great spirit. Genl. Tryon it is said commands these disgraceful expeditions.

I have the Honor &c,   G WASHINGTON

P.S. The Enemy have burnt Norwalk and another Town on the sound.

Dft (DLC: Washington Papers); in hand of R. H. Harrison and endorsed "Govr. Jefferson July 10: 1779. . . ." On THE PROCEEDINGS AGAINST GOVERNOR HAMILTON, &c., see TJ to Bland, 8 June, and the Virginia Council's Order, 16 June 1779, with references in notes there. Washington was later to qualify his approval of these proceedings.

William Phillips to John Jay

SIR   CharlottesVille July 11th. 1779.

The inclosed dispatch from me to Sir Henry Clinton contains copies of a variety of papers relating to Lieutenant Governor Hamilton a British prisoner of war now in confinement in Virginia. I have thought it my indispensable duty to give information to Sir Henry Clinton of the Lieutenant Governor's situation and of the means I have taken to endeavour at procuring his enlargement. I have imagined that transactions of so publick a nature must necessarily become known to all the parties concerned and my solicitude which is natural for the welfare of a brother Officer at present in great distress has induced me to be earnest in my hopes that some mode might be fallen upon between General Washington and Sir Henry Clinton for Lieutenant Governor Hamilton's release.

Upon my sending the inclosed dispatch with my other letters for the examination of Colonel Bland that Officer was pleased to sign his permission for all my letters to pass but the dispatch in question, observing upon it that he did not think himself authorised to sign his permission as it was a matter of a publick nature.

I take the liberty, therefore, of sending it to you, Sir, under

Colonel Bland's seal, requesting the favour of your Excellency to have the goodness to allow of its being sent into New York by Captain Edmonston who will have the honour of waiting upon you for that purpose. I have the honour to be, Sir, with great personal respect Your Excellency's most humble servant,   W Phillips

Tr (DLC: PCC, No. 57). In an unidentified hand and endorsed in two different hands: "M Genl. Phillips to the President of Congress July 11, 1779. desiring permission for E. to carry to Sr. H. Clinton an inclosed account of Hamilton."

THE INCLOSED DISPATCH: I.e., Phillips' letter to Sir Henry Clinton, dated 8 July 1779 (copy in DLC: PCC, No. 57), the contents of which are indicated in the letter above and its endorsement. Phillips' letter was referred by Congress to the Board of War, which reported on 7 Aug. that "the affair of Lieutenant Governor Hamilton . . . lies entirely with the Government of the State of Virginia, and Congress do not therefore now choose to take any measures therein" (report dated

5 Aug.). This report was referred to a committee of three, who in turn reported, and Congress voted, 21 Aug., "that as the imprisonment of Lieutenant Governor Hamilton was the act of the executive power of the State of Virginia, to whom it properly belonged to decide on the treatment suitable to his conduct: and as the American prisoners of war in New York have been hitherto denied the liberty of communicating to any public body within the United States the severities exercised upon them, Congress ought not to indulge Major General Phillips with forwarding his letters and papers respecting the said Hamilton" (JCC, XIV, 933-4, 985). On the Hamilton case generally, see TJ to Bland, 8 June, and references there.

From the Board of Trade, with Reply

[*Williamsburg*] *13 July 1779*. The proposals of Hunter & Co. concerning the cargo of the ship *Dolphin* seem exorbitant. From information respecting tobacco now owned by the state, it is impracticable to comply with the proposal. This commodity is rising daily and will probably soon reach £20 per hundred. Signed by Whiting, Ambler, and Rose. Countersigned with the following instruction: "In council July 13. 1779. This board concurs in opinion with the board of trade that the terms above referred to are so exorbitant that the purchase ought not to be made. Th: Jefferson."

RC (CSmH); 1 p. The proposals of Hunter & Co. have not been located, but see Board of Trade to TJ, 14 July 1780.

From William Fleming

SIR   Philadelphia 13th July, 1779.

My colleagues have requested me to transmit you the deposition of Ferrall Wade, on the subject of governor Hamilton's conduct at Detroit, which I inclose you accordingly.

A copy of the book of precedents in the war office shall still be attended to, tho' we have not yet been able to engage a man to undertake the business.

It is a matter of surprize and regret that Congress have not received a letter from their plenipotentiary, or either of their commissioners in Europe, for more than six months past; in which time the minister of France has received several dispatches from his court, and one very lately, the contents of which he has (in part) communicated to congress. I hope I shall not be suspected of affecting a mysteriousness when I tell you I am not at liberty to mention particularly the minister's communications, nor would it be prudent to risque them in a letter, under the present regulation of our post office: however, this much I can venture to say, that they are favourable—that the prospect of peace brightens, and that France seems to act on a very liberal scale, and has, in many instances, gone further in support of the common cause than she was, by the treaty, bound to go; notwithstanding which, it is to be feared, we are not all true friends to the alliance.

Nothing of consequence lately from headquarters. The enemy, on the night of the 4th. instant, made a sudden descent, with about 3000 men, at New Haven in Connecticut, and took possession of the town, but what damage they did we have not yet learnt. We have letters from Genl. Sullivan dated at Wyoming the 5th. instant; he complains of large quantities of damaged provisions, by which the progress of his army is much retarded. I have but little hopes from that expedition. Our cruisers in general are pretty successful, and I hope before this reaches you the enemy's privateers in Chesapeake bay will have met with a rub.

I am apprehensive we shall shortly be overun by committees. The original ostensible design of them was laudable, and under proper regulations might, perhaps, produce good effects; tho' I confess little or nothing salutary has yet been experienced by them here; and I am of opinion they are taking large strides towards the entire subversion of this government, the civil magistrates being, already, little more than mere cyphers. Adieu.

RC (DLC). Unsigned, but the handwriting is Fleming's. Enclosure (deposition of Ferrall Wade) not located.

COMMITTEES: No doubt a reference to the committee of Philadelphia citizens, radical in their point of view, organized to keep prices down; see R. L. Brunhouse, *The Counter-Revolution in Pennsylvania*, Harrisburg, 1942, p. 68ff.; also Meriwether Smith to TJ, 30 July 1779.

From Cyrus Griffin

DEAR SIR   [Philadelphia] July 13th. 79

It appears to me that Virginia will do her part in placing things
upon an adequate foundation; a large Income of Money, and a most
judicious taxation. Members of Congress highly applaud your
wisdom in demanding Indian Corn, Wheat, Tobacco &c. I wish to
heaven such measures had been adopted many months ago by
every State in the union. I have no doubt the Enemy are waiting
thus long to see the *downfall* of our paper Credit, but even that
calamitous affair would do them no essential Service; America can
never be reunited to Britain; and finances with our brave and
determined people are only a secondary consideration. The proceedings of Council relative to G. Hamilton &c. were received by
Congress with the utmost applause; the whole matter is beautifully
stated; the sentence judicious and spirited. That *peace* is a most
desirable object no man in his senses *ought* to deny, but then it
must be a peace honorable to America and grateful to our allies.
I hope such a one will take place before Christmas next. By the
violence of a giddy Multitude it would be highly disagreeable to
patch up even an *Independant* peace at the expence of public faith
and future salvation. Why are committees upon the establishment
throughout all America? They have almost *murdered* the French
Agent at Wilmington. Indeed *Fisheries* are too much of external
nature to be fought for at present; yet in a treaty of peace I would
not relinquish them, they should stand upon the common right of
Independant nations. But unhappily this will not answer the purpose. The bleeding Continent must bleed still further. When I say
my expectations lead to peace I do not mean that England will
expressly acknowlege our Independance; the pride of George will
not submit; but she may treat with us as an Independant people
notwithstanding provided our demands are not unreasonable, which
the French Court are in apprehension about, and therefore trust
that moderation and a well-guaranteed peace ought not to be
despised in our low circumstances. The Enemy with a body of five
thousand men have plundered and destroyed *New-haven*[NB] in
Connecticut; they carried off the wife and children of old Shearman
the member of Congress; yesterday he left this City full of anxiety
and trouble; I pity the Lady and Children exceedingly, but I have
no tender feelings for the old fellow on many accounts. & am Sir
Yours most affly.,   A. B.

NB Not ascertained to satisfaction. Two papers enclosed, because I do not know whether you get them regularly. I suppose you do not pay postage.

RC (DLC). The identity of the writer has been established from the handwriting and the content. Enclosures not identified.

From the Board of Trade, with Reply

[*Williamsburg*] *14 July 1779.* Upon consideration of the want of necessary supplies, it is proposed to offer Hunter & Co. "77½ for 1. for such Goods as will suit the State payable in Tobacco at the Market Price." Signed by Whiting, Ambler, and Rose. Countersigned: "In council July 16. 1779. Disapproved of, the price being thought too exorbitant. Th: Jefferson."

RC (CSmH); 1 p.
See Board of Trade to TJ, 13 July 1780.

From John Jay

Philadelphia, 14 July 1779. Circular letter to the state executives enclosing resolves of Congress of 9 July respecting persons employed in provisioning the army.

FC (DLC: PCC, No. 14); 1 p. Enclosure not located; printed in JCC, XIV, 812-15.

To ——— ———

July 15. 1779.

[Extract of?] a letter from A. Lee [to] Gov. Henry. Paris Dec. 14. 1778.

['I inclo]se the account of the paper which the Treasurer wrote for [. . . strike] the paper bills on which you will have the goodness to [. . . hi]m.'

[T]he inclosed paper and letter abovementioned came by [. . .] Genl. Washington. We have hopes that the paper (which [we . . . s]uppose to be laded with some military stores) will come to hand. I am Sir Your humble servt., TH: JEFFERSON

RC (Vi). Mutilated fragment. A printed text in *Official Letters*, II, 20-1, though inaccurate, supplies two or three words now chipped away from the MS. It is not possible to estimate the number of words missing in the remaining gaps. Enclosure missing.

THE TREASURER: George Webb, who succeeded Robert Carter Nicholas, 17 Dec. 1776 (JHD, 1776, 1828 edn., p.

100). In a letter to John Page, 27 May 1778, Arthur Lee mentions enclosing a specimen of the paper for the treasury desired by Webb (R. H. Lee, *Life of Arthur Lee*, II, 130; see also I, 419, and William Lee to TJ, 24 Sep. 1779). Since Lee's letter to Henry of 14 Dec. 1778 has not been found, the incident cannot be further clarified.

Credentials for Peter Penet

July 15. 1779

To all to whom these present Letters shall come Greeting:

Whereas the General Assembly by their resolution bearing date the 9th day of December 1778 did empower the Governor with the advice of the Council of State to take such measures as might be necessary and should seem probable for obtaining a Loan of Gold and Silver to this Commonwealth to such extent as they should think expedient, and that the said assembly would make good his Contracts for that purpose. And his Excellency Patrick Henry esqr. late Governor of this Commonwealth by his Commission bearing date the 22d. day of May in this present year did by and with the advice of the Council of State nominate constitute and appoint Peter Penett esqr. of Nante in the Kingdom of France to be agent for this Commonwealth for the purpose of obtaining a loan of Gold and Silver not exceeding the Term of one hundred thousand pounds Sterling for the use of the said Commonwealth and did pledge the faith of the said Commonwealth for the fulfilling and punctual performance of all such agreements as he might make and enter into relative to such loan of Gold and Silver: Now Know ye that I Thomas Jefferson Governor of the said Commonwealth of Virginia by and with advice of the Council of State, do ratify and confirm the said power and authorities so given to the said Peter Penet esqr. by the Commission from the said late Governor Henry and do solemnly pledge the faith of the Commonwealth for the fulfilling and punctual performance of all such agreements made or to be made by the said Peter Penet relative to the said Loan of Gold and Silver in the most full and ample manner. In Witness whereof I have hereunto set my hand and caused the Seal of the said Commonwealth to be affixed at Wmsburg the 15th. day of July in the 4th. year of the Commonwealth and in the year of our Lord 1779.

TH JEFFERSON

Tr in Board of War Letter Book (MiU-C).

Penet's mission proved fruitless; see his letters to TJ of 17 Mch., 20 May, and especially 22 Nov. 1780.

From George Mason

Cartwright's July 16th. 1779.

DEAR SIR

This will be deliver'd You by Mr. Hardy, one of the Officers of the Letter of Marque Ship General Washington, just arrived at Alexandria from Brest: She brought in with her a privateer Sloop Prize from New York, taken off the Coast of N. Carolina, as She was in Chase of a Virginia Sloop. Mr. Hardy comes to Wmsburg, with the Lieutenant of the Prize, in order to condemn her in our Court of Admiralty; and will inform You of any Particulars You may desire to know, respecting the french Fleet, with which he sailed from Brest. I believe it is pretty certain that the military Stores this Government has so long expected from France were on board two Ships in this Fleet; and as they parted with the Convoy off the Island of Madeira, and are not Yet arrived, there is Reason to fear they have miscarryed.

The Capt. and 22 Prisoners, taken in the Privateer Sloop, have been since her Arrival, and still are living at the Charge of the owners of the Ship General Washington: I shou'd imagine the Expence, since their being in Port, shou'd be charged to the Commonwealth. I beg the Favour of You Sir to give Orders for their Disposition and Maintenance.

Mr. Hardy has with him an advertisement of the principal articles of the Genl. Washington's Cargoe, with the time of the Sale: I have directed him to wait on the proper Boards (such as You will be pleased to direct) that they may see whether they will suit the Public; and am, with the greatest Esteem & Respect Dr. Sir, Your most obdt. Se[rvant],   G MASON

RC (CSmH). Addressed: "His Excellency Thos. Jefferson Esqr. Governor of Virginia." Endorsement and calculations on address leaf in an unidentified hand.

The GENERAL WASHINGTON sailed from Alexandria in the fall of 1778 for France, carrying dispatches. On its return in the spring of 1779, it captured a British privateer and brought her into Alexandria late in June (VMHB, XVI [1908], 176-7). Mason evidently had an interest in the ship, as he did in a later voyage (Rowland, *Mason*, II, 13). The cargo of the *General Washington* was advertised for sale in *Va. Gaz.* (D & N), 24 July 1779.

From the Board of Trade

Board of Trade July 17th. 1779.

Messrs. McCallum Osborne & Co. have made an offer of a new Brig just Launched of the undermentioned Dementions, her Sails Rigging &c. fitted and may be ready in three weeks the price

[37]

£30,000. We employed Capt. Maxwell, in whose Judgment we think we can confide, to go up and examine her; he Reports that it is his opinion she is a good Vessel and will sail fast. We are of opinion the said Vessel should be purchased, as the State will be under the necessity of having such and it is also our opinion that such a Vessel could not be built and got ready in this time of general scarcity for many Months and probably when built at much greater Expence.

THOM WHITING

J. AMBLER

DUN: ROSE

Dementions of a Brig belonging } to Messrs. McCallum Osborne & Co. }

	feet.	Inch.
Length of Keel	51	6
Breadth of Beam	22	6
Depth of Hold	9	4
Rake forward	20	
Ditto aft	7	6

RC (CSmH). Countersigned: "In council July 20. 1779. Approved. Th: Jefferson."

From the Board of Trade

[*Williamsburg*] *17 July 1779.* The owners of the cargo of the *Dolphin* propose to let the Board of Trade have such part of it as they wish, at the rate of fifty for one upon the sterling cost, payable in tobacco at £15 per hundred. It is recommended that such articles as are absolutely and immediately necessary be purchased, because the goods are better than any which may be offered for some time. The burden of payment will be somewhat lightened because the State has not paid more than £10 per hundred for tobacco on hand. Signed by Whiting, Ambler, and Rose. Countersigned: "In council July 17. 1779. Approved. Th: Jefferson."

RC (CSmH); 1 p.

Return of Arms, Stores, &c., Belonging to the State of Virginia

[17 July 1779]
[Text reproduced in illustration section following p. 254.]

Tabular MS (DLC); entirely in TJ's hand. See TJ's authorization to De Klauman, 12 June 1779.

To Richard Henry Lee

DEAR SIR   Williamsburgh July 17. 1779

This being post morning and many letters to write I must beg leave to refer you for some articles to my letter to the feild officers of Northumberland &c.. In order to render our miserable navy of some service orders were some time ago issued for two gallies on the seaboard of the Eastern shore to join the others; another galley heretofore stationed in Carolina (if not purchased by that government as proposed by our assembly) will be called into the bay. It seems we have few or none which can ride on the middle grounds. It is therefore in contemplation to keep them about the North cape for the protection of the North channel, and for the purpose of descrying such hostile vessels coming into the bay as they may be competent to attack. From a very early period of this contest it has been my uniform opinion that our only practicable defence was naval; and that tho' our first efforts in that way must be small and would probably be unsuccesful, yet that it must have a beginning and the sooner the better. These beginnings have indeed been unsuccesful beyond all my fears. But it is my opinion we should still persevere in spite of disappointment, for this plain reason that we can never be otherwise defended. Impressed with the necessity of this kind of defence, the assembly so long ago as October 1776 were prevailed on to direct two frigates and two large gallies to be built. Being ignorant of these things myself, but having great confidence in the British experience on the water, the proposition only referred as to the frigates to their method, and as to the gallies to the Philadelphia plan. I left the house soon after; some members vain enough to suppose they could correct errors in the construction of British vessels, got the plan changed: their plan was again ventured to be improved on by the navy-board, and the event was £100,000 laid out to not a shilling's benefit. I beleive now we should be gainers were we to burn our whole navy, and build what we should be able on plans approved by experience and not warped to the whimsical ideas of individuals, who do not consider that if their projects miscarry their country is in a manner undone. I am in hopes that Congress are about to correct their long continued habits of neglect to the trade of these Southern states, and to send us some aid. I shall refer to the Council the article of the bounty mentioned in your letter. My own idea is that the recruiting officer should apply here for such sum as he thinks he may want, lodging his bond and security for the due expenditure of it (without which we issue no money on account). As he is a standing officer, and will derive considerable advantage from his success, I think he cannot deem it hard to leave the application to be made by himself.

I am Dear Sir with much respect Your most obedt. & most humble servt., Th: Jefferson

P.S. The council approve of the above method of sending out the recruiting money.

RC (Stanley F. Horn, Nashville, Tenn., 1945). Addressed: "Richard Henry Lee esq. Chantilly in Westmoreland." Endorsed by Lee.

TJ's LETTER TO THE FEILD OFFICERS OF NORTHUMBERLAND is missing. The present letter, in answer to Lee's of 8 July, q.v., anticipates TJ's memorable and controversial interest as President in gunboats. THE PHILADELPHIA PLAN: Mr. M. V. Brewington in a personal communication to the editors (quoted further, below) suggests that TJ had probably seen and been impressed by the galleys of the Pennsylvania state navy, which had enjoyed some minor successes

on the Delaware. These vessels "were simply large open, or half deck, boats designed primarily for oar propulsion, but also equipped with one or two lateen sails. They carried usually three heavy cannon, a number of swivels, and small arms. . . . The shipwrights who built them also helped to build Arnold's fleet and it is likely his 'gondola' *Philadelphia* (still extant) represents the type." For a brief but useful account of naval affairs in Virginia in the Revolution, see Charles O. Paullin, *The Navy of the American Revolution*, Cleveland, 1906, ch. XIV; the Pennsylvania galleys are treated in the same, ch. XIII.

To George Washington

Sir   Wmsburg July 17th 1779

I some time ago inclosed to you a printed copy of an Order of Council, by which Governor Hamilton was to be confined in Irons in close Jail. This has occasioned a letter from General Philips of which the inclosed is a Copy. The General seems to suppose that a prisoner on capitulation cannot be put into close confinement tho his capitulation shall not have provided against it. My idea was that all persons taken in war were to be deemed prisoners of war. That those who surrender on capitulation (or convention) are prisoners of war also subject to the same treatment with those who surrender at discretion, except only so far as the terms of their capitulation or convention shall have guarded them. In the Capitulation of Governor Hamilton (a Copy of which I inclose) no stipulation is made as to the treatment of himself or those taken with him. The Governor indeed when he signs, adds a flourish of reasons inducing him to capitulate, one of which is the generosity of his Enemy. Generosity on a large and comprehensive Scale seems to dictate the making a signal example of this gentleman; but waiving that, these are only the private motives inducing him to surrender, and do not enter into the Contract of Colonel Clarke. I have the highest idea of the sacredness of those Contracts which take place between nation and nation at war, and would be among the last on earth who should do any thing in violation of them. I can find nothing in those Books usually recurred to as testimonials of the Laws and usages of nature and nations which convicts the opinions, I have above expressed, of error. Yet there may be such an usage as General Philips seems to suppose, tho' not taken notice of by these writers. I am obliged to trouble your Excellency on this occasion by asking of you information on this point. There is no other person whose decision will so authoritatively decide this doubt in the public mind and none with which I am disposed so implicitly to comply. If you shall be of opinion that the bare existence of a Capitulation in the case of Governor Hamilton privileges him from confinement, tho there be no article to that effect in the capitulation, justice shall most assuredly be done him. The importance of this question in a public view, and my own anxiety under a charge of a violation of national faith by the Executive of this Commonwealth will I hope apologize for my adding this to the many, many troubles with which I know you to be burthened. I have the honor to be with the most profound respect & esteem Yr. Excellency's mo: obedt. & mo: hble. servt.,   TH: JEFFERSON

P.S. I have just received a Letter from Colo. Bland containing information of numerous desertions from the Convention Troops (not less than 400 in the last fortnight). He thinks he has reason to believe it is with the connivance of some of their officers. Some of these have been retaken, all of them going northwardly. They had armed themselves with forged passports, and with Certificates of having taken the oath of fidelity to the State, some of them forged, others really given by weak Magistrates. I mention this to your Excellency as perhaps it may be in your power to have such of them intercepted as shall be passing through Pennsylvania and Jersey.

Your letter inclosing the opinion of the board of officers in the case between Allison and Lee is come safe to hand after a long passage. It shall be answered by next post.   TH: J.

RC (DLC: Washington Papers). Tr (DLC: Jefferson Papers). RC is in an unidentified hand but with the last paragraph of the postscript and both signatures in TJ's hand. Endorsed by Washington: "Govr: Jefferson July 17th: 1779 ansd 6 Augt." Enclosures: Phillips to TJ, 5 July 1779; Articles of Capitulation signed by Hamilton at Vincennes, 24 Feb. 1779 (copy in DLC: TJ Papers; printed in *George Rogers Clark Papers, 1771-1781*, p. 168).

On the Hamilton case generally, see TJ to Bland, 8 June 1779, and references

To the Board of War

In council July 22nd 1779.

Approved as to the gallies; and as to the ship Gloster it is recommended to the board of war to have a proper enquiry and report made whether it may not be more advantageous to convert her into a galley than to sell her, and on such report to reconsider the matter.

TH: JEFFERSON

Tr in Board of War Journal (Vi); printed in *Official Letters*, II, 23, where the source is incorrectly given as "Minutes of Navy Board."

On 5 July, the Board of War recommended that 5 galleys and the ship *Gloucester* be dismantled, their men consigned to other vessels, and their hulls sold at public sale (Board of War Journal, Vi).

From Daniel Brodhead

SIR   Head Quarters, Pittsburgh, July 22nd, 1779.

I have taken the liberty of enclosing you copies of sundry letters relative to the designs of the Enemy, in and about Detroit.

A great number of men must be discharged in the course of a few weeks, which will leave us weak on this frontier, and as no reinforcement of regulars can reasonably be expected for this district and the calling out some of the Militia from the States of Virginia and Pennsylvania may be indispensably necessary; I shall be glad of receiving such Authority from you for that purpose, as you may judge necessary.

About the fifth of next month I intend to make an excursion against some of the Seneca Settlements, they being the most hostile and warlike nation, and if I am successful it may establish the Tranquility of our frontiers for years to come.

I have the honor to be, with due regard, Your most Obed't Serv't,

DANIEL BRODHEAD,
Col. Commanding, W.D.

MS not located. Text from *Pennsylvania Archives*, 1st ser., XII, 140 (Brodhead's Letter Book). Enclosures not found.

Brodhead was the Continental officer commanding the "Western District"; his expedition against the SENECA SETTLEMENTS on the Allegheny was in cooperation with Gen. Sullivan's campaign in western New York State (DAB; Wis. Hist. Soc., *Colls.*, XXIII, *passim*).

From Archibald Cary

Sir   Ampthill July 22d. 1779.

Inclosed you have a State of Ballandines Account with the Country for the Works at Westham, also Ballandine and Reveley for the Buckingham Furnace.

You will also find Inclosed, his Deed to and Agrement with Mr. Richd. Adams and others for the Air Furnace and Canal.

I have also Sent as it will Save the Trouble of haveing recourse to the Journals of Assembly the Papers you Sent Containing their resolutions, with the report of the Gentlemen appointed to Settle the Inclosed Accounts.

As Ballandine is now Going down to wait on you I think it nesasary to Say Something as to a letter of his directed to My Self Messrs. Carrington and Southall. We Met the First day at Westham, and examined the whole Accounts but from the Finess, and I may Say the Villany of the Man, it was impossable to draw up a report and Coppy the Accounts and we Adj[ourned] to Richmond, the next day where he was to attend, but as you will see by his letter he did not.

He tells us we appeard determined not to assist in the repairing the Dam, and points out the Consiquence. For answer to that we refer to his Agreement, which I must observe he never comply'd with, as the Dam nor even the Canal so far as the Boaring Mill was ever Compleated, the Dam so little Secured, that I my Self told him it would not Stand a Common Fresh, and pointed out what was Wanting. This he Acknowledged and told me it Should be done, but the Dam Stood 12 Months, after and he never did what he Say'd was Nesasary to Secure it.

He also with much insolence says we did not attend to the letter of our appointment, and our principle View was to Ruin him. To this I shall say that he will ruin the Country had we the Wealth of Potosi to have recourse to, if we Go on with him. He Sets great Value on the Grant he made of the Land and use of the Water, but it is to be observ'd he Gave for the whole of what he possesses at the place not more than 5 or 6 pound, that what we paid him for 3½ acres and the Water was presisely what he demanded, and that when he had Compleated the Works the Country was to be at half the expence of repairs.

His last paragraph, was not in our power to do any thing about, as we had no power to purchase him out, but it is what I wish was done.

He talks of paying off the ballance due not according to Agreement, but With Iron at the high value it now is. To this I reply'd that at the Time the Money was Advancd, Lands had not rose, that the Accounts proves Labor was but little higher than Formerly, and that we Could have purchased Iron at the Value he was to deliver it.

The Assembly have determind to Allow more than his Agrement, they do not Say what. We allowed for what he furnished £30 pr. T: but it was Against my Opinion.

You will have (I have been told he Says so) a Troublesome business before you have done with him, or I mistake very Much. I have been more full than may be Nesasary, but Knowing the Man I could not help be[ing] so to put you on Your Gaurd. I have the Honor to be Sir Your Hble Servt.,   ARCHIBALD CARY

RC (DLC). Only one of the numerous enclosures has been found in TJ's papers, namely John Ballendine to Messrs. Cary, Carrington, and Southall, 12 July 1779; see below.

Cary was one of the commissioners acting for the governor in settling the accounts of John BALLENDINE, the iron and canal promoter with whom TJ was to have protracted negotiations set forth in a letter to Speaker Harrison, 30 Oct.

1779; see the note there, also the Bill for Establishing a Manufactory of Arms, printed under the same date. The chief immediate difficulty lay in the fact that Ballendine controlled water rights essential for operating the boring mill at Westham Foundry. His LETTER to the commissioners, without place, 12 July 1779 (DLC: TJ Papers, 4: 545), is a long wail of complaint about his mistreatment by the Virginia authorities.

To William Phillips

SIR   Wmsburg July 22d. 1779

Your Letter, on the Subject of Lieutenant Governor Hamilton's confinement, came safely to hand. I shall, with great chearfulness, explain, to you, the Reasons on which the advice of Council was founded, since, after the satisfaction of doing what is right, the greatest is that of having what we do approved by those whose opinions deserve esteem.

We think ourselves justified in Governor Hamilton's strict confinement, on the general principle of National retaliation. To state to you the particular facts of British Cruelty to American prisoners, would be to give a melancholy history from the capture of Colo. Ethan Allen, at the beginning of the war, to the present day; a history which I will avoid, as equally disagreeable, to you, and to me. I with pleasure do you the justice to say that I believe these facts to be very much unknown to you, as Canada has been the only Scene of your service, in America, and, in that quarter, we have

reason to believe that Sr. Guy Carleton, and the other officers commanding there, have treated our prisoners (since the instance of
Colo. Allen) with considerable lenity. What has been done in England, and what in New York, and Philadelphia, you are probably
uninformed; as it would hardly be made the subject of epistolary
correspondence. I will only observe to you, Sir, that the confinement, and treatment, of our officers, soldiers, and Seamen, have
been so rigorous, and cruel, as that a very great proportion of the
whole of those captured in the course of this war, and carried to
Philadelphia, while in possession of the British army, and to New
York, have perished miserably, from that cause only; and that this
fact is as well established, with us, as any historical fact which has
happened in the course of the War. A Gentleman of this Commonwealth, in public office, and of known and established Character,
who was taken on Sea, carried to New York and exchanged, has
given us lately a particular information of the treatment of our
prisoners there. Officers taken by Land, it seems, are permitted to
go on parole within certain limits on Long Island, till suggestions
shall be made to their prejudice by some Tory refugee or other
equally worthless person, when they are hurried to the Prevot in
New York, without enquiring 'whether they be founded upon
positive facts, be matter of hearsay, or taken from the reports of
interested men.' The example of enquiring into the truth of charges
of this nature, according to legal principles of evidence, has surely
not been set us by our Enemies. We enquired what these Prevots
were, and were told they were the common miserable jails, built
for the confinement of Malefactors. Officers [and men] taken by
sea are kept in prison ships [infected with malignant disorders
which have been brought on by the crowd put into them, and he
told us that the deaths among these, when he was there, were] from
five to ten a day. When therefore we are desired to advert to the
possible consequences of treating prisoners with rigour, I need only
ask where did those rigours begin? not with us assuredly. I think
you Sir, who have had as good opportunities as any British officer
of learning in what manner we treat those whom the fortune of
war has put into our hands, can clear us from the charge of rigour
as far as your knowledge or information has extended. I can assert
that Governor Hamilton's is the first instance which has occured
in my own country, and if there has been another in any of the
United States, it is unknown to me; these instances must have been
extremely rare, if they have ever existed at all, or they could not
have been altogether unheard of by me. When a uniform exercise

of kindness to prisoners on our part has been returned by as uniform severity on the part of our enemies, you must excuse me for saying it is high time, by other lessons, to teach respect to the dictates of humanity; in such a case, retaliation becomes an act of benevolence.[1]

But suppose, Sir, we were willing, still longer, to decline the drudgery of general retaliation; yet Governor Hamilton's conduct has been such as to call for exemplary punishment on him personally. In saying this I have not so much in view his particular cruelties to our Citizens, prisoners with him, (which, tho they have been great, were of necessity confined to a small scale) as the general Nature of the service he undertook, at Detroit, and the extensive exercise of cruelties which that involved. Those who act together in war are answerable for each other. No distinction can be made between principal and ally, by those against whom the war is waged. He who employs another to do a deed, makes the Deed his own. If he calls in the hand of the assassin, or murderer, himself becomes the assassin or murderer. The known rule of warfare with the Indian Savages is an indiscriminate butchery of men women and children. These Savages, under this well-known Character, are employed by the British nation as allies in the War against the Americans. Governor Hamilton undertakes to be the conductor of the War. In the execution of that undertaking, he associates small parties of the whites under his immediate command with large parties of the Savages, and sends them to act, sometimes jointly, sometimes separately, not against our forts, or armies in the feild, but the farming settlements on our frontiers. Governor Hamilton then is himself the butcher of Men Women and Children. I will not say to what length the fair rules of war would extend the right of punishment against him; but I am sure that confinement, under its strictest circumstances, as a retaliation for Indian devastation and massacre, must be deemed Lenity. I apprehend you had not sufficiently adverted to the expression in the advice of the Council, when you suppose the proclamation there alluded to, to be the one addressed to the Inhabitants of the Illinois, afterwards printed [in the public] papers, and to be affirm[ed to contain 'denunciations of vengeance against the Americans, calls for blood, or threats of general massacres of men, women and children.' The] Proclamation, there alluded to, contained nothing more than an invitation to our Officers and Soldiers to join the British arms against those whom he is pleased to call Rebels and Traitors. In order to introduce these among our people, they were put into the hands of the Indians; and in every house, where they

murdered or carried away the family, they left one of these proclamations. Some of them were found sticking on the breasts of the
persons murdered, one under the hand and Seal of Governor Hamilton came to our hands. The Indians being the Bearers of proclamations, under the hand and Seal of Governor Hamilton (no matter
what was the Subject of them) there can be no doubt they were
acting under his direction; and, as including this proof, the fact
was cited in the advice of the Council. But if you will be so good
as to recur to the address to the Illinois, which you refer to, you will
find that, tho' it does not in express terms threaten vengeance, blood
and Massacre, yet it proves that the Governor had made for us the
most ample provision of all these calamities. He there gives in
detail the horrid Catalogue of savage nations, extending from
South to North, whom he had leagued with himself to wage combined war on our frontiers: and it is well known that that war
would of course be made up of blood, and general Massacres of
Men Women and Children. Other papers of Governor Hamiltons
have come to our hands, containing instructions to officers going
out with scalping parties of Indians and Whites, and proving that
that kind of war was waged under his [express orders.] Further
proofs in abundance might be adduced, but I suppose the fact too
notorious to need them.

Your letter seems to admit an inference that, whatever may have
been the general conduct of our enemies towards their prisoners,
or whatever the personal conduct of Governor Hamilton, yet, as a
prisoner by capitulation, you consider him as privileged from strict
confinement. I do not pretend to an intimate knowledge of this
Subject. My idea is that the term 'prisoners of war' is a genuine
one, the specification of which is—1st. Prisoners at discretion: and
2d. prisoners on convention, or capitulation. Thus, in the debate in
the house of Commons of the 27h. November last, on the address,
the Minister, speaking of General Burgoyne (and in his presence)
says he is 'a prisoner' and General Burgoyne calls himself 'a prisoner under the terms of the Convention of Saratoga,' intimating
that, tho' a prisoner, he was a prisoner of a particular Species
entitled to certain terms.[2] The treatment of the first class ought to
be such as is approved by the usage of polished Nations; gentle and
humane, unless a contrary conduct in an enemy, or individual,
renders a stricter treatment necessary. The prisoners of the 2d
Class have nothing to exempt them from a like treatment with
those of the 1st. except so far as they shall have been able to make
better terms by articles of Capitulation. So far then as these shall

have provided for an exemption from strict treatment, so [far] prisoners on C[apitulation ha]ve a right to be distin[guished from those at discretion. I do not propose to rely at all on those instances which history furnishes, where it has been thought justifiable to disregard express articles of capitulation from] certain Causes antecedent thereto; tho' such instances might be produced, from English history too, and in one case where the King himself commanded in person. Marshal Boufflers after the taking of the Castle of Namur, was arrested and detained prisoner of War by King William tho by an Article in the Capitulation it was stipulated that the officers and Soldiers of the Garrison in general, and Marshal Boufflers by name, should be at liberty. However we waive reasoning on this head, because no article in the Capitulation of Governor Hamilton is violated by his confinement. Perhaps not having seen the Capitulation, you were led to suppose it a thing of course, that, being able to obtain terms of surrender, they would first provide for their own treatment. I inclose you a Copy of the Capitulation, by which you will see that the 2d article declares them prisoners of War, and nothing is said as to the treatment they were to be entitled to. When Governor Hamilton signs indeed, he adds a flourish, containing the motives inducing him to capitulate, one of which was confidance in a generous Enemy. He should have reflected that generosity on a large Scale would take side against him. However these were only his private motives, and did not enter into the contract of Colo. Clarke. Being prisoners of War then, with only such privileges as their Capitulation has provided, and that having provided nothing on the Subject of their treatment, they are liable to be treated as other prisoners. We have not extended our order, as we might justifiably have done, to the whole of this Corps. Governor Hamilton, and Captn. Lamothe alone, as leading offenders, are in confinement. The other officers and men are treated as if they had been taken in justifiable War; the officers being at large on their parole, and the men also having their liberty to a certain extent. (Dejean was not included in the Capitulation being taken 8 Days after, on the Wabache *150 miles* from St. Vincennes.)

I hope Sir that, being made more fully acquainted with the facts on which the advice of Council was grounded, and exercising your own good sense in cool and candid deliberation on these facts, and the consequences deducible from them, according to the usage and Sentiments of civilized Nations, you will see the transaction in a very different light from that in which it appeared at the time of writing your Letter, and ascribe the advice of the Council, not to want of attention to the sacred Nature of public Conventions, of which I hope we shall never, in any circumstances, lose sight, but to a desire of stopping the effusion of the unoffending blood of women and Children, and the unjustifiable severities exercised on our captive officers and soldiers in general, by proper severities on our part.

I have the honor to be with much personal respect Sir Your most obedt & mo: hble Servant.

Dft (Vi). Tr (WHi), in hand of Lyman C. Draper. The Dft, which is probably a corrected fair copy of a missing first draft in TJ's hand, is in an unidentified hand and is unsigned; it contains, however, numerous alterations interlined by TJ, and the more important of these are given in the textual notes below. The original is worn, and portions of the text at the foot of each page are missing; these have been supplied, in square brackets, from Tr, evidently made before mutilation of Dft.

Though this letter has been frequently printed, the addressee has hitherto not been correctly identified: in CVSP and in *Official Letters*, the addressee is given as "the Governor of Detroit"; in Ford, in the *Clark Papers, 1771-1781*, and in L & B, as "Sir Guy Carleton, Governor of Canada." The letter is manifestly a reply to Phillips' letter of 5 July, q.v. On the Hamilton case generally, see TJ to Bland, 8 June 1779, and references there. THE CAPITULATION of Hamilton, 24 Feb. 1779, is printed in *Clark Papers, 1771-1781*, p. 168.

1 The preceding sentence is substituted in TJ's hand for the following, deleted: "Can the Spirit of any Nation bear to carry on war on such unequal terms? And is not retaliation mercy in such a Case?"
2 The words "intimating . . . terms" are an interlined addition in TJ's hand.

Contract between the State of Virginia and Peter Penet, Windel & Company

[*Williamsburg*] *22 July 1779*. Contract entered into by the Governor and Council of Virginia on the one part and Peter Penet, Windel [or Wendel] & Company on the other part, by which the company pledges to establish "a Manufactory of Arms and Foundery of Cannon . . . on James river," to import artisans therefor, and to furnish 10,000 stand of arms annually to the state, while the state on its part pledges to obtain a proper site and water rights for the foundry, to exempt the artisans from military service, to secure supplies of iron, copper, and coal, and to purchase the arms made. Signed by TJ on the part of the state and by P. Penet "pour moy et Wendel & Co."; witnessed by Savarit (given name unknown) and Meriwether Smith.

Tr (Vi); 7 p.; in an unidentified hand but containing one insertion in TJ's hand; endorsed (in part) by TJ: "Penet Windel & c[o.] Articles of agreement (Copy) 1779"; the signatures are not in autograph. Another Tr is in Board of War Letter Book (MiU-C). Copies of a preliminary form of the contract and a series of "Observations" and "Answers" exchanged thereon between the company and the Governor and Council from 30 June to 16 July 1779, are also in Vi; 20 p. The contract of 22 July is printed in *Official Letters*, II, 23-8, but is only summarized here because it is given in full in the Bill for Establishing a Manufactory of Arms and Extending Navigation through the Falls of James River, printed below under date of 30 Oct. 1779.

For the history of attempts to establish a foundry to supply arms for the state, and to extend navigation around the Falls of the James, see TJ to Benjamin Harrison, Speaker of the House of Delegates, 30 Oct. 1779 (in which copies of all these papers were enclosed), with notes and references there, and also TJ's bill printed under that date.

From ——— Savarit

[*Without place, after 22 July 1779.*] Directed to the Governor and Council and written after the contract between the State of Virginia and Penet, Windel & Co. (q.v., 22 July) was signed. The writer considers the tenth and eleventh articles of the contract objectionable because they limit the exemption of arms makers from military service to twenty-one years and because the exemption applies only to imported laborers—a restriction which will "oblige the Undertakers to a perpetual importation of Artificers." He asks for amendment of these articles before the contract is submitted to the assembly for ratification.

Translation (Vi); 2 p.; attested by Charles Bellini. Enclosed in TJ to Harrison, 30 Oct. 1779, q.v. See also Penet to TJ, 17 Aug. 1779.

Orders for Defense of the Western Frontier

In Council July 23d 1779

The Act of General Assembly intituled an act for raising a Body of Troops for the defence of the Commonwealth, having directed that two battalions shall be raised for the Western and two for the Eastern Service, the Board advise the Governor to Order that the men to be raised according to the said act in the Counties of Yohogania, Monongalia, Ohio, Kentucky, Hampshire, Berkley, Frederick, Shenandoah, Rockingham, Rockbridge, Botetourt, Loudoun, Fauquier, Culpeper and Orange, be formed into one Battalion for the Western Service, The men to be raised under this same act in the Counties of Washington, Montgomery, Green Brier, Augusta, Henry, Bedford, Amherst, Albemarle, Fairfax, Prince William, Louisa, Fluvanna, Goochland, Cumberland, Buckingham and Pittsylvania be formed into one other Battalion for the Western Service. And the men to be raised in the Counties to the Eastward of those before named to be formed into two other Battalions for the Eastern Service. That the Western battalion secondly above named be divided and stationed the one half at such Posts and in such numbers as shall be proper for the defence of the Southwestern frontier and the other half at Fort Randolph and such other Posts and in such numbers as shall be proper for the defence of the North Western Frontier.

And in order that proper information may be obtained as to the Posts and Garrisons proper to be established, Genl. Lewis, Wm. Fleming and Wm. Christian Esqrs. are appointed to meet on the last day of August in the present Year at Botetour[t] Court House to concert together what Posts shall be taken on the So. Western frontier, and what number of Men stationed at each of the said posts not exceeding 250 in the whole and report the same to this Board for approbation. And for the same purpose, Sampson Matthews, Abraham Hite, and John Pierce Duvall Esqrs. are appointed to meet on the same day at Shenandoah Court House to concert together what posts shall be taken on the Northwestern Frontier (Fort Randolph to be one) and what number of men stationed at each not exceeding 250 in the whole and report the same to this Board for approbation. Joseph Crockett and James Knox are appointed Lieut. Colos. Commandants, Geo. Walls and Robt. Powell Majors, of the two Western Battalions, Wm. Cherry and Samuel Gill Capts., Thos. Walls and Peter Moor Ensigns in the same Battalions.[1]

The Governor Orders, as he is before advis'd by the Honle. the Council, and further he desires that the Feild Officers of the Counties herein after mentioned, will be pleased to assemble on the summons of their County Lieuts. or other Commanding Officer and recommend to the Executive persons proper for the Commands expressed against the name of their County respectively to wit,

Monongalia	a Capt.	a Lieut.	
Ohio			an Ensign
Kentucky		a Lieut.	
Hampshire	a Capt.	a Lieut.	
Berkley	a Capt.	a Lieut.	
Frederick	a Capt.	a Lieut.	
Shenandoah	a Capt.		an Ensign
Rockingham		a Lieut.	an Ensign
Rockbridge	a Capt.		
Botetourt	a Capt.		an Ensign
Loudoun	a Capt.	a Lieut.	two Ensns.
Fauquier	a Capt.	a Lieut.	an Ensign
Culpeper	a Capt.	a Lieut.	two Ensns.
Orange		a Lieut.	an Ensign
Fairfax	a Capt.		
Prince Wm.	a Capt.		
Louisa		a Lieut.	an Ensign
Goochland		a Lieut.	
Fluvanna		a Lieut.	
Albemarle	a Capt.		an Ensign
Augusta	a Capt.	a Lieut.	an Ensign

Green Brier		a Lieut.
Washington	a Capt.	an Ensign
Montgomery		a Lieut. an Ensign
Henry	a Capt.	an Ensign
Pittsylvania	a Capt.	an Ensign
Bedford	a Capt.	a Lieut. an Ensign
Amherst		a Lieut.
Buckingham		a Lieut.
Cumberland		a Lieut.

He moreover directs that the men to be raised in the Counties of Fairfax, Prince William, Louisa, Goochland, Fluvanna, Albemarle, Augusta and Green Brier and the Officers which shall be appointed on recommendation from the field Officers of those Counties as also one of the Capts. and both the ensigns appointed by the Council as before mentioned shall be allotted for defence of the posts which shall be established on the north Western Frontier and that the men to be raised in the Counties of Washington, Montgomery, Henry, Pittsylvania, Bedford, Amherst, Buckingham and Cumberland and the Officers which shall be appointed on recommendation from the field Officers of those Counties as also one of the Capts. before appointed by the Council shall be allotted for the defence of the posts which shall be established on the So. Western Frontier.

TH: JEFFERSON

MS (WHi); in an unidentified hand, signed by TJ; endorsed by Lyman C. Draper: "To Col. Wm. Fleming, Council Order, July '79. Western battalions & officers. Col. Crockett & Col. Knox. Gen. Lewis, Col. Fleming & Christian, commissioners &c."; this copy was presumably enclosed to Fleming in TJ's letter of 7 Aug. 1779, q.v. Dft (DLC), presumably in the hand of Archibald Blair, clerk of Council, attested by him. There is also a long amendment (Vi) to the Dft, written in TJ's hand, which calls for the deletion of the last five lines of the Dft text and supplies the remainder of the text as given in the copy sent to Fleming (see note 1, below).

THE ACT . . . RAISING A BODY OF TROOPS, passed 26 June 1779 (JHD, May 1779, 1827 edn., p. 65, 69) is in Hening, x, 32-4. See also the following document; TJ to William Preston, 7 Aug.; to John Bowman, 6 Nov. 1779.

1 The text of TJ's amendment to the Dft of this letter (see descriptive note, above) begins here and includes all that follows.

Notes and Plans for Western Defense

[23 July 1779 and after]

Plan for regimenting & stationing the two Western battalions.
Joseph Crocket & James Knox
   Lt. Colonels commandants
George Walls, Robert Powell. Majors.   } appointed by the Council
William Cherry, Samuel Gill. Captains.
Thomas Walls, Peter Moore. Ensigns.

no. of men supposed they will raise	Officers to be recommended by the feild officers of the respective counties			Destination.
	Yohogania.	a Captain.	a Lieutenant.	
40.	Monongalia.	a Captain.	a Lieutenant.	
12.	Ohio.	....	....	an Ensign.
	Kentuckey	....	a Lieutenant.	
41.	Hampshire	a Captain.	a Lieutenant.	
44.	Berkeley	a Captain.	a Lieutenant.	
41.	Frederick.	a Captain.	a Lieutenant.	
37.	Shenandoah.	a Captain.	....	an Ensign.
21.	Rockingham.	....	a Lieutenant.	an Ensign
25.	Rockbridge.	a Captain.		
31.	Botetourt.	a Captain.	....	an Ensign.
76.	Loudoun.	a Captain.	a Lieutenant.	two Ensigns.
45.	Fauquier.	a Captain.	a Lieutenant.	an Ensign.
69.	Culpepper.	a Captain.	a Lieutenant.	two Ensigns.
24.	Orange.	....	a Lieutenant	an Ensign.
506				

NORTH
WESTERN
POSTS

32.	Fairfax	a Captain.		for such stations on Northwestern frontier as shall be recommended by Col. Matthews, Abr. Hite & Duval, who are to meet at Shenandoah C. H. Aug. 31. one of the captains & both ensigns appointed by council to be of this division.
31.	Prince Willm.	a Captain.		
28.	Louisa.	.... a Lieutenant.	an Ensign.	
22.	Goochland.	.... a Lieutenant.		
12.	Fluvanna.	.... a Lieutenant.		
36.	Albemarle	a Captain.	an Ensign.	
61.	Augusta.	a Captain. a Lieutenant.	an Ensign.	
244 | 22.	Greenbriar	.... a Lieutenant.		

SOUTH
WESTERN
POSTS

38.	Washington.	a Captain.	an Ensign.	for such stations on South Western frontier as shall be recommended by Genl. Lewis, Colo. Fleming & Wm. Christian, who are to meet at Botett. C. H. Aug. 31. one of the captains appointed by council to be of this division.
25.	Montgomery.	.... a Lieutenant.	an Ensign.	
32.	Henry.	a Captain.	an Ensign.	
29.	Pittsylvania.	a Captain.	an Ensign.	
61.	Bedford.	a Captain. a Lieutenant.	an Ensign.	
24.	Amherst.	.... a Lieutenant.		
25.	Buckingham.	.... a Lieutenant.		
253 | 19	Cumberland.	.... a Lieutenant.		
497				

Plan for regimenting and stationing one of the Western battalions

Stations on the Ohio	No. of men proposed.	from what counties	Officers from each county	No. supposed each county will raise	Actual strength of the post	Feild officers to be stationed.
Fish creek	75.	Fairfax	a Captain. ...... *an Ensign	32. } 32.	} 75	
		Prince William	a Captain. ...... a Lieutenant.	31. 12 } 43		
		Fluvanna	...... *an Ensign	..		
Little Kanhaway.	75.	Augusta	a Captain. ...... an Ensign	61.	} 75.	
		Louisa.	a Lieutenant. a Lieutenant.	14		
Fort Randolph.	100.	Albemarle	a Captain. ...... an Ensign.	36. } 58.	} 94	Lieut. Col. Commdt. Crocket.
		Green Briar	a Lieutenant.	22		
		Goochland.	*a Captain. a Lieutenant.	..22 } 36		
		Louisa.	an Ensign.	14		
Guiandot[1] Sioto	50.		*a Captain.	11.	50.	
		Bedford		7. } 50.		
		Cumberland		7.		
		Buckingham	a Lieutenant.	7.		
		Montgomery.	an Ensign.	25. }		
Big Sandy river Great Salt lick	50.	Bedford	a Captain. ...... an Ensign	50.	50.	
Licking creek Kentucky	100.	Henry.	a Captain. ...... an Ensign.	32. } 50.	} 103	a Major.
		Buckingham	a Lieutenant.	18.		
		Pittsylvania	a Captain. ...... an Ensign	29. } 53.		
		Amherst.	a Lieutenant.	24		
Martin's cabbin in Powel's valley	50.	Washington	a Captain. ...... an Ensign	38. } 50	50.	
		Cumberland.	a Lieutenant.	12		

Falls of the Ohi...

Pittsburgh		Big Buffalo lick	390.
to Logstown.	18.	Large islands	410.
Beaver cr.	29¼	Little Miamis.	492.
Little do.	42.	Licking cr.	500.
Yellow cr.	52.	Gr. Miamis	527½
Mingstown	71¼	Elephant's bones	560½
Two creeks (Weeling)	72¼	Kentucke riv.	604½
Long creek (Fishg cr.)	123½	Falls of the Ohio	682
end of do.	139	Low country begins	837¾
Muskingham riv.	168.	Beginng of 5 islands	960.
L. Kanhawa riv.	182.¾	Wabache	999¾
Hockhocking riv.	186.	Big rock & cavern	1062½
Gr. Kanhaway	266¼	Shawanis riv.	1094.¾
Yandsto	308.	Cherokee riv.	1107.
B. Sandy cr.	321.	Fort Mansiack	1118
Sioto	366.	Mouth of Ohio	1164.

Lindsay says an intermediate post at Lawrence's creek 54 miles below Sioto and about 75 above Licking creek would be most essential. the principal war path crosses there from the Shawanese Wiandots & Northern Indians in general, and it is the only way a waggon road can be got from Kentucke up the Ohio.

A state of the Western posts & garrisons recommended by Col. Fleming

Augusta	Tyger's valley. on the headwaters of Cheat & the waters of little Canhaway.	60	Augusta	61
	Head of Green bryar - - -	40		
Greenbriar.	Fort Randolph. on Ohio at mouth Gr. Kanhaway	200.		
	Kelly's on the Gr. Kanhaway 20. m. abov. mouth of Elk.		Greenbriar	22
	Little meadows. on waters of Gr. briar abt 30. or 40. mi. from warm springs, more to Northward	100		
	Sinks on Gr. Kanhaway opposite mouth Bluestone.			
Montgomery	Head of Guyandot	100	Montgomery	25
	Culbertson's bottom. at mouth of Bluestone			
Washington	Sandy river	100	Washington	38
	Powel's valley. it is the valley betw. Kentucke & Clinch or			
	Blackmore's. is on Clinch 60. mi. above it's mouth.[2]			

Two tabular MSS and 2 pages of MS notes (DLC); entirely in TJ's hand; undated. In Vi there are 2 other pages of notes and estimates by TJ relative to the raising and stationing of the western battalions; these were written partly on the verso of TJ's amendment to the draft Orders for Defense of the Western Frontier, preceding, and partly on the verso of his draft letter to William Preston, 7 Aug. 1779. Since, with the exception noted below, the notes in Vi include no matter not found in the present Notes and Plans, they are omitted here.

The data here compiled with TJ's customary care obviously implement the Order of Council of 23 July 1779 and are therefore printed under this date. However, substantial portions of them must have been set down during the fall after TJ had received advice from Fleming and Lewis; see their letter to him of 31 Aug. 1779.

[1] This place, like "Big Sandy river" and "Licking creek" below, was enclosed by TJ in rectangular lines in the MS. The significance of the asterisks in this table is not clear, but they may represent the commissions that had been taken up.

[2] At the end of the fragmentary notes in Vi, mentioned in the descriptive note above, TJ wrote: "I am to direct the feild officers of each county for the 1st. Western battalion to recommend officers in proportion to the men they furnish as nearly as can be, so as to make up a compleat set of captains and subalterns for one battalion."

To George Washington

SIR   Williamsburgh July 23d. 1779

Your Letter of the 9th ulto. has been taken under Consideration, and I have now the pleasure to inform Your Excellency, that the report of the Board of Field Officers contain'd therein, meets with the intire approbation of the Executive of this State; I have therefore inclosed four blank Commissions, which it is requested You will be pleased to order to be filled up properly for the respective Officers intitled to them. I have been induced, Sir, to give You this trouble, lest any Mistake shou'd hereafter arise on Account of dating any of the said Commissions. I have the honor to be, with great respect Sir Your Most humble and Obedient Servant,   TH: JEFFERSON

RC (DLC: Washington Papers); in a clerk's hand, signed by TJ. Endorsed: "Govr. Jefferson 23 July 79. Inclg. Blank Commissions. acknd. 10th."

Washington's letter to Governor Henry of 9 June is printed in *Writings*, ed. Fitzpatrick, XV, 244-5. The opinion of THE BOARD OF FIELD OFFICERS, dated 29 May 1779 (Tr, DLC: Washington Papers), enclosed in the letter to Henry, recommended revoking standing commissions and issuing new ones to John Allison, John Lee, William Brent, and Thomas Meriwether to clear up a confusion in rank in the Virginia regiments. The BLANK COMMISSIONS were filled in and given effect in Washington's general orders issued 24 Aug. 1779 (*Writings*, ed. Fitzpatrick, XVI, 168).

To George Washington

SIR   Williamsburg July 23. 1779

I take the liberty of begging leave of your Excellency to forward the enclosed by the first flag which may happen to be going into

New York. They are addressed to [a] good man in distress which I am sure will apologize with you for my asking your intervention. I am with the greatest respect Your Excellencys most obt. & most hbl. servt.,   TH: JEFFERSON

Tr (DLC). Enclosure missing. The enclosure was a letter addressed to a Mr. Battora and was promptly for- warded, but the background and result of the incident are not known (Washington to TJ, 16 Aug. 1779).

From John Jay

SIR   Philadelphia 26th July 1779

I have the honor of transmitting to your Excellency sundry papers respecting the capture of a vessel of Portugal by a Captain Cunningham of the Privateer Phœnix the Property of Carter Braxton Esqr. and others.

Among these papers is a copy of an Act of Congress of the 21st. Inst., for the purpose of doing Justice to the Parties injured, and punishing the Aggressors, to both which Objects it calls your Excellency's Attention.

I have the honor to be with great Respect & Esteem Your Excellency's Most obedt: Servant.

FC (DLC: PCC, No. 14). Enclosures not found.

THE CAPTURE OF A VESSEL OF PORTUGAL: The snow, *Nostra Senhora de Carmo è Santo Antonio*, Capt. John Garcia Duarti (or Duarte) captured by the American privateer *Phoenix*, Capt. Joseph Cunningham, owned by CARTER BRAXTON and others. Congress on 21 July declared this an act of piracy and requested TJ as governor to compel Braxton to pay damages to the master and owners of the Portuguese vessel. The case dragged on for many months. See JCC, XIV, 838-42, 856-9; Edmund Randolph to TJ, 13 Nov.; TJ to Harrison, 23 Nov.; TJ to Huntington, 30 Dec. 1779.

From Edmund Randolph

Philadelphia, 27 July 1779. Detailed account of Wayne's capture of Stony Point on the Hudson, 15 July. Postscript reads: "You will oblige me much, by suggesting to me such reflections, as occur to you on the subject of peace: not on the propriety of making it, if possible, but on terms, necessary for America to insist on."

RC (DLC); 1 p. Printed in part: Conway, *Edmund Randolph*, p. 39-40.

From John Jay

Philadelphia, 28 July 1779. Circular letter to the state executives enclosing resolves of Congress of 23 July respecting, first, the better preservation of buildings belonging to the United States and, second, the delivery of horses, cattle, and other stores owned by the United States to proper officers.

FC (DLC: PCC, No. 14); 2 p. Enclosure (Vi); signed by Charles Thomson; endorsed by TJ; printed in JCC, XIV, 867-9.

From the Board of War, with Reply by John Page

Williamsburg, 30 July 1779. Because of the multiplicity of business, one clerk cannot attend to all the duties the office requires, including keeping a journal. Appointment of a second clerk desired. Signed by James Innes, Clerk. Countersigned by Lt. Gov. John Page: "In Council July 30th. 1779. The Council approves of the reasons above given by the board of War for the appointment of a second Clerk."

Tr in Board of War Letter Book (MiU-C); 2 p.

The Act establishing a Board of War was passed by the legislature 15 May 1779 (see Report of Committee of Revisors, 18 June 1779, Bill No. 8). James Innes, William Nelson, Robert Lawson, Samuel Griffin and James Barron were appointed by the House on 18 June to serve on that Board, and the appointments were confirmed by the Senate on 25 June (JHD, May 1779, 1827 edn., p. 55, 66). For the dispute between TJ and the Board of War over the appointment of a second clerk, see James Innes to Mann Page, 27 Oct. 1779, below.

Henry Hamilton to the Lieutenant Governor and Council of Virginia

GENTLEMEN   Williamsburg Jail July 30th 79

Mr. Pelham having very obligingly procured me the means of addressing you, I take this first opportunity of representing to you the Circumstances and situation of the two Gentlemen at present in confinement along with me.

I am to suppose they have been put in Prison for having acted under my orders. If there be any criminality in those orders Justice demands that I alone should be the sufferer. I therefore make it my request that I may suffer, alone.

The Health of these gentlemen is deeply impaired from the consequences of their restraint, as they are in want even of a change of linnen, highly necessary at this sultry Season.

As to my own Conduct, however misrepresented, I have a confidence (which will I hope hereafter appear well grounded) that it will support itself against the attacks which have been made upon it in this Country, and that it will abide the Test of That Enquiry, which I am to expect it will undergo, whenever, I shall be called upon by those Superiors whose orders I have endeavored to execute with Humanity and Moderation.

Gentlemen! Whatever may be the result of this applica[tion] I shall with patience wait for the day when I may more largely expose to the World the whole tenor of my Conduct, which I have all the reason imaginable to think has been discoloured and misrepresented.

I have the honor to be with all due Respect Gentlemen Your most obedient and very humble Servant, HENRY HAMILTON

FC (Brit. Mus.: Add. MSS 24,320). PELHAM commanded the prison guard. Hamilton in his Report of 1781 says that he addressed this letter to the lieutenant governor (John Page) because he was informed that the governor had left town, but the lieutenant governor "never deign'd an answer" (*George Rogers Clark Papers, 1771-1781*, p. 198-9). On the Hamilton case generally, see TJ to Bland, 8 June 1779, and references there.

From Meriwether Smith

Philadelphia, 30 July 1779. Quotes extracts from memorials to Congress from the French minister, Gérard, dated 26 and 28 July, demanding protection for M. Holker, the French consul, whose efforts to obtain provisions for the King's fleet have been publicly protested and interfered with by a committee of Philadelphia citizens. Smith then adds: "Thus, Sir, you see the good Effects of *Committees for regulating of Prices*; which have occasioned a great deal of Confusion without producing any Good that I can perceive. . . . I will take the Liberty of adding that I have it expressly from the Mouth of Mr. Gerard, that he beleives, from Circumstances the most convincing to him, that they are Instruments in the Hands of designing Men, who are not Friends to the Alliance, and wish to throw all Government into the Hands of the People by those Means, the better to enable them to attain their favourite Purpose."

RC (DLC); 4 p. At foot of text: "(Private)." Endorsed by TJ. Except for the extracts from Gérard's memorials, the text is printed in full in Burnett, *Letters of Members*, IV, No. 447.

The letter relates to the bitter popular protests in Philadelphia against the commercial transactions between M. Holker and Robert Morris, believed to be a cause of soaring commodity prices. Gérard's memorials are printed in Wharton, *Dipl. Corr. Amer. Rev.*, III, 258-60, 264, where will also be found numerous related documents; see also detailed references in Burnett, *Letters of Members*, IV, No. 487, note 2.

To Riedesel

[July 1779]

You mentioned the other day your wish to visit the several medicinal springs in Louisa, Berkeley and Augusta. You will be pleased in this to follow your own inclination, passing from one to another of them by such roads, and making such excursions while on the road or at any of the springs as may be agreeable to yourself, in doing which this shall be your passport, and shall dispense during your tour with so much of any parole you may have given as by prescribing certain limits might have restrained you from visiting these springs. You are perfectly at liberty to take with you such of your family as you chuse to be attended by, who shall be considered as included within the same dispensation. I shall be obliged to you however for their names at a time before you set out for the information of the commanding officer of the garrison, so as that I may be able to guard them from molestation by [writing?] and returning to you a certificate specifying with greater certainty to whom this protection is meant to be extended. A want of personal acquaintance in those quarters puts it out of my power by troubling you with letters to the particular gentlemen in your way [to?] give them an opportunity of paying their respects to you. I flatter myself however that without [. . .] the dispositions of our citizens will concur with my wishes and that they will avail themselves of every occasion of rendering you good offices. I wish you much health and satisfaction in your tour and have the honour to be with great respect.

Dft (DLC). Heavily corrected, but corrections are not noted here. On verso is a draft pass for Capt. Pelnitz [Poellnitz] enabling him to accompany Gen. Riedesel; a fair copy of this pass is printed under date of 25 Aug. 1779, below.

Recipient's name assigned from internal evidence. The date is uncertain. The general officers of the Convention army had expressed their intention of going to the Augusta and Berkeley springs about the middle of July (William Phillips to Theodorick Bland, 4 July 1779, *Bland*

Papers, I, 143; TJ to Riedesel, same date, above); but the passes issued by TJ to Riedesel's aides are dated 25 Aug. (see under that date, below). The several SPRINGS mentioned by TJ are best described in his own *Notes on Virginia*, Query VI (Ford, III, 121-2). Those in Berkeley co. are now in West Virginia; see Carl Bridenbaugh, "Baths and Watering Places in Colonial America," WMQ, 3d ser., III (1946), 160ff.; also Mme. Riedesel's *Letters and Journals*, ed. W. L. Stone, Albany, 1867, p. 157-9.

From the Board of War

[*Williamsburg, 4 Aug. 1779.* Minute in Board of War Journal (Vi) under this date: "This Board do recommend to his excellency the Governour and the honorable the Council, Mr. Theophilus Field as a proper person to be appointed a Lieutenant in the Navy of this Commonwealth." Not located.]

From George Washington

I have been honoured with your Letter of the 17 of July, upon
the case of Lt. Governor Hamilton. This subject, on more mature
consideration, appears to be involved in greater difficulty than I
apprehended. When I first received the proceedings of the Council
upon it, transmitted in Your Excellency's Letter of the 19th of June,
I had no doubt of the propriety of the treatment decreed against Mr.
Hamilton, as being founded in principles of a just retaliation. But,
upon examining the matter more minutely and consulting with several intelligent General Officers it seems to be their opinion that
Mr. Hamilton could not according to the usage of War after his
Capitulation, even in the manner it was made, be subjected to any uncommon severity under that idea. And that the Capitulation placed
him upon a different footing from a mere Prisoner at discretion.
Whether it may be expedient to continue him in his present confinement from motives of policy and to satisfy our people, is a question
I cannot determine; but if it should, I would take the liberty to suggest that it may be proper to publish all the Cruelties he has committed or abetted in a particular manner and the evidence in support
of the charges. That the World, holding his conduct in abhorrence,
may feel and approve the justice of his fate. Indeed, whatever
may be the line of conduct towards him, this may be adviseable. If from the considerations I have mentioned the rigor of his
treatment is mitigated; yet he cannot claim of right upon any
ground, the extensive indulgence which Genl. Philips seems to
expect for him, and I should not hesitate to withhold from him,
thousand priviledges I might allow to Common prisoners. He certainly merits a discrimination and altho the practice of War may
not justify all the measures that have been taken against him, he
may unquestionably without any breach of public faith or the least
shadow of imputation, be confined to a Room. His safe custody will
be an object of great importance. I have the Honor to be with Sentiments of great respect and esteem Yr. Excellencys Most Obed:
Servt.,   G: W.

P.S. Augt: 10. I have received Your Excellency's letter of the 19 of
July with the Blank Commission which I shall [. . .] fill up as the
Council requests.

Dft (DLC: Washington Papers). In   "To His Excellency Governor Jefferson
hand of R. H. Harrison and endorsed: Augt 6: & 10. . . ."

THE PROCEEDINGS OF THE COUNCIL: See the Council's Order, 16 June 1779, above; on the Hamilton case generally, see TJ to Bland, 8 June 1779. TJ's LET-TER acknowledged in the postscript was dated 23, not 19, July, and is printed above.

To Col. William Fleming

SIR   Albemarle Aug. 7. 1779.

The inclosed order will explain to you the general plan adopted for regimenting, officering, and stationing the two Western battalions. We are in hopes you will so far proceed in concert with the other commissioners as that the chain of posts to be recommended may form a complete Western defence, leaving no chasm in the middle. We wish you, when you report the stations proposed, to advise us also to what particular station it will be best for the men of each county respectively to go. As it will not be long before the men ought to be raised according to the directions of the law, it will be proper for the Executive to pay immediate attention to the procuring arms and camp utensils for them. I should therefore be glad if you will be so good as to lay before them a state of the arms in your possession or at any other convenient station: also for your opinion what proportion of the men should be furnished with rifles, where rifles are to be had and on what terms.

I am Sir Your very humble servt.,   TH: JEFFERSON

RC (NN). Endorsed: "Th: Jefferson Aug '79." "Col. Wm. Fleming" is written at the lower left front of the MS in another hand. Enclosure: Orders for Defense of the Western Frontier, 23 July 1779, q.v.

Col. William Fleming, county lieutenant of Botetourt, had been appointed one of three commissioners to superintend defense of the southwestern frontier; see orders dated 23 July, above, and also letter of Fleming and Lewis to TJ, 31 Aug. 1779, below.

To William Preston

SIR   Aug. 7. 1779.

You are desired to call together your feild officers and in conjunction with them to recommend to the Executive a Lieutenant and an Ensign to take command in one of the battalions to be raised for the defence of the Western frontier under an act of the late assembly intit[uled 'an] act for raising a body of troops for the defence of the Commonwealth.' The men to be raised in your county under the same act and the officers to be recommended by you, if appointed, are to hold themselves in readiness on the shortest warning to proceed to such post on the Southwestern frontier, or on such other Western service as shall be ordered by the Executive or the officer who shall be appointed to take command of them. Be pleased to transmit your recommendation to the Executive in Williamsburg by the earliest opportunity you can, and also to report to them from time to time your progress in raising your men. I am Sir Your very humble servt.,   TH: JEFFERSON

RC (Vi); at foot of text: "Montgomery"; addressed in a clerk's hand: "Col. Preston"; endorsed: "8 Sept Came to Hand." Another RC to the county lieutenant of Hampshire (Ben Bloomfield, N.Y., 1950). An undated Dft (Vi) of this letter was written by TJ on the same page with drafts of two other form letters to the lieutenants of all the counties named in the Orders for Defense of the Western Frontiers, 23 July 1779, q.v.; the terms of these three letters vary according to the terms of that order; each draft has a list of counties preceding it, and TJ placed a checkmark above the name of the county when the appropriate form letter was dispatched. On verso of Dft is part of TJ's calculations for estimates of troops for western battalions (see Notes and Plans for Western Defense, 23 July 1779).

From William Fleming

DR. SR.   Philadelphia, 10th Augt. 1779.

I am this moment told by Colo. Melchoir that a young gentleman will set out in half an hour for Charlottesville. By him I have just time to acknowledge the receipt of your favor of the 22d. of July, for which please to accept my thanks.

I find by your observations on the fishery that that matter is not yet properly understood in Virginia, nor have I time at present (were I at full liberty) to undertake the explanation of it—but this you may rely on, that there is not a state in the union, nor I believe, a member in Congress, that would relinquish the right; and Congress soon after I came here, passed a resolution (I believe unanimously) "that in no event should the common right of fishery be given up." Your former observation on the subject was communicated only to one gentleman besides the Virginia delegates.

A vessel arriv'd here yesterday in 17 days from Martinique and brought letters from Mr. Bingham, continental agent at that port, dated 22d. July advising that the day before a packet had arrived there in 31 days from France, with advice that the Spanish Minister at the court of France had declared his master ready to enter into a War with G. Britain, that court having refused the mediation of Spain And that 32 Ships of the line had sailed from Brest to Corunna, where they were to be joined by 20 Spanish ships of the line and proceed immediately to make a descent on Ireland with 25,000 men. The particular regiments for that service with the commander of the expedition are named, but I do not recollect them. My complimts to Mrs. Jefferson. Adieu.

I have procured all the books you wrote for except Erasmus, which is not to be had in this place. They will be sent to Wmsburg. I shall remain here 'til the 15th. of Sept. and hope to be favored with a letter by the gentleman who will be the bearer of this.

I enclose for your amusement Dunlap's paper of yesterday which contains some important news, and much private Scandal.

RC (DLC); unsigned. The hand is that of Fleming (the member of Congress, not the county lieutenant).

TJ's letter to Fleming of 22 July has not been located.

From William Phillips

SIR Colonel Carter's House August 10th. 1779

At the time the troops of Convention quitted New England the Officers, British and German, drew sundry Bills of Exchange in favour of Merchants and others at Boston for which they received the value in Continental Dollars and it so happened that by much the greater part of them were of the emissions which have since been called in by the American Congress which were regularly refused in payment upon the march and after the arrival of the troops of Convention in Virginia.

I gave direction that these dollars should be collected from the Officers, which was done to the amount of twenty thousand Dollars or thereabout, and I writ to the late Governor of Virginia, Mr. Henry, to request he would have the goodness to exchange them for me which, altho' he could not do at that time, he permitted to be received into the publick Treasury and a receipt was given for them to Mr. Geddes the Assistant Paymaster General to the troops of Convention who was going at that time to receive the publick money which had arrived in the Flag of truce.

I am now, Sir, to request the favour of your Excellency to permit Mr. Geddes or some other Officer to go to Williamsburg to receive good and proper Dollars in value for those delivered according to the resolution of the American Congress on that subject. I apprehend the time for repayment is considerably elapsed, and this money being the private property of Officers, for which they are in much distress, urges me to very earnestly solicit your Excellency's interposition.

I have been applied to by the Prisoners of war who were taken with Lieutenant Governor Hamilton for some relief, of which the inclosed copy of a letter will explain, and which I signified to Colonel Bland, requesting his permission for some Officer or non Commissioned Officer being allowed to carry them some money from me which request that Gentleman did not think himself authorised to grant. I should hope, Sir, however, you will have that goodness and allow me to assist those unfortunate men with money and Clothing in the manner your Excellency shall prefer.

I take the liberty to inclose you, Sir, a letter I have received in relation to some other prisoners of War which I refer with the other case to your consideration, not doubting but your humanity will allow me to afford them relief.

I have the honour to be, with great personal respect, Your Excellency's most obedient humble servant,   W Phillips

Tr (Vi), marked "Copy"; contains arithmetical calculations in TJ's hand on second page. The enclosures have not been identified.

On the case of Henry HAMILTON, see TJ to Bland, 8 June 1779, and references there.

From Richard Henry Lee

Menokin, 12 Aug. 1779. Arrival from France at Lee's house of Hezekiah Ford, late secretary to Arthur Lee. The writer has advised Ford not to go on to Congress but to ask a hearing on charges against him before the Virginia Council. Developments in the dispute between Arthur Lee and Silas Deane. If Congress does not publish Arthur Lee's vindication, then the writer will. Franklin's hypocrisy. Expected arrival of John Adams in America, and of La Luzerne, successor to Gérard. Prospects of European recognition of "our independency." Hopes to see TJ in the fall and to show him "all the papers relative to the innocence of Dr. Lee &c. and the wickedness of others." Encloses specimens, "displaying a most wicked plot to injure an honest man" in which Franklin's friends Chaumont and Schweighauser were concerned. Is at a loss what to do with recruits if any are procured under the late Act.

RC (DLC); 4 p. Printed: R. H. Lee, *Letters,* II, 112-15. Enclosures not identified.

On Hezekiah Ford, see Wharton, *Dipl. Corr. Amer. Rev.,* I, 539-40; *Official*

Letters, II, 35, 45. The Deane-Lee feud is summarized in Miller, *Triumph of Freedom,* ch. XVIII; the documentation is in Wharton, II-IV, and Burnett, *Letters of Members,* III-IV.

From William Phillips

Sir   Colonel Carters House August 12th: 1779

I am exceedingly sorry the Weather yesterday prevented me from having the pleasure of seeing you.

I return you my very sincere thanks for the answer to my letter of the day before yesterday. Mr. Geddes shall be sent in a very few days and I shall persue for the several Prisoners of War any mode of conveying money and Clothing to them you shall prefer.

The British Officers intend to perform a Play next Saturday at the Barracks. I shall be extremely happy to have the honour to attend you and Mrs. Jefferson in my Box at the Theatre should you or that Lady be enclined to go.

I am, Sir, with very great personal respect Your most obedient humble Servant,   W Phillips

RC (Lloyd W. Smith, Madison, N.J., 1946). Endorsed by TJ: "W Philips." TJ's answer to Phillips' letter of 10 Aug. has not been found.

From John Jay

Philadelphia, 14 Aug. 1779. Circular to the state executives. The expected arrival of 7,000 troops from Europe and 3,000 from the West Indies as reinforcements to the enemy is a matter of grave concern to Congress and "our Allies." The states are therefore to "prepare for the most immediate, and most vigorous operations" by filling up their battalions and by having the militia ready to march at shortest warning. Encloses a resolve of Congress of 12 Aug. denouncing John Douglass, late commander of the privateer *Hunter*.

FC (DLC: PCC, No. 14); 2 p.; printed in JCC, XIV, 953. Enclosure missing; printed in same, 950-1.

From John Page

Dear Sir   Wmsburg Augt. the 14th. 1779

I believe the Board had no Intention of removing the Convention Troops till you return; and wish to have a full Board, whenever the Propriety of that Measure shall be taken under Consideration, and every Inform[ation] which can be procured on a Subject of such Importance. Ayletts Letter [to] his Deputy was certainly unjustifiable. I will write to him on the Subject as he is not in Town. I hope no Inconvenience will arise from his writing as he did, as he informed us he had Provisions sufficient to last the Troops till the middle of Sepr. The Board approve of the Alteration you mention having made in their Plan. The Council and Board of War are at Loss how to fix on proper Places of Rendezvous for the Western Recruits. We would be glad of such Information on this head as you may be able to collect. I am dr. Sir your most obedt. Servt.,

JOHN PAGE

RC (DLC).

TJ left Williamsburg on 22 July and did not return until late in September; John Page, lieutenant governor, acted in his absence (Account Book for 1779).

Testimonial for Charles Clay

Parish of Saint Anne. Albemarle.   [15 August 1779]

The reverend Charles Clay has been many years rector of this parish, and has been particularly known to me. During the whole course of that time his deportment has been exemplary as became a divine, and his attention to parochial duties unexceptionable. In the earliest stage of the present contest with Great Britain, while the clergy of the established church in general took the adverse side, or kept aloof from the cause of their country, he took a decided and active part with his countrymen, and has continued to prove his whiggism unequivocal, and his attachment to the American cause to be sincere and zealous. As he has some thought of leaving us, I feel myself obliged, in compliance with the common duty of bearing witness to the truth when called on, to give this testimonial of his merit, that it may not be altogether unknown to those with whom he may propose to take up his residence. Given under my hand this 15th. day of August 1779.   TH: JEFFERSON

MS (Mrs. Nannie E. Steele, Cheyenne, Wyo., 1944); photostat in Vi. Entirely in TJ's hand, this is apparently the copy given to Clay.

It is not known whether Clay left Albemarle co. at this time; according to available records he remained the incumbent of St. Anne's Parish until 1785, when he transferred to Manchester Parish, Chesterfield co. (Goodwin, *Colonial Church in Va.*, p. 260). Clay had preached the fast-day sermon in Albemarle in July 1774 and the funeral sermon for TJ's mother in the spring of 1776; TJ organized a subscription for his support after the disestablishment of the Church in 1776, and paid a glowing tribute to Clay's patriotism (see TJ and John Walker to the Inhabitants of St. Anne's Parish, under date of 23 July 1774; TJ's Account Books, 5 Apr. 1777; Subscription to Support a Clergyman in Albemarle County, printed above at end of Feb. 1777). Bishop Meade quotes a fiery passage from one of Clay's patriotic sermons in 1777 (*Old Churches and Families*, II, 49).

From Rev. John Todd

I thank you for the favour you have done me in inclosing me the bill for establishing religious freedom. I had not seen it before—and teased with reports from the Assembly as people affected and were attached, that a general Assessment was to take place; again that the old detested establishment had warm advocates in the house, &c. Long have I been anxious for thoughts of mankind, sacred and civil—much I have feared on this head from the gross ignorance of Some on the Subject, and the little narrow soul'd bigotry and blind ungenerous attachment of others to the peculiarities of parties, which after long contention and disputing and endeavouring to set people right, many fears have attended my hopes of ever seeing the sacred and civil rights of mankind secured to them on a fair and catholic basis.

I have long thought our parties here were more inclin'd to do what is right than acquainted with what was right, that good information was the great thing wanting, to stem the Torrent of bigotry and prejudices that prevailed.

Now I have a peculiar pleasure, sir, in finding that we are blessed with men, some men at and near the helm with clear heads and honest hearts, zealous to bring to light and secure to all good men their rights without partiality. I guess at the author of the bill and I love and esteem the man. The Sentiments are the Sentiments of my heart, and therefore cordially approve them. It is my wish the author of the bill may find men of like Sentiments and abilities enough to pass it safely thro' the Assembly; and extirpate from our country all the rubish of contrary Sentiments: On so ample a basis what advantages may we expect from Church and State? The expulsion of many a Sordid wretch from the Sacred character of the gospel ministry: who Allured by a Sordid bait was only employed in disgracing christianity thro' the course of his ungodly life: and a ready Tool for the State that supported him in every design of Tyranny and oppression, &c.

The State on this free footing will undoubtedly flourish by so open a door for the arts, the Sciences, manufactures, Trade, &c. from all parts of Europe. In Short this is the safe plan for religion, and the best policy for the State.

For my own part, I can chearfully venture all upon it. I believe so large liberty will be abused; but what will not some men abuse? We must eat and drink tho' men abuse both meat and drink. Some are very British and think the Church will Sink: but it

Should be considered, there is a wide difference between religion sinking and some of its miserable Clergy sinking or taking themselves to business fite for them.

Besides the Sure promise of its supream head, that *the gates of hell Shall not prevail against it*; the experience of all the Churches Since *Constantine*, shew the absurdity of Establishments. *Virtue and pure religion* do better without earthly emoluments than with. They are not natural to an earthy soil.

I am also confident that people of all sorts of religion will be the real friends of the State that secures to them their rights religious and civil. I am not affrighted with tolerating papists in the State, but think they will be our true friends, and that people of different Sentiments in religion will be all one in their love and fidelity to the State which secures to them everything dear and valuable: and the more catholick and friendly one to another, and free from *pride* and *envy* when the State rewards all men alike according to their merit: not their hypocritical attachment to the favourite party for bread.

But I am afraid I have Scribbled on too long on a Subject So fruitful.

Wishing Success to the bill, and the certain Security of our Rights on so large and righteous a foundation, and that you may, Sir, long live to fill up the most important places in the State, and be blessed with every kind of happiness in all your tender connexions and public exertions, I have the pleasure of Subscribing my Self, your excellency's most cordial hble Servt,   JNO TODD

P.S. I have thoughts of taking a peep at Kentuckey in a short time. If your excellency has any commands to my Kinsman Col. Jno. Todd you may command Your hble Servt,   J. T.

RC (MoSHi).

Rev. John Todd (d. 1793), a graduate of the College of New Jersey, 1749, succeeded Rev. Samuel Davies as the leading figure in Hanover Presbytery, Va., and long strove for religious liberty in the state; he was uncle of COL. JNO. TODD, of Kentucky, county lieutenant of Illinois at this time, who is mentioned at the close of the present letter (Sprague, *Annals of the American Pulpit*, III, 144, note). THE BILL FOR ESTABLISHING RELIGIOUS FREEDOM is Bill No. 82 in the Report of the Committee of Revisors, submitted to the Assembly 18 June 1779, q.v.

From George Washington

West Point, 16 Aug. 1779. Acknowledges TJ's letter of 23 July enclosing one for Mr. Battora, which will be forwarded by the next flag.

Dft (DLC: Washington Papers); 2 p. Endorsed. Printed: Washington, *Writings*, ed. Fitzpatrick, XVI, 114.

From Peter Penet

Philadelphia August the 17th. 1779

I have received the five copies of the Contract which Your Excellency and the Honorable Council have been pleased to enter into with my Company, and I have fulfilled the necessary formalities to confirm it, waiting for the ratification of many Articles by the General Assembly in the next Session, where Mr. Savarit will attend for that purpose. This Contract, appears to me calculated for the general advantage of both parties; I have however observed in it several ambiguous phrases which make some restrictions without any particular object, which Mr. Savarit would not certainly have agreed to, had they not escaped his notice, or could he have foreseen a subsequent deviation from his demands relative to it. I have also reason to presume that they have been inattentions of the Copyist. As these objects are indifferent to your interest, contrary even to the views of the General Assembly, but are of the greatest consequence to us, I have not the least doubt of their being rectified by Your Excellency and the Honorable Council at the request of Mr. Savarit, and I am confident that they will be ratified by the General Assembly on the explanations which shall be given by Mr. Savarit intrusted with the particulars of this undertaking.

I shall set off in few days for France in order to execute the Commissions of the State, with all the zeal I am capable of, and take the necessary arrangements in consequence of the Contract.

I have the honour to be with a profound respect Your Excellency's Most humble & Most obedient Servan[t],   P. PENET

Translation (Vi); attested by Charles Bellini and endorsed by TJ: "Penet, Windel & co. Papers subsequent to agreement." Enclosed in TJ to Harrison, 30 Oct. 1779, q.v.

THE CONTRACT: See under 22 July 1779, above.

From John Todd, Jr.

Kaskaskia 18th. Augt. 1779

MAY IT PLEASE YOUR EXCELLENCY

By Letters which I had the Honor of writing to you by Col. Slaughter dated early in July, I gave your Excellency a full account of the situations of this Country, since which nothing important has happened here. Col. Clark I suppose is by this time at the Falls of Ohio, and as the Expedition against Detroit is declined, he will probably wait upon you in person. Col. Rogers has arrived from Orleans and will be the Bearer hereof, or send it by the earliest opportunity: I am uneasy in knowing that the Accounts he will render concerning the Quantity as well as the bad Condition of the Goods cannot be satisfactory. Who is to blame in it? The Batteau Masters who brought it up, The Person in whose care it was left at St. Louis or the Conductor of our Stores, or all of them, I cannot determine. The taking and disposing of them was (perhaps necessarily) planned, and in part executed before my Arrival. The Conductor's powers and Instructions were in no part derived from me, nor was he answerable to me for any Malfeazance in Office. Col. Clark will, I doubt not, satisfy you in this matter.

I wish the opportunity by Col. Rogers were safer; I have 15 or 20 thousand Dollars to send down on public account, I have required that all the money of the called in Emissions be sealed up and stopped from circulating, of which I expect we have in the Country, 20 or 30 thousand Dollars more. I have recommended that the People wait some future opportunity more safe for sending it down. The Resolve of Congress bears hard upon Illinois, where the risque is so great. If Congress have not yet made provision for the Reception of the money, I hope your Excellency will think proper to apply to Congress. I shall be cautious that none of the called in Emissions be brought into this Country or Certified which may come from any part of the States, where the Owners had an opportunity of exchanging it.

The visiting the different Districts of my Charge has so engag'd me, that I have not had time to prepare Answers to the Queries delivered me by some Gentlemen of your Honble. Board. As to Indian Grants, it may be necessary immediately to inform you, that they are almost numberless, only four of them are very considerable, the smallest of which will be near 1,000,000 Acres, and the whole between 7 and 8 Millions of Acres. The Grantees all reside in Philadelphia, London, Pensylvania and Virginia and are between 40 and 50, chiefly Merchants. How far it may be proper to make such Contracts binding upon the Indians I cannot say. I submit it to your Excellency. Whether it is not necessary to prevent Indian Grants, by other methods than making void the purchase; I mean by fines, and at the same time to prevent under-fines &c. the making any Settlements within the Charter Bounds of this State, except under certain permissions and Regulations: This I apprehend to be necessary immediately as some Land-Jobbers from the South Side of Ohio, have been making Improvements (as they call them) upon the unpurchas'd Lands on this side the River, and are beyond the reach of punishment from me. With the Arrival of new Adventurers this Summer, the same spirit of Land-Jobbing, begins to breathe here.

I expected to have been prepared to present to your Excellency, some Amendments upon the Form of Government for Illinois, but the present will be attended with no great Inconveniences 'till the Spring Session, when I beg your permission to attend and get a Discharge from an Office, which an unwholsome Air, a distance from my Connexions, a Language not familiar to me, and an impossibility of procuring many of the conveniencies of Life suitable; all tend to render unconfortable.

As to Military Affairs, Col. Clark will offer your Excellency Observations on that Head, which I wish to defer, being more his province.

Perhaps an additional Agent for supplying the Indians with Goods, may be necessary. Mr. Lindsay's Commission was for no more than 10,000 Dollars, which he will soon dispose of, to the Indians and our Soldiers, who I suppose will expect their Cloathing from him.

I have given a Letter of Recommendation as an Agent, to a Gentleman lately from Orleans, who set off with Col. Rogers, Monsr. Perrault.

If an Expedition shou'd be ordered against the Natchees, There cannot be any great dependance placed in the Illinois furnishing more than 100,000 ℔. Flour and supporting the Troops now here; and scarcly any Beef.

I have not heard from Williamsburg since January. I am, with the greatest respect, Your Excellency's most Obedient and very humble Servant, Jno. Todd jl. [jr.]

Tr (Brit. Mus.: Add. MSS 21, 844) of a captured letter.

Todd had been appointed first county lieutenant of Illinois co., 12 Dec. 1778; see Henry to Todd, 12 Dec. 1778, *Official Letters*, i, 341-4. His LETTERS . . . DATED EARLY IN JULY are missing, but were answered by Lt. Gov. Page on 20 Aug. 1779 (same, ii, 35-6).

From John Jay

Philadelphia, 24 Aug. 1779. Circular letter to the state executives enclosing a resolve of Congress of 17 Aug. relative to further provisions for the army.

FC (DLC: PCC, No. 14); 1 p. Enclosure missing; printed in JCC, XIV, 973-4.

Pass for David Geddes

The bearer hereof Mr. Geddes assistant Paymaster general to
the troops of Convention now within this commonwealth, is permitted to pass attended by his servant, from the county of Albemarle by the way of Richmond and of the honourable Archibald
Cary's along such direct roads as he shall chuse, to Williamsburg,
and to return by the same way, using reasonable dispatch, avoiding
communication with all prisoners of war, other than the Convention
troops, and still considering himself as under all the obligations of
his parole other than that which restrains him within certain limits,
with which restraint this passport is meant to dispense so far only
as is herein before expressed. Given under my hand this 25th. day
of August 1779.   TH: J.

MS (DLC). A retained fair copy, so labeled by TJ at foot of text.

Passes for Poellnitz and Others

VIRGINIA TO WIT   [25 August 1779]

The bearer hereof Capt. Pelnitz,[1] one of the aids de camp to
Majr. Gen. Riedesel of the German Convention troops now within
this commonwealth, has permission to pass, attended by his servant,
from the county of Albemarle along such direct roads as he shall
chuse to the Medicinal springs in the county of Berkeley there to
continue with Majr. Genl. Riedesel or his family and to accompany
them on their return to the county of Albemarle, or otherwise, at
his election, to remain there or within ten miles thereof, and to
return to the county of Albemarle by the way he went at any time
before the 1st. day of October next: he still considering himself as
under all the obligations of his parole other than that which restrains him within certain limits, with which restraint this passport is meant to dispense so far only as is herein before expressed.
Given under my hand this 25th. day of Aug.[2] 1779.   TH: J.

MS (DLC); actually a retained fair
copy and so docketed at foot of text by
TJ. Almost identical in text with rough
draft written on verso of TJ's draft letter to Riedesel, printed at end of July
1779, above.

PELNITZ: Julius Ludwig August Poell-
nitz, of the Regiment Riedesel in the
Brunswick corps (Riedesel, *Memoirs*,

Letters and Journals, Albany, 1868, II,
270). The pass actually issued to Burchsdorff (or Burgdorff; see note 1, below),
entirely in TJ's hand, is in the Century
Club, New York City.

[1] TJ added above this name that of
"Mr. Burchsdorff" (probably Lt. Ludwig Traugott Burgdorff, Regiment Rie-

desel), and below it that of "Capt. Cleve" (Friedrich Christian Cleve, Riedesel's adjutant). See Riedesel, *Memoirs*, II, 265, 270, and *passim*.

2 Inserted in square brackets by TJ: "Cleve 2d. September."

From William Phillips

August 25th. 1779.

I have reason to suppose that a Flag of truce may arrive at Hampton Road with passports from General Washington bringing wines, Rum, and other refreshments for the Troops of Convention. I am, therefore, to request your Excellency will have the goodness to allow such Flag of truce entrance into James River and that it may come up as high as the Bermuda Hundred or Warwick, that it be suffered to be unladen there and the Stores lodged in Storehouses and that permission may be granted for hiring waggons to transport the several Articles to the Barracks. Whatever expence may attend the transacting this business shall be defrayed as a private matter by me, it never having been my intention to mix charges of this nature with those of a publick kind, such as provisions, publick transport, &c., &c., and it leads me, Sir, to assure you that the charge for waggons for transporting the officer's baggage and Soldier's Cloathing from Richmond to the Barracks would have been settled by me as a private matter and paid accordingly had not orders been given for the American Quarter Master General's department taking it, and it became by that means a publick account in which I had no authority other than the sending it to His Majesty's Commander in Chief in America. I am particular in this explanation as Colonel Bland has been pleased to signify to me he should not grant any indulgencies to the Troops of Convention from my having refused paying the expence of the Transport I have described. I never did refuse it, for the plainest reasons in the world, the one that the account was never offered me, the other that I had explained to Colonel Harvie my intention of paying all that expence as a private matter, and it will appear, Sir, upon a clear investigation of the affair that Colonel Bland, exclusive of detaining the transport three weeks by forms and ceremonies, directed it into a different channel from that it had been first put into by Colonel Harvie, and it became, by that means, a publick charge and part of Mr. Milligan's Commission to whom I explained myself upon the subject previous to his departure.

I am earnest that you will be so good, Sir, to receive this as the real state of what relates to this particular matter, and I hope you will make the Executive power you are connected with acquainted of it. Be assured, Sir, I am incapable of subterfuge or of a concealed purpose in matters of business, particularly, where payments of money are concerned, but when my plain way of thinking and acting is opposed by particular orders and that, contrary to my wish or intention, matters of a private nature are directed to become publick charges you will, Sir, I am assured, be convinced it has been out of my power to act otherwise than I have done. I disclaim every principle but such as govern men of probity and honour.

Tr (CtY) of an extract, apparently enclosed in a letter not now identifiable. Endorsed: "August 25th. 1779. No. 9. Extract of a letter from Major General Phillips to the Governor of Virginia"; two earlier owners' names follow, the second dated 1846.

From Archibald Cary

DEAR SIR   Richmond 26th. [August] 1779.

I wrote you some time agon and Inclosed some Papers to you from Majr. Hay addressed to General Phillips. Mr. Hay was two days past at my House. I did not see him but he desired Mrs. Cary to Inform me he had received no Answer from Phillips and that the whole party were much distressed. A Few days after I wrote you I received from Williamsburg a letter from Phillips for Hay which Col. Bland had Sent down. In that he Informed Hay, Col. T: M: Randolph had promised to take charge of 4,000 Dollars and Send it to him, but Col: Randolph never received the Money from Phillips. If you think proper to Inform the General of this perhaps he may releive these People as in his Letter he promised.

We have had various Accounts respecting the Action between De Estange and Byron but I question whether we Yet know the Truth. The most Authentick Account at least I judge so, is that De Estange Faild in an attack on St. Lucia, he then Saild for Granade, which he took. Byron found him there, and being to Leeward Indeavourd to come up, in so doing his Fleet was a Good Deal dispersed, which Estange Seeing Bore down on 7 of his Head most Ships and engaged. He Shatterd them very much but took none; Byron Saild to St. Kitts, and was Followd by the Count, who lookd at Him and Saild of, Since which he has not been heard of, but it is Conjecturd he saild for Barbados. This Account we have by one of the State Vessels Arriv'd in a Few days, from Statia 13 days

[75]

passage, with Rum and Salt, &c. We are just told 5 or 6 French Ships with Large Car[goes] are Arriv'd in this State from old France. Since I began this letter Mr. Burk is Come to this place from Philadelphia, I shall see him. Dick Harvey who will deliver this does not go hence before the Morn. If Burk brings any thing of Importance you Shall have it in Continuance.

I have Seen Mr. Burk, the Grand Matter so long and oft debated, the Terms Congress are willing to make peace on, is at length agreed; he is not at Liberty to Say what they be, but thus much he Says, the Southern States prevaild, and unless Spain should have declared, he thinks peace may be had, on just and Honorable Terms. Why Spains declaring should retard it, he thinks to be, that England would not have refused Spains Mediation (which is not Authenticated) unless She had been Sure of Holland. A New Matter is Come out respecting Ar. Lee and Burkinhout [Berkenhout]. The French Minister long Suspecting Lee of Course had Letters Watch'd. After the Former returnd to England, Lee received a letter from him. It had the appearance of haveing been opend. This alarm'd him, and Satanlike he with a Good Grace producd it to the Minister. It had no Name but Lee to[ld] from whom it Came. It prov'd he was with us a Spy, and Inform'd that Honor and Ric[hes] awaited on Individuals. It prov'd a Setteld Corrispondence. He will be recall[ed.] It is thought the Navil affair less Honorable to Britain as the Ships were Equal and in the night their Fleet made the best of their Way. Estange and Barington encount[ered] the latter 10 Shot Through her. It is Said and beleived that the New Englanders have Taken and distroyd the Lodgment of the enemy at Ponobscot and that Sullavan has defeated the Indians. My Compliments to Your Lady and beleive me, Your Affte. Hble Servt.,   ARCHD CARY

Edmond Randolph returnd with Burk.

RC (DLC). Endorsed by TJ.
Cary's earlier letter and its enclosures are missing; one of the enclosures was no doubt Hay's letter to Phillips, 3 July 1779, concerning the distresses of the British prisoners at Chesterfield (*Bland Papers*, II, 12-13). The month omitted in the date line is established from the fact (among others) that BURK (i.e., Thomas Burke), North Carolina delegate, and Edmund RANDOLPH, Virginia delegate, had left Congress between 14 and 16 Aug. (Burnett, *Letters of Members*, IV, lx, lxvi).

From George Washington

West Point August the 26th 1779

Your Excellency I make no doubt has been made fully acquainted with the Ordinance established by Congress by their Act of the 23d of March for regulating the Cloathing department, and recommending the Respective States to appoint State or Sub Cloathiers. I addressed the Other States on this subject on the 22d of May, but deemed the measure unnecessary with respect to Virginia, as a Gentleman had been already appointed to act as such.

I have filled up Two of the Commissions transmitted by Your Excellency for John Allison, Gentn. as Lieutenant Colonel of the 1st State Regiment to rank as such from 1 Jany. 1779 vice Brent promoted and for Thos. Meriwether as Major of the same to rank from same date vice Allison promoted.

Dft (DLC: Washington Papers). In hand of R. H. Harrison and written on the back of Washington's circular letter of this date to ten state executives (whence the date at the head of the present letter is taken).

It is not clear from Harrison's memorandum on the draft whether this communication, addressed exclusively to Gov. Jefferson, preceded, followed, was accompanied by, or was sent instead of the circular letter addressed to the nine other governors. The circular itself, printed in Washington, *Writings*, ed. Fitzpatrick,

XVI, 173-4, points out that "there is but too much reason to apprehend, that unless the Respective States interpose with their exertions, our supplies of this essential Article [clothing] will be very deficient; and that the troops may again experience on this account a part of those distresses which were so severely and injuriously felt in past Stages of the War." Moreover, "the condition of the officers in this respect" is "in many instances painfully distressing." For THE ACT OF THE 23D OF MARCH recommending the appointment of state clothiers, see JCC, XIII, 356-60.

Proceedings of Commissioners to Settle the Pennsylvania-Virginia Boundary

Baltimore, 27-31 Aug. 1779. After presenting their respective powers, the commissioners for Virginia (Rev. James Madison and Rev. Robert Andrews; the third commissioner, Thomas Lewis, was absent) exchanged on the following days with the commissioners for Pennsylvania (George Bryan, Rev. John Ewing, and David Rittenhouse) a series of letters proposing and rejecting various lines as the southern boundary of the state of Pennsylvania beyond Maryland. The agreement at length reached on 31 Aug. and signed by the five commissioners proposed "To extend Mason's and Dixon's line due west five degrees of longitude, to be computed from the river Delaware, for the southern boundary of Pennsylvania, and that a meridian drawn from the western extremity thereof to the northern limit of the said state be the western boundary of Pennsylvania forever."

Tr (DLC); 8 p.; printed in Hening, x, 521-33. (The agreement as signed by all the commissioners, quoted above, is not in Tr, but follows the text of the Proceedings in Hening, x, 533.)

For the background of the Pennsylvania-Virginia boundary controversy, see several documents printed above, especially Virginia and Pennsylvania Delegates to Inhabitants West of Laurel Hill, 25 July 1775, and TJ's Memoranda on the Virginia, Pennsylvania, and Maryland Boundaries, printed under 5 Nov. 1776, with references there. On 18 Dec. 1776 the Virginia Assembly proposed a line yielding the Forks of the Ohio, and for more than two years there was desultory correspondence between the two states on the subject. In Dec. 1778 Virginia proposed that a mixed commission meet to settle the question. Pennsylvania agreed and nominated commissioners on its part. On 24 June 1779 Thomas Lewis, James Madison, and Robert Andrews were appointed commissioners by the Virginia Assembly. See *Penna. Archives*, 1st ser., V-VII, indexes under Virginia;

JHD, Oct. 1777, p. 116; same, Oct. 1778, p. 111-12; same, May 1779, p. 15-16, 35, 64 (all references are to the 1827 reprints); Paullin and Wright, *Atlas*, p. 77-8, and pl. 97G. For further developments on the boundary dispute during TJ's governorship, see Joseph Reed to TJ, 25 Nov.; Huntington to TJ, 30 Dec. 1779; and TJ to Huntington, 9 Feb. 1780.

From the Continental Board of War

[*Philadelphia, before 28 Aug. 1779*. A letter from Lt. Gov. Page to the Continental Board of War, 28 Aug. 1779 (DLC: PCC, No. 147, II; printed in *Official Letters*, II, 37, q.v.) answers a letter from the Board to TJ "on the Subject of the Muskets lately imported into this State for the use of United States." The Board's letter has not been found. For action by Congress on Page's letter, see JCC, XV, 1035-6, 1190-1; see also TJ to Huntington, 16 Dec. 1779. Page's letter was accompanied by a copy of a letter from the Virginia Board of War to the Virginia Executive Council, also dated 28 Aug. 1779 (DLC: PCC, No. 147, II), stating that the 5,000 stands of arms in question had been retained in Virginia by order of the Council.]

From Andrew Lewis and
Col. William Fleming

SIR   Botetourt Augt 31 1779

In compliance with the orders of Council of July the 23d, directing Genl. Lewis, William Fleming and Willm. Christian to meet for the purpose of fixing the Stations proper for the Troops designed for the Defence of the So. western Frontiers, Andrew Lewis and Wm. Fleming accordingly met, and on Maturely considering the order of Council, to Comply therewith, in forming as compleat a Chain of defence as the number of men allotted for that service will admit of. It is our oppinion that at, or as near the following places mentioned as a proper situation will suit: Fifty Men with the usual officers be stationed at or near the Mouth of Guayandot and Fifty Rank and File with the proper Officers at or near the Mouth of Big Sandy River, One hundered Rank and File at or near the Junction of Licking Creek with the Ohio. And Fifty at or near Martins Cabbin in Powels Vally. We imagine these posts occupied on the Ohio, will be of more service for the protection of the Frontier than stationing the Battalion nearer the Inhabitants. The Station at Licking is not a great distance from some Shawnese Town[s] and near the place they generally cross the Ohio. From these Towns, when they make inroads on our Southern Frontiers, it may be a proper Station for the Commandt. of the So. department, as he may at short notice command any detachment from Sandy, or Guandot Stations and Join'd with the Inhabitants of Kentucky conveniently carry on any Offensive Opperations against the Enemy on Meamee or elsewhere to the westward of Licking. The Station we make free to mention to Your Honorable Board in Powels Vally, will not only keep the communication open with Kentucky County but be a defence to the Western Frontier of Washington, by being near the path of the Northern Tribes in their way either to the Cherokees or Chuckamoga Indians. We think it would forward the Service for the Men raised in or near the Frontier Counties to be immediatly employed in the defence thereof and might save unnecessary marching. We therefor recommend it that the 50 Men we mention to be station'd at Guyandot and the 50 at Big Sandy River be raised from Montgomery, Botetourt and Rockbridge Counties. The 100 at Licking from Kentucky, Pitsilvania and Henry Counties and the 50 in Powels Vally from Washington and Bedford. And should the Districts of the above mentioned Counties be insufficient for the Men requir[ed] the Honorable Board may please to make up the deficiencies from Buc[k]ingham, Amherst or other convenient Counties. We beg leave to mention we think 5 Doz falling Axes. Eight broad Axes 1½ Doz Mattocks or Grubing hoes, 1½ Doz Agurs of different sizes. 1 D[oz] drawing knives Eight Fro's and Four Cross cut saws with some Spike Nails tenpenny Do. and Gimblets will be sufficient for the Southern Troops with one Camp kettle that hold two Gallons for each Six Men. These articles cannot be procured here and ought to be provided below. Riffles are the properest fire Arms for our Service. We wish the board to give an encouragement to the Volunteers to furnish themselves with Guns, Shot pouches and Powder horns. You will perceive Sir we have only turnd our Attention to the Southward of the Kanhaway, and make no doubt the Commissioners for the Northern District will establish a post of Communication between Fort Randolph and Green Brier County. We are Sir Your most obt. Humb[le] Servants,   ANDW. LEWIS

WILLM. FLEMING

RC (WHi); in hand of Fleming. Endorsed by Lyman C. Draper: "Col. Wm. Fleming Commissioners—Aug. '79." Addressee assigned from internal evidence.

THE ORDERS OF COUNCIL OF JULY THE 23D, with TJ's further instructions, are printed above under that date and were transmitted to William Fleming and his fellow commissioners for the southwestern frontier (Andrew Lewis, William Christian) in a letter of 7 Aug., q.v. TJ's Notes and Plans for the Western Defense, printed under 23 July 1779, q.v., obviously drew heavily on the advice furnished in the present letter.

From William Phillips

SIR   Colonel Carter's house, Sept. 3d, 1779.

I take the liberty of addressing your excellency, on the subject of a removal of part of the troops of convention, and that, should such a measure take place, it may be left in the option of the British to remain in their present barracks. I form this claim from the British having removed from Cambridge to Rutland, in New England, and that a removal now would be in regular turn given to the Germans. At any rate, sir, I will intercede that, should the British be ordered to move, the officers may still be permitted to remain in the present quarters, and present barracks, which they have hired and built at a great expense, except as follows: one field officer for the whole, one captain, and two subalterns each corps. These it would be proper should reside with the troops wherever they may be.

I will request your interposition in this as belonging to you, sir, and the executive power, to regulate and order. I have the honor to be, &c.

MS not located. Text from *Bland Papers*, II, 21. The original was enclosed in a letter from Phillips to Bland, 8 Sep. 1779 (same, p. 20).

Though there were at this time rumors that a part of the Convention army was to be moved elsewhere in order to solve the supply problem, no action was taken until Oct. 1780 and then for a different reason (A. J. Wall, "The Story of the Convention Army," N.Y. Hist. Soc., *Quart. Bull.*, XI [1927-1928], 94-5.)

To the Board of Trade

[*Williamsburg, 4 Sep. 1779.* Board of Trade Journal (Vi), under 19 Feb. 1780, records that upon application by the Board of Trade for a clarification of the terms under which the agent, commissary of stores, and his assistants were licensed to draw from the public store for their own use, TJ replied, 4 Sep. 1779, that "They have no objection to their drawing Goods out of the public Store, for their own private use, under this restriction, that they pay the current purchase advance of such Goods whether *imported* or *purchased*." Also, that upon a request by the Board of Trade for a further explanation, the Council answered, "that the necessaries to be supplied the Agent, Commissary of Stores and their Assistants were meant to be charged at the same rates which the State paid for Goods at the times the Necessaries were drawn." The letters thus recorded have not been located.]

From George Corbin

[SIR]   [Onancock Accomack Co September 4th 1779]

As I presume the important and weighty affairs of State, have altogether engrossed your Excellency's attention pardon me for calling to your recollection, the exposed situation of this County. Since my last to your Excellency (favored pr. Mr. Js. Henry) which I hope you received, I have had convincing proof that my fears, were not imaginary.

On the 15th. Ulto. a british privateer anchored off Wollops Island a few miles to the Southard of the Fort, sent a boat on shore with four french men, who were personally known to the Islanders, the french men under the character of traiding friends, invites an Island man who was a good pilot on board to recieve some small presents. The invitation being chearfully accepted of the Islander went on board, and as he says, the Captain of the privateer drew from him every circumstance concerning the Fort, and two vessels which lay near the fort, before he undecieved him. That night they landed 30 men marched to the back of the Island and surprised the fort having passed the centinals without interruption, being guided by the Islander. They then maned two crafts and under the character of fishermen rowed along side of the Sloop, being the only one of the two, that was armed, and boarded without opposition, made prize of both, and proceeded immediately down to the bar, but geting a ground with the Sloop. I went on the Island the next day with a party of the Militia took possession of the Fort, which the Enemy left (upon be[ing] informed by the Islander as he says that we were well arm[ed] with field peices) after spiking up the Guns. This was a very unluckly circumstance on our side. The Sloop and Schooner then lay within Musket shot of the fort with a strong tide a head, the wind also a head but very light. We proceeded to unspike the cannon as far as possible, which the Enemy perceiving immediately began to warp their Vessels down by their Anchors and Cables, and before we got one of the Cannon open, they were near a mile distant from the fort. Many guns were fired at them, but did them little damage except cuting some of their small riging. When the tide favoured them they went safe over the bar took the load out of the Schooner being chiefly flour, set her on fire and turned her a drift. The sloop they carried off, tho' they got no booty with the sloop she having just discharged her inward Cargo.

They took eight of the Substitutes in the fort, one of which made his escape. I passed a receipt to the Captain for the other seven, which he accepted of, and discharged them.

If I have done wrong in this particular please advise me. Altho' we were worsted as I have above mentioned together with the loss of a considerable quantity of stock; Yet the Enemy suffered a small loss. The boat they landed in with one Swivell 2 Muskets a brass blunderbus and several other small articles being left at a distance down the Island 6 men chiefly Islanders took and carried into the next Inlet to the Southward. The effects sold for upwards of three hundred pounds, which I agreed should be divided amongst the Captors. The Substitutes are very bare of cloths, and desire to know when they are to recieve their Wages, Cloths, and Blankets. You may depend they suffer much. Your Obedt. Servt.,

GEO. CORB[IN]

RC (Vi). MS mutilated; the date, place and salutation are lacking but have been supplied from CVSP, I, 326-7, where the letter is printed.

George Corbin was acting county lieutenant for Accomac co. (see George Corbin to TJ, 31 May 1781). MY LAST TO YOUR EXCELLENCY: This letter has not been located.

From Arthur Lee

DEAR SIR   Paris Septr. 4th. 1779

It was not until the 7th. of July 1779. that I received your favor of the 9th. of July 1778. It was open, without any seal, nor was the memorandum you mention enclosed. All this I suppose arose from Mr. Anderson and his Vessel having been captured by the Enemy.

It gives me very singular concern, that I was thus deprived of an opportunity of serving you which woud have given me the greatest pleasure. You will have heard of the declaration of Spain against our Enemy. The combined fleets of France and Spain, have been some time in the British Channel searching in vain for that of G. Britain, which has slipt out of the Channel and escaped. As it is not thought prudent to invade England till their fleet is beaten, the troops which were ready for that enterprise are not embarked. Two french frigates have taken the Ardent of 64 Guns, off Plymouth, after a very feeble resistance.

I am waiting here for the orders of Congress, after the very strange and unaccountable proceedings at Philadelphia. Your Letter relative to Mr. Ford, my former Secretary, has been transmitted to me. By this time he must be with you, to answer what he is charged with. I can only assure you, that I never had, nor heard, before, the smallest reason for suspecting him; and that it is impossible any man's conduct, both public and private, coud have been more exemplary and irreproachable while he was here.

The face of the war at present is favorable; but I entreat you to use your influence to prevent this from lulling our Countrymen into a security that may be fatal, or of relaxing their endeavors for putting our Country into the best possible posture of defence. The events of war are always uncertain; but it is most sure, that they who are best prepared for war, make peace upon the most advantageous terms. In my Letter to you of the 22d. of May, I mention that I had then disbursed for the State 86009 ℔. 12s. 12d. Upon casting up the account again, I find I made a great mistake against the State, for in fact what I have advanced is 75176 ℔. 18s. only; of which 71549 ℔. 3s. was out of the public money in my hands and 3627 ℔. 15s. out of my own Pocket. I shall take care to rectify this mistake, if payment shoud have been ordered here, before this reaches you. I have besides, as I have often written, engaged for the payment of the Artillery, Mortars, Bombs &c. and the freight of them, or interest at 6 pr. Cent till the payment can be made. The great seal I have paid for, and it is now in my possession. But it was finished too late to go by the french Minister, and I have had no opportunity since that I coud trust.

I shall be very happy to hear from you; and beg you will be assured, that you cannot do me a greater pleasure than putting it in my power to serve you. I have the honor to be with the greatest esteem Dear Sir, your most obedt. Humbl. Servt., ARTHUR LEE

RC (Vi); endorsed in a clerk's hand. TJ's letter to Arthur Lee of 9 July 1778, its enclosed MEMORANDUM, and the LETTER RELATIVE TO MR. FORD (i.e., Hezekiah Ford) are all missing; so also is Lee's letter to TJ of 22 May 1779. On the attempts to procure a GREAT SEAL for Virginia at this time, see Edward S. Evans, "The Seals of Virginia," published as part of the Virginia State Library *Report* for 1909-1910, p. 36-8.

From John Jay

SIR   Philadelphia 6th: Septr: 1779

You will receive herewith enclosed a copy of an Act of Congress of the 4th: Inst, giving Lieut. Colonel Simms leave of Absence from his Regiment until the 20th Novr. next, together with copies of two letters on that subject, one from General Washington of the 19th: Ulto. the other from Lieut. Coll: Simms of the 2nd: Inst. It is the wish of Congress that Coll: Simms may be enabled to join his Regiment as speedily as possible and that such measures may be taken relative to the business which calls him to Virginia as may render applications for like Indulgences from other officers under similar circumstances unnecessary.

I have the honor to be with great Respect and Esteem Your Excellencys Most Obedient Servant, JOHN JAY

Presid

RC (Vi); endorsed in a clerk's hand. FC (DLC: PCC, No. 14). Enclosures: (1) copy of a resolution of Congress, 4 Sep. (in Vi); printed in JCC, XV, 1025; (2) copy of George Washington to Congress, 19 Aug. 1779; printed in Washington, *Writings*, ed. Fitzpatrick, XVI, 129-30; (3) copy of Lt. Col. Simms to

Congress, 2 Sep. 1779; original in DLC: PCC, No. 78, XX.

Lt. Col. Charles SIMMS, of the 2d Va. Regt., had sought leave in order to survey his bounty lands; besides the references above, see JHD, Oct. 1779, 1827 edn., p. 11; JCC, XIV, 933; XV, 1018.

From Richard Henry Lee

DEAR SIR Menokin Septr. 6. 1779

The Chevalier D'Anmour who will have the honor of delivering you this letter, having been lately appointed Consul of France for this State, as he before was for Maryland, comes now to pay his respects to you. I have had the pleasure of being acquainted with this gentleman since early in the year 1777 and I have found in him the same unshaken attachment to our cause in times of its great depression as others are willing to shew in the day of its prosperity. The goodness of the Chevaliers head is by no means inferior to that of his heart, few men having more knowledge of books and the world than he possesses. It gives me pleasure to introduce such a person to your acquaintance.

I am yours dear Sir with most affectionate respect and esteem,

RICHARD HENRY LEE

RC (DLC).

The CHEVALIER D'ANMOUR: Charles-François D'Anmours, sometimes spelled D'Annemours, was appointed French vice-consul for Virginia, 27 July 1779 (Howard C. Rice, Jr., "French Consular Agents

in the United States," *The Franco-American Review*, I [1937], p. 368-70; JCC, XIV, 899-900; see also TJ to Benjamin Harrison, 23 Nov.; D'Anmours to TJ and enclosure, 7 Nov.; Proclamation concerning Consuls, 30 Dec. 1779).

From the Board of War

War Office Wmsburg Sep. 9th. 1779.

The Board of War have considered the case of Mr. Blunt of Sussex as Stated in a Letter to Colo. Starke, by Captain Edmundson, and have thereupon come to the following resolution. That Mr. Blunt has been forced to Stand the Draft unjustly and illegally, and therefore the Draft so far as it respects him, is not valid: Mr. Blunt having complied fully with the intent and meaning of the Law passed in 1778. by having sent an Able bodied man to serve in the continental army. During the time prescribed by Law, [he] is entitled to the exemption held out by that Law, and not the Substitute who was bribed to serve his country. The one acted in obedience to the Laws of this Commonwealth, the other was governed by mercenary motives. The Substitute is liable to the Draft, Mr. Blunt is exempt from it during the term of one year, to be dated from the time he was discharged; and that the Division out of which he was lately Drafted, ought to furnish another in his room.

JAS INNES

WM NELSON

SAML. GRIFFIN

GEO. LYNE

Tr in Board of War Letter Book (MiU-C).
TJ's answer was delayed until 13 Nov., q.v.

From the Board of Trade

[*Williamsburg*] *10 Sep. 1779.* Dean offers goods at sixty shillings for a livre, the money to be left at the loan office. Although the advance is very high, the pressing need for some of the articles should be considered. Goods are to be delivered at Smithfield and Portsmouth, at the risk of the state, as soon as the bargain is closed. The money will be put in the loan office as soon as it is received. Signed by Whiting, Ambler, and Rose.

RC (CSmH); 1 p. In an unidentified hand at the lower left front of the MS: "At a Conference with the Executive refd. to the Board of Trade Solely."

From the Board of Trade

[*Williamsburg*] *10 Sep. 1779.* Haywood offers 2,000 bushels of salt at £20 per bushel. Without salt it will be difficult to purchase tobacco because of the shortness of the present crop and the amazing depreciation of money. Without tobacco it will be impossible to procure goods. Signed by Whiting, Ambler, and Rose.

RC (CSmH); 1 p. Reply of Council, 11 Sep. 1779, written at bottom of page, expresses the opinion that only the best alum salt can be worth £20 per bushel; that no other can be bartered for tobacco; and £15 is a sufficient price for any other kind. Signed by Lt. Gov. John Page.

From William Phillips

Colonel Carters House Septr: 12th. 1779

Major General Phillips's Compliments wait on Governor Jefferson. He shall be greatly obliged to him to allow the inclosed letter being delivered to Mr: Hamilton.

Major General Phillips incloses a paper rather curious of its kind as a Parole for a Man of Rank merely travelling through a Country by a route he has already used: The letter of permission from Mr. Jefferson for the Major General making a Tour in Virginia was conceived in other terms.

Major General Phillips wishes Mrs. Jefferson and the Governor a pleasant journey to Williamsburgh.

RC (DLC). Enclosures: (1) letter from Phillips to Hamilton, missing; (2) see below.

On 11 Aug. 1779 Gen. Washington wrote Theodorick Bland that "Major General Philips and Major General Baron de Riedesel with his lady, and the Gentlemen composing their respective families, have permission to go into New York on parole. You will be pleased to notify them of this and furnish the Generals with a copy of the inclosed route" (*Writings*, ed. Fitzpatrick, XVI, 82; the permission to go into New York was countermanded while the party was en route; see later letters of Washington in the volume cited and JCC, XV, 1114). Phillips evidently enclosed to TJ a copy of the parole issued at this time to the Convention officers, together with an itinerary from Orange Court House, Va., to Elizabeth Town, N.J., prescribed by Washington and Bland; this document, without date, is in DLC: TJ Papers, 6: 1044-5. TJ's LETTER OF PERMISSION to Phillips has not been found, but its terms were no doubt the same as his letter to Riedesel printed under date of July 1779.

From George Washington

SIR   Head Quarters West Point Septr. 13th. 1779

I have the honor to inclose your Excellency the Copy of a Letter from Mr. Loring British Commissary of Prisoners to our Commissary of prisoners respecting the measures which have been taken in the Care of Lieutenant Governor Hamilton and the enemys intentions of retaliation in Consequence. By this your Excellency will be able to Judge how far it may be expedient to relax in the present treatment of Mr. Hamilton. Colo. Mathews, who will have the honor of delivering this, comes out at the request of the Virginia Officers in Captivity to solicit such indulgence for him and his companions, as will induce the enemy to relinquish the Execution of their threats. I have the honor to be With perfect Respect and Esteem Your Excellencys Most Obedt. Servt.,

G WASHINGTON

FC (DLC: Washington Papers). In hand of Caleb Gibbs and endorsed: "Governor Jefferson 13th: Septr. 1779. . . ." The enclosed letter from Joshua Loring (British commissary of prisoners) to John Beatty (American commissary of prisoners) unfortunately has not been found.

On the Hamilton case generally, see TJ to Bland, 8 June 1779, and references there.

From John Jay

Philadelphia, 14 Sep. 1779. Circular letter to the state executives enclosing resolves of Congress of 21 Aug. relative to an embargo; of 25 Aug. against restrictions on inland trade; and of 10 Sep. for providing clothing for the troops; also a copy of a circular letter from Congress to its constituents concerning finances.

FC (DLC: PCC, No. 14); 1 p. The three resolves and the circular letter (dated 13 Sep. 1779) that were originally enclosed but are now missing are printed in JCC, XIV, 986, 996; XV, 1044-5, 1052-62.

From Richard Henry Lee

DEAR SIR   Chantilly Septr. 20. 1779

I have the honor of inclosing you a letter that Mr. Mazzie formerly sent to me, and which having been mislaid among a number of papers, prevented me from returning to him so soon as he desired. It is at his request that I send it to you. I find by a letter that I received from Philadelphia by the last post, that some person has been representing a part of my letter to you by Mr. Ford in a manner not altogether fair. This freedom with your letter has been taken in your absence. It was by no means intended as a public letter, but written to my friend and tho I am sure there is no sentiment in it that I will disavow, or fact that I did not believe on good ground; yet, if the letters of one friend to another are to be subjected to malicious misrepresentation, there must be an end to all friendly correspondence. And the office of Governor will indeed be a painful pre-eminence if he is necessarily excluded from the communications of his friends. That letter was written when I was from home and no copy of it kept. I shall be greatly obliged to you for a copy of it.

I congratulate you on the accession of Spain to our warfare against great Britain. Without a miracle now, the Tyrant and his *friends* must quickly and humbly sue for peace. Three of our Continental frigates have taken 10 Jamaica men, of which 8 are safely arrived to the eastward with upwards of 5000 hhds. of sugar and rum. This capture will be sufficient to humble the british Merchants like falling ninepins. The loss of the enemies hopes to the west and south are additional circumstances [which?] promise the best consequences.

I am with very affectionate esteem and regard, dear Sir yours sincerely, RICHARD HENRY LEE

RC (DLC). Enclosures not located.
MY LETTER ... BY MR. FORD: Letter of 12 Aug. 1779, q.v.; on its alleged misuse, see Lee to TJ, 13 Oct. 1779.

From George Rogers Clark

DR SIR   Louisville Sepr. 23d 1779

I am happy to find that your Sentiments Respecting a fortification at or near the Mouth of Ohio is so agreable to the Ideas of Every Man of any Judgment in this Department. It is the Spot that ought to be strongly Fortified and all other garisons in the Western Cuntrey dependent on it if the ground would admit of it but the Misfortune is there is not a Acre of Ground nearer the point than four Miles up the Ohio but what is often Ten Feet under water. About twelve Miles below the point their is a beautifull Situation as if by nature designed for a fortification (by every observation that has been taken lays a Quarter of a degree within the State of Virginia). Its Ellevation is Such that a Small Expence would Render it very Strong and of greater advantage than one four Miles up the Ohio. In Case you have one built a few years will prove the propriety of it. It would Amedeately become the key of the whole Trade of the Western Cuntrey and well situated for the Indian department in general. Besides Many Salutary effects it would Render during the War by Awing our Enemies the Chicasaws and the English posts on the Mississippie, the Strength of the Garison ought not to be less than two Hundred men after built, A Hundred Families that might Easily be got to Settle in a Town would be of great advantage in promoting the place. I am Sensible that the Spaniards would be fond to Settle a post of Correspondence opposite to it if the Ground would admit but the Cuntrey on their

Side is so subject to Inundation that its Impossible. For the want of such a post I find it absolutely nessesary to Station an armed Boat at the Point So as to Command the Navigation of Both Rivers to defend our Trading Boats and Stop the great Concourse of Torys and deserters that pass down the River to our Enimies.

The Illinois under its present Circumstances is by no means able to Supply the Troops that you Expect in this department with provitions. As the Crops at St. Vincenes was so Exceedingly bad that upwards of Five Hundred Souls will have to depend on their neighbours for Bread. I Should be exceedingly glad that you would Commission Some person to furnish the Troops in this Quarter with provitions as the greatest part must Come from the Frontiers for the Ensuing year as I cant depend on the Illinois for greater supplys than will be Sufficient for two Hundred and fifty Men. Their is an Easy Conveyance down the Tennessee River and provitions more plenty on holston than the Neighborhood of Pittsburgh. Col. Jno. Campbell who promises to deliver this letter to your Excellency I believe would undertake the task at a moderate Sallery and a Gentleman of undoubted Veracity. But pray Sr. order as much provision down as will Serve the Troops you Intend Sending out at least Six months.

I am Sr. with the Greatest Respect your Hb Servt, G R CLARK

N.B. By my Letters of the 24th of August youl be made acquainted with my late disappointment in my Intended excurtion up the Ouabash. I have now a detachment of about two Hundred and fifty of French Volunteers Indians and a few Regulars on their March to attack a British Post at St. Josephs near Lake Mechigan Commanded by a Lieutenant and party where their is very Considerable Stores deposited for the purpose of Imploying Savages. The party is Commanded by Captn. James Shelby. Their is no doubt of his success as their Rout is such that their is but little probability of the Enemies being apprised of them untill its too late. His orders is to demolish the Fortification and Return with the Stores &c.

I am with Respect   G R C

RC (Brit. Mus.: Add. MSS 21,844); intercepted; endorsed: "Letter from Col. Clark 1779. 23d. Septr. Recd. 24th Novr. Copied." A copy is in Brit. Mus.: Add. MSS 21,757; endorsed: "Mr. Clark's intercepted letter." RC has this note at end of text: "NB. Serjeant Chapman reports that when Mr. Shelby endeavoured to raise his Volonteers they said they had no Shoes and therefore would not go to St. Josephs. At. S: DePeyster."

The fort proposed AT OR NEAR THE MOUTH OF OHIO was erected in the following year and was named Fort Jefferson; see TJ to Joseph Martin, 24 Jan.; to Clark, 29 Jan.; to Walker and Smith, 29 Jan. 1780; also *George Rogers Clark Papers, 1771-1781, passim.* Clark's LETTERS OF THE 24TH OF AUGUST have not been found.

From Richard Henry Lee

Chantilly, 23 Sep. 1779. This letter to be delivered by Messrs. Loyauté and Le Maire. The latter is in unfortunate circumstances. All his private effects are detained on board the ship on which he arrived until the state ratifies the bargain with the house he represents for stores he brought over. His accounts should be quickly settled. Virginia is now well supplied with artillery but lacks the knowledge requisite for its use. Some method should be devised to employ Loyauté for this purpose. His father has been active in procuring the best cannon and artillery stores, and the employment of his son in forming a corps for their use would be an agreeable return to him. Count d'Estaing's fleet of 5,000 men is reported at Charleston.

RC (DLC); 4 p. Addressed to TJ at Williamsburg; "favored by Colo. Loyeauté." Printed: R. H. Lee, *Letters*, II, 153-4.

From William Lee

Sir   Frankfort in Germany Sep. 24th. 1779

His Excellency Governor Henry was pleased in 1777, with the advice of the Council, to appoint me Agent in France for the State of Virginia and in 1778 by the same authority he sent me a power under the State Seal to obtain Arms, Artillery, Ammunition &c. of his Most Christian Majestys Ministers or any other persons to the amount of 2,000,000 of Livres, or to borrow money to that amount to purchase those articles with; Invoices for which were sent by the Governor for the Artillery Arms and Ammunition; by Mr. Smith the State Agent in Virginia for the linnens, Woollens and other merchandize; and by Mr. Webb the Treasurer for paper and printing materials. These Documents came to me last year when I was at Vienna in the Public Service, where I was fortunate enough to prevail with the French Ambassador at that Court, to solicit the Court of Versailles to grant us the Artillery, Arms and Ammunition and I also sent a power to my Brother Mr. Arthur Lee who was then at Paris to solicit the business for me at the Court of Versailles; and to try what cou'd be done in France towards procuring the other Articles. In consequence of these measures there was obtain'd from the French Ministry, Cannon, Mortars, Ball, Bombs &c. to the amount of £219489.7.4, and my Brother advanced the money for the purchase of swords, pick axes, hatchets &c., which with Capt. LeMaires and other expences amounts to about the sum of 45000 Livres. My Brother charter'd vessels to carry these articles to Virginia and I beleive they all were ship'd in the Governor Livingston Capt. Gale and the Hunter Capt. Robins. He also made a contract with Messrs. Penet D'Acosta freres & Compy. of Nantes for several thousand stand of Arms and some other Articles which they contracted to ship from France by the last of Septr. 1778, on the same terms which Mr. John King had agreed to in Octr. 1777, with these Gentlemen under the firm of Jas. Gruel & Co. for sundrie articles for the State. No part of the contract made with Mr. King was ever complyed with, nor was any part of the contract made with my Brother complyed with; which I now think a fortunate circumstance having lately had authentic information that several thousand muskets were in the course of last year sent from Leige to Nantes address'd to a clerk of that house, which were of such a base quality as to cost no more than £5. apeice. I hope none of these gun[s] will ever reach Virginia. Truth obliges me to say, that I have always found this house extremely ready to engage but never so to execute. My Brother has given Governor Henry advice from time to time of his proceedings and now he writes me that he has no more money to advance and the owners of the Ships in which the goods were ship'd are in extreme want of the money for the freight which amounts to about 27000 Livres.

Having no money myself to pay this freight with, we shall be greatly distress'd, unless you are good enough to hasten some remittances either in Bills or American produce which I most earnestly request of your Excellency to have done. 'Tis necessary that I shou'd inform you of what my Brother has before advised Govr. Henry viz, that the French Ministry did last Spring demand payment for the Cannon &c. furnish'd by them, but on its being represented to them that we were utterly unable to make this payment and that the State had not had time to make the necessary remittances, they agreed to wait sometime longer.

I have not received any letters from Congress for a long time but there are some private letters in Europe as I am inform'd which say that Congress has dispensed with my services, therefore my stay in this Country will not be long and when you are pleased to write to me be so good as to put your letter under cover directed A Monsieur, Monsieur Grand Banquier à Paris, if the conveyance is to any part of Spain, Portugal or France; and if the conveyance is by Holland put your Letter under cover directed A Messieurs Messieurs Jean De Neufville & fils negociants Amsterdam. If you remit any produce the Captain shou'd be directed to make the first Port in Europe that he can get to and let him address his Cargoe as follows, giving me notice of his arrival, under cover to Mr.

Grand. At Cadiz to Messrs. Rey & Brandebourg, at Lisbon to Mr. John Henry Dohrman; at Bilboa to Messrs. Guardoqui & fils; at Bordeaux to Mr. John Bondfield, at Nantes to Messrs. Schweighauser & Dobrée, at Amsterdam to Messrs. Jean De Neufville & fils.

As the Enemies Cruizers and Privateers have the Ports of Portugal to run into, they very greatly infest all the bay of Biscay from Gibralter to the English channel, so that it is very difficult indeed to escape them. Therefore I think the risk of being taken wou'd be much less to come round the North of Scotland to Holland or Embden in the Prussian Dominions where they wou'd be well received and find a better market for Tobacco than in France or Spain and cou'd get woollen and linnen goods better in quality and much cheaper. The want of money has prevented the Articles order'd by Mr. Smith, State Agent from being purchased, as well as the paper and printing materials order'd by Mr. Webb the Treasurer, which can only be got in London, for the types he orders cannot be purchased anywhere else in Europe. The first cost of Mr. Webbs order will amount to about £1500 Sterg.

I was last year flatterd with the hopes of obtaining a loan in France for the 2,000,000 Livres, but the large sums borrowed by their own Government from which the lender draws about 9 ℔ ct. interest, disappointed my expectations; tho' if this had not been the case, it cou'd not have been accomplish'd under my power, which only expresses the Governors authority by advice of the Privy Council, without any act of that Council to show its consent; and besides, they conceiv'd that the State cou'd not be bound without some formal Act, or resolution of the whole Legislature. I applyed also in Holland where money abounds and the terms were all agreed upon but when the power was sent, the same objections were made to it that had been made in France and farther—1st. as it specified that the money was to purchase *Arms and ammunition* such a loan cou'd not be negotiated without engaging their Government in a dispute with G. Britain, therefore the power shou'd only have expressed that it was to borrow so much money generally without naming to whom application was to be made for the loan; and after the borrowers had got the money they wou'd be at Liberty to lay it out as they tho't proper. 2dly. they desir'd some clear and certain information, by some public Act, how far any particular state was authorised by the terms and articles of the General association or Union of the 13 United States to borrow money on its own single security. But they rather wish'd to have the guaranty of Congress added to that of the particular State for which the money was borrowed as one State might be conquer'd by, or make some accommodation with G. Britain and the rest remain Independent.

They think themselves justified in this reflection by the history of their own Country, where their first association or union against Spain consisted of 17 Provinces; but 10 of them being conquer'd or seduced by Bribes and solemn contracts and promises which were never kept, submitted to the Tyranny of their old masters and are slaves to this moment, while the other 7 Provinces that were steady and true to themselves remain'd free, independent and happy.

Added to this, they look upon the State of Georgia as sever'd from the General American confederacy, and our Enemies spare no pains to persuade them, that it will be the same case with the Carolinas, Virginia and Maryland.

I have thus given you fully the objections which have been made to the power sent me, that you may take the proper measures to remove them, if the State still continues disposed to attempt a loan in Europe.

I am so far removed from the Port from whence this is to take its departure that I cannot send you any new publications or the public papers and as the Gentleman who is so good as to take charge of this letter is so fully inform'd of the State of Politics in Europe, 'tis unnecessary for me to say a word on that subject: I will therefore only add, that next to a speedy honorable and happy Peace, my most ardent wish is to hear that discord, intrigue and confusion are totally banish'd from America and that Union, harmony and good order prevail in full vigor. I have the Honor to be with the most perfect respect Your Excellencies Most Obliged & Obedient Hble Servant,   W: LEE

RC (Vi). Marked "Copy" at head of text. Addressed: "To His Excellency Thomas Jefferson Esqr. Governor of Virginia at Williamsbg. By favor of Thomas Lee Esqr." Endorsed by a clerk: "Mr. Wm Lee's Letter recd Feby 81. 1779

Septr. 24th. Copy." ("Copy" here probably means "Duplicate.")

MR. SMITH, STATE AGENT: Thomas Smith; see his letter of 22 Oct. 1779, below.

To John Jay

SIR   Williamsburg Sep. 25. 1779.

The various calamities which during the present year have befallen our crops of wheat, have reduced them so very low as to leave us little more than seed for the ensuing year, were it to be solely applied to that purpose. This country is therefore unable to furnish the necessary supplies of flour for the Convention troops, without lessening by so much as should be purchased, the sowing for another crop. I am therefore to submit to you Sir the expediency of ordering your Commissary general to send supplies of this article from the head of Elk or wherever else you may think best, to Richmond. Colo. Aylett informs us they will require about ten thousand barrels for a year's supply. We hope there will be a plenty of forage and of all other articles, necessary for their subsistence, raised within this state. I have the honour to be with great respect Sir Your most obedient & most humble servt.,

TH: JEFFERSON

RC (DLC: PCC, No. 71, I). Addressed: "His Excellency John Jay President of Congress." Endorsed: "Letter from Governor of Virginia Septr. 25. 1779 Read Octr. 7: Referred to the board of War. Supply of Convention Troops."
The Board of War reported on this letter on 18 Oct.; see JCC, XV, 1185, and Pres. Huntington's communication to TJ, 18 Oct. 1779.

Advice of Council respecting Henry Hamilton and Others

IN COUNCIL, *September* 29. 1779.

THE Board having been at no time unmindful of the circumstances attending the confinement of Lieutenant Governour *Hamilton*, Captain *La Mothe*, and *Philip Dejean*, which the personal cruelties of these men, as well as the general conduct of the enemy had constrained them to advise, wishing, and willing to expect that their sufferings may lead them to the practice of humanity should any future turn of fortune in their favour submit to their discretion the fate of their fellow creatures; that it may prove an admonition to others meditating like cruelties, not to confide for impunity in any circumstances of distance or present security; and that it may induce the enemy to reflect what must be painful consequences should a continuation of the same conduct on their part impel us to resort again to severities while such multiplied subjects of retaliation are within our power. Sensible that no impression can be made on the event of the war, by creating vengeance on miserable captives; that the great cause which has animated the two nations against each other is not to be decided by unmanly cruelties, on wretches who have bowed their necks to the power of the victor, but by the exercise of honourable valour in the field. Earnestly hoping that the enemy viewing the subject in the same light, will be contented to abide the event of that mode of decision and spare us the future pain of a second departure from kindness to our captives: Confident that commiseration to our prisoners is the only possible motive to which can be candidly ascribed in the present actual circumstances of the war, the advice we are now about to give: The Board does advise the Governour to send Lieutenant Governour *Hamilton*, Captain *La Mothe*, and *Philip Dejean*, to *Hanover* court-house, there to suffer them to be at large within certain reasonable limits, taking their parole in the usual form: The Governour orders accordingly.

Ordered, that Major ———— *Hay*, be also sent under a like parole to the same place. (A copy)   ARCHIBALD BLAIR, C. C.

Text from *Virginia Gazette* (Dixon & Nicolson), 9 Oct. 1779. A MS file copy, neither very faithful nor very legible, is in DLC. TJ enclosed another copy in his letter to Washington of 1 Oct. 1779.

Judging from the style, this paper was probably drawn up by TJ. On the Hamilton case generally, see TJ to Bland, 8 June, and references there. HAY: Jehu Hay, commissary of Indian affairs at Detroit; captured with Hamilton at Vincennes; appointed Hamilton's successor as lieutenant-governor of Detroit, 1782 (Peckham, *Guide to Manuscript Collections in the Clements Library*, p. 137).

From Samuel Huntington

SIR   Philada 30th Septr 1779

You will receive herewith enclosed a Copy of an Act of Congress of the 29th instant with Copys of the letters refferred to in it reccomending to the Executive of Virginia the stationing of and safe keeping of the Convention Troops in case of invasion and to advise the Board of War of their proceedings.

I have the honour to be with great respect your Excy's most obt & hble Servt,   S. H. President

FC (DLC: PCC, No. 14). Enclosures: see note below.

Samuel Huntington was elected president of Congress, in the room of John Jay, 28 Sep. 1779 (JCC, XV, 1114). The ACT or resolve of 29 Sep. concerning protection of the Convention troops is printed in the same, p. 1126, together with relevant letters from the Virginia delegates and the Board of War, copies of which were enclosed in the present letter to TJ.

Form of Parole Offered to Henry Hamilton

[1 October 1779]

I do promise on my parole of honor that I will not depart out of the limits which shall from time to time be prescribed to me by the

Governor of the Commonwealth of Virginia, or any other person having authority from him to prescribe or alter such limits: that I will not say or do any thing directly or indirectly to the prejudice of the United States of America or any of them: that I will hold no conference with any prisonners of War, other than those fixed at the same quarters with me, but in the presence of such person as the Governor or some one acting by authority from him shall appoint, nor send nor receive any Letter or message nor communicate any Intelligence to or from any person but with the privity and permission of the Governor, or other person authorized by him for that purpose, to whom all Letters or other papers coming to my Hands shall be delivered before their Seals shall be broken or they shall be otherwise opened: And this promise which I make on the faith of a Gentleman shall be binding on me untill I shall be enlarged from my Captivity by Exchange or otherwise with the consent of the Governor of the Commonwealth of Virginia.

Virginia Sct:

Under the faith of the above parole   is discharged from his confinement in the Public Jail, is to prepare himself immediately and to take his departure with such Gentleman as shall be appointed to escort him to Hanover Court House, where he is to continue untill further Orders, not going more than one Mile from the said Court House in any direction.

The County Lieutenant of Hanover has authority to inspect and licence all Letters to and from the said

signd. TH. JEFFERSON

A true Copy of the Original

HENRY HAMILTON

JEHU HAY

Tr (Brit. Mus.: Add. MSS 24,320). Endorsed: "Parole tendered to the Prisoners of War in confinement in the Jail of Williamsburgh Octr 2d. 1779." Another Tr is in DLC.

The date of the endorsement is in error, as is shown by TJ's letter to Washington, 1 Oct., and by Hamilton's own report in 1781, which states that this form of parole was offered on 1 Oct. (*George Rogers Clark Papers, 1771-1781*, p. 202). Hamilton gave this reason for his declining the parole: "As we had suffer'd already from the simple asservations of obscure persons, one of whom John Dodge was known by several Virginia[n]s to be an unprincipled and perjured renegado, and as we had experienced the inhumanity of the executive power, It plainly appeard that this parole was offer'd from no other motive than to lay us open to the malice of the first informer, when we should probably have been imprisoned as before, with the additional Stigma of having broken a parole, which it was next to impossible in all its parts" (same, p. 202-3). Sometime during this year presumably, TJ drafted another form of parole, perhaps used for officers of the Convention army, which is printed at the end of 1779, below. On the Hamilton case generally, see TJ to Bland, 8 June 1779, and references there.

To George Washington

SIR   Williamsburg Oct. 1. 1779

On receipt of your letter of August 6th. during my absence the Council had the irons taken off the prisoners of war. When your advice was asked we meant it should decide with us; and upon my return to Williamsburg the matter was taken up and the enclosed advice given. A parole was formed of which the enclosed is a copy and tendered to the prisoners. They objected to that part of it which restrained them from *saying* any thing to the prejudice of the United States and insisted on freedom of speech. They were in consequence remanded to their confinement in the jail which must be considered as a voluntary one until they can determine with themselves to be inoffensive in word as well as deed. A flag sails hence tomorrow to New York to negociate the exchange of some prisoners. By her I have written to Genl. Phillips on this subject and enclosed to him copies of the within; intending it as an answer to a letter I received from him on the subject of Governor Hamilton. I have the honour to be Sir Your most obedt: & most hbl. servt.,

TH: JEFFERSON

Tr (DLC). Enclosures (also in DLC): copies of Advice of Council, 29 Sep., and Parole offered to Hamilton, 1 Oct. 1779, qq.v.

TJ's letter to GENL. PHILLIPS is dated 2 Oct. 1779. On the Hamilton case generally, see TJ to Bland, 8 June 1779, and references there.

To William Phillips

SIR   Williamsburg Oct. 2. 1779.

I had just concluded what was requisite for the dispatch of the flag by which this comes, and was proceeding to inclose to you the within papers, when your letter of Aug. 20. on the same subject, that of Sep. 4. on the subject of Colo. Bland's conduct, and that of Sep. 15. containing your protest against the stoppage of some money in the Treasury for the transport of stores were put into my hands by post. The two latter I must refer for enquiry and future consideration. As to the first you must excuse me for still declaring that I cannot in the nature of the thing see any difference between a prisoner at discretion and a prisoner on capitulation, other than arises from the express stipulations in the articles; and that as to every circumstance not settled in the capitulation the two species of prisoners are on the same footing. Nor do I find any other distinction authorized by any of those books usually deemed authoritative on questions between nation and nation. I had however hoped that Govr. Hamilton's sufferings and of course this dispute were at length to be ended. The council about three weeks ago had the irons taken from off him, La Mothe and Dejean; and on the 29th. of the last month advised their enlargement on parole as you will see by the inclosed copy from their minutes. A parole was accordingly formed, of which the within is a copy, agreeing in substance with what has been generally signed by captive officers, restraining them from nothing which a man of honour enlarged by parole would do against a country wherein tho' a prisoner he was suffered to be at large.[1] They objected to that part of it which debarred them from *saying* anything to the prejudice of the United states and insisted on 'freedom of speech.' This being inadmissible and they persisting in their refusal to sign the parole, they were remanded to confinement in a room of the jail, without irons as before. In this confinement, which must be considered as a voluntary one they will stay until they can determine within themselves to be inoffensive in word as well as deed, which for their sakes I wish may soon take place, and do most heartily pray that no circumstance may again arise which may interrupt that benevolence to prisoners the want whereof so justly affects both personal and national characters. I wish with equal earnestness that when you shall have become acquainted with the occurrences of the place where this will find you, you may still be able to declare with that truth, from which I know you will not swerve, that 'there cannot be found any example of prisoners of war being loaded with chains, handcuffed and thrown into the common dungeon of a prison.' It would give me real pleasure to know that we had been misinformed on that subject, and to see the present become a contest of generosity as well as valour.

We have heard so many and so different accounts of the fortune of my former neighbor Mazzei, that, if you can with propriety give me certain information of him, you will oblige me.

I am made happy by your kind acceptation of the little attentions and civilities we were able to shew you while in this country. I wish they could have been as great as, in justice I must acknowledge, the propriety of your conduct called for. Your own good sense however would point out to you those circumstances which lessened the comforts of your situation and which could not be removed at our will.

Be pleased to present assurances of my great personal regard to

Majr. Genl. de Riedesel, Madame his lady, as also to Capt. de Geismer and your families, and beleive me to be with much respect Sir Your most obedient & most humble servt., TH: JEFFERSON

RC (MA). Addressed: "Major-General Phillips." The MS has something of the appearance of a corrected draft (the most important correction being noted below), but it is almost certainly the copy sent. Enclosure: Form of Parole, 1 Oct. 1779 (not now with the letter), printed above.

Phillips' letters of 20 Aug. and of 4 and 12 Sep. are all missing.

1 The highly significant words "agreeing . . . at large" were inserted by TJ in a minuscule hand between two lines of the completed letter.

To George Washington

SIR   Williamsburg Oct. 2. 1779.

Just as the letter accompanying this was going off Colo. Mathews arrived on parole from New York by the way of headquarters bringing your Excellencys letter on [t]his subject with that of the British Commissary of prisoners. The subject is of great importance and I must therefore reserve myself to answer after further consideration. Were I to speak from present impressions I should say it was happy for Governor Hamilton that a final determination of his fate was formed before this new information. As the enemy have released Capt. Willing from his irons the Executive of this State will be ind[uced] perhaps not to alter their former opinion. But it is impossible they can be serious in attempting to bully us in this manner. We have too many of their subjects in our power and too much iron to clothe them with and I will add too much resolution to avail ourselves of both to fear their pretended retaliation; however I will do myself the honour of forwarding to your Excellency the ultimate result of council on this subject.

In consequence of the information in the letter from the British commissary of prisoners that no officers of the Virginia line should be exchanged till Governor Hamiltons affairs should be settled we have stopped our flag which was just hoisting anchor with a load, of privates for N. York. I must therefore ask the favor of your Excellency to forward the enclosed by flag when an opportunity offers as I suppose General Phillips will be in N. York before it reaches you. I have the honour to be Sir With the greatest esteem your most obdt. & most hbl. servt.,   TH: JEFFERSON

Tr (DLC). Enclosure: see below. THE LETTER ACCOMPANYING THIS: TJ to Washington, 1 Oct. 1779, q.v. YOUR EXCELLENCYS LETTER: Dated 13

Sep. 1779. The letter of THE BRITISH COMMISSARY OF PRISONERS is missing. THE ENCLOSED: TJ to Phillips, 2 Oct. 1779. On James WILLING, an American agent on the lower Mississippi, taken captive in 1778, see James A. James, *Oliver Pollock*, N.Y. and London, 1937, *passim*. On the Hamilton case generally, see TJ to Bland, 8 June 1779, and references there.

From Samuel Huntington

Philadelphia, 3 Oct. 1779. Enclosing a resolve of Congress of 2 Oct., recommending to the Governor and Council of Maryland "to permit as much bread flour and wheat to be exported for the State of Virginia as the said State may want for its public Supply."

FC (DLC: PCC, No. 14); 1 p. Enclosure missing; printed in JCC, XV, 1137.

This action originated in "a representation from the executive of Virginia, to the executive of Maryland [Thomas Johnson], which was communicated to Congress by the delegates of Maryland" (JCC, XV, 1137); TJ's letter to Gov. Johnson, of uncertain date, is missing.

From George French

SIR   Fredericksburg 5th. Octbr. 1779.

Your Excellency's favour of the 24th. Ulto. came duely to hand, but being from home prevented me from writing you by last Post. Agreeable to Capt. De Curmars request I forwarded his Watch to Colo. Bland on the 20th. August, by Mr. Alexander Downie, and am surprised the Capt. did not receive her before his departure. On Receipt of Your Excellencys Letter I wrote Mr. Downie, if he had not delivered the Watch to Colo. Bland that he would instantly deliver her to him. As the Watchmaker in this place had not proper Instruments he could not repair her, Consequently there is no Charge. If you will take the trouble to write to Colo. Bland I make no doubt but he will deliver the Watch to your order. I am Your Excellencys Mo. Obt. St.,   GEORGE FRENCH

RC (DLC).   TJ's letter of 24 Sep. has not been located. CAPT. DE CURMAR: Doubtless Charles De Klauman (see TJ to De Klauman, 12 June 1779).

From the Board of Trade, with Reply

[Williamsburg] 8-9 Oct. 1779. Transmitting a requisition from the Board of War for the purchase of leather breeches for Maj. Nelson's corps of cavalry. Signed by Ambler and Rose. Below, in TJ's hand: "In council Oct. 9. 1779. There being a sufficiency of deerskins in Richmond for the purpose of this requisition from the board of war it is disapproved. Th: Jefferson."

RC (Vi); 2 p.; requisition of Board of War on recto of leaf; Board of War to TJ, and reply of Council on verso.

From the Board of Trade, with Reply

Board of Trade Octor. 8th 1779.

We tho't it prudent, before Mr. Smith's departure, that he should inform the Board what he expected would be allowed him for his Expences on his intended trip to Europe, that no difficulties might arise with respect to this matter on his return. He has consulted Mr. Beall on the occasion, who it seems lately made the same tour himself, and procured his Opinion, which is herewith submitted to His Excellency in Council. We have only to observe that, as by our Instructions Mr. Smith is to make no stay in France, his Expences there cannot be great.

Mr. Smith will certainly be entitled to have the most comfortable Provision made for him in case he should be so unhappy as to fall into the Enemies Hands: The Honble. Board will therefore be pleased to write such a distinct Letter to Doct. Franklin on this Head, as well as with respect to Soliciting his Interest to obtain his enlargement should he be taken, as they may think proper. Mr. Smith will want Money on his Arrival in France to bear his Expences to, and support him in, Holland, which we hope may be obtained by a Letter to Mr. Penet.
J. AMBLER
DUN: ROSE

Oct. 9. 1779.

The council approves of allowing to Mr. Smith five hundred pounds sterling for the trip and that they draw on Mr. Penett & co. for that sum accordingly.
TH: JEFFERSON

RC (CSmH); autograph authorization by TJ.
See also Thomas Smith to TJ, 22 Oct. 1779; Board of Trade to TJ, 29 Oct. 1779 (first letter of that date from the Board).

To George Mathews

SIR
In Council, Oct. 8. '79.

The proceedings respecting Governor Hamilton and his companions previous to your arrival here you are acquainted with. For your more precise information, I enclose you the advice of Council of June 16th of that of August the 28th. another of Sep: 19th. of the parole tendered them the 1st: instant and of Governor Hamilton's letter of the same day stating his objections in which he persevered: from that time his confinement has become a voluntary one. You delivered us your letters the next day when the post being just setting out much business prevented the Council from taking them into consideration. They have this day attended to them and found their resolution expressed in the enclosed advice bearing date this day. It gives us great pain that any of our countrymen should be cut off from the society of their friends and tenderest connections while it seems as if it was in our means to administer relief. But we trust to their good sense for discerning and their spirit for bearing up against the fallacy of this appearance. Governor Hamilton and his companions were imprisoned and ironed, 1st. In retaliation for cruel treatment of our captive citizens by the Enemy in general. 2d. For the barbarous species of warfare which himself and his savage allies carried on in our Western frontiers. 3d. for particular acts of barbarity of which he himself was personally guilty to some of our citizens in his power. Any one of these charges was sufficient to justify the measures we took. Of the truth of the first yourselves are witnesses. Your situation indeed seems to have been better since you were sent to New York but reflect on what you suffered before that and knew others of your countrymen to suffer and what you know is now suffered by that more unhappy part of them who are still confined on board the prison ships of the Enemy. Proofs of the second charge we have under Hamiltons own hand: And of the third as sacred assurances as human testimony is capable of giving. Humane conduct on our part was found to produce no effect: the contrary therefore was to be tried: If it produces a proper lenity to our citizens in captivity it will have the effect we meant: if it does not we shall return a severity as terrible as universal. If the causes of our rigour against Hamilton were founded in truth that rigour was just and would not give right to the Enemy to commence any new hostilities on their part: and all such new severities are to be considered, not as retaliation but as original and unprovoked. If those causes were not founded on truth they should have denied them. If declining the tribunal of truth and reason they chuse to pervert this into a contest of cruelty and destruction we will contend with them in that line, and measure out misery to those in our power in that multiplied proportion which the advantage of superior numbers enables us to do. We shall think it our particular duty after the information we gather from the papers which have been laid before us to pay very constant attention to your situation and that of your fellow prisoners. We hope that the prudence of the Enemy will be your protection from injury, and we are assured that your regard for the honour of your country would not permit you to wish we should suffer ourselves to be bullied into an acquiescence under every insult and cruelty they may chuse to practice, and a fear to retaliate lest you should be made to experience additional sufferings. Their Officers and soldiers in our hands are pledges for your safety: we are determined to use them as such. Iron will be retaliated by iron but a great multiplication on distinguished objects, prison ships by prison ships and like for like in general. I do not mean by this to cover any officer who has acted or shall act improperly. They say Capt. Willing was guilty of great cruelties at the Natches if so they do right in punishing him. I would use any powers I have for the punishment of any officer of our own who should be guilty of excesses unjustifiable under the usage of civilized nations. However I do not find myself obliged to believe the charge against Capt. Willing to be true on the affirmation of the British commissary because in the next breath he affirms no cruelties have as yet been inflicted on him. Capt. Willing has been in irons.

I beg you to be assured there is nothing consistent with the honour of your country which we shall not at all times be ready to do for the relief of yourself and companions in captivity. We know that ardent spirit and hatred for tyrany which brought you into your present situation will enable you to bear up against it with the firmness which has distinguished you as a soldier, and to look forward with pleasure to the day when events shall take place against which the wounded spirits of your Enemies will find no comfort even from reflections on the most [re]fined of the cruelties with which they have glutted themselves. I am with great respect Your most obedt. & most hbl. servt.,   TH: JEFFERSON

Tr (DLC) of an enclosure in TJ's letter to Washington of 8 Oct. 1779. The several enclosures mentioned are printed under their respective dates.

On the Hamilton case generally, see TJ to Bland, 8 June 1779, and references there; on Mathews, see especially TJ to Mrs. Byrd, 24 Oct. 1779.

Advice of Council concerning Prisoners

In Council Oct. 8. 1779.

The Governor is advised to take proper and effectual measures for knowing from time to time the situation and treatment of our prisoners with the enemy and to extend to theirs with us a like treatment in every circumstance. And also to order to a proper station the prison ship fitted up on recommendation from Congress for the reception and confinement of such prisoners of war as shall be sent to it. ARCH: BLAIR CC

Tr (DLC) of an enclosure in TJ's letter to Washington of 8 Oct. 1779.

To George Washington

SIR   In Council Oct. 8th. 1779

In mine of the second of the present month written in the instant of Colo. Mathews delivery of your letter I informed you what had been done on the subject of Governor Hamilton and his companions previous to that moment. I now enclose you an advice of Council in consequence of the letter you were pleased to enclose me from the British commissary of prisoners with one from Lord Rowden [Rawdon]. Also a copy of my letter to Colo. Mathews enclosing also the papers therein named. The advice of Council to allow the enlargment of the prisoners on their giving a proper parole has not been recalled nor will be I suppose unless something on the part of the enemy should render it necessary. I rather expect however that they will see it thei[r] interest to discontinue this kind of conduct. I am afraid I shall hereafter perhaps be obliged to give your Excellency some trouble in aiding me to obtain information of the future usage of our prisoners. I shall give immediate orders for having in readiness every engine which the Enemy have contrived for the destruction of our unhappy citizens captivated by them. The presentiment of these operations is shocking beyond expression. I pray heaven to avert them: but nothing in this world will do it but a proper conduct in the Enemy. In every event I shall resign myself to the hard necessity under which I shall act. I have the honour to be with great regard and esteem Your Excellency's most obdt. & most hbl. servant,   TH: JEFFERSON

Tr (DLC). Enclosures: Advice of Council concerning Prisoners; TJ to George Mathews, both dated 8 Oct. 1779.
The letters sent by Washington in his letter of 13 Sep. 1779 have not been found. On the Hamilton case generally, see TJ to Bland, 8 June 1779, and references there.

From Samuel Huntington

Philadelphia, 9 Oct. 1779. Circular to the state executives enclosing a resolve of Congress of 6 Oct. for promoting loans.

FC (DLC: PCC, No. 14); 1 p. The enclosure is actually part of the enclosure in the second circular of this date, which follows.

From Samuel Huntington

Philadelphia, 9 Oct. 1779. Circular to the state executives enclosing resolutions relative to Continental finance (see note below); asks promptness in payment and regrets that the state quotas are so large.

RC (Vi); 3 p.; signed: "Samll: Huntington President"; endorsed by a clerk. FC (DLC: PCC, No. 14). Enclosure: copy of a series of resolves of Congress signed by Charles Thomson (Vi): two resolutions of 6 Oct. fixing the additional sum of money for the Continental treasury required by 1 Oct. 1780 at $15,000,000, and encouraging private loans; three resolutions of 7 Oct. requesting state treasurers to make monthly returns of sums transmitted, fixing the state quotas (that of Virginia at $2,500,000), and declaring that this apportionment is not to be regarded as a precedent. These resolves are printed in JCC, XV, 1147-50. They were laid before the House of Delegates on 22 Oct. (TJ to Harrison, 22 Oct.).

From Richard Henry Lee

DEAR SIR   Chantilly October 13. 1779

I am very much obliged to you for your favor of the 28 of September and for the trouble you took in writing a copy of the letter I wrote to you by Mr. Ford. I was well apprized that nothing *in it which is mine* could be made an ill use of, but to remedy this, something not mine, and not in the letter, is substituted for the purpose of misrepresentation. As thus—that "R. H. Lee had written to the Governor of Virginia that Monsieur Gerard was recalled because he opposed Dr. Lee." My expression is "the latter (Gerard) being recalled, it is supposed for his factious support of Deane here." A very proper reason too, and which I verily believe to be true, and which would be as true altho Dr. Lee existed not. It is sufficient that there is no such thing, as is asserted, in my letter, and it serves further to shew that a certain Set neither regard truth or any thing else when opposed to their calumnious bad designs. I beg your pardon my dear Sir for having given you a moments trouble on this occasion. I did not mean to do so, my design was only to prevent in future this mode of misrepresentation, and it is effectually done by your information that writing "private" on the letters intended to be so, would prevent public inspection.

I hope, when the Assembly is preparing a system of law for our future felicity, that they will not neglect that noble and best foundation for public liberty, general diffusion of knowledge, for which you had left with the House so excellent a System. By the last post I am informed from Congress that an Embarkation of Troops from N. York had taken place with Teams &c. supposed for a secret

Southern expedition. In the last Baltimore paper it is said, that a Fleet for the Southward with Troops was returned to N. York. I took this account to mean the embarkation mentioned to me from Congress and that if they had put back, it was in consequence of hearing that Count D'Esteing was upon the Coast. I am satisfied that nothing else but his being here will prevent our being visited this Fall by these Devils (for I can call by no other name Men desperate in evil) from N. York. I wish we were better prepared to meet them. Mr. Le Maire told me that there were 8000 stan[d] of Arms belonging to our State in Nantes. They would be a glorious acquisition if we had them. There is already one Continental frigate in France (the Alliance) another (the Confederacy) will soon be there. Would it not be possible to obtain from Congress an order that one or both of these frigates should bring these Arms over and to Virginia? Such is the tardiness of people to engage in the Military that we have yet obtained but two men in Westmoreland upon both the acts "for raising a body of Troops &c." and that "concerning Officers, Soldiers, Sailors and Marines." The one obtained under the former law is delivered to me and I have prevailed with a Man to find him rations 'til further orders. I think there was in the Gazette some time ago an Advertisement from the Board of war mentioning Urbanna as the place of rendezvous for this County. Would it be proper for me to order these two men there, or wait until we see if more can be obtained? It will be some expence to get the men convoyed thither, and this will be nearly as great for one as for 20. I think that the accession of Spain to our Union must quickly close the Scene with o[ur] enemies. 'Tis merry enough to see how the score is changed already with them—The British kings proclamation to the Wardens of the Cinque ports to be watchful to drive away the Stocks &c. from the Sea coasts as he learns an invasion of the kingdom is meditated. He begins to taste the unpleasantness of that treatment which he has been so long inflicting upon us.

I have the honor to be with particular estee[m,] dear Sir your affectionate friend, RICHARD HENRY LEE

RC (DLC).
TJ's letter to Lee OF THE 28 OF SEPTEMBER has not been found. On the case of MR. FORD, see Lee to TJ, 12 Aug.

and 20 Sep. 1779. TJ's Bill for the more GENERAL DIFFUSION OF KNOWLEDGE is Bill No. 79 in the Report of the Committee of Revisors, submitted 18 June 1779.

To William Preston

Sir   Williamsburg Oct. 15. 1779.

Having heard the disagreeable news of your illness, and that there was a doubt whether you would recover in time to attend to the duties of the commission for settling the Western titles, and the executing that commission being of very great importence, the executive has been induced, considering the great distance and the delays that would occasion, to direct the inclosed commission to be made out. I take the liberty of inclosing it to you, asking the favor of you if you should find yourself unable to proceed on the commission, to deliver it to Mr. McDowell; otherwise to destroy it. I am Sir Your very humble servt.,   TH: JEFFERSON

RC (Vi). Endorsements and memoranda on address leaf in an unidentified hand.

For the appointment of other commissioners for settling western titles see Appointment of Commissioners for Kentucky, 26 June 1779.

To Samuel Huntington

Sir   Williamsburg Oct. 16. 1779.

I take the liberty of troubling your Excellency for some blank letters of marque for use in this state, those we have on hand (forty seven in number) bearing the signature of Mr. Jay your predecessor. I am in hopes a safe opportunity of conveying them may not be long wanting.

I have the honour to be with great respect Your Excellency's Most Obedient & most humble servt.,   TH: JEFFERSON

RC (DLC: PCC, No. 71, I). Addressed in TJ's hand; endorsed: "No. 57 From Govr. Jefferson Octor 16: 79 receivd 25th octor."

To Steuben

Sir   Oct. 16. 1779. Williamsburg.

Your letter on the general subject of the deficiencies in the Virginian quota of troops came to hand yesterday by post: but not attended by Colo. Davis's particular returns as the letter seemed to imply. This particular return is so essential that without it our legislature can do nothing towards supplying the deficiency and as they have just met I think it is important that there should be no failure of furnishing them this necessary information that I take the liberty by the return of post to inform you that no such return came. I hope it will state not only the Virginian regiments heretofore counted as of their quota, but all parts of other corps raised in this state for which we are entitled to credit by a resolution of Congress of Mar. 15. 1779.

I am but lately returned to this town after a considerable recess, during which your letter accompanied by your book of regulations came to hand. This has prevented my taking an earlier opportunity of acknowleging the receipt, which I now do with many thanks for it: and as I purpose to lay it before our assembly during their present session I have no doubt of their availing themselves of it's contents so far as to transfer into their militia law many useful matters from it.

I have the honour to be Sir Your most obedient servt.,

TH: JEFFERSON

RC (NHi). Addressed: "Major General Steubens, Head-quarters." Endorsed: "Mr. Jefferson Oct. 16 1779."

The two letters from Steuben mentioned in this letter have not been located. The BOOK OF REGULATIONS: *Regulations for the Order and Discipline of the Troops of the United States, Part I,* Philadelphia, Styner and Cist, 1779 (Evans 16627; Sabin 91395). TJ transmitted the volume to the House of Delegates on 22 Oct. (TJ to Benjamin Harrison, 22 Oct. 1779).

From Samuel Huntington

SIR   Philada Octr 18th 1779

In answer to your letter of the 25th. Septr last I have the honour of inclosing you an Act of Congress of this day.

The board of War to whom your letter was referr'd apprehend great inconvenience from removing or separating the Convention troops and damage to the public in supplying them with wheat flour in the manner pointed out in your letter. As indian Flour is equally wholesome they must be contented with that unless the Commander in chief of the British Forces will supply them with Wheat flour in the Manner prescrib'd by Congress.

I am Sir your Obedient hble Servant,   S. H. President

FC (DLC: PCC, No. 14).

TJ's LETTER OF THE 25TH SEPTR., q.v., was addressed to John Jay, who was succeeded as president of Congress on 28 Sep. by Samuel Huntington.

From the Board of Trade

[*Williamsburg*] *19 Oct. 1779.* Fifteen hundred additional hogsheads of tobacco have been purchased before a further rise in price, because it is feared that within a year goods may not be purchased for money. Signed by Ambler and Rose. Countersigned: "In Council Oct. 19. 1779. Approved. Th: Jefferson."

RC (CSmH); 1 p.

Parole to Philip Dejean

[*Williamsburg*] *19 Oct. 1779.* Parole accepted and signed by Philip Dejean, prisoner with Henry Hamilton. Identical in text with parole offered to Hamilton and others, printed under date of 1 Oct. 1779, above.

MS (Brit. Mus.: Add. MSS 21,885); in a clerk's hand; 1 p. Signed at foot by TJ.

From Samuel Huntington

Philadelphia, 20 Oct. 1779. Circular to the state executives enclosing a resolve of Congress of this day recommending that Thursday, 9 Dec., be appointed a day of public thanksgiving.

FC (DLC: PCC, No. 14); 1 p. Enclosure not found; printed in JCC, XV, 1191-3.

This letter and enclosure were transmitted to House of Delegates, 6 Nov., read, and ordered to lie on the table (JHD, Oct. 1779, 1827 edn., p. 45); letter of transmittal missing. TJ's Proclamation was issued on 11 Nov. 1779, q.v.

To Benjamin Harrison

SIR   In Council Oct. 22d. 1779

Since the date of my former letter to you, I have received the inclosed resolutions of Congress containing a requisition of additional supplies of money. The General Assembly in considering this Subject will naturally cast their eyes on the funds already provided for the Supply of their public treasury. As a principal branch of these was in some degree under the care and direction of the executive, I mean the proceeds of the estates of British subjects, it becomes my duty to guard the assembly against relying in their calculations for any great and immediate Supplies from hence. Facts have come to our notice which give great reason to believe that the traverse and other pleadings justly allowed by the law for saving the rights of those who have real or probable appearance of right is perverted to frustrate or delay its effects, by being put in on grounds either frivolous or false and by that means throwing the

Subject into a course of legal contestation which under the load of business now on the docquet of the general Court, may not be terminated in the present age. In one instance we are certified by the Clerk of the general Court that the estate is claimed by the Steward, tho' this very man undertook to act as Commissioner of the Estate under the sequestration law by our appointment, and has himself personally rendered annual accounts to us of the proceeds of the estate as the estate of a British Subject. Yet his claim, palpably false as it is, in order to obtain the ceremony of being adjudged so, is to go through all the formalities of regular litigation before the estate can be exposed to Sale. Perhaps the aids expected from this law might still be obtained however, and as perfect justice done to every individual by a legislative provision for determining these pleadings in a speedy way. I thought it my duty to guard the General Assembly against any deception in their expectations from these funds, that no disappointments may accrue in the measures they shall be pleased to adopt.

While on the Subject of Continental demands for supplies from this State I am to inform you Sir of an unfortunate delay in the settlement of the Continental accounts. Immediately on the rising of the General Assembly the Executive proceeded without intermission to put into a course of execution the several things made incumbent on them. It was the 17th. of July before, according to their arrangements, they could proceed to appoint a Commissioner to settle the Continental account. They then appointed a Gentleman fully qualified in every point of view to discharge this duty perfectly. His first Letter, dated three days after the appointment gave us reason to hope he would undertake the charge. Ill health however and other subsequent circumstances obliged him to decline; and the letter notifying that did not come to hand till the 10th. of the last month. Since this no person has been found competent to the business and willing to undertake it. We are in hopes that the more extensive acquaintance of the members of General Assembly may enable them to appoint a person equal to this very difficult business.

A Book of Military institutions written by Major General Steubens and recommended for general use by Congress has been transmitted to me. I take the liberty of depositing it with the General Assembly as on future revisions of their Militia laws they may be able perhaps to extract some useful Matters from it. Or it may be thought worth printing and dispersing among the officers of the militia.

I have the honor to be with the greatest respect Sir Your mo. obedt Hble Servt., Th: Jefferson

RC (Vi). In a clerk's hand; signed and addressed by TJ; endorsed: "Governors Letter October 22d: 1779. Referred to whole on Commonwealth." Enclosures: (1) Resolutions of Congress calling for additional sums of money; see Huntington to TJ, 9 Oct. 1779 (second letter from Huntington of that date). (2) Steuben's *Regulations*, Phila., 1779; see TJ to Steuben, 16 Oct. 1779.

To William Preston

Sir   Williamsburg Oct. 22. 1779.

Mrs. Byrd the other day inclosed to me copies of two entries under your hand, the one for 1000 acres at and near the Lead mines on both sides New river joining Forbes's and Herbert's land including the Mine hill, the other for 1000 acres at the big French Salt lick on the S. W. side of Cumberland river near the mouth of Stone's creek, both made by Colo. Byrd on the 1st. of March 1774 by virtue of Governor's warrants. Under the present land law the original warrants are indispensably necessary to obtain a grant of the lands, to the widow. I must therefore pray the favor of you to contrive me by a very safe hand and as soon as you can, the original warrants, as Mrs. Byrd, unacquainted with these things herself, has desired me to act in this matter for herself and children. I hope this letter will find you in better health than I lately heard you were. I am Dr. Sir with much esteem Your humble servt.,

Th: Jefferson

P.S. Should the change of counties or any other circumstance have put these warrants out of your hands you will oblige me by applying for them to the holder, as the distance will render repeated correspondence so dilatory as to defeat the widow's purpose.

RC (Vi). Endorsed.   On the TWO ENTRIES for land, see TJ to Mrs. Byrd, 24 Oct. 1779; her letter to TJ is missing.

From Thomas Smith

Williamsburg, 22 Oct. 1779. The scheme for a commercial negotiation in Europe has been abandoned after all necessary preparations were made. This decision causes almost ruinous personal consequences to the writer. Begs that an allowance be made as a restitution for disappointment and time. Signed: Thomas Smith. Minute in TJ's hand at foot of text: "In Council Oct. 25. 1779. Referred to the Board of trade to say what will be a proper Compensation. Th: Jefferson."

RC (CSmH).   See Board of Trade to TJ, 8 and 29 Oct. 1779.

From James Mercer

[Before 23 October] 1779

Mr. Mercer's most respectfull Compliments wait on the Governor. The Auditors say that the inclos'd order must have his Name to it before they can issue a Warrant on the treasurer. Mr. Mercer begs pardon for troubling him.

RC (Vi); without date. Addressed: "His Excelly Thos Jefferson." Docketed in a clerk's hand: "James Mercer £150, Octobr. 23d. 1779. On Account"; and in another hand, "Delegate in Congress." TJ used the bottom of the page for his reply. Enclosure not found.

To James Mercer

[Before 23 October 1779]

In the act establishing the board of Auditors the words are that they are authorised and required 'to give warrants on the Treasurer for the payment or advance of wages to our delegates in Congress, debiting each delegate' &c. The Auditors then and not the Governour are to give the warrant, as they will see on turning to the act.

TH: J.

RC (Vi); without salutation or date. Addressed: "Mr. Mercer." Written below the letter from James Mercer to TJ, preceding. The ACT ESTABLISHING THE BOARD OF AUDITORS was passed in the Oct. 1776 session and is in Hening, IX, 245-7.

To Maria Willing Byrd

MADAM   Williamsburg Oct. 24. 1779

Your letter of the last week found me much engaged or it should then have been answered. You were not truly informed as to the purpose for which Colo. Matthews came out of New York. The purpose expressed was that himself should be permitted to remain in Virginia on parole if Lieutt. Colo. Hamilton were permitted to go to New York on parole; and from this it was seen that he was pointed out as a proper exchange for Hamilton, their rank being the same. It was determined that Colo. Hamilton should not go to

New York, and Colo. Matthews was so sensible of the propriety of this that he rather advised it and returned perfectly satisfied. It is beleived that the capture and detention of Hamilton has solely prevented the laying our frontiers in blood this summer which might have been expected from the very extensive combination of Indians he had engaged in his service. I think he will not be exchanged on any terms during the war.

The two surveys which you were pleased to inclose me plats of, I filed in the Registers office. Grants will be made out as soon as the Register can be furnished with authentic evidence to whom the right has passed. If you will be so good as to inclose me a copy of Colo. Byrd's will, from which I suppose Mr. Harvie will see to whom they are devised or any other paper pointing out the title, I will have the grants issued accordingly. The two entries which were inclosed at the same time require a more troublesome process. The original governors warrants must be obtained on which these entries were founded, and on being delivered to the Register he will give other warrants in exchange for them, on which the surveyor will survey the lands entered for, and a grant issue. An opportunity occurring yesterday to Col. Preston the surveyor of Montgomery, I wrote to desire he would inclose to me by a safe hand the original warrants which I take for granted were lodged with him. As soon as I receive them, I will exchange them with the Register for others and do myself the pleasure of inclosing these to you. The copy of these entries is returned to you herin as it can be no further useful till the new warrants are obtained, and I was afraid it might get mislaid among my papers.

Mrs. Jefferson presents her respects to yourself and the young ladies. I am Madam with much respect Your most obedt. humble servt.,   TH: JEFFERSON

MS not located. Printed from a facsimile in William Hayden English, *Conquest of the Country Northwest of the River Ohio*, Indianapolis and Kansas City, 1896, II, 644-5; the original was then owned by Mr. English. Enclosures missing.

Mrs. Byrd's LETTER OF THE LAST WEEK has not been found. On the proposed exchange of MATTHEWS and HAMILTON, see TJ to George Mathews, and TJ to Washington, both dated 8 Oct. 1779. On the TWO ENTRIES for lands filed by Mrs. Byrd, see more details in TJ's letter to William Preston, 22 Oct. 1779.

To Samuel Huntington

SIR   Williamsburg Oct. 24. 1779.

Some time in June I received from Mr. Jay a letter desiring I would have evidence collected on the subject of some Frenchmen who were said to have been murdered in cold blood by the English during their invasion of this commonwealth in the Spring. Several disappointments have retarded this matter much more than I could have wished, tho' we have paid repeated attention to it. I now do myself the honour of inclosing you the depositions taken on that subject, and am with much respect Your most obedient & most humble servt.,   TH: JEFFERSON

RC (DLC: PCC, No. 71, i). Addressed in TJ's hand. Endorsed by Charles Thomson: "Letter from Govr. Jefferson of Virginia Oct 24. 1779 Read Nov 10." Enclosure: Transcript of testimony obtained in Norfolk co. in Sep.-Oct. 1779 from Peter and Mary Brown, John Cherry, and Alexander Bell respecting the killing of certain unnamed Frenchmen in the British raid on Portsmouth in May 1779. At foot of transcript TJ added a statement certifying the attestations signed by James Taylor and William Robinson, justices of the peace, and stating that "the foregoing depositions were taken . . . on my order."

A file copy of the LETTER from Pres. Jay to Gov. Henry, dated 26 May 1779, is in DLC: PCC, No. 14, p. 119; it enclosed a resolve of Congress of 24 May requesting the governor of Virginia to inquire into alleged British atrocities in Virginia (JCC, XIV, 640).

From John Randolph

London. Cannon Coffee House Spring Gardens

DEAR SR   October 25. 1779

The Letters, with which you some considerable Time ago, honourd me, got to Hand; tho', from their appearance, their Contents were known to many, before they reach'd the Person, for whom they were intended. The gloomy Cloud, which hung over our public affairs, and the general Suspicion, which prevail'd at that Time, recommended Caution, and prevented my answering them. But, as Matters *now* are fully understood, and the Ultimatum seems to be fix'd between the contending Parties; if You are not unwilling to read, *I* am under no Apprehension, in delivering my Sentiments to you.

Mr. J. Power, who is just arrived from Virginia, informs me, that you have been lately elected Successor to Mr. Henry, who presided over your Colony for three Years, the utmost successive Time allow'd for holding that office. I must take the Liberty to say, that your Constituents cou'd not have chosen a man of greater abilities to conduct their affairs, than you possess; and permit me to add my Hope, that Futurity may speak as favourably, of your Moderation.

If a Difference in opinion, was a good Ground for an Intermission of Friendship, Mankind might justly be said, to live in a State of Warfare; since the Imperfection of human knowledge, has render'd Mens Minds as various as the Author of their Being, has shap'd their Persons. The Man who condemns another, for thinking differently from himself, sets up his Judgment as the Standard of Conception; wounds the great Liberty we enjoy, of thinking for ourselves; and tyrannizes over the Mind, which Nature intended shoud be free and unconfin'd. *That* Tyrant, I cannot suppose You, to be. The Liberality of Sentiment, which ever distinguish'd you amongst your Acquaintance, when you were upon a Level with them, has not, I hope, forsaken you, since you have been rais'd to a Sphere, which has made you, superior to them. Shou'd I therefore be so unfortunate, as to make any observations, which may not meet with your approbation, for the Honour of your Understanding treat them with Benignity. I will allow you in such Case, to consider them, as the overflowings of a Mind, too zealous in the Cause in which it is engaged; but I must demand of you to admit, that they are the legitimate offspring, of an uncorrupted Heart. But, before you pass Sentence, I shall call on your Candour, to give them a fair Hearing.

When our unhappy Dispute commenc'd, (tho it arose from Circumstances, which left an opening for an honorable accomodation, yet) I saw that it was big with Mischief, and portended Ruin and Desolation, *Somewhere.* I thought that it behov'd me to reflect with the utmost Deliberation, on the Line of Conduct, which I ought to pursue, on so critical an Occasion. I clear'd every avenue to Information, and laid myself open to Conviction, let it come from what Quarter it wou'd. I read with avidity every thing which was publish'd on the Subject, and I put my own Thoughts in Writing, that I might see how they wou'd stand on Paper. I found myself embarrass'd by a thousand Considerations, acting in direct opposition to each other. In this Situation I had no Resource left but to submit myself Solely to the Dictates of my Reason. To that impartial Tribunal I appeal'd. *There* I reciev'd Satisfaction; and from her Decision, I am determin'd never to depart.

> Si fractus illabatur Orbis
> impavidum ferient Ruinæ.

Adversity is a School, in which few Men wish to be educated; yet, it is a Source, from whence the most useful Improvements, may be derived. When the Mind shrinks not from its approach, it offers a Season for Reflection, calls forth the Powers of the Understanding, fixes its Principles, and inspires a Fortitude, which shews the true Dignity of Man. In that School I have been tutor'd; from its

Tuition I have drawn those advantages, and I am unalterably re-solved, that all other Motives shall give Way, to the fullest and most *unequivocal* Enjoyment of them.

The Insults I reciev'd from a People, (whose Interest I always considerd as my own) unrestrain'd by the Influence of Gentlemen of Rank gave me much Uneasiness: But, the unmanly and illiberal Treatment, which the more delicate Part of my Family met with, I confess, fill'd me with the highest Resentment. As there is Nothing which I forget so soon as an Injury; and as animosity never rankles in my Bosom, I have cast the whole into oblivion. There let it lie buried; for Implacability belongs only to the unworthy.

Independance, it is agreed on all Hands, is the fix'd Purpose of your Determination. Annihilation is preferable to a Reunion with Great Britain. To support this desirable End, you have enter'd into an alliance with France and Spain, to reduce the Power of this Country, and make Way for the Glory of America. What Effect this Connection will have on you, or this Kingdom, Time alone can discover; But be it rememberd, that France is perfidious, Spain insignificant, and Great Britain formidable. The united Fleets of the House of Bourbon, lately cover'd the Seas, and paraded off Plym-outh. A Descent was threaten'd, and universally expected. The british Fleet was then in a distant Part of the Channel, and there was nothing remain'd to defend this Kingdom, but the internal Strength and Valour of its Inhabitants. The Space of three Days remov'd the Alarm, by producing a fruitless Departure of this mighty Squadron. Soon after this, the two Fleets came in Sight of each other, (a Great Superiority in Number lying on the Side of the Enemy) and a bloody barrage was expected to follow. The british Fleet in the Evening, form'd themselves into a Line of Battle and brought to, imagining that the combin'd Fleet, wou'd in the Morning begin the attack; but when that Period arriv'd, there was not an Enemy to be seen, from any one of our Ships. On which, our Fleet steer'd into Port, and there has continued unmolested, ever since. Individual Ships have been taken, but all our valuable Fleets from every Quarter of the Globe, for the present Year, are arriv'd in Safety; yet, our Ports are filled with French and Spanish Ships, and our Gaols with their Subjects.

Admiral Keppels Engagement off Brest about 15 Months ago, tho' a shameful one, as he had it in his Power to strike a Decisive Blow and omitted it, was converted into a meer Party Business here. His Conduct is now, very generally reprobated; The City of London has with-held the Golden Box, which the Rage of Party had prepared as a Present for him. Yet ill as he is supposed to have behav'd, the french fleet sustain'd such Damage on that Occasion, that it did not come out of Port, for near a twelve Month after. History does not furnish us with Instances of greater acts of Heroism, than have been exhibited in the Course of the last Summer, in some of our naval Engagements. National Party is very much on the Decline, and the Safety of the State, seems to supersede all other Considerations.

The Junction of the Spaniards, was more a Matter of Joy in England, than a Terror. The fingering of their Gold, is no small object with a commercial People. When his Catholic Majesty's Rescript was deliver'd at St. James's, and became known, instead of lowering, the Stocks immediately took a Rise. And the Dutch, who have already an immense Property in our Funds are still buying in, notwithstanding the various Difficulties, with which this Kingdom is surrounded. This Sir is a Short, but true Narrative of the State of british affairs, in Europe.

It must be confess'd, that the French have gain'd advantages in the West Indies; but it may be observ'd, that they have recover'd no more than what they lost in the last war. In Contests between great Nations, Events must be uncertain, and no Party can expect an uninterrupted Series of Success. Disappointments some times beget Exertions, which may give a new Face to Affairs. When the Troops, which are to be sent for the Protection of our Island, arrive, and the ships are on float, which the succeeding Spring will produce, these will unfold to us, Truths, about which, we at present, may form very different Ideas. The French may boast of their Prowess in Destaings Engagement with Barrington, but few think here, that the Glory of the british Navy was in any Degree diminish'd in that Encounter.

How far the French have been useful to you in Amer[ica], you must be better qualified to determine, than myself: Yet, I cannot avoid expressing my Wish, that you had never enterd into any Engagements with them. They are a People cover'd with Guile, and their Religion countenances the Practice of it, on all of a different Persuasion. They are educated in an Aversion to the English, and hold our Constitution in the utmost Detestation. They have the Art to insinuate, and the Wickedness to betray when they gain an admittance. Laws, they have none but such as are prescrib'd by the Will of their Prince. This is their only Legislature. They know your Coast, are acquainted with your Manners, and no Doubt have made Establishments amongst You. A Footing in the Northern

Provinces, is what they most devoutly wish to obtain. As a Means to effect their Purpose, they have sufferd you to run in Debt to them, and as a Security for the Payment of it, they say that your Lands are answerable. If you are not able to satisfy their Demands, how will you have it in Your Power to frustrate this Claim? But if you are able to discharge the Debt, how will you recompense them, for the Services, which they will urge that they have renderd to you. Your Trade is of no Consequence, it is not an object with them. Nothing but a Partition of your Country will silence them. When that happens, you may bid adieu to all social Happiness; the little finger of France will be more burthensome to you, than the whole weight of George the 3d. his Lords and Commons. Can it be imagin'd that a Prince, who is a Tyrant in his own Dominions, can be a Friend to the Rights and Priviledges of another People? Can it be Policy in him to waste his Blood and Treasure, in reducing one Rival, in order to raise another, more formidable perhaps, than his ancient Competitors? Your good Sense I am persuaded, will not suffer You to cherish such an opinion, and you cannot be so wanting in Discernment, as not to see the base Designs of this treacherous Nation. If France engaged in this Quarrel, for no other Purpose, than to fight your Battles, and vindicate your injured Rights, her Generosity will lead her to confer all the Benefit of her Conquests on you. When you become invested with the Possession of their acquisitions, you may then believe them to be your Friends; but until that happens, you ought to consider their Designs as dangerous, and not suffer yourselves to be deciev'd by such an artful and despotic People. But let us suppose in theory, what, facts I am convinced will not verify, that the Powers now contending with G. Britain are too great for it to withstand. What do you imagine will be the Sentiments of the other States of Europe on this Subject? These Potentates stand in such a Relation to each other, that as a Security to the whole, a Ballance of Power must be preserv'd amongst them. G. Britain has always held that Ballance. How dangerous a Neighbour would France become, if her principal opponent, and the great Arbiter of Europe shou'd be overwhelm'd? The Empress of Russia sees with a jealous Eye, the Strides which the french are taking towards universal Monarchy. The King of Prussia is too old a Soldier, to suffer a Rival to strengthen himself, on the Ruins of an old and natural ally. The Dutch are governd too much by their Interest, to see it in Danger, and never to make an Effort to preserve it. The Danes are the fast Friends of England. All these Nations wou'd have taken a decided Part long before this, had the Situation of G. Britain made it necessary: But the Truth is, our Councils are as vigorous, our Resources as great and the national Firmness as inflexible, as they have ever been, even in the most flourishing Periods recorded in the History of this Country. If you regard the assertions of a set of Men, who are distinguish'd by the appellation of *the Opposition*, you must I own form a different opinion, from that which I have endeavour'd to inculcate. They will tell you that the Glory of England is pass'd away, its Treasures exhausted, and that the Kingdom stands on the Brink of inevitable Destruction, owing to the Weakness and Wickedness of Administration. Believe not, my Friend, such Prophets. The Luxury of this Nation, and of Course its Expences, are unbounded. These Excesses must unavoidably make Mankind necessitous. The Department of a Minister is lucrative and alluring. The King, in order to silence the Clamour of Party, having frequently chang'd his Servants, has by this Means excited an Idea, that Noise will always procure a Removal of the Ministry. It is for this Reason, that they who have a Chance for the Succession, ring such alarms thro the Nation, in order to throw an odium on them, and get them out of their Places; yet these very People who are the Authors of so much Turbulence, don't think as they speak. Some join in the Cry; others suspend their opinions, till they recieve more convincing Proofs; and a third, thinking that Government ought to be supported strengthen as far as they can, the Hands of their Rulers. But still, the great Machine moves on, the Ministry Keep their Places, and look as if their Possession would be of long Duration. But a Change wou'd be of little Service to the Nation; for if it silenc'd one Party, it wou'd open the Mouth of another; and the Kingdom be just in the same Situation that it is in at this Time, and has been for many Years past.

If you form an opinion of our public affairs, by the Picture which is drawn of them in our daily Exhibitions, I acknowledge, that you must concieve my account of them to be, chimerical. But whoever wishes to avoid Error, must steer clear of an english Newspaper. There are of daily Papers publish'd in the Year, 27. Millions: The Types, the Ink, the Paper and a Stamp &c. distinctly pay a Duty to Government. Judge then, what a Revenue these Publications must produce. It is for this Reason that Ministry throw no Impediment in their Way; for punishing the Libels they contain, wou'd reduce their Number, and lessen of Course, the Emoluments arising from them. I have often thought, that the Toleration of such indecent Compositions, was a Reflection on Government, but it is a Maxim in England, that as soon as an Evil produces Good, it ceases to be an Evil.

The short Representation of the british affairs, which I have given you above, is intended to prepare you, for one important Question, momentous not only to America, and Great Britain, but also to Europe in General: Wou'd it not be prudent, to rescind your Declaration of Independance, be happily reunited to your ancient and natural Friend, and enjoy a Peace, which I most religiously think would pass all Understanding? I can venture to assure you, that your Independance, will never be acknowledg'd by the Legislative *Authority* of this Kingdom: The Nation would not agree to such a Concession; and your suppos'd Friends, who are so lavish in your Praise on other Occasions, wou'd on this, be against you. Every Immunity, which you can reasonably ask for, will be granted to you; the rapacious Hand of Taxation will never reach you. Your Laws and Regulations will be establish'd on the solid Basis of the british Constitution; and your Happiness will be attended to, with all the Solicitude, which belongs to an affectionate Parent. Reflect, I beseach you, on what I have said. Let not the flattering Possession of Power, which may be wrested from you in a Moment, stand in *Competition* with the Good of your Country, which you have now an opportunity of making, as lasting as Time itself. But if you still persist in your Resolution, never to listen to the voice of Reconciliation, Remember, that I, who know your Situation, and wish you every Degree of Happiness, tell you, that what you take to be the End, will be only the Beginning of your political Misfortunes.

I must now put a Period to a long Letter, the writing of which, is a very unusual Labour to me. How you may recieve it I know not. Be that as it will, I shall enjoy one Consolation, which is, a quiet Conscience. I see such Determination in Government, to proceed to the last Extremity with you; such a Disposition in the Powers of Europe to go to War; and such Mischiefs hovering over America, that I shou'd think myself an undutiful Son, and criminally guilty, if I did not impart to you, the Distress I feel on your Account. Let our opinions vary as they will, I shall nevertheless retain a very sincere Regard for you. How far your Politics may be blended with your Friendships, I cannot tell; but as I have ever preserv'd my esteem from improper Mixtures, I shall subscribe myself now as I always have done, Dr Sr, Your very affectionate Friend & humble Servt,   JOHN RANDOLPH

RC (ViW). Addressed: "His Excellency Thomas Jefferson Esqr. Governor of Virginia." The letter quite evidently never reached the addressee, for accompanying it is a memorandum reading: "I found this letter amongst the papers of Sir Edward Walpole K B. . . . J W Keppel April 23d 1840." Sir Edward Walpole (1706-1784) was the brother of Horace Walpole, the celebrated letter writer; his natural daughter Laura married the Hon. Rev. Frederick Keppel, later Bishop of Exeter, son of the 2d Earl of Albemarle (Walpole, *Letters*, ed. Toynbee, XVI, xxiii). How the letter came into Sir Edward's hands and stayed among his papers, is not explained. In 1912 it was purchased from

Maggs Bros. by Leonard L. Mackall, who published it, with valuable introductory comment, in Amer. Antiq. Soc., *Procs.*, new ser., XXX (1921), 17-31.

THE LETTERS . . . GOT TO HAND: The last letter now known to have been written by TJ to John Randolph is dated 29 Nov. 1775, q.v.; no reply is on record. MR. J. POWER: Probably Jack Power, lawyer, of Tappahannock, Essex co., Va., lawyer and loyalist, who left Virginia in June and reached London in Oct. 1779 (note by Mackall in the article cited above).

To Francis Taylor

SIR   In Council Oct. 25. 1779

When you wrote your letter of the 13th. inst. my last to you was on the road. I now send you one Captain's and three Ensigns commissions, so they will stand thus.

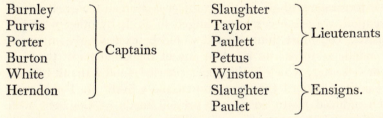

Burnley			Slaughter	
Purvis			Taylor	
Porter	} Captains		Paulett	} Lieutenants
Burton			Pettus	
White			Winston	
Herndon			Slaughter	} Ensigns.
			Paulet	

I am sorry to tell you that the throng of business peculiarly incumbent on the council puts it out of their power to do any thing with your requisition for necessaries more than to put it into the hands of the board of war. That board has not set these six weeks; but we are told they will set today and I hope will expedite your requisitions as well of the former as present letter.

I am Sir Your very humble servt,   TH: JEFFERSON

RC (O. O. Fisher, Detroit, 1950). At foot of text: "Colo. Taylor." Enclosures missing.

Francis Taylor, who had retired from Continental service in 1778, was named colonel of a regiment of guards for the Convention army, Dec. 1778 (*Va. Coun-*

cil Jour., II, 247). Taylor's LETTER OF THE 13TH and TJ's LAST TO YOU (Taylor) have not been found. In connection with the restaffing of the regiment of guards, see TJ's list of officers of that regiment, printed under date of 5 Nov. 1779.

James Innes to Mann Page

DEAR SIR   Fryday mor:g Octr. 27th 1779

I have meditated very deliberately on the Subject of our last nights Conversation, and the more I think, the more I wish that an accommodation produced by the force of rational Conviction, might banish the official Dispute, at present subsisting, between the Governor, and the Board of War. The refference of this matter for Settlement to the General assembly might perhaps produce Consequences, exceedingly disagreable to the feelings of one party, or the other. But believe me, Sir, I am not influenced to wish, that the principles of our Dispute may not appear before the legislature, because I am supposed the principal agent in the illegal proceedings of the Board of War. Conscious that every measure I have officially adopted was dictated by the most zealous and disinterested Love for my Country, I am ready to stand the Test of Inquiry before any earthly tribunal—or even the tribunal of Heaven.

It is the wish of my Colleagues, and with them I agree very cordially, that we should rather be induced to yield a willing obedience to the Regulations of the Executive from the persuasive powers of Reason, than from the arbitrary mandates of the legislature. But if to reason with us on this Subject is deemed too great a Condescention, we are necessarily obliged to abide by other modes of Decision. You must think, that it would be exceedingly improper, and indelicate for me to mention any of the Contents of the Gove[rnor's] Letter, which he has been pleased (and I thank him for h[is] polite Candor) thro you, to give me a Sight of. The reasons which induced us to adopt our present mode of Conduct, were stated in our letter to the Governor. These have never been officially answered. Consequently we remain not convinc'd, and to renounce an opinion which we think right from any motives of fear or Interest would manif[est] a pliability of Soul totally incompatible with that Stubborn virtue which should characterize the Citizens of republic[an] governments.

I assure you my Dear Sir, that the feelings of my heart are sensibly affected by this official altercation, which I fear from a number of Circumstan[ces] may become a personal one. I think the Spirit of personal[ity] breathes strongly in his Excellency's letter to the Assembly. I have ever loved and revered Mr. Jefferson as a virtuou[s] and wise Citizen, and beheld him with pleasure exalt[ed] to the high seat of Chief Magistracy, in this Commonw[ealth.] I too have been honor'd with an official Capacity, the Dignity of [which] I would not willingly tarnish by any subservient relinquishment [of] opinion. Yet I ever mean to keep open the Door of Conviction. Having long [. . .] to grow poor in the service of my Country, I should be unhappy to leave in [. . .] the last public office

I ever mean to hold in it. I thank you my Dea[r] friend for your benevolent mediation in this affair, and I have the honor [to] be yr affte

Js. INNES

RC (DLC). Endorsed by TJ: "Colo. Innes to Mann Page."

Innes' letter was evidently transmitted to TJ by Mann Page (a member of the House of Delegates), since it is endorsed by TJ and found among his papers. The GOVERNOR'S LETTER, shown to In-

nes, was probably that to Benjamin Harrison, 20 Oct. 1779, not located, but mentioned in TJ to Benjamin Harrison, printed under 20 Nov. 1779, q.v. For the OFFICIAL DISPUTE see Board of War to TJ, 2 Nov. 1779. OUR LETTER TO THE GOVERNOR is also missing.

From the Board of Trade

[*Williamsburg*] *29 Oct. 1779.* Transmitting a letter of Thomas Smith to the Board of Trade, 28 Oct. 1779, stating that in March of that year he was engaged by the Council to undertake a mission to Europe to purchase goods for the state; that he departed on 2 June but was captured and taken to New York and returned to Virginia about 25 July; that he was again ordered to be in readiness to depart with the first vessel to sail, but orders to proceed were not received until 8 Oct.; that shortly thereafter the scheme was abandoned; that the delay and confusion have resulted in great loss of business, and that restitution should be made. The Board, not competent to determine on circumstances which occurred before their establishment, recommend that, if the claim is valid, £2000 would be ample compensation. Signed by Ambler and Rose.

RC (CSmH); written below the letter of Thomas Smith to Board of Trade, 28 Oct. 1779, transmitted; 3 p. (includ-

ing both letters).

See Thomas Smith to TJ, 22 Oct. 1779; Board of Trade to TJ, 8 Oct. 1779.

From the Board of Trade

[*Williamsburg*] *29 Oct. 1779.* The salary of Mr. James Warren, assistant in the agent's office, has never been fixed. Forty pounds per annum, payable in tobacco at twenty shillings per hundred, seems an ample compensation. Signed by Ambler and Rose.

RC (CSmH); 1 p.; TJ's reply of the same date, q.v., is written on the lower portion of the page.

To the Board of Trade

In Council Oct. 29. 1779.

The Council concur in opinion with the board of trade that forty pounds per annum to be paid as they have said is a sufficient compensation for Mr. Warren's services, and approve of that stipend.

They will consent that he shall have from the public store necessary cloathing at the current advance paid or paying on the wholesale purchase by the state at the time they are drawn, proper precautions being taken to prevent more being drawn than is necessary for his own personal use.   TH: JEFFERSON

RC (CSmH); written below Board of Trade to TJ, same date, q.v.

To Benjamin Harrison

SIR   In Council Oct 29. 1779

The Executive in the Month of March 1778, in order to secure the acquisition and proper choice of a supply of Arms, Ordnance, and Military implements sent a Mr. Le Mair of the Kingdom of France their Agent express for that purpose to Europe. He executed his Commission with a zeal and assiduity which we have rarely met with, having traversed for fourteen Months those parts of Europe backwards and forwards where there was a hope of getting the Articles wanted, and after eighteen Months absence returned himself in the last of three Vessels which he charged with Ordnance and other necessaries. His reasonable expences we mean to pay and were about making him a proper pecuniary compensation for his time and great labour but he prays rather to be rewarded with Military rank unattended by either pay or command; expecting to reap greater benefit from this in his own Country to which he is about to return. The Executive apprehending they have no authority to grant brevet Commissions, refer to the general Assembly the expediency of authorising them to give to this Gentleman a Lieutenant Colonels Commission by way of brevet. They shall not indeed then think themselves discharged from making him some pecuniary compensation tho' a much smaller may be given than they had before proposed. I have the honour to be with great respect Sir Your most obedt & most humble servt.,

TH: JEFFERSON

RC (Vi). Addressed: "The honourable Benjamin Harrison esq. Speaker of the House of Delegates." Docketed: "Governors Letter Octor: 30th. 1779. about Brevet Commiss. to lie on table."
LE MAIR: Jacques Le Maire, commissioned by Virginia, 18 Mch. 1778, to procure military stores in France, landed in Boston, 30 Aug. 1779, on a vessel belonging to Penet, d'Acosta & Co. (CVSP, IV, 13). On 5 Nov. 1779 the General Assembly authorized TJ to grant Le Maire a brevet commission (JHD, Oct. 1779, 1827 edn., p. 42). His accounts were approved 13 Nov. (TJ to Board of Trade, 6, 9-12 Nov. 1779; Board of Trade to TJ, 9, 13 Nov. 1779); however, a satisfactory settlement was not concluded. Le Maire continued his appeals for a settlement of his claim, and was among the first to call on TJ upon the latter's arrival in France (TJ to Benjamin Harrison, 20 Aug. 1784).

To the Board of Trade

In Council Oct. 30. 1779

It is recommended to the Board of trade to take measures for the immediate purchase of necessary cloathing for the use of the Cherokee Indians wherever to be found within this state. Majr. Martin the agent with them will be able to give them information as to the articles and quantities.   TH: JEFFERSON

RC (Vi). Endorsed: "Recommendations from the Executive to furnish Sun-
dries for Cherokees."
    A MS (Vi) ccompanying this letter,

presumably in the hand of MAJR. Joseph
MARTIN, agent to the Cherokees, lists
the quantities of blankets, coats, shirts,
cloth and thread required.

To Benjamin Harrison

[*Williamsburg, 30? Oct. 1779.* JHD, Oct. 1779, 1827 edn., p. 30 (30 Oct. 1779): "The Speaker laid before the House a letter from the Governor, respecting the purchase of a frigate for the use of the State, which was read, and ordered to be referred to the committee of the whole House on the state of the Commonwealth." Not located.]

To Benjamin Harrison

SIR   In Council Octr. 30th. 1779

In pursuance of a resolution of the last session of General Assembly the Executive proceeded to form a Contract with Messrs. Penet Windel & co. for the establishment of a manufactory of fire arms and foundery of ordnance on James river and for extending navigation through it's falls. The several preliminary papers which passed between them are now transmitted to the General Assembly, that they may be enabled to judge of the obstacles the executive had to encounter, and to see the reasons explained which led them to the several conclusions. These articles also, as ultimately concluded, accompany this,[1] together with a subsequent letter from Mr. Penet and memorial from Mr. Savarit desiring some alterations in two of the articles.

The several objects of this Contract must be admitted of the last importance: The depending on the transportation of arms across an element on which our enemies have reigned, for the defence of our Country, has been already found insecure and distressing. The endeavours of five years aided with some internal manufactures

[125]

have not yet procured a tolerable supply of arms. To make them within ourselves then as well as the other implements of war, is as necessary as to make our bread within ourselves. The present contract seems really to afford a promising appearance of future supply. Should these Articles meet with ratification from the General Assembly, I must still inform them that obstacles are likely to arise of a very perplexing nature, from an unlucky connection of the public with a certain Mr. Ballendine who has entangled himself into every part of the subjects of this contract. Some of his rights are real, some only pretended. Unless they can be cleared away by legislative authority in a speedy mode, liberal compensation being first allowed him for such of them as shall be found just, the length of time which would be required to follow him through courts of justice in the ordinary course of proceedings, will defeat every hope which might be entertained from this contract. The duty imposed on the Executive by the resolution of assembly led them necessarily to an investigation of this mans rights and pretensions. That the assembly may have proper lights to conduct their enquiries I will analyse his claims as they have appeared to us. They refer to three several subjects, which I will endeavour to keep distinct, to avoid that confusion they might otherwise throw on one another. 1. to the Furnace in Buckingham. 2. to the Foundery at Westham. 3. to the construction of a navigable Canal at the falls of James river.

1. Mr. Ballendine with a partner Mr. Reveley received by order from the assembly £5000 in the year 1776 for the purpose of erecting a furnace in Buckingham and stipulated to repay it in pig iron at Seven pounds ten shillings the ton, which in fact amounted to a contract to pay the public 666⅔ tons of pig iron for it. In December 1777 he received a further sum of £2500. In may 1778 he petitioned the assembly to release him from the obligation of paying his debt in iron @ £7.10/ the ton, and to take it at the market price at the time of delivery of the iron. The assembly resolved that he should be allowed more than the £7.10. but not the market price at the *time of delivery*; thus signifying their sense that there was some intermediate ground on which they meant to take their stand, but not pointing out what that was. This led us to suppose that the market price of iron at the time of the *paiment of the money* to Ballendine might be what the assembly had probably in view. On settlement of his several accounts with the commissioners whom we appointed according to the resolution of assembly for that purpose and whose report is transmitted herewith, there

arose on one of them a balance in his favor for part of 3T-10C-2qr. of pig iron delivered. The commissioners had extended it in money at £30. the ton, and transferred the balance of £42-5 which that produced to the credit of his account for the £5000. or 666⅔ ton of iron. We think they should have credited so much of the 3T-10C-2qr. of iron at £30. as would have balanced that account and transferred the residue, in iron, to the credit of his debt due in iron. This error would have been too trivial to have noted to you, Sir, but as it tended to introduce a false principle into the account, and to prevent us from informing you precisely that of the 666⅔ tons due to the public for the £5000. there has been paid only 1T-3C and nothing paid towards discharging the additional £2500. To secure these balances the lands in which the money was invested were conveyed to the trustees themselves, but under an implied trust, that on payment of the debt conveyances should be made to Ballendine and Reveley: so that it is apprehended they amount in fact to nothing more than mortgages. There is little hope that this balance will ever be paid; an opportunity now occurs not only of making these securities produce to the public the real worth of what was advanced on them, but also of producing it in arms and implements of war, the very articles originally proposed to be obtained by it, and which of all others are most immediately essential to the public safety. But a bill for foreclosing the trust to pass through the usual forms of proceedings in a Court of Chancery will hardly bring us relief till I hope we shall not need it.

2. The General Assembly in May 1776 having determined to erect a foundery at Westham for casting ordnance appointed commissioners for that purpose. For the Sum of £242.10. which they paid Mr. Ballendine they purchased from him for situating the foundery three acres and an half of land adjacent to a canal he was opening from Westham, and a right to deduce water from the canal for turning a boring Mill and other works necessary for the finishing the cannon. They were also to have free navigation down the canal to the foundery on contributing one moiety to the repairs of that part of the canal; after it should have been once completed, as he bound himself to compleat it. They erected their foundery and found it necessary to make advances of money to Ballendine to enable him to complete his canal and dam on which alone they depended for water. The balance due the Commonwealth on these advances is £2051-2-5½ as appears by one of the accounts transmitted herewith: for securing which payments a mortgage had been taken on 46½ acres of land the whole of the real property of

the said Ballendine at that place. So that the public possessions and interests at this place are 3½ acres of land with the foundery on it, a right to draw off water for working their machines for completing the canon, a common in the navigation, paying one half the expence of keeping that part of the canal in repair, and a mortgage on 46½ acres of land for securing the paiment of £2051-2-5½. But for the state of Mr. Ballendine's dam and canal and the prospect of obtaining water as long as he is to be depended on for it, I beg leave to refer you to the report of the same commissioner.

3. The extending navigation from Westham to Richmond, besides it's other very general importance, being extremely requisite to promote the success of the proposed manufactory, by reducing the difficulty and expence attending the transportation of the bulky articles of coal, wood and other things necessary to be expended at it, and it's own very weighty produce, we were led to enquire by what means Mr. Ballendine had got foothold there and on what pretensions he founds a right of constructing the navigable canal. In 1764. the assembly passed an act authorising the opening the falls of James river by subscriptions of money from individuals and appointing Trustees to take such subscriptions. Some persons accordingly subscribed, but no appearance arising of the work's being ever compleated in this way, the assembly after waiting 8 years, to wit, in 1772. passed another act for putting the business into a different train. They directed that as soon as the former and subsequent subscribers or a majority of them should think a sufficient sum raised, any ten of them, being subscribers of £100. each at least, might appoint a general meeting at which a president and 11 directors should be elected, who should have power to agree with an undertaker to cut the canal proposed, provided such undertaker should first give sufficient security to perform his agreement: they gave to the adventurers authority to carry the canal through any person's lands, paying the worth of them, allowed them certain tolls, and pointed out the precise mode in which they might transfer their shares in the undertaking, to wit, by deed executed by the president, the subscriber having first tendered his share to the directors who were to have the refusal at the same price. Very considerable sums were engaged under this act: but there never was a meeting of the subscribers to elect a president and directors, nor an undertaker employed. While this was in agitation Mr. Ballendine proposing to clear the falls of James river and the falls of Potowmack set on foot subscriptions for enabling him to go to England to learn how to do it. Great sums were subscribed. He went;

returned, and brought some workmen. He purchased at the head of the falls of James river the 50 acres of land, three and a half of which were conveyed as before mentioned to the public for the foundery, and the other 46½ mortgaged to them. He opened a canal through this land and then of his own authority, without any act of assembly or even an order of court, as we are told, he made a dam across an arm of James river and drew off 50 feet width of water along his canal. In November 1777. by Petition to the assembly he informs them that the subscribers under the last act of assembly had transferred their interests to him, that he had made considerable progress in the canal, and should finish it if he met with no interruption from those through whose lands it must pass, and prays an act might pass vesting him with the powers of the former subscribers. Had the allegation in his Petition been true, that the former subscribers had transferred their interests to him, such an act would have been unnecessary, because he would have stood on their footing; but it could not be true, because the transfer being to be executed by the president, after a tender and refusal of the share to the company, and no president having ever been elected, there could have been no such transfer to him as he alledged. I have been thus particular Sir, in order to shew you that Mr. Ballendine has no legal right to the conducting the canal which can stand in the way of the present Contract. He has an equity of redemption in the 46½ acres of land before mentioned, and so far stands on the footing of every other landholder through whose lands the canal must pass. He prayed earnestly that their rights might be sacrificed to him, on his paying them the value: can he then with modesty now say that his rights shall not be sacrificed to others, paying him the value of the injury done him? It is now four years since he begun this canal; he has conducted it about one twentieth part of the whole distance: and this too while his workmen were with him, and his means, if he had any, were fresh. A very simple calculation then will inform us, that, in his hands the completion of this work will require near a century, and then a question arises whether Mr. Ballendine will live so long. I think we may fairly conclude that he will never complete it. It is right that in cases of such general importance, the interests of a few individuals should give way to the general good, full compensation being made them; and as right that Mr. Ballendine's should, as those of the others whose lands were to have been laid open to him. He has had a long enough trial to convince the whole world he never will complete it. Other gentlemen now offer to do it within a reasonable term. As the assembly then after an eight years trial and failure of the act of 1764. made another experiment in 1772. it seems reasonable, after other seven years patience, to try yet other means. It is possible the present Undertakers may not find it necessary to make use of Mr. Ballendine's canal at all, but may take out the water elsewhere. But should they find that it can be taken off no where else, it is submitted to the assembly, whether his having dug a canal along grounds thro' which the navigable canal must necessarily pass, shall privilege those grounds, more than the meadows and grounds of others are privileged, and for ever obstruct the opening that river, and whether there can be any sound objection to the having in his case, as well as in those of others, a just valuation made of the injury he will sustain by the use which shall be made of his canal, and after withholding the £2051.2.5½ due from him to the public, on that particular account, to pay him the balance if the injury shall be found to exceed that sum.

In stating to you the several obstacles which oppose themselves to the execution of the resolution of assembly, I have been necessarily led to mention circumstances which are to be found among your own journals and acts, and of which therefore you had knowledge before. They were necessary to continue the thread of the relation so as to render it intelligible, and are desired to be considered only as references to your own records for more authentic and precise information.

I have the honour to be with the greatest respect Sir Your most obedient & most humble servt.,   TH: JEFFERSON

RC (Vi); in a clerk's hand except for complimentary close, signature, address, and two or three small corrections in the text in TJ's hand; addressed: "The honble. The Speaker of the House of Delegates"; endorsed: "Governor Jefferson's Letter to the Speaker of the House of Delegats. 30th. October 1779. Copd. for the Executive." Dft (DLC), also bearing a clerk's endorsement (partly illegible) indicating that it was submitted to the House or a committee thereof. Dft contains numerous corrections, one of which is recorded below. The enclosures that have been located are also mentioned below.

The RESOLUTION of the Assembly referred to at the outset was that of 25 June 1779 empowering the executive to contract with Penet, Windel & Co. for the establishment of an arms manufactory on James River, and to cut a canal or open a road from Richmond or Man-

chester to the site of the manufactory (JHD; May 1779, 1827 edn., p. 66); the contract is summarized above under date of 22 July 1779, and is printed in full, as part of the bill for ratifying the contract, under the present date, below. Transmitted with the present letter were copies of the contract in its preliminary and final forms, together with a LETTER FROM MR. PENET of 17 Aug. (printed above) and one from MR. SAVARIT (summarized under date of 22 July 1779, above). The difficulties leading TJ into his long explanation sprang, as he states, FROM AN UNLUCKY CONNECTION OF THE PUBLIC WITH A CERTAIN MR. BALLENDINE. This was John Ballendine, an industrial promoter of Prince William co., who undertook many projects from 1755 onward, by no means always with success. His career and exceedingly involved dealings with the state of Virginia are summarized by Kathleen Bruce in *Virginia Iron Manufacture in the Slave Era*, N.Y. and London, 1930, ch. I, which provides an excellent background for the present letter as well as for the other documents printed here that relate to TJ's endeavors to establish a state foundry at Westham, a few miles up the James from Richmond. A memorandum in TJ's hand tabulating legislative resolutions and acts pertaining to the Buckingham works, the Westham foundry, and the canal around the Falls from 1772 to 1778, not printed here, is in DLC: TJ Papers, 3:446, and was evidently prepared as a partial outline of the present letter. At the same time (25 June 1779) that the House had empowered the governor to enter into a contract with Penet they had instructed him to appoint persons "to adjust and settle all matters and accounts between the Commonwealth and John Ballendine" (JHD, May 1779, 1827 edn., p. 67)—an assignment that did not prove easy; see Archibald Cary to TJ, 22 July

1779. In reporting on this topic as ealt with in TJ's letter of 30 Oct., Patrick Henry for the Committee of Propositions and Grievances stated the opinion that the validity of Ballendine's claims "is the proper object of the courts of justice" rather than of the legislature (JHD, Oct. 1779, 1827 edn., p. 62). Litigation respecting these claims was still pending in 1809 (Bruce, *Virginia Iron Manufacture*, p. 50, note). As to the further history of the contract with Penet, see the following document.

¹ In Dft the remainder of this sentence is interlined, and the following matter deleted: "So many of them are left open for the decision of the General assembly that it is quite in their power to decline the whole if they should be found disagreeable in the whole. No purchase has as yet been made nor a shilling otherwise expended in consequence of this contract."

Bill for Establishing a Manufactory of Arms and Extending Navigation through the Falls of James River

[30 October 1779]

Whereas in consequence of certain resolutions of General assembly the Governor with the advice of the council of state on behalf of this commonwealth hath entered into articles of agreement with Messrs. Peter Penet Windel and company of the kingdom of France, which articles are in these words following to wit.

Articles of agreement entered into and concluded on the twenty second day of July in the year of our lord one thousand seven hundred and seventy nine between the Governor of the commonwealth of Virginia with advice of the council of state on behalf of the said commonwealth on the one part, and Messrs. Peter Penet, Windel and company of the kingdom of France on the other part.

First. The said Peter Penet, Windel and company covenant and agree that they will establish at their own expence a Manufactory of arms, and Foundery of Cannon at such place on James river as they shall think suitable, that they will provide the same with able artists and workmen, that they will support and carry on the said Manufactory and Foundery for ever, and to such extent as that they shall at all times and so often as they shall be called on after the first nine years hereafter more particularly mentioned be able from the manufactory particularly to furnish ten thousand stand of arms complete and well made within one year after the same shall have been called for by the Governor and council for the time being.

Second. The said Peter Penet, Windel and company will begin to erect the buildings and other works necessary for the said Manufactory and Foundery as soon as the place shall have been fixed on and procured for them.

Third. They covenant and agree to make at the said Manufactory and Foundery and deliver to the Governour or order six thousand complete stand of arms each stand to consist of a musket, bayonet and scabbard, two hundred and fifty carbines, two hundred and fifty pair of horsemen's pistols, and two hundred and fifty swords within two years after the said place shall have been fixed on and procured for them, and the like number every year after for seven succeeding years, making in the whole forty eight thousand stand of arms two thousand carbines, two thousand pair of pistols, and two thousand swords reserving to themselves nevertheless a power of delivering the whole quantity before mentioned within such shorter time as they shall think proper. They will also make at the said Foundery such and so many Ordnance as shall hereafter be agreed on. The patterns for the muskets, bayonets and carbines shall be either the French model of one thousand seven hundred and sixty three or such as are now used in the British army at the election of the Governour and council to be declared at any time when such declaration shall be called for by the company such call not to be sooner than six months after the date of these presents the pattern of the pistols shall be the French model of one thousand seven hundred and seventy two or such as are now in use in the British cavalry at the like election of the Governour and council, to be declared as before provided in the case of the muskets. The swords shall be such as are used in the French cavalry, and shall be mounted with brass, there shall be duplicates of these patterns provided by the Governour and council, one of each to be deposited with the company, the other to be kept by themselves.

Fourth. The said Ordnance and fire arms shall be proved in presence of some person to be appointed by the Governour and council with a double charge of powder and ball three times repeated, the first proof to be at the expence of the company, the second and third proofs at the expence of the state. The Governor shall not be obliged to take any arms which fail under either of these proofs. The person so to be appointed shall attend at the Manufactory and Foundery at stated times to see the arms proved, and give certificates to the company.

Fifth. The Governour shall receive the said arms at the Manufactory and Foundery.

Sixth. The Governour and council shall have right once in every two years to direct any alteration in the form or materials of the said arms which they shall think proper, they taking such arms as shall be on hand, finished, at the time of the alteration directed, and paying such additional price for those to be afterwards made as shall be agreed on if the alteration should enhance the cost of the workmanship or materials. Such agreement to be made amicably between the parties before the alteration takes place.

Seventh. The Governour and council covenant that they will use their best endeavors to procure for the said company such situation within the description of the first article as the said company shall fix on, together with a right to the water and other conveniencies necessary for the said Manufactory and Foundery; also three thousand acres of land in one or more parcels in the neighborhood of the said situation. If they cannot do it without committing violations on private property which the laws will not authorize, or without giving such exorbitant prices as the importance of this contract will not justify they will report the same to the General assembly at their next meeting; and if the assembly shall not devise means of having it done, the whole contract shall become void.

Eighth. The said Peter Penet, Windel and company covenant and agree that the articles so to be procured for them by the Governor and council as stated in the preceding covenant shall be estimated by honest and judicious persons, to be chosen by joint consent of both parties according to their real worth in gold and silver at the time they shall be purchased, but if the public shall have paid nothing for the water nothing shall be required to be paid them for it, and the said company will repay the sum at which the said articles shall be estimated either in arms to be made at the said Manufactory or Foundery at the prices herein after agreed on for other arms, or in arms or other merchandize to be specified by the Governour, and imported from France by the Governour and council or, if they chuse it, by the said company at the risque and expence of the commonwealth. The right of determining in which of the said ways paiment shall be made or how much in the one and how much in the other shall be in the Governour and council: and so much as shall be called for by importation from France shall be ordered by the company so soon as the situation, land and other conveniencies before mentioned shall be procured for the company.

Ninth. The Governour and council agree that if the said Peter Penet, Windel and company shall fail in the execution of the preceding articles through too great difficulties or other unforeseen causes they shall not be liable to the commonwealth for damages for breach of contract. But in case of failure from any cause whatever the land water and other conveniencies procured for them with all improvements thereon shall become the absolute property of the commonwealth; the said commonwealth repaying to the said company the price which it shall have received under the eighth article for the said lands.

Tenth. The Governour and council will recommend to the General assembly the exempting for twenty one years the managers, artists and domestics imported by the company and employed in and about the Manufactory and Foundery from all public labors and from military service either in the militia or elsewhere. And in order to ascertain the persons entitled to this exemption, their several contracts with the company shall be exhibited to the clerk of the county in which the Manufactory shall be, to be by him copied and safely kept for the inspection of officers civil and military, courts of justice, and others concerned: if the assembly shall refuse such exemption the company shall be at liberty to declare the whole contract void.

Eleventh. The Governor and council will inhibit all officers from enlisting into military service before the determination of their engagements with the company, the artists and domestics which the company shall import and employ in and about the Manufactory and Foundery and which shall be ascertained as provided in the preceding article; and if enlisted, will have them discharged: and will recommend to the General assembly to make provision by law for preventing the citizens of this commonwealth from taking them into their service or seducing them away during the same term.

Twelfth. The Governour and council will recommend to the General assembly to make provision by law for enforcing the persons described and ascertained in the two preceding articles to a specific performance of their contracts for service, and to authorize the company to pass by-laws for the government of the said persons, inflicting penalties of fine and imprisonment where necessary: provided that such by-laws shall not be in force until approved by the General assembly.

Thirteenth. The Governour will receive the arms contracted for in the third article in time and manner as there specified; and the commonwealth within six months after receiving them shall pay to the company for every musket, bayonet and scabbard thirty livres ten sous Tournois money of France, for every Carbine mounted with brass, thirty eight livres ten sous of like money, for every pair of pistols for cavalry, forty livres ten sous of like money for every horseman's sword mounted with brass with it's scabbard twelve livres of like money.

Fourteenth. The Governour and council will undertake to purchase for the company one mine of iron, one of copper, and one of coal all of good quality if they can do it without committing violations on private property which the laws will not authorize, or if such mines can be found in unappropriated lands the company shall be entitled to a grant of one of each kind gratis: so as that they shall be entitled to but one of each kind by grant and purchase. They shall have liberty to search in any unappropriated lands for such mines, and the Governor and council will endeavor to get leave for them to search also in appropriated lands for the like mines. The Governour and council will undertake under the like reservation as to the rights of private property to purchase for, or grant to, the company five thousand acres of land adjacent to each of the said mines, and the streams of water necessary for working them. If any of the said mines shall become exhausted, the like shall be purchased or granted in the same manner and under the same reservation in lieu thereof. The said company covenants that the purchase money or cost of such mines, lands and streams of water shall be estimated by honest and judicious men to be chosen by joint consent of both parties according to it's real worth in gold and silver at the time the paiment of such purchase money or price shall become due from the state, and that it shall be repaid by the company as is before covenanted by them in the eighth article as to paiment for the matters stated in the seventh article. The state shall at it's own expence open a road from each mine to the river if that be practicable, or, if not, then to the nearest high road.

Fifteenth. The company shall have a right to conduct a canal from W[estham] to Richmond, and erect it's banks on and through any lands whether [of public] or private property with a saving only as to the rights of John Ballendine so far as they shall be maintaineable in law and equity. But as to the rights of the said

Ballendine the Governour and council are of opinion that there being no reasonable prospect that he will ever complete the canal, his rights ought not to obstruct the completing it for the public convenience by other hands any more than the rights of others, and will therefore refer to the General assembly the subjecting his property in like manner with that of other individuals and also that the lands of individuals which shall be occupied by the canal and it's banks, and damages sustained by them in consequence thereof shall be paid for by the commonwealth, and such paiment not re-demanded from the company. The breadth of the said canal and horseway on each side, and the depth of water for navigation, as also the toll to be allowed to the company and mode of levying it shall be as the General assembly shall prescribe. The company shall declare before the first day of January one thousand seven hundred and eighty one or so soon after as the General assembly shall have prescribed the circumstances just before mentioned whether they will undertake the canal or not, and at the same time shall declare within what term they will complete it. If that term shall exceed ten years the General assembly shall be at liberty to declare the several articles of this contract relative to the said canal, to be void. If they undertake and fail to complete it within the term agreed; their rights under the same articles shall vest in the commonwealth. It shall be lawful for the General assembly at any time after the year one thousand eight hundred and forty to take into the hands of the commonwealth the property of the canal, it's water locks, banks and other appendages, and the necessary privileges in the adjacent ground for repairing them, leaving to the undertakers the use of such portions of the water and in such places for working of their machines as they shall have applied to that use during the first twenty five years after their undertaking it, and paying to them the double of what the opening the said canal, building the locks, banks, and other the said appendages thereof shall have cost them; the amount of which cost shall be kept by the company separate and apart from that of their other works and shall annually with their vouchers be laid before persons jointly to be chosen by the Governour and council and the company, to be by them examined and certified so far as they find them just, and a copy of such certif-icate to be given each party and to be binding between them. Where such cost shall have been defrayed in paper money or com-modities the true worth thereof in gold and silver at the time of the expenditure and at the place where expended shall be estimated by the same persons, and the repaiment thereof, as also of all expenditures of gold and silver shall be made in double the quantity of gold and silver as before agreed. In consideration of this right of resumption reserved to the commonwealth, the Governour and council will recommend to the General assembly to take the same into their consideration when they shall proceed to establish the toll and to allow such toll as will with tolerable certainty reimburse the company within the term of fifty years, and also to give a right of passage toll free to all the productions of the Manufactory and Foundery and the necessaries for them 'till the year one thousand eight hundred and ninety.

Sixteenth. In case of the impracticability or too great difficulty of opening the canal aforesaid the state will at it's own expence prepare a firm and commodious road from the Manufactory and Foundery into the main road leading to Richmond, for transporting the Cannon and other productions of the Manufactory and foundery.

Seventeenth. The Governour and council will extend to the company all protection assistance and privileges which to them shall appear reasonable, and shall be within their power, and will recommend the same to be done by the General assembly.

Eighteenth. The Governour and council covenant and agree that the preceding articles shall be binding on them and their successors on behalf of the commonwealth, and the said Peter Penet, Windel and company covenant and agree that the said preceding articles shall be binding on them jointly and severally, their joint and several heirs, executors and administrators.

In witness whereof Thomas Jefferson esq. Governour of the commonwealth of Virginia, on the part of the commonwealth and with advice of the council of state and Peter Penet on the part of the said Peter Penet, Windel and company have hereto interchangeably set their hands and seals on the day and year first above written.

Now therefore for confirming the said Articles so far as the same were absolutely and completely ascertained and covenanted by the Governour, and for completing so much of them as were by him covenanted to be recommended or referred to the discretion of the General assembly, so far as is thought consistent with the public good;

Be it enacted by the General assembly that the first, second, third, fourth, fifth, sixth, seventh, eighth, ninth, thirteenth, fourteenth, sixteenth, seventeenth and eighteenth of the said articles shall be and the same are hereby absolutely ratified and confirmed on the part of this commonwealth and declared to be obligatory thereon.[1]

And whereas the Commonwealth is entitled to a trust in certain lands in the county of Buckingham for securing the paiment of certain large sums of money lent to a certain John Ballendine and John Reevely in pig iron at the rate of seven pounds ten shillings currency per ton; and are also entitled to a trust in three acres and an half of land in the county of Henrico adjacent to the falls of James river whereon is a foundery and other works, in absolute right, and have a mortgage on forty six acres and an half of lands adjoining to the said three and an half acres, from the said John Ballendine for securing to the commonwealth the paiment of certain other large sums of money lent to the said Ballendine; and it may the more effectually enable the Governour to carry into execution the seventh and fourteenth articles before confirmed if he shall be vested with power to transfer the public rights therein to the said Penet, Windel & company, be it therefore enacted that it shall be lawful for the Governour with advice of the council of state to agree with the said company on the mode of having the public right in the said lands estimated to convey the same to the said company in part towards performance of the said seventh and fourteenth articles, and to have paiment made of the said estimated value in the manner therein stipulated: and that the public may be availed of the opportunity of disposing of their interests in the said mortgaged lands in such manner as may save the advances made to the said Ballendine or Ballendine & Reevely in the said lands to await the ordinary delays of proceedings in equity and, reasonable time being allowed them for putting in their answers and other pleadings, and collecting their evidence, they will not have cause to complain merely for the expedition of justice; be it further enacted, that after a bill or bills shall have been filed against them or either of them for any the purposes beforementioned, and notice thereof actually served by a proper officer or left at the most usual place of their respective residences they shall be allowed one month and no more for filing their answer, plea, or demurrer respectively; within which time if there be a failure to answer, plead or demur, or if the answer, plea, or demurrer filed be adjudged insufficient or overruled, the bill shall be taken for confessed and a decree accordingly; and in like manner after a replication or any other pleading filed on the part of the Commonwealth and actual notice thereof served or left as aforesaid one month and no more shall be allowed to file the proper pleading in answer thereto, subject to the like condition of a decree as if the bill were confessed on failure to file the same within such time, or on it's being overruled or adjudged insufficient. And after issue in law or fact shall have been made up one month or on failure to answer or file any pleading in sufficient manner as before directed, a final decree shall be pronounced at the first court which shall be held after the expiration of the said month or failure as aforesaid, or at the court which shall be in session at the time of such expiration or failure: and in case of any appeal, such appeal shall be heard and finally determined by the court to which it is made at their first sitting after the said appeal prayed. And if any day after the decree pronounced shall be given to the said Ballendine or Ballendine and Reeveley for the redemption of any of the said lands, such redemption shall be allowed only on condition of specific performance of the agreement on which the monies were advanced, and the day given shall not exceed one month after that on which such decree shall have been actually pronounced. But as a part of the monies advanced to the said Ballendine and Reevely to be repaid in iron, were paid by the Treasurer after the price of iron had risen in some degree, it shall be lawful for any court before whom the said proceedings shall be depending to take into consideration the rise in the price of iron at the several times at which the said monies were paid out of the treasury, and to allow the said Ballendine and Reeveley to repay the said monies in iron at such advanced prices.

The managers, artists and domestics imported by the said company from any place other than any of the United states of America and employed in and about the said Manufactory and Foundery shall be exempted until the first day of January which shall be in the year one thousand eight hundred and one from all public labours and from military service as well in the militia as elsewhere: and in order to ascertain the persons entitled to this exemption, the contracts of such persons with the said company shall be exhibited to the clerk of the county in which the Manufactory shall be, to be by him registered in a separate book to be provided for that purpose and safely kept for the inspection of officers civil and military, courts of justice and others concerned. And if before the same day and during their engagements with the said company any of the said artists or domestics shall be enlisted into military service, or shall enter into the service or employment of any individual or of any body politic or corporate, it shall be lawful for the said company or any their agents or servants to retake such artist or domestic, or to make complaint to any justice of the peace in the county where such artist or domestic shall be, who thereon shall issue his warrant to the sheriff or any constable of his county commanding him to retake and deliver such artist or domestic to the person complaining: and moreover the person who enlisted him into military service, or took him into his service or employment, if he knew or had reason to beleive him to be an artist or domestic under engagements as aforesaid to the said company shall be liable to the said company for all damages they may sustain by the enlistment or employment of the said artist or domestic, and shall moreover be amerced.

And the more effectually to enable the said company to carry into execution the several covenants entered into on their part, all managers, artists, and domestics imported by them from any place other than any one of the United states of America and employed in and about the Manufactory or Foundery and ascertained and registered as before directed shall be compelled to a specific performance of their contracts for service until they shall have actually served seven years if their contract so long bound them to serve: and the said company shall moreover have full power and authority to pass by and for the government of the said managers, artists and domestics beforementioned, with clauses for inflicting penalties by way of fine and imprisonment; provided that such by-laws shall not be in force until approved by the General assembly and shall be subject at any time after to be repealed by them.

And whereas by an act of General assembly passed in the year one thousand seven hundred and sixty four and intituled 'an act for clearing the great falls of James river, the river Chickahominy, and the North [branch] of James river' certain trustees were appointed with powers to receive subscriptions of money for extending the navigation of James river from Westham downwards through the great falls and recovering the said monies, and to perform such other acts as were necessary for carrying the said purpose into execution, under which acts divers persons subscribed certain sums of money, but the said trustees surceasing to proceed on the said work afterwards, to wit, in the year one thousand seven hundred and seventy two, one other act of General assembly was passed intituled 'an act for opening the falls of James river and for other purposes,' enacting that as soon as the persons who had theretofore subscribed together with such as should thereafter subscribe, or a majority of them, should think a sufficient sum for effecting the work might be raised, any ten who had subscribed one hundred pounds each should appoint a general meeting of the subscribers in the manner therein specially directed, and that the subscribers so met should be impowered to elect a president and eleven trustees

and directors who should have authority to agree with an undertaker or undertakers for cutting the said canal, erecting locks and
other necessary works, with a proviso that such undertaker or
undertakers should first give sufficient security to perform his or
their agreement allowing certain tolls or duties for the passage of
vessels along the said canal to be demanded and received, vesting
the said canal with it's appurtenances in the subscribers, and their
heirs and assigns, authorizing them severally to sell and transfer
their right or interest in the said canal, tolls or duties by deed of
conveyance to be executed by the said President, such subscriber,
when desirous of selling, having first offered the same to the trustees, who it was thereby declared should have the preference in all
such sales if they would give the same consideration for which any
proprietor should really and bonafide sell; and declaring the said
canal when compleated should be open and common as a navigable
water to all leige persons of the state paying the tolls therein prescribed, together with many other particulars in the said act provided; under which act also other large sums of money were subscribed by divers persons: but a majority of the said subscribers
having failed ever to meet, and to give opinion that a sufficient sum
for effecting the work might be raised, and in consequence thereof
no ten qualified as the said act directed having appointed a general
meeting of the subscribers as therein directed, and no subscribers
met under such appointment, having elected a president and trustees and directors; no persons have ever been vested with authority
to agree with an undertaker or undertakers to execute the said work
or to take from such Undertaker or Undertakers sufficient security
for the performance of his or their agreement: and the said subscribers having never sold or transferred their right or interest in
the said canal, tolls or duties, and having for a long time altogether
surceased proceeding in the said undertaking, it becomes necessary
for the public good that the offers of emolument by the said work
made to them and[2] not complied with, should now be tendered to
others, in like manner as those made to the subscribers under the
first act abovementioned, and not complied with were transferred
to those under the second; be it therefore enacted that the two acts
of General assembly beforementioned shall be hereby repealed, and
that all right, title, interest and authority derived to any person
whatever under the said acts or either of them shall henceforth
cease and become void as if no such act or acts had ever been made.

And whereas the said Peter Penet, Windel and company have
in the fifteenth of the before recited articles proposed to undertake

to open or construct a navigable canal from Westham to Richmond on certain conditions therein pointed out and others to be prescribed by the General assembly, if such additional conditions shall be approved of by themselves; be it therefore enacted that the said Peter Penet, Windel and company shall have power and authority at any and all times before the first day of January which shall be in the year one thousand seven hundred and eighty one with proper engineers, surveyors and assistants to enter into any lands adjacent to James river between Westham or Beverley town and the town of Richmond, and to make such examination and surveys as may be necessary previous to their determining on the said undertaking, and if they shall determine to undertake the same, and shall make declaration thereof before the same day to the Governour by writing subscribed and sealed, then it shall be lawful for them to open or construct a canal for continuing the navigation to the said river from the said town of Beverley to the tide waters at Richmond, and to erect it's banks and locks on and through any lands whether of public or private property: that the breadth of the said canal shall be fifty feet, and the depth of water through the whole breadth and length thereof shall be   inches: that there shall be a horseway on each side twenty feet in breadth and of a convenient height above the water for the towage of boats and other vessels: that the property in the bed of the said canal when completed it's water horseways and banks to the extent of one hundred feet on each side measuring from the middle of the said canal, shall be vested in the said Peter Penet, Windel and company or such of them as shall then be citizens of this commonwealth and their heirs as tenants in common; subject nevertheless to the laws of escheat on their becoming aliens at any time after; and saving to all persons, bodies politic and corporate all mills and other engines already completed with their ducts of water and other necessary appendages as they now actually exist: that it shall be lawful for the said Peter Penet, Windel and company to erect a dam or dams in any part of the river for the purpose of diverting the water thereof into the said canal and to abut the same against and into the shores or banks in any part: and that they may demand and receive at such fixed place on the said canal or it's banks as they shall think proper for every hogshead one fourth of a dollar, every barrel one twelfth of a dollar, every bushel of grain or salt one seventy secondth of a dollar, every chaldron of coal one fourth of a dollar, every hundred pipe staves one sixth of a dollar, every hundred hogshead staves one eighth of a dollar, every hundred barrel staves one twelfth of a dollar, every hundred cubic feet of plank or timber one sixth of a dollar, every cubic yard of stone one twenty fourth of a dollar, every cubic yard of oar one twelfth of a dollar, and for every hundred weight of other merchandize whatsoever one twenty fourth of a dollar, and so in proportion for a greater or less quantity which shall enter the said canal and pass the place where the toll shall be demanded, in any boat or other vessel, and for every such boat or other vessel not laded (other than those which having passed upwards or downwards shall be on their return) five sixths of a dollar: which paiments shall be made in gold or silver or the worth thereof in paper bills of credit at such rate of exchange as shall have been last fixed for the purpose by the General assembly according to the true and actual difference at market between gold or silver and paper bills of credit and in case of neglect or refusal of paiment of such toll on demand, it shall be lawful for the said company to make distress on the said vessel which passed or the goods laden on board thereof, or the horses towing the same, and such distress to detain as a pledge till paiment in like manner as is allowed by the law in cases of distress for toll in a fair or market.

The said canal from the time of the first toll paid shall be deemed a navigable water and with the horseways on each side thereof shall be common to all the citizens of this commonwealth for the purpose of transporting along the said water their goods and merchandize paying the tolls herein before stated.

When the said company shall have determined on the course of the said canal and shall be ready to enter therewith the lands of any particular tenant, they shall make application after ten days previous notice to the proprietor if he be to be found in the county, and if not, then to his agent therein if any he hath that such application would be made to the court of the county of Henrico or to the General court who shall thereupon order a writ to be issued in the nature of a writ of Ad quod damnum directed to their sheriff commanding him to summon and impanel a jury of twelve fit persons to meet on the said tenement on a certain day to be named by the court and inserted in the writ, of which notice shall be given by the sheriff to the said proprietor or his agent as before directed, if neither of them were present in court at the time of the order made, which jurors taking nothing (on pain of being discharged from the inquest and immediately imprisoned by the sheriff) either of meat or drink from any person whatever, from the time they shall come to the said tenement until their inquest sealed, and being duly charged by the sheriff shall describe by certain metes and bounds the lands so to be occupied by the said canal, it's horseways and banks one hundred feet each way from the middle of the said canal except where they shall be restrained by mills or other engines or their appendages within the saving herein before provided: and shall estimate the true value thereof in so many different parts as there shall be different persons entitled thereto and according to their several estates therein, and shall also say to what damage it will be of the said several persons over and above the estimated value of their estate in the said lands, for the said Canal to be opened or constructed as so described: and if the said inquest cannot be completed in one day the sheriff may adjourn the jury from day to day until the same be compleated: which inquest sealed with the seals of the said jurors shall be returned by the sheriff to the court from which the order issued there to be recorded and a copy thereof shall be delivered by the clerk of the said court to each person found to have any estate in the said lands, who producing the same to the Auditors, and obtaining their warrant shall be entitled to receive from the Treasurer the value of his estate in the said lands and the damages estimated and assessed to him by the jury, in full satisfaction and bar of his right and title to the lands and to all damages which he may afterwards sustain by the opening constructing or establishing the said canal: which proceeding shall be repeated and observed with every several tenement whensoever the said company shall be ready to enter the same with the canal.

And whereas a certain John Ballendine is intitled to an equity of redemption in forty six and an half acres of land on the said river formerly the property of Patrick Coutts deceased and adjoining to the lands of the commonwealth whereon the Foundery was erected, the legal estate in which said forty six and an half acres of land is in Richard Adams, Nathaniel Wilkinson and Turner Southall in trust for the commonwealth as a pledge for the performance of certain covenants wherein the said John Ballendine is bound to the commonwealth and for the repaiment of certain monies advanced to him on the public behalf, and the said John Ballendine, giving out in speeches that he would open and construct a navigable Canal from Westham to Richmond, did, without authority from the legislature, without obtaining legal conveyances of the rights and authorities of the subscribers according to the act of assembly before mentioned passed in the year one thousand seven hundred and seventy two, and without order from any court of justice, begin a canal and open the same through the greater part of the tenement aforesaid, and erect a dam across an arm of the said river for the purpose of diverting the water thereof into the said canal, but hath now for a long time surceased doing any thing towards continuing the said canal and is visibly and notoriously unable to compleat the same had he authority so to do, yet nevertheless it will be just if the public convenience should require that the said canal or dam should be used for continuing the navigation proposed from Beverley town to the tide waters at Richmond, that the said John Ballendine should be allowed so much as the construction of the said dam and canal would cost under good management and oeconomy.

Be it therefore enacted that if the said company shall propose for the purpose of compleating the said navigation to make use of the dam or canal so begun by the said John Ballendine, the jury so to be summoned and charged as before directed for describing by metes and bounds the lands to be vested in the said company for estimating the value thereof, and saying to what other damage of the said John Ballendine it will be, shall in assessing such damage take into their consideration and allow as part thereof what the construction of the said dam and canal in the state in which they shall then be would cost under good management and oeconomy for which estimated value and damages the said John Ballendine shall have credit in the public account against him for monies lent and secured by mortgage of the said forty six and an half acres of land: or instead of a jury so to be summoned it shall be lawful for the Governour with the advice of the council of state in the particular case of the said John Ballendine if the said John Ballendine shall so elect and desire, to appoint five persons of judgment and integrity sworn to perform the duties which the said jury would otherwise have performed, having been first charged before a justice of the peace to do the same impartially and to the best of their skill and judgment, whose report shall be returned by them into the General court and have the force of a verdict rendered by a jury: and if any of the persons so appointed die, decline or delay to act, the Governour may in like manner appoint another in his stead as often as the case shall happen, provided that the said John Ballendine shall make election to have persons so nominated by the Governour instead of a jury and shall make application accordingly to the Governour within one week after the said company or some one on their part and by authority from them shall have required him to make such election, which requisition it shall be incumbent on them to make of the said John Ballendine one month before their application to any court for the empanelling of a jury to perform the said duties.

The said company at the same time and in the same instrument wherein they shall declare to the Governour their determination to undertake the said canal shall moreover declare within what term they will complete the same: and if the said term shall exceed ten years the General assembly shall be at perfect liberty at their first session next ensuing such declaration to disagree to the several articles of agreement before recited relating to the said canal, and to revoke all the powers and interests hereby given to the said Peter Penet, Windel and company in and about the said canal. If the said company undertake and fail to complete the said canal within the term declared, their rights under the same articles shall become forfeited to and vested in the commonwealth it shall be lawful for the General assembly at any time after the year one thousand eight hundred and forty to take into the hands of the commonwealth the property of the said canal, its water, locks, banks and other appendages, and the necessary privileges in the adjacent ground for repairing them, leaving to the said company of Undertakers the use of such portions of the water and in such places for working their machines as they shall have applied to that use during the first twenty five years after their undertaking it, and paying to them the double of what the opening the said canal, building the locks, banks, and other the said appendages thereof shall have cost them, the amount of which cost shall be kept by the company separate and apart from that of their other works and shall annually with their vouchers be laid before persons jointly to be chosen by the Governour with the advice of council and the company, to be by them examined and certified so far as they find them just, and a copy of such certificate to be given to each party and to be binding. Where such cost shall have been defrayed in paper money or commodities, the true worth thereof in gold or silver at the time of the expenditure and at the place where expended shall be estimated by the same persons, and the repaiment thereof, as also of all expenditures of gold and silver, shall be made in double the quantity of gold and silver as before mentioned. In case of such resumption of the said canal into the hands of the commonwealth the said company shall have a right of passage along the same toll free for all the productions of the manufactory of arms, and foundery before mentioned and the necessaries for them until the beginning of the year one thousand eight hundred and ninety.

MS (DLC); a fair copy in a clerk's hand and endorsed by the clerk: "A Bill for establishing a manufactory of Arms, and foundery: and for extending navigation through the falls of James river." The MS contains one long and significant paragraph inserted by TJ in a blank left by the clerk (see note 1, below) and also a number of small corrections and insertions by TJ (not individually noted here), indicating that he went over the fair copy very carefully. The composition draft of the last portion of the bill (see note 2, below), entirely in TJ's hand and much interlined and corrected, was written on three blank pages of Gen. Phillips' letter to TJ, 12 Aug. 1779 (letter owned by Lloyd W. Smith, Madison, N.J., 1946).

For the background of this bill see Contract between the State of Virginia and Penet, Windel & Co., 22 July 1779, and especially TJ to Harrison, 30 Oct. 1779. It is not known when TJ drew it up in such characteristic detail, though he must have done so after 12 Aug. and presumably about the time he submitted to Speaker Harrison all the papers pertaining to the proposed transfer of Ballendine's rights to Penet and his backers. On 13 Dec. 1779 Gen. Nelson reported for the Committee of Propositions and Grievances, and it was agreed by the House, that the proposed contract be referred to the consideration of the next session but that buildings be erected in Richmond for the accommodation of the workers expected from France (JHD, Oct. 1779, 1827 edn., p. 87-8). However, no workers ever sailed from France, for (as Penet reported to TJ, 20 May 1780) the French government had prohibited the emigration of munitions workers. This was the end of TJ's hopeful arrangements with Penet, but meanwhile

JOHN REEVELY (or Reveley), in spite of entanglements with Ballendine, was actually producing munitions and ordnance at the public foundry at Westham, which he succeeded in wagoning out; see Kathleen Bruce, *Virginia Iron Manufacture in the Slave Era*, N.Y. and London, 1930, p. 52-4. In Jan. 1781 the foundry was destroyed by Lt. Col. John Graves Simcoe, acting under Gen. Benedict Arnold's orders, together with such stores as the workers had been unable to ferry across the river; TJ himself had supervised the hurried and incomplete evacuation (same, p. 60-2; TJ's Diary of Arnold's Invasion, printed under date of 31 Dec. 1780, below; also TJ's correspondence of Jan. 1781). The Acts of 1765 (not 1764 as mistakenly cited by TJ) and 1772 for EXTENDING THE NAVIGATION OF JAMES RIVER will be found in Hening, VIII, 148-50, and 564-70, respectively. With the first of these TJ had himself been intimately connected (see his Project for Making the Rivanna River Navigable, 1771), but the canal around the Great Falls was not constructed until after the formation of the James River Company in 1785 (Hening, XI, 450-62; W. F. Dunaway, *History of the James River and Kanawha Company*, N.Y., 1922, ch. II).

1 The following paragraph is in TJ's hand, inserted in a long blank left by the copyist.
2 The surviving fragment of TJ's draft of the bill begins at this point and includes all that follows.

From Samuel Huntington

SIR   Philadelphia 30th. Octr. 1779.

You will receive herewith enclosed an act of Congress of this date, earnestly recommending to the State of Virginia to re-consider their late act of Assembly for opening their land office; And to that, and all other States similarly circumstanced, to forbear settling or issuing Warrants for unappropriated lands or granting the same during the continuance of the present war.

I am with sentiments of esteem and regard, Your Excellency's, Humble servant,   SAMLL HUNTINGTON President

RC (CSmH). In a clerk's hand and signed by Huntington. FC (DLC: PCC, No. 14); circular to the state executives.

Enclosure: Resolve of Congress, 30 Oct. 1779 (Vi); printed in JCC, XV, 1229-30. This letter and resolve were in turn transmitted by the governor to the House of Delegates; see TJ to Harrison, 19 Nov. 1779. The House thereupon formulated a remonstrance to Congress on the Vandalia and Indiana Companies' claims, 10 Dec. 1779 (JHD, Oct. 1779, 1827 edn., p. 83-4). For the background and consequences of this incident, see note on Huntington's letter to TJ, 10 Sep. 1780. Virginia's LATE ACT for opening its land office, passed in June 1779, is printed above under date of 8 Jan. 1778.

From Giovanni Fabbroni

AMICO, E SIGNIORE STIMATISSMO   Londra 1 9bre 1779.

Sento dal Sig. Digs [Digges] vostro amico, che voi siete stato recentemente eletto Governatore della Vostra rispettabil Provincia. Vi sia egli testimone del contento, che ne provai, e per voi e per tutta La Virginia, che invano cercherei d'esprimervi colla mia penna. Mi si presentano tutte ad un tratto alla spirito Le vostre belle qualità di cui è ripiena La Francia, ed anco L'Inghilterra, e ch'io particolarmente riconobbi, oltre le relazioni altrui, dalle due vostre lettere, colle quali mi onoraste in Francia. Vedo che tale elezione vi farà felice, perché vi pone in stato di render felici i vostri compatriotti con un paterno, e filosofico governo, confaciente all' indole vostro. Questa sola idea, tanto lusinghevole, m'eccita il più gran contento, e questo sarebbe immenso, se non venisse equiponderato dal dispiacere d'aver lasciata l'occasione di trovarmi adesso con Voi, d'esser suddito alle vostre savisse. leggi, e di partecipare anch'io della pubblica felicità di cotesti fortunati paesi, sempre fortunati benché devastati da delle armi inumane che vogliono contrastarvi il più prezioso tesoro della società. Combattete: La vostra causa è troppo giusta; il cielo benedirà assolutamente le vostre azioni. Nacqui in una parte d'Italia ove era motto men grave che altrove la servitù: Vissi, e vivo, sotto un Principe il più umano dell'universo, che con incessantí, e nuove Leggi ha abolito ogni segnio di dispotismo verso ai suoi sudditi, che egli ama e governa da vero Padre. Egli ha tolto ogni tassa arbitraria, ha reso libero affatto il commercio, e l'esercizio dell'industria, e lascia una più che sufficiente Libertà di coscienza ad ogni individuo. Queste circostanze mi fan sentire con molta energìa il beneficio di perfetta Libertà; sentimento ottuso, e nullo in quei, che nacquero, e vissero in perpetua schiavitù, e mi fan desiderare colla più grande ansietà di venire una volta à visitar cotesta felice Repubb. e conoscere personalmente in Voi un'uomo, che tanto stimo, ed amo sulle relazioni d'ogni uno.

Tutte si sono avverate le predizioni del mio amico Pryce [Price], vero profeta rispetto al successo delle imprudenti ed infelici dispute attuali di questo paese; presto spero di vedere effettuato altresì, che una tranquilla, e permanente pace assicuri per sempre quella Libertà or stabilita in cotesta parte del nuovo continente. Allora assolutamente spero, se il Cielo seconderà i miei voti di potere adempire ogni desiderio, e di venir costà con un Gentiluomo mio amico, amico dell'americana felicità, e possidente nella Vostra medesima provincia.

Vi prego a volervi valer di me in tutte quelle occasioni [in cui] mi crediate sufficiente, ed a volermi credere tale quale con sincerissima, e devoto ossequio mi pregio dirmi Vostro [Affettiso.?] ed obbedientisso. servo, ed amico,   GIOVANNI FABRONI

P.S. Ad ogni altro fuori che a Voi non avrei osato di scrivere in una maniera sì confidenziale, dopo l'esser stato voi medo. elevato giustamente a un tal grado di dignità; ma conosco il vostro bel cuore e son certo, che sarete Lontanissimo dal tenervene offeso.

Vi farò capitar da Parigi un piccolo sommario d'una parte delle leggi del mio Sovrano, che è stato ultimamente pubblicato in francese. Vi farò altresì pervenire un mio libercolo sull'agricultura, che all'istigazione de'miei amici consegnai alle stampe, ed una mia chimica dissertazione sull'arsenico. Si aduna ancora La vostra celebre accademia di Filadelfia? Potrei io indirizzarvi una mia teoria sugli effetti della polvere da cannone, per esser presentata alla medesima? Datemi, vi prego delle vostre nuove, e di quelle dell'amico Bellini, e dirigetemile, o a Firenze, ove sarò di ritorno fra due mesi, o in Parigi al mio amico Favi ministro di Toscana rue des Bons Enfans maison de Mr. d'Ennery o à Londra ai Signori Priestley, o Prayce [Price], o Waugham [Vaughan], o Paradisi membri della Società Reale, altrettanto miei buoni Padroni, quanto affezionati al ben essere dell'umanità, e partigiani della Libertà. Spero che vi saranno già pervenute due altre mie lettere, l'una scritta l'anno scorso di Francia, ed una 8 mesi sono dall'Inghilterra. La Filosofia non cessa, non ostanti le attuali turbolenze di far dei continovi e rimarcabili progressi. Voi sapete che Priestley indicò al mondo il principale uso della respirazione, ma la sua teoria non rendeva ragione della diminuzione dell'aria respirata. Il Dr. Leslie prova che lo sviluppo del flogisto dal sangue si effettua non solo nei polmoni, ma per tutto il corpo; Mr. Crawford dimostra, che questo sviluppo e cagionato dalla materia del calore, o fuoco elementare [ass]orbita dal sangue quando viene al contatto dell'aria nelle vescichette polmonari, e conciò si comprende da che derivi la diminuzione di volume dell'aria medesima. Priestley scoprì che il primo uso della vegetazione si è quello d'assorbire il flogisto che gli animali scaricano continuamente nell'aria, e col quale la infetta. Ingenhousz aggiugne che le piante depurano l'aria ma solo quando sono esposte all'azion della luce, ma che anzi la rendono più nocevole quando sono all'ombra, o nell'oscurità. S'intende dopo tale scoperta il perchè l'aria della campagna che è tanto salubre la mattina, sia poi malsana nella notte o anche verso sera. Il medo. filosofo ha altresì determinato, che le sole foglie, e fusto verde delle piante hanno la facoltà di migliorare l'aria alla luce, ed infettarla all'oscurità; ma [che] i fiori, le frutta, e le radici mai correggono l'aria, sia co[n] ajuto della luce, o senza, ma sempre anzi la rendono più flogisticata. Desidererei d'aver tempo e luogo da dettagliare queste scoperte importanti, che sono state fatte recentemente e che non saranno ancor conoscinte costà.

RC (DLC). Endorsed: "Fabroni Giovanni." The editors are indebted to Professor Archibald T. MacAllister, Princeton University, for the foregoing transcription and also for a translation on which the summary of contents, presented below, is based.

Fabbroni congratulates TJ on his election as governor. Regrets that he let slip the chance to become "subject to your most wise laws." The American cause is too just to suffer defeat. Fabbroni, who is fortunate in living under a prince who "has abolished every mark of despotism" and "rules as a real Father," still hopes to visit America with a friend who owns land in Virginia. The post-script apologizes for Fabbroni's writing in so informal a manner to so eminent a personage. He intends to send TJ a "summary of the laws of my Sovereign," lately published in French, also certain publications by himself on agriculture and arsenic. He inquires whether he might send to the American Philosophical Society "a theory of mine on the effects of cannon powder." Asks for news of Bellini. "I hope two other letters of mine will already have reached you, one written last year from France, and one 8 months ago from England." (Neither of these letters has been found.) Discusses recent chemical and physiological researches of Priestley, Leslie, Crawford, and Ingenhousz.

From the Board of War

SIR   War Office, Williamsburg. November 2nd 1779.

Your Excellency having inadvertently mistated to the Assembly, the nature of the Requisition, made by the Board of War, and approved by the Executive; for the appointment of a second Clerk to our Office; We take liberty by the inclosure accompanying this, to inform you more fully of the meaning of our Request. We had not in Idea, the space of two months, or any time, shorter than the duration of our Office, when we solicited the Aid of an additional Clerk. This may be easily discovered by the unlimited terms, in which, our Solicitation is expressed. Under the Sanction of the approbation of the Honorable the Lieutenant Governour in Council, we called to our Assistance, a young Gentleman, who enjoyed a permanent Provision in the Auditors Office, which it is hardly to be suppos'd he woud have relinquished, for the short Enjoyment of a two months Profit; and it surely woud have been treachery in us, to have seduced him so far from his real Interest, had we have thought our appointment woud have had so short an Existance. But independent of this, when the multifarious and extensive duties of our Office are properly understood, we are induced to believe, that the appointment we have solicited, will not be thought supernumerary. One Gentleman of the Honorable Council, at least, well knows from experiment, the trouble and business resulting from the naval department, and he, I dare say, can attest that the time of one Clerk was fully engrossed by a proper attention to maritime Affairs. And we trust, your Excellency and the Council will readily think, that the various Objects of Employment pointed out by Law, and referred to us by your Honorable Board, will form matter[s] of Business, sufficient to engage the Labor and assiduity of a second Clerk.

Conceiving the reputation of our official Characters, interested to support the appointment we made, under the positive approbation and Licence of the Supreme Executive, We have to request, that your Excellency will represent to the Assembly, the real State of this matter, which by the determination of the House of Delegates of yesterday, appeared to be exceedingly misconceived.

We have the Honor to be Your Excellency's most obt Servts.,

JAS INNES

SAMUEL GRIFFIN

JAS. BARRON

GEO: LYNE

RC (DLC). For the dispute concerning the APPOINTMENT of a CLERK, see above, James Innes to Mann Page, 27 Oct. 1779, and below, TJ to Benjamin Harrison, 20 Nov. 1779. The DETERMINATION OF THE HOUSE OF DELEGATES: On 1 Nov., the House of Delegates resolved that "the Governor, with advice of Council, be empowered to appoint an assistant clerk to the Board of Council" (JHD, Oct. 1779, 1827 edn., p. 33). This is undoubtedly a clerk's error and should read "Board of War"; see *Official Letters*, II, 56. Another resolution passed at the same time directed the Board of War to grant a certificate to Harrison Randolph for money due him as assistant clerk in proportion to the time he was employed, implying his dismissal.

Petition of Alexander Dick to the Governor and Council

Williamsburg, 2 Nov. 1779. The petitioner embarked on an armed brig in February 1777 as a part of the state regiment and was taken to England as a prisoner; having contracted a debt of 160 guineas while a prisoner and during escape, he requests that his pay as captain be made equal to hard money; he requests also a commission as major of marines.

RC (Vi); 2 p.   Dick's petition was transmitted to the House of Delegates in TJ's letter to Harrison of 8 Nov. 1779, q.v.

From Cyrus Griffin

Sɪʀ   Philadelphia Nov. 2nd. [1779]

My Colleague Mr. Mercer has charged himself with the naval Commissions mentioned a post ago in a letter from your excellency.

We have a report from the Eastward that a bloody Engagement has happend in English Channel, and that the admiral of his Britanic Majesty was met with sails and Colours flying; but we do not give the utmost credit to the Intelligence.

I have the honor to be, Sir, Your excellency's most obedient and humble servant,   C. Gʀɪғғɪɴ

RC (DLC).
The year, omitted by Griffin, must be 1779, since James Mercer attended Congress from 9 Sep. to 30 Oct. 1779 only, and returned to Virginia just at this time

(Burnett, *Letters of Members*, ɪᴠ, lxvi, and 505, note). TJ's letter to the Virginia delegates respecting naval commissions is missing.

From the Board of Trade, with Reply

[Williamsburg] 3 *Nov. 1779.* Submits requisitions from Board of War for shoes and for clothing for Col. Buford's battalion at Petersburg; also a memorandum of George Purdie offering sundry articles. Mr. Greenhow has 10 dozen men's large shoes which he offers at £12 per pair and 9 dozen small men's shoes at £10. Prices for all the articles are exceedingly high, but the need for them is pressing. Signed by Ambler and Rose. Instructions, in TJ's hand, on verso: "In Council Nov. 5. 1779. The board approve the purchase of shoes from John Greenhow and of the purchase of such articles from Mr. Purdie as the board of trade think proper, provided payment be accepted in money, not tobacco. Th: Jefferson." Also: "In Council Nov. 11. 1779. As to the purchase of necessaries for Colo. Buford's regiment this board must refer to the discretion of board of trade to conduct themselves according

to the necessities of the troops on the one hand and the prices of the goods on the other. Th: Jefferson."

RC (CSmH). Addressed: "His Excellency in Council." Enclosures not located.

From the Board of War

War Office Wmsburg Novr. 4th. 1779

Some men having arrived in Town who were enlisted under the Act for raising soldiers sailors and marines, The Board of War recommend to the Executive to Order the sailors on board of some of the armed vessells of this state, and the soldiers and marines to join the state Garrison Regiment which is very weak.

JAMES INNES

JAMES BARRON

GEO: LYNE

Tr in Board of War Letter Book (MiU-C).

From the Board of War

War Office Wmsburg Novr. 4th. 1779

The Board of War recommend to the executive to authorize the Commanding Officer of each County to review all the men recruited in their respective Counties under the Act for recruiting Soldiers Sailors and marines and to give certificates of review to the Officer, appoint a place of rendezvous if necessary supply the recruits with rations, and to make application for money to defray the expence.

The Board farther recommended that Officers be appointed to ride the circuits for the purpose of collecting the recruits, intended either for State or Continental Service and march them to such places of rendezvous as the Governor and Council shall appoint.

JAS. INNES

JAS. BARRON

GEO. LYNE

Tr in Board of War Letter Book (MiU-C). The ACT FOR RECRUITING SOLDIERS SAILORS AND MARINES was passed in the May 1779 session of the Assembly (Hening, X, 23-7).

To Benjamin Harrison

SIR   Wmsburg November 4th. 1779

According to the pleasure of the House of Delegates signified in their resolution of the 16th. of the last month, I now inclose you a

State of the armed Vessels belonging to this Commonwealth, and returns of the Garrison and Artillery regiments, and of such part of the four troops of horse for Eastern service as are raised. What progress is made in raising the four new battalions, is out of my power to say, the returns being very few. Probably the collected information of the Members of General Assembly may enable you to form a Judgment. A Considerable part of the Men for the Illinois troop of horse is raised. Orders were sent in June to Colo. Todd to purchase horses there. The present strength of the Illinois battalion under Colo. Clarke, I am unable to State with accuracy; but from information of Officers from thence not long since, its number was about three hundred.

I also inclose you Sir, returns of the Virginia troops now with the grand army, of Colo. Gibsons regiment at Fort Pitt, of so much of Colo. Baylor's regiment of horse as is with the grand army, and of Colo. Taylors regiment of Guards for the Convention troops. An Express has been sent to General Scott for a return of the new Levies under his command, which we may hope to receive very shortly, and shall be communicated to you the moment it comes. I am sorry that no returns enable me to give you an exact State of the residue of Colo. Baylors horse with the Southern Army, of Colo. Blands horse nor of two independant Companies of infantry under Captns. Ohara and Heath at Fort Pitt, for all of which you are entitled to credit as part of your Continental Quota, according to a resolution of Congress of March 15, 1779 to be found in the printed Journals, but of which no authentic Copy has been received by us. Colo. Taylors regiment on its present establishment seems not to come within the descriptions in the resolution, tho' in Continental service.

I have been much longer in collecting and transmitting to you these returns than I at first hoped. I beg you to be assured that I have not added a moment to those delays which the collecting them has unavoidably occasioned.

I have the honour to be with the greatest respect Sir Your most obedient and most humble servt., TH: JEFFERSON

RC (Vi); in a clerk's hand except for complimentary close, signature, and address in TJ's hand. Endorsed (in part): "Governor's Letter Novr. 4th. 1779. . . . Encloses Returns of Arms, Vessels & Troops." Enclosures missing, but TJ's drafts of these Returns remain among his papers and are entered under this date, below.

In a RESOLUTION of 16 Oct. 1779 the House of Delegates desired the governor to lay before the House returns of the land and naval forces of the state (JHD, Oct. 1779, 1827 edn., p. 11-12).

After this had been done, the Assembly on 20 Dec. passed an Act to regulate and ascertain the number of land forces to be kept up for the defense of the state, which substantially reduced the forces provided for under the defense Acts of May 1779 (same, p. 99; Hening, x, 215-16). For the RESOLUTION OF CONGRESS of 15 Mch. 1779 concerning state troop quotas, see JCC, XIII, 317-18.

Returns of Virginia Land and Naval Forces

[4 November 1779]

[Text reproduced in illustration section following p. 254.]

MS (DLC); entirely in TJ's hand.

Principally compiled in Oct. 1779 at the request of the House of Delegates, these memoranda are drafts of the returns actually sent in a letter to Speaker Harrison on 4 Nov., q.v., but contain additions made after receipt of Washington's letter to TJ of 26 Dec. 1779, q.v.; and other additions as late as 27 May 1780.

Board of War to Board of Trade

Williamsburg, 5 Nov. 1779. Recommends the immediate purchase of a list of articles needed for the officers and soldiers of the Virginia troops in the northern army. Signed by Innes, Griffin, Barron, and Lyne. Countersigned: "Approved. Th: Jefferson."

RC (CSmH); 1 p. Above the list of articles needed is a list of articles supplied to the northern army, dated 25 Oct. 1779, signed by Samuel Griffin.

Roll of Officers of the Regiment of Guards for the Convention Prisoners

[5 November 1779]

		Oct. 8. 1779.	Oct. 25. 1779.
Colonel	Francis Taylor.	Francis Taylor.	Francis Taylor.
Lt. Colonel.			
Major.	John Roberts.	John Roberts.	John Roberts.
Captains.	Garland Burnley.	Garland Burnley.	Garland Burnley.
	Ambrose Madison.	Ambrose Madison.	James Purvis.
	Benjamin Timberlake.	Benjamin Timberlake.	Thomas Porter.
	Robert Barrett.	Robert Barrett.	James Burton.
		James Purvis.	Richard White.
		Thomas Porter.	Edward Herndon.
		James Burton.	
		Richard White.	

Lieutenants.	James Purvis.	Edward Herndon.	John Slaughter. qu.
	Thomas Porter.	John Slaughter. resd.	John Taylor.
	James Burton.	John Taylor.	Richard Paulett.
	Richard White.	Richard Paulett.	Samuel O. Pettus.
	Edward Herndon.	Samuel O. Pettus.	
Ensigns.	John Slaughter.		John Winston.
	John Taylor.		William Slaughter.
	Richard Paulett.	.	Jesse Paulet.
	Samuel O. Pettus.		Nichols. Meriwether Nov. 5. 79

Nicholas Meriwether. appd. Ensign Nov. 5. 1779.

MS (DLC); in TJ's hand.
See TJ to Francis Taylor, 25 Oct. 1779, on restaffing the guard regiment.

To Benjamin Harrison

[*Williamsburg, 5? Nov. 1779.* JHD, Oct. 1779, 1827 edn., p. 42
(5 Nov. 1779): "The Speaker laid before the House, a letter from the
Governor, respecting sundry losses sustained by Mr. Martin, the present Indian agent, in the Cherokee country, and the propriety of making
him compensation for the same, which was read, and ordered to be
referred to the committee of Trade." Not located.]

From George Washington

SIR   Hd Qrs West Point Novr 5. 1779

I would take the liberty of addressing a few lines to Your Excellency, respecting such of the officers and privates of Blands and
Baylors Regiments of Dragoons and of Harrisons Artillery as
belong to the state of Virginia. Their situation is really disagreable
and discouraging; and it is perhaps the more so, from its being now
almost if not entirely singular. It is said, that under the idea of their
not having been originally a part of the Troops apportionned on
the State in September 1776, the State provision of Cloathing and

bounty for reinlisting their Men is not to be extended to them or at least that it is a doubtful point. This is the source of great uneasiness and indeed of distress among them; and it is the more felt, as most of the States, since the Resolution of Congress of the 15th of March last of which I have the honor to transmit Your Excellency a copy have made no discrimination between Officers and Men belonging to them, in the same predicament and those who were explicitly assessed on them as their Quota under the first mentioned Resolution; but on the contrary have permitted them to participate in every benefit and emolument granted others of their Troops. The Regiments of Artillery and Cavalry which in the whole amount to Eight as well as Many Companies of Artificers and other Corps have never been apportionned in a particular manner on the States, so as to show the exact proportion of Officers and Men which each should furnish but being absolutely essential to the public service, as they must be so long as the War continues, they have been raised in a promiscuous manner; and if the point was ascertained it is highly probable the proportion from each State, would be found not very unequal. I have mentioned this circumstance that the Officers and Men of the State in those three Regiments, may not be considered as a Quota furnished, over and above what is done by the Rest of the States. And I would take the liberty farther to observe that as several of the Regiments of Infantry apportionned on the State by the Resolution of Sept. 1776, have been reduced, a circumstance which has not taken place with respect to the Regiments of most other States, there appears to me the more reason, for the benefits of Cloathing and bounty granted by the State, being extended equally to them with any other of her Troops. They share with them in every danger, and in every burthen, both at home and abroad, and it seems but equitable that they should partake of every benefit. The terms of service for which the Men of these three Corps were engaged are expiring every day and if it should be the pleasure of the State to give the Men in them belonging to it the encouragements and benefits they have granted to their Infantry Regiments, the sooner the point is determined the better.

I have the Honor to be with the greatest respect & esteem Yr Excellency's Most Obed St,   G W

Dft (DLC: Washington Papers); in hand of R. H. Harrison; endorsed. Enclosure: Resolve of Congress of 15 Mch. 1779 (missing, but see below).

The RESOLUTION OF CONGRESS of 15 Mch. here brought to TJ's notice provided that those officers and soldiers commissioned and enlisted for three years or during the war, but not part of the eighty-eight battalions apportioned on the states, were to be assigned to the state quotas (JCC, XIII, 317-18). See TJ's reply, 28 Nov. 1779.

From the Board of Trade

Sir   Board of Trade Novr. 6th 1779.

We have considered the several letters and papers received from Messrs. Pollock and Lindsey referred by your Excellency to this Board, and beg leave to observe, that it appears therefrom that the late Governor Mr. Henry by virtue of an Act Assembly intituled "an Act for establishing the County of Ilinois" did, on the day of   in the Year one thousand seven hundred and seventy   Depute Mr. Joseph Lindsey to contract at New Orleans for sundry Goods, for the use of the Inhabitants of the said County of Ilionois, and that the said Lindsey was furnished with a Bill of Credit for 10,000 Dollars, on Account of the State, to enable him to make the purchase; in consequence of which, and the recommendations of Colo: Clarke and John Todd esquire, Mr. Pollock exerted himself in a very particular manner, and supplyed Mr. Lindsay with Goods to the amount of 10029. 1 Dollars; which Goods were shipped by Mr. Lindsay to Ilinois addressed to the commanding officer there. It appears also that Mr. Pollock has, at various times paid on Account of the State the Drafts of Colo. Clarke, Capt. O'Harra, and Mr. Linn, and the Expences of a Detachment of men to Ilinois, to the amount of 33,388 Dollars. It appears also that Colo. Clarke has drawn Bills on Mr. Pollock to the amount of about 25,000 Dollars, which from necessity Mr. Pollock was obliged to Protest. Concluding from the Papers before this Board, that the Persons drawing the aforementioned sums were legally empowered so to do by the late Governor, we think it highly expedient in justice to Mr. Pollock, and the Credit of our State, that the said sums should be reimbursed as expeditiously as possible, and therefore we beg advice from the honble Board with respect to the most eligible mode of making remittances to Mr. Pollock. It appears impossible, in our present circumstances, to remit in produce; and we beg leave to submit to the consideration of His Excellency in Council, whether it will not be practicable, under the engagements entered into by The Honble Board with Messrs. Penet & Co. of   , to impower Mr. Pollock to draw on that House for the amount of his advances, and Colo. Clarke's Protested Bills. As Mr. Pollock observes it will not be prudent to rest solely on a Credit in France, we beg leave to submit also to His Excellency in Council, whether, in aid thereof, as well as for securing a fund for any future contingencies, in that Quarter, it may not be advisable for the Honble Board to solicit a Loan of specie from the Governor of Orleans.

The War now carrying on by Spain against our common Enemy affords no unfavourable ground of Hope but that such assistance, on proper application, might be obtained.

Your Excellency was pleased to recommend to our consideration the disposition of the Goods sent by Mr. Lindsay to Ilinois: we are of opinion that if they are not disposed of before he reaches Ilinois, Instructions should be sent the Commanding officer to reserve them for the use of the Troops, and our friendly Indians, which now are or may hereafter be found necessary in that Quarter.

We have the Honor to be Yr. Excellency's Mo: Obed. Hble Servts., J. AMBLER

DUN: ROSE

RC (Vi). Addressed: "His Excellency Thomas Jefferson Esqr. in Council." TJ's reply of the same date, written below the Board's letter, follows.

To the Board of Trade

In Council Nov. 6. 1779.

The board are of opinion payment should be made to Mr. Pollock of all the articles of his account except the draughts by O'Hara, of whom they know nothing, nor by what authority he drew. They would recommend to the board of trade to desire from Mr. Pollock an explanation of O'Hara's draughts and to assure him that if it shall appear they were made on due authority, they shall be immediately replaced. They advise the Governour to write to the Governour of New Orleans for information whether their former application through him for a loan of money from the court of Spain has had success, and if it has, to desire him to pay the demands before allowed of Mr. Pollock; and they recommend to the Board of trade to authorize Mr. Pollock, if he shall not receive the money in that way, to draw on Messrs. Penet & company to that amount, and to take such measures as they can for procuring honour to the bills. They think it will be proper for the board of trade to give Mr. Lindsay a warrant for £2000 on account as agent of trade at New Orleans, notifying Colo. Todd thereof; and approve of the instructions they propose for retaining the merchandise sent to Illinois for the publick use. TH: JEFFERSON

RC (Vi). Written below Board of Trade to TJ, same date, to which this is n answer.

Board of Trade to Penet, D'Acosta Frères

[*Williamsburg*] *6 Nov. 1779.* The governor has written the Board to authorize Oliver Pollock of New Orleans to draw on Penet, D'Acosta Frères to the amount of 65,814⅝ Spanish milled dollars. This engagement was entered into by Peter Penet, and the order has been transmitted to Pollock. Signed (in clerk's hand) by "J. Answer" [error for Ambler] and Dun[can] Rose, and countersigned (in clerk's hand) by TJ.

Tr (CSmH); 1 p. At foot of text: "This is to certify that the above is true Copy taken from the Original New Orleans 20 Apl. 1782 William Smith."

To the Board of Trade

In Council Nov. 6. 1779

It is recommended to the board of trade to settle the expences of Capt. LeMaire stated in this account, and those incurred from his arrival at Boston until the 10th. instant.   TH: JEFFERSON

RC (CSmH); written on the final page of the account submitted: "Etat des Depenses faites en france par le Capitaine Le Maire a l'occasion de la Mission dont il a été chargé par L'Etat de la Virginie," signed by Le Maire and dated "A Williamsbourg le 2. Octobre 1779"; 3 p. (including both the account and the letter).

See Board of Trade to TJ, 9, 13 Nov.; TJ to Board of Trade, 9-12 Nov.; also TJ to Benjamin Harrison, 29 Oct. 1779.

To the Board of Trade

In Council Novr. 6th 79.

The Board of trade are requested to direct that Major Martin be furnished at the big island with 1000 ℔ iron 100 ℔ Steel and a Set of Smiths Tools for the Cherokee nation. Also 100 Gallons of good Whiskey or rum.

A Copy   ARCH. BLAIR CC

Tr (Vi).   See also TJ to Board of Trade, 30 Oct. 1779.

To John Bowman

SIR   Wmsburgh Novr. 6. 1779.

I am to ask the favour of you to give notice to the officer recommended by you for the Western Battalions, that as soon as one half his Quota of Men is raised and delivered by you, he shall be entitled to his Commission. These Men are to make part of a Battalion, which will be commanded by Lieut. Colo. Knox, and which is to be stationed this Winter in Powels Valley. As this station is so very far from you, your officer is to march his Men to the falls of Ohio, and there do duty under Major Slaughter this Winter, but he is not actually to march till he shall have heard of Major Slaughters arrival at the Falls; in the mean time let him employ them in the best manner he can for the public service. Money for their Subsistence from the time you deliver them to the officer till he shall have carried them to their Rendezvous, will be lodged with Major Slaughter. The Subsistence account previous to their delivery to the officer you will settle with the auditors here. I am Sir Yr. very hble. Servt.,   TH: JEFFERSON

RC (InHi); in a clerk's hand, signed by TJ. Addressed: "The County Lieutenant of Kentucky."

John Bowman was county lieutenant of Kentucky (Lewis Collins, *History of Kentucky*, Louisville, 1877, p. 476). On 4 Nov., the House of Delegates empowered the governor to raise 100 men to be stationed as a garrison on the southeast side of the Falls of the Ohio or to be employed as the governor and Council judge most expedient (JHD, Oct. 1779, 1827 edn., p. 40; see also TJ and Council, Orders for the Defense of the Western Frontier, 23 July; Notes and Plans for Western Defense, same date; TJ to William Preston, 7 Aug.; TJ to Certain County Lieutenants, 6 Nov.; TJ to David Shepherd, 13 Nov. 1779).

To Certain County Lieutenants

SIR   Wmsburg Novr. 6th. 1779.

I am to ask the favor of you to give notice to the Officers recommended by you for the Western Battalions that as soon as one half the quota of one of them is raised and delivered by you he shall be entitled to the Commission for which he was recommended. As soon as that quota is complete and half the next raised another shall be entitled to his commission: and so on where there are more. You will be so good as to decide between the Officers by Lot which shall be first called into Service, he upon whom the first Lot falls is to receive the men from you, til he gets his half quota. Then to march them to the Barracks in Albemarle, after which he who draws the second Lot is to receive the remaining half of the first quota and the half of his own quota when he will become entitled to his Commission and will march them on to the same rendezvous. The last half quota you must send on under a Sergeant as the Commissioned Officers will have left you. Lieut. Colo. Crocket is appointed to the Command of the Battalion of which your men will be. Money for their Subsistence from the time you deliver them to the Officer til he shall have carried them to their rendezvous will be Lodged with Colo. Sampson Matthews of Augusta. The Subsistence Account previous to their delivery to the Officer you will settle with the Auditors here. I am Sir Your very humble servt.,

TH: JEFFERSON

RC (Vi), in a clerk's hand, signed by TJ. Another RC (Mrs. Joseph P. Crockett, Alexandria, Va., 1949), in a clerk's hand, signed by TJ, omitting some details and with the words "the barracks in Albemarle" and "Crockett" inserted in the text in TJ's hand. Both are part of a series of circular letters to the county lieutenants; see TJ to John Bowman, this date, and TJ to David Shepherd, 13 Nov. 1779.

To Benjamin Harrison

[*Williamsburg, 6 Nov. 1779*. Cover only survives (in Vi), addressed in TJ's hand to Harrison as Speaker and endorsed: "Governors Letter Novr: 6th: 1779. Returns Military & Naval Referred to whole House on State of the Commonwealth." According to JHD (Oct. 1779, 1827 edn., p. 43), the letter was read the same day as sent and enclosed a return "of Maj. Nelson's corps of cavalry"; it was referred to the committee of the whole on the state of the commonwealth. See TJ to Harrison, 4 Nov. 1779.]

From D'Anmours, with a Memorial on the Status of French Subjects in Virginia

SIR [Williamsburg, 7 November 1779]

I have the honor of informing your Excellency and the honourable the House of Assembly that having received lately a Commission that appoints me Consul of France for his most christian Majesty in the State of Virginia, I accept it with the highest degree of pleasure. His Majestys Choice flatters me infinitely as I am entirely conscious with what particular Distinction he considers this State, and with what ardent desire he wishes to see the most constant harmony subsisting between his Kingdom and this Republic its Subjects and his. I leave it to you, Sir, and to the Honorable house to judge of the means of giving to that Commission the Authenticity it must have.

I have the honor to subjoin to this Letter, a Memorial Containing some eventual demands in favour of his Majesty's Subjects, and the french Nation in General that do, or will hereafter reside in Virginia, the importance of which I submit to your Excellency's and the honorable the House of Assembly's consideration.

I will always be ready to answer any objections that might be made to them, yet as an entire mistake of Principles as well as of Motives might give room to form some which I apprehend, I chuse to answer them before they are made, by an ample explanation of my Motives.

The Reason why I demand that the french Subjects that are settled, or will hereafter settle in Virginia, be entirely submitted to the authority of the Consuls of France, is, that being under their direct administration the Conduct of those same Subjects would be more known to them; and by that means they would be more able to stop or even prevent an immensity of Dissentions which might arise from the difference of language, manners &c. and propagate those ancient national prejudices, which every true Patriot of both Nations, strenuously endeavour to wipe off.

The Reason why I demand some privileges in favor of those same Subjects is to render that authority and administration agreeable and advantageous to them at the same time that those same priviledges would be useful to the trade of both Nations. For foreign Merchants will always prefer to trade with Countries where they shall be certain to find a protector, immediate and strict Justice, and priviledges with security for their Ships and their Commercial operations.

If I demand that the Government of Virginia would make all possible and proper regulations to stop all desertions and prevent emigrations from france and her possessions, it is not only because I think it an Act of Justice, but also because I conceive it to be one of prudence. By the nature of things every Man that will emigrate from every other Country but France will diminish the number of the Enemies of America; from France it would lessen the number of her friends, and such friends, that will always be ready to take up arms in her defence.

I take the Liberty, sir, to recommend to your Excellency the affair of Captain La Craix which I had the honor to communicate to you some time ago. The Situation of that man is really deplorable. The unjust manner in which he was used by the Judges of the Court of Accomack County, in depriving him of his Crew not only against the Laws of Nations but even against those of this Country has occasioned the loss of his Ship, and immense other Damages besides the loss of his Liberty: for he is still prisoner upon Bail. His Majesty's Minister has recommended that Affair most particularly to my protection. And I shall be glad to be able to give him an Account of it as soon as you have determined upon any Step on that Subject.

I have the Honor to be &c.,   LE CHEVR DANMOURS

ENCLOSURE

A Memorial Presented his Excellency Thomas Jefferson Esquire Governor in Chief of the State of Virginia, and the Honorable the house of Assembly, by the Chevalier D'Anmours, His Most Christian Majesty's Consul in the said State & in the State of Maryland

The Chevalier D'Anmours Consul of France for his most Christian Majesty in the States of Virginia and Maryland, has the honor to lay under the consideration of his Excellency the Governor, and the Honorable the House of Assembly of Virginia, the following Observations which he apprehends to be of the most essential importance to the good harmony and union that are now to subsist Between France and the Said State, and to the mutual prosperity of both.

As far as the nature of Things can allow human foresight to penetrate into futurity, any Statesman may perceive that for a long series of years, the French and American Nation on one side and the British on the other will be in a State of Constant enmity, either privately or openly. It behoves then the two first to be as constantly in a proper Situation of diffence, not only to oppose a foe in War; but also to force him to Abide by the treaties and conditions of peace. Therefore as the principal force with which his most Christian majesty can assist more effectually his Allies, is a powerfull and respectable Navy, the preservation of his Subjects and particularly his seamen of all classes, is a Capital point, which the Chevalier thinks, deserves the highest degree of Attention from his Excellency, and the Honorable House of Assembly.

The Chevalier begs leave to point out the materials of an act that might answer not only the desired object, but also that of Affording to his most Christian majesty one of the most evincing proofs of the sincerity of the Amity now subsisting between the State of Virginia and France. They are as follows. That by a Law of the State, all the subjects belonging to France either merchants Traders Seamen &c. be submitted to the immediate and entire administration and authority of his most Christian majesty's Consuls or their representants, as far as the said Subjects will not be criminally impeached by the Laws [of] the State, or apprehended for real Debts to its Subjects.

That the said authority and administration be always supported in the most Strenuous and effectual manner either by the Civil or military power, or the simple application of the Consuls or their representants to any of them notwithstanding all motives to the contrary except the two above mentioned ones.

That none of the said French Subjects but most Specially Seamen be at Liberty to withdraw themselves from the authority of their Consuls, not even on pretence of Naturalization.

[164]

Else what Ship would be sure to make her return in France, or what French merchant would intrust his interests to a man of his nation in Virginia that might by that Step elude to give any account of them. If in that case it is observed that the Laws of the Country wou'd see justice done to the first, it must be allowed also that the last might find a great many resources in them to procrastinate a conclusion to the ruin of a merchant particularly a foreign one, the fortune of which depends principally on immediate justice.

That by the same Law no Captain master of Ship Vessell, merchants or any other person of what nation so ever may be Allowed to engage in any manner or for what purpose so ever, any french Subject or Subjects un[less] they are provided with printed Signed and Sealed permissions from the Consul of France or his representants in this State under a considerable penalty; and that penalty double in case the said Subject or Subjects did at the time belong to some French Ship Vessel &c. Besides expences and Damages allowed by sentence to bring back the said Subjects to their Ships Vessels &c. and to atone for the loss occasioned thereby. This article ought also to be extended to men of all other nations sailing under his majesty's flag, since by the Laws of nations they are considered as Subjects belonging to the Flag they sail under. That on suspicion of some French Subjects belonging to the French flag, being received on board of some Ship Vessel &c. of what nation so ever in the ports or rivers of Virginia, the Consul of France or his representant will be at liberty to send a person to visit the same, accompanied by an Officer of the State, either Civil or Military, which will be immediately granted to him upon application to the magistrate of the place.

That no Ships Vessels Boats small embarkations &c. wearing French Colours can be visited by any of the State Officers without a permission from the Consul of France or his representant which he shall always grant, but which must be obtained, as it is generally practiced in all countries where the European Nations have Consuls. That to encourage Trade between the two nations, draw as many french factors in the State as possible and establish a necessary confidence from the merchants in France, a form of judicature be established to decide all commercial contests between French and American Subjects in a Short and peremtory manner without having recourse to the ordinary form of justice whose Lengths would be extreamly disadvantageous to Trade, and would particularly disgust foreign merchants from venturing their fortunes in that same trade. However the Chevalier demands that favour only in behalf of those merchants of his nation under the authority of his most Christian majesty's Consul or his representants in the State.

That all commercial contests between French Subjects residing in Virginia be submitted to the decision of the Consul of France or his representants, unless they have from him or from them a written permission to apply to the jurisdiction of the place.

That no french merchants Traders or any other Subjects belonging to his most Christian majesty, be not in any manner either directly or indirectly, constrained to take the oath of Allegiance to the State, nor pay any other duties or taxes but those that are or will be paid by the good and faithfull subjects of this State; and upon the same principle and in the same proportion that they do, or will do it. The Chevalier D'Anmours demands in this present memorial are presented by him as eventual and temporary ones. Circumstances Times or his Sovereign's future Orders may point him out some others for the welfare and advantage of both nations, which he then will have the honor to communicate to his Excellency the Governor and the honorable house of Assembly.

Wmsburg November 7th 1779

Le Chevalier D'Anmours
Consul of France for his
most Christian majesty in the
States of Virginia and Maryland

Tr (Vi). Enclosure: Tr (Vi); for docketing, see TJ to Benjamin Harrison, 8 Dec. 1779.

This letter, of which only a clerk's copy has been located, is dated by the clerk at the foot of the text as 8 Dec. 1779. However, it must have been written on 7 Nov., the date appearing on the enclosure. The clerk's error was doubtless occasioned by the fact that both the letter and its enclosure were

transmitted in TJ's letter to Benjamin Harrison, 8 Dec. 1779, q.v. TJ replied briefly to D'Anmours on 10 Nov. 1779, but held up the transmittal of the letter until D'Anmours' official commission had been received (see also TJ to Benjamin Harrison, 23 Nov. 1779). D'Anmours' earlier communication concerning CAPTAIN LA CRAIX [La Croix] has not been located. For the suits of La Croix against the Justices of Accomac County, see CVSP, III, 253-4.

To the Board of Trade

SIR   In Council Nov. 8. 1779

It has become necessary to advance an additional Sum of Money to Mr. Lindsay. The Board of Trade will therefore be pleased to issue a further Warrant in his favour for Six Hundred Pounds on Account.

I am Sir with much respect Your most obedt. humble servt.,

TH: JEFFERSON

RC (Vi). Addressed in another hand: "To the Honble Commissioners of the Board of trade."

From the Board of War

War Office Wmsburg Novr. 8th. 1779.

Lieut. Colo. Muter of the Artillery . . . Colo. State Garrison
                                              Regiment.
Major Matthews . . . . .Lt. Colo. Artillery
Captain Edmunds . . . . .Major Artillery
The Board having not in possession a Regular and proper Ros-

ter of the State Artillery, cannot certify precisely how far the chain of preferment occasioned by Colonel Muters removal may extend. We have specified the field promotions, and will notify those of a more subordinate nature as soon as we are acquainted therewith.

JAS. INNES
WM. NELSON
SAML. GRIFFIN
JAMES BARRON

In Council Nov. 8th. 1779. Approved. Th: Jefferson

Tr in Board of War Letter Book (MiU-C).

From the Board of War

Williamsburg, 8 Nov. 1779. John Peyton, clothier general to the state troops, should proceed to camp to receive from the Continental clothier general the proportion of clothing allowed by Congress and to issue it according to directions. His duty should be extended, with an increase in salary, to include the issuing of all supplies sent in by the Boards of War and Trade, because Mr. Moss, the state agent, is so occupied that he cannot attend to this task. Signed by Innes, Nelson, Griffin, and Barron.

Tr (Vi); 1 p. Also Tr in Board of War Letter Book (MiU-C). Printed in *Official Letters*, II, 58.

To Bernardo de Gálvez

SIR   Williamsburg November 8th. 1779

By Mr. Lindsay who was sent from our County of Islinois on the Mississippi to new Orleans and lately arrived here on his return by the way of Havanna, we hear that Col. Rogers had left New Orleans and proceeded up the Mississippi; We are anxiously expecting by him your Excellency's answer to the Letters of January 14 1778 by Col. Rogers and January 26th. 1778 by Captain Young from Governor Henry to whom I had the honor of succeeding on his Resignation. The Accession of his most Catholic Majesty, since the Date of those Letters to the Hostilities carrying on by the confederate powers of France and North America against Great Britain, thereby adding to their efforts, the weight of your powerfull and wealthy Empire, has given us, all the certainty of a happy Issue to the present Contest, of which human Events will admit. Our Vicinity to the State over which you immediately preside; the direct channel of Commerce by the River Mississippi, the nature of those Commodities with which we can reciprocally furnish each other, point out the advantages which may result from a close Connection, and correspondence, for which on our part the best Foundations are laid by a grateful Sense of the Favors we have received at your Hands. Notwithstanding the pressure of the present War on our people, they are lately beginning to extend their Settlements rapidly on the Waters of the Mississippi; and we have reason to believe, that on the Ohio particularly, and the Branches immediately communicating with it, there will in the Course of another Year, be such a number of Settlers, as to render the Commerce an object worth your notice. From New Orleans alone can they be tolerably suppl[ied] with necessaries of European Manufactures, and thither they will carry in Exchange Staves and Peltry immediately, and Flour pork and Beef, as soon as they shall have somewhat opened their Lands. For their Protection from the Indians, we are obliged to send and station among them, a considerable armed Force; the providing of which with cloathing, and the Friendly Indians with necessaries, becomes a matter of great Difficulty with us. For the smaller Forces we have hitherto kept up at Kaskaskia on the Mississippi we have contracted a considerable Debt at New Orleans with Mr. Pollock, besides what is due to your State for the Supplies they have generously furnished, and a Number of Bills from Col. Clarke now lying under protest in New Orleans. We learn by Mr. Lindsay that Mr. Pollock is likely to be greatly distress'd, if we do not immediately make him remittances. The most unfavorable Harvest ever known Since the Settlement of this Country, has put it out of our Power to send flour, obliging us for our own subsistence, to purchase it from the neighboring States of Maryland and Pensylvania to whom we have until this Year furnished large Quantities. The Want of Salt disables us from preparing Beef and Pork for your market. In this Situation of things, we cannot but contemplate the distress of that Gentleman brought on him by Services rendered us, with the utmost Concern. We are endeavoring by Remittances of Tobacco to establish a Fund in France to which we may apply to a certain extent: But the Casualties to which those Tobaccoes are liable in their Transportation; render the Dependence less certain than we could wish for Mr. Pollock's relief; and besides that we have other very extensive occasions for them. Young as we are in Trade and Manufactures, and engaged in war with a Nation whose power on the Sea, has been such as to intercept a great proportion of the Supplies we have attempted to import from Europe, you will not wonder to hear, that we find great Difficulties in procuring either money or Commodities to answer the Calls of our Armies, and therefore that it would be a Circumstance of vast relief to us, if we could leave our deposits in France for the Calls of that part of our State which lies on the Atlantic, and procure a Suspension of the Demands from Your Quarter, for supplies to our Western Forces one, Two, or three Years, or such longer Time as could be obtained; With this view Governor Henry in his Letters of January 14 and 26th 1778 solicited from Your Nation a loan of money which your Excellency was so kind, as to undertake to communicate to Your Court. The Success of this application we expect to learn by Col. Rogers, and should not till then have troubled you with the same Subject, had we not heard of Mr. Pollock's distress. As we flatter ourselves that the Application thro' the intervention of your Excellency may have been successful, and that you may be authorized to advance for us some loans in money, I take the Liberty of soliciting you in such Case, to advance for us to Mr. Pollock Sixty five Thousand Eight Hundred fourteen & ⅝ Dollars. Encompassed as we are with Difficulties, we may fail in doing as much as our Gratitude would prompt us to, in speedily replacing these Aids; But most assuredly nothing in that way within our Power will be left undone. Our particular prospects for doing it, and the time it may take to accomplish the whole, shall be the Subject of another Letter, as soon as I shall have the Honor to learn from You whether we can be Supplied, and to what extent.

By Col. Rogers I hope also to learn your Excellency's Sentiments, on the Other proposition in the Same Letters, for the establishment of corresponding Posts on Your Side and ours of the Mississippi, near the mouth of the Ohio, for the promotion of Commerce Between us. After returning our most cordial thanks to your Excellency for the friendly Disposition you have personally shewn to us, and, assuring you of our profound Respect and Esteem, beg Leave to Subscribe myself, Your Excellency's most obedient, and most humble Servant,   TH: JEFFERSON

FC (Vi). Endorsed: "8 Novr. 1779. Copy of Governor Jefferson's Letter to Governor Galvez—asking a loan of Money for the State." RC (a letter signed) sold at American Art Association, Varnum Sale, 20 Feb. 1928, lot 237; not traced.

Don Bernardo de Gálvez, Spanish governor of Louisiana, 1777-1783, was a warm supporter of American resistance to England; see John W. Caughey, *Bernardo de Gálvez in Louisiana, 1776-1783*, Berkeley, 1934. TJ was continuing the efforts of Gov. Henry to obtain aid from Spain, particularly in support of Clark's campaign in Illinois, which Oliver POLLOCK, American commercial agent in New Orleans was endeavoring to finance; see James A. James, *Oliver Pollock*, N.Y. and London, 1937, especially ch. X. Henry's letter of 14 Jan. 1778 by Col. David ROGERS is printed in *Official Letters*, I, 227-9; that of 26 Jan. by Capt. YOUNG, sent round by sea, has not been found, but see same, p. 235 and note, and p. 237 (Henry to Young, 26 Jan. 1778).

To Benjamin Harrison

SIR   In Council Nov. 8. 1779.

The matter of the inclosed petition being proper for the discussion of the legislature alone, I do myself the honour of transmitting it to them through you: and am Sir Your most obedient servt.,

TH: JEFFERSON

RC (Vi). Addressed: "The Honble Benjamin Harrison Esqr. Speaker of the House of Delegates." Docketed: "Governo[r's] Letter containing Capt. Dicks: Memorial November 8. 1779. referred to whole on the Commonwealth. Novr: 11th: 1779. Commee. of whole discharged herefrom & referred to Propositions. reasonable allowd. £2730." Enclosure: Petition of Alexander Dick to the Governor and Council of Virginia, 8 Nov. 1779. Dick's Memorial was dated 2 Nov. 1779 and is summarized above under that date.

The Committee of Propositions and Grievances made its report on the petition, 22 Nov. 1779 (JHD, Oct. 1779, 1827 edn., p. 66). The Journal under 8 Nov. also mentions the enclosure of an "extract of a letter from Col. Shepherd [to TJ], respecting intrusions on the Indian lands upon the Ohio" (same, p. 46), but this letter has not been found.

From the Board of Trade

SIR   Board of Trade Novr. 9. 1779.

We had the Honor of Your Excellency's Instructions respecting the settlement of Capt. Le Maire's Expences. We confess ourselves at a loss to know whether the several Articles stated in his Account have been admitted by The Executive or whether under the Engagements entered into with him by the late Governor in Council, We are authorized in making any deductions. We confess ourselves unable to judge likewise whether the Expences incurred were really necessary in the execution of his Commission, and in short being entirely ignorant of the whole of the transaction, We entreat Advice therein from Your Excellency.

We have the Honor to be Your Excellency's Obedt. & very humbl Servts.,

J. AMBLER

DUN: ROSE

RC and Tr (CSmH). TJ's reply of 9-12 Nov. 1779 is written at foot of RC. See also TJ to Board of Trade, 6 Nov. 1779 (first letter to the Board of that date); Board of Trade to TJ, 13 Nov. 1779.

To the Board of Trade

In Council Nov. 9. 1779.

The board are of opinion that Colo. Le Maire's expences of £15,545 livres 14 sous be paid in current money at the exchange of 20 for 1. and that £2000 be allowed him for his expences from Boston to this day. TH: JEFFERSON

In Council Nov. 12. 1779

On further consideration the board thinks Mr. Le Maire shoud be allowed 27. livres a day for 430 days to be paid in currency at a rate not exceeding twenty five for one. TH: JEFFERSON

RC (CSmH). The instructions of both 9 and 12 Nov. were written below the text of the recipient's copy of Board of Trade to TJ, 9 Nov. 1779.

See also TJ to Board of Trade, 6 Nov. 1779 (first letter to the Board of that date); Board of Trade to TJ, 13 Nov. 1779.

From the Board of War, with Reply

Williamsburg, 9 Nov. 1779. The prospects of procuring a supply of flour from Maryland are uncertain and expensive. The price in that state is already greater than in Virginia and the charge for freight immense. The extensive orders given to Col. Smith of Baltimore to purchase flour should, therefore, be immediately countermanded and a price limit set of £30 Maryland money per hundred. Purchasing flour in Virginia, besides being cheaper and safer, would have the added advantage of utilizing the seconds for ship bread, the bran and shorts for forage, and the screenings for distilling whiskey. Large quantities of wheat may now be engaged at £12 per bushel. Signed by Innes, Nelson, Griffin, and Barron. Countersigned: "In Council Novr. 9th. 1779. Approved and the board of War will be pleased to send an Express as proposed, and to leave necessary Orders here, and in Maryland. Th: Jefferson."

Tr in Board of War Letter Book (MiU-C); 2 p.

To the Board of War

In Council Novr. 9th. 1779.

The Board are of opinion that the sailors enlisted under the Act concerning Officers Soldiers Sailors and marines, Shoud be put on board such State vessels as the Board of War shall direct: that soldiers enlisted and to be enlisted under the same act, shall do duty in the garrison Regiment until further Orders, it being their

Idea that these men shall at a proper time be sent on to the grand Army towards supplying our deficiency in that: and that the marines enlisted and to be enlisted under the same Act do duty in the same Regiment until authority shall be given to Officer and embody them for their proper service.   TH: JEFFERSON

Tr in Board of War Letter Book (MiU-C).

To the Board of War

In Council Novemr. 9th. 1779

Mr. Peyton Clothier General is directed to repair to the Grand Army there to receive and issue to the Officers and Soldiers of the Virginia Line all Cloathing and Stores for them that shall be put into his hands either by the Continental Cloathier General or the Continental State Agents. If the salary annexed to his Office by the Assembly is insufficient, to them the application must be made.

THOS. JEFFERSON

Tr (Vi); also Tr in Board of War Letter Book (MiU-C); both written below texts of Board of War to TJ, 8 Nov. 1779.

From Samuel Huntington

SIR   Philada Novr 9th 1779

Your Excellency will receive herewith enclos'd an act of Congress of the 8th instant together with the Copy of a letter from Colo. Broadhead of the 26th Ultimo.

In pursuance of the orders contain'd in the act of Congress enclos'd I am to request your Excellency's endeavours to prevent a repetition of the trespasses mention'd in the letter from Colo. Broadhead. The evil tendency of such practices are too obvious to leave room for a doubt that proper exertions will be used on the part of Virginia to prevent the like in future.

I have the Honour to be with great respect your Excys hble Servt,   S.H. President

FC (DLC: PCC, No. 14). Enclosures: (1) resolution of Congress of 8 Nov. 1779 ordering that Col. Daniel Brodhead's letter to Congress from Pittsburgh, 26 Oct., be transmitted to TJ (copy in Vi, signed by Charles Thomson; printed in JCC, XV, 1249); (2) copy of the said letter from Brodhead protesting trespasses by Virginians on Indian lands beyond the Ohio in the region of the Muskingum River and Fort McIntosh (missing; original in PCC, No. 78, III; printed in *Penna. Archives*, 1st ser., XII, 176).

To D'Anmours

In compliance with the request which you were pleased to lay before us, I am now to authorize the forces of his most Christian majesty to land in such place, and his vessels to withdraw into such harbours within this commonwealth as the Admiral or other commanding officer shall think proper and to procure houses for the purpose of hospitals. In determining on the place of his debarkation and encampment, he will be pleased to follow his own judgment; receiving from us this information that the farther he can withdraw his vessels up our rivers into the country, the more it would be in our power to assist in defending them against any attack from the enemy. York river according to our present idea would offer itself as the most defencible but in this or any other we greatly apprehend the difficulties and distresses which may arise from the want of proper houses for hospitals. The board of war will issue orders for their immediate supply of provisions from our magazines, and will aid them with such of our vessels as may be necessary for procuring further supplies, landing their sick and other purposes.

These general measures seem to be all we can take for their present relief, till their wants shall be more particularly laid before us. We beg leave to take this early occasion to assure you that we shall receive into our state the forces of his most Christian majesty with the utmost cordiality and spare nothing which shall be within our power to aid and accomodate them in whatever situation they shall chuse.

I shall take great pleasure in shewing on every occasion which shall occur, my personal gratitude and affection to your nation, and the particular esteem with which I am Sir Your most obedient & most humble servt.

Dft (Lloyd W. Smith, Madison, N.J., 1946). Endorsed by TJ: "C. D'Anmour." Docketed in another hand: "No. 6. Novr. 1779. Recorded."

Ford (II, 273-4) printed this letter from a copy furnished by Elliot Danforth, but incorrectly identified the addressee as the French minister, La Luzerne. The same error has been made in L & B (IV, 312-14) and *Official Letters* (II, 61).

From the Board of War, with Reply

Williamsburg, 11 Nov. 1779. A restatement of the full duties of the commissary of stores. Signed by Innes, Nelson, Barron, Griffin, and

Lyne. Countersigned: "In Council Nov. 15th. 1779. Approved, except so far as relates to the establishment of pursers, which measure is still to be considered of. Th: Jefferson."

Tr in War Office Letter Book (MiU-C); 3 p.

From the Board of War

[*Williamsburg*] *11 Nov. 1779.* A statement of the duties of the state clothier. Signed by Innes, Nelson, Barron, Griffin, and Lyne. Countersigned: "In Council Novr. 15th. 1779. Approved. Th: Jefferson."

Tr in Board of War Letter Book (MiU-C); 2 p.

From the Board of War

SIR   War Office Wmsburg Novr. 11th. 1779.

We inclose to you for your approbation some arrangements which we think necessary to be adopted in the military and Naval departments. In the issuing the several portions of rum sugar Tea, and Coffee we have been regulated totally by the rank and rations of the several Officers, allowing to every rations as by Law directed one jill of Spirits, the other articles we have endeavoured to proportion in the same degree. The clothiers department We have assimilated as nearly as possible to the continental regulations. This appointment was made by the approbation, and under the sanction of the executive. Mr. Beverley Dickson at our instance hath hitherto exercised that Office with an Assiduity and integrity which ought to recommend him to public Attention. The institution of a commissary of Stores produces a division of duties with an augmentation of Officers, as Mr. Armstead one of the Agents in the commercial department executes that duty. The arrangements we recommend we will venture to Assert will prevent a vast Degree of embezzelment, fraud and confusion, which we are apprehensive have been too prevalent in some of our public departments. Colo. Nelsons report on some magazines, of which he has lately taken a Surveyor, we herewith communicate to your Excellency.

The Board after perusing Mr. Nelsons report have formed the following opinions, which are subjected to the consideration of the Executive. That a magazine be immediately built on the Land purchased by Messrs. Adams and Southall of Fortunatus Sydnor or else where for the reception of the gun powder at Richmond

Town, which daily receives the greatest injury from the bad situation of the house which at present covers it. If Sydnors widow and Executrix shoud persist in their determination not to suffer the magazines for powder and Arms to be built on the land of said Sydnor, that then the Attorney for the county of Henrico, be directed to bring suit to compel them to comply with the agreement entered into by Messrs. Adams and Southall with Fortunatus Sydnor, but in the mean time a house in a dry situation shoud be rented for the purpose of Storing the powder and properly arranging the arms. As there are many men in this State at present pensioned as invalids, who are still able to do centinels duty at magazines, and who it is probable might easily [be] induced to enlist for that purpose, the board recommend that a guard to consist of sixteen pensioners, be enlisted to Serve at each magazine for three years or for the War, and they further recommend that the command of these guards be given to such pensioners as have Served as Sergeants in the continental Army; this mode the board conceive will be infinitely preferable to the one hitherto pursued of hiring men from Day to day or from month to month, besides that the Business will be much better done by such men, as are accustomed to the Duty of Soldiers and a proper subordination.

We have the honor to be your Excellency's mo. Obt. Servts.,

JAS. INNES
WM. NELSON
SAML. GRIFFIN
GEO. LYNE

Tr in Board of War Letter Book (MiU-C). Enclosures not found.

To Richard Caswell

SIR   Williamsburg Nov. 11. 1779

I have lately received messages and informations from the Cherokee nation of Indians, painting their nakedness and general distress for want of European goods, so strongly as to call for pity and all possible relief. Their several settlements being contiguous to the two Carolinas and to Virginia they have at times received supplies I beleive from each of these states. Their great numbers however, and the extent of their settlements, when taken into view by any one of our states, bear a discouraging proportion to the moderate aids we can singly furnish, and render a general distribution of them very troublesome. These considerations have induced me to take the liberty of submitting to your Excellency a proposition (as I do to Governour Rutlege also by a letter of this day's date) to divide the trouble and task of supplying them among our three states. The division of those Indians into Southern, Middle, and Northern settlements, renders the apportionment of them obvious. The protecting from intrusion the lands of the Southern Cherokees and furnishing them with goods seems most convenient to South Carolina; the same friendly offices to the middle settlements seem most within your power, and the Northern settlements are convenient to us. The attachment which each settlement will by these means acquire to the particular state which is it's immediate patron and benefactor, will be a bond of peace, and will lead to a separation of that powerful people. If this distribution should happily meet the approbation of your Excellency and of Govr. Rutlege, we shall do every thing in our power for discharging our duties to the Northern settlement. Knowing your disposition to have these people protected in the possession of their unpurchased lands, I also take the liberty of mentioning to you that the old Tassel in a late message to me complains of intrusions on their lands, and particularly of some attempts to take from them the Great island. This, by the late extension of our boundary, falling, as I understand, within your state, removes the application for protection to your Excellency, whose power alone can extend to the removal of intrusions from thence. As to so much of their lands as lie within our latitudes, as well as the lands of other Indians generally, our assembly now sitting has in contemplation to authorize the Executive to send patroles of the military through them from time to time to destroy the habitations which shall be erected in them by intruders. The bearer of this letter is a Major Martin, our agent residing with the Cherokees, who will be able to inform your Excellency of any particulars you may wish to learn. We have reason to beleive him a good kind of man and worthy of credit.

Intending to fix a post and small garrison in Powell's valley, we have ordered part of a battalion thither to erect a stockade. But as it would be proper for them first to assemble together (being not yet embodied) at a nearer station, and there being a fort and houses at the Great island, we have taken the liberty of appointing their rendezvous at that fort, till there shall be so many embodied as may proceed with safety to Powell's valley. We have reason to expect that their stay at that place will be very short and hope it will not be disagreeable to your Excellency. The necessity of immediate orders, put it out of our power to apply for your previous approbation: we consider the measure still however subject to your pleasure and therefore take this early opportunity of acquainting you with it.

I have the honour to be with the greatest respect & esteem Your Excellency's most obedient & most humble servt.

Dft (CtY); endorsed by a clerk: "Govr. Caswell No 8. recorded Novr. 1779." RC (MeHi), in a clerk's hand, signed by TJ; endorsed: "No. 31. Letter from Govr. Jeferson dated WmsBurg Novr. 11th. 1779."

The MESSAGES FROM THE CHEROKEE NATION have not been located. For the difficulties encountered in securing supplies for the Cherokees, see Board of Trade to TJ, 12 Nov. 1779.

Proclamation Appointing a Day of Thanksgiving and Prayer

WHEREAS the Honourable the General Congress, impressed with a grateful sense of the goodness of Almighty God, in blessing the greater part of this extensive continent with plentiful harvests, crowning our arms with repeated successes, conducting us hitherto safely through the perils with which we have been encompassed and manifesting in multiplied instances his divine care of these infant states, hath thought proper by their act of the 20th day of October last, to recommend to the several states that Thursday the 9th of December next be appointed a day of publick and solemn thanksgiving and prayer, which act is in these words, to wit.

"Whereas it becomes us humbly to approach the throne of Almighty God, with gratitude and praise, for the wonders which his goodness has wrought in conducting our forefathers to this western world; for his protection to them and to their posterity, amidst difficulties and dangers; for raising us their children from deep distress, to be numbered among the nations of the earth; and for arming the hands of just and mighty Princes in our deliverance; and especially for that he hath been pleased to grant us the enjoyment of health and so to order the revolving seasons, that the earth hath produced her increase in abundance, blessing the labours of the husbandman, and spreading plenty through the land; that he hath prospered our arms and those of our ally, been a shield to our troops in the hour of danger, pointed their swords to victory, and led them in triumph over the bulwarks of the foe; that he hath gone with those who went out into the wilderness against the savage tribes; that he hath stayed the hand of the spoiler, and turned back his meditated destruction; that he hath prospered our commerce, and given success to those who sought the enemy on the face of the deep; and above all, that he hath diffused the glorious light of the gospel, whereby, through the merits of our gracious Redeemer, we may become the heirs of his eternal glory. Therefore,

Resolved, that it be recommended to the several states to appoint THURSDAY the 9th of December next, to be a day of publick and solemn THANKSGIVING to Almighty God, for his mercies, and of PRAYER, for the continuance of his favour and protection to these United States; to beseech him that he would be graciously pleased to influence our publick Councils, and bless them with wisdom from on high, with unanimity, firmness and success; that he would go forth with our hosts and crown our arms with victory; that he would grant to his church, the plentiful effusions of divine grace, and pour out his holy spirit on all Ministers of the gospel; that he would bless and prosper the means of education, and spread the light of christian knowledge through the remotest corners of the earth; that he would smile upon the labours of his people, and cause the earth to bring forth her fruits in abundance, that we may with gratitude and gladness enjoy them; that he would take into his holy protection, our illustrious ally, give him victory over his enemies, and render him finally great, as the father of his people, and the protector of the rights of mankind; that he would graciously be pleased to turn the hearts of our enemies, and to dispence the blessings of peace to contending nations.

That he would in mercy look down upon us, pardon all our sins, and receive us into his favour; and finally, that he would establish the independance of these United States upon the basis of religion and virtue, and support and protect them in the enjoyment of peace, liberty and safety."

I do therefore by authority from the General Assembly issue this my proclamation, hereby appointing Thursday the 9th day of December next, a day of publick and solemn thanksgiving and prayer to Almighty God, earnestly recommending to all the good people of this commonwealth, to set apart the said day for those purposes, and to the several Ministers of religion to meet their respective societies thereon, to assist them in their prayers, edify them with their discourses, and generally to perform the sacred duties of their function, proper for the occasion.

Given under my hand and the seal of the commonwealth, at

Williamsburg, this 11th day of November, in the year of our Lord, 1779, and in the fourth of the commonwealth.

THOMAS JEFFERSON

Text from *Virginia Gazette* (Dixon & Nicolson), 20 Nov. 1779.
    Issued in pursuance of the resolve of Congress here quoted; see Huntington to TJ, 20 Oct. 1779.

To John Rutledge

Sir   Williamsburgh Nov. 11. 1779

The bearer hereof Major Martin, our agent with the Northern or Upper Cherokees, comes to Charlestown to see if there be a possibility of purchasing there any goods to supply their wants. Give me leave to hope he will meet with your Excellency's patronage in the execution of this business. Their present distresses are so great that we have bought up every thing proper for them in our own country without regard to price. This however goes but a little way towards providing for them. Long accustomed to the use of European manufactures, they are as incapable of returning to their habits of skins and furs as we are, and find their wants the less tolerable as they are occasioned by a war the event of which is scarcely interesting to them. I am so far persuaded of the attention your Excellency has paid to these people and the supplies you have furnished them that the proposition I have the honour of submitting to your consideration (as I have done to that of Govr. Caswell also by a letter of this day's date) that we should divide this trouble among us, will be rather a matter of relief to you. The division of the Cherokees into Southern, Middle, and Northern settlements, points out a division of the cares and expences of patronizing them among the three states of South and North Carolina and Virginia. The protecting from intrusion the lands of the Southern Cherokees and furnishing them with goods seems most convenient to you, the same friendly offices to the middle settlements will be so to North Carolina; and the Northern settlements to us. The attachment which each settlement will by these means acquire to the particular state under whose patronage it is, perhaps will be a bond of peace, and will lead to a separation of that powerful people. If this distribution should happily meet the approbation of your Excellency and of Govr. Caswell, we shall do every thing in our power for discharging our duties, to the Northern settlement. Our assembly, now sitting, has in contemplation to authorize the executive to send patroles of the military from time to time through the unpurchased lands of the Indians within our own latitudes to destroy the habitations which shall be erected on them by intruders.

It has been matter of real mortification to me that the whole of the troops ordered from this state on the Southern service under Genl. Scott have not yet been marched on. The business of recruiting in this country being difficult, the assembly in their act under which these men were raised, as an encouragement, declared that they should receive every article of clothing enumerated in the act before they should leave the state, and that to march them out of it before they should receive them, should amount to a discharge. Finding it impossible to procure all these articles, we offered liberal compensation in money to those who would march on without their clothes. This prevailed with so many as composed the first division which went on to you in June. Our efforts since that enabled us to equip about as many more which accordingly marched the last month; but those still remaining are as yet unequipped. We are continuing our endeavours to procure the enumerated articles in order to make good the legislative engagements to them, and thereby authorize the marching of them also. I have the honour to be with great esteem Your Excellency's most obedt. & most humble servt.

Dft (Vi); endorsed by a clerk: "Govr. Rutlige No. 7. Recorded Novr. 1779."

From the Board of Trade, with Reply

[*Williamsburg*] *12 Nov. 1779*. In compliance with the requisition of 30 Oct. for the purchase of clothing for the Cherokee Indians, all the articles mentioned in Maj. Martin's list that were to be had were secured, but for want of money the goods are being held until payment for them can be made. Before the treasury is replenished the goods may be sold. Every effort has been made to secure the goods, but their procurement has been hampered by the restriction of their purchase within the state. If it is proper to purchase the goods in any other state, instructions should be issued to that effect. Without money, it would be prudent to furnish Maj. Martin with a letter of credit if he is appointed to manage the business. Signed by Whiting, Ambler, and Rose. Instructions, in TJ's hand: "In Council Nov. 13. 1779. It is the sense of the board that these goods be purchased in any state and particularly in South Carolina, and that the board of trade authorize the agent for this Commonwealth in Charlestown to draw bills on their board for payment. The Governour directs accordingly. Th: Jefferson."

RC (Vi); 3 p. Addressed: "His Excellency in Council." Endorsed: "Representation respecting furnishing Cloathing for Cherokees Nov. 13th 1779."

To the Board of War

The Governor is advised to appoint Frederickg., Petersbg., New London, Staunton, and Winchester places of rendezvous for New levies raised under the act of Assembly concerning Officers Soldiers Sailors and marines, and to direct an Officer to meet the recruiting Officers of the several counties at these places at certain times, to wit, Petersburg on the first Day of every other month, beginning in December at New London on the sixth of the same months, at Staunton on the twelve, at Winchester on the eighteenth, and at Fredericksburg on the twenty fourth then and there to review and receive such able bodied men as shall be produced to him by the said recruiting Officers. To appoint also Pittsburg and Wmsburg places of rendezvous for levies of the same kind, and an Officer of the Garrisons at those places to review and receive them at all times when produced to him.   TH: JEFFERSON

Tr in Board of War Letter Book (MiU-C). See Board of War to TJ, 4 Nov. 1779 (second letter of that date from the Board).

From the Board of Trade

[13 November 1779]

The State of Virginia,
                         to Jacques Le Maire Dr.

To Money laid out in France, as ℔ a former Account rendered, 5345 liv. 14 sous. at 25 for 1,	£5,846 15 6
To travelling expences, for 430 Days, at 27 livres ℔ Day at 25 for 1, or 11,610 livres	12,698 8 9
To Money allowed for Expences upon the Continent, to the 10th. Novr.	2,000
	£20,545 4 3

Board of Trade Novr. 13. 1779

The above appears to be what His Excellency in Council intends to allow Capt. Le Maire; if so they will be pleased to signify their approbation.   THOM. WHITING

                                         J. AMBLER
                                         DUN: ROSE

In Council Nov. 13. 1779. Approved. Th: Jefferson.

RC (CSmH). The summary of Le Maire's account is written in an unidentified hand; the letter of the Board of Trade is in the hand of Thomas Whiting and signed by the members of the Board.

See TJ to Benjamin Harrison, 29 Oct.; TJ to Board of Trade, 6, 9-12 Nov.; Board of Trade to TJ, 9 Nov. 1779.

To the Board of War

In Council Novr. 13th. 1779.

The board are of the opinion that Mr. Adams and Mr. Southall or any other persons who shall be appointed by the board of War, be desired to have proper proceedings in Law instituted to compel a conveyance of the Lands purchased from Fortunatus Sydnor and in the mean time proceed to erect the magazines, removing force by force, which the public necessity and Safety, and clear justice and right will justify. They approve of enlisting a guard of invalids, and recommend to the board of War to obtain from the Auditors a roll of the pensioners and to take other necessary measures to carry this into execution. TH. JEFFERSON

Tr in Board of War Letter Book (MiU-C).

To the Board of War

In Council Novr. 13th. 1779.

The act of May 1779. under which Mr. Blunt has been last Drafted refers to one of October 1778 as to the method of determining who were Subjects of that Draught. This act says the justices and the Field Officers shall lay Off the militia into Districts, each of which districts shall furnish a man. The justices and field Officers then are made Judges who shall be deemed to be of the Militia and of course Subject to the Draught, and no appeal is given to any other person or power whatever. The Board is therefore of opinion that the executive has no legal power of controuling the proceedings of the justices and Field Officers under these acts and advise the Governor accordingly. TH: JEFFERSON

Tr in Board of War Letter Book (MiU-C). This was an answer to a letter from the Board of War of 9 Sep. 1779, q.v.

From the Board of War

Williamsburg, 13 Nov. 1779. It is expedient to establish a small magazine in or near Staunton; Col. Sampson Matthews is to be furnished with money and implements to complete it as soon as possible. Rifles in his care should be repaired and he should have power to sell some arms to defray the expense of repairing the rest, if that seems more expedient than drawing money. He should also be empowered either to dispose of the cattle at Tyger's Valley or to have them driven to some place of rendezvous for the use of the western troops. Probably fifty recruits for the western service have been collected and must be outfitted. Shoes not being available in this quarter, someone in the back country should be furnished with public money to procure them there. Signed by Innes, Nelson, and Griffin.

Tr in Board of War Letter Book (MiU-C); 2 p.

From the Board of War

Williamsburg, *13 Nov. 1779.* Instructions desired as to whether a soldier's oath on his own behalf concerning his allowance of clothing shall be legal testimony for his compensation. The legislature at its last session elected a commissary of prisoners, who has declined serving, though the law constituting the Board of War vests that power in the Board. The Board proposes electing a proper person for that office. Signed by Innes, Nelson, and Griffin.

Tr in Board of War Letter Book (MiU-C); 1 p.

From the Board of War

Williamsburg, *13 Nov. 1779.* Upon consideration of the resolution of the House of Delegates of 1 Nov., it is recommended that two prison ships be prepared for the reception of prisoners of war and be moored in James River. One ship is now ready. Signed by Innes, Nelson, and Griffin.

Tr in Board of War Letter Book (MiU-C). 2 p. For the resolution concerning prison ships, see JHD, Oct. 1779, 1827 edn., p. 33.

From the Executive Council

SIR   In Council Wmsburg Novr. 13th 1779.

Sickness necessary Business and other Causes often preventing the Attendance of the members of this Board so as that no Council can be held, while many persons are waiting from great distances and at much expense on Business with the Executive; which inconvenience might in a great degree be obviated by a Standing Advice of the Board to the Governor to act during the intervals of their sitting in certain cases where the concurrence of the Council having generally been considered as a matter of course a Special advice woud be of little moment, The Board do Advise his Excellency during the intervals of their sitting to proceed without waiting for a special Advice on the case to countersign certificates from the Board of War for Cloathing due to soldiers under a resolution of the general Assembly, certificates from the same Board for Bounty money due to Soldiers, or enlisting money due or to be advanced to recruiting Officers, Orders from the Board of War for Cloathing to Officers Soldiers Sailors and marines, Orders from the Board of War or Board of Trade for provisions or other necessaries for vessels about to sail, Orders from either of the said Boards in consequence of resolutions approved by the Executive, to Issue military Commissions recommended by the board of War, to Issue commissions for public trading vessels on recommendation from the board of Trade, to issue blank Militia commissions to the County Courts, to Issue commissions of the peace, Inspectors Commissions and Sherifs Commissions on recommendation from County Courts, to order rations and small aids in money to deserters Captives and to discharged and disabled soldiers, to licence Attornies on the report of the commissioners to whom he may refer them for examination and to certify to the Auditors of Accounts where services upon which claims against the State are founded, were performed by Order of the Executive reporting from time to time to the Board his proceedings agreeable to the Above Advice.

RC (Vi); in Archibald Blair's hand?; unsigned. Endorsed by TJ: "General Advice of Council. Nov. 13. 1779."

From Edmund Randolph

Sir   Williamsburg Novr. 13. 1779.

I do myself the honor of returning to your Excellency the papers referred to me, respecting the Portuguese snow captured by Captain Cunningham while Commander of the privateer Phœnix.

The resolutions, entered into by Congress upon this Subject on the 21st. day of July 1779, call for public punishment, as well as private reparation; the former of which can be sought for upon no other principle than that Captain Cunningham was guilty of Piracy, and Mr. Braxton accessary thereto by virtue of his Instructions.

If those to whom letters of Marque are granted should instead of taking the ships and goods of that Nation, against whom the same were awarded, wilfully take or spoil the goods of another nation in Amity, this would amount to a direct piracy. See Molloy B.1. C.2d. §23d. For as the Animus furandi is a necessary ingredient in the crime of Piracy. 4 Black: 72—1 H. P. C. Pa: 100. I understand Molloy, as intending by the terms "wilfully taking or spoiling," a capture, accompanied with such Circumstances, as indicate a depravity of mind, or in other words an intention to steal. But Captain Cunninghams subsequent conduct seems to remove all suspicion. He does not appropriate the Snow to himself, upon the confidence, that more power constituted a right, but brings her before an american court of Admiralty, in order to obtain a regular condemnation. Upon these Grounds the persons deputed by George Carew, to execute certain Letters of reprisal, against the States general which were called in by Proclamation, were acquitted upon an Indictment for piracy; the reason assigned for such acquittal being, that the Caption was in order to adjudication. Molloy. B.1. C.4. §34.

If indeed there were any Evidence of a felonious and piratical Spoliation, before the Snow was brought into Court, the mere libelling of her there might not be a sufficient gloss for the act of Plunder. But I do not find any document transmitted by Congress, which justifies such a Charge.

Hence the Innocence of Captain Cunningham, the principal agent in this Affair, is assumed, and therefore Mr. Braxton cannot be criminal as an accessary.

But altho' Cunningham be in truth guilty of piracy, no tribunal exists in Virginia for the Cognizance of such an Offence. For a Jurisdiction for this purpose, can be derived from two Sourses only; the Statute of the British Parliament 28. H. 8. or our own act of assembly which erects the Court of Admiralty. The former, however, will be found to be merely local, and therefore not within the Law, by which the British acts, prior to the fourth year of James, the first, were adopted by our Legislature, and the latter in conformity I presume to the articles of confederation, interdicts the admiralty from the exercise of criminal authority. But at any Event the 28th Hen: 8. tho' it were not merely local, extends to principals only, not to accessaries. (3 Inst: 112.—H. P. C. B.1. ch:37. §7. How then can Mr. Braxton be amenable here? But I am persuaded that redress in a civil way is within the attainment of the owners of the Snow. For altho' this doctrine is somewhat contraverted by Molloy, B1. ch 4. §19. yet the adjudged Case there referred to, proves that the proprietors of the Privateer, are liable for damages. But under this limitation, that the Master of the Snow afforded no probable Cause of Seisure.

I am Sir with Respect Yr. Excellencys mo: obt. Servt.,

EDMUND RANDOLPH

Tr (Vi), in an unidentified hand, enclosed in TJ to Harrison, 23 Nov. 1779; endorsed: "Nov 13th. 1779." Another Tr (DLC: PCC, No. 71, I), in a different hand, enclosed in TJ to Huntington, 30 Dec. 1779; endorsed: "Copy of The Attorney's Letter to the Governor." Enclosures not located.

THE PORTUGUESE SNOW: On this case see John Jay to TJ, 26 July 1779, and references there.

To David Shepherd

SIR   Wmsburg Novr. 13th. 1779.

I am to ask the favour of you to give notice to the Officer recommended by you for the Western Battalions that as soon as one half his [quota] of men is raised and delivered by you, he shall be entitled to his commission and must march the men on to Fort Pitt, the remaining half you must send on under a Serjeant to the same rendezvous. Lieutenant Colo. Knox is appointed to take command of the Battalion of [which] your men will be. But your distance renders it impracticable to join them to their battalion till the Spring. They will do duty under Colonel Gibson this winter. The Subsistence Account previous to their Delivery to the Officer you will settle with the Auditors here. I am Sir Your very humble Servt.,   TH: JEFFERSON

RC (WHi); in a clerk's hand, signed by TJ.

To the Board of War

In Council Novr. 15th. 1779.

The board advise the approbation of the proposition from the board of War for building a small magazine at Staunton; but that it be paid for in money, and not by a sale of any of the rifles, these being already ordered to be delivered to the two Western Battalions now raising. They approve also of what is proposed as to the cattle. They advise that no particular supply of Clothing be sent for particular men, but that general supplies be sent to the places of general rendezvous appointed for the two Western Battalions. They approve of engaging Colo. Matthews to have shoes made in the

Western Country and furnishing him with money, on Account for that purpose.   TH: JEFFERSON

Tr in Board of War Letter Book (MiU-C).

To the Board of War

In Council Novr. 15th. 1779.

The Board are of opinion that a Soldiers oath is not sufficient testimony to entitle him to clothing or a compensation for it: It is their opinion also that the Board of War may proceed to appoint a commissary of prisoners.   TH. JEFFERSON

Tr in Board of War Letter Book (MiU-C).
See Board of War to TJ, 13 Nov. 1779

(second letter from the Board under that date).

To the Board of War

In Council Novr. 15th. 1779.

The Board advise that one prison ship agreeable to the resolution of Assembly be employed; that she be moored in James river above the windings thereof which form the Peninsula's in Henrico and Chesterfield Counties: that picquetts be erected on the South Side of the same river on such Spot as the Board of War or an Officer to be sent by them to examine grounds for that purpose shall direct; keeping in view the erecting them so near to the moorings of the prisonship as that the same Staff Officers may serve both. The height plan and dimensions of the picquets and block houses they refer to the board of War. The board will of course direct the materials to be of a durable kind, that country Abounding with Cedar proper for picquets.   THOS. JEFFERSON

Tr in Board of War Letter Book (MiU-C).
The RESOLUTION OF ASSEMBLY, 1 Nov. 1779, ordered the governor to erect a small picket and order proper

vessels to be moored in a convenient harbor for securing prisoners of war (JHD, Oct. 1779, 1827 edn., p. 33; see also third letter of Board of War to TJ, 13 Nov. 1779).

From the Board of War

War office Williamsburg November 16th 1779.

The Board of War have had under Consideration the present State of the Westham Foundery, and several papers to them referred relative to a Contract entered into between Mr. Henry the late Governour in Behalf of this State and Mr. David Ross to take of the said Ross two hundred and fifty tons of iron for the use of the public foundery.

Previous to their forming any opinion thereupon, they held Conference with Mr. Adams a Commissioner of the foundery, and Mr. Reveley the manager thereof. After which they adopted the following opinions, which they take liberty to present to the supreme Executive for Examination.

The manifest and various advantages, which must result to the State from the establishment of a work, capable of supplying a sufficient Quantity of Ordnance, not only for the purpose of public defence, but also affording such quantities thereof as will enable our merchants to protect their trade, thereby rendering our Commerce more certain and respectable, and ensuring a real Source of Revenue, if attainable, are objects of public expediency, too obvious to require comment.

It is necessary then, next, to consider, what are the peculiar Advantages appertaining to the Westham foundery from its local situation, which render the beneficial consequences to this Commonwealth, flowing from a proper establishment of it, almost demonstrative. Its situation is safe, convenient to ample Supplies of pig iron for Castings from the Buckingham and Oxford's furnaces, by water carriage.

Convenient to pit Coal, either by Land or water Carriage, most happily convenient to be supplied with a Species of Brick, known in England by the name of the sturbidge-brick, which alone is capable of standing the heat of the furnaces, from its adjacency to Coal mines—the Strata of earth, covering coal mines being the only proper earth, to form the Brick already spoken of. The Westham foundery too, besides all these local conveniences, not equalled by any Situation in America, that we have heard of, will shortly, it is hoped, be possessed of the advantages of conveying from the very door of the foundery by navigation, all its manufactures to any part of the Continent. We allude to the completion of the Canal, thro the falls to the navigable waters of James River.

We will next represent the solid Profits, which will clearly result to the State from the operations of the foundery if properly encouraged, and attended to.

Pig iron by estimation is accounted to be less valuable than Bar iron by two thirds. When Cast, which is effected by an easy and instantaneous Process, it is deemed equally valuable with bar Iron.

In the Process of Casting, it is generally supposed to loose one fifth. Nearly the same deficiency takes place, in reducing pig to bar Iron, but when pig iron is cast into Cannon, it receives the additional value of twenty five pr. Ct. In the form of Ball &c. &c. we find it, then, equal to bar iron, when modified into cannon, it exceeds bar iron in value twenty five pr. Ct. These Reasons serve to prove, that Iron manufactured in founderies yields the greatest Profit.

By the inclosed Scheme, furnished by Mr. Reveley, the foundery would be able annually to afford three hundred pieces of Ordnance, besides one hundred ton of Ball, shells, or other Castings, but if endowed with a sufficient number of proper artists and Labourers, it has Capacity to furnish three times that quantity, to which degree of perfection, shoud it ever attain, the public departments of this State woud not only be supplied with Ordnance Stores, but our merchants wou'd have the means in their power, of defending their trade. After which, the surplusage might be sufficient to supply the wants of many of our Sister States, which would render it an object of considerable Revenue to this Commonwealth.

There are several Reasons, which induce us to think it expedient to close with Mr. Ross's Proposition of furnishing two hundred and fifty tons of pig iron to the State.

Mr. Reveley informs that of the hundred ton purchased by the Board of Trade of Mr. Ballendine and company, not more than eighty ton can be furnished, of which the greatest part will be consumed in executing the orders for shot for the use of the Ships forts &c. &c., so that without a speedy supply, the foundery will be stagnated for the want of the implements of manufacture. By Reveley's Certificate herewith sent, Rosses pig iron has been tried, and will answer the purposes of the foundery. Mr. Reveley farther asserts that a mixture of iron, conduces to the goodness of the Ordnance, and that he thinks from observation on the Genus of Mr. Rosses and the Buckingham iron, they wou'd make a very happy mixture.

Governed by these Reasons, the Board of war recommend to the Honorable Executive to purchase of Mr. Ross two hundred and fifty ton of pig iron regulating the price thereof by the price of bar iron, at the time of payment, the pig iron to be delivered by Mr. Ross at Westham foundery. The Board farther recommend, that proper estimates shoud be made of the quantity and Species of Ordnance Stores which may be wanting for the ensuing year, proper regulations entered into for the government of the foundery, and a sufficient Quantity of provision, and other Stores, timously provided for the Support of it.

JAS. INNES

WM. NELSON

GEO: LYNE

RC (Vi). In a clerk's hand and signed by members of the Board. Endorsed: "Representation Board of War to the Executive—[*In another hand*:] to be heard on Wednesday the first of December 1779." At end of text is an answer in TJ's hand: "In Council Nov. 18. The consideration of this postponed until the Assembly shall determine whether to ratify, or not, the Contract with Penet & co. by which, according to a resolution of the last session, the foundery was to be conveyed to them. Th: Jefferson."

For the history of the public foundry at Westham, see the proposed Contract with Penet & Co., 22 July; TJ to Harrison, 30 Oct., and the Bill for Establishing a Manufactory of Arms, also under 30 Oct. 1779, with references there. On the contract with DAVID ROSS, see TJ to Board of Trade, 10 Dec. 1779. THE INCLOSED SCHEME, FURNISHED BY MR. REVELEY has not been found.

From the Board of War

War Office Wmsburg Novr. 16th. 1779.

The Board, from a variety of circumstances, think it probable that the British army may intend some Offensive operations against this State the ensuing Winter. Not only the exposed position of this Country, and its particular situation so favorable to the plans of predatory warfare, lead them to this opinion, but they are Strengthened in it, by the unsuccessful Attempt on the Savannah, and the departure of the french fleet from the American Coasts, whereby our enemies being left masters of the American Seas, may commence operations here, freed from the apprehensions of a superior maritime power. Influenced by these reasons the members of the Board of War recommend that measures be immediately taken, to throw this Country into as respectable a military posture as possible. To effect which the more speedily, that the necessary arrangements of defence, be immediately formed, and the necessary preparations made, to support, arm and equipt such numbers of the militia, as contingencies may render necessary to be called into the field; that twelve pieces of Field artillery be immediately mounted, proper harness secured, and sufficient number of Artillery horses, and ammunition Waggons, Baggage Waggons, forage Waggons, and Waggons for the commissariate be immediately furnished; that armourers be employed to put the arms in public magazines in readiness for immediate Service; that instant Attention, be paid to the five thousand Stands at Cumberland, three hundred at Richmond, and about one thousand at Petersburg which, for want of

Cleaning, and due attention are Spoiling and growing more and more unfit for Service every day; that to supply the want of leather Cartridge Boxes, of which there is a great scantiness, two thousand tin Boxes such as are used in the continental Army by Light Infantry, be immediately made, that recommendations be immediately sent out to the County Lieutenants to have the arms and military Stores in their possession, put into the best order; that they be urged to endeavour to furnish their several Counties with Cartouch boxes, for which purpose they may if necessary be furnished with money on account, provided the Cartouch boxes when made, be considered as belonging to the State and not to the several Counties, and be subject to the disposition of the Executive. That a small number of arms, be distributed to the several exposed Counties for their defence against marauding parties; that Stations of Observation be pitched on for Nelsons Corps of Dragoons; that look out Boats be kept constantly on the Watch, that our Ships and Galleys form a Line of Connection from the North to the South Cape, with orders to communicate the necessary informations of the approach of the enemy to the several garrisons and the Commandants thereof, hold in constant readiness, express Riders to communicate Intelligence to the Executive with all possible dispatch. The Board while they take liberty to make these several recommendations to the Executive, beg leave to mention, that nothing in their opinion woud conduce more to accelerate and give energy to military preparations, than the appointment of a general Officer to carry into execution the Orders of the Executive: Civil Bodies tho [they] may dictate to, are Illy calculated to direct military ones. The Vigor and dispatch, necessary in military movements, can only be derived from full powers concentered in one man, whose presence and exertion will give concerted plans, proper force and activity. The Board therefore recommends, that at this critical juncture a general Officer, be appointed, to direct such military operations as circumstances may call forth.   JAS. INNES

                                                                                        WM. NELSON

                                                                                        GEO. LYNE

Tr in Board of War Letter Book (MiU-C).

To Samuel Huntington

SIR   Wmsburg Novr. 16th. 1779.

   Colo. Bland being about to retire from his Command at the Barracks in Albemarle, and desirous to withdraw at the same time the party of his horse which has hitherto been Stationed there, wished that we should supply their place by sending thither about twenty or five and twenty of the horse of this State. Our horse being as yet not very well trained, the Officers represented that it woud much impede that work, and leave the remaining fragment in a very aukward situation should we divide a troop. We have therefore ordered a complete troop to that Station; but wish congress would be pleased to notify as soon as convenient whether they approve of this or not.

We have hitherto been unable to raise more than about the half of a Battalion of infantry for guarding the convention Troops at the same Post. The deficiencies have been endeavoured to be supplied with Militia. Congress have had too much experience of the radical defects and inconveniences of militia service to need my enumerating them, our Assembly, now sitting, have in contemplation to put the garrison regiment on such a footing as gives us hopes of filling it by the next summer. In the mean time a Battalion which we are raising for our immediate defence may be spared to do garrison duty this winter, and as but a small part of it is raised, as yet, and not probable that it will be completed within any short time, we suppose that with Colo. Taylors regiment it will not exceed the number required to guard the Troops. I woud observe to you that the Captains and Subalterns of this new Battalion are not to be called into service but as their men are raised; so that the burthen which has sometimes been incurred of paying Officers without men need not be apprehended in this instance. We have therefore Ordered this Battalion to rendezvous at the Barracks and do duty there this winter, and that the Battalion shoud be discharged in proportion as these come in. On this measure also we ask the pleasure [of] congress.

The appointment of a successor to Colo. Bland will give us great satisfaction and we hope congress will take it into early consideration. The duties of that post call for respectable Abilities and an uncommon vigilance and firmness of Character.

I have the honour to be with the greatest respect & esteem Sir your most obedient humble servt.,   TH: JEFFERSON

RC (PCC, No. 71, I). In a clerk's hand; complimentary close and signature in TJ's hand. Endorsed by Charles Thomson: "Letter from Govr Jefferson Novr 16. 1779 Read Decr. 7. Referred to the board of War."

A SUCCESSOR TO COLO. BLAND: On 14 Dec. 1779 Gen. Washington appointed Col. James Wood to succeed Bland as superintendent of the Convention troops (Washington, *Writings*, ed. Fitzpatrick, XVII, 260-1).

To Benjamin Harrison

[*Williamsburg, 17? Nov. 1779.* JHD, Oct. 1779, 1827 edn., p. 59 (17 Nov. 1779): "The Speaker laid before the House a letter from the Governor, on the subject of certain inquiries made by the executive, on complaints against justices of the peace for misfeasance in office, which was read, and ordered to be referred to the committee of the whole House on the state of the Commonwealth." Not located.]

To the Board of War

In Council Novr. 18th. 1779.

The Board are of opinion that until the numbers of an invading enemy and the proposed point of invasion known, neither the numbers of militia proper to be drawn into the field, nor the Counties from which they shall be called can be determined on. They approve of the making ready the Artillery harness's and horses for Artillery, Waggons for the baggage Ammunition forage and for the commissariate, and refer to the Board of War to propose the number proper, taking for granted that the Continental Waggons in this State may be freely called into the Service of the State in case of an invasion and may therefore be counted on as a part of the necessary number: they approve of the repairing immediately the arms in the public Magazines; and with respect to those at Cumberland particularly would recommend that five hundred Stand of them at a time be brought to this place to be repaired and be sent away before others be brought; they approve of having tin Cartridge Boxes made as proposed by the board of War: They approve of recommendations to the County Lieutenants of all the Counties below the blue ridge to have arms of their militia put into good [condition?] as required by Law; but disapprove of the method proposed of getting Cartouch boxes through their intervention: some arms have been heretofore put into the hands of the Lieutenants of the more distant Counties lying on the navigable Waters; the Executive are unwilling for very many reasons to part with more from the public Magazines, and more especially as the exposed Counties not heretofore furnished from them are so convenient as that they may be furnished on very short warning: they approve of the disposition of the three remaining troops of Cavalry, the lookout Boats and ships as proposed: and that express riders be held in readiness for the purpose mentioned by the Board of War. The Executive are of opinion they are not authorized by Law to appoint a general Officer till an invasion or insurrection has actually taken place, and three Battalions at least of the Militia embodied. They recommend to the Board of War to have two heavy Cannon mounted at Hoods on James river, two others at West point on the York river, two others at Hobb's hole on Rappahanock and two others at Alexandria on Potowmack: And if any position lower down the Potowmack can be found where cannon might obstruct the passage of vessels, they woud have two mounted there also: they further recommend that the most vigorous exertions be immediately used to withdraw from the reach of a sudden enterprize of the Enemy all cannon not necessary for the defence of the established batteries: At these Batteries also they wou'd have the Board of War reconsider the number of guns mounted, and where there are more than are necessary for the purpose of the Battery to withdraw in like manner those which are supernumerary: They woud also desire that the prisoners of War at this place, not being commissioned Officers, be removed immediately to the prison Ship and She repair forthwith to her moorings. TH: JEFFERSON

Tr in Board of War Letter Book (MiU-C).

From Samuel Huntington

Philadelphia, 18 Nov. 1779. Circular to the state executives enclosing resolves of Congress of 12 and 16 Nov. reorganizing the eleven companies of artificers raised by the quartermaster general, and other resolves of 16 Nov. requesting the state executives to issue writs, when applied for, compelling witnesses to appear and testify in courts-martial.

FC (DLC: PCC, No. 14); 2 p. Enclosures: resolves of Congress summarized above; copies (Vi), signed by Charles Thomson; printed in JCC, XV, 1261-2, 1276, 1277-8.

To Benjamin Harrison

In Council, 19 Nov. 1779. Transmits resolution of Congress, enclosed in letter from Samuel Huntington, requesting reconsideration of Act for reopening Virginia land office.

MS not traced; A.L.S., 1 p. and address, sold at American Art Association and Anderson Galleries, Terry Sale, pt. 1, 2-3 May 1934, lot 272. Huntington's letter, enclosed, was dated 30 Oct. 1779, q.v.; see also JHD, Oct. 1779, 1827 edn., p. 63.

Board of War to Board of Trade, with Reply

[*Williamsburg*] *20 Nov. 1779.* Approval, with the concurrence of the executive, of the purchase of cloth, to be paid for in part by cannon at the foundry. Signed by Innes, Nelson, and Lyne. Countersigned: "In Council Nov. 23. 1779. This purchase is approved: paiment to be made in Cannon as above proposed, so far as they will go towards full paiment; the balance to be paid in money as soon as the Treasury can furnish it. Th: Jefferson."

RC (CSmH); 1 p. Written below letter from Board of Trade to Board of War, same date, requesting approval of the transaction.

From the Board of War, with Reply

Williamsburg, 20 Nov. 1779. Alexander Stewart of Rockbridge co. has offered to supply the state with gunpowder. He should be engaged to supply as much as he is willing to contract for and should be paid as much as others receive for all he delivers to the magazine at Staunton. Signed by Innes, Nelson, and Lyne. Countersigned: "In Council December 1st. 1779. Approved on condition that Mr. Stewart and his partners shall let the State have the whole powder they shall make, except what they shall want for their own private consumption. By this it is understood that they are to sell none but to the State. Th: Jefferson."

Tr in Board of War Letter Book (MiU-C); 1 p.

To Benjamin Harrison

SIR   In Council November [20?] 1779.

The Board of War apprehending that the mention of the appointment of an assistant Clerk to them, as made in my letter to you of October 20th. was not accurately conformable to their resolution as approved by the Executive, have inclosed me the resolution with the approbation subscribed. This transaction happened in my absence, and the Clerk being otherwise engaged no copy was retained, so that I was informed of it from memory alone in general terms. It is observable that their Resolution goes only to the appointment of a Clerk, being perfectly indefinite as to the time during which he would be wanting. The Power of establishing a permanent Officer, being in the legislature only, and the Council, in their own office, having only made occasional appointments, when necessity required it, I was naturally led to suppose that the one in question was temporary. We stated therefore to the Assembly the time he had served, not presuming to give an Opinion, that a permanent officer of that kind was necessary, of which indeed we are not qualified to determine, and still less presuming to say we had made such permanent establishment ourselves. I take the liberty of inclosing to you the original Resolution and approbation, which I hope will place the transaction on its proper footing, if anything in my letter occasioned a misapprehension of it. I have the honour to be with the greatest respect Sir Your most Obedient humble Servant,   TH: JEFFERSON

Dft (DLC); in a clerk's hand, corrected and signed by TJ. In the date line the day was left blank, to be filled in later.

This letter, enclosing the RESOLUTION of the Board of War concerning the appointment of an assistant clerk and the APPROBATION of the Council (see Board of War to TJ, 30 July 1779), supplies the information concerning the controversy with the Board of War (see James Innes to Mann Page, 27 Oct. 1779; Board of War to TJ, 2 Nov. 1779) hitherto lacking because of the missing LETTER . . . OF OCTOBER 20TH. The date of the present letter has been supplied from a resolution of the House of Delegates of 20 Nov. 1779 authorizing the Board of War to appoint an assistant clerk and fixing his salary (JHD, Oct. 1779, 1827 edn., p. 65).

From Charles Thomson

SIR   Secretary's Office Novr 20th 1779

I take the liberty of transmitting you a duplicate of an Act of Congress passed the 16th of March 1779, the Utility of which is apparent: And as it may be proper and necessary that you should be informed of the several acts and proceedings of Congress I have herewith sent you a copy of their Journal from the 1st of January last and shall continue to send you from time to time their weekly publications. On the other hand as a communication of your acts may be advantageous, and lodging them in this office, for the information of the Delegates of the other states beneficial to the Union, and tend to facilitate the transmitting to posterity the rise and progress of these infant States, I take the liberty of requesting you to transmit to this office a copy of the constitution or form of government adopted by your State upon the declaration of Independence and of all the public acts passed by your legislature since that period. If you can add any Pamphlets or documents relative to the controversy and revolution they shall be carefully deposited and preserved and thereby you may do an acceptable service to posterity and oblige Sir your hum. servt.,   C: T.

FC (DLC: PCC, No. 18A). Enclosures not located.

To Benjamin Harrison

[*Williamsburg, 22? Nov. 1779.* JHD, Oct. 1779, 1827 edn., p. 66 (22 Nov. 1779): "The Speaker laid before the House a letter from the Governor, stating sundry matters for the consideration of the House, and enclosing several letters and papers on the subject thereof; and the same were read, *Ordered*, That so much of the said letter and enclosures as respects the public Cannon Foundery on James River be referred to the committee of Propositions and Grievances. *Ordered*, That so much of the said letter and enclosures as relates to other matters, be referred to the committee of the whole house on the state of the Commonwealth." Neither letter nor enclosures located.]

From Samuel Huntington

Philadelphia, 22 Nov. 1779. Circular to the state executives enclosing resolves of Congress of 19 Nov. recommending the enacting of laws for "a general limitation of prices . . . , to commence in their operation from the first day of february next."

FC (DLC: PCC, No. 14); 1 p. Enclosure: Resolves of Congress of 19 Nov. recommending limitation of prices and wages; copy (Vi), signed by Charles Thomson; printed in JCC, XV, 1289-92.

To Benjamin Harrison

SIR   [23 November 1779]

There is reason to believe that the appointment of a Consul to reside in this State on the part of his most Christian majesty either has been already or will shortly be made. I must submit to the general Assembly the expediency of considering whether our Laws have settled with precision the prerogatives and jurisdiction to which such a person is entitled by the usage of nations; and putting the Office on the footing they wou'd wish it to rest. The enclosed memorial from a Subject of the same prince is also perhaps worthy the Attention of the Assembly. The expediting judiciary proceedings wherein foreigners are concerned, who come to make only a short stay among us, seems expedient for the preservation of a good understanding with them and for the encouragement of Commerce. The Executive received from Congress some time ago copies of the several proceedings which had taken place between a Subject of the crown of Portugal and the Commander of an American privateer; a part owner of the privateer being a Citizen of this State. They were accompanied by some resolutions of congress

desiring that the executive would so far interpose as to have reparation made to the foreigner whose vessel had been taken, pyratically
as they supposed, and to have the Offenders proceeded against
criminally. The case with all the documents transmitted was submitted to the Attorney General for his opinion which he has lately
given us, and I now inclose it. From that you will perceive that if
the act complained of were piracy or should any future act of piracy
be committed by any of our Citizens, there is no judicature within
this State before which it could be tried. Whether the establishment
of such a judicature may not be necessary for the preservation of
peace with foreign nations is now submitted to the legislature.
I have the honour to be with the greatest respect,

TH: JEFFERSON

RC (Vi); in a clerk's hand and signed
by TJ; addressed to Harrison as Speaker.
Docketed: "Governors Letter Novr: 23d.
1779. 1st. to appoint Consul & ascertain
his powers. 2. respecting privateer phœnix & her case stated by the Atto. General. Refd. to the Whole on State of the
Commonwealth."

APPOINTMENT OF A CONSUL: The
Chevalier D'Anmours was appointed on
27 July 1779, but his commission was
not received until shortly after this letter was written (see R. H. Lee to TJ,
6 Sep. 1779; D'Anmours to TJ and enclosure, 7 Nov. 1779; TJ to Benjamin
Harrison, 8 Dec. 1779). The ENCLOSED
MEMORIAL was probably a copy of an
unsigned MS (DLC: TJ Papers, 4:
569-70), "Observations concerning the

appointment of a Consul of france in
Virginia," dated "Philadelphia July 31.
1779," and docketed "Observations of the
Minister of France on the subject relating to a Consul in Virginia." The enclosure has not been printed here because the Act passed by the Assembly,
cited hereafter, and TJ's Proclamation
concerning Consuls, 30 Dec. 1779, follow closely the "Observations." As a result of TJ's recommendation, the General Assembly passed, 24 Dec. 1779, an
Act for the protection and encouragement of the commerce of nations acknowledging the independence of the
United States of America (Hening, X,
202-3). For the OPINION of the ATTOR-
NEY GENERAL, also enclosed, see Edmund Randolph to TJ, 13 Nov. 1779.

From George Washington

DR. SIR   Head Quarters West-point 23d Novr. 1779.

I have been honored with your Excellencys favors of the 1st 2d
and 8th of October, and the several inclosures.

The measure of the council in remanding Governor Hamilton
and his companions back to confinement, on their refusing to sign
the parole tendered them, is perfectly agreeable to the practice of
the enemy. The particular part objected to I have always understood enters into the paroles given by our officers.

In regard to your letter of the 8th, I would hope with your
Excellency, that there will be no necessity for a competition in
cruelty with the enemy. Indeed it is but justice to observe, that of

late, or rather since Sir Henry Clinton has had the command, the treatment of our prisoners has been more within the line of humanity, and in general very different from that which they experienced under his predecessors. I shall not fail however as a matter of duty to pay proper attention to such deviations from this conduct, as may appear the result of mere wantonness or cruelty and that have not been incurred by the irregularities of our prisoners.

Dft (DLC: Washington Papers). In hand of James McHenry. At foot of text: "Governor Jefferson." On the Hamilton case generally, see TJ to Bland, 8 June 1779, and references there.

From the Board of War, with Reply

Williamsburg, 24 Nov. 1779. Col. Finnie, state quartermaster general, should be allowed a general order to employ workmen. Signed by Nelson, Griffin, and Barron. Countersigned: "In Council Novr. 24th. 1779. Approved for the present, but it is recommended to the Board of War to take Measures for setting apart a proper number of workmen in each Department who shall be subject to orders from the Quarter Master, while the residue shall be proceeding in other necessary works without being subject to interruption from him. Tho: Jefferson."

Tr in Board of War Letter Book (MiU-C); 1 p.

To Benjamin Harrison

[*Williamsburg, 24? Nov. 1779.* JHD, Oct. 1779, 1827 edn., p. 68 (24 Nov. 1779): "The Speaker laid before the House a letter from the Governor, enclosing a memorial of Mr. De Francey respecting a commercial transaction between the executive and his principal, Mr. De Beaumarchais, with other papers on the subject thereof, which were read, and ordered to be referred to the committee of the whole House on the state of the Commonwealth." Neither letter nor enclosures located.]

To Benjamin Harrison

[*Williamsburg, 24? Nov. 1779.* JHD, Oct. 1779, 1827 edn., p. 69 (24 Nov. 1779): "The Speaker laid before the House, a letter from the Governor, requesting that the vouchers returned by the commissioners of the Gun Manufactory at Fredericksburg, on the settlement of their accounts, may be furnished to the executive, to be by them used as vouchers in adjusting the account of the Commonwealth against the continent, which was read, *Ordered,* That the papers desired in the said letter be sent to the Governor." Not located.]

To Benjamin Harrison

[*Williamsburg*, 25? *Nov. 1779.* JHD, Oct. 1779, 1827 edn., p. 70 (25 Nov. 1779): "The Speaker laid before the House, two letters from the Governor, stating several matters for the consideration of the House, and enclosing several letters and papers on the subject thereof, which were read, and ordered to be referred to the committee of the whole House on the state of the Commonwealth." Neither letter nor enclosures located.]

From Joseph Reed

SIR   In Council Philadelphia November 25th. 1779

The Assembly of this State having ratified the agreement made between the Commissioners of the States of Virginia and Pennsylvania touching their disputed boundaries: I have now the honour and satisfaction to inclose the ratification, which I must request you to lay before the Honorable the Legislature of the State over which you preside.

Notwithstanding some difficulties and objections were made, the great desire of this State to preserve not only harmony and good correspondence with a Sister State so respectable, but to cultivate affection and an intercourse of mutual kind Offices so far prevailed as to induce individuals to wave private opinions and to agree in a unanimous vote on the occasion.

I am with very great respect and esteem Your Excellencys most obedient and very humble Servant,   JOS: REED President

RC (Vi). In a clerk's hand and signed by Reed. Enclosure (Vi): Resolution of the Pennsylvania General Assembly, 19 Nov. 1779, ratifying "the agreement entered into between Commissioners from the State of Virginia and Commissioners from this State which is in the following Words"; here follows text of agreement signed at Baltimore, 31 Aug. 1779; see under 27-31 Aug., above. Letter and enclosure endorsed: "Ratification of the boundary line between Pennsylvania and Virginia. Oct. Session 1779." The resolution of the Pennsylvania Assembly was in turn transmitted to Speaker Harrison, 11 Dec.; see under that date.

From the Board of Trade

[*Williamsburg*] 27 *Nov. 1779.* Transmitting proposals of Raleigh Colston for supplying the state with salt. The present and prospective stock of tobacco does not permit payment for any considerable quantity of salt in tobacco. It is hoped there is sufficient salt for the winter, and if the state's trading vessels escape the enemy they will bring a sufficient supply for the next summer. Although the Act establishing the

Board of Trade directs that salt shall be imported for civilians also, means are lacking to do so. A considerable share of tobacco has been used for purchasing salt even for the army. If this matter were submitted to the legislature, the expediency of allotting the Board a quantity of tobacco for the purchase of salt would be clearly seen. Signed by Ambler and Rose. Countersigned: "In Council Nov. 27. 1779. The board disapproves of the contract proposed. Th: Jefferson."

RC (CSmH); 2 p. Tr in Board of Trade Journal (Vi); printed in *Official Letters*, II, 69-70. The enclosed proposals of Raleigh Colston have not been located.

From Philip Mazzei

SIR   [Nantes, 27 November 1779]

It is 8. days since I arrived at this place from Rochelle, near which City I was set a-shore in an Island by a Portugueese vessel from Cork in Irland. The various circumstances, which have contributed to my liberty, and several other anecdotes since I left the Capes of Virginia; deserve I think that I should trouble you with an account of them; but an illness of 2. months and half, and the constant uneasiness of the mind during 5. months have reduced me so low, that I can scarsely write at all. I must therefore confine myself at present to that, which is most immediately necessary. I am at a loss what to do for want of my papers. I mentioned more than once to the late Governor, Mr. Page, and Col. Maddison the propriety of sending several duplicates of my Commissions and Instructions by the first opportunities. I even did remember it to Col. Maddison in one, or 2, of my letters dated on board the Johnston Smith in Rappahannack, or York River. I wish they had been sent to Mr. Penet in Philadelphia before the 7th. of August, as his letter of that date arrived at his house in this City about a month since. I could not with any degree of prudence attempt from New-York, or Long-Island, to write to Virginia. I had imagined to write to Mr. Bellini in such a manner, that you could understand my meaning; but having signified to those persons who under hand favoured me as much as possible, that I wanted to write to an Italian Gentleman in Williamsbourg about his domestick affairs in Italy, which he had recommended to me, they advised me not even to mention my desire of writing to any body. Indeed nothing but the necessity of drawing for money induced me to write twice to my Friends; and that, as I was told, could not give suspicion to my prejudice. The capture of Mr. Smith, who had set out for

Virginia before I was brought to New-York I expected would have
hurried the sending the duplicates of my papers with additional
commissions. There is one Col. Macballe at Paris, who wrote to
Mr. Penet's House, that he is charged by the Government of Virginia to cooperate with Mr. Smith &c. &c., that he was taken, of
course had threwn his papers over board; and desired to be supplied
with money. But far from supplying with money an unknown
person, who has nothing to shew to convalidate what he writes, or
says, it is not convenient for them even to supply me with the 300.
Louis mentioned in Mr. Penet's letter of credit in my favour, which
I had of the State to enable me to proceed as far as my native Country. They have however supplied me with some, and I hope they
will with a little more; but that I attribute to the very distressed
condition, in which I have come to them, and to the strong feelings
of Mr. da Costa in favour of America and her sons, as I have seen
the declaration of the Partners in Paris against making the least
further advance untill some remittances are received from America.
Indeed the exorbitant sums due to them from Virginia, South Carolina, Massachusets, and Congress, I am afraid may be of infinite
prejudice to their credit, if some remittances don't arrive pretty
soon; which would be a disgrace upon us. There is not the least
shadow of distrust, the American Independence is looked upon as
certain, the great internal resources of Virginia are well known, the
[de]sire of complying with our wishes is great, but the power I
fear is failing. As to my situation it is really precarious; I have
already drawn on my Friends, as mentioned; I am obliged to pay
here a debt of 58. guineas contracted in Irland; and shall probably
be obliged to expect here remittances from my Friends to enable me
to discharge it, and to proceed in my journey. As soon as I am in my
native Country I shall not want for my subsistance, but the unexpected multiplied heavy expences I have been at since I left Virginia will probably oblige me to an economy prejudicial to my
public duty, if I don't receive soon some assistance from you. Should
I recover my fortune in Tuscany you may depend that I will spend it
to the last farthing if necessary; but that will require time. The
affairs in Europe are as follows; England in mourning; France and
Spain triumphant; the Dutch determined to keep their neutrality;
Russia if joined to England will scarsely ballance the power of
France and Spain; and the other Powers seem determined to be
spectators. Should the Convoy not sail immediately I may perhaps
be able to write fully, and descend to particulars in a second letter
by the same vessel. I shall enumerate my origin[al] Letters 1, 2,

3, 4, &c.; and shall distinguish the copies by first Copy, 2d. Copy &c. I wish that the same method may be observed in the letters to me, and that I may be informed of every one of my letters, that are received, either copies, or originals, and by which vessel, if possible. I can write non more; I hope [to] be excused in consequence of my bad state of health; and I have the honour to be most respectfully, Sir, Your Excellency's most Obedt. & most Humble Servant,

PHILIP MAZZEI

RC (NN). Endorsed in an unidentified hand: "Mr. Madzei Letter recd Jany 81." At head of text: "1. 2d. Copy," i.e., second copy of first dispatch, as explained toward the close of the letter. Date supplied from Mazzei's notes

printed in Marraro, *Mazzei*, p. 10-11. In the same publication (p. 65-84) is printed "Mazzei's Relation of His Captivity," which provides full background for the present letter.

Form of Recruiting Commission

WILLIAMSBURG, [28 November] 1779

To   Gentleman:

Y OU are appointed, and forthwith are to proceed, to recruit men to serve in the *infantry* of this commonwealth. Each man is to receive at the time of enlistment a bounty *which with that heretofore received shall make*[1] seven hundred and fifty dollars to serve during the war, and the following articles of clothing, that is to say: A coat, waistcoat, a pair of overalls, two shirts, a pair of shoes, and a hat; to be delivered at the place of rendezvous, and with the like articles every year after during his service, to be delivered at his station; and will be entitled to the same pay and rations as are allowed by Congress to the like soldiers in continental service, and during his continuance in the service will be supplied with goods by this state, at the following rates, *viz.* Osnabrugs at 1*s.* 6*d. per* yard, coarse hats at 7*s.* 6*d.* each, coarse shoes at 8*s. per* pair, coarse yarn stockings at 5*s. per* pair, rum or brandy at the rate of 10*s. per* gallon, whiskey at the rate of 5*s. per* gallon, and such other imported articles as may be necessary at the rate of 120 *per centum* upon the first cost. At the end of the war he will be entitled to one hundred acres of unimproved land, within this commonwealth. All soldiers who may be disabled in the service will be entitled to receive pensions during life. You are to be allowed one hundred and fifty dollars for each able-bodied soldier you shall enlist and pass with the officer of review to be appointed for that purpose. You are to make return of your enlistments within   from the date hereof, in person, or by letter, and continue to make   returns thereof afterwards.[2]   *Th: Jefferson*

Printed form, filled in and signed by TJ (DLC: Washington Papers). Enclosed (with other copies) in TJ's letter to Washington of 28 Nov. 1779, q.v. Also Tr (DLC).

[1] Preceding seven words interlined by TJ in place of "of," crossed out.
[2] More than a line of printed text follows before the signature but has been heavily scratched out.

To George Washington

SIR   Williamsburgh Nov. 28. 1779.

Your Excellency's letter on the discriminations which have been heretofore made between the troops raised within this state and considered as part of our quota, and those not so considered, was delivered me four days ago. I immediately laid it before the Assembly, who thereupon came to the resolution I now do myself the honor of inclosing you. The resolution of Congress of Mar. 15. 1779 which you were so kind as to inclose was never known in this state till a few weeks ago when we received printed copies of the journals of Congress. It would be a great satisfaction to us to receive an exact return of all the men we have in Continental service who come within the descriptions of the resolution together with our state troops in Continental service. Colo. Cabell was so kind as to send me a return of Octob. 1779. of the Continental regiments commanded by Lord Sterling, of the 1st and 2d Virginia state regiments, and of Colo. Gist's regiment. Besides these are the following

Colo. Harrison's regiment of artillery:
Colo. Baylor's horse:
Colo. Bland's horse:
General Scott's new levies, part of which are gone to S. Carolina, and part are here:
Colo. Gibson's regiment stationed on the Ohio:
Heath's and O'Hara's independent companies at the same stations:
Colo. Taylor's regiment of guards to the Convention troops: of these we have a return.

There may possibly be others not occurring to me. A return of all these would enable us to see what proportion of the Continental army is contributed by us. We have at present very pressing calls to send additional numbers of men to the Southward. No inclination is wanting in either the legislative or Executive powers to aid them, or to strengthen you: but we find it very difficult to procure men.[1] I herewith transmit to your Excellency some recruiting commissions to be put into such hands as you may think proper for re-enlisting such of our souldiery as are not engaged already for the war. The act of assembly authorising these instructions requires that the men enlisted should be reviewed and received by an officer to be appointed for that purpose; a caution less necessary in the case of men now actually in service, and therefore doubtless able bodied, than in the raising new recruits. The direction however goes to all cases, and therefore we must trouble your Excellency with the appointment of one or more officers of review. Mr. Moss our agent receives orders, which accompany this, to pay the bounty money, and recruiting money, and to deliver the clothing. We have however certain reason to fear he has not any great sum of money on hand: and it is absolutely out of our power at this time to supply him, or to say with certainty when we shall be able to do it. He is instructed to note his acceptances under the draughts and to assure payment as soon as we shall have it in our power to furnish him as the only substitute for money. Your Excellency's directions to the officer of review will probably procure us the satisfaction of being informed from time to time how many men shall be re-enlisted.

By Colo. Matthews I informed your Excellency fully of the situation of Governour Hamiltoun and his companions. LaMothe and Dejean have given their paroles, and are at Hanover court-house: Hamiltoun, Hay, and four others are still obstinate. They therefore are still in close confinement, tho their irons have never been on since your second letter on the subject. I wrote full information of this matter to General Philips also, from whom I had received letters on the subject. I cannot in reason beleive that the enemy on receiving this information either from yourself or General Philips, will venture to impose any new distresses on our officers in captivity with them. Yet their conduct hitherto has been most successfully prognosticated by reversing the conclusions of right reason. It is therefore my duty, as well as it was my promise, to the Virginia captives to take measures for discovering any change which may be made in their situation. For this purpose I must apply for your Excellency's interposition. I doubt not but you have an established mode of knowing at all times through your commissary of prisoners, the precise state of those in the power of the enemy. I must therefore pray you to put into motion any such means you may have of obtaining knowledge of the situation of the Virginia officers in captivity. If you shall think proper, as I could wish, to take upon yourself to retaliate any new sufferings which may be imposed on them, it will be more likely to have due weight, and to restore the unhappy on both sides to that benevolent treatment for which all should wish.

I have the honour to be with the most perfect esteem & respect Your Excellency's Most obedient & most humble servt.,

TH: JEFFERSON

RC (DLC: Washington Papers). Addressed: "His Excellency General Washington Head-Quarters." Endorsed (in two or three different hands): "Wmsburg 28. Novr 1779 from Govr. Jefferson. answd. 18th recd 13 Decr Resolution of Assembly puttg All Officers & Soldiers on same foo[ting?]." Tr (DLC). Enclosures: (1) Resolution of Virginia General Assembly, 26 Nov. 1779, extending the bounty and other emoluments to certain officers and soldiers in the Continental service (copy in DLC; printed in JHD, Oct. 1779, 1827 edn., p. 71); (2) forms of a recruiting commission, one of which (DLC: Washington Papers) is printed above under the present date; (3) orders to John Moss, state agent for the Virginia Continental troops (missing).

YOUR EXCELLENCY'S LETTER: Dated 5 Nov. 1779, q.v. THE SITUATION OF GOVERNOUR HAMILTOUN: See TJ to Bland, 8 June 1779, and references there.

1 The remainder of this paragraph is enclosed in square brackets in the MS, but these were apparently added after the letter was received; they are not in the transcript.

Thomas Scott to Joseph Reed

DEAR SIR   Westmoreland November 29th. 1779

My indisposition of body of which I informed you in a former letter still continues so as to prevent my seeing Philada. altho (other obligations aside) the present circumstances of this county requires it in a more than ordinary way and hath made me conceive it my duty to dispatch the bearer Mr. Andrew Linn express to you, with the following intelligence vizt. In the latter end of July last the Assembly of Virginia passed a Law for selling their back lands, and adjusting Claims amongst the inhabitants on their frontiers in a summary way by a Board of Commissioners, appointed for the purpose with jurisdiction within certain districts; one of these districts is composed of what they call the Counties of Monongalia, Youghiogany, and Ohio, more than two of which pretended Counties, lie within the bounds of Westmoreland, and indeed include nearly the whole of it. However soon in October, the Commissioners for this district made their way out here, and set down at old fort bird within four miles of my house and at least thirty miles within the lines agreed upon by their and our Commissioners in order to determine Claims and grant certificates to such as are to obtain Patents. On hearing of this extraordinary Jurisdiction I conceived it was without the authority of the Legislature, since their own plan of settlement with Pennsylvania was yet depending, but on going to the place I was soon undeceived by the Commissioners shewing me the Act itself, which without reserve makes all claims within their district cognizable before them, and directs their Judgment on finding such and such circumstances attending the claims. I concerned no further with the business untill many of the subjects of this Government who had patents in their houses were summoned before this tribunal to answer such miscreants as were pleased to settle on, or set up claim to their lands, at or since Dunmores invasion on pretext that titles derived from Pennsylvania are invalid. And indeed where such intruders have been bold enough to raise corn on the premises they are sure of a Judgment under this Law. On these people and others who expected to share the same fate applying to me for Counsel in the case I went again to the Commissioners on the twenty second instant, and in the name of the People and Character of their Representatives queried with them by themselves what they meant by thus disturbing the peace of the people and County of Westmoreland and how far they meant to carry their prosecutions against such, letting them know that I was sent to them by the People in that character, and for that purpose, and further to let them know that these People would pay no regard to their summon or determination in consequence thereof.

They replied with great coolness that they were sworn servants of the State of Virginia for the express purpose of executing that Act of Assembly without restriction or reserve; That they had no further or other instructions than what was contained in the Act itself. That as faithfull servants to the State, they must and would carry the said law into full execution, and give the possession according to their determinations, without respect to persons &ca. except prevented by instructions from Virginia which they observed they could hardly expect since the Government was fully knowing to the Circumstances which I mentioned when the law passed and further said I might be assured Virginia was determined on protecting their subjects in this quarter and supporting the determinations they might make at all events, and accordingly the several causes depending were set for tryal at a day certain &ca.

From this relation your Excellency and all the powers of Government will easily gather the irksome, nay intolerable situation we are in in this County and that we need the interposition of Government for our protection; and that Government needs to stir, or Virginia will shortly sell the greater part of the lands contained in a scope of country sufficient for three large Counties, as it is provided in the Act aforesaid that if the proper owner doth not apply within the term of one year, any other person may have a patent for the spot; and numbers will be ready to avail themselves of this clause. The bounds I have mentioned lies all within the line settled by their and our Commissioners. I would have been larger on the contents of this extraordinary law, but that its like you have or can see it. Tryal by Jury is held sacred in their bill of rights and is totally taken away by this law.

I have the honor to be with the greatest respect Your Excellencys most obedient & very humble servant, THOMAS SCOTT

PS This day being the first of December these Commissioners are actually determining causes, I being present. T: S:

RC? (DLC: PCC, No. 69, II). Enclosed in Reed's letter to the Pennsylvania Delegates in Congress, 15 Dec. 1779 (printed in *Penna. Archives*, 1st ser., VIII, 46-7); a copy (now missing) was enclosed in Huntington to TJ, 30 Dec. 1779, q.v.

A LAW FOR SELLING THEIR BACK LANDS, AND ADJUSTING CLAIMS: Actually two laws: (1) Bill for Establishing a Land Office and (2) Bill for Adjusting and Settling Titles of Claimers to Unpatented Lands, both printed above, 8-14 Jan. 1778. In consequence of Scott's information and the resolve of Congress of 27 Dec., Reed published a proclamation, dated 28 Dec., embodying the resolve of Congress and assuring Pennsylvania settlers in Westmoreland of protection by the state (Reed to Scott, 28 Dec. 1779, *Penna. Archives*, 1st ser., VIII, 63-4; Reed's Proclamation, *Penna. Colonial Records*, XII, 212-14). See also entry for Reed to TJ, 8 Jan. 1780.

Proclamation of Embargo

By His Excellency THOMAS JEFFERSON, *Esq; Governour or Chief Magistrate of the commonwealth of* VIRGINIA:

A PROCLAMATION.

WHEREAS the exportation of provisions from this state will be attended with manifest injury to the United States, by supplying the enemy, and by rendering it difficult for the publick agents and contractors to procure supplies for the *American* troops, and will moreover give encouragement to engrossers and monopolizers to prosecute their baneful practices, I have therefore thought fit, by and with the advice and consent of the Council of State, to issue this my proclamation for laying an embargo on provisions; and I do hereby lay an embargo on provisions, *viz.* On all beef, pork, bacon, wheat, *Indian* corn, pease or other grain, or flour or meal made of the same; to continue until the first day of *May* next. And I do hereby strictly prohibit all mariners, masters, and commanders of vessels, and all other persons whatsoever within this state, from loading on board any vessel for exportation, and from exporting all or any of the above species of provisions, by land or water, from the date hereof, during the term aforesaid, under pain of incurring the penalties inflicted by the act of Assembly intitled *An act to empower the Governour and Council to lay an embargo for a limited time*, except as in the said act is excepted. And I do hereby strictly charge and command all naval officers and others, in their respective departments, to exert their best endeavours to the end that this embargo be strictly observed.

GIVEN under my hand this 30th day of November, 1779

THOMAS JEFFERSON.

Broadside (DLC: PCC, No. 71, I). Swem, "Va. Bibliog.," 7200; no copy located by Swem, and the broadside is not recorded in other bibliographies. Enclosed in TJ to Huntington, 30 Dec. 1779.

This proclamation anticipated the recommendation of Congress in a resolve of 15 Dec. 1779; see JCC, XV, 1383.

The ACT TO EMPOWER THE GOVERNOUR AND COUNCIL TO LAY AN EMBARGO was passed at the Oct. 1778 session and renewed at various times thereafter; see Hening, IX, 530-2, &c. TJ's Proclamation was reissued on 17 May, 17 July 1780, and 19 Jan. 1781, and was repeatedly printed in *Va. Gaz.*

From the Board of Trade

[*Williamsburg*] *1 Dec. 1779.* Requesting approval of the purchase of shoes and sugar. The articles are immediately wanted, but the prices are high. Signed by Whiting, and Rose. Countersigned: "In Council Decemr. 4th. 1779. Approved. Th: Jefferson."

Tr in Board of Trade Journal (Vi); 1 p.

From the Board of War

SIR   War Office, Williamsburg December 1. 1779.

We enclose Mr. Dickson's application to us, to annex a Salary to his Office. Conceiving it out of our Province to say what shall be his allowance, we take liberty to refer the Settlement of that matter, to your Honorable Board. We shall only beg leave to add that the Office of Cloathier is a very laborious and important One, the duties of which we can venture to assure your Excellency, Mr. Dickson has ever performed with Integrity and assiduity.

We have the Honor to be Your Excellencys

JAS. INNES

WM. NELSON

SAML. GRIFFIN

RC (Vi). Addressed: "His Excellency the Governour."

MR. DICKSON'S APPLICATION: B. Dickson to the Board of War, 25 Nov. 1779

(Vi), enclosed, states that he had held his office four months and would like a determination of his salary and that of his assistant.

From Richard Henry Lee

Falmouth [Stafford co., Va.] 1 Dec. 1779. Quotes a letter just received from a member of Congress in Philadelphia stating that "a capital embarkation" from New York is afoot and will undoubtedly proceed to the south, perhaps to Virginia. This is precisely what Lee has long apprehended.

RC (DLC); 2 p.; printed in R. H. Lee, *Letters*, II, 167-8.

To Pontdevaux

SIR   [Before 2 December 1779]

In hopes that by this time you will have discharged those attentions which the situation of your ship and men required on your arrival here, I take the liberty of expressing to you the satisfaction it would give me to have the honour of seeing you in our little capital. As such it would scarcely merit the notice of a stranger, but the exercise and change of air and element may perhaps be agreeable. If it should be convenient to you to take a dinner with me the day after tomorrow, my chariot shall attend you in York.

I am in hopes the several wants of your men have been supplied as far as our poor abilities enabled us to do it. I shall avail myself with great pleasure of every opportunity of testifying our gratitude to your sovereign and also of shewing you with how much respect and attention I am Sir Your most obedt. & most humble servt.

Dft (DLC). Endorsed: "Comte de Pont de Veaux. Marquis de Vaudreuil." The endorsement indicates that an identical letter was sent to Vaudreuil.

Pontdevaux was with D'Estaing at Grenada in July 1779 as lieutenant colonel of the regiment d'Auxerrois (*Va. Gaz.* [D & N], 19 Feb. 1780) and apparently accompanied Vaudreuil to Yorktown. Le Marquis de Vaudreuil, captain, under D'Estaing, of the ship *Le Fendant*, which was in York harbor from 20

Nov. 1779 to 25 Jan. 1780 (Ministère des Affaires Etrangères, *Les combattants français de la guerre américaine,* Paris, 1903, p. 76). See also TJ to D'Anmours, 10 Nov. 1779; to James Innes, 28 Dec. 1779.

From Pontdevaux

SON EXCELLENCE   a yorck le 2 xbre. 1779

J'ay l'honneur de vous remercier de l'invitation que vous avês la bonté de me faire. J'auray celuy de m'y rendre, ainsi que Mr. le chlr. de tarragon, qui vous est très respectueusement obligé: quant a Mr. le Mqs. de vaudreuil, je ne puis avoir sa réponse ce Soir. Je luy feray part demain des offres de votre êxcèllence.

Nous nous ferons un devoir de témoigner dans touttes les occasions notre respectueux attachement aux états unis, et a ceux qui les servent avec autant de distinction que votre êxcèllence; je suis avec respect Son êxcèllence Votre très humble et très obéïssant Serviteur,   PONTDEVAUX

RC (MoSHi).
LE CHLR DE TARRAGON: possibly Jean-Remy, Chevalier de Tarragon, who participated under D'Estaing in the siege of Savannah (Contenson, *La Société des Cincinnati de France,* p. 270).

From the Board of Trade

[*Williamsburg, 3? Dec. 1779.* Minute in Board of Trade Journal (Vi) under 3 Dec. 1779: "Ordered that Mr. Armisteads offer of Sundry Goods be submitted to the Executive. 'Fifty for one upon the West India Invoice payable in Tobo. is exceedingly high, higher than we have ever yet given. The Articles are such as are in great Demand. We wish advice from His Excellency in Council' " Not located.]

To Joseph Reed

SIR   Williamsburg Dec. 3. 1779.

Your acceptable present came duly to hand. Tho I had not the happiness of a personal acquaintance with your excellency, I never needed evidence of the propriety of your conduct on any occasion. A circumstantial development however of Governor Johnstone's essay cannot but have good effects in satisfying the world at large, that the same pure spirit of patriotism which produced this revolution, still directs it. It will further evince the baseness of our enemies with whom corruption and calumny supply the place of valour. I must however acknowledge myself under obligations to the Governour for having produced to me this occasion of assuring you of my great personal regard, and with how much esteem & respect I am Your Excellency's most obedient & most humble servt.

Dft (DLC). Endorsed: "President Reed." Deletions and corrections in Dft not noted.

The ACCEPTABLE PRESENT must have been Reed's pamphlet, *Remarks on Governor Johnstone's Speech in Parliament* . . . , Phila.: Francis Bailey, 1779 (Evans 16483), a defense of Reed's conduct in relation to overtures made to him by Charles Johnstone, a member of the British peace commission of 1778; see Van Doren, *Secret History*, p. 98-104.

From Riedesel

SIR   New York 4th. Decr: 1779

I should conceive it an instance of ingratitude, to leave Virginia without repeating to you my heartiest thanks for every mark of Friendship which you have so kindly testified to me from the first moments of our acquaintance; and for the Assistance and hospitality which you have shewn the Troops under my Command since you have assumed the Government of Virginia: I beg you will be assured that I shall ever retain a grateful rememberance of them and deem myself singularly happy, after this unnatural War is ended, to render you any Service in my power as a token of my personal regard for you and your Family.

Allow me to recommend to your farther protection the Brunswick Troops in your Province, now under the Command of Brigadier Genl: Specht; you have hitherto been satisfied with their Conduct and I am convinced they will ever behave so as to merit the continuance of your kindness.

I presume to request you will present my respects and Madame de Riedesels best Compliments to Mrs. Jefferson, whose very amiable Character and the many proofs which we have experienced of Her Friendship can never be effaced from out of our Memory, and she will ever possess a high rank among Madame de R's particular Friends.

I beg leave to inclose to Your Excellency a number of Letters received from Europe for several Officers and Soldiers of the Troops of Convention: As they are from individuals no ways interested in the Contest, I dare to ask after their passing your inspection, to have them sent by the safest conveyance to Brigr: Genl: Specht: Such Letters cannot have any influence in the general Cause but will give very sensible Pleasure to the Gentlemen to whom they are addressed; who have not heard from their Friends for a great length of Time.

Permit me to add in conclusion the perfect sentiments of respect and Esteem with which I have the Honor to be Your Excellencys most obedient humble Servant,   RIEDESEL M: G:

RC (DLC). Enclosures not identified.

From Philip Mazzei

[*Nantes, 5 Dec. 1779*. Mazzei's "Representation" of his conduct as agent for Virginia in Europe states that in a letter of this date, his second dispatch to TJ, "he foretold, that we ought not to expect any good from the Irish commotions, and signified his reasons for such a conjecture, which he confirmed in letter 11, dated Paris, April 10th 1780," q.v., below (Marraro, *Mazzei*, p. 88). Though four copies of this letter were sent, none has been found (same, p. 11); one copy certainly reached TJ, for it was acknowledged in TJ's letter to Mazzei of 31 May 1780.]

From the Board of Trade

[*Williamsburg*] 7 Dec. 1779. Transmitting offer of soap and candles, the purchase of which has been recommended by the Board of War. Signed by Whiting and Rose. Countersigned: "In Council Dec. 10. 1779. The purchase is approved. Th: Jefferson."

RC (CSmH); 1 p.

To Benjamin Harrison

In Council Dec. 8, 1779

I take the liberty of laying before the General assembly the enclosed letter and memorial from the Consul of his most Christian majesty in this state. That gentleman's letters of appointment came to hand soon after the date of my letter to you on the same subject.

MS not located. Extract printed from Anderson Auction Co. sale catalogue, 10 Jan. 1908 (Henry Goldsmith Sale), lot 134, a one-page A. L. S. The letter was resold at the American Art Association, 21-22 Jan. 1926 (Turner-Munn Sale), lot 430.

The LETTER AND MEMORIAL: Chevalier D'Anmours to TJ, and enclosure, 7

Nov. 1779, q.v. The docketing for this letter is found on a blank page attached to the enclosed memorial: "Governor's Letter 8th. Decr. 1779. enclosing Le Chevalier De Anmours Memorial &c. Referred to Commee. of whole on Commerce Bill." The bill for the protection and encouragement of commerce had been read twice in the House of Delegates and referred to a committee of the whole when TJ's letter was presented by the Speaker, 9 Dec. (JHD, Oct. 1779, 1827 edn., p. 82). MY LETTER . . . SAME SUBJECT: TJ to Benjamin Harrison, 23 Nov. 1779.

To the Board of Trade

In Council Dec. 10th. 1779.

The inclosed resolution for purchasing Slaves to carry on the West Ham Foundary is transmitted to your Board to be carried into execution, as the care of those works rests with you.

TH: JEFFERSON

P.S. Since writing the above another resolution of Assembly is come to hand for purchasing Iron of Mr. Ross. I inclose it to you with a Copy of his Letter proposing the supply, and Governour Henrys Answer.   TH. J.

Tr in Board of Trade Journal (Vi). Enclosures: Resolutions of Assembly of 3 Dec. 1779; these follow the text of the letter and are printed with the present letter in *Official Letters*, II, 74. The copies of the letter of David Ross and Gov. Henry's reply have not been further identified.

For the recommendations of the Board of War concerning the public foundry, see Board of War to TJ, 16 Nov. 1779, first letter from the Board of that date. As a result of these recommendations, the House resolved on 3 Dec. that the foundry should be continued and that the governor be empowered to purchase slaves for work there and carry into execution the contract with David Ross (JHD, Oct. 1779, 1827 edn., p. 78). TJ's reason for transmitting these resolutions to the Board of Trade instead of to the Board of War is not clear. The following minute appears in the Board of Trade Journals, immediately after this letter: "The Management of the Public Foundary at West Ham has ever been understood as under the direction of the board of War, but the Instructions above from the Executive being so pointed it becomes the Duty of the Board to carry them into execution in the best manner possible."

From Samuel Huntington

SIR   Philada Decemr 10th 1779.

By the act of Congress of this day herewith enclosed your Excellency will be inform'd, That Congress approve of the Measures taken by the Executive of the State of Virginia in providing Guards to the Convention Troops at Charlotte Ville, that those Guards all be considered in Continental Service and receive Continental pay and rations while doing duty at the Convention Barracks.

That the party of Colo. Bland's light Dragoons now at Charlotte Ville are to proceed to South Carolina and the Commander in Chief is directed to appoint a Successor to Colo. Bland resign'd.

I have the honour to be with the highest respect your Excy's hble Servt,

S.H. President

FC (DLC: PCC, No. 14). Enclosure (missing): resolution of Congress, 10 Dec. 1779, recommended by Board of War, approving arrangements for guarding Convention troops, &c.; printed in JCC, XV, 1366-7.

From the Board of War, with Reply

War Office Williamsburg Decr. 11th. 1779.

The Board of War recommend that a fast sailing Boat be kept as a look out at Smiths Island to give the alarm in Maggoty Bay on the approach of an Enemy; from thence an Express to be sent across the Country to Northampton Court House; the Boat then to proceed to York with the alarm. The Battery at Cheriton to be repaired, and the Guns there remounted immediately for the defence of that Inlet; That the Brass piece of Ordnance be brought over to the Western Shore, and that the Iron four pounders and the two pounder, with two Swivels be left with Colonel Corbin. That two Gallies be stationed between the South end of Hog Island and Chingoteague.

That the Continental Soldiers on the Eastern Shore which amount (as the Board of War are informed) to a compleat Company, be ordered to rendezvous at Bridge Town, and that a Captain &c. be ordered over to command them, with direction to canton them at the different Inlets and exposed places. That the Captain (to avoid the expence of a pay Master) be allowed to draw Money to pay the Company, first giving Bond and Security for the proper expenditure of it, that one of the Subalterns be empowered to do the Quarter Masters duty, and that a Commissary be also appointed. The Magazine to be removed to Bridgetown.

WILLIAM NELSON
JAS BARRON
GEO: LYNE

In Council Decr. 15. 1779.

The Board approves of the preceding Measures, but recommend to the Board of War to reconsider the same, so far as respects the number of Cannon proposed to be kept there, and to say whether it would not be better to remove all which may not be necessary for the defence of the Place.

THO: JEFFERSON

Tr in Board of War Letter Book (MiU-C).

To Benjamin Harrison

SIR   In Council Dec. 11. 1779.

The inclosed resolution of the General assembly of Pennsylvania with President Reid's letter came to hand by yesterday's post. I now do myself the pleasure of transmitting them to the assembly, and of assuring you that I am with the greatest esteem Your most obedient & most humble servt.,   TH: JEFFERSON

RC (Vi). Addressed in TJ's hand. Endorsed: "Governors Letter enclosing Pennsylvania Assembly's proceedings in ratifying Boundary line. December 11th 1779. Referred to Commee. of whole on State of the Commonwealth." Enclosure (Vi): Resolution of Pennsylvania General Assembly, 19 Nov. 1779, summarized in note to Joseph Reed's letter to TJ, 25 Nov. 1779.

The Pennsylvania resolution ratifying the boundary agreed on by the Commissioners at Baltimore, 27-31 Aug. 1779 (see under that date, above) was read in the House on 11 Dec., referred to committee of the whole, and on 23 Dec. deferred to following session (JHD, Oct. 1779, 1827 edn., p. 85, 106; see also TJ to Huntington, 9 Feb. 1780).

To Benjamin Harrison

[*Williamsburg, 11? Dec. 1779.* JHD, Oct. 1779, 1827 edn., p. 86 (11 Dec. 1779): "The Speaker laid before the House a letter from the Governor, enclosing one from the Board of War, respecting the attempts of a band of speculators to create an artificial scarcity of grain." Not located.]

From George Washington

SIR   Hd. Qrs. Morris Town 11 Decr. 1779

I inclose your Excellency a number of papers relative to a certain Richard Bird, and the money mentioned in Gen. Tylers letter. Col. Nevil takes charge of the prisoner. I give your Excellency this trouble as he appears to be the person some time ago advertised in a Virginia paper for the commission of some crime.

I am &c.

Dft (DLC: Washington Papers); in James McHenry's hand; endorsed. Enclosures missing.

RICHARD BIRD: See Washington to Brig. Gen. John TYLER, 28 Nov. 1779 (*Writings*, ed. Fitzpatrick, XVII, 203);

Tyler's letter to Washington has not been found. COL. NEVIL: John Neville, colonel, 4th Va. Continental line (Gwathmey, *Hist. Reg. of Virginians in the Revolution*).

From George Washington

SIR   Head Qrs. Morristown Decr. 11th. 1779.

I have the honor to inform Your Excellency that I have received advice from New York that a very large embarkation had taken place (said to amount to 8000) and that the fleet containing them was at the Hook on the point of sailing. Their destination *reported* to be for Chesapæk bay, on a combined operation in the 1st place against the French Squadron there, and afterwards to attempt the rescue of the Convention troops. Their naval force may consist of five sail of the line and two frigates of 44s. besides a 50 Gun ship. The Separation of the French Squadron mentioned by our last accounts from the Southward may have been a temptation to the enemy to undertake an enterprise against that part which had arrived. But it is not perhaps very probable that the Convention troops enter into the plan; nethertheless I think it prudent to communicate the intelligence to your Excellency, that you may have the goodness to direct Your attention towards their Security, and take any precautions which may appear to you necessary without conveying an alarm. For this purpose I request the favour of you to give immediate information to the Officer commanding at Charlottesville.

By the report of a deserter and the firing of Signal guns a great part of yesterday, I am led to conclude the fleet sailed at that time.

I have the honor to be With the greatest respect & esteem Yr. Excellencys Most Obedt Servt.

Dft (DLC: Washington Papers); in hand of Alexander Hamilton, with interlineations (not noted here) in Washington's hand. Endorsed.

On the British EMBARKATION see Washington to TJ, 25 Dec. 1779.

From Philip Mazzei

SIR   Nantes, Decr. 12th. 1779

A very good piece of intelligence, which I received yesterday, has been followed by very mortifaying news arrived in Town today. Yesterday I was informed, that 9. days since it was resolved in the King's council to lend Congress, in arms and such other things as they want, to the amount of 16. millions of livres. I must give you a clear notion of my authority to enable you to weigh with your own scales the probability of this intelligence, as well as the importance of other matters. I became lately acquainted in a Coffe-house with an elderly Gentleman, who appears to be prudent and wise, a deep politician, and a sound philosopher. He certainly knows mankind, and the characteres of European Nations. He is a stranger here, and I suppose him a resident in Paris. As I found his conversation pleasing and instructive I courted his acquaintance, and he seems to think himself well repayed by the satisfaction afforded by mine to his curiosity. I have reason to believe, that the person, from whom he has received the above intelligence, is well acquainted with what-ever passes in the council, and a regular correspondent of this gentleman. By 2 persons from l'Orient and letters from Brest we have heared the desagreable news of Count D'Esteings's defeat in America, supposed to have happened on Long-Island, where they say he has lost many men, and has been dangerously wounded himself in 2 places. The accounts are various and confused; but they all seem to signify, that the Count is furious against the Americans; that he has been betraied by them; that he was not joined by any thing like the number of our troops he had been promised; that at the first fire the Americans ran, and left him in the lurch; &c. &c. D'Esteing is reckoned a Hero, and is now the darling of France; but in this town they are downright mad for him. I never wanted the company of my judicious gentleman more than this day. We had 4 hours of a very interesting conversation, and every topick was maturely considered and thoroughly digested. He thinks that the accounts are too uncertain to hazard an opinion about the reception the Count is likely to meet with at court. He says however that courage is highly esteemed, and that the dissatisfaction proceeded from having done nothing in Europe with so powerful a fleet may reflect such a splendor on boldness as to eclipse many faults; that supposing the Count to the highest pitch of favour (as it may be the case) and so furious against the Americans (as reported) his anger would not produce any alteration in the adopted measure of lending Congress the said some [sum] as both honou[r] and good policy require now to go on. He looks with contempt on the popul[ar] voice, and with indignation on the expressions and clamours of the enthusiasts, of whom this Town is cheafly composed; and with his prudent and sound reflections has afforded some relief to my excessive uneasiness on some respects; but on the other hand the conversation has brougt me to the Knowledge of 2 things extremely disagreable. One is the want of subordination, order, and discipline in the marine of France, and the other a reigning opinion in Paris that should the French meet with bad success in the next campaign the Americans would settle their matters with Great Britain. What is called in France the Body of the Marine comprehends not only all the officers from the highest Commander to the youngest midshipman, but likewise those who have the direction of what belongs to the sea service and the Members of the King's council for that departement. They are of the rank called *Noblesse*; they form a powerful body by hanging together; and will disappoint and disobey a commander at sea if they don't like him, and for the same reason occasion delay and other inconveniencies on land and in the harbours to frustrate a good measure of the Minister. The evil is great, and very deeply rooted, owing in a great degree to the almost total neglect of the marine in the late reign. Many good officers, who of late have been taken in to the King's service from the commoners, are by the others considered as an inferior body; they are called intruders; and consequently often exposed to an ungenteel treatment. The evil is however something lessened, and they think seriously of applying good remedies to it; but a perfect cure (says this gentleman) cannot be obtained, as soon as is wanted, in this mild Government; it would be necessary, he thinks, to have a Minister of the Marine of Cromwel's character. The reigning opinion, that the Americans are too tired of the war to continue it much longer, and that they will make it up with England, if France was to be some thing unsuccessful in the next campaign, is generally entertained by the best politicians from the accounts constantly received from America, and the little patriotick spirit which (they say) has been commonly observed in those Americans, who have been, or are in France. The number of our Tories, and persons partial to the English Government has been much exagerated in France not only by frenchmen returned from America, but by many of our own people likewise through indiscretion, or villany. As I think the good opinion of this gentleman worth acquiring, I have mentioned to him a number of our good Patriots and Heros and several anecdotes, which would shine in the history of the best times of Rome. He observed that it would have been a very good thing if some such had been sent over. I noticed hi[s] hints relative to several persons in high posts, and on the bulk of th[ose] who have been over with publick commissions from the several states. I had already heared with mortification the character left behind by some, who have been over with commissions from our own state. As to a certain progeny I have convinced him of the necessity of supporting them at first, as the opposite party was composed of men, who thoug[h] unexceptionable in private life, were very dangerous for their political principles. As to a person who has made a great noice, and whom I don't know personally, I have observed that a Nation in infancy at the first entering on publick business could not pretend to a thorough knowledge of mankind, but that they had acquired experience, and things were about changing much for the better when I left America; and to the bulk of persons &c.; I have described as well as I could the situation of our country to prove that in many instances we cannot have our choice, and to convince him of the necessity we have been in till now of Keeping our best and wisest men at home for the forming and improving our new Governments, besides other reasons, which I have mentioned. He has been highly pleased with our new laws in favour of liberty, and is quite delighted with our barriers against Aristocracy. He is better reconciled with our conduct, but insists that some proper per[sons] ought to have been sent to Europe at any rate. He says that the Queen calls Dr. Franklin her Papa; that the whole Kingdom pay due regard to his great merit, the larned and scientifick body in particular; that he is an honour to his country; but that he was well known long time since, and it would have been as Well to have sent over some other good samples. He has likewise observed that the Dr. is old, and that an active insinuating person could have served his country much better in several instances. The merit of Mr. John Adams has not been known. You may remember that I foretold it in consequence of the account I had of him from you, and that I deplored the loss of that man in Congress to go where his talents would be lost. I heartly wish, that you had accepted the offer of congress yourself. The accounts I gave the Gentleman of the state of our affair[s] at several periods induced him to ask how it is come that the Americans have not applied for assistance to the court of France in Clear terms; and he seems to have no manner of doubt, that they could then, and can soon obtain what they want by proper application. I don't think I have succeeded to persuade him, that the Americans would never make peace with England without the consent of France. The least doubt of such a thing would make me shudder could I but harbour it. Besides the disgrace such a step would bring upon us, we would soon and bitterly repent on other accounts. Was even England to be successful in many instances, her ruin is unavoidable. France can bring her on her knees by only standing on the defensive. D'Esteing's defeat will be (I am afraid) of the worst consequence to us, and I heartly wish that that gentleman had never seen America; but should we lose our patience just when our enemies are at their last efforts? I shall trouble you again on this subject as soon as we receive more certain accounts, and I am most respectfully Sir, Your Excellency's most humble & most obedient Servant,

PHILIP MAZZEI

RC (NN). At head of text: "3 3d. copy." At foot of text: "His Excellency Ths. Jefferson Esqre. Govr. of Virginia."

A CERTAIN PROGENY: Unidentified. A CERTAIN PERSON WHO HAS MADE A GREAT NOICE: Probably Arthur Lee.

To the Board of Trade

[*Williamsburg*] *13 Dec. 1779.* Order to carry into execution a resolution of the Assembly of 8 Dec., empowering the governor to contract for clothing and provisions for the slaves and tradesmen at the Westham foundry.

Tr of executive order and enclosed resolution in Board of Trade Journal (Vi); 1 p.; printed in *Official Letters*, II, 76.

From the Board of War, with Reply

Williamsburg, 14 Dec. 1779. Since there is at present no commissary of prisoners, the vessel bearing a flag from New York should be committed to the care of Richard Barron, commanding officer of the state navy. If necessary, Capt. Barron will convey the ship to a place of safety on the western shore. Signed by Innes, Nelson, Barron, and Lyne. Countersigned: "In Council Decr. 15th. Approved and advised that the Flag be brought into James River. Th: Jefferson."

Tr in Board of War Letter Book (MiU-C); 1 p.

From the Board of War

[*Williamsburg*] *14 Dec. 1779.* After appointment to a majority, De Klauman refused to do duty as a captain and asked Col. Marshall to consider him no longer an officer in his regiment. The vacancy has been filled up. De Klauman, being at this time out of the line of preferment, should share the fate of the regiment to which he was appointed major. Signed by Innes, Nelson, Barron, and Lyne.

Tr in Board of War Letter Book (MiU-C); 1 p. See TJ to Board of War, 18 Dec. 1779.

From Samuel Huntington

Philada Decemr 14th 1779

Your Excellency will receive herewith enclos'd two acts of Congress of the 11th instant and one other of this Day by which you will be inform'd that Congress have determin'd to call upon the several States to furnish their quotas of such Supplies as may from time to time be wanted for carrying on the war taking due care to suit the conveniencies of the several States, and the articles by them respectively furnished shall be credited towards their quotas of the monies they are called upon to raise for the United States at equal prices for articles of the same kind and quality and for others in due proportion, and the accounts finally adjusted so as to do equity to all the States.

By the separate act of the 11th instant you will observe the Quantity at present requested from the State of Virginia is twenty thousand barrels of indian Corn. It is the desire of Congress that each State should use all possible œconomy and despatch in procuring the Articles requested of them.

So soon as Congress are inform'd that the several States can and will furnish the provisions necessary for the army, the many persons heretofore employed in the purchasing Commissaries department may be dismiss'd.

I have the honour to be &c S.H. President

FC (DLC: PCC, No. 14). Enclosures missing; these resolves of Congress are printed in JCC, XV, 1371-2, 1377-8.

From Samuel Huntington

Philadelphia, 15 Dec. 1779. Circular letter to the state executives enclosing a resolve of Congress of this date recommending an embargo on exports.

FC (DLC: PCC, No. 14); 2 p. Enclosure missing; printed in JCC, XV, 1383.

TJ had anticipated the recommendation of Congress in his Proclamation of 30 Nov. 1779, q.v.

To Thomas Sim Lee

Sir Williamsburg Dec. 15. 1779.

The inclosed letter which came by a flag of truce from New-York, will, I imagine, inform you that prisoners from your state are sent here for the purpose of exchange. A copy of a letter from the master of the flag I also take the liberty of inclosing, as it will give you further information of their arrival here and escape from the flag. The master is to await the return of the prisoners whom your Excellency may think proper to give in exchange for these.

After expressing my satisfaction at your Excellency's appointment to an office, a second time so worthily filled, I take this my earliest opportunity of asking leave to trouble you from time to time with such communications as may be for the good of either state, of praying that you will be pleased to render me instrumental to their common service by honoring me with your commands, and of assuring you how earnestly I wish to see a perfect cordiality maintained between two sister states to whom common interests, manners, and dispositions have rendered a cordial intercourse so easy and necessary.

I am with the utmost respect & esteem Your Excellency's most obedient & most humble servt,   TH: JEFFERSON

RC (MdHi). Addressed: "His Excellency Governor Lee, Maryland." Enclosures not located.

From the Board of War

Williamsburg, 16 Dec. 1779. When Col. Travis entered into a contract with Edward H. Moseley to build a ship of war for the state, Moseley refused, after the contract was written, to accede to the terms unless it was stipulated that if the vessel were destroyed by the enemy it would be the state's loss. Col. Travis agreed, but through haste the stipulation was not entered into the written agreement. The contract between the state and Col. Moseley ought to be void, the value of the hull of the vessel destroyed should be paid from money advanced to Moseley, and the residue paid to the public treasury. Signed by Innes, Nelson, and Barron. Countersigned: "In Council Decr. 16. 1779. Approved. Th: Jefferson."

Tr in Board of War Letter Book (MiU-C); 1 p.

From the Board of War, with Reply

Williamsburg, 16 Dec. 1779. In Feb. 1779 Mark Talbot agreed with Capt. Maxwell and Col. Travis, commissioners of the navy, to build a vessel of war for the state. Talbot, supposing he had a bad bargain, did not comply with the terms of the contract. When called on in June for delivery, he stated that the enemy had destroyed the vessel, though it appears that timbers for the hull had not been raised at the time he claimed it was destroyed. Talbot has been frequently urged to complete his contract and has received considerable money on account. Meanwhile he has built and sold several vessels to private adventurers. By a letter from Capt. Wilson, enclosed, it can be seen what prospect there is of Talbot's complying with his agreement. It appears he is appropriating public money for his own use. It would be expedient to purchase a similar vessel and commence action against Talbot for breach of covenant. Signed by Innes, Nelson, and Barron. Countersigned: "In Council Decr. 18th. 1779. The board approves of prosecuting Mark Talbot for breach of contract and the Attorney General is desired to prosecute him accordingly. Th: Jefferson."

Tr in Board of War Letter Book (MiU-C); 2 p. The enclosed letter of Capt. Wilson has not been further identified.

From the Board of War

Williamsburg, 16 Dec. 1779. There are three captains, two lieutenants and four cornets in Maj. Nelson's corps. Two gentlemen are appointed to recruit the quotas of a lieutenant. If they have not done so, they do not belong to the corps of horse, and the officers who have raised their quotas and are now on duty should be the officers of the three troops of horse and should rise according to seniority. Signed by Nelson, Barron, and Lyne.

Tr in Board of War Letter Book (MiU-C); 1 p.

To Samuel Huntington

Sir   Wmsburg Decr. 16. 1779.

We have information from our Delegates in congress that the detention of some continental arms by the executive of this State during the course of the last summer has given considerable umbrage to congress. I beg leave therefore, thro' you Sir, to lay before that honorable body facts, simply as they occurred hoping that these will satisfy them that, the arms being justly due to this State, necessity alone dictated the measure, and that no sentiment of disrespect to congress entered into the transaction. This State in an early part of the present contest raised at first two, and soon afterwards seven Battalions for its particular defence, finding however that the dangers of our being invaded became less, our legislature made a tender of these Battalions for the continental Service. The tender was accepted of by congress only on condition that We would permit them to carry their Arms with them. They were accordingly marched to the grand army, time after time, as we could get them armed. I think this condition was dispensed with as to two Battalions only which congress, induced by their increasing wants of men, permitted to march on with out their arms. This is one of the Articles of Debt in our Account of Arms against the continent, which I state particularly, in order to bring it into recollection with some of your honorable members, and because, being recollected, it will go far in our justification as to the number of arms retained with us. Since this however, at different times, and for different corps, many smaller parcels of arms have been sent to congress by us. It is a fact, which we are to lament, that, in the earlier part of our Struggles, we were so wholly occupied by the great Object of establishing our rights, that we Attended not at all to those little circumstances of taking receipts, and vouchers, keeping regular Accounts, and preparing subjects for future disputes with our friends. If we could have supported the whole continent, I believe we should have done it, and never dishonored our exertions by producing accounts; sincerely assured that, in no circumstances of future necessity or distress, a like free application of any thing theirs would have been thought hardly of or would have rendered Necessary an appeal to Accounts. Hence it has happened that in the present case, the collection of vouchers for the arms furnished by this State has become tedious and difficult. Our board of War has been Attending to this business a considerable time, but have as yet authenticated the loan of only 5664 Stand of Arms and 580 rifles. They seem however to believe that (exclusive of considerable numbers delivered where no receipts were taken and the Officers to whom delivered are dead or not to be found which of course we shall lose) they will be able to establish a right to 10,000 Stand. These arms were most of them of very best quality, imported from Great Britain, by the State, for its own use. After the loan of so many to the continent, the loss of a considerable number put into the hands of the militia during the short invasion of the last Spring, many of which we were never able to recover, and a very recent Loan of 1000 Stand, to be sent on, at the request of congress, to South Carolina, we were reduced to not more than 3000 Stand in all our Magazines. Rumors were spread of an intended invasion by the enemy for the purpose of rescuing the convention Troops; that body of men were in the heart of our Country under a guard not able to furnish centine[ls] for ordinary duty; congress had just recommended to us to prepare for the most immediate and most rigorous operations, and to have our militia ready to march at the Shortest warning; the knolege of the low State of our Magazines had by some means got abroad, and spread a general alarm among our people: in this situation of things a vessel, loaded with arms, seemed to be guided by the hand of providence into one of our harbours. They were it's true the property of our friend, but of friends indebted to us for those very articles. They were for the common defence too, and we were a part of the Body to be defended. An Officer came for the purpose of removing them out of the State. Would circumstances have permited a previous application to congress, tho' not present myself, I so thoroughly know the respect which the executive bears for Congress, that I am safe in affirming that such an Application would most certainly have been made. But had they awaited that ceremony, the arms would have been gone: the continent of course would have been at the expence, and the arms exposed to the injury, and risk of a double transportation: for I cannot but take for granted that congress would on such an Application, in the case of a State so reduced in her magazines, and reduced by Loans to them, have ordered the arms to be replaced. Time however did not Admit of this ceremony; the executive therefore retained 5000 Stand. We shall not draw examples of similar liberties taken by other States; we shall never recapitulate aids granted to, or taken by our brethren from the common Stock, because we wish it to be freely used for their service, and to draw nothing from it for ourselves unless our distresses should at any time be such as to point us out to them as objects needing the common Aid. But we will observe in general, that, between congress and this State, similar freedoms in other articles, had been repeatedly and mutually taken, on many former occasions, and never had been the cause of discontent to either party. This precedent then, strengthened by the existence of an actual Debt, seemed to give a Double sanction to the executive for what they did: nor did any instance occur to them of unreadiness at any time to spare freely on continental requisition any articles within their possession or power, which might expose them to experience in turn the disregard of congress: I flatter myself therefore that that honorable Body whenever this matter shall be the Subject of their deliberations will be of opinion that the proceedings of the Lieutenant Governor and council were substantially justifiable. They hope that no want of ceremony, or other smaller circumstance, may have been matter of Offence to congress. If in this they should be mistaken, feeling the most real respect for that body, impressed with the Idea that its authority can never be wounded without injury to the present union, they are to lament the misapprehension and wish to

remove it by assuring you, as they may with truth, that no sentiment of theirs, either on this, or any other occasion, has justified it.
A motive of duty and respect to the collective council of our union
has led me into this detail to remove all ground of discontent from
among us, and to Assure you Sir at the same time that I shall
consider as occasions of manifesting my zeal for our sacred cause,
those which shall occur of proving how sincerely, I am Sir their
and your most Obedient and most humble Servant,

TH: JEFFERSON

RC (DLC: PCC, No. 71, I). In a clerk's hand, signed by TJ. Endorsed: "No. 63. Letter from T. Jefferson Govr. of Virga. Decr. 16 1779 Read Jany. 13. 1780."

In the preceding summer the Continental Board of War had protested the retention in Virginia of 5,000 muskets intended for Continental use; see entry for the Board's letter under 28 Aug. 1779, above, and Lt. Gov. Page's reply of that date, *Official Letters*, II, 37. The Board transmitted Page's letter to Congress on 8 Oct. (JCC, XV, 1035-6), and a committee of three reported thereon, 20 Oct., saying (in part) "that in their opinion the State of Virginia had no right to detain the Arms imported on account and for the use of the United States, as thereby the safety and welfare of these States may be essentially endangered. Such conduct we conceive to be also pregnant with danger, because any State in the union undertaking to be its own Carver must consequently lay a foundation for anarchy and confusion" (same, p. 1190-1). Congress recommitted this censorious report, but the Virginia delegates (in a missing letter) informed TJ of Congress' disapprobation of the conduct of Virginia, and the present letter is TJ's explanation of the affair. Though read to Congress on 13 Jan. 1780, the letter was not acted on (same, XVI, 54).

From William Phillips

New York, 16 Dec. 1779. A flag-of-truce vessel brings this letter, together with food and stores for the Convention troops. To save expense it is desirable that the flag vessel "be permitted to go up the James River as far as possible to discharge her cargo." Capt. Farquhar of the 20th Regt., who comes with the flag, brings a supply of money and will need an escort from the vessel to Charlottesville. Farquhar wishes to spend some time with his friends among the Convention troops; and another passenger, the wife of Lt. Maxwell, comes to stay with her husband, who is a prisoner at Charlottesville. Letters for officers at the Barracks are enclosed for forwarding.

RC (DLC); 2 p. In a clerk's hand; complimentary close and signature in Phillips' hand. Enclosures missing.

To George Washington

SIR   Williamsburg Decr. 16. 1779.

I take the liberty of putting under cover to your Excellency, some
Letters to Generals Philips and Riedesel, uninformed whether they

are gone into New York or not, and knowing that you can best forward them in either case.

I also trouble you with a Letter from the Master of the Flag in this State to the British Commissary of Prisoners in New York, trusting it will thus be more certainly conveyed than if sent to Mr. Adams. It is my Wish the British Commissary should return his answer through your Excellency or your Commissary of Prisoners, and that they should not propose under this pretext to send another Flag, as the Mission of the present Flag is not unattended by circumstances of Suspicion, and a certain information of the Situation of ourselves and our Allies here might influence the Measures of the Enemy.

Perhaps your Commissary of prisoners can effect the former method of Answer.

I inclose to you part of an Act of Assembly ascertaining the quantities of Land which shall be allowed to the Officers and Soldiers at the close of the War, and providing means of keeping that Country vacant which has been allotted for them.

I am advised to ask the attention of your Excellency to the Case of Colo. Bland late commander at the Barracks in Albemarle. When that Gentleman was applied to, to take that Command, he attended the Executive here, and informed them, that he must either decline it, or be supported in such a way as would keep up that respect which was essential to his Command, without at the same time ruining his private fortune.

The Executive were sensible that he would be exposed to very great and unavoidable expence, they observed that his Command would be in a department separate from any other, and that he actually relieved a Major General from the same Service. They did not think themselves authorized to say what should be done in this case, but undertook to represent the matter to Congress and in the mean time, gave it as their Opinion that a decent table ought to be found for him.

On this he undertook the command, and in the course of it incurred expences, which seemed to have been unavoidable unless he would have lived in such a way as is hardly reconcileable to the Spirit of an Officer, or the reputation of those in whose service he is. Governor Henry wrote on the Subject to Congress. Colo. Bland did the same; but we learn that they have concluded the allowance to be unprecedented and inadmissable, in the case of an officer of his rank. The Commissaries on this have called on Colo. Bland for reimbursement. A Sale of his Estate was about to take place, when we undertook to recommend to them to suspend their demands till we could ask the favor of you to advocate this Matter with Congress so far as you may think it right, otherwise the ruin [of] a very worthy Officer must inevitably follow.

I have the honor to be with the greatest respect & esteem Your Excellency's Most obedt. & most humble servt., TH: JEFFERSON

RC (DLC: Washington Papers); in a clerk's hand, with complimentary close and signature in TJ's hand; endorsed (in part): "Recd. 16th. Jany. 1780. G W———n." Also FC (DLC); text defective. Enclosures missing except for the extract of the Act relating to north-western lands (see explanatory note, below), of which there are copies in both DLC: Washington Papers and TJ Papers.

AN ACT OF ASSEMBLY: "An act for more effectually securing to the officers and soldiers of the Virginia line, the lands reserved to them, for discouraging present settlements on the north west side of the Ohio river, and for punishing persons attempting to prevent the execution of land office warrants," agreed to on 1 Dec. 1779 (JHD, Oct. 1779, 1827 edn., p. 75) and printed in Hening, X, 159-62. THE CASE OF COLO. BLAND: See Washington's answer to TJ, 22 Jan. 1780, and also his letter to Congress, 26 Jan. 1780 (Writings, ed. Fitzpatrick, XVII, 445-7). In the MS there are square brackets enclosing the paragraphs relating to Bland, suggesting that at some time the passage was extracted.

From the Board of War

Williamsburg, 17 Dec. 1779. Workmen are needed for the next year at the shipyard. The commissioner should attend the sales of British property and purchase Negroes for that purpose instead of hiring them, because the hire is so exorbitant. A pair of sawyers would not cost less than £600 per annum. Signed by Nelson, Barron, and Lyne. Countersigned: "In Council Decr. 18th. 1779. Approved. Th. Jefferson."

Tr in Board of War Letter Book (MiU-C); 2 p.

From the Board of Trade

[*Williamsburg*] *18 Dec. 1779.* The public shipyard at Cumberland should be discontinued because of the enormous cost of maintenance. The trading department has only six vessels, and there is little prospect of increasing the number. These can be kept in repair at less expense than the present cost of the public yard.

Tr in Board of Trade Journal (Vi); 1 p.; printed in *Official Letters*, II, 76-7.

To the Board of War

In Council Dec. 18th. 1779.

Cap. De Klauman having sometime ago explicitly in the presence of the Board made his election to withdraw from duty in the Regiment of Artillery, and relied on his appointment to a majority in one of the Eastern Batalions and the vacancy thereby occasioned having been supplied by a new appointment, they are of opinion he cannot resume his command in that Regiment: the proposition to promote Cap. De Klauman to the Majority in the State Garrison Regiment renders necessary the determination of a previous general question whether established usage authorises the transferring a senior captain from one Regiment to the majority of another in preference to a junior captain of that other; or whether promotions are confined to the Regimental line only: reserving for future determination the question whether Cap. de Klauman is still entitled to the benefit of the Date of his former commission; The Board of war will be pleased to favour the council with their opinions on these points. Th: Jefferson

Tr in Board of War Letter Book (MiU-C).

From Archibald Cary

Dear Sir   Ampthill December 18th. 1779.

I have delay'd Answering your letter respecting the Goods Sent to Majr. Hay, in hopes of Giveing you Some Certain Account of the Theft, but as yet have not been able to Fix it with precision; I am however on a Good Sent [Scent], and hope Shortly to Give you an Account of the offender.

The badness of the Weather and a Cold which by Venturing out on a Damp day a Cought prevented my being in Town last Week. I do not know but it was Well for me I did not Come down, as I must have been exposed more than I am at Home. I understand the Assembly After Finishing many Nothings are this day to Adjourn, and notwithstanding Several attempts to prevent, are to meet at Richmond in May. Have they determind on which Hill to build; untill that is done no private Buildings will go on, and of Course so much the longer will those who are obliged to attend Publick business be put to Inconvenience; I understand many of the great officers, Intend to resign, no great Mark of a Patriotick Spirit, I Confess I have long known that Actuates to few, however I hope they will think better of it, and Consent to be put to Some difficultys as those have for Ages who live distant from Williamsburg.

I do not mean by what Follows to Complain to you so that you should take publick notice of it. I purchase and Grind wheat for the board of War, at their request Sent down in a Sloop belonging to the Mill 200 Barrills of Flower. They have detaind her at Collage landing untill the Demurrage will Come to as Much as the Fraight. It is Horrid to the Publick and it may also be of bad Consiquence should they be push'd for Flower, as we have 7 or 8 M. Bushels wheat at Richmond, no way to Git it to the Mill but by this Vessel, the Winter Seting in very hard and we may expect the river Frosen. A hint to some of them may Spur them up, but altho I Care not who I offend in a Just Cause, I wish not that my Name on this occasion be made use of.

I see by a list of Bills Sent me many or rather some of much Consiquence but have not heard the Fate of Any of them, and Judge According to Custom they have been left to be hurryd over at last; I wish it was otherways but Jobing in assembly will ruin us I fear; assure yourself that body begins to be held in very low esteem. In fact it is owing to their own Misconduct, Driking [Drinking] and Gameing it is Said not only Imploys them at Night, but the day also is oft spent in the Same Manner. I pray for better men but dispair of Seeing them dureing the little time I have to Stay. Had I a Turn for Publishing the Publick Papers should point out Such Men to their Constituents.

As I expect this will be handed you after the assembly is over have Ventured to Trespass on your Time with a long letter with nothing in it.

I am Dr. Sir with Compliments to your Lady, Your Hble Servt.,

ARCHIBALD CARY

RC (DLC). Endorsed by TJ.
TJ's LETTER to which this is a reply is missing.

From Philip Mazzei

SIR   Nantes, Decr. 18th. 1779.

We Know at last, that D'Esteing's melancholy affair happened in Georgia; that our few regulars there behaved very well; and we hear that it was the militia who did not Keep their ground; and that the pretended treachery did consist in the villany of one of our officers from New-England, who deserted and informed the enemy of Desteing's plan for the attack. We are convinced that D'Esteing's people, who adore him, have exagerated matters and accertained suppositions to magnify his actions, and render them more conspicuous; and that the accounts from the people on board have besides been ornamented in travelling with new additions. Nothing is Known from D'Esteing himself, and it cannot be otherwise, as the first intelligence must always be given to Government. It is still insisted, that the Count had been promised to be joined by 8000. of our troops, which being impossible in those parts makes me hope that all the reports to our disadvantage will dissipate like smoke as soon as we have a genuine account of the affair in the french gazette, which is retarded by the very slow travelling of the Count in consequence of his wounds. The future prospect of things in the southern states disturbs my mind as much as any unfortunate event ever happened since the beginning of the war. I am afraid for Charles Town, to apprehend another descent much worse than the first in our poor unarmed state. By the precipitation with which d'Esteing is come away, he must have left poor Lincoln in a very precarious situation; and by bringing home 12. men of war and troops, before the arrival of others, he has made the Enemies masters in the western seas, and has put the french Islands in great danger. There is at Brest, destined for that place, 16. men of war besides frigates and other smaller vessels, and 6000. men; but they won't be ready to sail in less than 3. weeks. They say, that when he found that 12. ships of the line, which ought to have sailed in Septr. were still here, he was struck by a fit of deep melancholy. His partisans say, that he had express orders to come away; that the state of his ships and the sickness of the soldiers did not permit him to stay any longer; that he was to have come home long ago; that he had been promised and disappointed too many times; that if he had been supported in the manner agreed, especially as to time, he would have done great things; that if he had not come the vessels for that station would not have been ready in 4. months hence; that he was much wanted at home for the reformation of the marine; and that he is come fully determined to have it done; or he will resign. Those, who in some respects are of a different opinion, especially as to his coming away before the arrival of other vessels, speak very softly, the other party being an impetuous torrent.

Jany: 9th 1780.

The Count has been by his wounds much retarded in his journey. He is lately arrived at Paris, and was received most gratiously at Court, and with transports of joy by the People. His wounds and generosity have probably contributed to it. He is not rich, and has given up to his people the share of his profits. He cannot yet stand without crutches and is now something worse on account of the prodigious number of visits he has been obliged to receive. The account of the affair at Savannah in the french gazette has been fully detailed; but I shall only give you an extract of a few particulars in as little compass as possible. "Count d'Esteing finding many of his vessels much damaged by a strong gale, resolved to go no further north, and to undertake the siege of Savannah with the troops he had on board to whom were joined 2000 men of the United States commanded by Genl. Lincoln. The combined army consisted of 5524. men; the besieged under Genl. Prevost were 7168, 4000 of which were negroes. The 24th. of Septr. the Enemy made a sally, and was repulsed with loss. Being impossible to continue the seige for reasons &c. the 9th of October the retrenchments were attacked. The Enemy informed of the plan of the attack by fugitives had prepared the defence accordingly. The french and americans attacked with the greatest vigour and returned 3-times to the charge, but the superiority of number obliged them to desist." I shall not say a word about the number of Killed &c. &c. The gazette takes notice of the great harmony, which subsisted between the french and Americans in the following words: *La plus grand union a subsisté entre les Troupes combinées.* I hope it has been so; but be as it will I have more than once been pleased with their prudence in endeavouring to destroy the credit of such reports, as are calculated to impress the people of the two nations against each other. I wish we would follow their example, and I think we never had more need of it than at present. The Enemy will have a good play now with our people to insinuate notions of their omnipotence, and the little value of the french alliance. The greater were the forces of this Hero, and the more his merit is magnified in France, the stronger will be in the minds of our people the impression of that nothing he has done in twice he has been with us. The French have in their power to lend us an effectual assistance, and I flatter myself, that was I in Paris I should not be a useless instrument towards contributing to it. The Gentleman mentioned in my letter 3. assured me; that Mr. de Sartine would be very glad to here from my mouth such relations and opinions, as I had communicated to him; he is personally acquainted with that Minister; and I suppose him to be some what intimate with him. He is now gone, and I have lost the only person in whom I could find some relief to my mind. He afforded me a very great satisfaction and a greater hope of being heared to some effect, by informing me that my bosom-friend Marquis Caraccioli is still at Paris Ambassadour from the King of Naples, as I left him. From the account you had very often of him in our conversations you cannot doubt his weight there, and especially at present, being in so high estimation with the King of Spain: It is probable that I shall not be suspected of partiality for America, as much as a native; though they may be mistaken in that. I have another great reason to hope of being heared to some effect, the Grand-Duke having certainly received a copy of the letter from a Citizen of the World to his American friend. I heared it at New-York from Mr. Bettoia, who had himself delivered it to that Sovereign according to my directions. When we read it together at Monticello I observed to you the probability (in case any one of the Copies should arrive to its destination) of its being communicated to the Kings of France and Spain. I am now fully persuaded it has been the case from the Minister of Tuscany's saying to Mr. Carmichael in Paris, that his Court had been of late much disappointed in not hearing from me, on whom they depended for the surest and most important intelligence. To be Kept in this place, and forced into inactivity, with such hopes, and so well founded, at a time which I consider the most critical we have had or will have during our troubles, I leave you (to whom my feelings are pretty well Known) to judge how tormenting my anxiety must be to my heart. I shall never trouble you by letter with a detail of my sufferings in this place for want of money. It would be now too mortifying. I hope it will be a subject of conversation at Colle, or monticello, in better times. I am however obliged to inform you (in order to shew reason for having not sent the narrative of my adventures, as promised in letter 2.) that for the want of 16. louis to pay for my passage from Ireland, my baggage has not yet been delivered to me. I have in a trunk several bundles of papers, in one of which are the rough copies of the letters I wrote in New-York to the Commodore and others, which it is proper you should see to judge of my conduct. I have applied for the liberty of taking my papers, as things of no value to any body but me, and in consequence incapable of securing any part of the debt; but have been denied. This specimen will be sufficient for you to form a notion of my misery, and pity me. I had at first almost determined to write to Tuscany for assistance, but have declined it. I could draw without prejudice while I was in captivity, but it could make an unfavourable impression to do it when among friends, on whom it is natural to suppose, that I ought to have been furnished with credit. It is often precarious and dangerous to attempt by letters what can effectually and easily be obtained in a conversation. I spoke fully on this subject to the late Governor and several members of the Council, expressing the necessity of being supplied with

3, or 400. Louis in this place, and the reasons I had to expect that I could raise in my native Country the rest of the sum necessary to answer the purpose of my mission. I don't Know yet what I shall, or can do. I shall inform you of it as soon as I find relief, and shall send you the copies of my correspondence on the subject with Mr. D'Acosta and Dr. Franklin. I hope you will not fail sending me some remittances as soon as possible. Necessity compells me to beg it of you most earnestly, in order that the publick service may not suffer. I am largely in debt here, and elsewhere; I cannot get a penny more from Mr. D'Acosta; and was he to pay me the ballance now, which is 246. Louis & 6 livres, it would be too inconsiderable a sum in my present circumstances. When it was resolved I should sail, I depended on the 300. Louis from Penet D'Acosta & Co; a bill of £.100. sterl. I bought of Col. Banister; the guineas I had received of Genl. Riedesel and the half jowls I had bought; and the assistance of my friends in Tuscany, besides what I expected to find in Mr. Bettoia's hands, on whom I had drawn only for the half of the value of the 2. last cargoes I consigned to him from Virginia, and nothing on account of my brig and her freight. But the case is now quite different. My good friends Mr. Bettoia and Capn. Woodford did manage my business so effectually, one in expences and the other in selling my goods to people who broke before the time of payment, that Mr. Bettoia acquainted me in New York, that I owe him a trifle, as the product of the brig, which he had sold, did not quite ballance the account. My friends have already assisted me with 200. guineas, 20 of which I lost in the exchange. That sum, and the cash I brought from Virginia, the bill of £.100. sterl; and almost every thing valuable I had with me, went off long since. I am indebted in Irland; I have not yet paid for my passage; I have about 200. Louis to pay here; and find myself disappointed in the credit I had of the State. I never received any thing towards the expences of my voyage, which have been immense. Even in Virginia they were considerable in journeys &c; 'though I was often with my friends. The 300. Louis (had they been paid) joined to the £.7000. currency I received, could not ballance my expences to the end of December last. I hope I shall not be suspected of venality. Could I recover my fortune soon enough, I would be proud of using it for the publick service; but that being almost impossible, I have thought it my Duty to acquaint you with my economical circumstances, in order to convince you, that notwithstanding the great desire of serving my Country, it is probable that I shall want the power of doing it, if you don't assist me. And in case you could not by any means, I wish you would send me at least some ostensible letters calculated to encourage my friends to do it, and even the Sovereign, by shewing the nobility of your sentiments, as well as the rectitude of your intentions, and some regard to the true zeal of your agent.

I hope you will be pleased with a piece of intelligence I had of the often-mentioned Gentleman just before he left this place; which is the very great probability, that Russia will preserve a perfect neutrality for powerful reasons, which hardly admit of a doubt. I shall give you another, which is a fact. The Irish after having made publick rejoicings, in consequence of the Liberty of trade, already obtained, now insist on liberty of Government independent of the british Parliament. The Ministry will be extremely puzzled. I think however, that America has given them a good lesson about the danger of refusing, but in one way or the other I expect no advantage from that quarter to our cause. I have the honour to be most respectfully, Sir, your Excellency's most Obedient & most humble Servant,   PHILIP MAZZEI

RC (NN). At head of text: "4 2d. Copy."

From the Board of War

SIR   War Office Wmsburg Decr. 20th. 1779.

To the previous general question from the Executive relative to Cap. de Klauman Whether established usage authorizes the transferring a Senior Captain from one Regiment to the Majority of another in preference to a junior Captain of that other. The Board Answer, in continental Service, the Cavalry, Artillery and Infantry are distinct and separate Corps and promotions take place accordingly paying regard to Seniority. Cap. De Klauman['s] proper Line of preferment is in the two Eastern Battalions ordered to be raised. Junior Captains and all Subalterns rise regimentally, the eldest Captain in the Line, is entitled in case of vacancy to a majority, all Field Officers rise according to Seniority in their proper Line, paying no regard to regiments. When we mention then proper Line we mean the Line of Cavalry Artillery and Infantry and consider them separate and distinct.

We have the honor to be Your Excellency's mo: Obt. Servts.,
WM NELSON
JAS. BARRON
GEO. LYNE

Tr in Board of War Letter Book (MiU-C).

From Giovanni Fabbroni

ECCELLENZA   Parigi 20 Xbre 1779.

Ho avuto già L'onore di congratularmi coll' Eccellenza Vostra,
per La giustizia resa al vostro carattere, e ai vostri talenti dai vostri
compatriotti elevandovi al grado di Loro Governatore. Io ne ebbi
La nuova dal Sige. Digs, e per mezzo di esso vi spedii La mia
Lettera. Il Sige. Lee mi favorisce adesso d'offrirmi una nuova
occasione di scrivervi, ed io non trascuro di profittarne. La mia
dimora in questa Capitale è per esser, ormai, troppo breve, per che
io intraprenda a trattenervi con novità scientifiche. Ma quando sarò
una volta ristabilito à Firenze, e ch'io conosca qualche facil mezzo
per farvi capitare le mie lettere, e ricever con sicurezza Le Vostre,
non mancherò di darmi ogni moto per ben riescire in quella Cor-
rispondenza Letteraria, che favoriste offrirmi coll' ultima Vostra
Lettera. Desidero con ansietà di ricevere delle Vostre nuove, e di
quelle di Cotesto Continente in generale, e degli Amici Bellini, e
Mazzei particolarmente, de' quali, malgrado le mie sollecitazioni
non so più niente fin da gran tempo. Sono ambiziosissimo dell'
onore che mi accordate di carteggiar con Voi, e non desidero adesso,
se non che di esservi conosciuto personalmente; il che spero sarà
per seguire forse fra non Lungo tempo. Si stampano adesso à
Parigi alcune mie riflessioni su' i principi generali dell' agricultura,
relative allo Stato in cui si trova in Europa: si stampa altresì à
Londra una mia Mineralogia sul testo di Cronstedt; e sarà mia cura
di farvi pervenire una copia d'ambedue colla prima occasione.

I preparativi bellici dell' Europa sono tremendi; e L'umanità deve
fremere nel veder gli Sforzi che si fanno dalle Nazioni per anni-
chilarne i più preziosi, e sacrosanti diritti.

Onoratemi dei vostri venerati comandi, e credetemi per sempre
qual mi dò L'onore di dirmi col più profondo ossequio, e perfetta
stima Dell' Eccellenza Vostra Umilisse. devotisse. obbligat Servi-
tore,   GIOVANNI FABRONI

RC (DLC). The editors are indebted
to Prof. A. T. MacAllister, Jr., Princeton University, for a transcription of
this letter, as well as for a translation
on which the summary below is based.

Fabbroni repeats his congratulations
to TJ on his elevation to the governorship. His own stay in Paris will be too
short to enable him to furnish TJ with
scientific news, but once he is reestab-
lished in Florence and finds an easy
means of sending and receiving American letters, he will make every effort to
carry out the literary correspondence offered by TJ. Is eager for news of America and of Bellini and Mazzei, from
whom he has not heard for a long time.
"A few considerations" on European agriculture and "a mineralogy of mine on
the text of Cronstedt" are being printed
at Paris and London, respectively; and
copies will be sent to TJ. The preparations being made for war in Europe
threaten the annihilation of "the most
precious and sacrosanct rights."

From Thomas Sim Lee

SIR   In Council Annapolis 20th. Decr. 1779

The enclosed is a Copy of Intelligence, this Moment received by this Board, from his Excellency the Chevalier De la Luzerne. We have taken the speediest Method of conveying it to your Excellency, under an Impression of the Propriety of giving you the earliest Intimation of the Design of the Enemy.

We have the Honor to be &ca.

FC (MdAA). Enclosure missing; see, however, La Luzerne to Gov. Lee, Philadelphia, 12 Dec. 1779, enclosing a (missing) report of a British naval threat to Vaudreuil's squadron in the Chesapeake (*Md. Archives*, XLIII, 383-4). See TJ to Benjamin Harrison, 23 Dec., transmitting the original of Lee's letter, and TJ to Thomas Sim Lee, 26 Dec. 1779.

From the Board of Trade, with Reply

[*Williamsburg*] *23 Dec. 1779*. The commanders of two vessels from Bermuda with salt to exchange for corn submit a proposal, enclosed. The terms agreed upon last July were bushel for bushel, but the price of corn has fallen and the price of salt doubled. It would be good policy to allow two bushels of corn for one of salt to induce others to bring salt. The captains are granted permission to purchase food for their crews. What disposal should be made of the salt? Benjamin Pollard offers a quantity of lump sugar, and the Board of War has recommended its purchase. Countersigned: "In Council Decr. 23d. 1779. Approved except as to the purchase of the Sugar which is thought too dear. Petersburg is a proper place to land the Salt. Th: Jefferson."

Tr in Board of Trade Journal (Vi); 1 p.; printed in *Official Letters*, II, 80. Enclosure not located.

From the Board of War

War Office Wmsburg Dec. 23d. 1779.

The Board advise that the most expeditious measures be immediately adopted, to remove to places of Safety both up James and York river all military Stores of any kind and Sort. That the Garrison Regiment hold itself in readiness to march to York at a momen[ts] warning, Nelsons Corps immediately to proceed to the same place. One third of the Militia of York, Warwick, James City, New Kent and King William, to be immediately embodied regimented and accoutred to act on the South side of York river. That six hundred Stands of arms be sent over to the Gloster Shore to equip the militia from Caroline, King and Queen and Gloster, who shall immediately rendezvous at Gloster Town, to defend the North side of York river. The numbers of the militia on both sides York river may be augmented or diminished proportionately as the numbers of the invading enemy will be ascertained. Should York appear the object of the enemy, the detachment of Artillery at Hampton, immediately to retreat to York, a Chain of redoubts to be thrown up from the back of York to extend in a circular form to Ballards Creek. Should the enemy incline to make Portsmouth their Strong hold, and from thence carry on an incursive war, which we think more than probable, the detachment of Artillery under Col. Matthews to retreat immediately to great Bridge, to endeavour to Effect a Stand to cooperate with the militia's of Princess Anne, Nansemond, Isle of Wight, Surry, one third of which to be ordered to be held in readiness, to be armed from the Magazine at *Broad water* and rendezvous at the Great Bridge; That a plan of operations should be immediately settled with the state of North Carolina. Auxiliary Troops from that state to the defence of our lower Country on the South side of James river, can only be obtained thro' the channel of the North West Landing. To this place, Col. Matthews, should he not be able to make his stand good at the great bridge with all the Troops under his command to retreat. From whence when reinforced by Aids from Carolina, he may Attempt to regain his post at the Great Bridge, the only Station capable of covering and protecting the fertile counties of Norfolk and Princess Anne. That all the counties below the ridge should hold the third part of their respective Militia's ready to march at a moments warning. The Two small armed boats, we conceive would answer the purpose of Look outs much better than the ships, which are not only slow sailors but improper from their Structure to be exposed to the Sea at this tempestuous Season. We think it would be most expedient first to apply them to the purpose of removing the military Stores to some places of safety up York and James rivers where they might afterwards be useful in covering the passage of Troops which it may be found expedient occasionally to throw across these rivers. The Board farther advise that the Regiment of guards at the Barracks near Charlottesville be reinforced by five hundred men from the neighbouring Counties. The Board have in a cursory manner advised what they thought the most expedient measures on a supposition that York or Portsmouth would be the most probable objects of the enemy: after all they confess that when they consider the extensiveness and accessibility of our Coasts, the Situation of this Country desected and separated as it is by great Navigable Waters, which lead into the Heart of the State, and the few regular forces that are now within this state, that no place is defensible against a considerable force of the enemy. York is the only one where the experiment ought to be made til the militia are collected in considerable force, as we may there receive the Assistance of our great and good Allies, and we consider this State bound by every tie of national Honor to render their utmost exertions for their protection. If necessity should require it we advise the sick to be removed to West Point, or some convenient place up Pamunky or Mattapony river, and the necessary measures for their comfortable support to be adopted and executed by the Director General.

The Board are exceedingly alarmed at the impoverished State of the commissariate, and recommended that the commissary's be forthwith instructed to provide sufficient Stores of Pork, Beef, Flour, Indian Corn &c. for the subsistence of ten thousand men.

JAS. INNES

WM NELSON

GEO. LYNE

Tr in Board of War Letter Book (MiU-C); 3 p.

To the Board of War

In Council Dec. 23d. 1779.

The Board approves of the whole of the foregoing measures except as follows. They think the particular works of defence [to] be constructed at York had better be referred to the Engineers of this State and of our Allies on view of the ground; and under the controul of Col. Marshall and the commanding Officer of the French. They are of opinion that the application to the State of North Carolina should be deferred til the invasion actually takes place; and that the five hundred militia to be called to the barracks should be from the nearest counties above the blue ridge, which number should be augmented to two thousand if the enemy shall actually enter our capes. They recommend the immediate removal of the prisoners of war from the Barracks according to the resolutions formerly taken.   TH: JEFFERSON

Tr in Board of War Letter Book (MiU-C).

Written in answer to the preceding communication. COL. MARSHALL: Thomas Marshall (1730-1802), father of Chief Justice John Marshall and colonel of the Virginia state regiment of artillery (Beveridge, Marshall, I, 489-90).

To Benjamin Harrison

SIR   In Council Dec. 23. 1779.

The inclosed letter from Governor Lee and intelligence (from the French Minister) accompanying it, gives reason to apprehend that the enemy meditate an invasion of this state. The reasons which support this opinion as well as those which oppose it will occur to the General assembly. It is our duty to provide against every event, and the Executive are accordingly engaged in concerting proper measures of defence. Among others we think to call an immediate force from the militia to defend the post at York, and to take a proper post on the South side of James river, but the expence, the difficulties which attend a general call of the militia into the feild, the disgust it gives them more especially when they find no enemy in place, and the extreme rigor of the season, induce us to refer to the decision of the general assembly, whether we shall on the intelligence already received and now communicated to them, call a competent force of militia to oppose the numbers of the enemy spoken of; or whether we shall make ready all orders and prepare other circumstances, but omit actually issuing these orders till the enemy appear or we have further proof of their intentions? The assembly will also please to determine whether, in case the enemy should make a lodgment in the country, it would be expedient to avail ourselves of the laudable zeal which may prevail on their first landing and enlist a sufficient number to oppose them and to continue in service during the invasion or for any other term. Perhaps it may not be amiss to suggest to the assembly the tardiness of collecting even small numbers of men by divisions, that if any better method should occur to them they may prescribe it. The present state of the Treasury in more points of view than one, will no doubt be thought an absolute obstacle to every military endeavor which may be necessary.

I have the honor to be with due regard & esteem Sir Your most obedient & most humble servt.,   TH: JEFFERSON

RC (CtY). Addressed in a clerk's hand to Harrison as Speaker. Endorsed. Enclosures missing, but a file copy of Gov. Lee's letter is printed above under 20 Dec. 1779.

The House on 24 Dec. passed a long series of resolves in response to TJ's letter and then adjourned; see JHD, Oct. 1779, 1827 edn., p. 106-7.

To ⸻ ⸻

Williamsburg Dec. 25. 1779.

The difficulties, which you proposed to me as to the commission of the peace I will endeavor to answer, as a private friend, for the satisfaction of your own judgement: the regular determination of them belongs to the judiciary department between whom and the executive should be a sacred barrier.

Under the regal government, the office of a justice of the peace was held during the pleasure of the crown only. Lawyers know that either estates or offices held during will are determinable by the slightest acts *implying* only, without positively *expressing*, a change of will. Hence the issuing a new commission of the peace determined the offices of those named in the former. Such of them therefore as were meant to be continued, were of necessity to be named again in the new commission; and a new qualification became necessary. On the establishment of the republican government, the office of justice was made to continue during good behavior, and the justices, then actually invested, were confirmed in their offices. The Executive not attending sufficiently to this change in the nature of the office, continued the old practice of repeating in every new commission the names of the former members intended to be continued, and of omitting others. Since this, they have considered the subject and altered their practice, by issuing a commission now to the additional members only. To form a true judgment therefore of the present state of the commission of the peace for your county, you must consider the justices actually in office at the time of forming the constitution, as making the ground work. The subsequent commissions so far as they added new members were legal and authoritative, but where they omitted or repeated the name of a former member they were so far mere nullities. The omission of a name could not deprive a justice of his seat, because he no longer held during pleasure, but had a free hold in his office from which he could not be ousted but on a regular prosecution. The repeating his name again was of course nugatory; and did not even infer on him a necessity for qualifying anew. This is the sum of the reasoning which induced the Executive to issue new commissions to the new members only, and not to meddle with the former members at all, but leave their situation altogether to the construction and operation of the law. I am aware that a difficulty arises as to the manner in which a justice shall vacate his seat. This however is not chargeable on the executive, whose duty is to act under the law as they find it. I was in hopes the legislature would have pointed out precisely the mode of disqualifying. Were I a justice myself, and desirous to withdraw, I should make my resignation in open court and of record, and repeat it by letter or deed sent to the executive, as I think these two acts together would amount to so certain a divestiture of the office, as to leave no doubt remaining, which might not be the case if one alone of them was relied on. I am Dr. Sir Your friend & servt.,   TH: JEFFERSON

RC (Andre deCoppet, N.Y., 1949).
The addressee of this letter, evidently a personal friend, has not been identified.

From George Washington

SIR   Head Quarters Morristown 25h. Decr. 1779

I had the honor of addressing your Excellency on the 11h: inst. I then informed you it was reported that the fleet, which had been some time preparing at New York, had sailed the day before. I have since found the account was premature; or, that if any Vessels went out at that time, they were but few. I have now certain information that a fleet of about one hundred sail, under convoy of a 74, a 40 and a ship of 36 Guns left the Hook the day before yesterday. It is said they have no troops on Board, and it is imagined that they are Empty transports and private Vessels bound to Europe. The Fleet with the troops remained yesterday at the watering place and are not expected to sail till the fore part of next Week. As I have had no intelligence which contradicts that which I communicated to your Excellency in my last, I would recommend a continuation of the precautions which I then pointed out.

I have the honor &c.

Dft (DLC: Washington Papers); in hand of Tench Tilghman; endorsed.

To Thomas Sim Lee

SIR   Williamsburg Decr. 26. 1779.

I am much obliged by your friendly communication of the intelligence from the Chevalier de la Luzerne. It was delivered to me on the 22d. Instant, two days after the date of your letter, and three days sooner than I received it by Express in the ordinary way, a Time very precious if the Enemy should really visit us. I was sorry that the Master of the Vessel returned before I could send to him, as the Expence of his Journey was in Honour and Justice ours.

I shall omit no opportunity of performing the like friendly Offices to your State, and of cementing by every other means that union so necessary to the general good and happiness of us all, nor of assuring you with how much respect, I am Your Excellencys most obt. & most humble servant,   TH: JEFFERSON

RC (Lloyd W. Smith, Madison, N.J., 1946). In a clerk's hand, signed by TJ. Addressed: "His Excellency Governor Lee, Annapolis. (public Service)." Endorsed: "26 Decr. 1779 Thos. Jefferson Gr. of Virga."

Lee's letter was dated 20 Dec., q.v.; see also TJ to Harrison, 23 Dec. 1779.

From George Washington

SIR   Head Qrs: Morris Town Decr the 26 1779

On the 13th. Instant I had the honor to receive your Excellency's Letter of the 28th Ulto. with a copy of the Resolution of the assembly to which it referrs. The proceeding is founded in a generous and just liberality with respect to the Officers and soldiers who had not been provided for by the Act alluded to and will I hope at least have a happy operation in alleviating their distresses which were exceedingly great if in nothing more.

I transmit your Excellency the best state I am able to give of the Virginia Troops. I have no return by me of Baylors Horse nor of the New Levies gone and going to the Southward with Genl. Scott. A Return however of the former agreeable to the Resolution of Congress of the 15 of March has been transmitted, as I have been informed, to the Honourable the Board of War and also of Harrison's Regiment of Artillery. I have never received a Return of the New Levies; nor have I had one of Bland's Regiment since the Middle of summer so that I cannot give your Excellency the information I could wish with respect to them. The Returns of Gibsons Regiment and of Heaths and OHara's Companies stationed at Fort pitt are old and as they do not contain a state of the Mens Inlistments they may convey a very imperfect idea of their strength at this time and it is probable they have undergone or may soon suffer great diminutions. Besides the Corps mentioned by your Excellency I believe there are some Virginians in Moylan's Dragoons and I have written to him to make me a Return which I shall take the earliest occasion to transmit after it is received. At present the Regiment is quartered at a considerable distance from hence. Your

Excellency will I am persuaded, have often reflected upon the inconveniences of short and temporary Inlistment[s]. The state of the Virginia troops now forwarded will place the disadvantages and impolicy of the measure in a very striking light and shew how difficult at least it is for us to provide for any military arrangements and operations either offensive or defensive with a tolerable prospect of success. This unhappily has been pretty much the case through the whole of the Contest and it would give me great pleasure as I am sure it would you if I could tell you that this state of the Virginia line was not a pretty just picture and representation of the state of the rest of the army.

Your Excellency it is probable will have heard before this reaches you, that the Virginia troops are on their march for the Southward in consequence of the pressing situation of affairs in that Quarter and from the apprehension that they may become more so. The Troops had marched two or three days before the receipt of your Letter, which circumstance left it only in my power to transmit an Extract of it, with the recruiting Commissions to General Woodford. This I did and requested him to nominate such Officers as he should deem best qualified to answer your Excellency's views of reinlisting the Men. The Sub Inspector would be the proper officer to review and receive the Men who reinlist; but as Congress have determined that it will not be worth while for the Troops to proceed whose services will expire by the last of March and as the Sub Inspector will go on with the Others I desired General Woodford to appoint one of the Officers who would be left with these, to act in his stead. Indeed Any of the Old Troops that can be reengaged, will be liable to little if any objection as they are very generally a fine body of Men. The difficulty will be to bring them to reinlist and not in passing them. It is probable the Men who do not proceed to the Southward will remain at Trenton or Philadelphia. How the attempts to reengage them will succeed I am not able to determine.

I beg leave to refer Your Excellency to the Letter I had the honor of writing you the 23d Ulto., on the subject of prisoners of War and their treat[ment.] I have not heard the least complaint since on this head and I should hope there will be none. Your Letter to Genl. Phillips was transmitted and besides this the Enemy must have seen the Public prints, in which the reasons for remanding Govr. Hamilton &c. were fully assigned. They can never make, I should think, his obstinacy and refusal to comply with a common and invariable condition of parole either expressed or implied a ground for imposing hardships upon any of our Officers. In this conte[st] I [believe] the condition required of Govr. [Hamilton] has been always expressed in paroles taken by the Enemy.

I have the Honor to be with sentiments of great respect & esteem Yr Excellency's Most Obed. St., GW

The Returns inclosed are The Virginia Infantry (including the two State Regiments) serving with the main Army, specifying the terms of service of the Men.

Return of Harrison's Artillery, specifying do.

Return of 9h. Regiment and two Independent Companies at Fort Pitt.

Dft (DLC: Washington Papers), in hand of R. H. Harrison, with appended list of enclosures (which are now missing) in hand of Tench Tilghman; endorsed by Washington.

STATE . . . OF THE VIRGINIA TROOPS: This was requested by TJ in his letter to Washington of 28 Nov., q.v.; though the returns sent with the present letter are missing, they are incorporated in TJ's memoranda of Returns of Virginia Land and Naval Forces, 4 Nov. 1779, q.v., wherein the originals are said to have been signed by Col. Carrington. YOUR LETTER TO GENL. PHILLIPS: Dated 2 Oct. 1779, q.v.

To James Innes

SIR   In Council Dec 28th. 1779.

The Board has taken into consideration the several parts of Colo. Marshalls Letter, and I now do myself the pleasure of communicating to you their opinions. It seems proper you should immediately call on Eaton and Brown, the commissaries and have the most decisive measures taken to have provisions brought into place. Perhaps the Board of Trade may be able to give you some assistance as to the means of transportation, in which they will be justified by the Executive. If the present want of provisions on the Spot has proceeded from any default in any Officers whatever, We think it should not be passed over without enquiry. The proceedings of the Tartar and her Orders, are too little known to us to give any opinion on them. I have no doubt you will do what is right and necessary to enforce an observance of duty if the Officer has swerved from it. The throwing up proper works at York, and providing fuel should be done by the Soldiery aided by as many negroes as will be necessary and can be procured. In this we think not a moment should be lost, and that to this object Colo. Marshall should point his particular exertions. The proper place for laying up the Stores you will please to direct or refer to the commanding

Officer as you think best. If insurmountable difficulties in barracking the militia in York should occur you will be pleased to consider whether the placing them here would keep them near enough to that post to give them timely Aid. As to the council proposed, my Attendance on it would be perfectly insignificant or I should Attend it without a moment's Delay. But the determinations should rest with those only Skilled in Works of defence. I do not think however that so long as the ships are there any question should be admitted whether the place can be defended or not, but only how it is to be defended.

The Marquis de Vaudreuil wishes to have vessels along side, ready to take off his sick on the first intimation of the enemy's Approach. You will be so good as to take measures for this immediately, and to procure from the Board of Trade such aids as they can give. Necessaries for the sick, or at least such necessaries as are to go from hence, should be ready on board the Vessels of transportation. Perhaps it would give satisfaction to the Marquis de Vaudreuil were he to be consulted as to the best means of getting information of the enemy's approach in our present circumstances and his Advice to be taken on that head.

If the Commanding Officer should wait on every minute occurrence for precise orders from this or your Board it will greatly retard our preparations. Will it not be better to give him extensive discretionary powers, and only to require an immediate communication of what he does, so that if it should be greatly different from what might be thought right, his measures might be countermanded in time. I am Sir Your mo. Obt. & very huml. Servt.,

TH: JEFFERSON

Tr in Board of War Letter Book (MiU-C). COLO. MARSHALLS LETTER has not been further identified (see TJ to Board of War, 23 Dec. 1779). For the MARQUIS DE VAUDREUIL, see TJ to Pontdevaux, printed under 2 Dec. 1779.

To James Innes

SIR   In Council Decr. 28th. 1779.

Since writing to you on the subject of the council proposed by Colo. Marshall, General and Colo. Nelson have called on us from York. The measure is further pressed and shewn to be expedient. We have concluded to ask the favor of yourself to proceed to York tomorrow and hold a conference with the Marquis de Vaudreul Count Pont de Veaux and such of their Officers as they may think proper, General Nelson and Colo. Marshall, on the General means of defence best adapted to our actual force and situation. I have asked the favor of the Marquis and Count to Assist at the conference. Your presence may be peculiarly usefull as you can communicate the measures heretofore proposed, the probable force we may collect, the State of our Arms provisions &c. From the Letters received by Colo. Finnie we have reason to expect every hour 2000 Virginia forces down the Bay. 800 Carolinians come down the Bay also but go to Suffolk. Baylors regiment of Light horse about 200 are said to be on their Way, but where abouts we know not. I have the Honor to be Sir Your mo. Obt. Servt., TH: JEFFERSON

Tr in Board of War Letter Book (MiU-C); bears notation of address: "The Honble James Innes Esquire."

To the Board of War

In Council Dec. 30th. 1779.

The Board are of opinion that Capt. de Klauman cannot regularly be promoted to the Majority in the State Garrison Regiment; but considering him as a very good Officer and as having resigned his command in the Artillery Regiment on being nominated to a majority in one of the Eastern Battalions then intended to be raised, a nomination which could not then be considered as exposed to disappointment, they recommend him to the Attention of the Board of War to be employed in any Office now vacant or which may hereafter occur, which Lies within the Line of his qualifications.

TH: JEFFERSON

Tr in Board of War Letter Book (MiU-C).

From Samuel Huntington

SIR   Philada Decr 30th 1779

Your Excellency will receive herewith enclos'd the copy of a letter from Thomas Scott to the President of Pennsylvania of the 29th of Novemr. last with a copy of the proceedings of the President and Council of Pennsylvania of the 15th of Decemr., as also an act of Congress of the 27th Instant consequent thereon recommending to the contending Parties not to grant any part of the disputed lands or to disturb the possession of any persons living thereon and to avoid every appearance of force until the dispute can be amicably settled by both States or brought to a Just decision by the intervention of Congress, That possession forcibly taken be restored to the original possessor and things in the situation they were at the Commencement of the war, without prejudice to the Claims of either party.

I have the honour to be &c.   S.H. Pt.

FC (DLC: PCC, No. 14). Enclosures: (1) Thomas Scott to Joseph Reed, 29 Nov. 1779 (printed above); (2) Joseph Reed to Pennsylvania Delegates in Congress, 15 Dec. 1779 (DLC: PCC, No. 69, II; printed in *Penna. Archives*, 1st ser., VIII, 46-7); (3) resolve of Congress, 27 Dec. 1779, requesting Virginia and Pennsylvania to refrain from granting lands in the area in dispute between them until the dispute is settled (not located; printed in JCC, XV, 1411).

On the boundary dispute, see Proceedings of Commissioners, 27-31 Aug. 1779, and references there; also TJ's answer to Huntington, 9 Feb. 1780.

To Samuel Huntington

SIR   Wmsburg Decr. 30th. 1779.

Your Letter inclosing the resolutions of congress relating to the capture of the Portuguese Snow by Captain Cunningham has remained hitherto unanswered because I hoped Daily to be enabled to write more fully on that subject. The resolutions, and documents accompanying them, as soon as received, were put into the hands of our Attorney General, for his opinion, with intention to have such proceedings at Law instituted as he should advise. You will see that, by his opinion, which I do myself the honor of inclosing you, the Offence could not be prosecuted here criminally; our act of Assembly, establishing a Court of Admiralty, having, in conformity with the Articles of confederation, expressly inhibited it from criminal jurisdiction. The General Assembly being then to meet in the month of October, I reserved the subject to be laid before them, which was accordingly done. A great variety however of other Business, which would not Admit of being postponed, occasioned them to pretermit this til their next session. So that if the Offenders be within the cognisance of the criminal Law at all (which the Attorney seems to doubt) we have as yet no court wherein they may be prosecuted. A Civil action for Damages may be instituted; and if the sufferers shall think proper to direct it, the countenance and protection of Government here shall not be wanting so far as propriety will Admit or justice require.

I am to acknowledge the receipt of your Letter of December 10th, inclosing resolutions of Congress of the same Date, approving our measures for guarding the convention Troops, and accepting the resignation of Colo. Bland. I hope that, ere this, his place has been supplied, as the constant Attention of an Officer of knowlege and understanding is requisite there. Perhaps his troubles might be lessened, and his Office more fully discharged, by residing at the Barracks, rather than at Charlottesvile; these posts being five or six miles apart.

The resolutions of the 11th. and 14th. inst. inclosed in your Letter of the 14th. unfortunately came not to hand til two Days after the rising of the General Assembly, which was on the 24th. and they will not meet again before the period for the delivery of the Indian Corn will be passed. They had however, early in the present year, laid a Tax payable in specific commodities; and, in their late session, directed the executive to raise from the proceeds of that Tax, six hundred thousand pounds towards making up the quota's of money for which they were called on by Congress. The Articles Specified were Wheat, Indian Corn, rye, Barley, Oats, hemp and Tobacco at the option of the payer but it is conjectured that paiment will be made almost wholly in Indian Corn and Tobacco. I am in hopes that, on these acts of the legislature, we shall be enabled to comply with your requisition as to the specific article and quantity required, as we may retain the Tax in its specific form instead of converting it into money: but we shall fail in point of time; because it happens, that the ultimate term of paiment allowed for this Tax is the Day on which your resolutions require delivery of it to your commissary at such places as he shall appoint. In this point then will be felt the misfortune of the legislature's separation before receipt of the resolutions; the Executive having no powers to shorten the Day of paiment. I thought it my duty to give you this early notice of the particular part of that requisition, with which, from these circumstances we shall be unable to comply, that the ill effects of disappointment may be lessened by other timely measures.

The resolution of the 15th. Instant recommending the continuance of embargoes is also received, that measure had been adopted some time ago as you will see by the proclamation inclosed.

I shall hereafter according to the desire of your Secretary transmit you copies of our acts of Assembly by which you will receive more minute information of the measures taken in consequence of your recommendations from time to time than the compass of a Letter would admit.

I have the honor to be with every sentiment of respect & esteem Sir Your most obedient & most humble servt., TH: JEFFERSON

RC (DLC: PCC, No. 71, I). In a clerk's hand; complimentary close and signature in TJ's hand. Endorsed by Charles Thomson: "No. 62 Letter from T. Jefferson respectg Portuguese Snow Decr. 30. 1779 Read Jany 13. 1780." Enclosures: Randolph to TJ, 13 Nov.

1779, q.v.; and Proclamation of Embargo, 30 Nov. 1779, q.v.

The LETTER . . . RELATING TO . . . THE PORTUGUESE SNOW: I.e., Jay to TJ, 26 July 1779, q.v., with references there pertaining to this episode.

Proclamation concerning Consuls

By his Excellency THOMAS JEFFERSON, *Esq; Governour or Chief Magistrate of the commonwealth of* Virginia.

WHEREAS the General Assembly by their act intitled "An act for the protection and encouragement of commerce of nations acknowledging the independence of the United States of America" have authorized the Executive to receive and admit into this commonwealth, a Consul or Consuls from any state which shall have acknowledged the independence of the United States of America, have given them jurisdiction to determine all controvercies between the subjects or citizens of their own state, and exempted them from all personal services required from the citizens of this commonwealth, and further to prove their regard to justice and the interests of those in amity with them have provided a summary mode of decision for all controvercies arising between citizens of this commonwealth and subjects or citizens of any state so acknowledgeing their independence, and more effectual means for preventing desertions of sailors, seamen or marines from the vessels of such states: And his Most Christian Majesty, our great and good ally, having been pleased after declaring and supporting our independence farther to manifest his willingness to cultivate friendship, commerce, and free intercourse with these states, by establishing Consuls to be resident therein, and hath appointed the Sieur Chevalier D'Anmours, to exercise that office within this commonwealth. I have therefore thought fit, by and with the advice of the Council of State, to declare that the said Chevalier D'Anmours is received and admitted within this commonwealth as Consul, on the part of his Most Christian Majesty, and that he is entitled to all the exemptions, prerogatives and jurisdictions belonging to the said office; and hereby to notify and promulgate the premises; strictly charging and enjoining all good citizens of this commonwealth, and all subjects of his Most Christian Majesty, and others within the same, duly to respect the prerogatives and jurisdiction of the said Consul established by law, as they will answer the contrary at their peril.

GIVEN under my hand, and the seal of the commonwealth, this 30th day of December, in the fourth year of the commonwealth, and in the year of our Lord 1779. THOMAS JEFFERSON

Printed from *Virginia Gazette* (D & N), 8 Jan. 1780. Tr in Board of War Letter Book (MiU-C).
For AN ACT FOR THE PROTECTION AND ENCOURAGEMENT OF COMMERCE, see TJ to Benjamin Harrison, 23 Nov. 1779.

To Charles Thomson

SIR   Williamsburg Dec. 31. 1779.

   Your letter of Nov. 20. 1779. came safe, tho lately, to hand. The future acts of our assembly I shall take care regularly to transmit, as also such of those past since the institution of the commonwealth as can be procured: for they are become scarce. I have in my own collection of pamphlets some few duplicates which I will also forward to you as soon as I shall be able to examine them, for they are not at this place, and shall be ready to do every thing else in my power which it may be thought can in future cast the feeblest beam of light on the feild of science. This satisfaction will be increased by the opportunities it will give me of assuring you how truly I am Your most respectful & obedient servt.,   TH: JEFFERSON

RC (DLC: PCC, No. 71, I); addressed: "Charles Thompson esq. Secretary of Congress Philadelphia"; endorsed: "Letter from Govr. Jefferson to Secy of Congress Decr. 31st. 1779." Dft (DLC).

Notes on Threatened British Invasion

[December 1779]

INVASION

Pro	Con.
1. French ships.	1. Too unimportant.
2. Convention troops.	2. Impracticable.
3. Forage.	
Pilot taken away.	Length of time and the winds.
	Season too severe.
	They give out this as their object.
	Danger of being blocked up by French fleet.

PREPARATIONS

Look-out boats.

Remove cannon.

Remove prisoners from jail and barracks.

Remove public records and treasury.

Navy. To be withdrawn up to Fendant.

Militia. Call ⅓ from counties below Blue ridge. This will be 8000 of those who will actually come. Send Garrison regiment to York. Call down Knox's men from Lynch's ferry. Deliver orders to Colo. Bland for stopping Genl. Scott should he be ready to march.

Convention troops to be ready to move over Blue ridge. ⅓ of Militia from nearest counties above Bl. ridge, amounting to 2000. to come to barracks. Colo. Bland to be in readiness to repair there. Qu. whether better to march Conventioners in a body directly Westward, or disperse them in parties of 50 each, in different directions beyond Bl. ridge.

Quarter master. Have waggons and boats ready. Have expresses ready.

Commissaries.

Assembly to enable us to enlist men to serve during invasion. Provide money. Inform them we mean to call lower militia to York instantly and neighborhood of Portsmth. Take their sense whether other militia shall be called in before actual invasion. Mention tardiness of calling in by divisions.

N (DLC); entirely in TJ's hand; undated.

These notes may be confidently dated from internal evidence, since they correspond in many details with the exchanges between TJ and the Board of War in Dec. 1779 respecting a British invasion threat, of which both Gen. Washington and Gov. Lee of Maryland had warned TJ. See Washington to TJ, 11 Dec.; T. S. Lee to TJ, 20 Dec.; Board of War to TJ, 23 Dec.; TJ's answer of same date; and Washington to TJ, 25 Dec. 1779, which contradicted earlier reports of an invasion threat. Very likely these memoranda were set down for discussion with the Council of State toward the end of this month; the invasion scare was over by mid-January (see TJ to Bland, 18 Jan. 1780). The FENDANT was a French naval vessel in Virginia waters from Nov. 1779 to Jan. 1780 (see TJ to Pontdevaux, 2 Dec. 1779).

Form of Parole for Captive Officers

[1779?]

I promise on my parole of honour and on the faith of a gentleman that I will continue within such limits as shall be assigned to me by his excellency the Govr. of Virga. or such other person acting in that particular by authority from him; that I will not directly or indirectly deliver or cause to be delivered nor receive for the purpose of conveying to or from any person not being a citizen of the United states of America any letter or written or printed paper whatever which shall not have been previously examined by the Governor or other person having authority from him, or any verbal message or matter which is not merely of a private nature and unrelative to the war now subsisting between the confederated powers of France Spain [Ame]rica and Gr. Britain, that I will not put in prac[tice] a[ny] means for obtaining intelligence as to the force, finances, posts, harbours, naviga[tion] or other circumstances of the state of Virga. or of any other of the United states of Ame[rica,] that I will not carry on nor treat on the subject of carrying on any commerce with any citize[n of] the said United states nor buy nor sell any thing to or from any of them further than is necessary for my perso[nal] subsistence or accomodation while among them nor otherwise say or do any thing to the prejudice of any of the said states and this [pa]role shall be binding on me so long as I remain within the state of Virga.

Dft (DLC). Deletions and corrections not noted here.
Perhaps prepared for the use of officers of the Convention army at Charlottesville. Compare this Form of Parole with the more stringent one prepared for Henry Hamilton (1 Oct. 1779, above), which Hamilton refused to accept.

Form of Commission to Militia Officers

[1779]

The COMMONWEALTH of VIRGINIA.

T O   GREETING:

KNOW you, that from the special Trust and Confidence which is reposed in your Patriotism, Fidelity, Courage, and good Conduct, you are by these Presents, constituted and appointed
of Militia in the County of   . You are therefore carefully and diligently to discharge the Duty of
of the Militia, by doing and performing all Manner of Things thereunto belonging; and you are to pay a ready Obedience to Orders and Instructions which from Time to Time you may receive from the Governour, or executive Power of this State, for the Time being, or any of your superiour Officers, agreeable to the Rules and Regulations of the Convention or General Assembly. All Officers and Soldiers under your Command are hereby strictly charged and required to be obedient to your Orders, and to aid you in the Execution of this Commission, according to the Intent and Purport thereof.

Returns of Arms, Stores, etc., Belonging to the State of Virginia

State of the Virginia forces in the Continental army as by return. Oct. 1779. Sam.l Calcel

The Continental Virg.a regiments commanded by Maj.r Gen.l L.d Stirling

Time of service																						
Spring 1780	..	..	..	..	..	..	..	..	..	..	..	6	5	1		1	86	15	556	670	
Fall 1780	..	..	..	..	..	..	..	..	..	..	..	..	1	2	36	9	255	303			
Spring 1781	..	..	..	..	..	..	..	..	..	..	..	..	..	9	8	57	74				
During war	..	..	..	..	..	..	..	..	..	..	3	3	5	3	59	67	1099	1229			
Officers	10	8	9	56	8	102	28	2	9	9	9	9	6	..	..	..	..	265	2551		
Deficiencies	..	2	1	4	2	..	56	..	1	1	1	1	4	1	2	3	4	80	81	3073	3357
Establishment	10	10	10	60	10	102	84	2	10	10	10	10	10	10	10	10	10	270	180	5040	5808

Return of the 1.st & 2.d Virginia State regiments

Spring 1780	..	..	..	..	..	..	..	1	2	1	1	43	15	388	454				
During war	..	..	..	..	..	..	..	1	1	1	10	10	134	157	608				
Officers	2	2	2	18	..	29	..	2	2	2	2	..	..	61	669				
Deficiencies	..	..	..	..	7	18	..	..	2	..	19	11	702	729					
	2	2	2	18	8	36	18	2	2	2	2	2	2	2	72	36	1126	1430	

Return of Col.o Gist's regiment

Spring 1780	..	..	..	..	..	..	..	1	1	..	11	3	83	99
Fall 1780	..	..	..	..	..	..	..	..	..	..	7	1	45	53
During war	..	..	..	..	..	..	..	..	..	..	3	3	62	70	222
Officers	1	..	1	7	..	6	2	..	1	1	..	..	6	11	314	344	21	243
Deficiencies	1	1	1	7	1	9	9	..	1	1	1	1	27	18	504	587

Col.o Gibson's regiment stationed at Fort Pitt. July 15. 1779

1	1	1	5	1	3	..	1	1	1	1	1	22	12	244	287

Heath's & O'Hara's independent companies. at Fort Pitt.

Draughts embodied under Gener.l Scott & ordered to Southward. Nov. 18. 1779.
Related with Col.o Parker 280. Do with Col.o Heth 250. at Petersburgh 272. = 1002.

Col.o Harrison's regiment of artillery about 300.

Cavalry. The third regiment of light dragoons commanded by L.t Col.t Baylor. Oct. 13. 1779.

Col.o Taylor's regiment of guards to Convention prisoners.

172	25	25	322	727

Returns of Virginia Land and Naval Forces, page 1

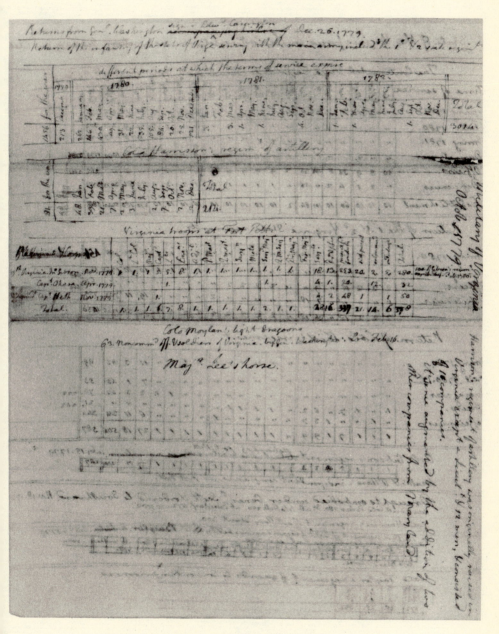

Returns of Virginia Land and Naval Forces, page 2

Return of the regiment of artillery. Virginia Oct. 1. 1779

Col.	Lt.Col.	Maj.	Capt.	Capt.Lt.	1.L.	2.L.	Chap.	Adj.	2.Mast.	Serj.	Serj.Mat.	Corpl.	Mus.ft	Matross.
1	1	1	12	10	11	7	1	1	2	2	2	3	110	373

Return of the Garrison regiment Virginia Oct. 1. 1779

Lt.Col.	Maj.	Capt.	1st.L.	Ens.	2.Mast.	Adjt.	Serj.	S.major	M.Smith	Priva.			
1	..	3	8	4	1	1	1	1	22	138			

The Illinois regiment under Colo Clarke

Four battalions now raising

The Illinois troop of Cavalry now raising

Four Eastern troops of Cavalry now raising. Oct. 30. 1779.

Maj.	Capt.	2.Lt.	Corn.d	Adj.t	Serj.M	Serj.t	Trum.	R.&file	Horses
1	3	1	2	1	.	5	3	81	60

A State of the Armed vessels of Virginia Oct. 30. 1779.

Names	kinds	Guns	Swivels	Comd. Offic.	Warrt. Offic.	Petty Offic.	Seamen	Total
Tartar		16	2	2	5	14	57	78
Dragon		16	..	3	5	14	81	103
Tempest		16	..	3	5	14	69	91
Jefferson	brigg	14	..	2	5	5	13	25
Accomack	galley	6	..	1	5	4	34	44
Diligence	galley	6	..	2	3	4	29	38
Henry	galley	10	..	1	3	4	14	22
Manley	galley	4	..	..	1	..	4	5
Liberty	boat	..	8	..	3	..	19	22
Patriot	boat	..	6	..	3	..	19	22
Nicholson	transport	..	..	..	1	..	4	5
Thetis	Ship	..	..	1	..	..	..	1
Gloucester	Friendship	..	..	2	..	..	..	2
		..	..	..	..	..	..	
Total		13	88	14	20	39	59	343	458

Returns of Virginia Land and Naval Forces, page 3

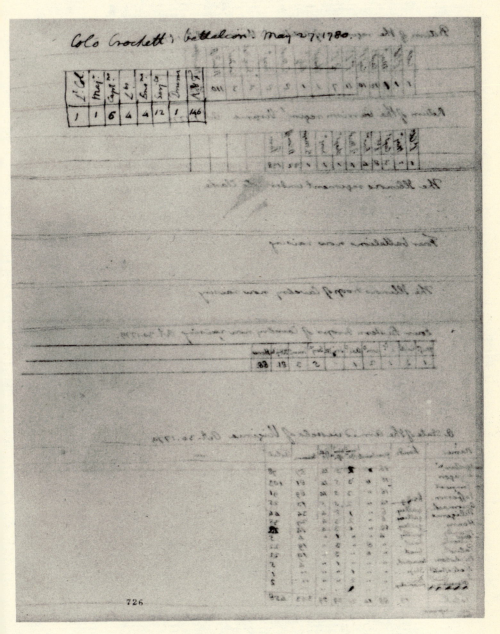

Returns of Virginia Land and Naval Forces, page 4

Calculations and Returns of Virginia Battalions, page 1

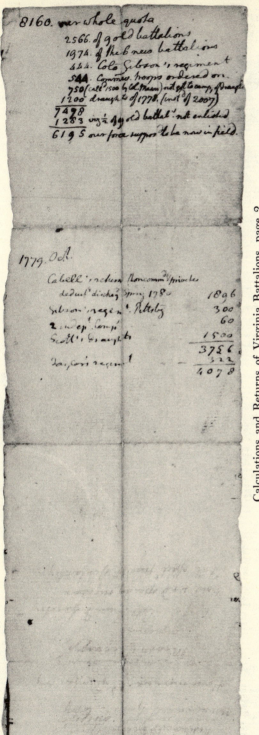

Calculations and Returns of Virginia Battalions, page 2

Calculations and Returns of Virginia Battalions, page 3

PORT

TO all the Faithful in CHRIST, to whom these Presents may come: I THOMAS JEFFERSON, Esq; Governour and Chief Magistrate of the Commonwealth of Virginia, in Williamsburg, in the Dominion aforesaid, greet you well.

WHEREAS it is pious and honourable to bear Testimony to the Truth, and that no Errour, Mistake, or Deceit happen, subverstive thereof; and Seeing now at

the good _____ called the _____ Guns, Master Name, Norfolk, Burthen _____ Tons, carrying _____ and is now ready under GOD, is to sail from the said Port, GOD willing for and other Foreign Ports, with her Compliment of Mariners: We by these Presents declare and pledge our Honours, that Praise be ascribed to ALMIGHTY GOD, no dangerous, pestilential, or contagious Distemper at Present existh within the Dominion of Virginia. IN WITNESS whereby, I have affixed my proper Seal, given at the Office of the Commonwealth, at Port Norfolk aforesaid, on the

Day of _____ according to the Computation of the Commonwealth,

Church, One Thousand Seven Hundred and Seventy Nine, and in the fourth Year of the Virginia State.

a forgery

Bill of health. replete with nonsens & falshood drawn by some tory

Counterfeit Bill of Health

Witness *Thomas Jefferson*, Esquire, Governour or Chief Magistrate of the Commonwealth aforesaid, at *Williamsburg*, this
Day of   in the   Year of the Commonwealth,
Annoq. Dom. 17

Th: Jefferson

Printed form, signed (DLC); signature partly torn away.

Calculations and Returns of Virginia Battalions

[1779]

[Text reproduced in illustration section preceding this page.]

MS (DLC); entirely in TJ's hand. Most of these notes and calculations were apparently made in 1776, either for or following the Bill for Raising Six Battalions of Infantry (q.v. under date of 28 Oct. 1776). To them, however, TJ added returns of Virginia troops in the fall of 1779; see Returns entered under date of 4 Nov. 1779, above.

Notes and Queries concerning Proposed Removal of Convention Troops

[1779?]

General heads of enquiry.
Situation of barracks.

Their distance from navigation. The roads leading to them. Their direction, soil or bottom. The water courses to be crossed. What obstruction. What circumstances when troops came. 3[. . . .][1] Is there any other situation accessible by roads which cannot be worked into mire or waters which cannot be raised. Did one night's rain ever render impassable 2 days. Is there any water course to obstruct if Q.M. will avail himself of navigation. Health. Deaths among prisoners. Garrison. Water. Wood. Soil.

Provisions.

Flour. Whence supplied. Westward. How much. By whom brought. Eastward. From what places. How much. Might not all from this quarter be supplied from Richmond.
Pork. How much necessary. Whence.
Beef. How much necessary. Whence.
Forage. How many waggons necessary for flour if navigation

neglected. How many if navigation used. How many officers entitled to forage. And how many waggons will supply it. How many waggons will furnish wood to garrison. Are Convention troops furnished with wood ready waggoned. How many waggons would do this. For what other purposes waggons wanted, and how many. Whence is forage supplied. What has been general price this year wheat, corn, rye, oats. By whom extravagant prices given. What prospect as to forage in the neighborhood this year. As to quantity—compared with last year. As to price.

Will this year's crop be short in any article necessary for troops but flour. What ought the transportation of that to amount to at this post. Would difference between transportation to this post, and to any other equal expence of removal and new bar[racks.] Can they be removed to any country not liable to the accident of a short crop, and from which same cause may not drive them. Is it best to send flour to another country and then send the troops after it to eat it, or to deliver it here at short hand. Could the forage, now applied to their support, be [. . .]ed to the grand army, if these troops are removed.

Expence of removal.

Cost of new barracks. Picquets. Transportation.

Garrison.

How many enlisted during continuance in Albemarle. How many during continuance in Virginia.

Inconvenience to Convention troops.

Gardens. Are there many. How furnished with vegetables. Are the prisoners attentive to them.
Poultry.
Officers. Those who have rented houses &c. What expences have they been at. Those who have built or purchased barracks. Would they (Officers and men) wish to remove.

Advantage of their being here, to this Commonwealth.

What sum of money weekly is expended by the Convention troops. What is the amount of the weekly pay and subsistence of the Garrison.

Mr. Aylett.

What provision did he make for troops on their road.
What provision had he made against their arrival here.

By whom has the provision been purchased on which the troops have subsisted.

Is he chargeable with any circuity of transportation of the provisions.

Has he had provisions brought by cheapest methods. Particularly on the hoof?

Has he directed or forbidden any particular feilds of purchase.

How has he laid off his districts of purchase and to what places do the supplies from each go.

How often has he been at this post.

What have been the losses of provision. Through what causes.

Have his proceedings encouraged or discouraged the vicinities of the post to raise forage &c. Particularly has he not constantly kept up the idea of speedy removal of troops.

What are his present orders for purchase. For bringing from his stores.

What stock of provision on hand.

What prospect of immediate supply.

Mr. Finnie

What number of waggons does he employ for this post.

How many are Continental. How many on daily hire.

What number of batteaux or canoes does he employ.

How often has he been at this post. What stay has he made each time.

Does his personal knowlege of the vicinities of the barracks enable him to give an opinion as to the supplies of forage they may yeild.

N (DLC); entirely in TJ's hand.

These notes appear in some respects to be a kind of outline for TJ's long letter to Gov. Patrick Henry dated 27 Mch. 1779, q.v., protesting the proposed removal of the Convention troops who had recently been interned in Albemarle co. But it is not likely that such a full and formal "enquiry" as TJ outlined here was undertaken before he himself became governor; and furthermore some of the language used here suggests a considerably later date for this paper, perhaps as late as the spring of 1780.

[1] Two or three words illegible.

Counterfeit Bill of Health for Ships Clearing the Port of Norfolk

[1779]

[Text reproduced in illustration section following page 254.]

Printed form (DLC: Broadsides Collection), with TJ's notation at head of text: "A forgery" and, on verso, "Bill of health. replete with nonsense and falshood drawn by some tory."

No satisfactory explanation of this document can at present be given, though several authorities on maritime and medical history have been consulted and have offered helpful suggestions. One view (with which the editors cannot agree) holds that this was a serious counterfeit, designed to obtain clearance for tory vessels from Norfolk; but nearly all of the authorities consulted (and the editors) agree that it is a burlesque aimed at TJ on account of his known hostility to the Anglican religious establishment in Virginia. Expressions like "To all the faithful in Christ," "Whereas it is pious and honourable," and "according to the Computation of the Commonwealth Church," are more pious and stilted than even 18th century custom required. The statement that "no dangerous, pestilential, or contagious Distemper" exists in Virginia could be medical fact but is more likely intended as political irony. And it is clear that the forgery *did* succeed in irritating TJ. Very little, unfortunately, is known about contemporary practice in requiring and issuing bills of health. No colonial legislation on this point is found in Hening, though by an Act of the Oct. 1776 session of the Assembly, 5 shillings was fixed as the fee for obtaining a bill of health; in May 1779 the fee was altered to two dollars and a half; by an Act of 1783, the master of an incoming vessel ordered to perform quarantine was required to deliver to the port officer "the bills of health and manifests he shall have received during the voyage" (Hening, IX, 188; X, 122; XI, 330).

To George Rogers Clark

SIR   Williamsburg Jan. 1. 1779. [i.e., 1780]

The late assembly having made some alteration in the Western force as stated to you in my former letter, I think it necessary to apprize you of it. They have directed your battalion to be completed, 100 men to be stationed at the falls of the Ohio under Majr. Slaughter, and one only of the additional battalions to be completed. Major Slaughter's men are raised, and will march in a few days, this letter being to go by him. The returns which have been made to me do not enable me to say whether men enough are raised to make up the additional battalion; but I suppose there must be nearly enough. This battalion will march as early in the spring as the weather will admit.[1] I hope that by this time the Spaniards have releived us from the Natchez and Mansiack. I know therefore of but two objects between which you can balance for your next summer's operations. These are 1. an expedition against Detroit. or 2. against those tribes of Indians between the Ohio and Illinois rivers who have harrassed us with eternal hostilities, and whom experience has shewn to be incapable of reconciliation. Removed at such a distance as we are, and so imperfectly informed, it is impossible for us to prescribe to you. The defences at Detroit seem too great for small arms alone. And if that nest was destroyed the English still have a tolerable channel of communication with the Northern Indians by going from Montreal up the Utawas river. On the other hand, the Shawanese, Mingoes, Munsies, and the nearer Wiandots are troublesome thorns in our sides. However we must leave it to yourself to decide on the object of the campaign. If against these Indians, the end proposed should be their extermination, or their removal beyond the lakes or Illinois river. The same world will scarcely do for them and us. I suppose it will be best for the new battalion to act with you all the summer, aided by a considerable part of Slaughter's men, and in the fall to fortify the posts we propose to take on the Ohio, and remain in them during the succeeding winter. The posts which have been thought of are the mouth of Fishing cr., Little Kanhaway, Gr. Kanhaway, Sioto, Great Salt lick, and Kentucky. There being posts already at Pittsburg, the mouth of Weeling, and the Falls of Ohio, these intermediate ones will form a chain from Pittsburg to the falls. I have then only to wish that your post was at the mouth of Ohio, which would complete the line.

I am Sir with great respect Your very humble servt.

Dft (Miss Ellen M. Bagby, Richmond, 1946). Endorsed by TJ: "lre. to Colo. Clarke Jan. 1. 1780." The endorsed date is manifestly correct for this hitherto unpublished letter; see TJ to Clark, 29 Jan. 1780, which mentions a letter of 1 Jan. The principal passage excised in the draft is noted below.

TJ's FORMER LETTER to Clark is missing and cannot even be precisely dated. THE NATCHEZ AND MANSIACK: Fort Panmure at Natchez and Fort Bute at Manchac, below Baton Rouge, British posts on the lower Mississippi that had been captured by Spanish forces under Gálvez in Sep. 1779 (J. W. Caughey, *Bernardo de Gálvez in Louisiana*, Berkeley, 1934, p. 154ff.; Wis. Hist. Soc., *Colls.*, XXIV [1917], 129-30; *Atlas of Amer. Hist.*, N.Y., 1943, pl. 77).

1 Following this TJ first wrote and then deleted: "I think the most important object which can be proposed with such a force is the extermination of those hostile tribes of Indians who live between the Ohio and Illinois who have harrassed us with eternal hostilities, and whom experience has shewn to be incapable of reconciliation. The Shawanese, Mingos, Munsies and Wiandots can never be relied on as friends, and therefore the object of the war should be their total extinction, or their removal beyond the lakes or the Illinois river and peace."

To Richard Henry Lee

DR. SIR   Williamsburg Jan. 2. 1780.

The inclosed letters which came to hand yesterday from France I do myself the pleasure of forwarding to you. I have had in my possession for you, two months, four numbers of the parliamentary register, containing the whole correspondence between the ministry and Sr. Wm. Howe, and Burgoyne from the time of Howe's coming to America till the Convention of Saratoga. I kept them at first in hopes of seeing you here. That failing, I forgot to send them by your delegates, and am afraid the post would be too precarious and expensive. How shall I contrive them to you? We are informed, and I think so as to merit confidence, that Pensacola is taken and St. Augustine invested by the Spaniards. I hope we shall see you in the next assembly. I would advise you to procure lodgings in Richmond in time as they will be scarce. We had some intelligence lately that the enemy meant us an immediate visit. We are preparing for them, but I cannot say that I expect them. I am Dr. Sir Your friend & servt., TH: JEFFERSON

RC (ViU). Addressed: "Richard Henry Lee esq Westmoreland." Endorsed in a later hand. Enclosures not identified.

To Samuel Huntington

SIR   Williamsburg Jan. 3. 1780.

A large packet directed to the President of Congress with other dispatches for the Chevalier de la Luzerne and others, coming to my hands two days ago, I thought it proper to forward them to you by express. He should have set out yesterday but it was too tempestuous. I have the honor to be with all possible respect Your Excellency's most obedient & most humble servt.,

TH: JEFFERSON

RC (DLC: PCC, No. 71, I). Addressed: "His Excellency Samuel Huntington esq President of Congress Philadelphia." Endorsed by Charles Thomson: "Letter from Govr. of Virginia Jany 3. 1780. Read 19." Enclosures not identified.

The Journals record no action on this letter when it was read on 19 Jan. (JCC, XVI, 72).

From Benjamin Lincoln

SIR   Chas. Town January 7. 1780

I am informed that the Virginia Line are ordered from the Main Army to reinforce the one here. Unless they have more than a common stock of shoes and socks, they will soon be barefooted, which will at this inclement season, prevent their continuing the march. I have, therefore, to request that these articles may be provided for the troops and supplied them, if necessary, on the march. And as this reinforcement will augment the army to a number beyond our ability to clothe from our present Magazines (though clothing is indeed sent for from the West Indies, yet it's arrival depends on so many circumstances, that it would be unsafe and imprudent to depend solely thereon). I wish, as Congress have desired the several States to attend to the clothing of their own troops, that a supply might be sent on for yours. Blankets, shoes, and shirts, are now exceedingly wanted here. Many of your Officers are in real want of cloth for themselves, and cannot be supplied here, as it cannot be obtained either from the public or private Stores in this Town.

I have the honor to be with great esteem your Excellencys most Obedt. servant,   B. LINCOLN

RC (NHi). Endorsed by a clerk: "Genl Lincoln to the Governor Feby. 7th. 1780. [*In another hand:*] Respecting Clothing for the Officers & Soldiers of the State at the South." Below the text TJ wrote: "Referred to Board of War. Th: Jefferson."

From James Mercer

DEAR SIR   Fredericksburg. St. James's. Jany. 8th 1780.

The severity of the weather obligeing Colo. Mason to continue with me for three days, he among other things communicated to me the powers the General assembly had vested your Excellency with respecting the settlement of this State's accounts with the united States, and your Inclination that I shou'd undertake this business. Considering the Recess I have had from the fatigues of public Service and my late resignation of my Seat in Congress it gave me not a little uneasiness that I must again and so shortly decline a business I know is of importance to Virginia and the more so as your Excellency wished me to undertake it. I mentioned to Colo. Mason my peculiar Domestic Situation and he writes your Excellency on that Subject by this Conveyance, but how much he has said I know not, and his last request being that I shou'd write your Excellency on the Subject, I presume he has left something for me to say without being guilty of a Repetition. I must therefore in my justification assure your Excellency that nothing but the frequent and critical Situation of my Wife shou'd have induced me to quit Congress where so much was to be done, this Cause continuing till the first of May next, I cou'd not accept the new Business intended me, nor can I now say nor how soon after I cou'd be from home for any length of time. All that I can say is that I shou'd gladly undertake my share of Service in these critical times and that nothing but necessity shou'd induce me to refuse any employment (as to solliciting any I never did nor ever shall) and cou'd I foresee the extent of the business proposed and know how soon it must be done, my will is to undertake it, tho' of all that cou'd be offered it must be the most hazardous in pleasing and the most difficult to accomplish with Justice to Virginia. For entre nous, I am sure the prejudice of Congress against Virginia on account of the Land office is now so great that I cou'd not expect *Justice* at their Hands, and if I mistake not, the Nature of Virginia's Demand, is such as to require Chancellors, not prejudiced Judges at Common Law to settle them. From Colo. Masons information I understand this demand commences from the beginning of this War. If so there can be no precedent to govern me or bind Congress, and I remember so much of this business which occurred during my being of the Committee of Safety, as to know that liberality of Sentiment is really necessary in adjusting so complicated affairs of business; tho' I think now as I did then, that the plan adopted by that Committee and the account stated by Mr. Everard ought to be approved; and I hope since then that more Leisure and knowledge of the executives may have rendered such matters more certain.

I have heretofore forbore intruding on your Excellency's time, but as I have taken up my Pen I can't lay it down without expressing the high Sense I have of the Services rendered my Brother. Colo. Mason gives me such a favourable detail of his Life, that I can but rejoice that I ever thought of it, and that there was a power on Earth capable of working such a Change, as your Excellency has, in a Relation I have much Interest in. I have the honour to be, with great esteem Yr. Excellency's most obedt. & much obliged humble Servant,   Js. Mercer

RC (ViWC).

James Mercer and George MASON were first cousins. THE FREQUENT AND CRITICAL SITUATION OF MY WIFE: Mercer's wife, Eleanor Dick, daughter of Charles Dick of Fredericksburg, died 28 Mch. 1780 (WMQ, 1st ser., XVII [1908-1909], 209). Mercer had served only three weeks in Congress, and the letter that he wrote to the Speaker of the House of Delegates, which was a remarkably blunt attack upon the character of his colleagues in Congress, did not mention his wife's health as being a cause of his resignation (Mercer to Speaker, 1 Oct. 1779, Burnett, *Letters of Members*, IV, No. 571; MS in possession of Lloyd W. Smith, Madison, N.J., 1946). Mason's letter to TJ on Mercer's PECULIAR DOMESTIC SITUATION has not been found. Mercer's BROTHER was John Francis Mercer, who had been an aide-de-camp of Gen. Charles Lee, had resigned his commission and returned to Virginia in the autumn of 1779, and had thereupon —presumably at James Mercer's suggestion—entered upon a year's study of law under TJ (DAB).

From Joseph Reed

[*Philadelphia, 8 Jan. 1780.* From "Minutes of the Supreme Executive Council of Pennsylvania," *Penna. Colonial Records*, XII, 224: "A letter was sent to his Excellency Thomas Jefferson, esquire, Governor of the State of Virginia, enclosing the Proclamation of the Council of the twenty-eighth day of December last, with an attested copy of the resolution of Congress of the twenty-seventh of December. Also, a duplicate of a letter from Council to the Governor of Virginia, and the resolution of the Honourable House of Assembly of the nineteenth day of November last, on the subject of the disputed Territory between Pennsylvania and Virginia." Letter and enclosures not located. Reed's proclamation is printed in same, p. 212-14; the resolution of Congress was enclosed in Huntington to TJ, 30 Dec. 1779; and the original letter from Reed, dated 25 Nov. 1779, of which a duplicate was here enclosed, is printed above. See also Thomas Scott to Reed, 29 Nov. 1779.]

To Theodorick Bland

SIR   Williamsburg, Jan. 18, 1780.

The most timid being now satisfied that the enemy will not pay us a visit, Baptiste is relieved, after a delay which seems to have been very painful to him. This should have taken place much sooner, but I wished and hoped daily to send by him orders for taking off the suspension of General Scott's march, which it was thought not proper to do, till we received satisfactory information of the enemy's movements. It seems tolerably certain that they left New York about the 27th of December, so that they must be gone somewhere else. I am, sir, your most obedient, humble servant, &c.

MS not located. Text from *Bland Papers*, II, 31, where it is printed without signature and said to be addressed to Bland at Petersburg. RC sold by C. F. Libbie & Co., Boston, 26 Apr. 1904

(Kennard Sale), lot 675 (an A.L.S. with address leaf).

BAPTISTE was an express rider, according to a note in *Bland Papers*.

From Samuel Huntington

SIR   Philada Jany 18. 1780

Your Excellency will receive herewith enclos'd two Acts of Congress of the 13. and 14. Instant.

The former containing the regulations adopted relating to prisoners of War whether taken by Continental Troops or captured by the arms of any particular State either by sea or Land.

Many difficulties have frequently occurred for want of such a general regulation too numerous to be recited. It is proper to observe that the first paragraph of the Act recommending to the Executive of the several States to transmit with all possible Expedition to General Washington the names and rank of all Officers and the number of privates belonging to the Enemy held as prisoners of War in each State and the places they are at &c. should be complied with as soon as possible by those States that have any number of prisoners.

The other act of the 14th Instant recommending to the Legislature of the several United States to make provision where not already made for conferring like privileges and Immunities on the Subjects of his most Christian Majesty as are granted to the Subjects and Inhabitants of these United States by the recited Article in the Treaty of Amity and Commerce will no doubt be chearfully complied with by each of the States.

His most Christian Majesty as soon as the Treaty became known published an Edict conformable to that Article Exempting the Subjects and Inhabitants of these United States from the Droit d'Aubaine &c. I have the honour to be &c.   S.H. Prest.

FC (DLC: PCC, No. 14). At head of text: "Circular." Enclosures missing; printed in JCC, XVI, 48-52, 56-7.

To the Board of War

SIR   Wmsburg Jan. 19th. 1780.

On a conjectural view of the money likely to come in to the Treasury between this and the 15th. of June, and on estimates of the several demands on the public for money with in the same period we find it will be necessary to restrain the amount of Warrants to be issued hereafter to about two thirds of what would have been a full supply. We Allot therefore as follows.

To the Commissaries	£250,000.
Quarter Master	100,000.
Recruiting money	250,000.
Pay Master of the Army	24,000.
Ditto of the Navy	16,000.

The above coming within the superintendence of your board I thought it proper to State it to you. When warrants are issued for the reenlistment of the Soldiers it should be calculated on the supposition that two thirds only may be engaged of those whose times will expire by the ensuing Spring. I am Sir with great respect Your most Obedient Servant,   TH: JEFFERSON

Tr in Board of War Letter Book (MiU-C).

From the Board of War

Williamsburg, 20 Jan. 1780. Because of the dissolution of the fourth troop of Nelson's corps of cavalry, a dispute concerning the lieutenancy of the third troop has arisen between Mr. Nicholson and Mr. Read. It is recommended that the decision be referred to a board of officers "as the most proper Tribunal to determine all military disputes." Signed by Innes and Barron.

Tr in Board of War Letter Book (MiU-C), 1 p.; also Tr in War Office Letter Book (Vi), 1 p., the text of which varies somewhat from that presented here.

See TJ's reply under 25 Jan.

From the Board of War, with Reply

Williamsburg, 21 Jan. 1780 [misdated 1779]. A recent regulation enables captains of artillery in the Continental army to keep horses, which makes boots necessary equipment. A request for boots from the public shops at the reduced price seems reasonable, but, being unusual, the approval of the executive is desired. Signed by Innes and Barron. Countersigned: "In Council Jan. 24th. 1780. The Board are of opinion that the above Officers may be furnished with boots agreeable to the opinion of the board of War, the souldiers being first provided with shoes. Th: Jefferson."

Tr in Board of War Letter Book (MiU-C); 1 p.

From George Washington

Morristown, 22 Jan. 1780. Acknowledges TJ's letter of 16 Dec. 1779, which did not come to hand until 16 Jan. Will give proper consideration to applications from the enemy for flag-of-truce vessels to the Chesapeake. Has communicated Col. Bland's case to Congress.

Dft (DLC: Washington Papers); 2p. In hand of James McHenry; endorsed. Printed: Washington, *Writings*, ed. Fitzpatrick, XVII, 430. For the action by Congress on Theo-dorick Bland's case, see a resolution of 11 Feb. 1780 (JCC, XVI, 154), a copy of which (in Vi) was transmitted to TJ in a letter now missing.

To Joseph Martin

Sir   Wmsburg Jany. 24. 1780

We are very desirous of having a fort at the mouth of Ohio which together with other posts meant to be established on the Ohio may form a chain of defence for our Western frontier and at the same time protect our Trade with New Orleans. But the ground at the Mouth of Ohio on the South side belonging to the Cherokees we would not meddle with it without their leave. We wish you therefore to treat with them for as much as will do for this purpose and for a few settlements round it for the support of the post. Indeed if they should shew a disposition to part with it you may treat for all their lands between the Mississippi, Ohio, Tanissee and Carolina boundary the whole being of but small extent. I think not exceeding 20 miles square if reduced to that form. If they do not discover a willingness to part with the whole, get ground for a fort and as much as you can round about it to make corn, furnish wood &c. Obtain them on as good terms as possible to be paid for in goods, which we will have provided for them. The whole when sold at our Land Office price will not bring in more than three thousand pounds Sterling. I think the goods must be got from New Orleans. I am in hopes they will not insist on our not beginning the fort till the delivery of the Goods, but if they do we must submit to it. Make your bargain, if you can, subject to our approbation or disapprobation, because this matter having never been proposed to the Assembly we should wish to have it in our power to decline it if they should so advise. Communicate without delay what you do to Colo. Geo: Rogers Clarke at Kaskaskias or the falls of Ohio and also to Sir Your very hble Servant,   TH: JEFFERSON

RC (WHi). In a clerk's hand, signed by TJ. At foot of text, in TJ's hand: "Majr. Martin."

For a biographical sketch of Joseph Martin, a native of Albemarle co., Va., who became a frontier fighter and agent to the Cherokees, see Thwaites, *Descr. List of MS Colls. of the State Hist. Soc. of Wis.*, p. 82-3; his papers are in the Draper Coll. and have been calendared in Wis. Hist. Soc., *Publs., Calendar Ser.*, III (1929).

Proclamation Requiring Settlers Northwest of the Ohio to Vacate

By his Excellency Thomas Jefferson Esqr. Governor or chief Magistrate of the Commonwealth of Virginia:

A PROCLAMATION

Jany 24. 1780

Whereas the General Assembly by an act passed at their Session in October 1779, intituled 'An Act for more effectually securing to the officers and soldiers of the Virginia line the Lands reserved to them, for discouraging present Settlements on the north west side of the Ohio river, and for punishing persons attempting to prevent the execution of Land Office Warrants' reciting that 'altho no lands were allowed by law to be entered or warrants to be located on the north west side of the Ohio river until the farther order of the General Assembly, several persons are notwithstanding removing themselves to, and make new settlements on the lands upon the north west side of the said river, which may probably bring on an indian war with some tribes still in amity with the United American States, and hereby involve the Commonwealth in great expence and bring distress on the Inhabitants of our Western frontiers,' did declare end enact 'that no person so removing to, settling on the said lands, should be entitled to or allowed any right of preemption or other benefit whatever from such settlement or occupancy, and authorized the Governor, with the advice of the Council of State to remove with armed force all such settlers and occupants, with an exception and saving to all French, Canadian, and other families or persons heretofore actually settled in or about the villages near or adjacent to the posts reduced by the forces of this State.' I have therefore thought fit, by and with the advice of the Council of State, to issue this my Proclamation hereby requiring all persons settled on any lands on the north west side of the Ohio within the chartered limits of this Commonwealth, and not described in the exception or saving before recited, immediately to remove therefrom and do strictly inhibit and forbid all others to settle thereon in future until they shall be permitted by act of the General Assembly; and I do moreover make known that military patroles will be ordered from time to time and more especially at those times when the labours of the year may be destroyed in the field, to waste all settlements which may be found within the Limits before described, and to remove the settlers by force of arms. Given under my hand and the seal of the Commonwealth this 24th. day of Jany. in the year of our Lord 1780. and 4th. of the Commonwealth.

TH: JEFFERSON

Tr in Board of War Letter Book (MiU-C); French translation (Arch. Aff. Etr., Paris, Corr. Pol., E-U, vol. 2). The ACT . . . FOR DISCOURAGING PRESENT SETTLEMENTS ON THE NORTH WEST SIDE OF THE OHIO RIVER and other purposes (Hening, X, 159-62) was passed by the General Assembly 1 Dec. 1779 (JHD, Oct. 1779, 1827 edn., p. 75). No printing of this proclamation has been found in the *Virginia Gazette* or elsewhere. However, the fact that a French translation of the proclamation exists among the papers of the French minister, La Luzerne, indicates that it was circulated.

To Evan Shelby, Jr.

Sir Wmsburg Jany. 24. 1780

Before the receipt of your Letter, the assembly having empowered us to raise one troop of horse for the Illinois, we had commissioned Captain Rogers for that purpose who raised his men and proceeded some time in the fall to join Colo. Clarke, who was not informed of any of these measures at the date of his Letter to you. We have therefore no authority to direct the raising any more. After thanking you for your readiness to serve the public, I subscribe myself Sir Your hble Servant, Th: Jefferson

RC (WHi); in a clerk's hand, signed by TJ. Endorsed: "His Excellency the Governr. to Capt. Shelby, Jany. 24 1780." Bears also a notation on cover: "This is the governers Letter to Me Wen I applied as you Desierd Me," indicating that the letter was sent on to G. R. Clark, who probably added the further endorsement: "Captn. Shelby Dated Holston." Neither Shelby's LETTER to TJ nor Clark's LETTER to Shelby has been located; see, however, TJ to Clark, 29 Jan. 1780.

From the Board of Trade, with Reply

[*Williamsburg*] *25 Jan. 1780.* Requests advice of Council concerning purchase of spirits and other commodities from De Francy for the use of the several garrisons. Reply follows: "In Council January 25th 1780. The Board disapproves altogether of the proposed purchase of Rice and Salt; and refer to the Board of Trade to determine whether the sum to which the State of the Public Treasury will of necessity reduce them as was mentioned in Council to one of their board, will admit of their purchasing Rum as well as Cloathing and other Necessaries. If it will, there can be no objection, to the purchase of Rum, if it will not, it is thought adviseable to restrain their purchases to those Articles only which they shall deem most essentially necessary. Th: Jefferson."

Tr in Board of Trade Journal (Vi); 2 p. The Board's communication is printed in full in *Official Letters*, II, 86-7.

To the Board of War

In Council Jan. 25th. 1780.

Mr. Randolph having been at first appointed a Lieut: of horse, and declined accepting it Mr. Reid was then appointed. He therefore is conceived to Stand on a footing of an original appointment. He raised his whole quota within a few Days after receiving notification from the executive. This then not being a case of vacancy by

Death, resignation or removal, where regular succession takes place, and Mr. Reid claiming his Lieutenancy on the same footing of original appointment as Mr. Nicolson claims his command of cornet, the board is of opinion it is improper to refer it for decision to a Board of Officers as it would have been to have referred the original appointment to them: and are of opinion that Mr. Reid is entitled to receive a Lieutenan[t's] Commission.

TH: JEFFERSON

Tr in Board of War Letter Book (MiU-C).
See Board of War to TJ, 20 Jan.

Instructions to Inspector
of Stores and Provisions

SIR   War Office Wmsburg Jan. 25th. 1780.

The Board of War have appointed you to act a[s] inspector of all the military Stores and provisions in the several Magazines of this State. You will make the inspection every three months and make report the[re]of to this board. All commissaries of provisions and milita[ry] Stores and all the Superintendants of the public magaz[ines] are under your directions and controul. To them you will issue such orders from time to time as you may think expedient. You are to employ as many armourers and Labourers as are necessary to repair and arrange the arms at the different magazines. You are empowered to erect armourers Shops at the Magazines. You are from time to time as you find it necessary to send the damaged powder to mills most convenient to be r[e]claimed. You are empowered to rent houses for the purpo[se] of Storing powder and arms and to grant certificates [for] Regimental Hospitals to be established at Williamsburg York Hampton and Portsmouth.

Each Hospital to be furnished with two nurses one orderly man one cook one washing woman.

The Hospital in Williamsburg to be superintended and managed by the Surgeon and mate of the State Garrison Regiment.

The Hospitals at York Hampton and Portsmouth to be under the direction of the Surgeon of the Regiment of Artillery, who is to detach a mate to Hampton and Portsmouth, and take care that they do their duty.

One Surgeon of the Navy to be Stationed at Hampton to take care of the sick seamen.

The Surgeon of Nelsons Corps to Attend them at their Station, and his mate be dispatched to any Hospital where any part of them may be sick.

The Apothecary, to prepare proper medicine chests and issue them together with chirurgical instruments to the Regimental Surgeons, who are faithfully to account with him for the safe keeping and expenditure thereof.　　　　　　　　　　JAS. INNES

JAS. BARRON

Tr in Board of War Letter Book (MiU-C). Countersigned in TJ's hand: "Jan. 28th. 1780. Approved. Th: Jefferson."

From the Board of Trade

[*Williamsburg*] *26 Jan. 1780.* Recommending purchase of the whole or part of a tract of escheated land near the public foundry at Westham, as it would "probably furnish Wood, Grain and other necessaries for the use of that Work," these items now being purchased at very extravagant rates.

Tr in Board of Trade Journal (Vi); 1 p.; printed in *Official Letters*, II, 88.

TJ's reply has not been located, but the following minute appears in the Journal under the same date: "The Executive approving of the Purchase of the Tract of Land convenient to the Foundry Ordered that a letter be written to Colo. T. Southall and Mr. James Buchanan."

To the Board of Trade

In Council Jany. 26. 1780.

The Governor is advised to recommend to the Board of Trade to draw Bills of Exchange on Messrs. Penett & Co. to the amount of £4,000. Sterling payable to Colo. Geo. Rogers Clarke, to be by him disposed of to the best Advantage, and the proceeds paid, four fifths to Colo. Legras, and one fifth to Capt. Lintot in part of the debt due to them, and to take Measures for procuring other Bills of Exchange from Congress to be remitted to the said Penet & Co. in order to enable them to comply with the said Drafts on them; and to give the said Legras and Lintot written Assurance that the Balance which shall be still due to them shall be paid by the Public within the Term of one Year. The Board also advise the Governor to recommend to the Board of Trade to take Measures for providing on the public Account Lumber and Beef on the Ohio to be carried to New Orleans for payment of the public Debt and providing a Fund there, and that he give Sanction to such Measures when ready to be carried into Execution. Extract from Minutes.

A BLAIR, C. C.

Tr in Journal of the Board of Trade (Vi).

There is no record in the Journal of a reply to this letter, but on 27 Jan. the following minute was entered in the Journal: "Tho the Board, on maturely considering the Instructions of the Executive of yesterday, relative to Colo. Legras and Capt. Lintot, are of opinion the Business does not come with propriety within their Department; they are willing, however, to contribute all in their power to the service of the State, and therefore in Obedience to said Instructions it is Ordered that Bills of Exchange be drawn on Messrs. Penet & Co."

To the Board of Trade

GENTLEMEN   Williamsburg Jan. 28. 1780.

I find that the recommendation of council to have bills of exchange drawn and sent to Colo. Clarke that the proceeds may by him be divided between Colo. Legras and Capt. Lintot will not answer, as I now understand the latter does not mean to return to the Illinois but to take a trip to France. The bills must therefore be made separate here. I think also that those which shall be sent to Colo. Clarke will be negotiated to greater advantage if drawn in livres, with which the people of Illinois are acquainted, and in small bills. Perhaps if your whole draughts were to amount to 75,000 livres only and these be divided into bills of 5000. livres each, it might answer. Three sets of these I should deliver to Capt. Lintot and twelve sets to Colo. Legras. Colo. Legras leaves town on Sunday. I am Gentlemen Your most obedt. servt.,

TH: JEFFERSON

P.S. On further consideration perhaps it will suffice to draw the bills for Legras only at present, as Lintot will be here some time, perhaps long enough to get bills from Philadelphia to which place I write by an express going tomorrow.

RC (Vi), addressed and endorsed. Tr in Board of Trade Journal (Vi).

To John Todd?

SIR   Wmsburg. Jany. 28th. 1780

By Colo. Legras I have written to Colo. Clarke fully as to the military affairs in the Western department. Among other things

I have advised him to withdraw to the Eastern side of the Ohio all the forces not absolutely necessary to sustain the Spirits of the Inhabitants of the Illinois, and for their real defence.

This necessity has been inforced by the impossibility of our supporting an armed force where our paper money is not current. We have no hard money among us, and are not able to establish in Europe funds sufficient to cloathe and arm our Soldiers. This puts it out of our power to pay hard money Debts with bills, and renders it necessary to press you to purchase nothing beyond the Ohio which can be done without, or which may be got from the Eastern side where paper money will pay for it.

The establishment of a post at the mouth of Ohio which will take place this summer will be a convenience to the Trade of the Illinois and near enough to furnish them aid. Should any tribe of indians commit hostilities against them, Colo. Clarke will of course take on him the war, and endeavour to chastize them. We are in hopes you are endeavouring to introduce our Laws and form of Government among the people of Illinois as far as their temper and disposition will admit. I am satisfied of the difficulties attending this and the address necessary. We wish for their own good to give them full participation of the benefits of our free and mild Government. It is also essentially necessary that all who are parts of the same body politic should be governed by the same laws: and the time to introduce this identity of laws with least inconvenience to themselves, is while they are few. Nothing else can so perfectly incorporate them into the general American body.

I find that the Justices of the peace appointed among them [ex]pect to be paid. This not being the practice under our laws, there is no provision for it. Would it not be expedient to restrain these appointments to a very small number, and for these (if it be necessary) to require small contributions either from the litigants or the people at large, as you find would be most agreeable. In time I suppose even this might be discontinued. The Clerks and Sheriffs perhaps may be paid as with us, only converting Tobacco fees into their worth in peltry. As to the rules of decision and modes of proceeding I suppose ours can be only gradually introduced. It would be well to get their Militia disciplined by calling them regularly together according to our usage. However all this can only be recommended to your Discretion.

Tr (WHi); unsigned and without indication of addressee. Bears a docketed summary, probably in hand of Lyman C. Draper. Recipient tentatively identified as John Todd in *Ill. Hist. Colls.*, v, 143, no doubt correctly. Todd was county lieutenant of Illinois.

To George Rogers Clark

Your letters of October 26 and 28 and Novr. 6 came safely to hand and lastly that of August 24. I am glad the proposition of establishing a post at or near the mouth of Ohio is likely to answer as well in practice as to us, who judged on theory only, it seemed likely to do. I have therefore written to Messrs. Walker and Smith, as you will see by the enclosed copy of my letter to them, to take observations of the latitudes thereabouts that we may proceed on the surest grounds. You will please to furnish assistants, guards and all necessaries. I expect the description of the Cliffs &c will be so minute as that when you see them you will know them in the plat and of course know their latitude. The choice of the ground for your fort must be left to yourself. It should be as near the mouth of Ohio as can be found fit for fortification and within our own lines. Some attention will be proper also to the circumjacent grounds as it will probably become a Town of importance. The nature of the defensive works and their extent you will accommodate to your force. I would reccommend your attention to the wood of which you make your stockades, that it be of the most lasting kind. From the best information I have had, I take for granted that our line will pass below the mouth of Ohio. Our purchases of the Cherokees hitherto have not extended Southward or Westward of the Tanissee. Of course the little tract of country between the Missisipi, Ohio, Tanissee and Carolina line (in which your fort will be) is still to be purchased from them before you can begin your works. To effect this I have written to Major Martin our Cherokee agent of which letter I inclose you a copy. If the new fort should fall within this territory and it can be purchased we may grant lands to settlers who will fix round about the fort, provided the Assembly should approve of it, as from its reasonableness I think they will. The manner in which the lots of land are laid off about the french villages I have thought very wise and worthy of imitation. Perhaps besides guarding your promises of lands to settlers with the conditions above mentioned it would be well to add also the mode of laying them off. I send you recruiting instructions for having your Battalion filled up with men to be inlisted for the war, as I wish to avoid receiving any on any other terms. Your instructions for recruiting which were communicated to us by some of your officers in the fall, we took in and gave them such as are now sent you. Instead of bounty money I send you three hundred Land warrants for five hundred and sixty acres of Land each, which at forty pounds the hundred being the Treasury price, amounts to the bounty allowed by Law. These we think more likely to induce men to enlist than the money itself. I also send you twenty four blank commissions which will be necessary to officer eight companies the present plan of the continental army having that number in a battalion and a Captain, Lieutenant and ensign only to each company. The officers of your Battalion when commissioned will stand on a footing with the officers of the other State Battalions. The state of the public finances obliged the late assembly to reduce very much their military establishment from what they had proposed at their session in May. They discontinued raising both the additional Eastern Battalions and one of the Western, so that there will be one Battalion only to send to you, to which is to be annexed Major Slaughter's hundred men who have already marched as I expect for the falls of the Ohio. I wish that one Battalion may be raised in time to join you in the spring. Very few returns having been made to me I cannot say what number is raised probably not more than half. However whatsoever number may be raised by that time shall march as soon as the season will admit. By them we will send such stores as to us occur to be necessary such as powder, lead, flints, hoes, axes, saws, gimblets, nails, hammers, augers, drawing knives, froes and Camp-Kettles. If there be any other articles necessary I must get you to write me on the subject, also to settle the best route of sending those articles hereafter there being no guards to be had but militia for conveying them from the frontiers and no dependance on collecting militia. Cannot you point out to us some place on the frontiers where they may be safely lodged from time to time and from whence you can send for them with a proper escort. I would wish you also to inform me to what post I shall order the Battalion which is to join you.

We received letters from Mr. Pollock in the fall informing us of our debts at New-orleans and his distresses. We had just taken measures by shipping tobacco to France to procure necessaries for our army. Having no other means of relieving Mr. Pollock we were obliged to give him draughts on France which took the whole of that fund and has distressed us exceedingly. The demands of Colo. Legras and Capt. Lintot coming on us now and it being impossible to raise hard money to discharge them we are utterly at a loss what to do with them, indeed we shall not be able to determine them absolutely as to the sum we shall pay them till we know from you what proportion of the dollars for which they have draughts, were expended at the depreciated prices or in other words till we know from you what sum in hard money would reimburse their advances for which your draughts on us were made, which we should be glad you would inform us of by the first opportunity and send a duplicate by some second conveyance. The difficulty of answering demands of hard money renders it necessary for us to contract no debts where our paper is not current. It throws on us the tedious and perplexing operation of investing paper money in tobacco, finding transportation for the tobacco to France, repeating this as often as the dangers of capture render necessary to ensure the safe arrival of some part, and negociating Bills, besides the expensive train of agents to do all this and the delay it occasions to the creditor. We must therefore recommend to you to purchase nothing beyond the Ohio which you can do without or which may be obtained from the east side where our paper is current. I am exceedingly glad you are making such timely provision of your next year's subsistence. A Commissary for the Western department was appointed in the fall with orders [to purchase] provisions on the frontiers for one Battalion. His instructions shall be enlarged and a notification sent him to comply with your requisitions. Besides this we leave to yourself to commission Mr. Shannon to act as commissary of purchases, issues, stores, Quarter-Master or whatever else you may find him useful in. I suppose you will employ him principally about the posts, while the one acting in the frontiers will be providing thereabouts. We shall use all our endeavours to furnish your men with necessary clothing but long experience renders it proper to warn you that our supplies will be precarious. You cannot therefore be too attentive to the providing them in your own quarter as far as skins will enable you to do it. In short I must confide in you to take such care of the men under you as an œconomical householder would of his own family, doing every thing within himself as far as he can, and calling for as few supplies as possible. The less you depend for supplies from this quarter, the less will you be disappointed by those impediments which distances and a precarious foreign commerce throw in the way. For these reasons it will be eligible to withdraw as many of your men as you can from the West side of the Ohio, leaving only so many as may be necessary for keeping the Illinois settlements in spirits, and for their real defence. We must faithfully attend to their protection, but we must accomodate our measures for doing this to our means. Perhaps this idea may render doubtful the expediency of employing your men in building a fort at Kaskaskia. Such fort might perhaps be necessary for the settlers to withdraw into in time of danger, but might it not also render a surprize the more dangerous by giving the enemy a means of holding a settlement which otherwise they could only distress by a sudden visit and be obliged to abandon. Of this you must be ultimately the judge. We approve very much of a mild conduct towards the inhabitants of the French villages. It would be well to be introducing our laws to their knowledge and to impress them strongly with the advantage of a free government. The training their militia, and getting it into subordination to proper officers should be particularly attended to. We wish them to consider us as brothers, and to participate with us the benefits [of] our rights and Laws. We would have you cultivate peace and cordial friendship with the several tribes of Indians (the Shawanese excepted). Endeavour that those who are in friendship with us live in peace also with one another. Against those who are our enemies let loose the friendly tribes. The Kikapous should be encouraged against the hostile tribes of Chickasaws and Choctaws and the others against the Shawenese. With the latter be cautious of the terms of peace you admit. An evacuation of their Country and removal utterly out of interference with us would be the most satisfactory. Ammunition should be furnished gratis to those warriors who go actually on expeditions against the hostile Tribes. As to the English, notwithstanding their base example, we wish not to expose them to the inhumanities of a savage enemy. Let this reproach remain on them, but for ourselves we would not have our national character tarnished with such a practice. If indeed they strike the Indians, these will have a natural right to punish the aggressors and we none to hinder them. It will then be no act of ours. But to invite them to a participation of the war is what we would avoid by all possible means. If the English would admit them to trade and by that means get those wants supplied which we cannot supply, I should think it right, provided they require from them no terms of departing from their neutrality. If they will not permit this I think the Indians might be urged to break off all correspondence with them, to forbid their emissaries from coming among them and to send them to you if they disregarded the prohibition. It would be well to communicate honestly to them our present want of those articles necessary for them and our inability to get them, to encourage them to struggle with the difficulties as we do 'till peace, when they may be confidently assured we will spare nothing to put their trade on a comfortable and just footing. In the mean time we must endeavour to furnish them with ammunition, to provide skins to clothe themselves, with a disposition to do them every friendly office, and to gain their love. We would yet wish to avoid their visits, except those who came with Capt. Lintot. We have found them very hard to please, expensive and troublesome and they are moreover exposed to danger in passing our western countries. It will be well therefore (especially during the war) to waive their visits in as inoffensive a way as possible.

In a letter to you of the 1st. instant I supposed you would in the ensuing summer engage either in the Shawanee war, or against Detroit, leaving the choice of these and all other objects to yourself. I must also refer to you whether it will be best to build the fort at the mouth of Ohio before you begin your campaign or after you shall have ended it. Perhaps indeed the delays of obtaining leave from the Cherokees or of making a purchase from them, may oblige you to postpone it till the fall.

I have received letters from Capts. Shelby and Wotherington, the former acquainting me he had received your instructions to raise a troop of horse, the latter that he had raised one. From the date of your letter to Shelby, I knew you could not have been apprized that the Assembly had authorized us to raise a troop for you and that we had given a commission to Rogers by whom you sent us information of the capture of St. Vincennes. Rogers accordingly raised his men, got all accoutrements and marched to join you in the fall. As to Captain Wotherington who sais he has raised his men, you must state to us the necessity for your having two troops that we may lay it before the assembly who alone have a power of giving sanction to the measure. The distress of the public treasury will be a great obstacle, so that it will be well for you to take measures for reserving to yourself the benefit of Captain Wotherington's men in some other capacity, if they should be disapproved of as horsemen.

I am Sir Your very humble Servt., TH: JEFFERSON

Tr (DLC). At foot of text: "A copy of a document filed in a suit pending in the Superior Court of Chancery for the Richmond Circuit between George Woolfolk administrator with the will annexed of George Rogers Clarke deceased, plaintiff, and James E. Heath auditor of Public accounts of the State of Virginia; Teste Wm. G. Sands C C August 5th 1843." Two other transcripts, one of them dated 2 May 1831 and taken from the original in the hands of Gen. William Clark, St. Louis, are in WHi: Draper Collection. The copy in DLC is more faithful to TJ's spelling and capitaliza-tion than the others, though one omitted phrase has had to be supplied in square brackets, two misspelled words have been silently corrected, and several sentences have been repunctuated, TJ's habit of using lower-case letters at the beginning of sentences having confused all three copyists.

Clark's LETTERS to TJ of 24 Aug., 26 and 28 Oct., and 6 Nov. are all missing. TJ's letter to MESSRS. WALKER AND SMITH is dated 29 Jan., and that to MAJOR MARTIN 24 Jan. 1780. THE NEW FORT, built this year near the mouth of the Ohio, was called Fort Jefferson. TJ's

LETTERS FROM CAPTS. SHELBY AND
WOTHERINGTON (i.e., Capt. Edward
Worthington; see *George Rogers Clark*
Papers, 1771-1781, passim) have not
been found, though an answer to Shel-
by's appears under date of 24 Jan. 1780.

To Thomas Walker and Daniel Smith

SIR   Wmsburg Jany. 29th 1780

As we propose this Spring to take possession of and fortify some post as near the mouth of Ohio as the ground will admit, it becomes very important for us to know the exact latitude thereabouts. I take it for granted that your present Line will be stopped before you get there by unpurchased Lands. We therefore wish extremely that one of you would take a trip to the mouth of the Ohio with your instruments immediately on finishing your present work. I suppose it will be best for you to go to the falls of the Ohio where Colo. Clarke has orders to furnish you with Assistants, an Escort and all necessaries. You will first find the point at which our Line strikes the Missisippi or Ohio, and fix it by some lasting immoveable natural mark if there happen to be any on the spot, or if not, then by its course and distance from some such natural mark, noting such course as corrected from the errors of variation, and the distance reduced to horizontal measure. The reason of requiring this accuracy in fixing the point where our Line strikes is, that in future, with common instruments it will be easy to find it which may perhaps be of importance. When you have found this point if it be on the Missisippi run from thence along up the river to the mouth of Ohio, and by protraction fix the point of the forks or if it be on the Ohio, run up that river to where good Clifts for fortification shall make in and as you go along note the high ground points or Clifts on the river which appear to you capable of Works of defence and at the same time to command a view of the river. This done I would ask the favor of you to return one plat of your work to Colo. Clarke and another to me. Colo. Clarke has in his eye a particular Cliff on the Missisippi which he expects is the nearest good ground for fortification. This he will describe to you, and you will please to note it particularly. I am in hopes that it will suit one of you to undertake this business. We think to have the fort begun, which cannot be till we are assured that the ground we should pitch on is within our own Country. The disappointment will therefore be of the greatest moment should you decline the Service.

I am Gentl. with the greatest respect Your most obedt. Hmble Servt.

RC? (WHi); in a clerk's hand, presumably signed by TJ, but signature has been cut out. At foot of text, in TJ's hand: "Messrs Thomas Walker & Daniel Smith." Bears a docketed summary in a later hand. This or another copy of TJ's letter to the commissioners to extend the Virginia-North Carolina boundary was enclosed in TJ's letter to George Rogers Clark of the same date, q.v.

The fort erected near the mouth of the Ohio in pursuance of these orders, implementing a favorite scheme of Gov. Henry and of Clark himself, had a short and stormy history. It was located, under Clark's supervision, at the "Iron Banks" five miles below the mouth of the Ohio and was named Fort Jefferson; efforts were made to attract settlers, and the place was named "Clarksville." In the fall the post was attacked by hostile Indians. Their grievance was that the fort and settlement had been located on their land without their consent (TJ's orders to purchase the site from the Indians—see his letter to Joseph Martin, 24 Jan. 1780—having been overlooked). It proved impossible to supply the post adequately, and it was abandoned in June 1781. (See John Dodge to TJ, 1 Aug. 1780, and James, *G. R. Clark*, p. 195-7, 215-16, 244-5, and references there.) TJ was early blamed by historians for this unsuccessful venture, and he justified himself by amplifying Girardin's account of these events before it was published in 1816. In PPAP there is an undated paper in TJ's hand reading as follows: "pa. 174. l. 13. from bottom. Delete 'ever attentive &c. ———' to 'emissaries' in the bottom line and insert 'with a view to secure, on that principle, by actual possession, the right of Virginia in it's whole extent to the Missisipi, sent proper persons, under an escort, to ascertain by celestial observation, the point on that river intersected by the latitude of 36½ degrees, the Southern limit of the state, and to measure it's distance from the mouth of the Ohio. And Colo. Clarke was directed, as soon as this should be done, to select a strong and commanding position on the river, near the Southern limit and there to establish a fort and garrison: in the mean time to advance his establishments towards the lakes, erecting forts at different points, which might be an actual possession, as well as protection of that portion of the country also. Under these orders Fort Jefferson, on the Missisipi, a few miles above the Southern limit, was erected and garrisoned. This measure gave great umbrage to the Chickasaws, a friendly and faithful tribe of Indians, who claimed these as their hunting grounds. But full explanations being given of the object of the measure, and of it's necessity as well for their own security as for that of Virginia, they became satisfied; insomuch that when the fort and garrison were afterwards beleaguered by hostile Indians, the Chickasaws came to it's relief, and drove off the besieging force. The place was afterwards restored, and is still held by them. On the Northern quarter, Clarke proceeded with his usual judgment, combining policy with enterprize, encouraging peace among the friendly tribes, and directing, against the hostile, the force of those who could not be persuaded to remain inactive.' It was thus that the Kickapoos &c."

This correction of Girardin's MS was adopted in full by him and will be found in Burk-Girardin, *Hist. of Va.*, IV, 371-2.

To Thomas Sim Lee

SIR   Wmsburg Jan. 30th. 1780.

A most distressing harvest in this State having reduced us to the necessity of either disbanding our military force or seeking subsistence for them else where we asked permission from Governor Johnson to purchase a quantity of flour in your State. He was pleased to grant it to the extent of two thousand Barrels. Mr. Smith who was intrusted with the purchase informed us at different times of purchases to the amount of sixteen hundred Barrels, of which about two hundred Barrels I believe have been forwarded to us. By a Letter from him of Jan. 12. we are now informed that the residue not forwarded has been seised by your State. Should it be detained we shall be in very great distress having absolutely no other means of supporting our military till harvest. The object of the act (of which Mr. Smith inclosed a Copy) is patriotic and laudable. But I refer to your Excellency to consider whether the supply of the troops of the several states may not be considered as comprehended in the spirit of the act. The defence of the States severally makes up the general defence, no matter whether fed and paid at the generall or separate charge. Indeed I am induced to hope your Excellency will think our Stores not seizable within the Letter of the Law. At least I may say that according to the rules of exposition in use here, and derived from the common source of English Law, the clause which defines the subjects of seizure, enumerating, by way of example, what should be found in the hands of traders, farmers planters millers and others, would be construed to mean others ejusdem generis only, that is individuals, and not to extend to States which cannot be reduced into such a group. A further proof that individuals only were within the scope of your legislature is that they direct a sufficiency to be left for the consumption of the *family of the person* from whom taken, terms in no wise applicable to a State. However Sir it is not my Office to expound your Laws. I am sure your Excellency knows much better how to infer their true sense, and that in doing this, in the present instance, you will give weight to the purpose of our purchase, as well as to *the circumstance* of our being led into such an expenditure of our money by permission from your State. I am the more induced to hope an exemption from the operation of this Law, as I find it has given your Excellency a discretionary power to direct the conduct of the commissioners. Accustomed at all other times to furnish Subsistence to others, it is the first instance wherein providence has exposed us to the necessity of asking leave to purchase it among our friends. Assured that whatever your Excellency does on the present occasion will be right, I have the honor to subscribe myself with the most perfect esteem and respect Your Excellency's most Obt. & most huml. Servt.,   TH: JEFFERSON

RC (MdAA); in clerk's hand, signed by TJ.

MR. SMITH: Probably Samuel Smith of Baltimore; see Maryland Council to Samuel Smith, 24 Nov. 1779 (*Md. Archives*, XLIII, 24-5). See also Lee's answer, 23 Feb. 1780.

To David Shepherd

Sir   Wmsburg Jany. 30th. 1780

I find that the execution of the Commission for determining disputed titles to land, so far as the same has taken place in the controverted territory, has given great alarm and uneasiness to the State of Pennsylvania, who have applied to Congress on the occasion, and produced their interference. I hope no other Act has taken place subversive of the quiet of the Settlement. I must intreat you to exert the whole of your influence and to call in that of the Captains and subordinate Officers under You, to keep the inhabitants on both sides in good temper with each other, and to induce ours rather to neglect little circumstances of irritation, should any such happen, than by embroiling their two Countries to Shipwreck the general cause and bring on events which will destroy all our Rights. I put great confidence in your discretion on the present occasion and the effect of your recommendations to the people to be temperate in word and deed with their brethren of Pennsylvania. I am with great respect Sir Your most humble servt.,   TH: JEFFERSON

RC (WHi); in clerk's hand; complimentary close and signature in TJ's hand.

Shepherd was county lieutenant of Ohio; this letter, though without indication of addressee, is from Shepherd's papers in the Draper Collection. See Thomas Scott to Joseph Reed, 29 Nov. 1779, and references there; also the entry for Reed's missing letter to TJ, 8 Jan. 1780.

From Fielding Lewis

Honble. Sir   February the 2d. 1780.

I have advanced upwards of Two Thousand pounds for the use of the Gun factory under the care of Mr. Dick and myself, and Money daily wanted which I shall continue to furnish untill a supply can be obtained from the Treasury; Majr. Alexander Dick informs me that he shall shortly return to this place and has promised to bring up any Money you will please to send me, about Ten Thousand pounds will serve for some time as the Provisions are all purchased except about eighty barrs. of Corn which will shortly be provided.

I am Honble. Sr. with the greatest respect Your most Obedt. Humble Servant,   FIELDING LEWIS

RC (CSmH). At foot of text: "Feb. 5. 1780. In council. Referred to board of trade. Th: Jefferson."

Lewis' GUN FACTORY was at Fredericksburg; his partner in this important enterprise was Charles DICK (Kathleen Bruce, Virginia Iron Manufacture in the Slave Era, N.Y. and Lond., 1930, p. 29-42; also Charles Dick to TJ and enclosure, 23 Jan. 1781).

[281]

From James Wood

Sir   Charlottesville 3d. Feb. 1780.

I find it altogether Out of My Power to engage Any of the Tradesmen Among the German Troops to go to Richmond; by Some Means or Other they have found Out Our Distress for Tradesmen to do Our Public Work, and their Officers have Contrived to get so Considerably in their Debt for Work, Besides their Pay and Cloathing, that they are Afraid to go without their Consent, least they shou'd be returned Deserters, and by it lose the whole that is Due them.

I am with Great respect and Esteem, Sir, Yr. Excellency's Very Obt. Servt.,   JAMES WOOD

RC (Vi). Addressed: "His Excellency Governor Jefferson. Richmond." Endorsed in several clerks' hands.

From the Board of Trade

[*Williamsburg*] *4 Feb. 1780.* The agent has secured all of the deficient supplies for the new levies of Col. Buford's battalion as recommended, with the exception of 152 shirts. Proper linen not to be had and shirts exceedingly high-priced; therefore, decision to purchase them is left to executive.

Tr in Board of Trade Journal (Vi); 2 p. Printed in *Official Letters*, II, 96.

To the Board of Trade

In Council Feby. 4. 1780.

The Board are of Opinion that exorbitant as the Price is these Articles must be bought to complete the cloathing which will authorize us to march Buford's Battalion out of the State. A few day's subsistence and pay (if detained for want of Shirts) will exceed the price demanded.   TH. JEFFERSON

Tr in Board of Trade Journal (Vi).

From the Board of Trade

[4 February 1780]

The exhausted State of the Treasury rendering it impracticable to make the Purchases of Slaves, Tobacco and Land which have from time to time been recommended to this Board, We wish, as the only Means left us to comply with those recommendations, to have a Letter from his Excellency in Council to the Escheators of those Counties where the Purchases can be made, authorizing them to admit of our Assumpsits to the Treasurer for what We shall purchase in behalf of the State.

THOMS. WHITING

J. AMBLER

DUN: ROSE

Tr in Board of Trade Journal (Vi).

TJ's reply has not been located, but the following minute appears in the Board's Journal under 5 Feb.: "The Executive approving of the Escheators admitting of the Assumpsits of this Board to the Treasurer for such Purchases as are of escheated Property on behalf of the State, Ordered that Letters be written to the several Escheators agreeable to the recommendation of the Executive."

Board of War to County Lieutenants and Recruiting Agents

WAR OFFICE, Williamsburg, *Feb.* 4, 1780.

THE inclemency of the season having prevented the officer appointed to review and receive the new recruits raised under the act of Assembly concerning officers, soldiers, sailors, and marines, to perform the duties there prescribed on the days advertised in the gazette of *December* the 11th. The Board of War have changed the days of general rendezvous in the following manner, *viz*. At *Petersburg* on the 1st instant, *New London* on the 26th, *Staunton* on the 6th of *March*, *Winchester* on the 12th, *Fredericksburg* the 20th, and *Williamsburg* the 1st of *April*. The County Lieutenants and recruiting officers are most earnestly requested to use every possible exertion to have the recruits falling under their several directions, at the places and at the times above specified.

T. JEFFERSON

JAMES INNES

JAMES BARRON

MS not located. Printed in *Virginia Gazette* (Dixon & Nicolson), 12, 19, 26 Feb. 1780; also in *Official Letters*, II, 97.

FOR THE INCLEMENCY OF THE SEASON, see TJ to Philip Mazzei, 4 Apr.

1780. DAYS ADVERTISED IN THE GAZETTE OF DECEMBER THE 11TH: The orders of the Board of War, dated 1 Dec. 1779, appointing places to receive and review troops "beginning in January" were published in *Va. Gaz.* (C & D), 11 Dec. 1779.

From the Board of Trade

[Williamsburg] 5 *Feb. 1780.* Requests advice for the disposition of six Negroes purchased for the state.

Tr in Board of Trade Journal (Vi); 1 p.; printed in *Official Letters*, II, 96.

TJ's reply has not been located, but the following minute appears in the Board's Journal under the same date: "The Executive recommending the six Negroes, mentioned above, to be employed in the Armourer's Shop, Ordered that the Agent deliver them to Mr. James Anderson Superintendant of said shop."

From the Board of War

War Office Wmsburg Feb. 5th. 1780.

As the removal of the public Boards and Public Shops to Richmond may be Attended with very great inconvenience for the want of houses, The Board recommends to his Excellency the Governor to direct that all the escheated houses in Richmond be purchased for public use.

JAS. INNES

JAMES BARRON

Tr in Board of War Letter Book (MiU-C).

From the Board of War

[5? February 1780]

A plan for new modelling the Quarter Masters department in this State.

The Quarter Master General, taken from the Line, to draw three rations four forages and receive six hundred dollars ℔ month in Addition to his pay in the Line, be allowed the use of three public horses.

Two assistant Quarter Master Generals to draw each one ration two forages and receive four hundred Dollars ℔ month equivalent the pay and privileges of a Major in the Line.

Each regiment or Corps to have a Quarter Master from the Line, who shall be forage master to the same and to receive two hundred Dollars monthly in Addition to his pay in the Line and that such Regimental quarter Master be allowed one or more quarter Master Serjeants to Assist him, each to have an Additional pay of thirty Dollars ℔ month.

All the Waggons and horses assigned to each Garrison or Corps to be under the immediate direction and care of the quarter Master for the same. One Waggon master and one horse master be appointed under the immediate direction of the Quarter Master General as exigencies may require. The Waggon Master to draw one ration and receive two hundred Dollars ⅌ month and the horse master one ration and one hundred and fifty Dollars ⅌ month. One Deputy Quarter Master General be appointed to reside at Richmond to draw one ration two forages and receive four hundred Dollars ⅌ month, Equal the Assistants above and to be allowed an Assistant to receive two hundred Dollars monthly and to draw one ration. That all persons in the Quarter Masters department when called on public Business from their respective Stations, be furnished with a horse, and reasonable expences paid them. Assistant Quarter Master Generals' deputies and regimental Quarter Masters be Allowed a horse and forage also, the Waggon and horse master to be allowed the same. All appointments in the Quarter Masters department to be made by the Quarter Master General and the persons so appointed to be responsible to him for their conduct.

JAS. INNES

JAS BARRON

In Council Feb. 5th. 1780. Approved. TH: JEFFERSON

Tr in Board of War Letter Book (MiU-C).

From Richard Henry Lee

Chantilly, 7 Feb. 1780. Acknowledges letter and enclosures of 2 Jan. Intends to go into next Assembly and will early procure lodgings in Richmond. Hopes the southern news is true. A letter from Arthur Lee of 28 Sep. brings news of naval fighting in European waters. Arthur Lee may not be able to leave Europe because he stands pledged for 300,000 livres which he has no means of paying.

RC (DLC); 2 p. Printed in R. H. Lee, *Letters*, II, 174-5.

From Philip Mazzei

Nantes, 8-12 Feb. 1780. Is still at Nantes but has been obliged to beg personal financial assistance from Tuscany. Action of the Spanish and British fleets off Cadiz; capture of numerous Spanish merchantmen by Admiral Rodney. French success under M. LaMotte Picquet at Martinique. Encloses extracts from French *Gazette* to show "the monstrous contrast" between the published accounts in Spain and France, which are characterized by "the scrupolous regard paid to truth . . . the decency of their expressions, and the dignity preserved . . . ," and "the low, mean, dorty impudent false assertions of the Enemy." Will write again in a few days.

RC (Vi); 2 p.; dispatch No. 5, "1st. Copy." A "2d. copy" of the same is in NN. Printed in CVSP, I, 335-7; also in Marraro, *Mazzei*, p. 26-9. Enclosures missing.

To Samuel Huntington

SIR   Wmsburg Feby 9th 1780

Your Excellencys letter inclosing that of Mr. Scott to President Reed, and the President's to the Delegates of Pennsylvania in Congress, together with the resolutions of your honorable body recommending to both States to forbear granting lands within their disputed territory came safely to hand. I immediately availed myself of an opportunity, which occurred at that time, to Pittsburg, of taking measures to prevent any disorders on the part of our people. Having had no other information on the subject than what was communicated in the letters beforementioned I am uninformed whether any actual breach of the peace has taken place. As Mr. Scott however mentions nothing but the proceedings of the Commissioners for settling disputed titles under this Commonwealth, I rather hope that that is the only act which has been the subject of uneasiness. Our assembly finding that, in defiance of their endeavours to discourage and prevent the settling our Western Country, people were removing thither in great numbers, appropriating lands of their own authority, and meditating to hold them by force, after propositions, made and rejected at several sessions, for legalising those settlements, at length found it necessary to give way to the torrent, and by their Act of may 1779 to establish a land office. The irregular claims and settlements which in the mean time had covered that Country were become so extensive that no prudent man could venture to locate a new claim, and so numerous that in the common administration of justice it would have engrossed the whole time of our ordinary courts for many years to have adjusted them. So multifarious were they, at the same time, that no established principles of law or equity could be applied for their determination; many of them being built on customs and habits which had grown up in that Country, being founded on modes of transmission peculiar to themselves, and which, having entered almost into every title, could not be absolutely neglected. This impressed on the minds of the assembly the necessity of sending special Commissioners to settle, on the spot, and without delay, those various claims, which being once cleared away wou'd leave the residuary Country open to the acquisition of other adventurers. The Western Counties were accordingly laid off into Districts for this purpose, and the arrangement, being general, included the territory on the Waters of the Ohio claimed by the State of Pennsylvania. Whether the assembly did not advert to this Circumstance, or took for granted that the Commissioners would never consider a law of this State as meant to be applied to those who professed themselves the Citizens of another, and had been freely admitted so to profess themselves by our Government, or whether they relied that the term of one year, within which they provided that no grant should issue on any judgment of the Commissioners would give them time for the settlement of our disputed territory, or at least to provide for the peace of their Citizens within it, is not within my province or power to say. This however I can say, that from an intimate knowlege of their cordial desire to settle this claim with them amicably, no motive, inconstent with that, entered into the transaction. In fact the execution of this Commission, guarded as it's effects are by a twelvemonts delay of the grants, appears to be as peaceable and inoffensive as the mission of so many astronomers to take the longitude or latitude of the several farms. There is indeed a clause in the act of assembly which might, on first view, be thought to leave an opening for the introduction of force. It is that which sais that, judgement being rendered, if possession be *forcibly detained* by the party against whom it is, restitution may be made by the Commissioners or by any justice in like manner as might be done in the case of lands holden by grant actually issued: a Clause very necessary in our other Western Country, but not at all applicable to that part of it claimed by the State of Pennsylvania. By the laws of this Commonwealth (the same in this instance with the English law) even in the case of lands holden under actual grant, no restitution can be made after three years peaceable possession, a term much shorter than that of any bonâ fide possessions in the disputed territory. The latest of these must be of six or seven years continuance, the present dispute having so long subsisted. The expediency and necessity therefore of the general measure of establishing this temporary Court, I doubt not but Congress will percieve, and tho' it is to be wished that the disputed territory had been exempted from this jurisdiction, in order to avoid every thing which might give jealousy or uneasiness to a Sister State, or which might lead them into an apprehension that we meant to do any act which should wound the amity between us; yet I hope when Congress contemplates it's effects, they will be sensible that it only amounts to a settlement on paper of the rights of individuals derived from this State, and that no mans possession or quiet can be disturbed in consequence of any proceedings under it, until our Legislature, which meets in May next, shall have had time to settle finally with them this unfortunate dispute, or otherwise to provide against the evils they have apprehended. On my part nothing has been, or shall be omitted for preservation of the peace of that Country. Besides the injunctions which, as far as the laws would authorize, I have urged to those, the exercise of whose offices might lead to any thing disagreeable, or whose personal character and influence might aid in the preservation of peace, I shall avail myself of such other measures as may tend to the same object. The law having admitted grants to be sued out in cases where there were no contending claims of individuals, I inquired at the proper office whether, previous to the receipt of the resolutions of Congress, any such might have issued for lands in the Counties of Yohogania, Monongalia, and Ohio, they being the Counties part of which are claimed by the state of Pennsylvania. I found that eight such had issued. Under what particular circumstances they are, I am not able to discover. I am happy however that the law has left it in my power to comply with the recommendations of Congress, by witholding my signature from any other grants within those Counties, which I shall strictly do, and rest its approbation on the general assembly and the motives which led to it.

President Reed seems to think that this State has affected delays in the settlement of the right to the disputed territory. A review of the proceedings of our assembly on that subject will so fully convince you of their earnest and unremitting endeavours to procure an amicable settlement, that without giving you further trouble, I may take the liberty of referring you to the inclosed State of their proceedings for full justification from this suspicion. The novelty of the line proposed for the Western boundary of Pennsylvania, by the joint Commissioners, may well account for a hesitation to confirm it, until probable information can be obtained of it's actual location. At the same time I must not leave unnoted that the joint Commissioners have not attended to the settlers under either State, who may by this new line fall within the other, nor made any proposition for quieting their possessions. Yet it is surely an object, worthy the attention of us all, to provide that a tract of country, derelict by the State under which they wished to live, should not be urged into a secession from the common union, and into an assumption of independance by fears that their actual possessions may be made to give way to mere paper titles. Should the reference of the proposition to our next session of assembly give time to avoid this evil alone, I am persuaded it will be thought conducive to the quiet of both States.

I shall take care to lay before our assembly the resolutions and letters you have been pleased to communicate to me on this subject, not doubting that they will supply those efforts beyond the limits of my power which are necessary to remove the present and prevent all future uneasiness. I can say nothing to whatever looks like menace on the part of our brethren. The choice of terms would be delicate and difficult, and their construction hazardous, which would express a proper sensibility on this tender point, and not produce sentiments repugnant to that sincere love I shall for ever strive to cultivate with all our Sister States. To history therefore I must refer for answer, in which it would be an unhappy passage indeed, which should shew by what fatal indulgence of subordinate views and passions, a contest for an atom had defeated well founded prospects of giving liberty to half the globe. That no such blot shall wipe out the sequel of our glorious struggle I trust as well in the approved zeal of the Gentleman who adorns the administration of the other State, as in the resolutions of our own Government to postpone to the great object of Liberty every smaller motive and passion. In every Circumstance, Sir, the kind attentions of your body will be remembered and approved, and no occasion omitted of assuring you with how great respect and esteem I am Your Excellencys Most obedt. & most hble Servt.,   TH: JEFFERSON

RC (DLC: PCC, No. 71, I). In a clerk's hand and signed by TJ. Endorsed: "Letter from Gov. of Virginia 9th. Feby 1780. read 28th." Enclosure: MS digest of proceedings of Virginia Assembly relative to the Virginia-Pennsylvania boundary, 5 July 1776 to 23 Dec. 1779 (same location); 10 p.; in a clerk's hand, with some dates inserted by TJ.

Huntington's LETTER to which this is a reply was dated 30 Dec. 1779, q.v., with note on enclosures therein; also Thomas Scott to Gov. Reed, 29 Nov. 1779, and TJ to David Shepherd, 30 Jan. 1780. THIS UNFORTUNATE DISPUTE: See entry for Proceedings of Commissioners, 27-31 Aug. 1779, above; on 23 Dec. 1779 the House of Delegates resolved to defer until the next session consideration of the agreement reached by the Commissioners, and, meanwhile, "General Lewis, Thomas Lewis and James Innes of Yohogania, Esquires, or any two of them, be appointed to inquire in what manner the rights of this Commonwealth and of its citizens will be affected by the terms of the agreement" (JHD, Oct. 1779, 1827 edn., p. 106). On 23 June the House at length accepted the agreement in respect to the boundary line but made certain reservations about title claims; see entry for TJ to Reed, 17 July 1780.

From Samuel Huntington

SIR   Philadelphia Feby 10. 1780

Your Excellency will receive herewith enclosed an Act of Congress of the 9th. Instant ascertaining the number of men exclusive of Commissioned Officers for the Continental Army the next Campaign to be 35. 211. which Congress deem necessary for the service of the present Year the Quota of each State being specified in the Act.

You will observe that all the Men belonging to each State respectively now in the public service and whose time of Service does not expire before the last day of September next, whether they compose the Battallions in the line of the several States, those of the additional Corps including the guards, the artillery and horse, or the Regimented artificers in the department of the Quarter Master General and Commissary General of Military Stores are to be credited to their respective States and accounted as part of their Quotas and each State is required to furnish their respective Deficiencies of their Quotas as above stated on or before the first Day of April next.

You may expect to receive as soon as possible from the Commander in Chief or his order, an accurate return of the Troops now in service belonging to the state which will ascertain the deficiency to be furnished by the States respectively agreeable to the act enclosed.

As the Quotas apportioned to each State may be supposed not to be exactly Just you will observe Congress have made provision to pay the Expence any State hath incurred or may incur by furnishing more than their Just proportion of men.

It is recommended to each State respectively in the strongest Terms punctually to comply with this Acquisition by furnishing their respective Quotas of Men compleat without loss of Time.

Many powerful motives too obvious to need enumeration conspire to urge the propriety, policy, and necessity of having a respectable Army ready to take the field early in the spring.

Vigorous exertions and a respectable Army in the field are the most sure means to prevent the necessity of another Campaign on the one hand, or on the other to crown it with the desired success and put a period to the Contest upon honourable Terms.

I have the honour to be &c.   S. HUNTINGTON President

FC (DLC: PCC, No. 14). Circular to the state executives. Enclosure (missing): Resolve of Congress of 9 Feb. 1780, printed in JCC, XVI, 150-1.

From Riedesel

SIR   New York 10th: February 1780

For your very polite recollection and kind Compliments as well, as those from Your Lady, to whom please to present my best respects, myself and Madame de Riedesel return you our most perfect thanks, requesting you will be persuaded that nothing can ever efface from our Memory the Esteem we have for so respectable a Family from whom we received so many instances of Friendship. Madme: de Riedesel, whose sentiments are united with mine, charges me with Her Compliments to Yourself and Mrs. Jefferson; and believe me to hear of the Continuation of the Health and Happiness of you and Yours will ever be most pleasing to us both.

Permit me Sir to trouble you with the inclosed and to beg you will have it sent to Brigr. General Specht at Stantown, as no other safe oppertunity presents itself to convey a Letter to Him.

I have the Honor to be with the most perfect Esteem and Consideration, Your Excellencys most obedient humble Servant,

RIEDESEL, Maj: Gen:

RC (DLC); in a clerk's hand, signed by Riedesel. Enclosures not further identified. Riedesel's letter was evidently transmitted to TJ by Gen. Washington; see Washington to TJ, 16 Feb. 1780.

To George Washington

SIR   Williamsburg Feb. 10. 1780.

It is possible you may have heard that in the course of the last summer an expedition was meditated by our Colo. Clarke against Detroit; that he had proceeded so far as to rendezvous a very large body of Indians (I beleive four or five thousand) at Saint-Vincennes; but being disappointed in the number of whites he expected, and not chusing to rely principally on the Indians, was obliged to decline it. We have a tolerable prospect of reinforcing him this spring to the number which he thinks sufficient for the enterprize. We have informed him of this, and left to himself to decide between this object and that of giving rigorous chastisement to those tribes of Indians whose eternal hostilities have proved them incapable of living on friendly terms with us. It is our opinion his inclination will lead him to determine on the former. The reason of my laying before your Excellency these matters at present is that it has been intimated to me that Colo. Broadhead is meditating a similar expedition. I wished therefore to make you acquainted with what we have in contemplation. The enterprizing and energetic genius of Clarke is not altogether unknown to you. You also know (what I am a stranger to) the abilities of Broadhead and the particular force with which you will be able to arm him for such an expedition. We wish the most hopeful means should be used for removing so uneasy a thorn from our side. As yourself alone are acquainted with the whole circumstances necessary for well informed decision, I am to ask the favor of your Excellency, if you should think Broadhead's undertaking it most likely to produce success, that you would be so kind as to intimate to us to divert Clarke to the other object, which is also important to this state. It will of course have weight with you in forming your determination, that our prospect of strengthening Clarke's hands sufficiently is not absolutely certain. It may be necessary perhaps to inform you that these two officers cannot act together; which excludes the hope of ensuring success by a joint expedition.

I have the honour to be with the most sincere esteem Your Excellency's Most obedient & most humble servt., TH: JEFFERSON

RC (MH). Tr (DLC); text defective. See Washington's reply, 5 Mch. 1780.

From the Board of War, with Reply

Williamsburg, 15 Feb. 1780. Encloses a roster of Col. Marshall's officers, together with a recommendation of some cadets and others for commissions to complete officers for the corps of artillery, and requests that commissions be issued according to the dates specified. Signed by Innes and Lyne. Countersigned: "Feb. 17th. 1780. The Board Advise that commissions be issued accordingly. Th: Jefferson. [*Postscript:*] The Board of War will be pleased to fill up the commissions, to prevent mistakes or misunderstanding the Above mentioned Roster."

Tr in Board of War Letter Book (MiU-C); 1 p. Enclosures not located.

From the Board of War, with Reply

Williamsburg, 15 Feb. 1780. Encloses a letter from Lt. Col. Porterfield stating objections to the new quartermaster's arrangement; these objections seem proper and will be given consideration if the executive approves. Signed by Innes and Lyne. Countersigned: "In Council Feb. 16. 1780. The board approve of giving Colo. Porterfield 200. Dolls. ♉ month in Addition to the 600 Doll. ♉ month formerly proposed. Th. Jefferson."

Tr in Board of War Letter Book (MiU-C); 1 p. Enclosure not located. For the new arrangement of the quar-termaster's department, see Board of War to TJ, 5? Feb. 1780.

From Patrick Henry

DEAR SIR   Leatherwood Feby 15h. 1780

I return you many Thanks for your Favor by Mr. Sanders. The kind Notice you were pleased to take of me was particularly obliging, as I have scarcely heard a Word of public Matters since I moved up. In the Retirement where I live, I have had many anxietys for our Commonwealth, principally occasioned by the Depreciation of our Money. To judge by this, which some Body has called the Pulse of the State, I have feared that our Body politic was dangerously sick. God forbid it may not be unto Death. But I cannot forbear thinking the present Increase of prices, is in great part owing to a kind of Habit, which is now of four or five Years Growth, and which is forstered by a mistaken avarice, and like other Habits, hard to part with. For there is really very little Money here abouts. What you say of the Practices of our disguised Torys perfectly agrees with my own Observation. And the Attempts to raise prejudices against the French, I know were begun while I lived below. What gave me the utmost pain was to see some men indeed very many who were thought good Whigs keep Company with the Miscreant Wretches who I am satisfy'd were laboring our Destruction. This Countenance shewn them is of fatal Tendency. They should be shunned and execrated, and this is the only way to supply the place of legal Conviction and Punishment. But this is an Effort of Virtue, small as it seems, of which our Country men are not capable. Indeed I will own to you my dear Sir, that observing this impunity and even Respect which some wicked Individuals have met with, while their Guilt was clear as the Sun, has sicken'd me, and made me some times wish to be in Retirement for the rest of my Life. I will however be down on the next Assembly if I am chosen. My Health I am satisfy'd will never again permit a close Application to sedentary Business, and I even doubt whether I can remain below long enough to serve in the Assembly. I will however make the Tryal. But tell me do you remember any Instance, where Tyranny was destroyed and Freedom established on its Ruins among a people possessing so small a Share of Virtue and public Spirit? I recollect none; and this more than the British Arms, makes me fearfull of our final Success, without a Reform. But when or how this is to be effected I have not the Means of judging. I most sincerely wish you Health and Prosperity. If you can spare Time to drop me a Line now and then it will be highly obliging to dear Sir yr. affectionate friend & hble Servant, P. HENRY

RC (DLC). TJ's FAVOR BY MR. SANDERS has not been found.

From the Board of Trade

[*Williamsburg*] *16 Feb. 1780.* Requesting approval of purchase, from Henry Brown, of "10 hhds of Rum at £25. ℔ Gall. in exchange for Cordage at 40/.℔ lb.—the price . . . is extravagant, but . . . Troops cannot be marched on to the Southward without this Article. . . ."

Tr in Board of Trade Journal (Vi); 1 p.; printed in *Official Letters*, II, 101-2. TJ's reply has not been located, but this minute follows in the Journal: "Which being approved by the Executive, Ordered that the Agent be directed to purchase the same."

From George Washington

SIR Head Qrs: Morris Town Feby 16th 1780

I have the pleasure to transmit Your Excellency a Letter from Major Genl. de Riedesel which only came to hand Two days ago.

I would now inform Your Excellency, that agreeable to my Letter of the 18th of December I have obtained a Return of Moylan's Regiment of Light Dragoons and find as I apprehended that there are Sixty three Non Commissioned Officers and Privates in it, who belong to Virginia. Of this number Two only are inlisted for the War and the service of the Rest will expire in December next. Having given Your Excellency an account of those Men I have only to observe, that with the Returns transmitted in my Letter of the 18th of December, You now have the fullest and most accurate state of the Virginia Troops that I can furnish and of those to be applied to the credit of Your Quota. By these and the information Your Excellency may have received with respect to the Levies under General Scot and Blands and Baylor's Regiments You may perhaps be able to form a pretty just estimate of the force of the State employed in the Army and to govern Yourself with tolerable certainty as to the deficiency of the State's Quota, which Congress, as Your Excellency will no doubt be informed by the President, have required to be levied for the ensuing Campaign by an Act on the 9th. Instant.

I have the Honor to be with the most perfect esteem & respe[ct]
Yr Excellency's Most Obed Sevt,   Go: WASHINGTON

Dft (DLC: Washington Papers); in hand of R. H. Harrison, including signature; endorsed. The LETTER FROM MAJOR GENL. DE RIEDESEL is doubtless that of 10 Feb. 1780, q.v. MY LETTER OF THE 18TH OF DECEMBER actually refers to Washington's letter of 26 Dec. 1779, q.v.

From the Board of Trade

SIR   Bd. of Trade Feby. 17th 1780

We have the honor of your Excellency's Letter of the 7th. inst. recommending the necessity of an immediate remittance to Arthur Lee Esqr. who is, and has for a long time been considerably in advance for the state. The repeated references both of Letters and Accounts, from France which We have received from time to time from your Excellency in Council since our establishment have distressed us greatly for so far from ever having it in our Power to make a remittance to France, our finances have been so low from the time of our coming into Office as to put us to the greatest difficulties in providing even the temporary supplies which were indispensably necessary and loudly called for; and at this instant our credit is suffering extremely by reason of our inability to replace Monies which our friends have advanced for payment of Shoes, and the Goods for the Cherokee Indians; purchases which we were urged to make at all events. We entreat Your Excellency and the honorable Board will consider our circumstances which when duly weighed must satisfy the Honorable Board and our Country that our embarrazements deprive us of the Power of rendering the Services we anxiously wish. We have &c.   T W.
                                                           J. A.
                                                           D. R.

Dft (CSmH).
A minute in the Board of Trade Journal (Vi) under the present date ordered that a letter be written to TJ in reply to his LETTER OF THE 7TH, but neither the text of TJ's letter nor the reply is present in the Journal.

From the Board of Trade

[*Williamsburg*] *17 Feb. 1780.* The adjustment of the business with Col. Legras and Capt. Linctot not coming properly in their jurisdiction, as they have previously observed, the Board requests instructions concerning any alterations or additions therein, for their justification as well as their guidance.

Tr in Board of Trade Journal (Vi); 2 p. Printed in *Official Letters*, II, 102. See TJ to Board of Trade, 26 Jan. 1780.

Commission to D. M. G. Linctot as Indian Agent

Form of Majr. Lintots Commission, 17th. Feby. 1780

The Commonwealth of Virginia to Daniel Morice Godefrey Lintot Greeting: Know you that in consideration of your courage, zeal and attachment our Governor with the advice of the Council of State, constitutes and appoints you to be agent on behalf of this Commonwealth with the indians in the northwestern department with the pay of five shillings in silver money by the day and the rank and rations of a Major. In testimony where of these our Letters are sealed with the Seal of the Commonwealth and made patent. Witness Thomas Jefferson esqr. our said Governor at Wmsburg on the 17th day of Feby. 1780. Th Jefferson

Tr in Board of War Letter Book (MiU-C).
    There is a detailed sketch of the frontiersman and soldier Daniel Maurice Godefroy de Linctot (Lanctot, Lintot) in Wis. Hist. Soc., *Colls.*, XXIV, 176; he ordinarily signed his name "Godefroy" or "G.f."

To George Washington

Sir   Williamsburg Feby 17. 1780

I inclose you according to desire our approbation of the military appointments you recommended. You will please to forward it to the proper power for obtaining the Commissions as we are strangers to this arrangement.

We have with great concern received information of the numbers of our soldiers whose times are expiring, and with the greater because of the extreme poverty of our Treasury. Impressed with the importance of reinlisting them, we have determined to postpone to this every other application of the public money, and shall furnish for this use every shilling possible.

General Scott has just forwarded to me a Letter from Major Clarkson dated Newbern, Feby. 7th. informing him that the army which embarked at New York on the 26h of Dec. had arrived at

Savanna and pressing his utmost dispatch to Charles town. Other undoubted intelligence received before had convinced me they were destined for Charles town. The distresses I hope they experienced on their passage rendered necessary probably to go to Savanna to refresh. We shall immediately send forward all the little aid in our power. Tho' satisfied that no spur could be added to your natural desire of pressing forward to action, my duty would not permit me to pass over this altogether unnoticed. I am Sir Your mo: obedt hble Servt.,   TH: JEFFERSON

RC? (DLC); in a clerk's hand, signed by TJ. Endorsed: "Govr. Jeffersons Letter 17th Feby. 1780." Though it is now in the TJ Papers, this appears to be a recipient's copy. Enclosure missing.

The LETTER FROM MAJOR CLARKSON (probably Matthew Clarkson of Massachusetts, aide to Gen. Benjamin Lincoln; see Heitman) to Gen. Charles SCOTT has not been located.

From the Board of Trade

[18 February 1780]

The Act of Assembly establishing this Board directs, that it shall be subject to the advice and controul of the Executive, in every instance; and shall be held when and where the Governor, with advice of Council shall appoint: Now, tho' we clearly see the propriety of the Board's being fixed under the immediate inspection of the Executive, and it is what the Commissioners wish for, We are, nevertheless, apprehensive it will be impracticable to remove it to Richmond so soon as the Executive are under the necessity of going there, for the following reasons.

It appears to us that it will be to very little purpose to remove the Board unless the several Appendant officers, as the Agent, Commissary of Stores &c. and their Assistants could also accompany it, for these being the persons to whom the execution of the most important business of the Trade is necessarily committed, it is essentially requisite that the Commissioners should be present to superintend them; and tho' perhaps we may be able, at very great expence and uncertainty, to procure accommodations at Richmond during the Session of Assembly there is good reason to believe it will be impracticable to accommodate all the necessary officers, and absolutely impossible to procure the proper Houses for the reception and securing the Public Stores; and without these, most of the Officers in the trading department would be useless. It appears to us also at this time of pressing call for supplies for the state, that our present situation will afford us much better opportunities of making advantageous purchases of such cargoes as may arrive; if at Richmond our distance from the Sea Ports will be so great as still to add much to the advantages which the Speculators and Monopolizers have over us. If to these considerations we may presume to add, that should it be found expedient or necessary at the next Session of Assembly, either to abolish the Board, or return it to Williamsburg until a more favourable time for removal shall offer, the expence to the State, to say nothing of our own, which an immediate removal would unnecessarily incur, must be enormous. The only inconvenience we can at present foresee in the boards being seperated for a short time from the Executive is our not being able to procure their immediate approbation of any purchase we may think it prudent to make; but the opportunities of making considerable purchases seldom occur, and when they do we have generally for [four] or five Days given us to determine, which will afford us time sufficient for procuring it from Richmond. This matter appearing to us of very great consequence we think it our duty to submit our sentiments respecting it to His Excellency in Council not doubting such advice and direction therein as maybe most for the Interest of the State.

Tr in Board of Trade Journal (Vi). For the removal of the government to Richmond, see Notice of Removal of the Executive Office, 25 Mch. 1780. The Board of Trade Journal ends with the minutes of 7 Apr., and the Board itself was discontinued by an Act of Assembly passed 6 July 1780 (Hening, x, 291-2).

To the Board of Trade

In Council Feb. 18. 1780.

The Board, in order to give Satisfaction as far as they are able to Colo. Legras and Major Lintot, recommend to the Board of Trade to convert into Tobacco such of the Bills of Exchange formerly recommended to be drawn as they shall be able to do on reasonable terms, such Tobacco to be delivered in payment in lieu of the Bills; they do not doubt the Board of Trade will endeavor to negotiate at the same time a suspension of the transmission of the Bills a certain time to give them leisure to provide for their acceptance.   TH: JEFFERSON

Tr in Board of Trade Journal (Vi).

From the Board of War

Williamsburg, 18 Feb. 1780. Encloses a plan of forming the detachment of troops to be sent to South Carolina, with an estimate of camp apparatus needed. This plan proposes augmentation of garrison regiment to man the forts intended to be erected, and retention of part of artillery regiment for a laboratory, which must be established to equip artillery in the field. Two letters are enclosed to the commanding officers of the corps of cavalry and artillery, for countersignature. Signed by Innes and Lyne. Countersigned: "Feb. 19th. 1780. Approved. Th: Jefferson."

Tr in Board of War Letter Book (MiU-C); 1 p. Enclosures not located.

From the Board of War

Williamsburg, 18 Feb. 1780. Col. Wells has purchased pork costing over £340,000 for the use of the troops; he has been furnished about £118,000; for much of the difference he has been obliged to give his private notes, and he says he will have to sell some of the pork to support his credit. The pork must be had for the troops, but the treasury is so low it will not admit of a draft. Northern speculators are purchasing all the pork in Nansemond at any price. "The Honour and Credit of an honest Man is at Stake and the Pork must be had for the Troops. It seems utterly out of the Power of the Board of War to remedy the Evil. They therefore request the Advice of your Excellency."

Tr in War Office Letter Book (Vi); 1 p.

From Philip Mazzei

SIR   Nantes, Feby: 18th. 1780.

I send you the inclosed copies, containing my corrispondence with Mr. D'Acosta and Dr. Franklin, being the most satisfactory proof I can give of having done what I prudently and decently could do to find the means for proceeding on the important business so strongly recommended to me. My delay to write to Dr. Franklin, and the distance between the first and second letter have proceeded cheafly from the reports we often had of the arrival of the confederacy in one of the spanish Ports, Mr. D'Acosta having often repeated to me that as soon as Mr. Penet arrived, or the least remittance was received from America, or even a letter to satisfy the minds of his Partners, my letter of credit would be paid. Your not writing to the House has been a great charge against you, as well as against congress the states of south Carolina and Pensilvania.

He often said that the government *of the state of Boston* have been more regular. To this I answered, that in New-Egland they have always been Merchants; but we are beginners and cannot as yet be acquainted with all the rules of the counting-House of a Merchant; that perhaps you had written, and the letters were lost; or Mr. Penet being on the spot it was probably thought superfluous to write to his House, since he made his contracts, received the necessary acknowledgements, and could have as many copies as he thought expedient of all interesting papers. We have repeatedly written, says he, that they must write to the House; Mr. Penet may die, and we have nothing to shew; and then hinted, more by motions than words, that Mr. Penet was not in danger of losing any thing. As he might easily suppose, that I must have heared enough of that already, I answered as if he had spoken in clear terms, and said, That Mr. Penet being the first mentioned in the firm of the house it was natural for us to believe him to be the person of the first consequence in every respect; and as one of his clerk's had said on change (I suppose by his order to support the honour of the house) that they were not obliged to pay Mr. Penet's letter of credit, because he had drawn on his private account, I observed that I had made some objections to Mr. Penet in Williamsburgh about his signing his own name only, and that I had acquiesced on his assertions of its being the same; but now I clearly comprehended the mystery (expressing this *more with motions than words* in conformity to the fashion.) I assure you, Sir, that I have been greatly and often mortifyed by a continuance of complaints and reproaches against us (some of which, as I thought them ill founded, I had thoroughly confuted) and always in the same words, like the repetition of a Parrot. One day when I could hold it no longer, I told him, that in consequence of our Constitution our feelings for whatever regards the Community differ from the feelings of those, who live in a monarchical Government; that I was wounded by his reflections; and beged he would decline the subject. His behaviour to me, since the first 8, or 10 days, has been inconsistent, unequal, and sometimes provoking to a degree, that I incline to think, that he wanted to riduce me to go out of temper, in hope of prejudicing my character here where he knows I am a stranger, and to raise from that some plausible pretence for not paying the 300 Louis. To oppose his views, and for other good reasons, I have behaved in a manner as to leave him to guess whether I have been sensible, or not, of his undelicacy and indecency in speaking, evasions in writing, and mean dirty shuffling way of proceeding in every respect. Only the day before yesterday I was forced to make him understand on change, that I should be obliged to preceed legally, after he had declared with such a roguish impudence, as has shocked all who have heared it, that he would return me my receits when I should return him the 53 Louis and 18 livres, but would keep the letter of *recommendation* (so it was termed by him instead of letter of credit) with which I had no business, being a letter directed to his house. He came however to his senses in the after-noon (I suppose out of fear after reflecting on the consequences of such a denial) and sent the letter of credit with my receits by 2 clerks, to whom I returned the money and certificates, but could not prevail on them to take the interest, which I was sorry for. In the interim of the 3 last letters he promised an answer in writing twice to me on change, and once to a Gentleman, by whom I sent the 2d; but never did. Was I to call him to account (which I would certainly do had I not publick business on hand) I firmly believe that he would deny having refused me the letter of credit on my returning the money. You will please to observe, that I made no answer to his 2d. letter and certificate, because I could not do it without expressing my just resentment for his repeated scandalous evasions, or affecting not to understand him and pass for a simpleton, or a pusillanimous wretch. The field is large, but shall say no more about it untill I see Mr. Penet, or hear from him. I shall set out for Paris before morning, and am most respectfully, Sir, Your Excellency's most Obedt. and most humble Servant,   PHILIP MAZZEI

RC (NN); endorsed in clerk's hand. At head of text: "6 [i.e., 6th dispatch]. 3d. Copy." Enclosures missing.

To George Muter

SIR   Williamsburg Feb. 18. 1780.

I have spoken with the board of war on the subject of the battery at Hood's, and they concur with me in wishing to avail themselves of your services there, and will give orders accordingly. This together with similar batteries on the other rivers will probably take some time, tho' considering their great importance to the security and quiet of the country above them, we are assured you will freely lend us your aid in seeing them planned and executed. We ask this the rather as the distresses impending over our sister state of South Carolina urge us to send forward the whole of our regiment of artillery (whom we have a power of sending out of the state) and a detachment from yours of about 80. under the command of Colo. Porterfeild, with the two state troops of horse. Your battalion, after this detachment is withdrawn, we think to divide among the several batteries and have reason to hope that the recruits for the two Eastern battalions will enable us to compleat it, so that on you we shall rest for this campaign the burthen of our military cares, endeavoring to procure a readiness of such aids of militia as may be suddenly called for by you. I must ask the favor of you to communicate to Colo. Porterfeild orders to prepare immediately for marching, and to concert with him the best means of obtaining voluntarily the number of men required from your battalion. We understand a greater number of them have reenlisted under the act concerning officers, souldiers, sailors and marines, who of course are obliged to go: but we would rather call the willing into this service.

I am Sir with great esteem Your friend & servt.,

TH: JEFFERSON

RC (PHi). Addressed: "Colo. Muter Williamsburg." Endorsed: "The Governour Feby 18, 1780 Respecting Hoods and volunteers to goe to the southward of State Garrison & other Regts." Heretofore printed without name of addressee.

Concerning THE BATTERY AT HOOD'S, on James River in Prince George co. opposite Weyanoke, see a useful note in *Official Letters*, II, 103.

To James Innes

SIR   Wmsburg Feb. 19th. 1780.

Colo. Crocketts Battalion is now rendezvousing at the Barracks in Albemarle from whence it is to proceed to join Colo. Clarke as soon as the season will admit them to march. I therefore refer to your consideration whether measures should not be immediately taken for furnishing them with Clothing, Blankets &c. Arms Ammunition and other necessaries to last them through the summer, as also for Colo. Clarkes own Battalion, as it is possible they may go on duty to such a distance as that supplies from time to time cannot be sent them. After recommending this to your immediate attention, I have the honor of Subscribing myself Sir Your mo. Obt. Servt.,

TH: JEFFERSON

Necessaries said to be requisite for each Battalion.
60 falling Axes. 8 Broad Do. 18 Mattocks. 18 Augers.
12 Drawing knives. 8 Froes. 4 X Cut Saws. Nails. Gimblets.
80 camp kettles of 2 Gallons—Crockets Battalion has orders for

170 Rifles from Colo. Matthews, who has about as many more.
Flints will be wanting.
Cannon in the Illinois.
1 Brass 6 pounder mounted on a travelling carriage & compleat.
4 double fortified Iron 4 pounders ⎱ destitute of
11 Swivels of different sizes ⎰ every necessary
Ball &c. Should be sent for the 6 & 4 lbrs. & Swivels.

Tr in Board of War Letter Book (MiU-C).

From Thomas Sim Lee

Sir   In Council Annapolis 23d. Feby. 1780.

We had the Honor to receive your Excellency's Letter of the
30th. Jany. The Necessity which constrained our Assembly to enact
a Law, the extensive Operation of which has interfered with the
Purchases made by your Agent, for the Subsistence of the Military
of your State, we must deplore, and can assure you that an anxious
Solicitude for the Welfare of the United States and an Opinion that
nothing short of the most vigorous and sudden Exertions, could procure an immediate and full Supply for our distressed Army, were
the only Motives which prompted them to make it so general. We
are satisfied it is not the Intention of the Act, to provide Supplies
for State Troops, because, when it was made, it was not known that
the Military of any particular State was in Distress. The Object of
the Assembly being an immediate and full Supply for the Army, we
cannot admit your Exposition of the Law, because it would, in some
Degree, counteract the Purpose of it and because we think the
Word "others" was inserted with a View of including every Person in whose Possession any Flour or Wheat was found and may
well comprehend the Agent of Virginia; and that, unless such
Construction is made, as there is no other Person except the Agent
of the Marine of France (whose Flour is also deemed seizable) to
whom it can relate, that Word would be deprived of its Effect, and
a well known Principle in expounding Act of the Legislature,
would be infringed, that a Law ought to be so construed that no
Word should be rendered void or insignificant if it can be prevented.
We must further observe that the Intention of the Assembly ought
to prevail, which is to be collected from the *Cause* or *Necessity*
which induced them to make the Law. We cannot esteem it necessary to enter into a minute Discussion of the present Question or to
resort to nice and subtil Reasoning to justify an Exertion which

was requisite to prevent the numerous Calamities which must result from the Dissolution of the Continental Army. We are sensible it is the mutual Interest of both States to preserve the Harmony that subsists between them which, added to our Desire to contribute all we possibly can to the Relief of your Distresses, make us wish to receive Information from Congress or His Excellency General Washington, that the Army is supplied, that we may have it in our Power to restore your Flour, before you feel any Inconveniencies from the Seizure of it. Our Assembly will meet the second Day of March, when your Excellency's Letter will be laid before them for their Consideration. We are &c.

FC (MdAA).

From Geismar

Sir   N. York febr: 26th. 1780

I take the liberty to send Your Excellency a parcel of letters for the Regiment of Hessen Hanau. Though I have not opened them, I beleave I may assure that they Contain nothing which concerns public Affaires, nor anny thing prejudicial to the Americans. I flatter myself that You will be kind enough to order them, opened or not, to be delivred Save [safe] to Brigadier General de Gall. There is an other letter for Gen: Gall with a news paper containing some letters of Gen: Bourgoyne, which if Your Excelency has no objection I wish to be delivred to him. An other to our paye master Lieut. Sartorius, concerning some private business of my one [own], and which I sealed for fear a Small Bill might been dropt.

I am not exchanged yet and therefore may have the Pleasure to meet Your Excellency in Virginia once more, where and under what-ever Condition it may by [be]; I will be happy to see my friends; and among which I am particularly indeted to Your Excellency for the Civilitys and Kindness shown to me during my stay there.

I hope Madame and the little family are well. To all I present my Respects and beg in particular to be remembered to my little friend Paty.

I have the honour to be with great Respect, Sir! Your Excelencys Most Obed: Very humbl' Servant,   DE GEISMAR

RC (DLC). Enclosures not identified.
For Geismar's subsequent relations with TJ, see Kimball, *Jefferson, War and Peace*, p. 40-5.

From Samuel Huntington

Philadelphia, 26 Feb. 1780. Circular letter to the state executives enclosing a resolve of Congress of 25 Feb. "by which the several States are called upon to procure their respective Quotas of Supplies for the ensuing Campaign in the Articles and Quantities specified." The states' undertaking to furnish and deposit the supplies called for "will supersede the Necessity of purchasing Commissaries and Quarter masters in the several States." The states are, moreover, excused from paying into the Continental treasury "two thirds of the Monies which they were called on to raise monthly . . . by the Resolution of the 6th of October last." Any change in the kind or quantity of the articles called for will be duly indicated by the commissary general.

FC (DLC: PCC, No. 14); 3 p. Enclosure missing; printed in JCC, XVI, 196-201. See further Gen. Washington's circular letter, 26 Mch. 1780.

From William Phillips

New York, 1 Mch. 1780. Introduces Mrs. Maxwell and asks TJ's "Notice and Protection" in conveying her to her husband, Lt. Maxwell of the Convention troops. Compliments to TJ and Mrs. Jefferson.

RC (DLC); 2 p. Enclosed in Maria Maxwell's letter to TJ, 15 Mch. 1780, q.v.

From Philip Mazzei

SIR   Paris, March 2d. 1780

I arrived in this metropolis 8 days since; have been at Dr. Franklin and Marquis Caraccioli frequently and have seen several others who are likely to influence those in power; but have not as yet been introduced to any of them myself. Marquis Caraccioli was for us already, and will do all his endeavours to put me in the way of being useful. Marquis de la Fayette, the bearer of this, truly deserves our esteem love and gratitude. I was with him 2. hours yester[day] and he is a going to set out to morrow for America, where I wish him safe with all my heart and soul. He is sensible and clever, lively smart and modest, and all together one of the most amiable characters I eve[r] saw. His attachment to us and our cause cannot be greater. We conversed cheafly in English, but whenever I mentioned a anecdote apt to reflect honour upon us, he repeated it to the company in French with a surprising joy. He took leave of the King three days past in his america[n] uniform, and in the afternoon being at the Duke of Choiseul in a numerous Company one

Mr. Ths. Walpole, grand nephew to the Minister of the same name, having expressed a surprize at it, and reflected on the neckedness of the Americans, he replied with the coolness of a Socrates, that we had various uniforms, which he described; owned that all the troops were not equally well dressed; and concluded by saying that those, who took Burgoyn[e]'s Army, were almost all necked. Marquis Caraccioli, who was present, says that while all the Company whe[re] a laughing, and Walpole confused and mortified, that wonderfu[l] young man preserved a most serious and surprisingly modest contenance. As I know personally that proud and insolent englishman I have warned the Marquis, with whom I dine 2 or 3 times a week, that if I should meet him in his house I will produce my contract with General Riedesel, as a proof that notwithstanding the war I have in a short time made such inprovements on my land as to render the living on it convenient to that German General and his family.

As a continuance of the intelligence contained in letter 5 I must inform you, that Rodney had really been forced by the weather into the Mediterraneum, but had time to return and go into Gibraltar before the arrival of Gaston; that the 2d. of February having prepared to sail, the Spaniards posted in different places made signals for the Spanish fleet in Cadix to go out, which was done by both Cordova and Gaston; that he must been sensible of the danger, as he stood at anchor till the 13th, when he took the opportunity of a night favourable to his views, and went off unseen; and that the spaniards are gone after him, but I am afraid to no porpose, as he can make the best of his way, having sent the transports, under convoy, to the Islands previous to his entering the streghts. It is supposed that 12. men of war in all are gone to the Islands, and that the other 9 are in their way back to England. Out of the 17 French, wich sailed from Brest the 2d. of Feby. with 6000. more troops, as mentioned in said letter 5, one returned having suffered by the weather; but will sail again with 12 more and 6000. more troops in a few days. Count d'Estaing is certainly to command the grand fleet in Europe, and they speak of sending more troops and more men of war to the Islands, or the Continent, in a few weeks. Mr. Girard is not yet arriv[ed] from Madrid; therefore I don't know wether Mr. Penet will come here, or go first to Nantes. In returning to Mr. D'Acosta the money he had paid me in part of my letter of credit I had in view my honour and the *decorum* of the state, which I hope will appear from my corrispondence with him inclosed in letter 6. I wish that my conduct may meet with your

approbation. I have known in this place that Mr. Bettoia is a bankrupt. The circumstance joined to what I said in letter 4th. relative
to my economical circumstances will I hope seriously engage you
to assist me with some remittances as soon as possible. If you could
send to Leghorn, or Genoa, a gargoe of the best tobacco under
french colours the consequences mig[ht] be exceedingly advantagious. I suppose, that you might ha[ve] the necessary papers for
that purpose from the french minister in Philadelphia. I am sure
that I could send you very good returns. I wish that you may not
have neglected sending the duplicates of my Commissions and
Instructions by Mr. Penet. I cant help being very uneasy about it;
and I am most respectfully Sir, Your Excellency's most hum[ble,]
and most Obedient servant, PHILIP MAZZEI

RC (NN). At head of text: "7 [i.e., dispatch No. 7]. 1st Copy."

From the Board of Trade

[*Williamsburg*] *3 Mch. 1780.* Submits for approval a requisition
from the Board of War for clothing for 60 volunteers of the S.G.R.
for the expedition to Carolina; 132 non-commissioned officers and privates, viz.: 126 hats, 50 uniform coats, 50 vests, 219 shirts, 219 pairs
of shoes, 264 overalls, 132 stocks, 132 knee garters.

Tr in Board of Trade Journal (Vi);
1 p.

It appears from TJ's Account Book
that he was absent from Williamsburg
from 20 Feb. to 14 Mch. 1780. On 4
Mch. Lt. Gov. John Page replied to the
present letter as follows: "The Board of
Council wish to leave the Board of Trade
to the free Exercise of their own Judgment, of their Office, and think them the
proper Judges of the Prices of the articles to be purchased by their Agent"
(Tr in Board of Trade Journal). S.G.R.:
State garrison regiment; see Board of
War to Charles Porterfield, 29 Mch.
1780, below.

From the Board of War

Williamsburg, 3 Mch. 1780. Capt. Weasy of the vessel from Bermuda awaits a final determination of his case which was submitted to
the executive some days ago. He seems to have been influenced by his
compassion for the American prisoners of war to come under a flag of
truce. It seems proper to allow him the privileges of trade hitherto
permitted to the Bermudans by acts of Congress and resolutions of the
state in return for his efforts. The Bermudans in general are well disposed to the American cause and it would be good policy to increase that
friendship with a moderate quantity of grain and, in return, procure
salt for the state. Receipts will be given for the prisoners delivered and
it is recommended that privateers and others of the same kind be exchanged. Signed by Innes and Lyne.

Tr in Board of War Letter Book (MiU-C); 2 p.

In TJ's absence John Page made the following reply, which was copied into the Board's Letter Book: "In Council March 4th. 1780. The Board approve of the Steps taken by the Board of War with respect to the prisoners brought in the Flag of Truce Captain Weasey from Bermuda. But are unanimously of opinion that a flag ought not to be permitted to carry any kind of merchandize not only as being contrary to the Law of nations but as tending in our situation to establish a precedent, which may be attended with mischievous consequences, and that therefore the Flag vessel from Bermuda should not be permitted to unlade or deliver out any of her Salt; but as it was brought here under the denomination of Ballast it should be actually returned in her as such." CAPT. WEASY: i.e., Vezey, see TJ to Board of Trade, 22 Mch. 1780 (second letter to the Board of that date).

To James Wood

SIR   Monticello Mar. 3. 1780.

A Doctr. John August Leonhard Kohly, chaplain to Brigadr. Specht's regiment complains that a considerable sum of money is due to him from a German Doctor Smith who he says is a tavern keeper on the road to Richmond. As he cannot maintain an action for it I have recommended to him to call on Smith personally as the most likely way to sustain his right, and have referred him to you for leave. He also prayed to be allowed to visit some Lutheran brethren citizens of this commonwealth, in Culpepper and Rockingham. My Answer to him was in these words, 'Your own good sense will suggest to you that the license to take this latter journey must be attended with some difficulties. Your visit is intended to persons not natives of our country, nor personally known to Colo. Wood or myself. Your profession will of course give you influence with them. Your discourses to them will be in a foreign language, and tho' held in public, will yet be, in effect, as if private. Your present situation would, primâ facie, bespeak your political sentiments to be different from ours. Should this be really the case, it will be in your power to do an injury. However, you may be able to remove these difficulties. I trust you will excuse my mentioning them with candor, as it will be impossible for you to remove objections unless they are made known to you: and I shall be pleased if, by removing them, you may put it in Colo. Wood's power to gratify you.' I think he wishes that this latter application not be made known to any person. This with some other passages of his letter induced me to suppose it possible he might be able to take away the force of the objections to the permission he asks. Of this you will be a judge when he shall call on you, which I suppose he will endeavor to do when you shall be alone. I am Sir with great esteem Your most obedt. servt.,   TH: JEFFERSON

RC (Lloyd W. Smith, Madison, N.J., 1946); text damaged by water stains. Addressee identified from internal evidence.

No correspondence between TJ and KOHLY has been located.

Executive Council to Board of Trade

Williamsburg, 4 Mch. 1780. If the accounts of Col. Legras and Maj. Linctot cannot be settled in the manner last proposed, they should be paid by bills of exchange drawn on Penet & Co. at Nantes. Signed by John Page.

Tr in Board of Trade Journal (Vi); 2 p. Printed in *Official Letters*, II, 105.

From the Board of Trade

[4 March 1780]

The Commissioners of Trade are sorry to be understood by the Honorable Board as intending to free themselves from any part of their duty by submitting the Requisitions of the Board of War for their determination; We conceive it our Duty to do So, as the Act establishing this Board runs thus

"The Duty of the said Board shall be to see to the procuring by importation or otherwise all Military Stores, Cloathing, accoutrements, utensils, materials and necessaries which shall be required by *the Governor with the advice of the Council*, for the publick use, or for the use of the Officers, Soldiers &c."

It appears from hence that all Requisitions to this Board should at least be approved by the Executive, if not directly made by them; and it was this that induced us to lay the requisitions of the Board of War before his Excellency in Council; for We could not legally comply with them untill approved; and this mode We have constantly observed ever since our establishment.

Tr in Board of Trade Journal (Vi).

Executive Council to Board of Trade

[*Williamsburg*] *4 Mch. 1780.* The reasonable expenses of Col. Legras and Maj. Linctot to the sixth of the present month will be paid by the public, and an account should be submitted to the auditors for settlement. Signed by John Page.

Tr in Board of Trade Journal (Vi); 1 p. Printed in *Official Letters*, II, 106.

Executive Council to Board of Trade

[*Williamsburg*] *4 Mch. 1780.* Upon reconsideration of the case of Col. Legras, he is to be furnished with 50 hhds. of tobacco in addition to the bills of exchange already delivered to him as part of his demand against the state; and 10 hhds. are to be furnished to Capt. Linctot as part of his demand. Copy attested by H. Randolph, Clerk of Council.

Tr in Board of Trade Journal (Vi); 1 p. Printed in *Official Letters*, II, 106.

From Philip Mazzei

SIR   Paris, marh 4 1780

From Rappannack, or york River, I wrote to Col. Maddison, that the season being so far advanced I had a mind not to wait untill I got to Italy to propose the exchange of goods on the terms expressed in my Instructions, and that least I should be taken, and of course be obliged to throw my papers over-board, I had inter-lined in some of my private old papers the cifer and the substance of the business intrusted to me (so as to give no suspicion) in order that I might (in Case I should make my escape) prepare things as far as possible by the time I should receive the duplicates of my commissions, so long time being past when I arrived at Nantes, and knowing that Mr. Smith had not come to Europe, my desire of purchasing the goods wanting for our army was very great. I proposed the bargain to many, several of whom declared it im-practicable for reasons, which appeared to me well founded. Four of them made each a calculation, and gave it me, of which the most advantagious for us is inclosed, the other 3 fixing the freight more or less higher, and the insurance at 60 ℈%. You will observe that I was not impowered to agree on such termes, and it was impossible for me to obtain any better. According to the inclosed plan the adventurer has about 26 ℈% profit for his trouble and the interest of his money; but he must run several risks, as the freight and insurance may be higher, and the sale of the tobacco lower; he cannot recover the total from the Insurerers in case of loss; the Insurers may breck; and the result of the profit is not extraordinary considering how small is the capital sum, which cannot be in-creased unless the Adventurer would have part of his effects in Virginia; and I even think that the supposed 300 hogsheads of tobacco could not go in a Vessel of 200 tuns. I am convinced that such a thing cannot be undertaken but by People, who would reduce the freight by sending valuable cargoes, and leave the greater part of their effects in our funds; which I think may be obtained in Italy sooner than in France. I am now about proposing a plan here to encourage the people of the several states of Italy to become adventurers. I have only mentioned it to Dr. Franklin, who approves of it, and has promised me his assistance in it.

In letter 6. the 8th of February I said that I had been obliged at last to ask relief from Tuscany, and the 12th. that I had found it in the place, and prepared for my journey to Paris. I shall now tell you how that came about. Mr. Mark Lynch Merchant in Nantes came to me with a bill I had drawn in Irland on Penet and Co., D'Acosta having refused to accept it. My noble creditor Mr. John Cotter of Corke had ordered that in case of not payment the bill should be returned without protest, or molestation. Mr. Cotter's Generous and delicate behaviour had probably prepared Mr. Lynch in my favour, and the sight of my situation compleated the business. His countenance expressed his sensibility at the bad usage I had met with in that Town, and in the most genteel manner offered me the assistance I was in so great need of on the security I had proposed to others. As he had not the whole sum at the time, he advanced me enough for my present exigencies, one of which was the recovering of my baggage, and took 10, or 12 days to collect the rest. During that time I made a point to frequent and study the man, because I had imagined that he could be of service to my friends and the state, and some people had described him to me as a man of a suspicious principles. I found in him intelligence, attention, and the utmost integrity. As I flatter myself, that you have frequently observed that I am not easily mistaken in judgeing of men, I dare to propose him to you as the only man *to my knowledge* in that place capable of doing you justice, and as such I shall recommend him to all my Virginian Friends, conscious that I serve them while I perform my duties of gratitude towards him. I hope that he will in time be your corrispondent for the affairs of the state, but will not descend to particulars on that head untill I have seen Mr. Penet. As I apprehend from certain people in Nantes every thing that is roguish and infamous, I send you the inclosed 2. letters, as an antidote to what could be written to the disadvantage of Mr. Lynch. Our Capn. Rt. Barron is acquainted with him. My letters must be put under cover to Mr. Lynch or Dr. Franklin. It is a matter of fact that a letter to me at Nantes from the Minister of Tuscany is disappeared; and that I have been robed of many here, and more there, cannot be doubted. I have the honour to be most respectfully, Sir, Your Excellency's most Humble and most Obedient Servant, PHILIP MAZZEI

RC (Vi). At head of text: "8 [i.e., dispatch No. 8]." Another MS, labeled "1st. Copy," is in Board of War Letter Book (MiU-C); discolored and worn. The "3d. Copy" is in NN. Enclosures not found.

From George Washington

SIR Head Quarters March 5th 1780

I had the honor to receive by last nights Post Your Excellencys favor of the 10th Ultmo. I am not certain I ever heard that Colo. Clarke had meditated an expedition against Detroit but I have thought it probable enough that he might turn his views that way. The reduction of this Post would be a matter very interesting from it's situation and consequent importance to the tranquility of the Western Country. I have long wished to effect it, but hitherto unhappily our force and means at the Westward have not appeared sufficient to authorise an attempt. These are now from the expiration of the enlistments of many of the Men stationed at Fort Pitt, more incompetent than they were, and I have no prospect of directing an Enterprise to be undertaken. Your Excellency will hen[ce] be able to determin on the measures bes[t] for Colo. Clarke to persue. I have thought the Icy season when the Enemy's Ships and other armed Vessels are confined in the Harbour would be the most eligible time to attempt the Post if the Preperations and Provisions necessary for such an opperation could be then ma[de] as the Garrison would not only be precl[u]ded from a retreat but if it were happily to be reduced, it would also involve the loss of the Vessels, an event of great moment.

I have the honor to be with the greatest respect & esteem Your Excellencys Most Obt Servant, G W

P.S. If the Expedition against Detroit is undertaken and I am advised of the time it may possibly be in my power to favor it in some degree by directing a movement of part of the Troops at Fort Pitt by way of diversion.

I beg leave to inform Your Excellency, that besides the Men in the Regiments and Corps of which You have had Returns There are 52 Non Commissioned Officers and privates belonging to the State in the partizan Corps commanded by Major Lee.

Dft (DLC: Washington Papers); in hand of George Augustine Washington; postscript in hand of R. H. Harrison.

From Samuel Huntington

Philadelphia, 6 Mch. 1780. Encloses a resolve of Congress of this day requesting the governors of Virginia and North and South Carolina "to use their utmost Exertions in filling up their Continental Battallions, and in the mean Time to raise a Body of Militia to supply the Places of the Battalions." Reinforcements for the southern army are urgently needed. TJ's dispatches of 9 Feb. have been received and laid before Congress.

RC (Vi); in a clerk's hand, signed by Huntington; endorsed. FC (DLC: PCC, No. 14). Enclosure (Vi): copy, attested by Charles Thomson, of resolution of Congress, 6 Mch.; printed in JCC, XVI, 234.

From the Board of Trade

[*Williamsburg, 13 Mch. 1780.* Minute in Board of Trade Journal (Vi): "Thomas Smith esq. having purchased three negroe men Slaves of the Escheated property in Hanover in compliance with our request Ordered that the Executive be informed thereof and that they be requested to instruct us into what department they choose to have them disposed of." Minutes also show that the cost of these slaves was £13,544. Letter not located.]

From Samuel Huntington

Philadelphia, 14 Mch. 1780. Circular letter to the state executives enclosing resolve of Congress recommending that Wednesday, 26 Apr., be set apart as a day of fasting, humiliation, and prayer.

FC (DLC: PCC, No. 14); 1 p. Enclosure (missing): Resolve of Congress, 11 Mch., printed JCC, XVI, 252-3.

From Maria Maxwell

Hampton Road [Va.], 15 Mch. 1780. Encloses a letter of introduction from Gen. Phillips, and requests that liberty be granted her husband, Lt. Maxwell of the Convention army, to come and meet her.

RC (DLC); 1 p. See entry for Phillips' letter, enclosed, 1 Mch. 1780.

From the Board of War, with Reply

Sir   War Office Wmsburg Mar. 16th. 1780.

Captain Minnis of General Mulenburgh's family, who belongs to the 1st. Virginia Continental Regiment, being destitute of active

employment, owing to the deficiency of the Virginia Line, has been called on to resume his command in his Regiment, and his company therein being extremely thin, he requests to be honored with the charge of a proportion of the recruits raised under the act concerning Officers Soldiers sailors and marines. We are inclined, with your Excellency's approbation, to indulge Captain Minnis (who is an enterprizing deserving Officer) in his request. There are about thirty of the Levies above mentioned at the Barracks in the Vicinity of this Town. The Captain Sollicits the appropriation of half that number to his company which he purposes immediately to march on to join General Woodfords Brigade. Should you approve of this measure we will give the necessary directions thereon. We have the honor to remain with respect &c.   JAS. INNES
                                                          JAS. BARRON

Williamsburg Mar. 17. 1780

I approve of the sending forward to join the Virginia forces under General Woodford all soldiers within the commonwealth enlisted under the act concerning Officers Soldiers Sailors and marines, and not already incorporated into the Virginia Line. But not being sufficiently informed of the State of the Several Regiments and companies in our Line, and supposing it possible that some of them may have greater need of supplies of men than Captain Minnis's company, I think it better that the appropriation should be made by General Woodford. I think it would be well that Captain Minnis take charge of as many of these levies as can be immediately put into motion, and march them to the Southward, which will probably place his application for them on a favorable ground with General Woodford.   TH: JEFFERSON

Tr in Board of War Letter Book (MiU-C). Another Tr, lacking TJ's reply, in War Office Letter Book (Vi).

From the Board of Trade, with Reply

[17 March 1780]

It appears from an Act of the last Session of Assembly that the Executive are empowered to make Sale of sundry State Vessells therein mentioned with this proviso that they shall have power also to retain for the State such of the said Vessels as can consistently with the Public Interest be employed in the Commercial concerns of this Commonwealth.

The Commissioners of Trade beg leave to inform His Excellency and the Honble Council that we are unable to procure a sufficient number of Craft to transport the Tobaccoes formerly engaged by the Executive to be delivered in York River to Mr. Defrancey in proper time and that the State must unavoidably incur an enormous expence by the delay of said Tobaccoes unless We can be assisted immediately with the Ship Dragon or Tartar.

March 18th 1780. In Council

The Ship Tartar is transferred to the Board of Trade.

TH: JEFFERSON

Tr in Board of Trade Journal (Vi). AN ACT OF THE LAST SESSION OF ASSEMBLY: "An Act to regulate the Navy of this commonwealth" (Hening, x, 217). See further, TJ to Board of Trade and Council Order respecting State Naval Vessels, both dated 25 Mch. 1780. Immediately on receiving approval of transfer of the Tartar, the Board of Trade

"appointed Capt. Will. Saunders Commander thereof," and directed the agent to furnish Captain Saunders with orders for receiving as much tobacco as the vessel would carry, together with such "Money and other Necessaries as are immediately essential for said Ship" (Board of Trade Journal, 18 Mch. 1780).

From Peter Penet

SIR   Nantes 17th. March 1780

I have the Honor to acquaint you with my arrival here. As I am to set off to Paris and Versailles immediately to have a Conference with the Ministry respecting the Plans and Operations I am intrusted with by your State &c. you will in a little time hear the good success of my Engagements with your Commonwealth.

I am with Gratitude & Respect Sir Your most obedient & very humble Servant,   J. P. PENET

RC (Vi). Addressed: "To His Excellency Ths. Jefferson Esqre Governor of Virginia." Endorsed by a clerk: "Peter Penets Letter recd Jany 81."

To the Board of Trade

GENTLEMEN   [18? March 1780]

Mr. Nathan having taken up Bills drawn on us to a considerable amount payable in N. Orleans, and having occasion for ten thousand Livres in France in part paiment, I am to desire you to furnish him with Bills of Exchange to that amount, carrying them to his debit; also that you will be pleased to take back the Bills you gave Colo. Legras on Penet & Co. He having received Satisfaction for them from Mr. Nathan to whom he delivered Clarke's and Todds on general draughts in exchange for Mr. Nathan's Bills.

Tr in Board of Trade Journal (Vi); received 18 Mch.

The BILLS OF EXCHANGE issued to Simon NATHAN, drawn on Penet & Co. for 10,000 livres, were the cause of a long-drawn-out controversy between Nathan and the Commonwealth of Virginia which extended at least through 1791. In the May 1783 session of the legislature, Nathan presented a petition for payment of his claim to the House of Delegates. The committee appointed to review the claim reported on 21 June (the documents on the case to this date are printed in the report); the House disapproved the recommendation of the committee that the claim be paid and ordered that the claim, "together with all papers and testimony relative thereto, be referred to any two gentlemen in the State of Maryland, . . . who shall have power to arbitrate and finally determine all disputes and controversies arising upon the said claim" (JHD, May 1783, 1828 edn., p. 15, 72-5, 81-2; see also TJ to George Rogers Clark, 19 Mch. 1780, and TJ to Edmund Randolph, 18 July 1783). In 1791 William Alexander, agent for the attorneys of Simon Nathan, again petitioned the governor for payment of the claim (CVSP, V, 259-60).

To the Board of Trade

[18? March 1780]

It is recommended to the Board of Trade to procure for Colo. Bufords Officers now under orders to march to Charles Town

50 yds. Cloth blue and white Cloth, 16 Suits Tremings, 40 Shirts with buttons, 30 ℔ of Thread Hose, 40 Handkerchiefs, 44 Summer Vests and Breeches.

Also for the Officers of Colo. Bland's Regiment 60 Shirts 45 Summer Vests and Breeches, 30 Handkerchiefs, 30 ℔ Thread Hose.

Also for the Officers of Colo. Parker's Regiment 60 Shirts 45 summer vests and Breeches, 30 Handkerchiefs, 30 ℔ thread Hose, Cambrick and Thread for the Shirts.

Tr in Board of Trade Journal (Vi); received 18 Mch.

Ambler and Rose immediately issued orders to the agent to procure "as soon as possible" the articles named in the requisition (Board of Trade Journal, 18 Mch.).

To George Rogers Clark

SIR   Williamsburg Mar. 19. 1780.

Since my last to you by Capt. Shannon informing you that draughts from yourself and Colo. Todd to the amount therein mentioned had been presented by Colo. Legras and Capt. Lintot, a Mr. Nathan merchant from the Havanna has presented us with others which he had taken up in New-Orleans to the amount of near 50,000 dollars. These two parcels added to those before presented from Mr. Pollock and being all demanded in hard money or commodities at their hard money price which is more than we are able to pay has demolished our credit at that port. In order therefore to re-establish it so far as may enable us to furnish necessaries for your troops, we are obliged to have a regular correspondence opened by our board of trade with some person at Orleans, to remit proper funds there, and that no draughts may go till provision is made for them to desire that you will always notify the articles of clothing and military stores you will want that the board of trade may have them provided either by remitting to you their bills on New Orleans, or sending them immediately to that place. Provisions we put out of the question as well as whatever else the country will furnish, meaning that they shall be purchased on the South side of the Ohio, where our money is current. In the mean time I must desire you to send us a list of all the bills you have drawn on us, specifying where they are drawn in dollars whether silver or paper dollars were intended, and if paper at what rate of depreciation they were estimated. The known price of commodities in hard money or peltry will serve as a standard for you to fix the rate of depreciation. I must put you on your guard not to confide too much in Shannon as he has proved here that it would be misplaced.

Many reasons have occurred lately for declining the expedition against Detroit. Want of men, want of money, scarcity of provisions, are of themselves sufficient, but there are others more cogent which cannot be trusted to a letter. We therefore wish you to decline that object, and consider the taking post on the Missisipi and chastising the hostile Indians as the business of this summer.

There is reason to apprehend insurrection among some discontented inhabitants (Tories) on our South-Western frontier. I would have you give assistance on the shortest warning to that quarter, should you be applied to by the militia officers, to whom I write on the subject. Nothing can produce so dangerous a diversion of our force, as a circumstance of that kind if not crushed in it's infancy.

The withdrawing the whole of your men from the Illinois country seems very expedient and necessary unless there be powerful reasons against it unknown to us. Colo. Todd I hope will get their militia into such training and subordination as that they will be in no danger from the Indians.

I am Sir with great respect Your most humble servt.,

TH: JEFFERSON

[317]

RC (Brit. Mus.: Add. MSS 21,835).
Endorsed: "1780 Intercepted Letter to
Colo. Rogers [sic], from Thos Gesserson
[sic], dated Williamsburg 19th. March."
On William SHANNON, one of Clark's
commissaries, see *George Rogers Clark
Papers, 1771-1781*, and *1781-1784, pas-*
sim. On MR. NATHAN, see TJ to Board of
Trade, 18 Mch. 1780. For a discussion
of the settlement of the claims for furnishing supplies to Clark, see Temple
Bodley, *George Rogers Clark*, Boston
and N.Y., 1926, ch. XXII.

To John? Harris

SIR   Wmsburg Mar. 19. 1780

The Patsy flag of truce fr[om] York having arrived at Hampton with cash, Stores and refreshments for the Officers of convention, and being to proceed as far up James river as her commanding Officer shall think proper, I am to request of you to take charge of her. You will apply to Capt. Wright for a guard of eight men under a commissioned Officer who will be subject to your directions. You will also withdraw her pilot from on board and if he be not a citizen deliver him to the care and superintendance of Captain Wright till the flag returns down the river. Another pilot of our own must of course be provided to carry her up and down the river, at the expence of the flag. Your Objects will be to see that no person from the Shore has any communication with those on board but on written permission from us; for which purpose principally the guard is furnished that there may be two centinals on constant Duty. Mrs. Maxwell her child and servants are permitted to leave the vessel or remain in her, to perform her journey by land or water as she pleases and when she pleases. Cap. Farquhar, Mr. Coffin and any other commissioned officer may go a Shore for air or exercise on such cautions as you think necessary. The crew will be governed in the same circumstance as you will. When the Officers who will be permitted to come from the Barracks to receive the Stores shall attend to that purpose, you will be pleased to be present at all their conferences. I have required of Cap. Farquhar that he receive yourself and guard on board his vessel. Nevertheless if it should be disagreeable to you and the purposes of your charge can be as effectually answered by your going on board another vessel, apply to Cap. Barron for one who is hereby authorised to furnish you with such one as may answer your purpose and may be best Spared, with necessary hands for navigating her. Still it seems best that your centinals should do duty on board the flag. Apply to the commissary at Hampton or Portsmouth for provisions and necessaries for yourself, guard and crew during your passage and stay on duty, they being hereby required to furnish you. I am to urge an immediate Departure from Hampton up the river and to effect this hope that all Officers from whom any necessaries may be required for your dispatch will furnish them without waiting for a particular order from me.

I am sir Your very humble servt.,   THO. JEFFERSON

Tr (Vi). Endorsed: "Copy Lre Cap. Harris. Mar. 19th. 1780."

The addressee may be tentatively identified as John Harris of Hampton, a captain in the Virginia navy from 1776; he had been captured in 1777 and was apparently exchanged in 1779 (W. D. Mc-Caw, "Captain John Harris of the Virginia Navy," VMHB, XXII [1914], 160-72). It is not known whether John Harris reentered service after his captivity, and there was at least one other Captain Harris in the Virginia navy, i.e., James Harris, whose record is obscure (Gwathmey, *Hist. Reg. of Virginians in the Rev.*, p. 352, q.v., also for John Harris).

From Philip Mazzei

[*Paris, 19 Mch. 1780*. Mazzei's "Representation . . . of His Conduct, from the Time of His Appointment to Be Agent of the State in Europe untill his Return to Virginia," written in 1784 and printed in Marraro, *Mazzei*, q.v., p. 86, states that in his 9th dispatch, of this date, he sent the Governor of Virginia a "narrative of Mr. Mazzei's captivity." No copy of the 9th dispatch has been located, though four copies were sent by different vessels (same, p. 11). The "Relation" of Mazzei's captivity thus transmitted does, however, survive and has been printed more than once, most accurately from the MS in NN (photostats in TJ Editorial Files) by Marraro, *Mazzei*, p. 65-84. The vessel in which Mazzei had sailed from Virginia for Nantes in June 1779, a brig named the *Johnston Smith* owned by Peter Penet, had been captured off the Virginia capes and was brought into New York, one of the vessels which captured her being owned by the notorious Goodriches. After various adventures, including the seizure of "5 of Mr. Jefferson's proposals to the Assembly relative to criminal laws, liberty of religion &c., which I had not thrown overboard, as I had a great desire to keep them, and did not think that they could be of prejudice to me," Mazzei contrived to sail in the Cork fleet in August, and from there he soon obtained passage in a Portuguese vessel for France.]

To John Todd

SIR   Williamsburg. Mar. 19. 1780.

Your letter from the falls of Ohio of Dec. 22. came safely to hand. You mention therein that you have not in a twelvemonth received any letters from hence. I know not what were written before the 1st. of June last, but since that time I have written several to you.

The expences attending the support of our troops in the Illinois have obliged us to call them all to the South side of the Ohio, where our paper money is current. Hard money is not to be had here, and we find the difficulty of sending commodities to New Orleans very great. The draughts from Yourself and Colo. Clarke on Pollock, those presented us by Le Gras and Lintot, others for about 50,000 dollars presented by a Mr. Nathan of the Havanna who took them up at New Orleans, being all claimed in hard money or commodities at the hard money price, have rendered us bankrupt there; for we have no means of paying them. Mr. Beauregard's bill for 30,000 dollars will be on a footing with these; we will accept it, promise paiment, and make it as soon as we shall be able. We have no bank in France nor any other foreign place. There being an absolute necessity to obtain from New Orleans supplies of clothing and military stores for Colo. Clarke's men, we shall endeavor that our board of trade shall send commodities there for that purpose. But to prevent the injury and disgrace of protested bills, we think that in future all bills must be drawn by them, in which case they will take care to make previous provision for their paiment. I am therefore to desire you hereafter to notify to us your wants which shall be provided for as far as we shall be able by bills from the board of trade sent to you or to New Orleans. Provisions and all other articles which our country affords will be purchased on the South side of the Ohio. I must beg the favor of you to send me a list of all the bills you have at any time drawn on us, specifying where they are drawn in dollars whether silver or paper dollars were intended, and if paper, at what rate of depreciation they were estimated. The known price of commodities in hard money or peltry will serve as a standard for you to fix the rate of depreciation. We chearfully exert ourselves to pay our debts as far as they are just but we are afraid of imposition, for which the rapid progress of depreciation has furnished easy means. Yourself alone and Colo. Clarke can guard us against this by timely and full information in what manner your several draughts ought in justice to be paid.

I am sorry you think of resigning your office in the Illinois. The withdrawing our troops thence will render the presence of a person of established authority more essential than ever. Your complaints concerning your allowance we think but too well grounded; and will lay them before the assembly in May, who we doubt not will remove them. The other objections I am in hopes you can get over. It would give us much concern should any necessity oblige you to leave that country at all and more especially so early as you speak of. I am Sir with great esteem Your most humble servt.,

Th: Jefferson

RC (Brit. Mus.: Add. MSS 21,835). Endorsed: "1780 Intercepted Letter to Coll. Todd, from Mr. Gessennon [*sic*], dated 19th. March Williamsburg." No doubt intercepted with TJ's letter of

same date to George Rogers Clark.

Todd's letter of 22 Dec. 1779 is missing. Only one earlier letter from TJ to Todd has been found, that of 28 Jan. 1780.

To George Washington

Sir   Williamsburg Mar. 19. 1780.

Since writing to your Excellency on the subject of the expedition against Detroit, the want of men, want of money and difficulty of procuring provisions, with some other reasons more cogent if possible and which cannot be confided to a letter, have obliged us to decline that object. I thought it therefore necessary to notify this to your Excellency that no expectations of our undertaking it may prevent any enterprize of that kind which you may have had in contemplation. That nest is too troublesome not to render the relinquishment of the attempt to destroy it very mortifying to us.

I have the honor to be with all possible esteem and respect Your Excellency's Most obedient humble servt.,   Th: Jefferson

RC (CSmH); endorsed.

It may be that the OTHER REASONS alluded to so mysteriously by TJ in this and in the letter to George Rogers Clark

of the same date included the deteriorating military situation to the southward of Virginia and the fear of invasion from that quarter or from the sea.

From Samuel Huntington

Philadelphia, 20 Mch. 1780. Circular letter to the state executives enclosing a resolve of Congress of 18 Mch. "calling upon the several States to bring in the Continental Currency by monthly taxes, or otherwise as shall best suit their respective Circumstances, . . . and making provision for other Bills to be issued in Lieu thereof." Requests that there be no delay in submitting this resolve to the Assembly, which should be convened if not now sitting in order to enact laws to carry out this measure. Encloses also a resolve of Congress of this day "recommending the revision of such Laws as may have been passed making the Continental Bills a Tender in Discharge of Debts &c."

FC (DLC: PCC, No. 14); 2 p. Enclosures missing; printed in JCC, XVI, 262-6, 269.

Congress' RESOLVE of 18 Mch. was the important and controversial "new plan

of finance": it called for the redemption of the old Continental currency at one-fortieth of its face value and an emission of new currency to be fully supported by specific taxes levied by the states. In effect a declaration of bankruptcy, it was a bold attempt to undercut speculators and make a fresh start on a sound footing. In Virginia the plan met with strong opposition, was first rejected, and then, under strong pressure from the more nationally minded Virginia leaders both in Congress and at home, was accepted by the Assembly on 12 July upon condition that a majority of the other states first adopt it. See Burnett, *Continental Congress*, p. 426-7; Hening, x, 241-54 (an Act for calling in and redeeming the money now in circulation, and for emitting and funding new bills of credit); JHD, May 1780, 1827 edn., p. 84 and *passim*; frequent references in TJ's correspondence in the following months; see especially letters to Madison, 26 July; to Huntington, 27 July; from Huntington, 4 Aug.; and from Charles Lee, 7 Aug. 1780.

To James Wood

Williamsburg 20 March 1780

This express brings some packets of letters for Generals Specht, Hamilton and Gall,[1] which came by the Patsy, flag of truce, just arrived from New York with money and stores for the Convention Troops. You will please send on the Express to the first two named gentlemen. The flag is to go up the James River as far as she can. When her arrival there shall be notified to you, you will be pleased to give permission to Mr. Geddes, Mr. Clark and Mr. Hoakerly to go the Flag and receive their several charges. A proper guard of horse you shall also be pleased to furnish to Mr. Geddes with to carry up the money. Let him name the day on which they shall attend at the flag. I think it will be well that Mr. Geddes himself should attend with the guard thro' the whole journey up. . . . The Continental Board of War having referred to us to give final orders on the subject of the Convention horses you will be pleased to obtain and send us a report of the officers who keep horses, and the number kept by each.

MS not located. Printed from extract in American Art Association, sale catalogue, 30 Nov. 1927 (Henry Goldsmith Sale), lot 2. Recipient's named assigned on the basis of internal evidence.

[1] Extract in sale catalogue erroneously reads "Sall."

Orders to the Board of Trade

[21 March 1780]

One hundred and ninety Dollars are allowed for the within Services (Monsr. Francois Bosserons) in hard Money, The payment of which the Board of Trade is desired to negotiate.

Orders to draw in favour of Mr. Nathan a Bill on Penet & Co.

for fifteen thousand Livres on Account of Major Lintot in part of his demand.

To deliver Mr. Nathan ten hogsheads Tobacco in part of his own debt.

Also a warrant to the Agent for £7125 Currency.

Another Warrant to ditto for 3345.17.3 Currency in part of his own debt allowing the difference of Exchange between Specie and Paper Money at present.

Also an Order to deliver to Mr. Nathan three setts of Exchange for twenty thousand Livres each in part of Colo. Legras's Bills.

The Board of Trade will be pleased to draw the Bills of Exchange and warrants abovementioned and direct the Agent to deliver the ten Hogsheads Tobacco to Mr. Nathan.

The Board of Trade will be pleased to direct their Agent to pay Mr. Dickson (his Account) and charge the Sum in Account to Colo. Legrass.

The Board of Trade will be pleased to direct their Agent to pay the above (Wm. Nicholson's Account) and charge the sum in Account to Colo. Legrass.   THO. JEFFERSON

Tr in Board of Trade Journal (Vi). The enclosures of the accounts of Bosseron, Dickson, and Nicholson, which evidently accompanied the above orders, have not been located.

For the accounts of Simon NATHAN, see TJ to Board of Trade, 18 Mch. 1780, first letter of that date. The Board of Trade on 21 Mch. also, at the direction of TJ, ordered the agent to discharge a bill of exchange drawn by Oliver Pollock "on the late Governor for three thousand five hundred Spanish Mill'd Dollars, which Bill is endorsed to, and this day presented by, Saml. Griffin Esqr. and accepted by His Excellency."

To the Board of Trade

March 21. 1780.

The Council having explicitly guarded against admitting purchases from the Public Store by Mr. Armistead and Mr. Day but "on the current purchase advance" in their original Agreement, and these Gentlemen being secured against Depreciation by receiving their Stipend in Tobacco at a fixed rate it is thought that no alteration should be made in the Original terms.

TH. JEFFERSON

Tr in Board of Trade Journal (Vi). The letter to which this is a reply has not been located. A minute preceding the letter in the Journal states: "The following was handed from the Executive in Answer to the Agent and Commissary's Letter." William ARMISTEAD was commissary of stores (Va. Council Jour., II, 40), and Benjamin DAY was state agent (same, p. 260; Hening, XII, 420). On the subject of the present letter, see TJ to Board of Trade, 4 Sep. 1779.

Board of War to Board of Trade

Williamsburg, 21 Mch. 1780. Recommendation of the purchase of a suit of colors from Jesse Taylor. Signed by Barron and Lyne. Countersigned: "Approved. Th: Jefferson."

Tr in Board of War Letter Book (MiU-C), 1 p.; printed in *Official Letters*, II, 109.

Board of War to Board of Trade

Williamsburg, 21 Mch. 1780. Mr. North has arrived with a valuable cargo. Order to purchase "all that part of the cargo that will be serviceable to the Troops"; also recommendation of purchase from Abraham Jones of 31 hats, 30 firkins of butter for the navy, "also a thousand weight of Rice." Countersigned: "Mar. 21st. 1780. Approved except as to the butter, which is supposed not to be included in the ration. Th: Jefferson."

Tr in Board of War Letter Book (MiU-C), 1 p.; another Tr in Board of Trade Journal (Vi); printed in *Official Letters*, II, 109.

The Board of Trade had already learned of North's cargo and had in fact, on the preceding day, ordered "that the Agent be directed to treat with Mr. North for such part of the Cargoe as may suit the State" (Board of Trade Journal, 20 Mch.).

From the Board of War

Williamsburg, 21 Mch. 1780. Agreement with Mr. Moody for himself and others for compensation for labor in the service of the state for five years. Signed by Innes and Barron. Countersigned: "Mar 23. 1780. The Executive agree to the Articles of contract proposed by the Board of War with Mr. Moody restraining the determination of the term to five years or the end of the war if it shall sooner happen; instead of board to himself and men, allowing him three rations and one forage, and his men one a piece; and explaining the price of goods taken by him from the public Store to be the Average price which they shall have cost the public. Signed, Th Jefferson."

FC (Vi), 2 p.; Tr in Board of War Letter Book (MiU-C), dated 20 Mch., 2 p. Printed in *Official Letters*, II, vi-vii. A transcript of an identical agreement with James Anderson, public armorer (See *Va. Council Jour.*, II, 459), 20 Mch., with the same authorization by TJ, is in Board of War Letter Book (MiU-C), 2 p.

MR. MOODY: He had a shop in Williamsburg that was burned by the British in Jan. 1781 (CVSP, I, 496); he is often mentioned as a supplier of military equipment and wagons, and may be the Philip Moody who accounted for "public negroes" in Dec. 1781 (same, II, 641).

To William Preston

I am sorry to hear that there are persons in your quarters so far discontented with the present government as to combine with it's enemies to destroy it. I trust they have no greivance but what we all feel in common, as being forced on us by those to whom they would now join themselves. Had any such grievances existed complaint and refusal of redress should have preceded violence. The measures they are now taking expose them to the pains of the law, to which it is our business to deliver them. We must therefore avoid any irregularity which might give them legal means of withdrawing themselves from punishment. I approve much of your most active endeavors to apprehend the guilty and put them into a course of trial. The carrying them out of the county before an examining court is had on them, if their safe custody requires it must be yeilded to: but if they can be kept safely without it, I should rather approve it. I suppose this may be done by strong guards of militia, which must be summoned, and subsisted and paid at the public expence. You seem to expect that writings may be found about them which will convict them of treason. Should your evidence however not be such as the law requires in cases of treason where the punishment is capital, perhaps it may be sufficient to convict them of a misprision of treason which is punishable by fine and imprisonment at the pleasure of the court. I suggest this to you that you may not suppose them absolutely cleared if the evidence will not support the charge of treason.

I think it necessary that you should take the most immediate measures for protecting the lead mines. For this I know none so likely to be effectual as your calling on a sufficient number of the newly recruited soldiers (no matter for what service engaged) from the counties round about, which you are hereby authorized to do, rendezvousing them at the lead mines and putting into their hands the arms taken from the malcontents. The commissary in that department will subsist them. Should you find it necessary a guard of militia must be called on in the mean time. Harrassing the militia however is what I would wish to avoid if possible. By the time these new recruits are wanted to join their corps I am in hopes the danger with you will be over.

Nothing which I have heard gives me reason to fear any disturbance in your quarter with the Indians. Colo. Clarke will be employed this summer in preserving peace with them. He will aid you if called on either in the case of invasion or insurrection. Should the Indians molest you, your militia must be embodied according to the invasion law, till Colo. Clarke can go to your assistance. I am Sir with great respect your most obedt. humble servt.,

TH: JEFFERSON

RC (WHi). Endorsed: "Governours Letter 21st. March 1780." Though the MS does not indicate the addressee, the letter is from the Preston Papers in the Draper Collection and has been hitherto assigned, no doubt correctly, to this recipient.

From the Board of Trade

[*Williamsburg*] 22 *Mch.* 1780. There is little prospect of procuring supplies absolutely necessary for the army in the state. It is proposed to send a trustworthy person, John Moss, to Philadelphia with tobacco notes in the amount of 300 hhds. to purchase supplies there. Signed by Ambler and Rose. Countersigned: "Mar. 22. 1780. Approved. Th: Jefferson."

RC (CSmH), 1 p.; Tr in Board of Trade Journal (Vi), printed in *Official Letters*, II, 112.

On the same day that the above letter was written and approved the Board of Trade ordered "that Mr. John Moss be requested to attend the Board on Saturday next to propose his terms if he will undertake the business" (Board of Trade Journal, above). There was evidently a subsequent letter from the Board of Trade to TJ, reporting the result of the conference with Moss, which has not been located (see TJ to Board of Trade, 25 Mch. 1780). On 1 Apr. the Board ordered that a letter of instructions be written to Moss and that another be sent to the Virginia delegates in Congress requesting them to aid him in his purchases for the state.

To the Board of Trade

Mar. 22. 1780.

The Executive will not interpose to favor such a commerce (referring to a proposal contained in a Letter from Mr. Thoroughgood Smith of Accomack Mar. 16. 1780 with respect to exchanging Corn for Salt with a Bermudian Vessel) with Individuals as is herein proposed; but as great Quantities of Salt are wanting for public use and an immense Quantity lately required by Congress the Board of Trade will please to consider whether it may be beneficial to purchase the within Salt, giving not more than two Bushels of Corn in exchange for one of Salt. THO. JEFFERSON

Tr in Board of Trade Journal (Vi). The letter has cross lines drawn through it and "countermanded" written below it. Before this was done, the Board of Trade had decided to purchase the salt and had directed a letter to be written to Thoroughgood Smith requesting him to contract with Captain Vezey "upon the most advantageous terms he can, to be paid for in Corn, at no rate exceeding two Bushels of Corn for one Bushel of Salt." This also had lines drawn through it;

the reason for the countermanding of the order appears to be that given in TJ's letter to the Board, following.

To the Board of Trade

[22 March 1780]

It occurs to the Executive that the Mr. Vezey at the Eastern shore with Salt is the Person who came to this State with a flag for the Exchange of Prisoners, who applyed for leave to sell some Salt which he had brought for Balast, and to whom it was refused by the Executive on Account of the Mischief of the Precedent permitting a flag to trade. It is therefore recommended to the Board of Trade to decline making any Proposition to him.

TH: JEFFERSON

Tr in Board of Trade Journal (Vi).
This entry has been crossed out in the Journal. See Board of War to TJ, 3 Mch. 1780.

To the Board of Trade

[22 March 1780]

The Board of Trade will be pleased to direct their Agent to State an account in his Books with Colo. Legras, Major Lintot and Mr. Anthy Gamilin, charging them therein with the Money Tobacco, or other things they have received from the State in part of their Demands, the same with Mr. Nathan.   TH JEFFERSON

Tr in Board of Trade Journal (Vi).

From the Board of War

War Office Wmsburg Mar. 22nd. 1780.

The Board of War wish to be informed by his Excellency whether the Henry Galley now at Hampton under repair and one side finished, shall be completed, and furnished for the protection of that post. As Vessells bound to Sea frequently make that their Harbour when wind bound and if not protected by a Galley or some other vessell of force they must, if chased up by the enemy, fall into their hands as the Situation of the Fort cannot Afford them any relief. There is a small Galley laying at back river, which is useless for the Service but if sold soon may fetch something. Cap. Barron is going down in a day or two and if approved by your Excellency, may give the necessary Orders.

JAS. INNES

JAS. BARRON

GEO. LYNE

Tr in Board of War Letter Book (MiU-C); Tr in War Office Letter Book (Vi).

Board of War to Board of Trade

Williamsburg, 22 Mch. 1780. Enclosing a charge to be paid to Col. Harrison for clothing furnished for his regiment. "The articles . . . appear to have been well bought, and we hope you will not think the Colo's. Zeal, which has led him to expend his own money, and risque his own interest, to promote the public weal, an improper one." Also requesting the purchase of clothes for Capt. Ragsdale in accordance with his order on the clothier. Signed (twice) by Innes, Barron, and Lyne. Countersigned: "In Council Mar. 25. 1780. Referred to the Board of trade to originate such resolution on as to them shall seem proper. Th: Jefferson."

RC (CSmH), 2 p.; the requisition for Col. Ragsdale is written below the first signatures and again signed; TJ's instruction is on verso. Addressed: "The Board of Trade"; docketed. Tr of portion concerning Harrison is in War Office Letter Book (Vi). Enclosed accounts not located.

Although the letter was written to the Board of Trade, TJ's instruction and the Board of Trade minute (below) indicate that it was first sent to TJ and transmitted by him to the Board of Trade. The following minute is entered in the Board of Trade Journal (Vi) under 25 Mch. 1780: "The Law requiring all requisitions for purchases to originate with the Executive, or at least have the approbation of that Board; the Commissioners of Trade therefore cannot, consistently with their duty, determine on Colo. Harrisons and Capt. Ragsdale's Cases, referred by His Excellency in Council to this Board." There is no record of further action on these cases.

From J. M. P. LeGras

MONSIEUR   Ouilliambourque Le 22e. Mars 1780

L'équité avec Laquelle votre honnorable assemblée Rend Justice aux fideles Sujets des Etats m'enhardit a vous Réprésenter le tord que les papiers dont Mr. Simon Nathan Est Chargé, Vá nous faire Si votre Bonté n'en ordonne le payement; les Domicilliers de st Vincenne Et pays des Ilinois ignorant l'ordonnance du Congrés ont Vendû Leurs Darées [denrées] a L'armée de Mr. le Colonel Clark et ont Reçûe En payement Des piastres du Continant Sur le pied et pour la Valeur Des piastres Espagnoles, les personnes En place (par vos ordres), les ont faites Circuler Comme telles et nous ont assurés authentiquement qu'il ny avoit Rien a perdre ils en ont même fait passer des fausses; En qualité de Magistrat pour ce District, Mon Devoir Et La Charité m'oblige a vous Supplier de vouloir Bien avoir pitié D'un peuple qui par pareille perte Se trouvera Réduit aux Necessités les plus Urgentes; D'ailleurs il a Eté Battû un Bân Dans les Rües de st Vincennes par ordre du Colonel Jean Tood pour Contraindre Les Domiciliers a Recevoir cet argent Comme piastres Espagnoles; et plusieurs ont Eté mis En prison pour les avoir Refusés; quelque tems aprés le Susdt. Colonel Jean Tood ma Requis (Comme il apparoitra par Sa Lettre) d'en arretter la Cour; Vu la quantités des fausses ordonnances que plusieurs faisoint Circuler Ce que J'ai fait; Esperant Bien que les Etats DéDommageroit le public Des fausses et de Celle de Mauvaise Datte; J'ai L'honneur d'etre Tres Respectueusement Monsieur Votre tres humble Et tres obeissant Serviteur,   LEGRAS Colo.

RC (Vi). Translation in Chicago Hist. Soc., *Colls.*, IV, 328-9.

LeGras (variously spelled) was a merchant of Vincennes who held a com-

mission under G. R. Clark. See *George Rogers Clark Papers, 1771-1781*, and *Ill. Hist. Colls.*, V.

From Duncan Rose

Williamsburg, 22 Mch. 1780. During the severe winter weather when there was a pressing demand for spirits and when an invasion was hourly expected, Rose made a contract with De Francy for rum, salt, and rice, all of which were badly needed for the army, and a portion of the supplies thus procured have been used for the troops. The Board of Trade refuses to take notice of the transaction without instructions from the executive. Countersigned: "In Council Mar. 25. 1780. It is recommended to the board of trade to carry into execution the preceding contract. Th: Jefferson."

RC (Vi); 3 p. Printed in *Official Letters*, II, 114.

On 25 Mch. the Board of Trade ordered the contract between Rose and DeFrancy to be executed in accordance with the following terms of exchange

(Board of Trade Journal):
"100.℔ Tobo. for every Bushel salt.
150 ℔ Do. for every hundred weight
     of rice
100.℔ do. 2½ Galls. french rum
100 ℔. do. for 1½ Galls. Jamaica rum."

To ――― ―――

SIR   Williamsburg Mar. 22. 1780.

I have laid before the Council Mr. Griffin's letter recommending the annexation of the cavalry of this state proceeding to the Southward to the regiment you are to command. But as our act of assembly has made them an independant corps we think we have no power to consolidate them with any other. Considering however the right of command which will result to yourself as a superior officer whenever you act with Majr. Nelson, we are in hopes all the substantial advantages of such an annexation will arise to the public.

I am sorry that the business of removing our servants furniture &c. to our new seat of government, in which we are now engaged puts it out of my power to have the pleasure of entertaining you at the palace[, a] respect I was desirous of paying as well to your merit as to Mr. Griffin's letter. Should you pass on any occasion through the place of our future residence, I must be permitted to ask that favor of you.

I am Sir with great respect, your most obedt. servt.,

TH: JEFFERSON

RC (Lloyd W. Smith, Madison, N.J., 1946).

MR. GRIFFIN'S LETTER: Doubtless a letter from Cyrus Griffin, a Virginia delegate in Congress; it has not been found, and the Continental officer to whom the present letter was addressed has not been identified. REMOVING . . . TO OUR NEW SEAT OF GOVERNMENT: See Notice of Removal of Executive Office, 25 Mch. 1780, below.

From the Board of War, with Reply

SIR   War Office Wmsburg Mar. 23rd. 1780.

The Quarter Master General informs us, that for want of proper Offices and Store houses, The State not only incurs a considerable expence for rents but that the public property from the impossibility of procuring proper accommodations for Storage suffers very great detriment. We take liberty to recommend that your Excellency would direct such houses on the lot purchased by the Executive of Mr. Hornsby, as are suitable to the Quarter Masters purpose to be appropriated to his use.

We have the honor to be your most Obt. Servants,

JAS: INNES
JAS: BARRON
GEO: LYNE

In Council Mar. 25th. 1780.

The Western room below Stairs and passage in the dwelling house and the Grainery are assigned to the Quarter Master, and

after the Eighth Day of April the Coach house is likewise assigned
to his use.   TH: JEFFERSON

Tr in Board of War Letter Book (MiU-C); another Tr in War Office Letter Book
(Vi).

To the Board of Trade, with Reply

[25 March 1780]

The Act of Assembly having directed a Sale of the Ships Tartar
and Dragon, the Gallies Henry, Manly, Hero, Page, Lewis and
Safeguard, except such of them as may consistently with the public
Interest be employed in the commercial Concerns of this Commonwealth, it is recommended to the Board of Trade to declare which
of the said Vessels they are of Opinion should be retained under
that exception.   TH JEFFERSON

[*Reply follows:*]

The Ships Tartar and Dragon if immediately put under our
direction will be a means of saving several thousand Pounds to the
State in the freight of the Tobaccoes which The Executive engaged
to deliver to Mr. Defrancy in York River.

In Council Mar. 25. 1780

The Ships Tartar and Dragon are transferred to the Board of
Trade.   TH JEFFERSON

Tr in Board of Trade Journal (Vi).
See Board of Trade to TJ, 17 Mch. 1780.

Council Order respecting State Naval Vessels

In Council Mar. 25th. 1780.

The act of Assembly for regulating the Navy of this Commonwealth having directed the executive to sell for ready money at
public vendue the Ships Tartar and Dragon the Gallies Henry,
Manly, Hero, Page, Lewis and Safe Guard retaining such only of
them as may be requisite for the purposes of the state, and such
of the guns and other materials of those which shall be sold as they
should judge usefull and for the Advantage of the commonwealth,
the board is of opinion that the Ships Tartar and Dragon be retained for the commercial purposes of the State, and transferred
to the Board of Trade; and that the others of the said vessels be

sold by the board of War as directed by the said act, the said board of war retaining such guns and other materials of the vessells so to be sold as they shall think usefull to be kept. They are of opinion however that the sale of the Henry Galley may be postponed til they may State the matter to the Assembly, and take their sense whether she may be retained for the defence of Hampton, and in the meantime that her repairs be completed. TH: JEFFERSON

Tr in Board of War Letter Book (MiU-C).
See TJ to Board of Trade, 17 and 25 Mch. 1780.

To the Board of Trade

[25 March 1780]

The Board approves of the allowance to Mr. Moss of thirty five hundred Pounds for his trouble and expences.

TH JEFFERSON

Tr in Board of Trade Journal (Vi). See Board of Trade to TJ, 22 Mch. 1780.

From the Board of Trade, with Reply

SIR   Board of Trade March 25th. 1780

Your Excellency's letter of the 23d. was this day laid before the Board; there is a Vessel now at the Capitol Landing which we shall have detained till the 7th of next month, in order to take in those Articles directed to be removed to Richmond; unless it should be thought better to order her round to the College Landing to receive them: The other instructions contained in the Letter shall be duly attended to. We wish to know the opinion of the Honble. Board with respect to the removal of the Agent and Commissary of Stores; if the Board of Trade should be continued, it will be very inconvenient to be so far distant from those officers.

We are Your Excellency's Most Obed. Servants, J. AMBLER
DUN: ROSE

In Council Mar. 25. 1780.

It is thought adviseable that the vessel come round to the College landing immediately. The board of trade can best judge at what place it will be most convenient for their Agent and Commissary of stores to reside. To them therefore this board refers it.

TH: JEFFERSON

RC (Vi). Addressed: "His Excellency in Council." TJ's reply is written at bottom of page. FC (CSmH). Tr of TJ's reply in Board of Trade Journal (Vi). TJ's LETTER OF THE 23D has not been located.

From the Board of War, with Reply

Williamsburg, 25 Mch. 1780. Before issuing orders for the privateersmen at King William Courthouse to be delivered to the flag from New York, the Board wish instructions concerning the British prisoners of war. Signed by Innes and Lyne. Reply follows: "In Council Mar. 25th. 1780. The Board are [of] opinion that all the prisoners of War belonging to this State (excepting only Governor Hamilton, Major Hay and those who are now returned by the Mary Anne Flag in exchange for prisoners received) be given up to Congress and ordered as desired in their resolutions. This transfer to Congress is meant to include Governor Rocheblave now in this City. Th: Jefferson."

Tr in Board of War Letter Book (MiU-C).
ROCHEBLAVE: Phillippe de Rastel de Rocheblave, an influential resident of Kaskaskia who threw in his lot with the British and was commandant at that post (under the style of "lieutenant governor") when it was captured by Clark in 1778; he escaped from Virginia in April 1780. See Rocheblave to Haldimand, New York, 9 Sep. 1780, for some account of his adventures (*Ill. Hist. Colls.*, v, 173-80); also TJ to Washington, 26 Sep. 1780, and *George Rogers Clark Papers, 1771-1781*, p. lxii-lxiv, 203.

From the Board of War

SIR   War Office WmsBurg March 25. 1780

We return your Excellency the Letters from Governour Rutledge which you did us the honor to send for our Perusal. No exertion of ours has been wanting to accelerate the march of the Detachment of Troops intended for Charles Town. But we must take Liberty to assure your Excellency that unless the Board of Trade receive your peremptory Orders to comply with the Schedule of Necessaries furnished that Board by our [. . .].

Tr in War Office Letter Book (Vi); fragment. Enclosures not found.

Notice of Removal of Executive Office from Williamsburg to Richmond

[25 March 1780]

Notice is hereby given, that the business of government, in the executive department, will cease to be transacted at *Williamsburg* from the 7th of *April* next, and will commence at *Richmond* on the 24th of the same month. The Governour will be in *Richmond* during the interval, to do such business as may be done by him, without the concurrence of the publick boards. ARCH: BLAIR, C.C.

Printed from *Virginia Gazette* (Dixon & Nicolson), 25 Mch. 1780.

The following note summarizes information available on TJ's removal as governor from Williamsburg to Richmond. His last communication "In Council" in Williamsburg is dated 7 Apr. 1780; on 4 Apr. he had written to Mazzei: "The seat of government is removed from this place to Richmond. I take my final departure hence within four or five days." The following entries in his Account Book for 1780 tell something of his movements: "[Mar.] 28. pd. ferrge. at Cowles 48/. . . . Mar. 29. pd. ferrge. at Richmond £3-12. . . . [Mar.] 30. gave servt at Ampthill 30/ gave workmen at Foundery £10-10. . . . Apr. 2. pd. ferrge. at Cowle's 48/. . . . [Apr.] 3. pd. household expences by Mrs. Jefferson in my absence £30-12. . . . [Apr.] 9. pd. ferrge. at Cowle's £10-4. . . . [Apr.] 14. pd. household expences at Richmd. £20-8." Cowle's [Cole's] ferry, on the Chickahominy River, was on the route between Williamsburg and Richmond (Christopher Colles, *Survey of the Roads of the U.S.*, N.Y., 1789, pl. 78). The difference in the amounts TJ paid in ferriage on 2 Apr. (48s.) and on 9 Apr. (£10-4) suggests that on the second trip he was accompanied by the members of his household or that the amount included ferriage for baggage.

Among TJ's papers (DLC: TJ Papers, 7: 1196, 1198) there are duplicate, undated inventories of household goods that were doubtless made at this time or a little earlier. Both are in unidentified hands. The first has the caption "List of Packadges sent from the Palace"; and the second "Invoice of Goods sent from the palace." The lists enumerate forty-nine boxes of furniture, books, pictures, lamps, and other household equipment. Though not identical in form, the lists include the same items. The recollections of Isaac Jefferson (one of TJ's household slaves), as dictated to Charles Campbell (MS in ViU), contain the following account of the Governor's removal: "It was cold weather when they moved up. Mr. Jefferson lived in a wooden house near where the Palace (Governor's house) stands now. Richmond was a small place then: not more than two brick houses in the town. . . . It was a wooden house shedded round like a barn on the hill, where the Assembly-men used to meet, near where the Capitol stands now. Old Mr. Wiley had a saddler-shop in the same house." For TJ's residence in Richmond, rented from his uncle, Thomas Turpin, see Turpin to TJ, 22 Dec. 1780, with reply, and references there. His first communication "in Council at Richmond" is dated 11 May (Agreement with DeFrancy).

From George Washington

Morristown, 26 Mch. 1780. Calls attention to resolve of Congress of 25 Feb. 1780 assigning state quotas of supplies for the army and directing them to be deposited at places designated by the Commander in Chief. The quotas and places of deposit for Virginia are listed as follows:

Places	Bbls. Flour	Gals. Rum	Tons Hay	Bu. Corn
Alexandria		40,000	80	40,000
Fredericksburg	300	30,000	100	40,000
Richmond	100		70	20,000
Petersburg	878	30,000	150	100,000
	1,278	100,000	400	200,000

As to beef and salt, the time and place of delivery and also the proportions must be governed by the occasional requisitions of the Commissary General.

Dft of circular letter to the state executives, 3 p., in hand of R. H. Harrison; Dft of table of quotas for all states, 4 p. (DLC: Washington Papers). Text of letter, but not of table of quotas, is printed in Washington, *Writings*, ed. Fitzpatrick, XVIII, 159-60.

See Huntington to TJ, 26 Feb. 1780, enclosing resolve of Congress of 25 Feb.

From James Madison

DEAR SIR   Philadelphia March 27th. 1780

Nothing under the title of news has occurred since I wrote last week by express except that the Enemy on the 1st. of March remained in the neighbourhood of Charlestown in the same posture as when the preceding account came away. From the best intelligence from that quarter there seems to be great encouragement to hope that Clinton's operations will be again frustrated. Our great apprehensions at present flow from a very different quarter. Among the various conjunctures of alarm and distress which have arisen in the course of the revolution, it is with pain I affirm to you Sir, that no one can be singled out more truly critical than the present. Our army threatened with an immediate alternative of disbanding or living on free quarter; the public Treasury empty; public credit exhausted, nay the private credit of purchasing Agents employed, I am told, as far as it will bear, Congress complaining of the extortion of the people; the people of the improvidence of Congress, and the army of both; our affairs requiring the most mature and systematic measures, and the urgency of occasions admitting only of temporizing expedients and those expedients generating new difficulties. Congress from a defect of adequate Statesmen more likely to fall into wrong measures and of less weight to enforce right ones,[1] recommending plans to the several states for execution and the states separately rejudging the expediency of such plans, whereby the same distrust of concurrent exertions that has damped the ardor of patriotic individuals, must produce the same effect among the States themselves. An old system of finance discarded as incompetent to our necessities, an untried and precarious one substituted and a total stagnation in prospect between the end of the former and the operation of the latter: These are the outlines of the true picture of our public situation. I leave it to your own imagination to fill them up. Believe me Sir as things now stand, if the States do not vigorously proceed in collecting the old money and establishing funds for the credit of the new, that we are undone; and let them be ever so expeditious in doing this, still the intermediate distress to our army and hindrance to public affairs are a subject of melancholy reflection. Gen. Washington writes that a failure of bread has already commenced in the army, and that for any thing he sees, it must unavoidably increase. Meat they have only for a short season and as the whole dependance is on provisions now to be procured, without a shilling for the purpose, and without credit for a shilling, I look forward with the most pungent apprehensions. It will be attempted I believe to purchase a few supplies with loan office certificates; but whether they will be received is perhaps far from being certain; and if received will certainly be a most expensive and ruinous expedient. It is not without some reluctance I trust this information to a conveyance by post, but I know of no better at present, and I conceive it to be absolutely necessary to be known to those who are most able and zealous to contribute to the public relief.

March 28.

Authentic information is now received that the Enemy on their passage to Georgia lost all their Horse, the Defiance of 64 guns which foundered at sea, three transports with troops, although it is pretended these troops and the men of the Defiance were saved, and 1 transport with Hessians of which nothing has been heard. By a letter from Mr. Adams dated Corunna 16 December there seems little probability that Britain is yet in a humour for peace. The Russian ambassador at that Court has been lately changed, and the new one on his way to London made some stop at Paris whence a rumor has spread in Europe that Russia was about to employ her mediation for peace. Should there be any reality in it, Mr. Adams says it is the opinion of the most intelligent he had conversed with that the independance of the United[2] would be insisted on as a preliminary: to which G. B. would accede with much greater repugnance than the cession of Gibraltar which Spain was determined to make a sine qua non. With respect and regard I am Dr Sir. Yrs sincerely,   JAMES MADISON JR

RC (DLC: Madison Papers). Endorsed by TJ: "Madison Jas. Mar. 27. 1780." The word "Extract" appears at head of text, and square brackets and quotation marks have been placed around the main body of the letter, excluding the part added by Madison 28 Mch. These markings are the work of Henry D. Gilpin, who edited The Papers of James Madison, 1840, and who took other liberties beyond selecting extracts from the originals, for he occasionally silently suppressed words and phrases within the extracts he selected; an instance in the present letter is pointed out in note 1, below. Unfortunately, Gaillard Hunt, whose edition of *The Writings of James Madison* appeared in 1900-1910, followed Gilpin's printed texts rather than the MS originals, for the collection of Madison Papers listed as Accession 1081 did not come to the Library of Congress until 1910. Burnett, who points out the facts here restated (*Letters of Members*, v, No. 118), prints much more faithful texts of Madison's letters than Gilpin or Hunt, but he in turn, for legitimate and stated reasons, omits matter found in the originals. Hence some matter in Madison's letters to TJ, nearly all of which were re-turned to Madison after TJ's death (see Madison to Nicholas Trist, 26 Jan. 1828; Madison, *Writings*, ed. Hunt, IX, 301) has never hitherto been printed.

This is the earliest letter so far found in a correspondence that was to continue uninterruptedly for forty-six years and that documents the most important collaboration between two great statesmen in American history. See Adrienne Koch, *Jefferson and Madison: The Great Collaboration*, N.Y., 1950.

1 The phrase from "from a defect of adequate Statesmen" through "right ones" was omitted by Gilpin (and by Hunt following Gilpin).
2 Thus in MS.

From Duncan Rose

[*Williamsburg, before 28 Mch. 1780.* Minute in Board of Trade Journal (Vi), under 30 Mch. 1780: "A Letter laid before the Board from D. Rose Esqr. to His Excellency the Governor acquainting him that he had contracted with Saml. Beale Esqr. for twenty one pieces of Ozenbrigs at the rate of twenty pounds Tobacco ℔ yd." Not located.]

To the Board of Trade

Williamsburg 28. Mar. 1780.

The Expence to this State in particular which is occasioned by every day's detention of these troops, and the Danger impending over Charles Town renders it expedient for the public Good to approve of the above contract however exorbitant the price. I do therefore approve of it.   TH. JEFFERSON

Tr in Board of Trade Journal (Vi), subjoined to minute concerning Duncan Rose's communication to TJ, preceding. Immediately following this Tr there is an order directing the agent to pay Samuel Beale "agreeable to the Instructions" from TJ.

Board of War to Charles Porterfield

Williamsburg, 29 Mch. 1780. Appointment to command the detachment of Virginia troops, consisting of "volunteers of the State Garrison Regiment, The greater part of Marshalls Corps of Artillery and two Troops of Nelsons horse," to be under Porterfield's "absolute controul and Command" and to be prepared "to march on the Shortest notice" to

Charleston, S.C.; also instructions for procedure. Signed by Innes and Lyne. Countersigned: "In Council Apl. 6th. 1780. Approved. Th: Jefferson."

Tr in Board of War Letter Book (MiU-C); 2 p.
See Estimate of Troops for South Carolina, following.

Estimate of Troops for South Carolina

[ca. 29 March 1780]

	for the war	till Sep. 30 1780.	terms not specifd	Total	exp. befr. Sep. 30. 80.
Detachmt. from the State garrison regimt. under Colo. Porterfeild.	46.	39.		85.	1
Detachmt. from Artillery regiment under Majr. Matthews	30	104		134	176
1st. troop of Cavalry under Capt. Fear	26	3		29	2
2d. do. Majr. Nelson	16.	17.		33	
				281	

N (DLC), in TJ's hand, written below a memorandum from the Board of War; see below.

Immediately above TJ's calculations appears this memorandum: "Ordered to the Southw[ard]. From Marshalls Regmt. —350 R. From Muiters—100. 2 Troop of Horse 64 [Total] 514. Officers proportionate to the above numbers." Signed by Innes, Barron, and Lyne. The paper obviously refers to the expedition to which Col. Porterfield was commissioned (see the preceding document) and has therefore been assigned to this date. In DLC: TJ Papers, 5: 718, is a more extended and detailed "Return of the Southern Detachment April 6th. 1780," signed by Charles Porterfield, and giving the total rank and file as 427.

From Riedesel

New York, 30 Mch. 1780. Cannot "refrain from once more addressing Your Excellency, and repeating my invariable Esteem for you, your Lady, and amiable Family, also testifying the lively rememberance I, and all mine have of your many Civilities and particular politeness to us." Announces "the happy recovery of Madame de Riedesel after having presented me a fourth Daughter, near three Weeks ago .... we both beg leave to reiterate our assurances that it will ever give us much pleasure, not meerly from gratitude but our real personal attachment, to hear of your and Mrs: Jeffersons uninterrupted Happiness." Asks conveyance to Charlottesville for enclosed letters to Gen. Specht.

RC (DLC); in a clerk's hand, signed by Riedesel, 2 p. Enclosures not further identified.

To Francis Taylor

SIR   Richmond Mar. 31. [1780]

As to the examination of the German letters I know no better method than what Colo. Bland took, which was to get a discreet German officer of the Conventioners to examine them on parole. The answers they shall return by the flag should be examined in the same way. The English letters which come or go by her you will be so good as to examine and indorse. I shall not be living at this place till the 12th of April so dispatches from you will be addressed accordingly.

I am Sir with great esteem Your most humble servt.,

TH: JEFFERSON

RC (Lloyd W. Smith, Madison, N.J., 1946). Addressed: "Colo. Taylor Charlottesville." Endorsed: "Govr. Jefferson 31st. Mar. 1780."

Notes on Council Proceedings

[March 1780?]

What station of vessel during stay? Cherryton's.

What relief shall be furnished and how? Let him state his wants.

What rules of intercourse with natives? Leave it on footing of my letter on officers.

What guard? The boat to continue.

Who correspond with them as Commissary of prisoners? Recommended to Colo. Innes to get Porterfeild to act pro hac vice— Capt. Barron.

What done with letters to Maryland and No. Carolina? Send by post or any earlier conveyance with copy of [Stalker's?] letter.

Shall any thing be done to So. Carolina? Write by Savarit to Govr. of So. Carolina.

What notice be taken of the Captain's not giving earlier notice? Desire him to assign his reasons for it.

Shall Robins's receipt of prisoners be admitted? Shall not; but we will account for any which may hereafter appear.

Shall delay be affected and by what means? It will be proper.

What shall be said to [Colo. Ro]bbins for not communicating? Desire him to say why he has permitted it, and whether there has been intercourse?

What shall be done with letter to Commissary of prisoners N. York? Send it to Gl. Washington to be communicated by flag, and write the latter that we do not chuse to admit flags to come on small occasions and they must send answer through [. . . .] Desire from board of war copy of their receipt for prisoners.

N (DLC); entirely in TJ's hand; without date or caption.

These notes, apparently recording decisions and deliberations in council, must have been written between Aug. 1779 and Mch. 1780, for in the former month Charles Porterfield became colonel of a state regiment (Gwathmey, *Hist. Reg. of Virginians in the Revolution*), and early in Apr. 1780 he marched south in command of a detachment of Virginia troops (see Board of War to Porterfield, 29 Mch. 1780, above). They may refer to the arrival of the flag about the middle of Mch. (see TJ to John? Harris, 19 Mch. 1780).

From William Preston

Montgomery County [*Va.*], *Mch. 1780.* Has received circumstantial information that "a Number of Men dissafected to the present Government had combined to disturb the Peace of this unhappy Frontier as soon as the Season would Permit and the british Troops could gain any Footing in So. Carolina." There are now fifteen British commissions in this county and that of Washington. Nor is this the first information of the kind that has been received. Has sent out a party "to Sieze three of the Ringleaders and bring them well tied before Justice to be dealt with as the Law directs," and plans to post a guard at the lead mines, which are a principal object of the tories. There will be difficulty in securing witnesses and evidence against the conspirators. Desires advice on this point and on further measures for frontier defense.

Dft (WHi); 2 p. Signed with initials and endorsed "Lr. to the Govr. Mar 1780." Printed in Wis. Hist. Soc., *Colls.*, XXIV, 143-4.

See further, Preston's undated memorandum on this conspiracy (same, p. 144-5).

From John Hay, with Jefferson's Instructions

Richmond, 1 Apr. 1780. In consequence of executive's request in reply to Hay's previous application to borrow 500 lbs. of powder from the state, John Fisher has been sent to Williamsburg for a final answer. The powder is wanted for an "armed vessel now lying at four Mile Creek"; she will sail in about eight days. Powder will be replaced in a reasonable time. Signed by John Hay. Countersigned: "In Council Wmsburg Apl. 1780. Deliver to Mr. John Fisher for use of Mr. Jno. Hay 500℔ powder, taking his Note for the repaiment thereof. Th: Jefferson."

RC (Vi). Addressed: "His Excellency Thomas Jefferson Esqr. Williamsburg. favd. by Mr. Fisher." Instructions, in a clerk's hand and signed by TJ, written below the letter; addressed by the clerk: "To Captn. Maupin." This address has been crossed out and corrected by TJ: "To the Keeper of the magazine (at Richmond)." Printed in *Official Letters*, II, 116.

From Samuel Huntington

Philadelphia, 4 Apr. 1780. Encloses a resolve of Congress of 27 Mch., "by which you will be informed that the Recommendation of Congress of the 17th of August 1779 in their Opinion makes Provision for the Case of the Widow and Children of the late Lieut. Colo. John Sayer [Sayres, Seayer, Seayres]." Also a resolve of 30 Mch. requesting the State of Virginia to supply provisions for the Convention troops, such supplies to be credited to the quota assigned by Congress' resolution of 25 Feb. 1780.

RC (Vi); 2 p.; in a clerk's hand, signed by Huntington. FC (DLC: PCC, No. 14). Enclosures (Vi): Resolves of 27 and 30 Mch., printed in JCC, XVI, 290, 318.

To Philip Mazzei

DEAR SIR   Williamsburg Apr. 4. 1780.

The Fier Rodrique being to sail within about three weeks, I think it a safe opportunity of writing to you, and of sending you according to your desire the two bundles of papers indorsed 'fogli da estrarne principj di governo libero' &c. and 'pamphlets, newspapers, fogli stampati,' which with this letter will be addressed to the care of Penet & co. of Nantz. I have heard nothing certain of you since your departure except by letter from Genl. Phillips in N. York that you had been taken, carried into that place, and permitted to take your passage for England. All the progress has been made in complying with your memorandums which my situation would admit. Some of your accounts (of the smaller kind) have been denied; others are paid, and some still to be paid. I have put into the hands of Mr. Blair and into the loan office for you since your departure as follows;

1779. July. 1.	£261-10-6
Sep. 27.	£609.
1780. Mar. 16.	£384-18.
	£1255- 8-6

being all I have received for you. I wrote to Mr. Phripp to press a final settlement. His death however has prevented it. I shall renew my endeavors with his executors when known to me. Generals Phillips and Riedesel with their families were permitted to go to N. York on parole last September. Majr. Irving succeeded at Colle and still continues. There is reason to beleive a part of those troops

[341]

will be exchanged; but whether the lot will fall on the Major is unknown. Your vines and trees at Colle have suffered extremely from their horses, cattle and carelessness. I sent my people there this spring under the direction of Anthony, and had the young trees in your nursery transplanted. But I think you need not count on the possibility of preserving any thing of that kind under present circumstances. There have been applications to purchase it; which will await your orders. Madame de Riedesel was at the Barclay springs when the permission came for her to go to New York. She of course went from thence. I expect she had with her the other books you had lent her, as none but Candide were returned. Giovannini went with them as far as the state of New-York, but not being permitted to go in, he returned, and is now in my service, as is also Anthony. Giovanni also lives with us, working for himself. Anthony is still desirous of returning, and I shall endeavor to procure him a passage. Pellegrino took his departure in some vessel, was taken, carried into N. York, and is now in Philadelphia, from which place he wrote me this information, desiring to get back to this country. I have not yet sent on Fontana's works to Philadelphia, expecting the plates from you. Should I be able to remit some tobacco to France to enable you to comply with my commissions to you I will give you notice of it: tho' should any merchant undertake to fulfill them as mentioned in the paper I shall be glad of it, settling the price in tobacco; in doing which the worth of tobacco must be estimated from the European market, making proper deductions for risk and transportation: for with us there is no such thing as settled prices. I wish not to receive any of the people I wrote for these two years. I would also have the Encyclopedie, Buffon, and Belidor omitted. All the other things, adding a pair of stays, are ten times more desireable than when you were here. Indeed you can form no conception how much our wants of European commodities are increased tho' the superiority of the French and Spanish fleets in Europe, and their equality here have reduced the risk of capture to be very moderate. Hearing of Mr. Bettoia's captivity and distress in New York, I wrote to him making a tender of any services I could render him. But I have since heard he had left that place before my letter could have got there.

The seat of government is removed from this place to Richmond. I take my final departure hence within four or five days. The principal military events since you left us are the evacuation of Rhodeisland by the enemy; the surprize of Stoney point (a post about 30 miles above N. York) by our general Wayne attended with the capture of upwards of 1000 prisoners; the defeat of the joint forces of Count d'Estaing and our Genl. Lincoln before Savanna with the loss of about five hundred killed on the side of the allies; the reduction of the English posts on the Missisipi by the Spaniards and about a thousand prisoners taken in them; and a late expedition of the enemy from N. York against Charlestown. About 7000 men, commanded by Clinton and Cornwallis left N. York for the invasion of South Carolina. What number arrived safely we know not. They experienced in their passage a month of continual tempest, so dreadful as to bear full comparison with the hurricanes of the West Indies. We learn certainly that they were obliged to throw all their horse overboard. They are now on James's island, which is separated from Charlestown by a water of a mile and a half broad. Genl. Lincoln defends the town (which is rendered amazingly strong) with about 5000 men, of whom 2000 only are regulars. The Virginia and North [Carolina] lines of regulars under generals Woodford, Scott, and Hogan, are on their march thither; part of them probably there by this time. They will add 3500 excellent souldiers to Lincoln's strength. No blow had been struck on the 5th. of the last month, which is our latest intelligence. That is likely to be the only active scene in the ensuing campaign. We have had all over N. America a winter so severe as to exceed every thing conceivable in our respective climates. In this state our rivers were blocked up to their mouths with ice for six weeks. People walked over York river at the town of York, which was never before done, since the discovery of this country. Regiments of horse with their attendant waggons marched in order over Patowmack at Howe's ferry, and James river at Warwick.

Not knowing how far this letter may travel post, I do not over-burthen you with paper or words. The handwriting and matter will make known to you the writer, without his signature, who therefore bids you Adieu!

RC (NhD); unsigned. Addressee identified from internal evidence.

THE FIER RODRIQUE: In DLC: TJ Papers, 6: 1072, is an undated memorandum docketed by TJ "sent for by the Fier Rodrique" and listing, in another hand, "5000 Muskets of the French model of 1763. . . . 25 Tons Musket Powder. 1000 Reams Canon Cartridge Paper. 1000 do. Musket do. 30,000 Musket Flints." The several letters here mentioned—from PHILLIPS and PELLEGRINO and to PHRIPP and BETTOIA—have not been found.

From Philip Mazzei

Paris, 4 Apr. 1780. Abstract, with liberal quotations, of Edmund Burke's speech in Parliament on Economical Reform, delivered 11 Feb.

1780. Sends text of Louis XVI's message to the widow of Capt. Couedic, which Mazzei hopes will be translated for the "perusal of our people." Enlarges on the good qualities of the French king.

RC (NN); in a clerk's hand, signed by Mazzei; 4 p. At head of text: "10 [i.e., dispatch No. 10]. 1st. Copy." The "3d Copy" of the same letter is also in NN, in a different hand, and is printed in Marraro, *Mazzei*, p. 35-8; see notes there.

From the Board of Trade, with Reply

[5 April 1780]

The following Slaves have been purchased for the use of the State agreeable to the Instructions given this Board by His Excellency in Council

Gabriel	cost £6305.	Ned, cost	4210
Solomon	3675	Sam	4700
Kitt (a Boy	3640.	Charles	3115
Tom	3755	Sawney	3190
David	3820	James	3510
James	4000	Argyle	3820
George	4135	Jupiter	2100
Peter	3160.	Cæsar, Aggy, Fanny, Calah, Will, Sukey, Harry	15050.
Of Mr. Bristow's Estate.		John	5070
		Phill	6250
		Sambo	7950
		Joe	6010

Of Harmer & King's Estates.

We beg the Hono. Board will direct us how the above Slaves are to be disposed of. J: AMBLER

DUN: ROSE

In Council April 7th. 1780.

The board of War being not likely to meet for some time it is thought best to continue these slaves with the board of Trade until the division may be taken up at Richmond. TH: JEFFERSON

Tr in Board of Trade Journal (Vi).

From the Board of War

Williamsburg, 5 Apr. 1780. Encloses Maj. Quarles' return of men raised in his last tour; Quarles "complains extremely" of inattention of county lieutenants to the execution of laws which fall within their departments. He has also applied for compensation for his services; six hundred dollars per month is recommended. Signed by Innes and Barron. Countersigned: "April 5. 1780. I approve of the allowance of six hundred dollars per month. Th: Jefferson."

RC (Vi); 2 p.; printed in *Official Letters*, II, 115-16. Addressed. Enclosures not located.

From the Board of Trade

[*Williamsburg*] *6 Apr. 1780*. In order to comply with pressing requisitions for linen, 100 pieces of Irish shirting have been purchased, allowing a rate of 50 for 1 on the sterling cost, payable in tobacco at £15 per hundred, if approved by the executive.

Tr in Board of Trade Journal (Vi); 1 p. TJ's reply has not been located, but a minute following the letter in the Journal instructs the agent to purchase the linen, "The above being approved."

To the Board of Trade

[*Williamsburg, 6? Apr. 1780*. Minute in the Board of Trade Journal (Vi) under date of 6 Apr.: "In compliance with Instructions from the Executive Ordered that the Agent be directed to pay Doctr. McClurg the sum of nineteen hundred and eighty Pounds for Mr. Rutledges Draught on the Governor of South Carolina which draught must be remitted to Maurice Simonds, Esqr. of Charles Town to be passed to the Credit of the state." Letter not located.]

From the Board of Trade

[*Williamsburg*] *7 Apr. 1780*. Requesting approval of the purchase of articles listed in enclosure and recommended by the Board of War, also medicines received by Dr. Galt. Signed by Whiting, Ambler, and Rose. Countersigned: "In Council Apr. 7. 1780. Approved. Th: Jefferson."

RC (CSmH); 1 p. Enclosed list of articles has not been located.

To the Board of Trade

[*Williamsburg, 7? Apr. 1780*. Minute in Board of Trade Journal (Vi) under date of 7 Apr.: "In compliance with a requisition from the Executive Ordered that the Agent replace a Hogshead of Rum borrowed of Mr. Roe Cooper for the use of the Garrison at Hampton or make such other Satisfaction as may be agreed on." TJ's requisition not located.]

Inventory of Supplies for the Virginia Line, with Jefferson's Instructions

[7 April 1780]

Inventory of necessaries to compleat the Officers and soldiers of fifteen Regiments on continental establishment with Clothing for 435 Officers, 6810 non Commissioned Officers and privates.

	Yds
Seven Quarter Cloth fit for Regimentals	2610
Linen Allowing 6 shirts each	9035
Stockings one half Silk 6 pair each	2610 pair
Stuff fit for summer Vests and Breeches	7430
Best shoes 870 Pr. but twice the number will not be too many	870
Hatts of the best kind	435
Cambrick for Stocks	652½ yds
Ditto for Ruffles	652½
Handkerchiefs	2610
Blanketts	435
Trimmings for Suits	870

For Non Commissioned Officers & Privs.

Hatts	6810
Coats Regimental blue if to be had	6810
Vests and Breeches Pr. of each of Blue	6810
Overhalls Allowing 2 pr. to each man	13620
Shirts Allowing 3 to each man	20430
Shoes Ditto ...... Ditto	20430
Blanketts and black Stocks each	6810
Handkerchiefs	13620

Necessaries for 6 Regiments on State establishment and four Troops of horse.

For 227 Officers	Yds
seven quarter Cloth & trimmings for the same	1362
Linen for Shirts	4767
Cambrick for Stocks	340½
Stockings one half Silk	1362 pair
Shoes	908 Do.
Stuff fit for summer Vests and Breeches	3986 yds
Hatts of the best kind	227

Handkerchiefs 1362
Blankets 227

Necessaries For 3480 non Comd. Officers & Privates

Coats 3480
Vests 3480
Breeches pair of 3480
Overhalls allowing 2 pair to each man 6960
Shirts allowing three to each man 10440
Shoes pair of 10440
Blanketts and black Stocks each 3480
Hatts 3480
Handkerchiefs allowing 2 to each man 6960

JAS. INNES
JAS. BARRON

In Council Apl. 7th. 1780.

This Schedule is calculated on a supposition that we have 6810 non commissioned Officers and Soldiers in fifteen Regiments in continental [. . . .] We have in continental Service in all our Regiments of infantry and troops of cavalry (including the detachment under Colo: Porterfield) only 4175 non commissioned Officers and Soldiers: which it will be our duty to raise as soon as we can to 6070 that being our whole quota required by congress. To these must be added about 200 State Troops detained in the Eastern department and about 700 which we suppose will be acting on the Western and the Navy. We therefore recommend to the board of Trade to reduce by this Scale the Schedules, and then procure the articles enumerated, endeavouring to get first those which are most wanted.   TH. JEFFERSON

Allowance for 60 Officers in Service at Charlestown.

180 yards of Broad Cloth & Trimmings for 60 suits of Clothes
300 yards of Linen for Shirts
  50 yards of cambrick for Ruffles
  60 pair of shoes
  90 Handkerchiefs
270 yards of Jeans for summer Vests & Breeches
  60 Hatts

In Council Approved. TH: JEFFERSON

For twelve Officers in the Navy.
72 yards of Blue broad Cloth & trimings for 12 Suits
Linen for 72 Shirts Cambrick for Stocks & Ruffles
72 Handkerchiefs.
24 pair of shoes.
12 Fine Hatts.
54 yards of Jeans for summer Vests and Breeches.
72 pair of Stockings half of them Silk.

March 7th. 1780.
Jas. Innes
Jas. Barron.

In Council Apl. 7th. 1780. Approved. Th: Jefferson

Schedule of Necessaries for the Army & Navy, for 1780.
10,000 Wt. Brown Sugar. 5000 Wt. of Coffee. 1000 Wt. of Tea.
2000 Wt. Loaf Ditto. 10,000 Gallons of Rum.

Jas. Innes.
Jas. Barron

In Council Apl. 7th. 1780. Approved. Th: Jefferson

Deficient for the Virginia Troops in Continental Service by
returns from John Moss Esquire
737 yds Cloth, 697 Shirts, 191 yds Cambrick, 635 Stocks
1416 Handkerchiefs, 789 pair of Silk Hose, 209 pr. Stocking[s]
587 pair of Shoes, 150 Hatts, 1761 summer Vests & Breeches

By a requisition from the Board of War of Mar. 29th. 1780.
800 compleat suits of Clothes.

By requisition of the Board of War of 30th. of Mar. 1780.
100 Suits of Clothes, 200 Shirts, 100 pair of Leather Breeches
100 pair of Boots, 100 Horsemens Caps, 1000 suits of Regimentals
for soldiers in Scotts Brigade, Clothing for five hundred Sailors
viz. Jackets, shirts, Breeches, Overhalls, shoes, stockings, Hatts,
Caps, &c. &c.

Jas. Innes
Jas. Barron

In Council Apl. 7th. 1780. Approved. Th: Jefferson

Tr in Board of War Letter Book (MiU-C).

Several of the requisitions from the Board of War are undated, while others are dated in March. Since all were approved by TJ in Council on 7 Apr., possibly they were accumulated and transmitted by the Board of Trade on that date. Or they may have been held up in council and signed in a group in order to complete business before the recess occasioned by the removal of the government from Williamsburg to Richmond (see Notice of the Removal of the Executive Office, 25 Mch. 1780).

From John Page

DEAR SIR Wmsburg April the 7th. 1780

I have often mentioned to you My Intention of resigning my Seat at the Council Board, on Account of my Inability, from the particular Situation of my Affairs, to give that Attendance at the Board which I ought and wished to give; and that I had therefore determined to send in my Resignation to the General Assembly at the latter End of their last Session; but that the Report which then prevailed of an Invasion had determined me to wait till I might resign without incurring the Suspicion of retiring to avoid the Dangers which then appeared to threaten us. As I find the Obstacles to my Attendance on the Board greatly increased, and the only Objection which I think could be reasonably made to my Resignation removed; I must now beg Leave to retire from it, and beg you will be assured that nothing but the particular Situation of my private and domestic Affairs which have suffered extreme[ly] by a four Years and an half almost total Neg[lect] of them could induce me to retire from the Service of my Country during the War; and that it gives me Pain to do so at present, and particularly during your Administration. I am my dear Sir with the greatest Respect & Esteem your sincere Friend & most obedt. hble S[ervant,]

JOHN PAGE

P.S. I have taken the Liberty of inclosing my Resignation to the General Assembly, contained in a Letter to the Speaker, to whom you will be so kind as to have it transmitted at their first meeting.

J. P.

RC (DLC). Enclosure: Page to Benjamin Harrison, same date (letter of resignation, endorsed, in part: "May 9, 1780 to lie on table"); printed in *Official Letters*, II, 116-17.

On 24 May 1780 the House and Senate jointly elected Andrew Lewis, George Webb, and Jacquelin Ambler members of the council of state in the room of John Page, Thomas Blackburn, and David Meade, resigned (JHD, May 1780, 1827 edn., p. 21; for Blackburn's resignation see his letter to TJ, 4 May 1780).

From Philip Mazzei

Paris, 10-19 Apr. 1780. Russia has confirmed her strict neutrality, dashing England's hopes, and has insisted as well that her trading vessels are not to be visited. This declaration has been well received in Europe; and hence "I hope . . . soon to see the friends and allies of Great Britain limited to the inhabitants of the Coast of Barbary, with whom they can't help sympathising from a Similitude of sentiments and trade. I think I can see in the behaviour of the northern Powers a silent intimation to England, that *America shall be independent*, and a Salutary advice to make peace on the best terms she can." English outrages on neutral shipping in the Mediterranean. In an addendum of 19 Apr.: Exchanges of French and British prisoners are resumed; the British loan; a crisis brewing in Ireland. Growing strength of the opposition in Parliament; Mazzei, however, wants the present ministry to have the entire credit for defeat in America. Movements of English, French, and Spanish naval forces. P.S.: George III has issued a proclamation denouncing all treaties with Holland. 2d P.S.: Will send this letter by "our brave Paul Jones," who is still in Paris. Sends extract from Leyden *Gazette* exhibiting Dutch satisfaction in Russia's declaration. The affair of Count Byland. American resistance has "created almost all over Europe, a kind of Sympathetic affection in our favour, which is not a little increased by the unaccountable insolence of Great Britain."

RC (NN); 4 p.; in a clerk's hand, signed by Mazzei; at head of text: "11 [i.e. dispatch No. 11]. 2d: Copy." The "3d: Copy" is in Vi; an unnumbered copy is in CtY. Second copy printed in Marraro, *Mazzei*, p. 39-43. Enclosure missing.

Proceedings of a Court-Martial and Remission of Sentence of George Ennis

Albemarl Barracks April the 10th. 1780

At a General Courtmarshal held for the Tryal of Such prisoners as shall come before them:

Major Geo. Walls President

Members

Capt. Purvis	Lt. Glenn
Capt. Porter	Lt. Carney
Capt. Cherry	Ensn. Slaughter
Capt. Young	Ens. McGavock
Lt. Brent	Ensn. Pollet
Lt. Taylor	Ens. Meriweather

The Court being duly sworn Proceeded to the Tryal of George Ennis of Capt. Millan's Company, in Colo. Crockets Battalion for Disertion. The prisoner being brought before the Court pleads Guilty of Enlisting and disarting three times. The Court are of Oppinion that the Prisoner is guilty of a breach of the 1st. and 3rd. Article of the 6th Section of the Articles of War, and Sentence him to suffer Death. John Smith a soldier in the 8th. Virginia Regiment was brought Before the Court for disartion. Pleads guilty. The Court are of Oppinion that the prisoner is guilty of the

1st. Article of the 6th. Section of the Articles of War, and Sentence him to run the Gantlet once thro the Brigade.

James Cragy being brought before the Court for disartion pleads not guilty, and no evidence appearing the Court are of Oppinion that the prisoner be Releas'd from his confinement.

GEO. WALLS Majr.
President

In Council May 19. 1780

The sentence of the court martial on George Ennis is remitted.

TH: JEFFERSON

MS (MHi); in a clerk's hand, signed by Walls. TJ's instruction is in his own hand. Endorsed in an unidentified hand: "Proceedings of Genl Court Martial Apl. 10th. 80."

To J. P. G. Muhlenberg

SIR   Richmond Apr. 12. 1780.

The state of the recruiting business in this country is as follows.

There are some draughted soldiers in different parts of the country, but they are so few, so dispersed, and enlisted for so short a term that we have not thought them worth the expence and trouble of gathering up.

There are recruits raising under a standing law concerning officers, souldiers, sailors and marines. These are enlisted for the war, by a person resident in each county. We have an officer appointed who rides the circuit of the country once in two months to receive these men at certain places of rendezvous. He has just finished a circuit and we have sent on about fifty of these recruits under Capt. Minnis to the Southward.

All the officers of the Virginia line now in the state who have (according to a request of the executive) applied for recruiting instructions and money, have received them. These have been given with a particular view to the re-enlisting such souldiers of their respective regiments as are discharged or entitled to discharge. I hear they are tolerably succesful. As to the 1st. and 2d. state regiments particularly, there not having been in the treasury money enough to re-enlist them at the time they became entitled to discharges, their officers (as I am informed) postponed paying them off, gave them furloughs to visit their friends till the 1st. of May, at which time they were to rendezvous at Williamsburg and Fredericksburg, and it was hoped money would then be ready for re-enlisting them. In the mean time considerable sums have been furnished the officers, and more will be provided; and there is good reason to hope this judicious measure of their officers will enable us to recover most of them. Colo. Harrison's regiment of artillery is very considerable recruited.

Under the preceding state of things I do not know of any immediate services with which we need to trouble you. Perhaps you could be instrumental in procuring orders, from the proper authority for such of the above regiments as are not yet ordered to the Southward, to march thither by fifties as fast as they are recruited. We had such orders for all other new recruits not yet regimented, but I do not consider those as authorising the march of men raised by the officers of a particular battalion for their battalion, and that not under marching orders.

I have the honor to be with great respect Your most obedient & most humble servt., TH: JEFFERSON

RC? (DLC: PCC, No. 148, I); this is presumably the "copy" sent by Muhlenberg to the Continental Board of War, mentioned in Muhlenberg's letter to George Washington, 8 May 1780 (DLC: Washington Papers), and so it may be a duplicate of a lost RC. It is, however, entirely in TJ's hand and is probably the original sent to Muhlenberg (PCC, No. 148 consists of Continental Board of War papers). Tr (DLC: Washington Papers); in a clerk's hand and bearing notation of address at foot of text: "To Genl. Muhlenberg at Richmond." Tr is dated "April 10th. 1780," but the "10." is heavily written over another date (perhaps correcting a mistake in the date by TJ); the presumed RC is very clearly dated "Apr. 12." Text of presumed RC and that of Tr are identical except for copyist's errors. Ford (II, 301-2) printed the letter from the Tr and therefore under the date of 10 Apr., but he added to the confusion by stating that the recipient was George Washington; Ford has been followed by *Official Letters*, II, 117-18. Hence this letter has hitherto been printed only from a defective text, with an erroneous date (or at least not the date TJ gave it), and assigned to a wrong addressee.

Brig. Gen. John Peter Gabriel Muhlenberg of the Virginia Line was in command in Virginia from Mch. to Dec. 1780, when he became second in command to Steuben (DAB). Acting under instructions from the Continental Board of War, his initial task was to fill up the Virginia Line and speed the recruits to the southern theater of war (Washington to Muhlenberg, 20 Apr. 1780, *Writings*, ed. Fitzpatrick, XVIII, 285-7; Muhlenberg to Washington, 8 May 1780, cited above; the latter letter summarizes a number of early exchanges between TJ and Muhlenberg no longer surviving).

From George Washington

SIR   Head Quarters Morris Town 15. April 1780

The probability of a continuance of the War to the Southward, which will of course draw the troops of the State of Virginia to that quarter, makes it essentially necessary that every measure should be taken to procure supplies of Cloathing for them, especially of Shoes, Stockings and linen. The distance and the difficulty of transportation would render a supply of those Articles, from hence, extremely precarious, even were our Continental Magazines well stocked, but this is so far from being the case, that I can assure your Excellency there never was greater occasion for the states to exert themselves in procuring Cloathing for their respective troops. General Lincoln has, he informs me, already written to you on this subject, but as he could not be acquainted with our present circumstances and prospects in regard to Cloathing, I thought it expedient to communicate our situation to your Excellency that You might the better perceive the necessity which the State of Virginia will be under of supplying the troops to the Southward more particularly with the Articles which I have before enumerated.

I have the honor to be &c.

Dft (DLC: Washington Papers); in hand of Tench Tilghman.

To Joseph Reed

Sir   In Council, April 18, 1780.

I have had the pleasure to receive your Excellency's favor of March 27 and am to return you our sincere thanks for your interposition in favor of the operations carrying on by General Clark, operations which I hope will result equally to the benefit of yours as of our State, and which if successful will give us future quiet in our western quarter. I beg you to be assured that Colo. Broadhead has been altogether misinformed as to any restriction having been laid on a Mr. Wilson or any other person in purchasing within this State cattle for the use of Fort pitt, or that if such a restriction actually took place, it was a private act in those who presumed to impose it, unauthorized by government and which would have been censured and rectified had it been made known. We are so sensible of the evils which would result from such a line of conduct, and so sincerely disposed to render the union of the States more perfect that we shall on all occasions endeavor to render to our neighbors every friendly office which circumstances shall bring within the compass of our powers.

I am further to thank your Excellency for the kind dispositions you entertain and the aids you were pleased to render to the expedition under the Marquis of Fayette which was intended for the immediate relief of this State in particular, as well as for those furnished to General Greene for the southern service in general. Such is the present aspect of the war, that it does not seem very probable its circumstances should be so reversed as to place us in a situation of returning the favor in kind. However we trust that while the contest was northwards our contributions of men, arms and other necessaries were such as to prove we should not be wanting to our friends under a change of circumstances. With respect to your State particularly we shall take very great pleasure in cultivating every disposition to harmony and mutual aid; that policy would be very unsound which should build our interest or happiness on any thing inconsistent with yours.

I have the honour to be with very great respect your Excellency's mo ob Serv't,   THS. JEFFERSON

MS not located. Text from *Penna.* Reed's FAVOR OF MARCH 27 is miss-
Archives, 1st ser., VIII, 196 (slightly ing.
repunctuated).

To George Rogers Clark

SIR   Richmond April 19. 1780
Your Letter from Louisville of February 22'd —80 came safely to Hand. In Answer to your Observations on the Spot proper to take Post on at the Mouth of Ohio we can only give our general Sentiments leaving the Ultimate Determination to your Prudence on view of the Ground, as we can neither make the particular spot we would elect to be what we should wish nor recommend to you to take Post on it if Nature has rendered it unfit.

The Point of Land at the Mouth of the Ohio on the South side is the precise spot which would have been preferred had nature formed it capable of Fortification but this we were apprised was subject to inundation. How deep the Waters may occasionally be there, we are quite uninformed, and therefore are unable to decide on your Proposition for banking them out as at New-Orleans. In general, undertakings of that nature are expensive, and not without great Danger that Floods of unexpected Magnitude may overwhelm the Works and Garrison, or that an enterprizing Enemy may find Means to let in the Water. Yet if those Lands lie so high as to be very little under Water, these objections become small in proportion, and may perhaps be less than that of taking the Post at a situation less favorable for vigilance over the Trade of the two rivers. Of this you will judge when you see the Lands and know the height of Inundation they are subject to. If this Place should be rejected, and we were to decide between two Posts one of which should be on the Ohio, the other on the Missisipi below the Mouth of Ohio equally near the Mouth, and equally proper in every other respect, we should prefer the one on the Missisipi because it would command a greater Part of the Trade than the other; for I take for granted more Trade will go down the two Rivers to Orleans than down one river to the Mouth and up the other. If the question is between two Situations on the North and South side of the Ohio, equal in other respects, the one on the South side would be greatly preferred. Indeed this circumstance would weigh against a good Degree of other Superiority for Reasons which cannot be trusted to a Letter: Yet it would not so far weigh as to prefer a Post which cannot be made tenable to one which can. You describe a high Ground on the North side of the Ohio, three or four Miles above its Mouth, yet the Missisipi, so near in that Part as that a Town might reach from the one to the other and a small river mouthing at the same Place and forming a commodious Harbor for Vessels. This indeed is tempting, as in such a case the Navigation of both rivers would lie under your Eye as effectually as at the Mouth of Ohio, and holds out such advantages as may get the better of the objections to its [being on] the North side. However you must finally decide on view [of the] whole. As to the kind of Fortification I imagine you proposed in the first Place to build a Stockade for temporary Purposes. The Post is so important really as to merit Works of the best Kind, but on this it would be necessary to consult the Legislature who would be to provide for the Expence. In the mean Time I imagine you will think it well first to plan and lay off the good works you would propose, and then build your temporary Fort so as to encompass them and protect those who should be working on them, or, if this would be too large to be manned by your Force, the temporary Work might be built within the Lines laid off for the good. When you shall have determined on your spot we should be glad to receive a minute description of it with a plan of the good works you would [pr]opose to erect not meaning however thereby to suspend the temporary works.

I am Sir Your very humble servt.,   TH: JEFFERSON

RC (WHi); in a clerk's hand, with complimentary close and signature by TJ. Addressed: "Colo. George Rogers Clarke at the Falls of Ohio." Endorsed: "[Jeffer]son April 19th 1780." Enclosed in TJ's second letter to Clark of this date, following.

Clark's LETTER FROM LOUISVILLE OF FEBRUARY 22'D is unfortunately missing. On the plans for and subsequent history of Fort Jefferson, see TJ to Thomas Walker and Daniel Smith, 29 Jan. 1780.

To George Rogers Clark

Sir   Richmond [April 19] 1780.

I have received information of many Murders recently committed by the Indians in Washington, Montgomery, Green-Briar, Kentucky and the neighborhood of Fort Pitt. Tho the Nations by whom co[mmit]ted are not specified in the Information, the extent of the Mischief [indicates an?] extensive combination. Incertain whether you were near enough at Hand to afford relief, and indeed rather expecting from your last Letter received that you are now at the Mouth of the Ohio, satisfied at the same time that any Plan of enterprize determined and minutely directed here would prove abortive from want of Information and unforeseen Difficulties and Events, I have directed the Lieutenants of the Counties of Washington, Montgomery, Botetourt, Rockbridge, and Green-Briar to assemble and concert, and immediately with a Portion of their Militia carry an Expedition into the Indian Country: To communicate their determinations to the Lieutenants of the Counties Northward of them between the Blue-Ridge and Allegany who are also to assemble, concert, and execute similar offensive Measures with their Militia either by concurring in the same, or undertaking a separate Expedition; and these again to call for Aids from the Counties West of the Allegany. They are to give Notice of their Plans to yourself, and should the combination of the Enemy appear still formidable for their Force I have desired them to ask such Assistance as you can give them, and in such way as you shall Think most effectual. Since the Conduct of the Indians has precipitated our meditated Chastisement of them, it seems to have determined on which of the Objects formerly submitted to you the first Efforts of the campaign are to be directed. Nothing is more desirable than total suppression of Savage Insolence and Cruelties, and should your Affairs be in a condition to admit your going in Person, and taking command of the whole expedition, the object is of sufficient Importance to require it, yet unacquainted as I am, with the present State of your forces, where they are, and how employed, I am afraid that your distance from the Scene of action, or other unknown circumstances might produce a greater Measure of Injury to the Public by interrupting your present operations than they might derive of good from your co-operation. I therefore leave to your Discretion and Zeal for the good of your Country to determine whether, and in what manner, to concur [in] this Expedition, still considering it as so important as to recommend it to you, if very great injury to the public may not attend the calling you off on that Business. I also write to Major Slaughter (as he is probably so distant from You) to lend his Aid if called on in the Manner I have mentioned to him. I have it not in my Power to give you precise Information of the numbers recruited for Col. Crockett, or time of their March. I experience Mortification on every enquiry by finding that every Enquiry lessens my Hope both as to Numbers and dispatch. Nothing shall be left undone to forward them, and I do not Despair all together of their participating in the projected Expedition. I am Sir Your very humble servt., TH: JEFFERSON

P.S. Inclosed is an answer to your's of Feb. 22.

RC (WHi); in the same clerk's hand as the preceding letter to Clark, with complimentary close, signature, postscript, and address in TJ's hand. Addressed: "Colo. George Rogers Clarke at the Falls of Ohio." Endorsed: "Govr. Jefferson April the 19th: 1780. Received at the Falls July 11th 1780."

I ALSO WRITE TO MAJOR SLAUGHTER: This letter has not been found. The ANSWER mentioned in the postscript is the preceding letter to Clark of the present date, q.v. Clark's letter of 22 Feb. has not been found.

From Samuel Huntington

Philadelphia, 20 Apr. 1780. Circular letter to the state executives enclosing a resolve of Congress of 15 Apr. allowing the states credit with the United States "for such Clothing as they may furnish to the Officers of the Hospital, and medical Staff."

FC (DLC: PCC, No. 14); 1 p. Enclosure missing; printed in JCC, XVI, 366-7.

From Philip Mazzei

SIR   Paris, April 20th. 1780

It is about a month Since Mr. Penet came here from Nantes. I got intelligence of it next day, went to See him, had a Short conversation, and Spoke very a little, as I was determined to find out his Sentiments before he could know mine. He appeared to be confused irresolute and discontented both from his discourse and countenance; complained of your drafts to a large amount in favour of a Spaniard, by paying which very a little would remain to his house of the produce of your tobacco arrived in 2. large Vessels at Lorient and Nantes in February, mentioning the large orders you expected to have executed, and the heavy debt which it Seemed as if you had forgotten; attempted to exculpate Mr. D'Acosta for having not paid the letter of credit, observing that the house had letters from you, or Mr. Jameson, or both, in which the operations respecting Mr. Smith and me were countermanded; Said that the purport of my mission had been written from Virginia to Philadelphia, and Some of our Delegates had been instructed to inquire after the probability of Success from persons, whom he was not at liberty to mention; and endeavoured to make me understand (though not in clear terms) that it was believed in America, that I had Settled my matters with the Enemy, and gone to England. Four, or five days after we met for the 2d. time by appointement; he treated me like an intimate friend, and with a distinguished kindness; informed me of his Success with his Partners here, whom he had persuaded into his plan; Said that your drafts should be paid and your orders executed; blamed very much Mr. D'Acosta's unaccountable behaviour to me, which he Said to have heared of by Some of the Clerks in Nantes, and to have had Some words with him about it already; expected that the brothers D'Acosta Should not be long his Partners; asked if I had his letter of credit, and When I Should want the money, &c. &c. I answered that I would raise the money whenever he pleased; I had studiously avoided to mention a word about it myself; I took notice, but very gently, of his attempts in the first conversation to exculpate Mr. D'Acosta, to which he replied in a manner as if he had been certain I would approve his direction in Speaking of a Partner; and I did not give the least hint of remembering any thing of his confusion, irresolution, and inconsistence, which I dare Say he remembered nothing of himself. Mr. Penet's Situation must have been very disagreable the first time I Saw him. I had already been informed in Nantes that he is not a man of capital, which you must have observed in letter 6; and am now certain it is the case. He knew, that his Partners here were in bad humour, and that all his engagements in America must fall to the ground, and he himself be reduced to nothing, if he did not Succeed to persuade them into his views. This, I think, accounts fully for the monstruous difference between his first and Second conversation. He paid me the 300 Louis the 6th. instant, and is now gone back to Nantes. While he was here I Saw him often, as he Shewed a great regard for me, attachement to the american Cause, and even procured me the acquaintence of a person, who is in the way of giving a lift in matters of importance for us. But we ought notwithstanding to be on our guard for the following reason. I know that his Partners would make a great deal of their money on the Spot, and have reason to believe what has been suggested to me by an old acquaintence, who is a banker in Paris, that they would not have embarked in Such affairs, unless they had been assured of extraordinary profits. A mixture of ambition and vanity extravagance and generosity must rise Mr. Penet's expences to a considerable amount. His Show gave offence in Nantes and has been ridiculed in Paris. Count Kaunitz, who was here in his way to Madrid Ambassadour to the King of Spain from the Emperor, asked me if I knew a person lately come from America (whom from his description I found to be Mr. Penet) who (the Count Said with a Smile to the whole company) had taken great pains with his tongue and by Showing his rings the night before at the play to be taken particular notice of. The whole must come out of the profits in the American affairs, as he has got no others. Therefore we ought, I repeat, to be on our guard. And as you cannot See these things from Such a distance, I think it incumbent on me to inform you. I hope that my character is Sufficiently known to take for granted, that I am induced to give Such informations merely from my regard to the public interest. I wish however that interest may never be prefered to gratitude and delicacy. Both these are due to Mr. Penet by what I heared of the late Governor and the Gentelmen of the council. First of all you will easily See by the quality and price of the goods you receive, and the accounts of Sale of your tobacco, whether you are imposed, or not. If not, the informations I give you can do no harm. And if you Should be imposed, I wish that the paying of your debt may always precede your complaints. Of the 2 evils I would prefer the being imposed to the risk of hurting the credit and honour of the State. My greatest apprehensions are on account of the £100,000 Sterling he is empowered to borrow. He has avowed to me, that he never expected to raise a farthing on that commission, but that he had taken it merely as a Security, principally to Satisfy the minds of his Partners. If then from the nature of his Commission he has in his power to make the State answerable for that Sum without any further formality from you, I wish that you will withdraw it from him as soon as possible, and that it may be done with great precaution and delicacy. Indeed his extravagant expences would hurt the credit of any rich merchant, and it is prudent to be afraid of those who have So great a thirst for appearing So much higher than their Station. I have the honour to be most respectfully, Sir, Your Excellency's most obedient & most humble Servant,

PHILIP MAZZEI

RC (MiU-C); in a clerk's hand, signed by Mazzei; at head of text: "12 [i.e., dispatch No. 12]. 1st. Copy"; endorsed by a clerk: "Philip Mazzie Apl. 20th. 1780." The "2d. Copy," in a different hand, is in CtY; the "3d. Copy," in still another hand, is in NN.

From J. P. G. Muhlenberg

[*Place not known*, *20 Apr. 1780*. In a letter to Gen. Washington from Fredericksburg, 8 May 1780 (DLC: Washington Papers), Gen. Muhlenberg states: "On the 20th. of April I wrote to the Governor, proposing Rocky Ridge a town opposite Richmond for the place of General Rendezvous, and Winchester and Fredericksburg as by posts for the recruits to collect in small numbers. I further proposed as there was a favorable prospect of Recruiting . . . I should call in all the Officers of the Virginia Line on Continental establishment, who were at present off duty, appoint their districts and send them out to recruit and collect the Deserters, provided the Treasury could furnish Money." Not located. See, however, TJ's answer to Muhlenberg entered under 1 May 1780.]

From Philip Mazzei

SIR   Paris, April 21st. 1780.

The first time I spoke, according to my Instructions, to Dr. Franklin on the purport of my mission, he observed that so many People had come to Europe from every State on that kind of business, that they had ruined our credit, and made the money-men shy of us. I said that Virginia should not partake of the blame on my account, as I would not let them know my business, unless I was pretty well sure of success. Having since taken the opportunity of mentioning the subject several times to him, he never failed giving some marks of disapprobation and displeasure. About 3. weeks past (that is to say about a month since I had first mentioned the matter to him) his reflections induced me to observe, that while Congress called on the several States to supply their men in the Continental Army with things, which must be got from Europe, it became a necessity for them to seek for credit and money; that the persons sent by the States on that errand may perhaps have not proceeded with all the discretion required in such cases; but as to the dishonour and discredit, which you think, says I, that they have brought upon us by spreading such an idea of American poverty, I must beg leave to differ from you, Sir; since all Europe knows, that we want a great many things from hence: that we have no species: and that we cannot, during the war, remit enough of our produce to pay the debts. The only 2. points to gain are, I continued, the persuading them of the solidity and resources of the States, and that we are firmly determined to keep our Independence; and then mentioned the reasons I have to expect that I shall be believed, particularly in Florence and Genoa. We have tried in Genoa, he said, without effect. As I had informed him of my views there from the beginning, his defering so long to acquaint me with that unlucky trial, made a sudden and disagreable impression on my spirits for a double reason. But that was nothing in comparison to what I have felt to day. He has at last signified to me that 6. ♆ cent was offered. But, Sir, says I, at the very first conversation on the subject I informed you that I was impowered to give only 5; had I known this at that time I could have given notice of it by *Marquis la Fayette*, and the Assembly could have been informed of it in the Spring-Session. "I din't think of it," said he with a true philosophical indifference, "it never came into my head."

I have lost no time, Sir, to come and write you the intelligence, with which I have been most disagreably surprised this day, knowing that there is at *Nantes* a vessel ready to sail; and I heartly wish that you may receive one of the 4. copies before the Assembly rises. You will, I hope, excuse my blundering more than usual, as I am really disconcerted. In coming from the Doctor, who lives 3 miles out of Town, I was a thinking what to do. I have resolved to proceed on my journey as soon as I can raise money, and to go and lay a foundation for executing the orders I may receive hereafter. It is requisite to observe, that however great my success may be in infusing notions of our solidity and resources, and a desire of entering into our views, I cannot with any degree of prudence mention the terms expressed in my Instructions, as Dr. Franklin's offer is certainly known every where, the experiment having been tried by the medium of public Bankers. The offering less than it has already been offered, would be ridiculous, and perhaps injurious to the credit of Congress. If the State should not like the terms, I might act for Congress, and probably succeed, although others have failed. I intend to mention it to the Doctor, and if I should meet with more philosophy than zeal, I have a mind to explain the whole matter to Mr. John Adams (if he affords me an opening to do it) and avail myself of his advice and assistance. The established character of his great abilities and patriotism all over the Continent would, I hope, sufficiently warrant my step, besides what I know of him from the late Governor, and still more from yourself. I hope soon to entertain you with some favourable accounts of European affairs, and I have the honour to be most respectfully, Sir, Your Excellency's most Obedient & most Humble Servant,

PHILIP MAZZEI

RC (CtY); at head of text: "13 [i.e., dispatch No. 13]. 3d. Copy." An unnumbered duplicate of the same dispatch is in PHi. Both versions are entirely in Mazzei's hand, attesting his agitation and haste in informing TJ of the unpleasant result of the conference with Franklin.

From Samuel Huntington

SIR   Philada April 23. 1780

Your Excellency will receive herewith enclosed an Act of Congress of the 18th Instant with Copies of sundry Papers therein referred to No. 1. and No. 2. by which you will be informed that a Suit at Law is said to be instituted in Yoghogania County against Colo. Broadhead Commanding Officer at Fort Pitt, in Consequence of Orders given by him to some of the Troops under his Command to take Possession of a House occupied by Edward Ward and Thomas Smallman Esquires which he judged necessary for the Safety of that Post.

You will observe that by the Act enclosed Congress have resolved Colonel Broadhead shall be supported in any Acts or Orders which the Nature of the Service, and the Discharging his Duty as Commanding Officer at Fort Pitt hath made or shall make *necessary* with which I have no Doubt the supreme Power of Virginia will concur, and that proper Measures will be adopted to prevent Colo. Broadhead his being unjustly vexed on Account of any Orders or Act by him given or performed, in the necessary Discharge of his Duty as Commanding Officer.

I have the honour to be &c.,   S. H.

FC (DLC: PCC, No. 14). Enclosures (missing): (1) copy of Daniel Brodhead's letter to Richard Peters, secretary of the Continental Board of War, Pittsburgh, 27 Feb. 1780, printed in *Penna. Archives*, 1st ser., VIII, 119-20; (2) copy of resolve of Congress, 18 Apr., declaring that Brodhead will be supported in discharging his military duties, printed in JCC, XVI, 373.

Brodhead's letter of 27 Feb. related the difficulties he had encountered in attempting to fortify a house on an eminence near Fort Pitt against an expected attack by a strong body of Indians. The occupants of the house, Ward and Smallman, after being evicted by troops from the Fort, commenced a suit against Brodhead in the court of Yohogania co., Va., and he was served by the sheriff of that county with a summons to appear in that court or accept judgment in default. Huntington's reply to Brodhead, 22 Apr., is in DLC: PCC, No. 14; and a letter similar to that sent to TJ was sent to Gov. Reed of Pennsylvania, 23 Apr. (same).

From Paulus Æmilius Irving

Monday Morn [April? 1780]

Major Irving's Compliments to the Governor. He sends him a few Pease. He is very sorry his stock will not admit of a Larger proportion.

Majr. Irving will esteem it a very particular favor if the Governor will be so good as to Purchase him a few Barrels of fine flour no Matter as to the Price.

RC (MHi). Addressed: "Governor Jefferson." Endorsed by TJ: "Irving." On the date, see below.

Maj. Paulus Æmilius Irving of the 47th British Foot (later a baronet and general; see DNB) occupied Mazzei's plantation Colle after Gen. Riedesel's exchange in 1779. The date assigned to the present letter is tentative, but early peas ripened in April in Albemarle, and Irving's letter of 2 May 1780 acknowledges the receipt of a barrel of flour. TJ's Account Books yield no information on this affair.

To J. P. G. Muhlenberg

[*Richmond?*, *before 1 May 1780*. In a letter to Gen. Washington from Fredericksburg, 8 May 1780 (DLC: Washington Papers), Gen. Muhlenberg states that "I received the Governor's Answer (to Muhlenberg's letter of 20 Apr., q.v.) on the first of May, approving my proposals as far as related to the recruiting Business, but Objected to having Rocky ridge appointed for a General Rendezvous, it being unhealthy and too near the Seat of Government, and proposed Chesterfield as a healthy and convenient Situation." Not located.]

From Paulus Æmilius Irving

SIR   Collé May 2d. 1780

I receiv'd the Barrel of flour you was so kind as to send me, for which I am greatly obliged to you, but I am vastly concern'd you have had so much troubles. The weight of the flour and cask is 242 ℔.

I am sorry to hear that the negociations for the exchange of prisoners has faild, but we must make use of a little Philosophy and live in hopes the next trial will prove more successfull.

My Most respectfull Compts. to Mrs. Jefferson & I am Sir Your very Humble Servant,   P Æmilius Irving

RC (DLC).

State of the Virginia Forces

State of the Virginia forces in Continental service, including the rank & file & Non-commissioned officers only	Temporary enlistments not expiring before Sep. 30. 1780.	Enlistments for terms not specified in the returns	Enlistments for the War.	Total counted as of our Quota	Enlistments expiring between dates of returns & Sep. 30. & therefore not counted as of our Quota
Infantry with the main army, including the 1st & 2d. state regiments, as by return from Genl. Washington of Dec. 26. 1779.	181.		1456	1637.	1377
Colo. Gist's regiment; as by Colo. Cabell's return of Oct. 1779.	53		70	123.	99.
Recruits sent to the Southward under Genl. Scott, as by his return Nov. 18. 1779.		1002.		1002.	
Colo. Porterfeild's detachment of Infantry to South Carolina, as by his return May 2. 1780.	134.		84.	218.	*171[1]
Colo. Harrison's regiment of artillery, as by Genl. Washington's return Dec. 26. 1779.[2]	4.		81.	85.	129.
Colo. Hazen's regiment, as by return from Continentl. War office Feb. 23. 1780.		12.		12	
Majr. Caleb Gibbs's corps of guards, as by return of War office Feb. 23. 1780.		37		37.	
Virginia troops at Fort Pitt as by return from Genl. Washington Nov. 1779.		308		308	100

	395.	1781.⁴	2029	4205	1876.
Colo. Taylor's regiment of guards to the Convention troops, enlisted during the stay of those troops in Albemarle			297.	297.	
Colo. Moylan's horse, as by letter from Genl. Washington of Feb. 16. 1780.		63		63	
Reid's troop of Majr. Nelson's horse on service with the Convention troops Albemarle		29		29.	
Two troops of Majr. Nelson's horse detached to S. Carolina undr Colo. Porterfeild, return, May 2. 1780.	23				
Colo. Baylor's horse (exclusive of those in Carolina at the date of the return) as by return Oct. 13. 1779.			41.	64.	
Colo. Bland's horse, no return: but said by the commanding officer to be about		138.		138.	
Majr. Lee's horse as by letter from Genl. Washington Mar. 9. 1780³		140		140.	
		52		52.	

MS (DLC); entirely in TJ's hand.

This memorandum could not have been completed before 2 May 1780 (see the fourth and twelfth entries). In DLC: TJ Papers, 5: 723, is "A General Return of the Southern Detachment of State Troops under the comd. [of] Lt Colo. Porterfield, Specifying the expiration of their service, May 2nd 1780," signed "Cs. Porterfield" and directed to "His Excelcy. Thomas Jefferson." The total there given is 433.

1 Below this column is a corresponding asterisk followed by a note reading: "these enlistments do not expire till Aug. & Sep. 1780."

2 At this point occurs a marginal note which applies to the first five entries in the table: "Marched, or or[dere]d to South Carolina."

3 At this point occurs a marginal note which applies to the last four entries in the table: "[M]ar[che]d t]o S. Carolina."

4 Below this column appears the following note: "Scott's brigade serve through the campaign of 1780. The cavalry is increased in numbers. Reid's troop is for the war."

From Thomas Sim Lee

S<small>IR</small>   In Council Annaps. 2d. May 1780

A Detachment of 3000 Troops is already embarked at the Head of Elk, in a Day or two, to proceed down the Bay of Chesapeake to your State, to reinforce the Southern Army. We esteem it highly necessary that every possible Precaution should be used to prevent any Part from falling in with the Enemy's Cruisers and have, to that End, communicated to your Excellency the Intelligence we have received from one of our Lookout Boats that returned last Night from the Mouth of Potowmack. The Captain informs us that there are several small Privateers in the Bay and one or two as high up as Wiccomico in Virginia. We shall keep our Boats out constantly, to give us Information, that we may apprize the Commanding Officer, of every Movement of the Enemy, to intercept the Troops. We have the Honr. &c.

FC (MdAA).

From Philip Mazzei

S<small>IR</small>   Paris, May 3d. 1780.

In letter 7, the first of which I sent by Marquis de la Fayette, I took the liberty to propose to you the sending to Leghorn, if possible, under french colours a cargo of the best tobacco. I have since been informed by the Tuscan Minister (who is American in the heart, and is of some service to me) that good Indigo would be likewise a very profitable article there, and especially at present. I was not acquainted with it before, but he has proved it to me very clear, and is so sanguine in it that he would, if practicable, take some interest in the cargo himself. I therefore wish that you could and would make a trial. You will remember that one of the points I always had in view, for the good of our Country in these difficult times, was the persuading the Italians to send us on their account and at their risk such goods as we are in most need of. I have observed to the said gentleman, Marquis Caraccioli, and other Italian ministers and travellors the advantages, which would result to the States of Italy from their entering earley in commercial corrispondence with America. I have seen already from various symptoms that seeds scattered in such a manner are apt to vegetate. A cousin to the present first Minister of the King of Naples came purposely to converse with me on the subject, and before he parted from this place made me promise that I would write my notions about it, as soon as I have leisure; and send them to him. He and another person of high rank and *abilities* engaged me much to go to Naples myself, which I intend to do, if my purse will bear it. That King may become a useful friend to us, particularly on account of the barbarians, as he intends to have soon a respectable marine, consisting of 12. ships of the line fregates and other vessels sufficient to protect a free navigation in the Mediterraneum. But at present the States of Italy cannot act openly for several reasons. I will mention one, which is not perhaps so very obvious. They cannot prudently take the lead of Prussia Russia and the Emperour. The only way for the Italian adventurers would be, after having their cargoes ready for America, to take their dispatches for France, where they ought to be furnished with french passports, letters of mark, and every thing requisite. I mentioned it earley to Dr. Franklin, desiring that he would procure me an interview with the Minister, as I wanted to carry with me the certainty of having executed here what I might propose to them. He undertook to do it, and the week after told me that he had not been at Versailles. The Foreign Ministers go there only on tuesday, unless there are particular reasons, as pressing business, &c. The next time he could not mention it, having had too much to do. The 3d. week it had gone quite out of his head; and as he expressed not remembering well what it was that I wanted to propose, I repeated it. He then proposed that I would write it, and he would give it to the Minister. I observed that the point in question could probably be well digested and determined in one conversation; that the writing upon it would be too tedious and too difficult a task; and in short that it could not be done with any propriety without being thoroughly acquainted with their marittime laws and regulations, and some of their Treaties, especially those with the Barbarians. He advised me to go to one Mr. Chaumont, a good friend of his, and a gentleman from whom I could have, he said, all the informations I might wish relative to the french national affairs. I could get none however but was favoured with an advice to persuade the Italians to what they probably would not, and prudently should not do. I had made many trips, and lost many days after the desired informations when I returned to the Doctor, mentioned the impropriety of the advice, and repeated my desire of having some thing done in an affair, which I conceived might be of great utility to us. The day before yesterday I spoke again to him on the subject; said that the only way to do some thing was the going to the fountain at once; and expressed again a desire of his assistance to enable me to serve our Country. He had often complained in our conversations of the multiplicity of business; he repeated the same on the occasion; and said that the best thing the Italians could do was, in his opinion, to follow Mr. Chaumont's advice. I therefore determined to go to work some other way, and not to trouble him any more on that score. I asked him if he had found certain papers relative to the money, which Congress want to borrow, and others, all which I was to peruse, and to take copies of such I thought may be of use to me. He had had no time to look, he said, but he would do it, and send them to me. In my last letters before I leave Paris I shall perhaps be more explicit. Till then I intend to say nothing more, than what is necessary to convince you that I am, as I have always been and shall be, as active and as zelous as possible in my endeavours to promote the good of our Country through every means. I am most respectfully, Sir, Your Excellency's most Obedient & most Humble Servant, PHILIP MAZZEI

RC (NN); at head of text: "14 [i.e., dispatch No. 14]. 3d. Copy"; endorsed by a clerk. The "2d. Copy" of this dispatch is in Vi, but is in a clerk's hand.

FC (DLC: Mazzei Papers).
Mazzei's LETTER 7 was dated 2 Mch. 1780, q.v.

To Riedesel

SIR   Richmond May 3. 1780.

Your several favors of Dec. 4. Feb. 10. and Mar. 30. are come duly to hand. I sincerely condole with Madame de Riedesel on the birth of a *daughter*, but receive great pleasure from the information of her recovery, as every circumstance of felicity to her, yourself or family is interesting to us. The little attentions you are pleased to magnify so much never deserved a mention or thought. My mortification was that the peculiar situation in which we were put it out of our power to render your stay here more comfortable. I am sorry to learn that the negotiations for the exchange of prisoners have proved abortive, as well from a desire to see the necessary distresses of war alleviated in every possible instance, as that I am sensible how far yourself and family are interested in it. Against this however is to be weighed the possibility that we may again have a pleasure we should otherwise perhaps never have had; that of seeing you again. Be this as it may, opposed as we happen to be in our sentiments of duty and honor, and anxious for contrary events, I shall nevertheless sincerely rejoice in every circumstance of happiness or safety which may attend you personally, and when a termination of the present contest shall put it in my power to declare to you more unreservedly how sincere are the sentiments of esteem & respect (wherein Mrs. Jefferson joins me) which I entertain for Madme. de Riedesel & yourself & with which I am Sir Your most obedt. & most humble servt.

Dft (DLC). Printed by Ford (II, 302-3) under date of 13 May 1780 from RC in possession of Thomas Addis Emmet but now not located. The date "May 13" may appear on the recipient's copy, since Ford calls attention to the "erroneous" date of 3 May given in HAW, I, 240-1; but the draft clearly reads "May 3."

From Thomas Blackburn

Prince William County, 4 May 1780. Acknowledges a (now missing) letter from TJ by Henry Lee notifying Blackburn of his appointment to the executive council. Feels a due sense of the honor intended for him by the Assembly but must decline because of "a Deafness with which I have been long afflicted, and which I fear is too considerable to allow a proper Attention to the Duties of the Office."

RC (Vi); 2 p.; signed "T. Blackburn"; addressed: "His Excellency Thomas Jefferson"; endorsed by a clerk. Enclosed in TJ's letter to Harrison, 8 May 1780, q.v.

Thomas Blackburn of Ripon Lodge, Prince William co., lt. col., 2d Va. line, 1776, had been wounded at Germantown, 1777 (WMQ, 1st ser., IV [1895-1896], 266). See note on John Page's letter of resignation from the Council, 7 Apr. 1780.

From James Madison

DEAR SIR   Philada. May 6th. 1780

I am sorry I can give you no other account of our public situation than that it continues equally perplexed and alarming as when I lately gave you a sketch of it. Our army has as yet been kept from starving and public measures from a total stagnation by draughts on the States for the unpaid requisitions. The great amount of these you may judge of from the share that has fallen to Virginia. The discharge of debts due from the purchasing departments has absorbed a great proportion of them, and very large demands still remain. As soon as the draughts amount to the whole of the monthly requisitions up to the end of March, they must cease according to the new scheme of finance. We must then depend wholly on the emissions to be made in pursuance of that scheme which can only be applied as the old emissions are collected and destroyed. Should this not be done as fast as the current expenditures require, or should the new emissions fall into a course of depreciation both of which may but too justly be feared a most melancholy crisis must take place. A punctual compliance on the part of the States with the specific supplies will indeed render much less money necessary than would otherwise be wanted, but experience by no means affords satisfactory encouragement that due and unanimous exertions will be made for that purpose not to mention that our distress is so pressing that it is uncertain whether any exertions of that kind can give relief in time. It occurs besides that as the ability of the people to comply with the pecuniary requisitions is derived from the sale of their commodities, a requisition of the latter must make the former proportionally more difficult and defective. Congress have the satisfaction however to be informed that the legislature of Connecticut have taken the most vigorous steps for supplying their quota both of money and commodities, and that a body of their principal merchants have associated for supporting the credit of the new paper, for which purpose they have in a public address pledged their faith to the Assembly to sell their merchandise on the same terms for it as if they were to be paid in specie. A similar vigor throughout the Union may perhaps produce effects as far exceeding our present hopes as they have heretofore fallen short of our wishes.

It is to be observed that the situation of Congress has undergone a total change from what it originally was. Whilst they exercised the indefinite power of emitting money on the credit of their constituents they had the whole wealth and resources of the Continent within their Command, and could go on with their affairs independently and as they pleased. Since the resolution passed for shutting the press, this power has been entirely given up and they are now as dependent on the States as the King of England is on the parliament. They can neither enlist pay nor feed a single soldier, nor execute any other purpose but as the means are first put into their hands. Unless the legislatures are sufficiently attentive to this change of circumstances and act in conformity to it every thing must necessarily go wrong or rather must come to a total stop. All that Congress can do in future will be to administer public affairs with prudence vigor and œconomy. In order to do which they have sent a Committee to Head Quarters with ample powers in concert with the Commander in chief and the Heads of the departments to reform the various abuses which prevail and to make such arrangements as will best guard against a relapse into them.

The Papers inclosed herewith contain all the news we have here. With great regard I am Dr Sir Yr Obt Servt,

JAMES MADISON JR

RC (DLC: Madison Papers). Enclosures not identified.

To J. P. G. Muhlenberg

[*Richmond?, before 7 May 1780.* In a letter to Gen. Washington from Fredericksburg, 8 May 1780 (DLC: Washington Papers), Gen. Muhlenberg quotes from a letter received from TJ on 7 May, as follows: "As to the pay of the Officers left in this State, the poverty of the Continental Treasury shall not prevent their receiving it, if You will procure Authority for them to apply to the General Paymaster here or any other single person, whose receipt shall be so authoritative as to vouch our paying him Monies for that purpose and charging them to the Continent." Further, the sick troops at Petersburg should be moved to Chesterfield, which is healthier. TJ's letter not located.]

To Benjamin Harrison

SIR   May. 8. 1780.

I this day received the inclosed letter from Mr. Blackburn, appointed by the last assembly to be of the council of state, but declining to act in that office. Incertain whether he may have given the same information to the general assembly immediately, or may have relied on my doing it, I do myself the honour of inclosing it to you and am with the greatest esteem & respect Sir Your most obedient & most humble servt.,   TH: JEFFERSON

RC (NjP). Addressed by TJ to Harrison as Speaker. Endorsed: "Governors Letter May 8th: Enclosing Thos Black- burnes resignation as Councillor. May 9th: 1780. to lie on table." Enclosure: Blackburn to TJ, 4 May 1780, q.v.

To Benjamin Harrison

[*Richmond, 9? May 1780.* JHD, May 1780, 1827 edn., p. 4 (9 May): "The Speaker laid before the House a letter from the Governor, enclosing several others addressed to the executive, and sundry resolutions of Congress, with other papers, and stating several matters for the consideration of the General Assembly; and the said letters, papers and resolutions being read, were ordered to lie on the table." Later the same day: "*Ordered*, That the letters and papers from the Governor, which were ordered to lie on the table, be referred to the committee of the whole House on the state of the Commonwealth." Letter not located and enclosures not clearly identifiable, though one of the subjects of TJ's letter was certainly the withdrawal of G. R. Clark's forces to the Ohio; see TJ to Harrison, 14 June 1780, referring to the missing letter.]

Agreement with De Francy

[11 May 1780]

Articles of agreement entered into this eleventh day of May in the year 1780, between his Excellency Thomas Jefferson on behalf of the Commonwealth of Virginia of the one part, and Lazarus Defrancy of Paris of the other part Witness: that whereas an importation of Goods from France for the use of the State of Virginia, has been proposed by the said Defrancy to the Executive of the State; It is therefore agreed by the parties,

First That the goods to be imported shall be delivered at Bermuda hundred along side of the Ship if required on the arrival, and provided the Ship can go so far up James river.

Secondly, that six Days shall be allowed to the State for loading the Ships after the Demand made by said Defrancy or his Agent for the Tobacco; and the Demurrage, in case of any, shall be settled by a reference to two persons chosen by the parties, and if a Difference in opinion should arise, a third person shall be chosen whose opinion shall be final.

Thirdly, That the goods shall be paid for in Tobacco, which shall be delivered along side of the Ship, in equal proportions on each river, that is to say, at the port of Bermuda hundred on James river; york, on york river; Hobshole on Rappahanock; and Alexandria on Potowmack, at the rate seven shillings Sterling Per hundred pounds of Nett Tobacco.

Fourthly, That the first payment shall not exceed four thousand hhds. of Tobacco; and that the remainder shall be paid within the term aforesaid, after notice being given that the Ships are ready to receive the same, or on their being required to be delivered provided the said remainder shall not be called for, within six months after the delivery of the Goods.

Fifthly, That the goods shall be charged at their first Cost at the Manufactories, the expences of transportation from the place of purchase, to the port where they are shipped and the Duties payable thereon in France, shall be added thereto and considered as part of their prime Cost; and well authenticated accounts thereof shall be rendered.

Sixthly, That the amount of Goods and Charges agreeable to the foregoing Article shall not exceed the Sum of thirty thousand pounds Sterling, but any lesser Quantity shall be received on the aforesaid Terms, the articles being proportioned according to the Invoic[es] that may be delivered. And if any unforeseen accident or event, shall prevent the said Defrancy from complying fully with this Contract on his part, he shall not be subject to Damages; neither shall the State be obliged to receive any of the Articles which may be tendered under this agreement after the expiration of twelve month from the Date hereof.

Seventhly, That if Hostilities shall cease, or peace take place between the united States, France and Great Britain, before the Shipping of the said Goods, the said Defrancy shall receive in payment thereof in manner aforesaid after the delivery, Tobacco at the rate of ten Shillings Sterling ⅌ hundred pounds of nett tobacco.

Eighthly, That Salt, wine and other Liquours are excepted out of this Agreement.

In Witness whereof the parties have hereunto set their hands and affixed their Seals the day and year above written.

                              Signed TH: JEFFERSON
In presence of   L DEFRANCY
Alexr. Wylly

Tr in Board of War Letter Book (MiU-C).

For the complicated transactions of De Francy, agent for Beaumarchais, with the State of Virginia, see Meriwether Smith to TJ, 24 June 1779; see also entry for TJ to Benjamin Harrison, 24? Nov. 1779 (first letter); and resolution of the House of Delegates of 6 Dec. 1779 concerning TJ's transactions with De Francy (JHD, Oct. 1779, 1827 edn., p. 80). There is also a Tr (Vi) of a statement of TJ dated 12 May 1780, certifying that there is due De Francy from the state a balance of £161,603 and 13 shillings, with interest at 6%, from 1 July 1778 (printed in *Official Letters*, II, 121-2).

From Samuel Huntington

SIR   Philada. May 11. 1780

Inclosed your Excellency will receive an Act of Congress of the 9th Instant with a Letter from P. Legras and other Papers therein referred to which I am directed to lay before the Executive of the State of Virginia as proper for the Consideration of the Assembly of that State.

I have the honour to be &c.   S. H.

FC (DLC: PCC, No. 14). Enclosures missing; the resolve of Congress of 9 May is printed in JCC, XVII, 416-17; see also XVI, 362. The present letter and enclosures were transmitted to Speaker Harrison in a missing letter of 5? June 1780; see under that date.

From Philip Mazzei

Paris, May 12, 1780. De Ternay's fleet with 6,300 troops under Lt. Gen. Rochambeau sailed from Brest on 2 May; a second division, with 3,000-4,000 men is expected to sail in about three weeks. The Spanish fleet, with 11,460 men, sailed from Cadiz on 28 Apr. Observations on the comparative naval status of the three powers. France is fast winning the confidence of the other European powers; England has lost it through "an immodest thirst of Empire, joined to an unbearable insolence." In France "liberal sentiments" make rapid progress in all ranks; "it seems as if the whole nation were turned true citizens of the world." Ruthless impressment in England will have bad results. Eagerness of the French to join the army under Rochambeau. Mazzei intends to propose a plan to John Adams. Postscript: French naval strategy in European waters; the English continue to capture Dutch vessels, and a protest by Russia will probably follow; the French troops who sailed are 6,000, including the marines, and the Spanish above 12,000.

RC (Vi); 4 p.; in a clerk's hand, with signature and postscript in Mazzei's hand; at head of text: "15 [i.e., dispatch No. 15]." The "2d Copy" of this dispatch is in CtY; 4 p.; in a clerk's hand, signed by Mazzei. The version in Vi is printed in CVSP, I, 348-50, and from there by Marraro, *Mazzei*, p. 49-52; the postscript is not in either printing.

To Francis Taylor?

Richmond, May 13, 1780

Permission having been granted by Sir Henry Clinton to two American officers to come out on parole on condition that the same indulgence should be granted to Lord Ingstricken and Lieut. Hannon of the Convention prisoners, and these gentlemen desiring of going to New York in the flag Patsy, now lying at this place, you will be pleased to furnish them with passports and take proper paroles.

MS not located. Printed from A. H. Joline, *Catalogue of Autographs and Portraits of Members of the Continental Congress* . . . , N.Y., December, 1897, p. 44. An A.L.S.; the body of the letter is probably printed entire. Without much doubt it was addressed to Col. Francis Taylor, commandant of the Albemarle Barracks.

Neither INGSTRICKEN nor HANNON has been identified; their names are perhaps mistranscribed.

To Anthony Walton White

Sir   Richmond May 14. 1780.

I do myself the pleasure of transmitting to you the inclosed advice of Council and order, in answer to your application to us. The board of trade inform me they have and shall immediately forward to the Southward such stores as will amount to about half the annual allowance.

I am Sir Your most obedt. Servt.,   Th: Jefferson

RC (A. Phillippe von Hemert, New York City, 1947). Addressed by TJ: "Colo. White of the Virginia horse in South Carolina. recommended to the particular care of Colo. Porterfeild"; franked: "Th: Jefferson." Endorsed: "Publick Letter from Governor Jefferson. Virginia [*and, in a different hand:*] May 4. 1780 No. 11."

"Colo. White" was Anthony Walton White of New Jersey, col., 1st Continental Dragoons, who served with the Virginia cavalry in South Carolina; he had been defeated by Tarleton on 6 May (Heitman; Gwathmey, *Hist. Reg. of Virginians in the Revolution*; Burk-Girardin, *Hist. of Va.*, IV, 382-3).

From George Washington

Sir   Head Quarters Morris Town 15h: May 1780

I have the pleasure to inform your Excellency confidentially that a French Fleet may in the course of a few Weeks be expected upon this Coast, and as it is uncertain what part of the land they may first make, Gentlemen are to be stationed at different points to give them Signals and to make them some necessary communications immediately upon their arrival. Major Galvan who will have the honor of delivering this to your Excellency is appointed to go down to Cape Henry for the purposes above mentioned, and as He will have occasion to keep one or two Boats in constant readiness to go off upon the appearance of the Fleet, I shall be much obliged by your giving an order to the person who has the superintendance of the public Vessels and Craft in Virginia to supply him with the necessary number. Should the public have none of the proper kind in their possession, you will be pleased to recommend to Major Galvan the most certain and speedy methods of procuring them. One or two skilful and trusty pilots will also be necessary, that if any of the ships should have occasion to enter the Bay, they may not be at a loss.

Your Excellency will no doubt see the prop[riety] of keeping the object of Major Galvans mission as much a secret as possible, lest the importance of the dispatches with which he is charged might be an inducement to some of the disaffected to take him off. It would add much to his security, if your Excellency would be good enough to introduce him to some Gentleman in the neighbourhood of Cape Henry, in whom he may confide and with whom he may remain while in that quarter.

It is essentially necessary that Major Galvan should be constantly informed of the operations in South Carolina, and as he will be out of the common track of intelligence, I have desired him to keep up a communication with your Excellency. Yo[ur] acquainting him therefore with what comes to your knowledge either officially or sufficiently authentic to be depended upon may be productive of most salutary consequences. I would beg leave to recommend Major Galvan generally to your Excellency for every public assistance of which he may stand in need, and particularly to your personal Civilities.

I have the honor to be with the greatest Respect and Esteem Sir Yr.

Dft (DLC: Washington Papers); in hand of Tench Tilghman; endorsed.

William Galvan, a Frenchman serving in the South Carolina Continental line, was appointed major and inspector in the Continental army, Jan. 1780; on the present occasion he bore a letter from Lafayette to Rochambeau, who was expected to arrive with his forces at Cape Henry, Va., or Newport, R.I. (Rochambeau landed at the latter). See Heitman; Lasseray, *Les français sous les treize étoiles*, I, 225-7; also TJ's Instructions printed under 31 May 1780.

To the Board of Trade

GENT.   Richmond May 16. 1780.

By a letter from Mr. Mazzei dated Nantes Nov. 27. 1779 I am informed that he had not then received any copy of the commission and instructions with which he was charged. As the Fier Rodrique offers a very secure opportunity of conveying them, I send you copies of his commissions and instructions which with a copy of the invoice and additional instructions from your office and whatever else may be proper you will be so good as to forward by the Fier Rodrique, Mr. De Francy having been so kind as to offer to take particular charge of them.

I am Gent. Your most obedt. humble servt.,

TH: JEFFERSON

RC (CSmH). Endorsed: "Duplicate of Letter to P. Mazzei Esq. sent. J[acquelin] A[mbler]." Enclosures missing.

To James Wood

Richmond May 17. 1780.

I take up your letters of Apr. 12. and 23. to answer at this very late day, having never been able to get a council since the 7th. of April till four or five days ago, so that I was unable to give you an effective answer. The council think it better to leave to yourself altogether the enforcing the order you inclosed me and which I now return. They rather advise that it should not be printed, it being out of the ordinary course to use that mode of publication in such cases.

Capt. Cherry's complaint about his rank is just and has apprised us of an error which we had run into without being sensible of it. I shall beg leave to explain it to you by stating facts. When the two eastern and two Western battalions were to be raised, the council determined that they would provide for the supernumerary officers in preference to all others as far as they would go, advancing them also one step if the commands to be given would admit of it. Sensible that in appointing new officers, and giving new appointments to old ones we should be in danger of justling their rank, we determined that the commissions to the supernumerary officers should all bear date the same day, so that where two of the same former rank received the same new appointments their seniority should be decided by their former commissions. It was found necessary also to prevent an undue preference of these officers to those of our old state regiments (Marshall's and Muters) that their commissions should be dated the 8th. of Nov. some general regulation taking place that day in those two regiments. As to the new officers to be appointed it was proposed that their commissions should give them rank from the time their half quota was raised, but still it was meant that they should not go back beyond the 8th. of November, that no new officer might take place of one of the same rank who had been in service before. This arrangement appeared to us to be just, and it so appears now. Inadvertently however we find that in some instances counting back on their recruiting rolls for the date of the half quota raised; the commission had been filled up with that date without observing that it carried him back beyond the 8th. of November. This inadvertence has given rise to the present derangement, which we think it just to rectify by inclosing to you five new commissions to be delivered to the gentlemen to whom they are directed, and their former ones to be taken in being now revoked. These are all the instances we can find on the council books where the inadvertence happened. There may be others in the books of the board of war of which we cannot at present be informed. As soon as we are these also shall be rectified. I hope this full explanation will satisfy the gentlemen whose commissions are exchanged that it proceeds from no motive derogatory of their personal worth or rank; but that principles of justice alone have led to it; and I am persuaded that their acquiescence will be the more chearful as true military delicacy revolts as much at the idea of incroaching on the just rank of another, as having their own incroached on. I think the justice of the original arrangement of council cannot be questioned.

With respect to the clothing of your guards, it will not come so soon as their necessities call for; but it shall come. The troops going to the Southward and Colo. Crockett's going to the Westward are called on by dangers too pressing to the general union, to delay them longer than necessary. The order in which we have directed the clothing to be distributed as fast as it can be bought is 1st. Porterfeild's detachment. (This is complete and marched on.) 2. Harrison's new recruits, about 80. 3. Crockett's men supposed 200. 4. Gibson's and Brent's new recruits about 200. 5. Some remains of Woodford's and Scott's brigades, about 80 or 100. All these are now detained from pressing duty till they can receive clothing. After those, the guards of Colo. Taylor's regiment shall be next served. I hope it will not be long before their turn will come.

Mr. McNiell of the British has permission to go to the warm springs and to remain there as long as his health may call for. You will be pleased to regulate his parole accordingly. I am sorry that this part of your letter has escaped me so long as I might have answered that without waiting, but I had put the letter by without attending to the part particularly relating to Mr. McNiell.

I am Sir Your very humble servt.,   TH: JEFFERSON

RC (NN). Enclosures missing.
Wood's LETTERS OF APR. 12 AND 23 have not been found.

From Samuel Huntington

SIR   Philada May 19. 1780

Congress have received authentick Information that his most Christian Majesty is preparing to send a powerful Naval and land Force to some Part of the Continent of North America. This Force generously calculated, either to produce a Diversion in our Favour, or to forward the Operation of our Arms by being directed to the same Object, may either by our Exertions be made the happy Means of delivering our Country in the Course of the Campaign from the Ravages of War, or being rendered ineffectual thro' our Supineness, serve only to sully the reputation of our Arms, to defeat the benevolent Intention of our great Ally, and to disgrace our Confederacy in the Eyes of all Europe.

Every State that reflects upon the Depreciation of the Currency and their own Deficiency in the Payment of their Taxes must necessarily conclude that the Treasury is exhausted. The military Departments are at a Stand for the Want of Money to put them in Motion. Congress have no Resources but in your Spirit and Virtue, upon these they confidently rely. You know the Value of the Prize for which you contend, nor need you be informed how much you are interested in a speedy Termination of this distressing and expensive War.

But as the smallest Disappointment in the requisitions they make may be attended with the most serious Consequences they have endeavoured so to limit their Demands as not exceed your Power to comply with them.

The Sum for which you are called upon by the within Resolution they flatter themselves you will furnish to the Treasury by the fifteenth of June at farthest without neglecting to discharge the Orders that have been drawn upon you, for the whole of which you will receive Credit on your Account of Taxes due on the first of March last.

As this Money is absolutely necessary to put the Army in Motion, independant of the Purchase of Provisions, we trust you will by no Means remit your Attention to the Forwarding your Quota of Supplies, which the present Exigency renders more requisite than ever.

It may not be improper to suggest to you, that if a strict and immediate Collection of Taxes should be insufficient to procure the necessary Sums within the Time limited, it may perhaps be more speedily obtained by Loans.

Congress for the greater Despatch have thought it expedient to appoint a Committee to assist the Commander in Chief in drawing out Supplies. As their Powers will be inadequate to the Purposes of their Appointment unless they shall derive Force from the States to whom they will be under the Necessity of applying. They most earnestly request you, if you should find it inconvenient to continue your Sessions, to lodge such Powers in your Executive, or some part of your legislative Body, as will enable them at this interesting Period on the Application of the Committee to call forth the Resources of your State.

Congress trust that these requisitions will not appear unnecessary, when compared with the Information on which they are grounded. In the Importance of which they doubt not you will find a sufficient Appology for the Demand and the Warmth with which they intreat you to carry these Measures into immediate Execution.

By Order of Congress   S. HUNTINGTON   President

FC (DLC: PCC, No. 15). At head of text: "To the several States from New Hampshire to Virginia inclusive." Enclosure (missing): Resolve of Congress of this date; printed in JCC, XVII, 437-9.

THE WITHIN RESOLUTION of 19 May called upon the ten states in question "to collect and pay into the continental treasury, immediately, if possible, and, at all events, within thirty days from this time, ten million dollars." Virginia's quota was $1,953,200. The money was to be "applied solely to the bringing the army into the field, and forwarding their supplies"; and the Committee of Congress at Headquarters was designated to expedite drawing out the supplies required of the states by Congress' resolution of 25 Feb. 1780 (see the Committee's first letter of 25 May, below). For Virginia's action, see TJ to Harrison, 8 June 1780, and references there; also TJ to Huntington, 9 June 1780.

From Philip Mazzei

SIR   Paris, May 19th. 1780.

It is obvious that the European adventurers cannot, during the war, fetch from America but a Small proportion of their Capital. My intention has always been to persuade them to leave the Greatest part of it in our funds; which would be the means of interesting them in our welfare, and of taking a great deal of paper money out of circulation. The late resolutions of Congress tending to so great, and I hope advantagious, alteration in our finances, put me now intirely at a Stand. I am not only unfit to propose any thing, but likewise unable to give Satisfaction to any question on the Subject, untill you favour me with a clear and thorough information of the whole, which I heartily wish may soon be the Case. I Suppose that the States will adopt the plan recommended by congress, and I wish that the collection of the monthly taxes may prove as easy near the end as I hope it will be at the beginning. It appears to me that the redemption of the currency of individual States becomes unavoidable at the Same time; and if I dont mistake, our state is pretty well loaded with it. I hope however that the Sale of our back-lands, and british property will greatly alleviate the heavy burden. The Silence of congress respecting the money borrowed by them from Individuals at 6 ℔ cent interest, payable in paper-money, induces me to believe that they had not as yet agreed on the resolution they should take about it. I expect that our State will follow their Steps in regard to our Loan office. It is highly necessary that I should be acquainted with it, as well as with any other new establishment of the kind, if there Should be any hereafter in the Country. I shall take it as a particular favour if you will be at the trouble of informing me with the new laws relative to emigrants, and in short with every article of our constitution and new Code of Laws apt to satisfy the minds of those, who may incline to become our Countrimen. I have already been applied to on this particular by Several french and two young Italian gentlemen, who were here in their travels. One of them is a Young brother of the Prince of Ottaviano of Naples, an old branch of the Medicean family, who assured me that with a moderate fortune and families of Labourers and Machanicks, he will bring to Virginia true Republican Sentiments. The notions of Equality among mankind have made of late a most rapid and Surprising progress in Europe. All judicious and Sensible people agree that this happy and noble improvement is chiefly owing to our Glorious cause, by the noise of which the minds of the people have been shakened and awakened. Great Britain only has been So far from partaking of the benefit, that it seems as if the prejudices, which are obliged to fly from other Countries, were accumulating in that disgraced Island. How pleasing and comfortable such reflections must be to true American hearts! I have the honour to be most respectfully, Sir Your Excellency's most Obedient & most Humble Servant,

PHILIP MAZZEI

RC (CtY); in a clerk's hand, signed by Mazzei. At head of text: "16 [i.e., dispatch No. 16]. 1st. Copy." The "3d. Copy" of this dispatch, also a letter signed, is in NN.

From William Armistead

Williamsburg, 20 May 1780. Submitting his resignation as "Commissioner of Loans for the States" (i.e., commissioner of the Continental loan office for Virginia), and recommending his assistant, John Hopkins, for that post.

RC (Vi); 2 p. Addressed: "His Excellency the Governour of Virginia ℔ Mr. Hopkins"; endorsed in a clerk's hand. Transmitted to Harrison in a letter of 3 June 1780, q.v.

The writer was William Armistead,

who continued as state commissary of stores (JCC, XVI, 289; *Official Letters*, II, 117, note). On 7 June 1780 John Hopkins was elected his successor (JHD, May 1780, 1827 edn., p. 38).

From Philip Mazzei

Paris, 20 May 1780. Gives a sketch of the plan of operations by the French land and naval forces recommended by Mazzei in influential quarters. Has sent a copy of his plan to Rochambeau by the Comte de Deux-Ponts, "to whom I gave a letter of recommendation for you dated March 27th." Postscript: John Adams before sailing for America made "the first and *strong* motion towards sending us effectual assistance," and Adams has been "warmly seconded in his absence" by Lafayette.

RC (Vi); 4 p.; in a clerk's hand, signed by Mazzei; endorsed by a clerk; at head of text: "17 [i.e., dispatch No. 17]. 1st. Copy." The "2d. Copy" of the same dispatch is in CtY; 3 p.; also a letter signed. First copy printed in CVSP, I, 350-2.

Mazzei's LETTER OF RECOMMENDATION for Guillaume, Comte de Deux-Ponts, addressed to TJ and dated 27 Mch. 1780, has not been found.

From Peter Penet

GENTLEMEN   May 20, 1780.

You have no doubt been informed of the misfortunes that have befallen us in the Confederacy, and of the retard occasioned by them. We left Philadelphia on the 25th Oct: ult: I arriv'd at Nantes only in march. From this place I sat off immediately to execute without delay the orders I received from you, that I might at the same time negotiate a loan, according to the Instructions and Powers which were delegated to me by your Honourable Council. I apply'd directly to the Gentlemen deputed by the different Cantons of Switzerland to the Court of France; but before I enter[ed] into discourse with them concerning that negotiation, I try'd to know their sentiments about your actual circumstances: they appear'd not to consider them in a favourable light. The miscarriage of the Count Destaings' Expedition in Georgia, the Discredit and undervalue of your paper money, the Commotions in Philadelphia about salt and other objects, having been communicated by Public newspapers, all those things, and the immense losses the Europeans had sustained in their Trade, with your Continent stopt on a sudden all Business. When I saw the Merchants of this Country were disheartened; that for all I could plead against their prevention, Financeers would no longer speculate; in that dilemma, I thought it was best to propose the proposal of the Loan. A conversation on that subject pass'd between me and the Honble Doctor Franklin: I was told by him that a great number of people having been Commission'd by different States to raise such Loans, far from succeeding happily in their negotiations, they prevented other Gentlemen to obtain success, on account of the prejudices they had excited in being importunate.

By this time several men of war with transports, and six thousand land forces must be near the Coasts of America. In about two months, a reinforcement is to be embark'd, in order to Joyn the first Army. I do not in the least, question but that fleet landing the Troops on your Continent, your affairs will wear another face, and the Credit of your paper money will be re-establish'd. The Super-Intendent General of the Fleet and Army bound to your parts, being a Nobleman concern'd in my Company, whom the King has promoted to that Post; I had many conferences at Paris with him relative to the affairs of America, and Cheifly to the power, Riches and Resources of your Common-wealth, the Harmony in your Councils, good order in your General Meetings and Strict Equity in your Dealings.

I caus'd to be recommended to the Commissioners and other Gentlemen named to provide supplies for the French Army in America, to take from the State of Virginia, the corn, flower, fodder, Horses and salt meat they shall want. The Treasurer of the army is directed to pay every thing with good Bills on France: and as that Gentleman is one of my Friends if you have a mind to procure some Bills either for yourselves or others, please to write to him: he was so obliging as to promise me the preference for your State. In case you treat with him, the Exchange is to be in Proportion of your currency. I think it should be an important Business, if you could contract to furnish all the supplies to the French army, which consists in Provisions only: your Province is abundantly stock'd with them.

My House at nantes, in Conformity to my advice, has Just dispatch'd a vessel call'd the Committee, loaded with an assortment of Goods and ammunitions as pr: your Order. At present it is impossible to provide ships and still less Sailors. I have employ'd my friends at Court near the ministers: but notwithstanding my Influence and Expostulations to get some ships that are detain'd in Harbours for Transports releas'd, I met with no success. They say the Royal navy is in want of them, and for that Reason none can be expedited. As a special favour I obtain'd only five and twenty men for the Committee. You may depend Gentlemen, that no opportunities shall be neglected by me, to perform my engagements with the State of Virginia. I expect in a short space of time, to see our Commerce more free and active. I am about to prepare adventures for you, suitable to the season. From this month to September, I will forward the articles that are fit for winter. I am on the point of concluding a Treaty for eight hundred thousand livers Tournois: it respects the cloathing of your troops, and all their accoutrements: also the armaments, with all the necessaries for the fitting out of your vessels. I earnestly wish I may be able to perform such a Treaty for the Best of your Interest. The payment of said eight hundred thousand livres is propos'd to be made in following manner—Twelve thousand Guineas ready money. The remainder to be paid in six, nine, and twelve months. Our House wants no Credit, we might afford several millions if we could depend on exact remittances, every nine or twelve months. I say I expect remittances, because in France, had any body the misfortune not to pay due honor to his engagements, which are held sacred, in a moment His reputation, His Credit are lost. As we shall be considerably in advance, it is then highly necessary that you should make remittances on all occasions to Europe. I paid to Mr. Mazzie in Paris, three hundred Louis d'or agreeable to the Order, I receiv'd from the Council of State whilst I was in Williamsburg. I spoke many times with him and got him introduced to some Gentlemen, that may be serviceable to him at Court. I wish with all my heart, his Projects may meet with a favourable Issue; but I must own freely in the conversation I had with several great men on that Topick, I was ascertained such Projects were not Practicable. However, Mr. Mazzie is a man of parts. If his Projects miscarry it shall not be for want of good zeal in the service of the State: Consequently his conduct cannot be blamable.

During the time I staid in Paris, I had frequent Opportunities to discourse with Several Farmers General, touching Tobacco Trade, which in Peace, will become most Considerable. None have more facilities than the State of Virginia, to undertake supplying them with that commodity. The Traffick of Tobacco might produce four millions at least annually. Many Persons of Virginia and Maryland design to have staples at L'Orient and at Dunquerque. Should the State venture on that Plan, I will be answerable on account of the Great Connections I have found with the Farmers General, theirs will be prefer'd to others. In France the best Tobacco is not sought for: that of your second quality sells as well as the first: but In future they will know the difference, and I shall endeavour to obtain the most advantageous price in the distinction of them.

When peace is come, it will be an easy matter for the State to procure ships and load them with great quantities of Tobacco. By these means large sums might be held at their disposal in Europe. You might even establish a Bank between Virginia and France to improve the Stocks.

I have the Honour to Inform You Gentlemen, that next place you may be supply'd with one to thirty six-pounders cast in a Royal Foundry well finish'd and try'd before the delivery. It is requir'd I should give four pounds of unwrought Iron, for one transmuted into a Cannon: so that with sixteen hundred pounds of Iron, you can have a Gun well made and prov'd weighing four hundred pounds wt:

The Foundry is establish'd on the river Loire two Leagues from Nantes. As soon as peace is proclaim'd, if you be willing to expedite some ships to this place, you might have them Ballast with Iron, and in return ship the Cannons that are necessary for your Armories, Coasts and fields. The Manufacture of small arms, hand guns &c., which was intended to be established in Virginia, cannot be founded in time of the war between France and England. The pain is capital, at the peril of one's life, it is forbidden to give passage to any workmen employ'd in such manufactories. By that Prohibition, we suffer a great loss, on account of the Dispositions that were already taken for that Establishment: Above all we regret to be compelled to suspend it.

I flatter'd myself on my departure from America, to be able coming back, after the Expiration of one year: but when I consider the state of things, it is a duty incumbent upon me to prolong my sojourn in France. My Presence is indispensable to discharge faithfully the trust you were so good as to repose in me: and to conduct at the same time your business with good Order and dispatch. Would you be pleas'd to communicate my letter to the Honorable Members of the Board of Trade. You have herewith some Public news papers for your perusal. I have the honor to be Very Respectfully Gentlemen, Your most obedient & devoted, humble servant, &c. &c.

MS not located. Text from *Calendar of Virginia State Papers*, I, 352-5.

MY HOUSE AT NANTES: Penet, D'Acosta Frères & Cie. (see Board of Trade to Penet, D'Acosta Frères, 6 Nov. 1779); letters from them to the Virginia Board of Trade respecting supplies sent in the company's schooner *Committee* are in TJ Editorial Files, 24, 31 May, 6 June, and 19 Nov. 1780, from originals in Vi, Executive Papers, 1779-1780. In his paragraph relating to the PROHIBITION on exporting munitions workers from France during a time of war, Penet dashed to the ground TJ's plans for a great armament factory on the James; see Contract with Penet, Windel & Co., 22 July 1779, and TJ to Harrison, 30 Oct. 1779. There is unfortunately no clue as to when TJ received this disappointing news.

From Alexander Sinclair,
with a List of Funds Collected for the State

Sir   Staunton May the 21st. 1780

Colo. Sampson Mathews not having imediate use for the money that he detained, (which was taken in in consiquence of your adress to the people) have desired me to send it down to you I have therefore embraced this oppertunity by Mr. Smyth Tandy for that Purpose. Please Sir, to give Mr. Tandy recepts for it and when Colo. Mathews gos down he will receve the loan Office Certificates. The list of the money is inclosed, with the dates it was received, and the time it was put in for. I am Your Excellencys Mo. Humle. Servt,   Alexr. Sinclair

ENCLOSURE

An Acct. of cash received of sundry persons in Consiquence of the Governors adress to the people Viz

1780.		£	s	d		
March 15th	John Vance	100			for 12 months	
"	Charles Donaley	1864	4		to the 1d of August	
18	Robt Dunlap	550				
21	Charles Donaley	135	16			
22	Capt Robt Brattan	633	14		for 3 years	
"	Adam Brattan	480			for do.	
	Capt Robt Brattan	600	16		for do.	
April 4	William Matear	560			for one year	
March 30	Andrew Ramsey	300			for 3 years	
	Hugh McClure	225			for one year	
A.S. April 1d.	James Crawford	200			for 3 years	200
A.S. — 3	Elijah McClenachan	120			for one year	120
A.S. — 8	James McNut	400			for 3 years	400
11	William Finley	800	14		for one year	
A.S. —	Jno. Ramsey	1220			for 3 years	1220
A.S. 18	Jacob Lerew	90			for 1 Year	90
A.S. 18	Ruben Lerew 150	140	00		for do	150
A.S. 18	Abram Lerew	150			for do	150
18	Thomas Scott	400	02		for 2 Years	
18	Walter Davis	417	9		1 Year	
A.S. May 16	James Campbell	1336	16		for 6 months	1336:16
5	Andrew Hamilton	1123	8	0	1st January 1781	
		11848	3	0		
			16			
A.S. 27th	William Lewis	1017	2		for three years.	1017:2
	Joshua Perry	1000			one year	

RC (Vi); addressed "His Excellancy Thos. Jefferson Governor of Virginia." Docketed in an unidentified hand: "Letter from Alexr. Sinclair to his Excellency. wt. Public Money." The following memoranda, in another hand, also appear on verso of letter: "1. delivery. 2. Accident excuse. Tan[dy] answerable for not counting money. Who wd. serve public. Took same care of his own. Delivered to bar-keeper." Also, interlined in the docketing, is the figure "[£]4376.-13," which is the amount of money missing. Enclosure: "An Acct. of cash received," printed herewith.

YOUR ADRESS TO THE PEOPLE has not been located, but this address was probably issued in pursuance of the Act passed at the Oct. 1778 session authorizing the treasurer to borrow from individuals any sum of money in specie, paper money issued by Congress, or bills of credit issued by the state in amounts not less than $300 for periods not less than one year nor more than three years, since, as stated in the preamble of the Act, "it has been proved by experience that it is more beneficial to this commonwealth to borrow money on interest than to make large emissions of paper money" (Hening, IX, 481). The Act does not authorize the governor to issue an appeal to the public, but it is possible that one was issued and that Sinclair is referring to an address issued by Gov. Henry before TJ took office. It is much more likely, however, that the address was one issued by TJ, for not only is Sinclair's letter addressed to him by name, but also the receipts of money as listed in the enclosure are all dated after 15 Mch. 1780. On MATHEWS (or Matthews), TANDY, and the case of the missing money, see George Brooke to TJ, 14 June 1780, and Advice of Council concerning Money Collected, same date; the note on the latter document explains the docketed memoranda quoted above.

To Jacquelin Ambler

SIR   In Council May 23. 1780.

During your absence the Speaker Harrison applied to me to let him be furnished with some guns from the foundery, a note of which he furnished Mr. Reeveley and afterwards Colo. Fitzgerald applied for the within; I promised both provided it was not inconsistent with any contracts, orders, or purposes of your board; the Speaker to be first supplied and Colo. Fitzgerald next. You will be pleased to direct a compliance with these engagements as far as they were meant to be absolute. I am Sir with great respect Your most obedt. servt.,   TH: JEFFERSON

RC (Vi). Addressed in TJ's hand; endorsed: "Govr. Jeffersons Letter to J. Ambler of the Bd. of Trade May 1780." Enclosure missing.

Memorial of the Officers of the
Virginia Line in Captivity

Long Island May 24th. 1780.

To His Excellency Thomas Jefferson Esquire, Governor of Virginia.

The Memorial of the Officers of the Virginia Line Prisoners of War here.

Most respectfully represents, That your Memorialists have endured a long, many of them a very long and irksome confinement, subject not only to those disagreeable sensations inseperable from a State of Captivity, but finally find themselves unfortunately left to struggle, with all the calamities of indigency and want. A whole year has now elapsed since they have received the smallest supply, and the scanty pittance then handed them, was barely sufficient to pay their Debts, and furnish them with the then absolutely necessary articles of Cloathing. That your Memorialists in conjunction with the rest of their Fellow prisoners on this Island, have lately made repeated applications to the Honorable the Continental Congress for relief, without having received even the promise of any immediate redress. Thus circumstanced, your unfortunate Memorialists and Captive Officers belonging to Virginia, a List of whose names are hereunto annexed, find themselves under the necessity as their last resort, of taking this method to lay their unhappy situation before you, and earnestly intreat your aid and assistance in relieveing or at least in alleviating their present complicated distresses.

They trust they have hitherto supported themselves with a patience and perseverence becoming the Soldier and the Citizen, and that the same line of conduct will still continue to mark their Character. They however on the present occasion cannot forbear mentioning their uneasiness and great anxiety, at the painful and tedious length of many of them near Three and some almost Four Years Captivity which they have endured, And although they have the most perfect confidence, both in the wisdom and humanity of the powers, by which their enlargement by way of Exchange depends, yet they humbly take occasion to mention, that amidst the great multiplicity of important business to be transacted, they fear their unfortunate situation has not been attended to, in such a manner as their fond wishes have led them to expect. This sentiment they are in some measure led to adopt, when they consider the great number of British Prisoners who are held in a state of Captivity similar to theirs, and the assurances they frequently have from the Friends of those Prisoners, of their great desire to exchange them. These the suggestions of your Memorialists, they submit to your feelings, without enlarging further on that head.

It was the earnest desire of your Memorialists that this their Memorial, might have been transmitted to y[ou] through the Hands of some of their unfortunate Brethren, who would have been able [gener]ally to explain at large, both their wishes and their wants; and fully to have communica[ted] To you many particulars, which are to them so very interesting; but as this was a priviledge that could not be admitted, they are left to content themselves out of the many material Matters that might be enumerated, of only Further imparting the following: That in consequence of, and on the Faith of a Resolve of Congress, to supply the Wants and exigencies of the Officers Prisoners of War from time to time, as their occasion might require, your Memorialists as well as other Prisoners obtained on Credit, those necessaries that their most poignant wants demanded, and although patriotism as well as prudence and Interest conspired to render them as frugal as possible in their expenditures, yet they have the mortification to find themselves considerably indebted, few or none of them less than Fifty Pounds, and many of them more than that sum, exclusive of the sum of Forty one Pounds Twelve shillings due from each Officer for one Years Board. That superadded to these inconveniencies, they are not only almost left destitute of the common necessaries, but their feelings are wounded with frequent and almost daily applications, attended with Threats on account of failure in payment, and what their situation will be unless speedily redressed, your Memorialists had rather you should conceive, than that they in their restricted State should now attempt to describe.

Should the General Assembly be sitting when this reaches you, it is the desire of the Memorialists that this their representation should be laid before them, and in that case they beg leave to observe to you, that it is intended to be addressed to that respectable Body as well as to yourself.

Your Memorialists with the most firm attachment and duty to their Country, for and in behalf of the Officers of the Virginia line and for themselves have the honour to be with the most perfect Esteem and Respect Your Excellency's Most Obedient And Most Humble Servants,

Geo Mathews Col.	Tarlton Woodson Majr.
Wm. Darke Major	Smith Snead Captn.
Oliver Towles Major.	Nathl Pendleton Jr. Lieut.

ENCLOSURE

A List of the Officers of the Virginia Line Prisoners of War to the British Army. Referred to by their Memorial, May 24. 1780.

NAMES AND RANK	REMARKS
Colo. George Matthews	On Long Island
Colo. George Baylor	On Parole in Virginia
Major William Darke	On Long Island
Major Levin Joynes	On Parole in Virginia
Major Oliver Towles	On Long Island
Major Tarlton Woodson	do. do.
Captains	
Moore Fauntleroy	On Parole in Virginia
John Willis	On Long Island
John Hays	do.
John Poulson	do.
Smith Snead	do.
George Gilchrist	do.
Robert Higgins	do.
Thomas Thewait	do.
John Spotswood	On Parole in Virginia
Joseph Scott. Brigade Major	do.
Lieutenants	
Thomas Parker	On Long Island
Robert Woodson	do.
Charles Snead	do.
Joseph Rogers	do.
Robert Randolph	On Parole in Virginia to return next July to L. Island
Severn Teacle	On Long Island
Thomas Payne	do.
Thomas Martin	do.
Reuben Field	do.
John Clarke	do.
Samuel Findlay	do.
William George	do.
Nathaniel Pendleton jr.	do.
Thomas Warman	do.
Henry Bedinger	do.
Edward Smith	do.
Adjutant William Robinson	do.
Ensigns	
Charles Stockley	do.
Nathaniel Darby	do.
Thomas Coverley	do.
Joseph Payne	do.

NAMES AND RANK	REMARKS
John Robins	On Long Island
John Scarborough	do.
Jonathan Smith	do.
Robert Foster	do.
Citizens or Volunteers.	
Thomas Brittle	do.
Thomas Granberry	do.
Josiah Riddick	do.
John Meals	do.
Officers omited in their place.	
Lieutenant Erasmus Gill	do.
Hancock	City New York with others supposed to be about two or three more whose names are unknown to us, so that the amount of Officers is 44. which with the 4 Citizens or Volunteers, and the unknown Names will make the total amount about 50 or 51.

MS (Vi); in Oliver Towles' hand (including the tabular enclosure), with autograph signatures. Addressed: "His Excellency Thomas Jefferson Esquire Governor of Virginia"; the address leaf (now separated from the letter) bears calculations and notations in several hands, not noted here.

For the Assembly's action on this Memorial, see entry for TJ's letter to Harrison, 22 June 1780, in which the Memorial was transmitted.

From the Committee of Congress
at Headquarters

SIR   In committee of Congress, Morristown, 25th May, 1780.

Yesterday we were honored with a despatch from Congress, conveying to us their resolutions of the 19th instant, (see page 3) together with a copy of their circular letter of the same date, to the several States, from New-hampshire to Virginia, inclusive.

By one of the former we are appointed to assist the commander in chief in drawing out supplies for the Army, and the line of conduct we are to pursue, is pointed out in those subsequent: The whole having been transmitted to your State, together with the circular letter, it is unnecessary to inclose your Excellency a copy. Immediately on the receipt of these papers, we laid them before the commander in chief, and entreated him to signify what supplies were immediately necessary to enable him to move the Army; and to put it in a condition to co-operate vigourously with the shortly expected succour of the great and generous ally of these States. This request we candidly avow, was made more with a view to preserve form in conducting business, than for want of competent information on the subject, that having already been fully detailed us by the General, and others, on former conferences, when acting as a committee of arrangements, he, consequently, had only to refer us to what had been before delivered us, by him and others, and which was in substance as follows. That the Army was five months pay in arrears; That it had seldom, or ever, since it took this cantonment, had more than six days provision in advance; That at present, it is without meat, and has been on half, and on quarter allowance, for some days past; That the commissaries cannot give any assurances of doing more than barely subsisting the troops, from day to day; That even then, they apprehend a want of meat will frequently prevail; That the Army is greatly deficient in camp equipage; That it is destitute of forage, for the few horses which indispensible necessity has required should be maintained in Camp; That it will require several thousand horses to move the Army, so as to promise any effectual operation from it; That the sick in hospitals, have not a sufficiency of *those* articles necessary for their comfort; That carriages in considerable numbers are wanted; That the quarter master general has not a competent number of boats for the use of the Army, in case any offensive operations should take place; That he has no materials for constructing new boats, and carriages, nor even for repairing the old; That as every department of the Army is without money, and not even the shadow of credit left, consequently no article, however necessary, can be procured; That the transportation even of the inadequate supply of flour, forage, and other articles hitherto furnished by the States, is at a stand; That very few of the recruits required by the act of Congress, of the 9th of February last, have arrived; That from information received, there is no prospect that any considerable number will *timely* engage in the service, on voluntary inlistment; That by the expiration of the *terms* for which men were engaged, deaths and desertions, the Army is so greatly reduced, that it does not afford a probable prospect of its acting with any degree of efficacy on merely defensive operations; That the patience of the soldiery, who have endured every degree of conceivable hardship, and borne it with fortitude, and perseverance, beyond the expectations of the most sanguine, is on the point of being exhausted;

That a spirit of discontent is encouraged by the arts of the enemy, whose emissaries hold up in printed papers, distributed among the soldiery, the most flattering prospects and promises, to enduce them to desert their coulours: The evidence given us in support of this detail of facts, has been fully corroborated by our own observations and enquiry; and painful as the contemplation of the distresses our country labours under, may be; we conceive it would have been inconsistent with our duty to have palliated, or disguised them, in an address to the constituents of that body under whose authority we act; as *they* ought, in our opinion, to be fully informed: For it is to them, this committee is directed to apply, and on them every reliance for relief and assistance must rest, in this very critical and important moment: But so far are we from desponding under this variety of embarrassment, that we reflect with satisfaction, the result of conviction, that the country is not destitute of the resources necessary to enable its Army to act with vigour, and to second the views of our illustrious ally; and that the legislative and executive powers of your State, impressed, as they are, with a just sense of the magnitude of the object, are equally desirous, as capable, of drawing them forth.

Congress, in their circular letter, has pointed generally at the measures necessary to be adopted by the States: We conceive it incumbent on us, in discharge of the trust reposed, to point more minutely at particulars, and in some measure to enter into a detail of *them*. We are encouraged to this, under a persuasion that the States will impute to our zeal, and affection for the interest and weal of our country, the liberty we take; and not to a spirit of dictating, which would be, equally improper, as presumptuous.

In a letter we had the honor to address Congress on the 16th instant, (see page 22) but which had not reached Philadelphia, when the circular letter and resolutions we have alluded to, were passed, we stated the little probability (which from the information we had obtained) there appeared to be, of completing the quota's of men, called for by the act of Congress, of the 9th of February last, by voluntary inlistment; and we conceived it requisite, to propose a set of resolutions, calculated to draw forth the intended complement of men for the Army, together with a state of the deficiencies—copy of which we have the honor to inclose (see page 303.) persuaded that the States can with more facility, and much less expense, make drafts to serve during the campaign, than to engage men to serve during the war, and convinced, from repeated experience, that no reliance is to be made on gaining a sufficient number by voluntary inlistment, should the mode, we have proposed, be as agreeable to the sentiments of the legislature of your State, as it is to those of the commander in chief, we cannot entertain a doubt but that the measure will be adopted with alacrity, and executed with energy.

From the state we have made of the distressed condition of the Army, in point of provision, we are persuaded that every argument to induce the utmost exertions to fill the magazines, which the commander in chief has directed to be formed, would be needless, as a matter of such importance will certainly claim the most immediate attention of the legislative and executive powers of the States.

Congress, in their act of the 25th of February last, have not called on the States for the transportation of any of the articles of supply, enumerated in that act, beyond the limits of the State furnishing the same. If the officers, whose business it is to direct the transportation, were, or could be furnished in *time*, with money, for that service, it would probably supercede the necessity of any intervention of the State: As they are not, nor is it probable they can *be*, even with the best exertions of the States, we humbly recommend, that authority be given by your legislature, to the executive authority, or to such other persons, as they may think proper, to furnish such carriage to the officers acting under the authority of Congress, or their committee, as may be needful, to convey those supplies, or any other, for the public use to the Army, or to such posts and places where they may be required: And that until the public officers shall have cash in hand to pay for the same, we intreat the legislature of your State, to give assurances to its citizens, that speedy and effectual measures will be taken to make payment of the debts which may be thus incurred, and remain unpaid, with an interest of 04 ⅌ cent, ⅌ annum, as stated in the resolutions of Congress, of the 19th instant.

It is more than probable necessity will require, that some States should be called upon for additional supplies to those apportioned to them in the Act of Congress of the 25th of February last; both because our Army, and that of our ally, may take such a position, as that supplies from remote States cannot be brought; and because some States are so exhausted, that they cannot even furnish the quota's assigned them: It therefore becomes essential that similar powers to those stated in the preceding paragraph, should be lodged in the executive authority, or other persons, for furnishing such extra-supplies, on the application of this committee, or officers appointed for that purpose: And to this matter we also intreat permission to draw the attention of your legislature. As it would be hazarding too much to depend on the precarious supply of horses and carriages, which might be furnished by the inhabitants occasionally, to move the artillery, baggage, and stores immediately attached to the Army; and as the aid of the States to procure the horses and carriages in the present exhausted State of the public Treasury, is evidently necessary, we are also constrained to intreat the attention of your legislature to this capital object, and to request that the executive authority, or other persons, may be empowered to comply with the requisition of this committee, or persons by them authorized for that purpose, on the condition mentioned in the paragraph next preceding the last.

Having, Sir, stated the most material articles of the many which are wanted, we beg leave to urge the indispensible necessity of investing your executive authority, or such other persons as your legislature may judge proper to intrust, with ample power to comply with the requisitions of the committee, or other persons by them appointed, for that variety of articles necessary for an Army, and its appendages, and of which, no perfect enumeration can be made; and to rely for reimbursement out of the monies called for from the States. Had it been practicable to have stated the particular extra-supplies, which necessity will induce us to call for, from each State, for the support of the Army, and its operations, it would have been our duty to have done so: As it was not, we wish your legislature to believe, that the committee will pay every possible attention, in making requisitions for supplies, so as to render the burden as equal in proportion to the ability of each State, as their situation, and the nature of the service will by any means admit.

It is possible, Sir, that should even the deficiencies to complete the quota of troops apportioned to the States, in February last, join their corps as early as the exigency of affairs certainly require, aid of militia may nevertheless be called for by the commander in chief, and as so much depends on dispatch in offensive operations, we beg leave most earnestly to recommend, that such measures may be adopted as will, effectually draw forth this invaluable resource with as little delay as possible.

Having stated what appears to the committee absolutely requisite to be adopted and pursued by the States, permit us, Sir, to add we are authorized to communicate, *that* the naval and land force alluded to by Congress in their circular letter, was to have sailed so early from France, that they may be daily expected to arrive on this coast; That the orders given by the court of Versailles, for the line of conduct to be observed by their officers, in combining their force with ours, to operate against the common enemy, clearly evince the most unbounded confidence, and the most unequivocal determination, that it should be directed by *American councils* and rendered subservient to the interest of these States. This generosity, on the part of our illustrious ally, strongly points at the necessity of taking every precaution in our power, that his views may not be frustrated, nor his arms disgraced. Indeed we should be left without the shadow of an excuse, should we through inattention, or indecision, neglect to avail ourselves of the advantages to which such a capital succour is capable of being improved. We should degrade our character, disgrace our Arms; and evince to all the world, that we were either destitute of resources, wanted exertion to draw them forth; or wisdom to apply them; and either would tend to discredit our cause, and stamp these States with indelible stains of infamy: But Americans are incapable of such folly: They will see the necessity of risking possible evils, nay even suffering certain, but temporary *ones*, with fortitude, and sacrificing a portion of property, if such sacrifice is necessary, rather than by withholding it involve themselves and their posterity in misery too painful to be contemplated without the deepest anxiety.

You, Sir, and the legislature of your State, we are fully convinced will, on this occasion, display with additional lustre that virtue and wisdom which have hitherto so emminently distinguished your councils, and, by taking the lead in exertion, will stimulate your citizens to such laudable acts as will amply intitle them to the invaluable blessings of that liberty, peace, and independence, for which they have fought, and bled.

The committee have only to add their wishes, that you, Sir, will be pleased to convene the legislature of the State with as much dispatch as possible, and to lay these our applications before them.

We have the honor to be, with the greatest respect, Your Excellency's, most obedient servants,

PHILIP SCHUYLER
JOHN MATHEWS
NATHL. PEABODY

FC (DLC: PCC, No. 11). At head of text: "Circular. No. 1. (N.B. From New-Hampshire to Virginia inclusive.)" The page references in the text are to the MS volume of the Committee's Proceedings, whence the present letter derives and where a copy of the enclosure ("state of the deficiencies" of the army) will also be found.

On 3 Apr. 1780 Washington wrote a long letter to Congress setting forth the deplorable state of the army, and on 6 Apr. Congress resolved "That a committee of three be appointed to proceed to headquarters, to confer with the Commander in Chief on the subject of his letter of the 3d instant," &c. The Committee's instructions were agreed to on 12 Apr., and the three members (those who signed the present letter) were elected next day (Washington, *Writings*, ed. Fitzpatrick, XVIII, 207-11, and especially Fitzpatrick's note; JCC, XVI, 332-3, 354-7, 362). By their resolves of 19 May, Congress assigned to the Committee, along with its other broad powers, the task of drawing out supplies from the states in order to put the army on a footing to cooperate with the French forces expected to arrive shortly (see Huntington to TJ, 19 May 1780).

From the Committee of Congress at Headquarters

Morristown, 25 May 1780. Circular to the state executives enclosing copy of Gen. Washington's letter of same date to Committee. Signed by Schuyler, Mathews, and Peabody.

FC (DLC: PCC, No. 11); 1 p.; at head of text: "Circular, No. 2." Enclosure: Washington to Committee, 25 May 1780, approving recommendations in the Committee's first circular letter (preceding) and urging filling up the state battalions by draft; printed in *Writings*, ed. Fitzpatrick, XVIII, 416-19.

From Abner Nash

DEAR SIR   Newbern May the 25th. 1780

I have this day received a letter from Governor Rutledge a copy of which, I send inclosed for Your perusal; by this and a Letter I received from Col. Laurens dated at Wilmington containing a paragraph of a letter he received from one of the Council of So. Carolina it seems reasonable to conclude that Charles Town is in the hands of the Enemy and yet the post rider who comes from George town three days after the date of these letters says the Current report and belief there was that Chs. town was not taken. A few days will no doubt relief us from our present doubts. I also inclose for Your Excellencys perusal a copy of an intercepted letter from Mr. Simpson, Genl. Clintons Secretary to a German Minister by which You will perceive the Secret means the Enemy are employing to effect their ends. I have also two intercepted letters from a Mr. Mitchell to Some of the leaders of the disaffected in our back Country incouraging the people to go down and Saying in express terms that Charles Town Surrendered on discretion, the ninth instant, this we know is not true and I own it leads me to hope that the whole is false and Spread by the Enemy to Intimidate the people in the Country. It seems very strange if the Garrison did

Capitulate as it is said that it should not be known of a certainty the 19th. following at George Town the place the Express came from. However, Sir, I will not tire you with more of my reasoning or Conjectures on the Subject. As soon as I know the fate of Charlestown with Certainty I will immediately send an express to Your Excellency.

Since I had the Honor of receiving your favor of the 4th. instant, I have not heard a word to be depended on of the Maryland and delaware troops. Should Chas. Town fall, Sir you may depend we shall want them and an aid also from Virginia of men and Arms for the immediate defence of this State. I take the Liberty of Inclosing to You my dispatches for Congress and intreat You Sir to forward them by Express. With the Highest esteem and regard I remain Sir Your Excellencys most obdt. & Hble. Servant,

A: NASH

RC (Vi). Addressed: "on pub. Service To His Excellency Thomas Jefferson Esqr. Governor &c. of Virginia." Enclosures: (1) copy (Vi) of letter from Gov. John Rutledge of South Carolina to Gov. Abner Nash of North Carolina, place not indicated, 16 May 1780, informing him of the surrender of Charleston on 12 May; (2) copy (Vi) of a letter from James Simpson to the Rev. Mr. Weikhman(?), "Headquarters Chas Town Neck May 5. 1780," commending the loyalty of the inhabitants of interior North Carolina and promising them British arms and provisions; (3) a dispatch or dispatches from Nash to be forwarded to Congress (read in Congress, 5 June; JCC, XVII, 486). TJ transmitted the letters of Nash and Rutledge to Speaker Harrison on 30 May; see under that date.

The report of the surrender of Charleston on the 12th was correct. TJ's FAVOR OF THE 4TH. INSTANT to Nash has not been found.

To Benjamin Harrison

[*Richmond, 26? May 1780*. JHD, May 1780, 1827 edn., p. 24 (26 May): "The Speaker laid before the House a letter from the Governor, enclosing one from a council of officers, held at Botetourt courthouse, and their determination on the subject of an offensive and defensive war with the Indians; which were read, and ordered to be referred to the committee of the whole House on the state of the Commonwealth." Neither the letter of transmittal nor its enclosure has been located.]

To George Muter

SIR   Richmond May 27th. 1780

You will be pleased to give orders to Mr. Moody to employ immediately such artificers as he has skilled in making Cartouchboxes, in that way, and to direct the QrMaster to procure leather.

As far as the public has or is entitled to leather let that be used and the deficiency be supplied by purchase. If a sufficient stock can be procured for covering in the best manner let them be so covered: if this article is very scarce, they must have flaps only. As the number wanted will be very great he may continue making till further orders.

Be pleased also to order the persons having custody of the ordnance, arms and other military stores, provision Waggons, horses, geer and other public property to make returns of what they have on hand, and the condition of the several articles: and that they hereafter make such return monthly. The Commissary has received these orders from me twice but has never obeyed them.

We want also Wooden Canteens to be made immediately. If Mr. Moody has no Artificers who can do this it could be best for him to employ some on Wages; if this cannot be done to a sufficient extent, he must procure them to be made by the piece. We should possess from eight to ten thousand Canteens in the whole. I am Sir Yr. very hble Servt.,   TH: JEFFERSON

Tr in Board of War Letter Book (MiU-C).

On 12 May 1780 the House appointed a committee to prepare, and on 6 July the two houses agreed upon, "An act to repeal an act establishing a board of war, and one other act establishing a board of trade, and authorizing the governour and council to appoint a commissioner of the navy, a commissioner of the war office, and a commercial agent" (JHD, May 1780, 1827 edn., p.

8, 75; Hening, X, 291-2). No record has been found of the exact date of Muter's appointment as commissioner of the war office, but the Board of War functioned very little after the removal of the government to Richmond in March, and Muter's correspondence with TJ indicates that the former may have been acting in the capacity of commissioner before TJ was authorized to make a formal appointment.

To William Galvan?
With a Summary of Affairs at Charleston

State of things at Charlestown.
Force of the enemy between 11,000 and 12,200
    viz. between 7000 and 8000 under Clinton in the lines before the town on the neck of land and between 4000 and 5000 under Cornwallis on the N. side of Cooper ri[ver.]
    Cornwallis has overrun the whole country South of Santee river, which is the whole of what is valuable except the district of Georgetown on the No. side of Santee, has burned all the grain and killed all the cattle which he could not carry off.

His posts on Cooper river prevent all communication with the town and have rendered the blockade complete.

Clinton had on the 27th. of Apr. (the date of our latest intelligence) advanced by regular approaches to within 6 feet of the wet ditch which has been cut across the neck from river to river. This ditch is 30 f. wide, the water 4. f. deep, and from the water to the surface of the ground 3 f. Within the ditch is a strong Abbatis; then 100 yards of open ground, then another abbatis. Behind this pitfalls thus ⬚◠⬚◠⬚ to break their columns. Then a dry ditch with two rows of Palisades and on this a rampart of earth with a plenty of guns mounted on carriages, and not embrazured. The whole is flanked by a battery of cannon at each end reaching from the wet ditch to the rampart of earth. These flank batteries are half a mile asunder and command perfectly the whole ground lying between the wet ditch and rampart of earth. On the 27th. of Apr. the enemy attacked a redoubt on the left flank but were repulsed with the loss of between 300 and 1000 men.

Ashley river is possessed by the enemy's shipping. They have been able to get only some gallies into Cooper river, the main channel of which is obstructed by a chain and forts.

The town is defended by Gen. Lincoln with between 4000 and 5000 men. Of these about 1000 are militia, 1000 sailors, and the rest regulars. Clinton demanded a surrender, leaving the lives and properties of the towns people uninjured. This was rejected. After the batteries had been opened about 10 days, Lincoln offered to surrender the town on condition that he should be permitted to march out with the honors of war, have ten days truce for removing public stores, weighing and sending out the armed vessels, and the inhabitants be allowed a twelvemonth to remove. These terms were rejected with a declaration that none but the first proposed would be granted, and that none so favorable would be offered again. On the 25th. or 27th. Lincoln sent a confidential officer to Governor Rutlege with a verbal message that it was the unanimous opinion of the engineers that the works were not tenable and would be carried if the enemy should make an attack in full force, and advised the beginning to form an army of militia and what regulars could be collected to save as much of the country as could be. The provisions in the town will last to the 1st. or perhaps 10th. of July.

Governor Rutlege is endeavoring to form a camp on the North side of Santee, with a view to force Cornwallis's posts on the north of Cooper river and throw provisions into the town. He had with him on the 27th. of Apr. only 400 militia and 300 regular infantry with about 2. or 300 horse. The succours going on to him are

420 infantry and 60 horse under Colo. Porterfeild, regulars, who will join the governor about the last day of Ma[y.]

200 horse under Col. Armand who are a little behind Porterfeild.

1900 Maryland and Delaware regulars under the baron de Kalb, who will join Govr. Rutlege about the 28th of June.

4000 N. Carolina militia (but call them only 2000) who will not be before Charlestown till about the 10th. of July.

2500 Virginia militia (call them 1250 or 1000) who cannot be there before the last of July.

Sir   Richmond May 28. 1780.

The preceding is a summary state of things at Charlestown as they stood on the 27th. of April. The whole (except the description of the works) was communicated to me by Majr. Harlstone who was sent by Governor Rutlege to Congress and the intermediate states. The Governor not chusing to commit it to paper referred me to Majr. Harlstone as a person of particular confidence on whose information I must rely as most authentic. Part of these circumstances had been before communicated to me by Genl. Woodford who is next in command to General Lincoln. The description of [the works] was given me by Mr. Bee heretofore the Governor of S. Carolina lately gone on to Congress who was personally acquainted with the works. What occurrences come to my knolege hereafter you shall know within 24 hours after they are made known to me, by expresses which shall be posted between this place and Cape Henry.

N, followed by Dft of letter (DLC). There is no indication of the addressee of this letter, but it was with little doubt intended for Maj. Galvan, then on his way to Cape Henry to keep a lookout for the French fleet (see TJ's Instructions printed under 31 May 1780). Washington had particularly requested TJ (letter of 15 May 1780) to keep Galvan informed of the operations in South Carolina; and it may have been TJ's hope that the French fleet and army could be diverted at once to the rescue of Charleston. MAJR. HARLSTONE: Isaac Harleston, maj., 2d S.C. Line. Heitman asserts that Harleston was captured at Charleston on 12 May, a logical assumption in view of the fact that Harleston's regiment was captured. But, since Harleston left that city on 27 Apr. and since he gave a verbal report to TJ in Richmond some days afterwards, while he was on his way "to Congress and the intermediate states," it is obvious that he could not have been present at the capitulation on 12 May.

From Samuel Huntington

SIR   Philada May 29 1780

Your Excellency will receive herewith enclosed two Acts of Congress of the 26th and 27th Instant. The former recommending to those of the States where Debts are due to their Inhabitants from the Quarter Masters and Commissary's Department by Notes or Certificates given as mentioned in the Act; to make Provision for discounting and discharging such Debts by empowering the Collectors to receive them in Payment of the Taxes due to the first of March last in the Manner prescribed in the Act. It is hoped this Mode may prove beneficial in those States where considerable Debts are due under the Circumstances beforementioned; and in those States only can the Act be properly applied.

By the other Act of the 27th you will be informed of the Measure adopted by Congress to equip for Sea the naval Force of the United States with the utmost Expedition, as also their recommendation to the several States for promoting Harmony, and forwarding the common Views of France and America as expressed in the resolutions enclosed; which it is not to be doubted will meet with due Consideration and Attention from the several States, and receive the necessary Aid of the Legislatures to carry the same into Execution as speedily as the Nature of the Case will admit.

I have the honour to be &c.,   S. H.

FC (DLC: PCC, No. 15). Circular to the state executives. Enclosures missing; printed in JCC, XVII, 463-6, 468-9.

To the Commissioners of the Specific Tax for Augusta County

GENTLEMEN   Richmond May 30. 1780

Be pleased to deliver for the use of this State to Messrs. Eaton and Brown, or order, whatever indian corn, oats rye, or barley you may have received for the public. Your wheat you will please to have properly manufactured and packed. No return being yet received from your County I shall hope to receive one without delay. I am Gentlemen Yr. hble Servt,   TH: JEFFERSON

RC (Vi); in a clerk's hand signed by TJ. Addressed below text: "The Commissioners of Specific tax for Augusta County."

By an Act "for laying a tax, payable in certain enumerated commodities" (Hening, x, 79-81), passed in the May 1779 session, a tax payable in wheat, corn, rye, barley, oats, hemp, or tobacco was levied on all persons over sixteen years of age, and two commissioners were appointed in each county to col- lect the levies and to make annual re- turns to the governor on or before 15 May.

To Benjamin Harrison

In Council, Richmond, 30 May 1780. Transmitting letters and intelligence concerning the surrender of Charleston.

RC (Vi); mutilated. Addressed by TJ to Harrison as Speaker. Endorsed: "Governors Letter. May 30. 178[0.] Inclosing Govr. Nash & Rutledge's respecting Surrender of Charles town. Referred to Committee of whole on the State of the Commonwealth." Enclosures: Abner Nash to TJ, 25 May 1780, q.v., and John Rutledge to Nash, 16 May, enclosed in Nash's letter.

From Abner Nash

DEAR SIR   Newbern May 30th. 1780

Inclosed your Excellency will receive a Copy of the Articles of Capitulation agreed on between Genl. Lincoln and Genl. Clinton. Mr. Laurens in his Letter to me dated at Wilmington the 26. Inst. has the following paragraph "I am informed and I fear from too good authority that Govr. Martin at the head of a large body of Infantry and Cavalry is actually on his way for this Country, his rout to be thro Cherraws and Cross Creek. Another Body of the Enemys Infantry and Cavelry are penetrating South Carolina towards Cambden under Lord Cornwallace, a Junction may be formed and a formidable army soon appear in the heart of North Carolina." We are preparing for them in the best manner we are able and hope shortly to see the Maryland and Delaware Troops so long expected in this State together with the aid voted lately by the Assembly of Virginia. With the highest respect I remain Dear Sir Your Obdt. & very Hble servt.,   A NASH

RC (Lloyd W. Smith, Madison, N.J., 1946). Endorsed in a clerk's hand: "Nash to Gov. Jefferson May 30. 1780. informing of the approach of the enemy." Enclosure (missing): copy of Articles of Capitulation of Charleston, 12 May 1780, entered into by Generals Lincoln and Clinton and Admiral Arbuthnot; printed in *Va. Gaz.* (D & N), 7 June 1780, and in Tarleton's *History of the Campaigns of 1780 and 1781,* Lond., 1787, p. 61-4. The present letter was transmitted in TJ's letter to Harrison of 5 June 1780, q.v., the day this first certain intelligence of the fall of Charleston was received in Richmond.

Instructions to Express Riders between Richmond and Cape Henry

[ca. 31 May 1780]

To

You are to proceed immediately to Hood's[1] and be there in constant readiness, never absenting yourself a moment from your quarters, nor suffering your horse to be out of your instantaneous command.

Whenever you shall receive from the express who will be placed next to you any letter or paper from me to Majr. Galvan you will proceed without a moment's delay by night and by day and without regard to weather to carry it down to the next express stationed at   .[2] And when you receive a letter or paper from Majr. Galvan to me you are to proceed in like manner with it to this place; always returning to your station, after the delivery, moderately but without delay. You are to give a receipt specifying the hour and minute at which you receive any such paper, and to take a like receipt from the express to whom you shall deliver it.

You will continue in this duty till you shall be notified by Majr. Galvan or myself that you may return from your station.

Dft (DLC) of a circular order to the several express riders appointed and stationed in pursuance of Washington's letter introducing Maj. Galvan, 15 May 1780, q.v.

Galvan arrived at Cape Henry on 31 May and reported on 2 June that "his Excellency Governor Jefferson has concurred in my Mission with a zeal and an activity deserving the highest praises, tho' all his orders have not yet been brought to execution"; the next day he wrote that "The guard of twelve men, which his Excellency Governor Jefferson ordered from Portsmouth, arrived last night, and, this morning, was posted at the light house" (Galvan to Washington, 2 and 3 June 1780; in TJ Editorial Files, from originals in DLC: Washington Papers). See also TJ's letter to Galvan, 28 May 1780.

[1] The words "Sandy point" are crossed out.

[2] The words "Sleepy hole" are crossed out.

To Charles Lynch

SIR   Richmond May 31. 1780.

Deliver to the order of Governor Nash for the use of the state of North Carolina two thousand weight of lead. TH: JEFFERSON

RC (Vi). At foot of text: "Colo. Charles Lynch. Manager of the Virginia lead mines." On verso: "2000. [and in TJ's hand:] Govr. Nash."

To Philip Mazzei

Dear Sir   Richmond May. 31. 1780.

The Fier Rodrique has waited till now, and therefore gives me an opportunity of acknowleging the receipt of your letters No. 2. 3. 4. 7. The intermediate ones 5. and 6. have not come to hand. An express now setting out to carry letters to the ship supposed to be on her departure leaves me leisure to say but little in answer to yours.

I am sorry an idea should prevail in France that if they should be unsuccesful this campaign we should make terms with England. Beleive me no opinion can have less foundation. The disinterested exertions of France for us have not only made real impression on the leaders of the people, but are deeply felt by the people themselves, and the sentiment of making separate terms with England is so base that I verily beleive no man in America would venture to express such a one. It is an unfortunate truth that we were left so long to struggle alone that our resources had become exhausted, and Great Britain has been so lucky as to encounter her adversaries as the surviving Horatius did the Curiatii, one after another, and not all together. Our money has almost lost it's circulation. A new system is adopting for raising the expences of the year annually: but as we find it necessary at the same time to call in the whole of our old money by taxation within the period of a year, you may judge that we shall be able to raise very little more for current expences. The period too which will intervene between abolishing an old and establishing a new system of finance, will be distressing to the last degree. Yet I am thoroughly satisfied that the attachment of the people to the cause in which we are engaged and their hatred to Great Britain remain unshaken. Wherever the French and American troops have acted together the harmony has been real, and not given out merely to influence the opinion of the world. There has been no instance of the smallest bickering except between some French and American sailors at Boston, who had a fracas, such as eternally happens among people of that kind, and I beleive one life was lost.

As for news, a report has been among us that Charlestown was taken, it is again contradicted and we are all in suspence as to the truth. It is certainly in danger. The French fleet and troops you mention are hourly expected by us and by the enemy. New York is alarmed, and we are not without hope that Clinton will be obliged to relinquish his Southern enterprize to go to the defence of New

York. The Marquis Fayette is safely arrived and was the bearer of this good news. The express waiting, I can add no more than that I am truly Your friend & servt.,   TH: JEFFERSON

RC (NhD). Addressee's name assigned from internal evidence.
Mazzei's LETTERS NO. 2. 3. 4. 7. were dated 5, 12, 18 Dec. 1779, and 2 Mch. 1780, respectively; No. 5 and 6 were dated 8 and 18 Feb. 1780.

From Carter Braxton

[*May? 1780?*] Has heard from the skipper of one of his vessels now at Annapolis that a number of cartouche boxes for Col. Finnie have been received there, but Braxton had already given orders to sell the vessel, even though at a loss, because of the lack of a convoy through Chesapeake Bay. (The vessel had gone to Annapolis loaded with public corn under convoy of the *Jefferson*, and had been promised the same protection on her return.) This and similar disappointments and losses have determined Braxton to sell all his vessels; it is to be feared that hereafter no vessels will venture to go up the Bay. Memorandum at foot of text by TJ: "Referred to Colo. Muter to take measures for saving and bringing hither the Cartouch boxes."

RC (Vi); 2 p.; partly in third person and unsigned; dated only "Monday Morng." Addressed: "His Excellency Governor Jefferson." The hand appears to be that of Carter Braxton, who was a shipowner. Below TJ's notation at foot of text is the following in an unidentified hand: "A letter from Colo. Braxton to his corrispondent in Annapolis for the delivery of the boxes, was delivered to the Governeur." The paper contains no good clue as to date beyond the fact that George Muter began to perform his duties as commissioner of the war office about this time, but see TJ to Benjamin Harrison, 29 Jan. 1781.

From the Committee of Congress
at Headquarters

SIR   In Committee of Congress Morris Town June 2d. 1780.

In a letter of the 31st Ulto. from the commander in chief, which we had the honor to receive the same day, his Excellency observes, "That in the expected co-operation with the force of our ally against that of the common enemy; it is of great moment that we should proceed with circumspection and on the surest ground. Before we can determine what aught to be undertaken, we should be able to appreciate the means we shall have it in our power to employ on some precise scale. To begin an enterprise against any point in possession of the enemy on a general presumption of sufficient resources in the country and proportionable exertions in the respective governments to bring them forth, would hardly be justified by success, could never be defended in case of misfortune, to say nothing of the fatal consequences that might ensue. It appears to me necessary to ascertain the number of men, and the quantity of supplies which the States are capable of furnishing in *a given time*, and to *obtain assurances* from them, founded on experience of their continuing supplies in the same proportion. I esteem the plan adopted by the committee in their circular letter an extremely good proparatory one; but I think it of *indispensible importance*, in the next place, to come to something fixed and determinate. I therefore take the liberty to submit to the committee the necessity and propriety of calling immediately upon the States, for *specific aids of men, provisions, forage*, and the means of transportation."

His Excellency next states the enemies number, and position mentions the points against which the combined arms will probably be directed, and furnishes us with an estimate of the forces which America ought to draw into the field with others, exhibiting a state of the provisions, horses, carriages, and a variety of other articles indispensibly necessary to give vigour and a probable prospect of success to our operations. The result was a determination, specifically to apportion to and request from the states referred to in the resolution of Congress of the 19th. Ulto. to furnish the requisite supplies by the first day of July. In estimating these we have paid all possible regard to the probable resources of each and to their relative position to those scenes of operation, which are at present in contemplation. We shall accordingly annex the kind and quantum of supplies which are monthly expected from your State; and which we have the honor to make, and that they will be kept up, in the same proportion until the last of November, if necessity should induce us to continue the application to that period, even although any of the articles now called for, should exceed the quota assigned you by the act of Congress of the 25th. of February last: and you will please, Sir, to signify to us, without delay, the determination of your State on this important subject.

Here it becomes our duty to advise you, as upon examination you will perceive, that we have stated your quota pr. month, in some articles, beyond what it would have been, could we have strictly adhered to the proportion on which the allotments made by the act of the 25th of February last, were adjusted; but this was found impracticable, because of the exhausted condition of some of the States, in which the army and its principal detachments have wintered. But as these, in the course of the campaign, will be enabled to afford more than they can at present, your quota as now stated, will of course diminish. The requisition, Sir, is large but it is barely competent. It is the least adequate to the intended operations, as it is calculated on the most limited expenditures, without the smallest allowance for accidental losses or extra consumption.

Having given the States a fixed point to regulate themselves by, their measures will be equal to it, and their exertions competent to the magnitude of the object. In matters of such high import it appeared to the General and to us, essential that there should be a proper understanding on all hands. That the States should know the wants of the army and what is expected for it. That the General and the Committee should be clearly and explicitly advised of their abilities both individually and collectively and to have determined with precision, what may be expected. We do not fear to discourage by the largeness of the demand, as we conceive it impossible they should not bear with the knowledge of the wants of the army and because knowing them we are persuaded their wisdom and patriotism will impell them to every exertion fully to afford the supplies.

The supplies allotted to be furnished by your State are sixty thousand pounds of Bacon in three equal parcels monthly to the last of September and sixty hoggsheads of Bacon pr. month, to be transported and delivered where the Commissary General shall direct, also twenty nine thousand seven hundred and fourteen Bushels of Grain for forage pr. month to be transported to and delivered as the quarter Master General shall direct. The first monthly quota of supplies to be delivered by the first day of July next, and the subsequent ones monthly within the months succeeding, as the Quarter Master or Commissary General may direct. The Bacon is an additional article to those stated in the act of Congress of the 25th February last, but the requisition on your State as on others for supplies could not be dispensed with, and the amount thereof together with the transportation of any must be charged in account with the United States.[1]

As the object against which the military operations will be directed cannot be positively ascertained we have it not in our power to call on you for a determinate quantum of transportation, but beleive it will be considerable.

The continental troops already engaged and with the army together with the addition requested by the Generals letter of the 25th. Ulto. to compleat the battalions to five hundred and four rank and file will still in his opinion and in our own be inadequate to insure success in the intended operations.

In our circular letter of the 25th. Ulto. we intreated your legislature to adopt measures for drawing forth your militia on the shortest notice. We have now to request that such arrangements may be made as that your quota of militia which with the concurrence of the commander in chief we state at four thousand seven hundred and twenty five rank and file shall rendesvous at the army or at such posts as the General shall direct by the 15 day of July next at furthest and to continue in service for the term of three months computing from the day of their arrival at such rendesvous as aforesaid. We have not apportioned to your State any flour beef salt or hay as we were apprehensive that calls might be made on you from the southward; should that not be the case you will forward as much beef and flour monthly as will amount to about a fifteenth part of the quota assigned you of those articles by the act of Congress of the 25 of February last.

Such of the supplies herein required as make part of the quota assigned to your State by the act of Congress of the 25 of February last, and which it is requested you will transport to and deliver where the Quarter master Genl. or Commissary Genl. shall direct, will be receipted for by the continental officers appointed for that purpose before they or your agents convey or transport the same beyond the limits of your State. If however such continental officer should not be present you will give directions that the weight or quantity of the articles may be estimated and an account or invoice transmitted with each parcel. We have to observe that in the beef requested, hides and tallow are not included. Allowances must therefore be made for these when cattle are sent to the army. If drivers are sent with the draft horses and cattle requested of your State we wish to have one for every four horses or oxen.

We have the honor to be with great respect and esteem Your Excellys. most Obedt. Hble. Servt.,   PHILIP SCHUYLER
JOHN MATHEWS
NATHL PEABODY

P.S. We do most earnestly entreat that the requisition now made on your State for the quotas of militia may not be suffered on any consideration whatever to retard the completion of the continental Battalions, as recommended in our second circular letter of the 25 Ulto. The necessity of that measure becoming daily more striking and important. When the militia of your State is drawn forth, they must subsist on the beef and flour called for from your state by the act of Congress of the 25 Ulto.

FC (DLC: PCC, No. 39, I); at head of text: "Virginia." Another FC (DLC: PCC, No. 11); captioned "Circular, No. 3"; in this copy the particular instructions to each state are inserted successively in the text. The order of the paragraphs is somewhat different in the two copies. The Committee's letter was transmitted by TJ to Speaker Harrison on 19 June; see under that date.

Washington's letter of 31 May to the Committee is printed in his *Writings*, ed. Fitzpatrick, XVIII, 455-9.

¹ FC (DLC: PCC, No. 11) contains at this point the following not in the text of FC (DLC: PCC, No. 39, I): "We believe it would be advantageous to the States in general, that the carts, oxen, and horses, should be procured by hire, in preference to purchase, as the drivers who will then accompany them will be more careful of the cattle; should your State adopt that mode, we recommend that the contracts may be made payable in specie, or in paper money equivalent, and that the value of the carts, waggons, oxen, and horses, should be appraised, on oath, and a return of the appraisement be made to the quarter master general."

Resolution of the General Assembly
Appointing Jefferson Governor

VIRGINIA SCILICET.
  IN GENERAL ASSEMBLY.

Friday the 2nd: of June 1780

Resolved

that Thomas Jefferson Esquire, be appointed Governor or Chief Magistrate of the Commonwealth, for one Year, he having been elected to that Office by joint ballot of both Houses of Assembly.

ARCHIBALD CARY   S.S.

BENJA HARRISON   Sp H D

MS (PHi); engrossed copy on parchment, signed by the speakers of the two houses and endorsed: "resoln: of Ass: appt. of Govr." Another MS (Vi), headed "Virginia to wit. In the House of Delegates" and bearing the attestation of John Beckley, in whose hand it is drawn as clerk of the House; also bearing on its face the following: "June 2d. 1780 Agreed to by the Senate Will Drew C S"; endorsed: "Reso. &c. appointing Thoms. Jefferson esqr. Governor 2d June 1780."

The House on 1 June resolved that it would on the next day proceed by joint ballot with the Senate to the choice of a governor, to which the Senate agreed. The House nominated "a person proper to be ballotted for" and the Senate (still on 1 June) notified the House that it had "added another person to the nomination." On 2 June the election took place in form, and TJ was found to have "a majority of votes"; neither the number of votes cast nor the name of the Senate's nominee is known (JHD, May 1780, 1827 edn., p. 29, 30, 31).

From James Madison

Dear Sir   Philadelphia. June 2d 1780

I have written several private letters to you since my arrival here, which as they contained matters that I should be sorry should fall into other hands, I could wish to know had been received. If your Excellency has written any acknowledgements of them, they have never reached me.

Mr. Griffin tells me he has seen several letters just received by Mr. Bingham from Martinique which give information that three successive engagements have taken place between the Fleets in the W. Indies the two first of which were indecisive but that the third was so far in favor of the French that the English had gone into port and left the former entirely master of those Seas: that they were gone in consequence of that towards Barbadoes, and that the general expectation was that both that Island and St. Kitts would speadily be in their possession.

It appears from sundry accounts from the Frontier of N. York and other N. States that the Savages are making the most distressing incursions, under the direction of the British Agents, and that a considerable force is assembling at Montreal for the purpose of wresting from us Fort Schuyler, which covers the N. Western frontiers of N. York. It is probable the Enemy will be but too successful this campaign in exciting their vindictive spirit against us throughout the whole frontier of the United States. The Expedition of Genl. Sullivan against the six nations seems by its effects rather to have exasperated than to have terrified or disabled them. And the example of those nations will add great weight to the exhortations addressed to the more Southern tribes.

Rivington has published a positive and particular account of the surrender of Charlestown on the 12 Ulto: said to be brought to N. York by the Iris which left Charleston five days after. There are notwithstanding some circumstances attending it which, added to the notorious character for lying of the Author, leave some hope that it is fictitious. The true state of the matter will probably be known at Richmond before this reaches you.

We have yet heard nothing further of the Auxiliary Armament from France. However anxiously its arrival may be wished for it is much to be feared we shall continue to be so unprepared to cooperate with them, as to disappoint their views, and to add to our distress and disgrace. Scarce a week, and sometimes scarce a day, but brings us a most lamentable picture from Head Quarters. The

Army are a great part of their time on short allowance, at some-times without any at all, and constantly depending on the pre-carious fruits of momentary expedients. General Washington has found it of the utmost difficulty to repress the mutinous spirit engendered by hunger and want of pay: and his endeavours cou'd not prevent an actual eruption of it in two Connecticut Regiments who assembled on the parade with their arms and resolved to return home or satisfy their hunger by the force of the Bayonet. We have no permanent resource and scarce even a momentary one left but in the prompt and vigorous supplies of the States. The State of Pennsylvania has it in her power to give great relief in the present crisis, and a recent act of its Legislature shews, they are determined to make the most of it. I understand they have invested the Executive with a dictatorial Authority from which nothing but the *lives* of their Citizens are exempted. I hope the good resulting from it will be such as to compensate for the risk of the precedent. With great respect I am Yr. Excellency's Most Ob & humb servt,

JAMES MADISON Junr.

RC (DLC: Madison Papers); endorsed by TJ: "Madison Jas June 2. 1780."

From Philip Mazzei

SIR   Paris, June 2d. 1780.

It is 8 days since we heared another anecdote of british wild barbarity, which I really did not believe. It comes however authen-ticated to day in the Spanish gazette, the extract of which is in-closed. The english Commander is supposed to have been Com-modore, *alias* Govr., Johnstone, or his Lieutenant. I must repeat what I said in letter 15. "What a happy circumstance for us to have divided in time from those wretches!" We hear that the french Commodore is gone from Cadix with his 5 ships of the line to cruise about the latitude of Lisbon. It would be a glorious affair if he was to meet with our old friend Johnstone. I have thought proper to send you likewise here inclosed a paragraph, copied from the Leiden gazette, about the demand and declaration of Sueden to the Court of London. I hope soon to hear that the Envoys from Russia Sueden Holland and Danmark have been in a body to demand the restitution of the Dutch vessels. Poor old England, it is high time to prepare thy crutches! The english affairs begin to take a bad turn even in the Est-Indias. Mr. Yelverton in the Irish

House of Commons the 18th. ulto. silenced the ministerial majority by signifying that the People were determined to support their rights, and that they should have him with them, not with only his voice, but *with all his faculties.* As it was evident that nothing but fear made the ministerial party give way, that precedent may perhaps induce the Irish to make hereafter a proper use of the spirit, which came to them across the Atlantic from America, as the Dutch received their present courage from Russia in the manifest of the Empress. Fifteen russian ships of the line are soon expected in the Texel, and the second division, they say, will soon be ready. I wish that our Tories (if any such mortals should now exist in America) and our moderate and timid men may be asked, whether they think that those vessels are intended to convoy 40000 russians to our Continent, or to administer physic to english piracy.

In regard to the preparations necessary to be made here for the encouragement of Italian adventurers, I have done what in letter 14. I said I would do. I have been to work some other way, and not in vain. The reasons I have alledged to prove the good policy of seconding my views have been approved, and especially that of showing the Americans the propensity of France to contribute to their relief even by facilitating their trade with other nations, while the English are constantly insinuating that her avidity is insatiable, and her reigning system of moderation and equality a mere imposture. But I don't see now a chance of doing any thing, untill I receive the necessary informations relative to the alterations made, and to be made, in our Finances. I am sorry to find that the resolutions of Congress on that head have already occasioned in France some unpleasant, and I am afraid disadvantagious, if not dishonorable reflections. A sensible elaborate justification to the World appears to me highly necessary. I have asked Mr. Adams if he will write it, saying that we may get it translated and published in several languages. He approves the idea, and wishes it was done, but observes that it would be dangerous to attempt such a thing before we are certain of the event, and know the whole of it.

Having in several letters mentioned my good and noble friend Marquis Caraccioli, I must do him the justice to say, that I have received from him the most friendly and effectual assistance. He has taken me with him and introduced me to all those, with whom I thought some thing could be done for us; he has produced my writings; has spoken favorably of my notions; and in short has promoted my views for the American service in every respect. He has even introduced me to the King's Levee, since our American

Minister has thought proper to circumscribe his civilities to me within the walls of his abitation, where as an acquaintance I have been well treated.[1] Mr. Adams who knew, since the first time he was in France, the Marquis's great merit and reputation, has desired of me to be introduced to him; I think I should have succeeded in it, notwithstanding the political obstacles, and hoped that such an acquaintance could be of great service whenever the subject of peace should come on the carpet; but he is soon to leave this country, the King of Naples having lately made him Viceroy of Sicily. Marmontel and other great men having told him at table, when that news came, that they would now go and see the Country of Archimedes &c. &c., I replied that I would go and see what kind of trade could be established between us and his new subjects.

I shall conclude this letter with some reflections on the possible duration of the war, which I think our people ought to be made sensible of, to prevent the discontented imposing on the quiet in case it should last longer than is expected. The situation of british affairs is now such, that any other nation in a like case would buy the peace almost at any price, provided it could be had immediately. But the british Ministry cannot make the sacrifices, necessary to obtain it, without running the risk of losing their heads. And as they would see the whole british Empire in ashes before they give up their places, what will they not do for their heads? Their policy is now to let things go to a point, that the nation must be alarmed and cry for peace on any terms; and they hope that it will be easy for them to preserve their heads, and even their places, in the general consternation. It depends on circumstances the time it will take to come to that. I look on this to be the last campaign; but should it be otherwise, I hope we shall bear our difficulties with less uneasiness when we see our enemy going to perdition without hope of redemption. I have the honour to be most respectfully, Sir, your Excellency's most Obedt. & most Humble Servant,

PHILIP MAZZEI

P.S. It will be thought, perhaps, that in letter 14. I ought to have mentioned the nature of Mr. Chaumont's advise, as I so much disapproved of it. It was to persuade the Italians to send their goods to be landed in France, and afterwards shipped on french vessels going to America.

Rodney's defeat at the Islands has been metarphosed in the London extraordinary gazette into a *defeat of the french fleet*. I shall say nothing more about it, as the news from the Island are sooner with you than with us.

RC (CtY); at head of text: "18 [i.e., dispatch No. 18]." Enclosures (also CtY): extracts in Mazzei's hand, in French, from newspapers mentioned in text, that from Cadiz being headed "le 6 May 1780" and that from Leyden bearing the caption "Extrait des nouvelles de Londres du 19 May." This let-ter was not located or printed by Marraro in his *Mazzei.*

Mazzei's LETTERS 14 and 15 were dated 3 and 12 May 1780.

¹ One line has been heavily inked out, so that it is impossible to read any of its words.

From John Rutledge

SIR   Salisbury June 2. 1780.

I think it proper to acquaint you that, intelligence being received last Saturday morning at Cambden that 3900 men under Ld. Cornwallis had crossed and taken post on the North side of Santee river about 57 miles below Cambden, and that they were to be soon joined (as they have been since) by 1200 more from the opposite side of the river, who were to rendezvous at that town, and proceed higher up the country. Genl. Huger who commanded the No. Carola. troops under Genl. Caswell, and the Virginia Continentals under Colo. Buford, ordered them to retreat, the former to Pedee river, and the latter to this place. Genl. Caswell has I understand, made good his retreat, but Colo. Buford was attacked last Monday on his march and totally defeated, with the loss of 2 feild peices, his baggage &c. Colo. Porterfeild thinking his force insufficient to oppose the enemy, retreated yesterday from this town and crossed the Yadkin, meaning however to return and join the militia here, if they turn out in such numbers as may probably be able to prevent the enemy's getting higher up the Country.

Tr in TJ's hand (DLC: Washington Papers), captioned "Extract of a letter from Govr. Rutledge" and presumably enclosed in TJ's second letter to Washington of 11 June 1780, q.v. A later Tr, in a clerk's hand, is in DLC: TJ Papers.

Rutledge's original letter has not been found. It was entered by TJ under the erroneous date 1 June 1780 on the first page of his early, fragmentary Epistolary Record.

From John Todd

MAY IT PLEASE YOUR EXCELLENCY   Richmd. 2nd June 1780

On Consulting with Col. Clark we found it impracticable to maintain so many petty posts in the Ilinois with so few men and concluded it better to draw them all to one post. The Land at the Junction of the Ohio and Missisippi was judged best Situated for the Purpose as it would command the Trade of an extensive Country on both sides of each River and might Serve as a Check to any Incroachments from our present Allies the Spaniards whose growing power might justly put us upon our guard and whose fondness for engrossing Territory might otherwise urge them higher up the River upon our side than we would wish. The Expences in erecting this new Post and victualing the men would have been Obstacles unsurmountable without a Settlement Contiguous to the Garrison to support it whose adventurers would assist the Soldiers in the heavy Work of Building their Fortifications. I therefore granted to a certain Number of Families four Hundred Acres to each family at a price to be settled by the General Assembly with Commissions for civil and Militia-Offices and the Necessary Instructions, Copies of the principal of which I herewith send you, the Others being agreeable to the printed forms heretofore delivered me by the Governor and Council. Lest the withdrawing our Troops from St. Vincenne might raise suspicions among the Citizens to our disadvantage, I have sent to Majr. Bosseron the then district Commandant blank Commissions with powers to raise one Company and put them in possession of the Garrison with assurance that pay and rations should be allowed them by the Government.

I inclose you also a Return of the Cloths &c. which I sent down by Mr. Clark to Capt. Dodge whom I appointed Agent agreeably to your Excellencys Letter as Mr. Lindsay desired to be discontinued. When Col. Clark left the falls his Officers and Men to the amount perhaps of 120 were well Cloathed except in the article of Linens. Mr. Lindsay had not arrived the 8th of May last from Ilinois and I have not heard whether the Goods from Orleans were yet arriven. Capt. Dodge was also to receve them from Lindsay.

Mr. Isaac Bowman with 7 or 8 men and one family set off from Kaskaskia the 15th Novr. last in a Batteau attended by another Batteau with 12 Men and 3 or 4 families in it bound to the falls of Ohio. I judged it safer to send to the Falls many articles belonging to the Commonwealth by Bowman than to bring them myself by Land. Bowmans Batteau fell into the Hands of the Chickasaw Indians and the other arrived in March or April at the French Lick on Cumberland with the Account that Bowman and all the Men except one Biddle were killed and taken. I inclose your Excellency a List of such Articles as belonged to the State as well as I can make out from my Detached Memorandums. My Books and Many necessary papers being also lost.

Many necessary Articles of Intelligence yet remain unmentioned. I will enjoy no Leisure until I shall have fully acquainted your Excellency with the Situation of Ilinois.

I have the Honor to be with the greatest Respect Your Excellency Most Obedient & humble Servant,   JNO TODD Jr

RC (Vi). Addressed: "His Excellency Tho. Jefferson Esq; Governor of Virginia." Endorsed by TJ: "Colo. Todd." Enclosures missing. The letter was transmitted to Speaker Harrison in a letter of 14 June 1780, q.v.

To Benjamin Harrison

SIR   June 3. 1780.

The inclosed letter of resignation from Mr. Armistead Commissioner for the Continental loan office I beg leave to lay before the General assembly by whom that officer was appointed.

With sentiments of the highest respect I have the honor to be Sir Your most obedt. & most humble servt.,   TH: JEFFERSON

RC (CtY). Addressed by TJ to Harrison as Speaker; John Beckley's endorsement concludes: "to lie on table." Armistead's letter of resignation, enclosed, is dated 20 May 1780, q.v.

From Samuel Huntington

Philadelphia, 3 June 1780. Circular letter to the state executives enclosing a resolve of Congress of 1 June respecting supplies to be furnished over and above quotas fixed by Congress' resolve of 25 Feb. 1780.

FC (DLC: PCC, No. 15); 1 p. Enclosure missing; printed in JCC, XVII, 480.

To the General Assembly

[4 June 1780]

I receive with great satisfaction this testimony of the public approbation, and beg leave through you gentlemen, to return my sincere thanks to the General Assembly. I shall cheerfully again encounter the anxieties and assiduities inseparable from the important office to which you are pleased a second time to call me, and only wish to be able to call forth those effectual exertions of my country, which our friends expect, and the present emergency requires.

No MS located. Printed from *Journal of the House of Delegates*, May 1780, 1827 edn., p. 34.

This message was conveyed to the House by Patrick Henry, who had wait-

ed on TJ with other members of a joint committee of the House and Senate to notify him of his election on 2 June (same).

To Benjamin Harrison

[*Richmond, 5 June 1780.* JHD, May 1780, 1827 edn., p. 35 (5 June): "The Speaker laid before the House a letter from the Governor, enclosing one from Governor Nash of North-Carolina, containing intelligence from Charleston." Not located, but see the letter from Nash, 30 May, which was enclosed, and TJ to Huntington, 9 June, which states that the first certain information of the surrender of Charleston on 12 May reached Richmond twenty-four days later, i.e., 5 June.]

To Benjamin Harrison

[*Richmond, 5? June 1780.* JHD, May 1780, 1827 edn., p. 35 (5 June): "The Speaker laid before the House a letter from the Governor, enclosing one from the President of Congress, together with a resolution of that body, concerning a Monsieur Legrass of Illinois, and several letters and papers on the subject thereof." Not located, but see Pres. Huntington's letter to TJ, 11 May 1780, which was enclosed.]

From Samuel Huntington

Philadelphia, 5 June 1780. Encloses a resolve of Congress and asks that orders for executing it be carried out.

FC (DLC: PCC, No. 15); 1 p. Caption reads "To Governor Lee," but at foot of text is the notation "The like verbatim to Gov Jefferson." Enclosure (Vi): see below.

The RESOLVE enclosed was one adopted by Congress on the day this letter was written (see JCC, XVII, 489) and reads as follows in the copy attested by Charles Thomson and sent to TJ: "That the Governors of the States of Virginia

and Maryland be requested immediately to engage trusty persons in those States respectively at proper distances from each other on the main road from Cape Henry in Virginia to Philadelphia to hold themselves in readiness should the french fleet be discovered off that Cape or the Adjacent Coast to forward intelligence thereof, and any dispatches that may be received from them to Congress in the most expeditious manner."

From James Madison

DEAR SIR   Philadelphia Jun 6th. 1780

A Vessel from West Florida has brought to the President of Congress intelligence from Govr. Galvez of the surrender of Mobile. No other particulars than that contained in the inclosed paper are mentioned, except the verbal report of the Capt. that the Garrison consisted of about 800 including inhabitants &c. Seven or eight vessels have just arrived from the W. Indies as you will also observe in the inclosed paper but they bring no satisfactory information concerning the late engagements between the two fleets. The Address from the General Assembly was yesterday immediately on its receipt laid before Congress and referred to a special Committee, on whose report it will probably be considered in a committee of the whole. I flatter myself that the arrival of the French Armament which is hourly expected will place our affairs in a less melancholy situation than their apprehensions seem to paint them. There is little doubt but the Conquest of the Southern States was the object of the operation of the present Campain, but I can not think the Enemy will pursue that object at the manifest risk of N. York. It is more probable they will leave a strong Garrison in Charleston, and carry back to N. York. the residue of their forces. If they shou'd endeavour to extend their acquisitions in the Southern States, it must proceed from an Assurance from England that a superior naval force will follow the french fleet to frustrate their views on the American Coast. I cannot suppose that however intent they may have been on taking port at Portsmouth, that they will venture in the present prospect to spread themselves out in so exposed a situation. With great respect & sincerity I am Dr Sir Yr. friend & Servt.,   JAMES MADISON Junr

RC (DLC: Madison Papers). Endorsed: "Madison Jas   June 6. 1780." Enclosure missing.

THE ADDRESS FROM THE GENERAL ASSEMBLY: A memorial to Congress from the General Assembly of Virginia, dated 24 May 1780, concerning defense of the southern states; MS in DLC: PCC, No. 71, I, endorsed by Thomson (in part): "Read June 5. 1780   Referred to Mr Henry Mr Armstrong Mr Holten"; printed in JHD, May 1780, 1827 edn., p. 20; see also Burnett, *Letters of Members*, V, No. 226, note 3.

Proceedings of Council concerning Purchase of Horses

[8 June 1780]

The Governor laid before the board a resolution of General assembly of this day for purchasing horses and accoutrements for the Continental light dragoons raised in this state, and a return of the number of the said dragoons from Capt. Jones whereby it appears they are 70 in number; whereupon the board advise the Governor to furnish Capt. Jones with 70 pr. of pistols, to authorize him to purchase on the terms mentioned in the resolution saddles, bridles, holsters, sword belts, and spurs; and to appoint Wm. and Herbert Claiborne esqrs. to purchase on the like terms 40 horses and William Randolph of Chestfd. to purchase 30. others, not to cost more than £2000 each, to allow them for their trouble £60 for each horse purchased and the expences of feeding the said horses from the time of their purchase till they shall be delivered to Capt. Jones, whose receipts are to be requisite to entitle them to the said premium. Neither mares nor white horses are to be purchased, nor any others above the age of eight years.

MS (Vi), in TJ's hand, on verso of an attested copy of the resolution of Assembly, 8 June 1780, for purchasing horses for Baylor's dragoons (printed in JHD, May 1780, 1827 edn., p. 39).

Proceedings of Council concerning Western Defense

In Council June 8th. 1780.

The Governor laid before the board the resolution of the General Assembly of May 27th. 1780 and a Letter from the Lieutenants of the Northwestern Counties beyond the blue ridge on the plan of defence for the Western frontier most eligible at present which together with the Letters formerly written or received, on the same [subject] the board proceeded to take into consideration and thereupon advise the Governor to direct that posts be taken at the mouths of little Kanhaway, Gr. Kanhaway, Sandy and Licking; that the little Kanhaway be garrisoned with so many of the militia from the Counties of Yohogania, Monongalia, and Ohio as the County Lieutenants of those Counties shall think proper to be furnished proportionally from that militia; that Gr. Kanhaway be garrisoned with 164 men, Sandy with 100 and Licking with 200. That [for these] purposes 254 militia be raised from the following Counties and in the following proportions viz. Botetourt 22, Rockbridge 18, Greenbriar 16, Augusta 43, Rockingham 15, Frederick 30, Hampshire 30, Berkeley 30 and Kentucky 50, that the garrison at Gr. Kanhaway be composed of militia from Hampshire, Frederick,

Berkely, Rockingham Augusta and Green Briar, that at Sandy of Militia from Rockbridge and Botetourt and a detachment from Colo. Crockets battal[ion and] that at Licking of the residue of Col. Crockets battalion and the militia from Kentucky, that a post be taken at Kelly's on the Gr. Kanhaway to be garrisoned with twenty six men from the County of Shenandoah, that these militia remain in service until relieved from their respective Counties, that the whole of these Garrisons be subject to the order of Colo. Clarke, and that it be recommended to him to draw from them from time to time when circumstances shall render it proper so many as are not essentially necessary for the preservation of their post with such Volunteers as he may [eng]age and proceed on such active enterprizes against the Indians and particularly the Shawanese as the [force] shall be adequate to.

They also advise that a post be taken at or near Martins Cabbin in Powells valley to be garrisoned with 30 militia from the County of Washington and 20 from the County of Montgomery to continue until relieved in like manner as the former Garrisons, that so soon as Colo. Crockets battalion be ready to march he be directed to proceed by the way of the Great Kanhaway.   (A Copy)

ARCH: BLAIR C.C.

Tr (Vi); signed by Blair. Another Tr (WHi) varies slightly in phrasing and contains a correction added at the end: "On the 23d of June the numbers mentioned above from Augusta and Rockingham were altered. Viz.: Augusta to furnish 35 men and Rockingham 23" (*George Rogers Clark Papers, 1771-1781*, p. 424).

THE RESOLUTION OF THE GENERAL ASSEMBLY OF MAY 27TH. 1780: This resolution approved the recommendations of a council of officers held at Botetourt Courthouse "on the subject of an offensive and defensive war with the Indians" (JHD, May 1780, 1827 edn., p. 24). The LETTER FROM THE LIEUTENANTS OF THE NORTHWESTERN COUNTIES, which doubtless embodied the plan of defense, has not been identified.

Memoranda concerning Western Defense

[ca. 8 June 1780]

I

Write to Colo. Bowman.
> order on Colo. Fleming to send 1000℔ powd[er.]
> do. Lynch 3000℔ lead.
> Commanding officer of Clarke's to receive, escort, go to Kentucky deliver to Bowman, call on Baker to aid in transportn.
> order on Lynch 1000℔ lead for Chuckamogga expedn.

[421]

	detamt. Crockett	⎫	
22.[1]	Botetourt	⎬ Sandy	100
18.	Rockbridge	⎭	
16.	Gr. Brier	⎫	
43.	Augusta		
15.	Rockingham	⎬ Fort Randolph	150
30.	Frederick		
30.	Hampshire		
	Berkeley	⎭	
50	Kentucky	⎫	
	Colo. Crockets	⎬ Licking	200
26.	Shenandoah.	Kelly's	

II

The Powder in Botetourt under the care of Co[l. . . .] may be
sent to Kentuckey with Lead from the Mines to be escorted by
100 Men sayed to be held in readiness to march from Washington
under the command of Colo. Ar. Campbele. Any further supplys
for the relefe of Kentuckey must be had from Colo. Broadhead and
our three Countys near Pitsburg. A Letter to Colo. Broadhead, and
orders to the County Lieutenants may be of singular service.[2]

150 men from Washington ⎱ to join N. Carolinians in expedn.
100 Montgomery   ⎰ agt. Chuckamogga.

    500 ℔ powder from this place
    1000 ℔ lead from the mines

the men from the mines to go to Kentucky
    to carry 1000 ℔ powder from Colo. Fleming
        3000 ℔ lead
        1000 ℔ powder to be sent now to Colo. Flemg. to replace
        2100 ℔ do. to go by Colo. Crocket.
        3000 ℔ lead to go by Crocket.

write to Colo. Broadhead and County Lts. Yohoga., Mononga.,
    Ohio to send [men?]
        to Broadhead to furnish ammunition if we have none, & to
        repay.

a guard of militia of Montgomery for lead mines long as necessary.

MS (DLC); 2 p.; in TJ's hand, with
the exception noted below.

These notes were evidently prepared
by TJ in connection with the Proceedings of Council, preceding. See also TJ
to William Preston, 15 June 1780, and
TJ to William Campbell, 3 July 1780.

[1] There is in the MS another and
parallel column of figures, evidently an
earlier estimate, which varies slightly
and has not been printed here.
[2] The preceding paragraph is in an
unidentified hand.

To Benjamin Harrison

SIR   In Council June 8. 1780.

According to the advice of the General Assembly we have proceeded to take Measures for selling six hundred thousand weight
of the public Tobacco. To do this as readily as possible we determined to allot for this purpose the Tobacco at the nearest Warehouses, and particularly four hundred thousand at the Warehouses
at or near the Falls of James River and on Appamottox.

We have now an offer for this Quantity to be paid for at the
Market price of the crop Tobacco on the 19th instant, the transfer
in Bills on Philadelphia, to be drawn now, but not payable till
six weeks hence. As it was probably the Sense of the Assembly,
that this Sale should be for ready Money, we have not concluded
this Agreement, till we know whether it will be approved, nor
should we have entertained such a Negociation but that we have
no prospect of selling for ready Money. The Credit of the Gentlemen proposing to purchase is such in Philadelphia, as will probably
render their Bills immediately negociable there. It is necessary for
us to give them a definitive Answer to day.

I am Sir Yr. very hble. Servt.,   TH: JEFFERSON

RC (Vi); in a clerk's hand, signed by
TJ; addressed by the clerk. Endorsed:
"Governors Letter June 8th. 1780. respecting Sale of part of public tobacco.
to lie on table."

ADVICE OF THE GENERAL ASSEMBLY:
The sale of the public tobacco was part
of the Assembly's program in response
to the appeal of Congress for emergency
grants of money by the states to put the
army on a footing to cooperate with the
French army imminently expected. See
Huntington to TJ, 19 May 1780, and
JHD, May 1780, 1827 edn., p. 28-30
(1 June), p. 39-40 (8-9 June).

Council Order for the Security
of the Convention Prisoners

In Council June 9th. 1780.

It having been reported that the Enemy are advancing thro the
interior Country of No. Carolina, and a doubt arising whether they
may not mean to attempt a rescue of the Convention troops, the
Governor is advised to instruct Colo. Wood immediately to call
in all the said Officers and Soldiers to the barracks; that he have
every thing in readiness to move them over the blue ridge at a
moments warning; that he post some of his light horse at proper
intervals from the barracks to the neighbourhood of the hostile

army with orders to convey to him from time to time intelligence
of their movements and particularly whether they advance towards
his Station; that whensoever he shall find it necessary he embody
such proportion of the militia of the County of Albemarle and of
the Counties adjacent thereto as he shall think necessary; that it be
submitted to him whether it may not be immediately proper, without further intelligence to embody and draw to the barracks so
many of the militia of Albemarle as may suffice to guard the prisoners on their march, and embody and draw to Rockfish gap so
many of those of Augusta as may secure that pass. And that if it
should become necessary to remove the said prisoners the removal
be in such Direction as Colo. Wood in his discretion shall think
most likely to withdraw them from danger.   A Copy.

                                        ARCH: BLAIR C.C.

Tr (Vi); signed by Archibald Blair;   oners."
endorsed: "In Council 9th. June 1780   See TJ's letter to James Wood of
relative to security of Convention Pris-   same date amplifying this Order.

From Cyrus Griffin

SIR   Philadelphia June 9th [1780.]

I have the mortification to inform you that the Enemy are
parading the Jerseys in great force, at least with six thousand
Infantry and the General says with a large body of horse also. In
consequence of this movement the commander in chief requests
that major Lee may be ordered to the main army, and I suppose
this morning Congress will prevent his proceeding to the southward.

A Committee of Congress who have been many weeks at head
quarters with very extensive powers, in concurrence with G.
Washington and the marquis de La Fayette, think proper to call
upon the different states for a considerable quantity of specific
supplies in addition to a former resolution of Congress, and also
for 22,000 militia immediately to join the northern army, but
whether Congress will send forth the requisitions to the state of
Virginia I cannot determine, as the neighboring states will demand
your utmost exertions.

I suppose the great plan of finance is already happily executed;
indeed the resolutions of Congress should be complied with, as a
General scheme, for without unanimity upon these important points
our confederation will break to pieces. What ever may have been

the opinions of some states in Congress, a large majority of that body ought to be regarded especially in critical times like the present.

Congress have no objection that I should sit in the Court of appeal, notwithstanding my resignation be not accepted, but my attendance must be dispensed with whilest acting in that commission—it is probable I shall not act in that commission long.

There has been skirmishing in the Jerseys. The militia behaved well—as yet no great mischief. The army are moving towards the enemy.

No MS located. Printed from Burnett, *Letters of Members*, v, No. 231, "From the collection of the late Adrian H. Joline of New York." Joline's *Catalogue of Autographs and Portraits of Members of the Continental Congress . . . ,* N.Y., 1897, p. 31, states that the letter is an A.L.S. of 4 quarto pages and quotes one sentence or paragraph not in Burnett, given above as a concluding paragraph. It is not certain whether the body of the letter contains more than is given in our combined text. At head of text: "(public)."

THE COURT OF APPEAL (Appeals) was established by Congress in Jan. 1780 for the final trial of appeals from the state courts of admiralty in cases of capture; Griffin had been elected a judge of this court in the place of George Wythe, who had declined to serve (see Huntington to Wythe, 2 Feb. 1780, Burnett, v, No. 33, with references there).

To Benjamin Harrison

SIR   In Council June 9. 1780.

The inclosed letter from Governor Nash with the articles of Capitulation entered into between Generals Lincoln and Clinton, having just come to hand I beg leave to communicate them to the General assembly.

I am with great esteem & respect Sir Your most obedient & most humble servt.,   TH: JEFFERSON

RC (DLC). Endorsed by John Beckley: "Governors Letter June 9th: 1780. enclosing Govr: Nashs Letter of 30th. May & Capitulation of Chas:ton. Refd. to Commee of whole on State of the Commonwealth." For the enclosures, see Nash to TJ, 30 May 1780.

To Samuel Huntington

SIR   Richmond June 9th. 1780

I had the honor of receiving your requisition for 1,900,000 Dollars and of laying the same before the General Assembly then sitting. They immediately took measures for complying therewith. As we had not the money in our treasury it became necessary to raise it partly and principally by a sale of property, and partly by borrowing. These operations requiring some time it is absolutely impracticable, however earnest their desires have been to place it in Philadelphia by the day proposed. I hope however I shall not be disappointed in my expectations of being able to send from hence by the 20th. inst. nearly the whole sum or perhaps the whole in money, or in good bills on Philadelphia paiable on such short day as will render them equal to money.

On receiving from the board of war notice of the aids which would be necessary to forward on the Maryland and Delaware Lines, I consulted with your Deputy Quarter Master in this State, and gave him every aid and power which he asked. He left me with the most confident assurance that waggons to move the whole corps should be with them in two days from that time. Why he quitted his station and State at the moment when every exertion was called for to forward a respectable body of troops to the relief of a sinking State and army should seem to be worth enquiring. The Mortifications I have experienced from the repeated disappointments which flowed from the devolution of his duties on Deputies acting without a head, without concert, or communication with one another, have been as great as if they had been really the cause of those unfortunate events they were calculated to produce. The artillery and 1st. division mov[ed] after a few days delay only; but the second division are but just now enabled to proceed.

Our information from the Southward has been at all times defective, but lamentab[ly] so on the late occasion. Charlestown had be[en] in the hands of the enemy 24 days before we received information of it. Their movements since that event are handed to us very imperfectly. The inclosed intelligence from Governor Nash seems to indicate an intention to penetrate as far Northward as they can. Whether under these appearances it may be expedient to send further aids to the Southern States can alone be decided by Congress on a view of the operations which they may have in contemplation elsewhere. I have no doubt such aids will be sent unless greater good to the general union will be produced by employing them where they are. In either event great supplies of military Stores are immediately requisite here. North Carolina has none at all, those of South Carolina are in the hands of the enemy and ours inadequate to the arming our own Militia. As far as they will go, they have been, and will be chearfully submitted to the common use. Some members lately of our executive, but now of your honourable body, are able to give you a State of our Stores, which I consider as a more safe communication than by confiding it to paper. Of musket-cartridge paper, and cartouch boxes particularly we are so destitute that I must pray Congress to send us an immediate supply. These articles are so light too, that a single waggon if sent without delay may furnish a timely and considerable relief.

About Seventy new recruits for Colonel Washingtons horse, being now in this State and utterly unfurnished, will be provided with all necessaries by us. We are informed that the greater part of the continental horse to the Southward are reduc[ed] to the same helpless condition. Some infantry also have applied for military furniture. Gibson's and Brent's battalions which went into continental service full armed were disarmed when returned to us. They are now recruited to about 200 men, and will be modelled for service. We shall again put arms in their hands, as no motives will induce us to let the general good labour even a moment for want of any thing we have. But it would be very satisfactory to us to receive the pleasure of Congress as to the mode of authenticating any advances of this kind which we shall make for them: some of the applications having been necessarily made by subordinate officers.

The removal of our Seat of Government to this place has withdrawn us from the post road. A rider employed by some private Gentlemen furnishes a precarious conveyance to Hanover town the nearest place on the post road. This has rendered all our communications with Congress and the other States very incertain and our Southern ones particularly circuitous and slow. I believe there can be no doubt but that were the post directed to pass from Hanover Courthouse immediately through this place, by Petersburg &c. it would shorten the distance and save still more time by crossing James river and Roanoke where they are narrow and always passable; whereas the present post road crosses where they are wide and tempestuous. I beg leave to submit the expediency of this alteration at this time particularly to the wisdom of Congress assuring them it is considered as very desireable here.

With sentiments of the highest regard & esteem I have the honor to be Your Excellency's Most obedt. & most humble servt.,

TH: JEFFERSON

RC (DLC: PCC, No. 71, I). In a clerk's hand except for TJ's complimentary close and signature. Endorsed: "Letter from govr Jefferson June 9. 1780 Read 16. Referred (except what relates to the post Office) to the Board of War. [In another hand:] Acted upon."

Enclosure missing; probably a copy of Nash's letter to TJ, 30 May.

YOUR REQUISITION: See Huntington to TJ, 19 May 1780. For the Assembly's MEASURES in response, see TJ to Harrison, 8 June 1780.

To Simon Nathan

SIR   June 9th. 1780.

Your obliging offer of serving the State in the purchase of Supplies for the Officers and Men stationed at Pittsburg is accepted, and a Memo of such Supplies as are now wanted is herein inclosed.

I am Sir Your most obedient Servt.,   TH: JEFFERSON

RC (Vi); in a clerk's hand, signed by TJ. Addressed by the clerk: "Simon Nathan Esqr." Endorsed in several hands, probably upon or after being turned in by Nathan in support of his claims against Virginia. Enclosure not further identified.

To James Wood

SIR   Richmond June 9th. 1780.

The progress of the enemy with a very considerable body of cavalry from South to North, tho' not perfectly known, is yet reported here on such grounds as are thought sufficient to render it prudent to be on our guard. This has given occasion to the inclosed resolution of assembly for calling in all the absent officers and soldiers of the conventioners to the barracks, and the advice of council for further measures. This order is not meant to be intended to those beyond the blue ridge, as they are already where they should be. It may perhaps be proper, if they are scattered, to collect them at Staunton. The advice of Council pretty fully explains itself, yet I will give you my ideas of the best mode of executing it, submitting them to your judgment. I think the most essential measure is to procure a judicious, sensible officer, not likely to listen to idle tales nor to take alarm at specious dangers. Consider Cross-creek in North Carolina as the further end of your line of communication for the present. Inform yourself of its distance from the barracks. Send your officer on upon the best road with a sufficient number of horsemen to leave one at every 40 miles distance, reserving one to be always with himself at the other end of the line for the purpose of conveying his letters from himself to the horse man at the first post. Let him remain as near the enemy as he can safely and shift his position as they shift theirs, always sending proper instructions to the horsemen to make the necessary changes in their stations in order to streighten the line of communication. Let him through these communicate to you from time to time every important movement of the enemy. Let the horsemen go their distance from post to post by night and by day without regard to weather, taking receipts of the hour and minute at which they deliver to each other their dispatches. In this way a letter may pass with ease the distance of three stages, that is 120 miles every 24 hours, without injury to their horses. Let them always take two days to return back to their post. It is further necessary that as speedy communication should be established between you and us. For this purpose Station a horseman at Rutherfords ordinary in Goochland, who may as occasion shall require hand your intelligence to me or mine to you with the like dispatch. I mean that you should communicate to me all the intelligence you shall receive thro this channel.

As the Officer who will go to the Southward and the more distant horsemen (especially those who will be out of our Country) must be at considerable expence in living even plainly, I send you by Captain Read two thousand pounds on account for this purpose. You will of course give them notice to provide Vouchers of its expenditure.

Should emergencies render it absolutely necessary and you think such a measure would contribute to safety, the officers must be separated from their men, tho' this should be done only in case of dangers approaching near. It may be well for the present to soothe them with assurances that they shall be permitted e'er long to return to their quarters.

If your horsemen are sent on immediately to gain intelligence it should seem that they might obtain and communicate it to you very early, if the enemy should really approach your post. Taking this circumstance into consideration as well as the State of your provisions you will determine whether it be necessary or not to embody the militia of Albemarle and Augusta, until you have further notice. It is adviseable to avoid every measure which might tend to diffuse a panic among the people.

I am Sir with great respect Your most obedient servt.,

TH: JEFFERSON

RC (Lloyd W. Smith, Madison, N.J., 1946); in a clerk's hand except for TJ's complimentary close and signature. Endorsed: "Govr. Jefferson 9th. June 1780." Enclosures (missing) as follows: (1) copy of resolution of General Assembly, 9 June 1780, requesting the governor to issue orders summoning all absent Convention prisoners to their barracks (JHD, May 1780, 1827 edn., p. 40-1); (2) copy of Council Order for Security of the Convention Prisoners, 9 June 1780, q.v., above. Addressee identified by his acknowledgment of 15 June 1780.

From James Innes

I this morning arrived in Town from Williamsburgh charged with some dispatches for your Excellency, which I herewith transmit you.

On my arrival, I was astonished to be informed, that a Report had been industriously handed to you, of intentions in me, to impeach your Excellency before the general assembly, of illegal conduct relative to the palace furniture. I would fain flatter myself, that your knowledge of me, will not permit you hastily to harbour suspicions so injurious to my character. Had Instructions to that purport been laid upon me, by my Constituents, or had such an insane measure been the spontaneous production of my own Brain, I should surely have been called upon by every Tie of Honor, and fair Dealing, to have candidly apprized your Excellency thereof. But I am happy that, I stand in neither of those predicaments. I declare to the eternal God that this Report, which I suppose some *busy go between* has communicated to you, is foundationless and void of truth. If I know my own Heart, there is no man upon earth would more heartily oppose, than I would, the measure alluded to, which would inevitably tend to excite bitter animosities, tarnish the Dignity of Government, and expose the Character of a fellow Citizen (whom I have ever thought meritoriously exalted) to Cowardly and Envious attacks, without affording him the Opportunity of Exsculpation.

That I have, among others, censured some principles of your administration, I will not hesitate Candidly to Confess to you. As the Citizen of a free State, I thought myself at liberty to express my sentiments, of the Conduct of those magistrates into whose Hands are committed the Reins of Government. I deemed the Dismantling the Forts and the Removal of so great a proportion of military stores from the Eastern Frontier impolitic, because it not only rendered the exposed Country incapable of defending itself, until it might be succoured, but because too, it made a very evil Impression on the minds of the people below, and induced them to believe, they were consigned to a State of dereliction. I spoke of this measure, as the act of the Executive collectively, and did support a motion in the House of Delegates that your Excellency might be advized to adopt a System, which I thought (and the major part of the House concurred with me) a Salutary one.

If either an involuntary warmth of temper, or excited feelings, have hurried me into Indiscretions, of which I am not at present sensible, I shall with pleasure when reminded of them, make the necessary Concessions. This is not the first time, I am apprehensive, that attempts have been made to foment Discord between us. I own I shall be unhappy if such machinations ever succeed. I know your attachment to the great cause of Liberty. I know your abilities, and repose a firm confidence in your virtues, my Respect for which a Difference of opinion shall never shake, tho' it may induce me to declare my sentiments, which I wish to be ever charitably construed.

I have the honor to remain with high Regard and Esteem yr Excellency's obt. Sert., JAS: INN[ES]

RC (DLC). Enclosures not identified. TJ's CONDUCT RELATIVE TO THE PALACE FURNITURE: Nothing further is known of this bit of gossip. A MOTION IN THE HOUSE OF DELEGATES: This motion of censure, if it was such, has not been identified; early in the session Innes was appointed a member of a committee to form a plan of defense for the eastern frontier, and an Act was passed for this purpose near the end of the session in July, after long debate (JHD, May 1780, 1827 edn., p. 6, 86; Hening, x, 296-9). DISCORD BETWEEN US: For a supposed earlier instance, see above, Innes to Mann Page, 27 Oct. 1779, and references there. TJ and Innes seem to have remained on excellent terms; see especially a letter to Innes, 13 Mch. 1791, urging him to run for Congress.

From Thomas Sim Lee

Annapolis, 10 June 1780. Notifying TJ that a line of expresses has been established by the State of Maryland "on the Main Road, leading from Young's Ferry on Patowmack River to Philadelphia," in accordance with Congress' resolution of 5 June.

FC (MdAA); 1 p.   See Huntington to TJ, 5 June; TJ to Gov. Lee, 14 June; Lee to TJ, 17 June 1780.

To James Monroe

DEAR SIR   In Council June 10. 1780.

The Executive have occasion to employ a gentleman in a confidential business, requiring great discretion, and some acquaintance with military things. They wish you to undertake it if not inconsistant with your present pursuits. It will call you off some weeks, to the distance of a couple hundred miles. Expences will be borne and a reasonable premium. Will you be so good as to attend us immediately for further communications. I am Dr. Sir Your friend & Servt., TH: JEFFERSON

RC (NN). Endorsed in two (presumably) later hands. No indication of addressee, but it was doubtless Monroe, for the original is among the Monroe Papers in NN, and Monroe, a few days later, undertook an important mission fully described in TJ's letter to him of 16 June, q.v.—in all probability the mission outlined above.

To George Gibson?

Sir   Richmond June 11. 1780

Understanding from Mr. Dixon that yours and Col. Brent's men will be clothed in two or three days, so that there will be no necessity for their being delayed when they come up, and Chesterfield Court-house being out of their way, I am to desire that they be carried to Petersburg, by which they will be enabled [to] join the Corps now marching or about to march to the Southward. I shall be very glad of your assistance and Col. Brent's in modelling them on the Continental plan which the board of War require before you will be received. I am Sir Your most obt. Servt.,

THOS. JEFFERSON

Tr (Francis Richard, Erie, Penna., 1946). Addressee not indicated, but the owner has always understood that the letter was addressed to George Gibson (col., 1st Va. state regiment), and Gibson's regiment was acting at this time in conjunction with Col. William Brent's 2d Va. Continental regiment, also mentioned in the letter; the forces under the command of both officers were about to be sent south (see Council Orders of 13-24 June, below; also *Va. Council Jour.*, II, 261).

To George Washington

Sir   Richmond June 11th. 1780.

Majr. Galvan as recommended by your Excellency was dispatched to his station without delay, and has been furnished with every thing he desired as far as we were able. The line of expresses formed between us is such as will communicate intelligence from one to the other in twenty three hours. I have forwarded to him information of our disasters in the South as they have come to me.

Our intelligence from the Southward is most lamentably defective. Tho' Charlestown has now been in the hands of the enemy a month, we hear nothing of their movements which can be relied on. Rumours are that they are penetrating Northward. To remedy this defect I shall immediately establish a line of expresses from hence to the neighborhood of their army, and send thither a sensible judicious gentleman to give us information of their movements. This intelligence will I hope be conveyed to us at the rate of 120 miles in the 24 hours. They set out to their stations tomorrow. I wish it were possible that a like speedy line of communication could be formed from hence to your Excellency's head quarters. Perfect and speedy information of what is passing in the South might put it in your power perhaps to frame your measures by theirs. There is really nothing to oppose the progress of the enemy Northward but the cautious principles of the military art. North Caroline is without arms. We do not abound. Those we have are freely imparted to them, but such is the state of their resources that they have not yet been able to move a single musket from this state to theirs. All the waggons we can collect have been furnished to the Marquis de Kalb, and are assembling for the march of 2500 militia under Genl. Stevens of Culpeper who will move on the 19th. inst. I have written to Congress to hasten supplies of arms and military stores for the Southern states, and particularly to aid us with Cartridge paper and Cartridge boxes, the want of which articles, small as they are, renders our stores useless. The want of money cramps every effort. This will be supplied by the most unpalateable of all substitutes, force. Your Excellency will readily conceive that after the loss of one army our eyes are turned towards the other, and that we comfort ourselves that if any aids can be furnished by you without defeating operations more beneficial to the general union, they will be furnished. At the same time I am happy to find that the wishes of the people go no further, as far as I have an opportunity of learning their sentiments. Could arms be furnished I think this state and North Caroline would embody from ten to fifteen thousand militia immediately, and more if necessary. The following is a state of the force in and about to be in motion.

Colo. Buford's regulars (of Scott's and Woodford's men)	400.	
Colo. Porterfeild's do. of Virginia state troops	500	
Colo. Armand's horse	190	
The remains of White's and Washington's as is said about	200	
The Maryland and Delaware troops and artillery	1900	3190
Virginia militia	2500	
North Caroline militia under Genl. Caswell in the feild	400	
Do. embodying under Govr. Caswell if they can be armed	4000	6900

I hope e'er long to be able to give you a more certain state of the enemy's as well as our situation, which I shall not fail to do. I inclose you a letter from Majr. Galvan, being the second I have forwarded to you.

With sentiments of the most perfect esteem & respect I have the honor to be your Excellency's Most obedient & most humble servt.,

TH: JEFFERSON

RC (DLC: Washington Papers); endorsed (in part): "No. 10. Richmond 11th: June 1780 from Govr: Jefferson. Ansd. 29h." Tr (DLC: TJ Papers); text defective. Enclosure: presumably Galvan's letter to Washington, 3 June (*Cal. Wash. Corr. with Officers*, II, 1354). The present letter was enclosed in a further note to Washington of this date, following.

To George Washington

SIR   Richmond June 11th. 1780.

Since sealing the within to your Excellency I received a letter from Govr. Rutlege of which the inclosed is an extract. As it will correct and supply some parts of my letter I do myself the honor of transmitting it, and of again subscribing myself, Your Excellency's most obedt. servt.,   TH: JEFFERSON

RC (DLC: Washington Papers); endorsed: "Extract of a letter from Govr. Rutledge." Tr (DLC: TJ Papers). Enclosures: (1) TJ to Washington, same date, preceding; (2) extract of John Rutledge's letter to TJ, 2 June 1780, q.v.

From the Committee of Congress at Headquarters

In committee of Congress, Morristown,
SIR   June 12th, 1780.

We have the honor to inclose you copy of a letter addressed to us by the commander in chief (see page 211). The contents will advise you to what an alarming crisis our affairs are reduced. The General observes with great propriety, that this committee "need no arguments to evince the danger." Indeed we do not: our own observations have led to the fullest conviction that unless the force stated in our second letter, of the 25th ultimo, is drawn into the field with a celerity equal to the urgency of the occasion, the period which is to end our liberty, and commence the most disgraceful state of slavery, which human nature has ever experienced, is not far distant: But dark and gloomy as the prospect is, America has it in her power to dispel the cloud, by those exertions of which she is abundantly capable, and to which it is her duty to rouse, from every consideration which can affect the human heart.

We are, most indubitably, possesed of the means wherewith to expel the enemy from every part of the continent; but it requires a display of that virtue which distinguished the Citizens of Rome when their State was, as ours now is, on the brink of ruin, and we trust Americans, impressed with a proper sense of the blessings of peace, Liberty, and Independence, will follow the bright example, and evince to future ages, what great minds are capable of, when driven to the extremity of distress.

We dare not suppose, Sir, that efficient measures have not been adopted, by your state to complete your Battalions to the establishment recommended in the letter above referred to; on the contrary, we believe that the men are raised, or raising, but we have to conjure you to hasten them on to the Army, without a moments delay. We intreat you likewise, to give the most pointed direction, to induce an unremitting attention to forward the supplies allotted to your State to be furnished, as specified in our letter of the 2d. Instant.

Had the Enemy on wednesday last, pursued what we generally beleived to be their object, Our heavy Cannon and stores, would inevitably have fallen into their hands, as our Military force was incompetent to their protection, and the means of conveying them to places more distant, for want of horses and Carriages, out of our power.

Since writing the above, a second letter, from the General, has been handed us, a copy whereof we inclose, (see page 212). Previous to our recommendation to compleat the battalions to five hundred and four rank and file, we had a conferance with the general on the subject, in which the matter was thoroughly canvassed, and the necessity of the augmentation clearly evinced; The reduction of Charles Town, was then problematical; we had even hopes that it would have been saved, and the Maryland and Delaware lines, have returned to this Army, which then, with the quota requested of the states would have amounted to about Twenty five thousand men, the number which Congress had promised our illustrious ally, should be brought into the field, to co-operate with his troops. It is now beleived, that Charles Town is reduced, and the troops which defended it, prisoners, consequently we shall not have the Maryland and Delaware troops: hence those in this quarter will be less, by nearly three thousand men, than our estimate, we therefore most earnestly intreat that no deduction may be made from the numbers we have stated as necessary.

We have the honor to be, with the greatest respect & Esteem, Your Excellency's, Most Obedt. Hble Servts.,

PHP. SCHUYLER

JNO. MATHEWS

NATHL. PEABODY

FC (DLC: PCC, No. 11). At head of text: "Circular. No. 4." The page references in the text are to the Committee's journal of proceedings, whence the present text is derived; the letters from Washington enclosed were dated 11 and 12 June 1780, respectively, and are printed in his *Writings*, ed. Fitzpatrick, XVIII, 504-6; XIX, 2.

THE ENEMY ON WEDNESDAY LAST: This refers to the raid on Connecticut Farms, N.J., by 5,000 British troops under Knyphausen, 7 June (Carrington, *Battles of the Amer. Revolution*, p. 498-9; see also Cyrus Griffin to TJ, 9 and 13 June 1780).

To Benjamin Harrison

[*Richmond, 12? June 1780*. JHD, May 1780, 1827 edn., p. 44 (12 June): "The Speaker laid before the House a letter from the Governor, enclosing several others from the President of Congress, with sundry acts and resolutions of that body." Not located. Enclosures not clearly identifiable.]

To James Wood

SIR   Richmond June 12. 1780.

I have heard with real concern the sufferings of the guard and prisoners at your station, for want of provisions, and the more as it has been out of my power to afford relief. There is no exertion I would not put in practice, to help you. I am told the assembly are taking measures to enable us to carry on government: and I think that the late motions of the enemy begin already sensibly to revive the public spirit of the people, whom long quiet had diverted from all attention to the war. They lend money, and other aids now with considerable freedom. Till our treasury shall be enabled to supply money for the purchase of fresh provisions (which is much the most eligible) I have directed the Quartermaster to encrease his number of waggons that you may be supplied with salt provisions. This he supposes he can do by raising his hire to £15. a day.

By what you mention as to the prisoners in close confinement I suppose you have not been able to execute my recommendation for removing them to the Northward. At present it would certainly be improper to spare a guard to go to such a distance. We must therefore leave altogether to your discretion the measures necessary to relieve them in point of health. Confinement should not be carried so far as to produce mortal effects. I know no objection to the letting such of them go at large within proper bounds, whose health really requires it. And if these behave well why not extend the indulgence to all others whose term of confinement has been already such as to amount to a sufficient punishment of their offence.

The enemy had not entered N. Caroline on the 29th. of the last month. In the directions given you on that subject you will no doubt have been sensible of the effect of popular influence on public councils. Nothing less could be done; more was proposed. The measures for obtaining true and speedy intelligence of the enemy's movements were wise and proper. As soon as you shall know from the person you send on that business their true situation and that it does not respect your quarter, or cannot affect you but on sufficient previous notice, you will of course permit the officers to return to their quarters. I hope it will not be long before you obtain that intelligence. I am Sir Your most obedt. servt,

Th: Jefferson

RC (CSmH). Addressee identified from internal evidence; see TJ to Wood, 9 June; Wood to TJ, 15 June 1780; TJ to Nash, 16 June.

From Cyrus Griffin

Philadelphia, 13 June [*1780*]. Griffin is about to retire from Congress. Hopes governor approved intelligence he has forwarded. Confesses that, duty aside, he had "pride and pleasure in corresponding with a great character." Stirling reports British in New Jersey considerably reinforced. They have built a floating bridge to retreat to Staten Island if necessary. Two or three "little battles" have taken place. Probably object of enemy was "to try the force of General Washingtons regular Troops—unluckily by the experiment they find our illustrious commander unable to meet them without the aid of militia—and what next?" Fears they will remain in Jersey until Clinton returns from Charleston and then make a bold attempt on the Continental stores. About fifty sail of merchantmen arrived at Philadelphia a few days ago.

RC (DLC); 4 p. Body of letter printed in full by Burnett, *Letters of Members*, v, No. 245, who conjectures that it was written originally as a postscript to Griffin's letter to TJ of 9 June 1780, q.v.

To Benjamin Harrison

Sir   In Council, June 13, 1780.

The supplies of cloathing and other necessaries actually procured for the officers of the Virginia troops having been very far short of what an act of the legislature had authorised them to call for, and it being evident to the Executive from a view of the supplies on hand provided by the board instituted for that purpose, and of the means now in their hands for making future provision, that there is no prospect that those allowances can be fully procured, I beg leave to bring the subject under the consideration of the legislature. Whether, on a revision of the allowance, it may or may not be found greater than is necessary, is a question for them alone to decide. The difference however between that allowance and what is actually received by the officers had produced a claim for compensation which is the subject of the within letter and requires legislative explanation. These differences have been the cause of very real sufferings to the officers, of much discontent, and have produced the most distressing applications to the Executive. They have been more severely felt by the gentlemen serving within the state than by those engaged in more active scenes of duty, the latter having been supposed more exposed to wants with less means of supplying them.

MS not located. Text from Ford, ii, 310-11, who prints it without signature and who gives his source as Virginia State Archives.

This letter, with one enclosed from George Muter to TJ (also missing), was laid before the House on the same day and referred to the committee of the whole on the state of the commonwealth (JHD, May 1780, 1827 edn., p. 45).

From Samuel Huntington

Sir   Philadelphia June 13. 1780

By the Act of Congress of this Day herewith enclosed your Excellency will be informed that Major General Gates is ordered to take the Command in the southern Department.

This Order is in Consequence of Intelligence received that seems to place it beyond a Doubt, the Enemy are in Possession of Charles town and the Garrison there made Prisoners, although the Intelligence received is not official.

I have the honour to be with very great Respect your Excelly's most obedt servant,   SAM. HUNTINGTON President

RC (Vi); endorsed in a clerk's hand. Enclosure (Vi): copy of unanimous resolution of Congress of 13 June, appointing Gen. Gates to take immediate command of the southern department; printed in JCC, XVII, 508. FC of letter is in DLC: PCC, No. 15.

Council Orders to George Muter

[13-24 June 1780]

Order in answer to Colo. Muters Letter of 30th May 1780.

In Council June 13th 1780

Gibson's and Brent's men are to be armed from Petersburg as far as the good arms there will go, deficiencies to be supplied from Richmond. Colo. Muter will be pleased to instruct Majr. Quarles and such assistant Officers as may be procured to go through the Country and collect the draughts dispersed in different parts, writing at the same time to the County Lieutenants to aid in collecting them. Also to obtain from the auditors a list of the military pensioners, and call on them to engage as Guards at the various small posts for which they are fit, giving pay rations and clothing instead of their pension, but no bounty. The Executive know at present no other means of supplying necessary guards and garrisons. Colo. Muter will take such measures for finishing the prison ship as may not interfere with the preparation of more important Vessels.   TH: JEFFERSON

Order in answer to Colo. Muter's Letter of March 8th 1780.

In Council June 13. 1780.

The Board are of opinion that Colo. Muter have measures immediately taken for having the framing provided at Sydnor's removed to and erected on the ground destined for that purpose near the foundery and that proper workmen be engaged for this business.   THO JEFFERSON

Order in answer to Colo. Muters Letter of June 14. 1780.

In Council June 14. 1780

The board approves of employing Doctor Foushee on the terms abovementioned and more fully explained on a former paper.

THO JEFFERSON

Order in Answer to Colo. Muters Letter of June 15. 1780.

In Council June 15th. 1780

The board approve of Captain Pierce being appointed, a warrant is sent for £1000. on account for expences, and despatches shall be ready by tomorrow morning.   TH JEFFERSON

Order in answer to Colo. Muter's Letter of June 23rd 1780.

In Council June 24. 1780.

The Board advise that orders be given to the Quarter master, to hire a house properly situated for a hospital, or if that cannot be done to build one with logs for temporary use and that he have cradles provided by the public artificers; that Dr. Foushi be authorized to hire a nurse occasionally, or if one can be got on moderate terms, a standing one; that the issuing commissary and commissary of stores be directed to provide and issue on application from Dr. Foushi, rice, homony, molasses, sugar, vinegar, spirit, fresh meats and vegetables, and to provide a cow.   TH JEFFERSON

Transcripts, in various hands, in Board of War Letter Book (MiU-C). These Orders in answer to various requests for instructions by Col. Muter are, for some reason, gathered together on two pages of the Letter Book and are therefore printed here collectively. The letters of Muter to which they reply are all missing; the date "March 8th" (preceding the second Council Order) is suspect and in all probability is an error for 8 June.

From Riedesel

New York, 13 June 1780. Acknowledges TJ's kindness in forwarding earlier letters to officers of the Convention army and encloses others to be so forwarded. Begs his own and Mme. de Riedesel's remembrance to Mrs. Jefferson. The Riedesels have moved for the summer to a house a few miles out of town on the East River. The children are well and have not forgotten Mrs. Jefferson's kindnesses.

RC (DLC); 2 p. Enclosures not identified.

From John Todd

[*Richmond?*, *13 June 1780.*] TJ's letter to Speaker Harrison, 14 June 1780, q.v., states that Todd had addressed TJ on 13 June asking for indemnification for losses in connection with the proposed settlement at the mouth of the Ohio. Todd's letter was transmitted to the Assembly but has not been located (JHD, May 1780, 1827 edn., p. 46).]

From John Walker

Dear Sir   Philada. June 13th. 1780

I hoped before I had been here so long, to have had the pleasure of a few lines from you, if it was merely to inform us of your health and that of your Family, in which you know we are so deeply interested.

My Family is perfectly recovered from the small-pox, which to them was so favorable that they never lay'd by for it. Mrs. Walker had only two pustules and Milly one for each of the united States. We are comfortably enough lodged and but for the exorbitant expences of the place, might do well enough. As there is no provision made by our State for furnishing us with the needful and the Continental Treasury is empty, our situation is disagreeable. I found one Man (Levi Hollingsworth) who agreed to advance me 10,000 dollars for which sum I have taken the Liberty of drawing on our Treasury and hope my Bill will be honored; otherwise judge what will be our situation. We wish our State would fall on some expedient to furnish such Supplys as may be inte[nd]ed for us, as we find it extremely difficult to get Cash here.

General Gates was this day appointed to take command in the Southern department. The further arrangements &c. for that Quarter are yet unfinished for want of the necessary information, having as yet received no Accounts of our Misfortune there, but by way of New York. Is not this astonishing when Chas. Town is said to have surrendered on the 12th Ult?

The inclosed paper will inform you of the Enemy's late incursions in New Jersey, which is the only news here. This and the neighboring States are making the most vigorous exertions to oppose their operations. Pensylvania is about to fill up their Continental Line by subscription and I believe they will effect it, so great and laudable is their Zeal. The very Ladi[e]s contributing large sums on the inclosed plan, drawn up by the Minister of France's Secretary.

Virginia's conduct in rejecting the scheme of March the 18th Appears to give as great uneasiness here, as the Loss of Chas. Town. I believe it is prety generally approved in the Eastern states and already adopted by most of them. My Family desires to be affectionately remembered to Mrs. Jefferson and Miss Patsey And I am My dear Sir Your affectionate Friend & humble Servt.,

Jn. Walker

RC (DLC). Enclosures not found, but see below.

THE INCLOSED PLAN: A plan to collect funds among the women of America for clothing the Continental troops; François Marbois, THE MINISTER OF FRANCE'S SECRETARY, was one of those closely associated with this forerunner of modern charitable "drives"; see William B. Reed, *Life and Correspondence of Joseph Reed*, Phila., 1847, II, 260 and *passim*; also Mrs. Jefferson to Mrs. James Madison, Sr., 8 Aug. 1780, printed below. THE SCHEME OF MARCH THE 18TH: The proposal to call in all outstanding Continental bills and substitute a new emission; see Huntington to TJ, 20 Mch., and Joseph Jones to TJ, 30 June 1780. Virginia later complied; see TJ to Madison, 26 July; to Huntington, 27 July; TJ's Proclamation, 28 Aug. 1780.

From George Brooke

SIR   Richmond June 14. 1780.

Upon examining the money transmitted by Mr. Sinclair the undermentioned bundles were missing, which Mr. Smith Tandy who received the money says was taken out of his bags on his way down. Inclosed is the list sent by Mr. Sinclair.

I am with due respect Sir Your most obt. servt,

GEO BROOKE

Bundles missing vizt.

Mar. 18[1]	Robert Dunlap	£ 550		£18[2]			
Apr. 4	William Matear	560		9	6	8	
Mar. 30	Andrew Ramsey	300		6			Certificates
Do.	Hugh Mcclure	225		4	8		issued
Apr. 11	William Finley	800	14	13	6	10/2	July 12.
18	Thomas Scott	400	2	6	13	4	1783
18	Walter Davis	417	9	6	19	2	
May 5	Andrew Hamilton	1123	8	18	14	5/2	
		£4376	13				

RC (Vi). Addressed: "To His Excellency Thomas Jefferson esqr." Endorsed by TJ: "Colo. Matthews." Enclosure missing, possibly a duplicate of the list of sums of money received enclosed in Alexander Sinclair's letter to TJ, 21 May 1780, q.v. On verso: Advice of Council concerning Money Collected by Sampson Matthews, following.

George Brooke was at this time state treasurer (JHD, May 1780, 1827 edn., p. 64).

[1] The dates in this column are in a later hand, possibly added when the matter was under consideration and certificates were issued in 1783.
[2] The amounts in the last three columns are in a different hand and probably represent accrued interest.

Advice of Council concerning Money Collected by Sampson Matthews

In Council June 14. 1780.

The board are of opinion that Colo. Sampson Matthews having acted as their agent in receiving the money borrowed from the people, the lenders are in no wise concerned or to be affected by whatever happened to the money after they paid it to Colo. Matthews; and therefore clearly that the lenders are entitled to loan office certificates. Mr. Sinclair's letter of May the 21st. is an acknolegement that he had received the money from Colo. Matthews and so far clears Colo. Matthews and leaves the dispute only between Sinclair and Tandy. It should seem therefore proper that the money should be charged by the Auditors to one or both of these gentlemen, who should be called on to account for it, and failing, that it should be referred to the General court for decision in due course of law whether these gentlemen have been guilty of such negligence as will charge them in law with the money lost.

The board conceive their interference at present to be not strictly within their line, but that it rests with the Auditors and treasurer to determine how they will proceed. They are induced to give their opinion from a sense of the meritorious motives which induced the lenders (who are said to be farmers, not monied men) to supply monies to their country in the hour of her distress, and from reflection on the discouragements which would follow on all future applications to the people, were the miscarriages which happen in other hands to bring loss on them. Th: Jefferson

MS (Vi); in TJ's hand, written on verso of George Brooke's letter to TJ, preceding. Although this is an "Advice of Council," there can scarcely be any doubt that TJ was its author.

Two resolutions of the House of Delegates throw light on the case of the money collected by SAMPSON MATTHEWS and transmitted by Alexander SINCLAIR in a letter to TJ of 21 May 1780, q.v. On 27 June 1780 the House amended and agreed to a report on a memorial of Smyth TANDY which stated in part that a considerable sum of money had been collected in Augusta co. and by order of Matthews had been paid to Sinclair for transmittal to the governor (JHD, May 1780, 1827 edn., p. 64). Sinclair sent the money to TJ by Tandy, and TJ referred Tandy with the money to the state treasurer, George Brooke, who, when he examined the packet, found £4376/13 missing (Brooke to TJ, preceding). Tandy returned home and found one small bundle of money among the papers in his desk. As a result of its investigation the House rejected Tandy's petition "praying that he may not sustain the loss." From a resolution of the House of 24 June 1783 it appears that Matthews had sued Tandy for the missing sum, that he had been nonsuited, and that he now sought reimbursement for the sum lost by Tandy and for the costs of the suit. The House found his plea reasonable, the Senate agreed, and he was accordingly reimbursed (JHD, May 1783, 1828 edn., p. 79-80, 82).

To Benjamin Harrison

Sir   In Council June 14th 1780.

In a Letter, which I had the Honor of addressing you on the meeting of the present General Assembly, I informed you of the necessities which had led the Executive to withdraw our western troops to the Ohio. Since the date of that Letter I have received the inclosed of the second instant from Colo. Todd communicating the measures he had adopted in Conjunction with Colo. Clarke to procure such a Settlement contiguous to the post which shall be taken as may not only strengthen the garrison occasionally, but be able to raise provisions for them. As the confirmation of these measures is beyond the powers of the executive, it is my duty to refer them to the General Assembly. It may be proper to observe that the grant of Lands by Colo. Todd was made on a supposition that the post wou'd be taken on the north side of the Ohio whereas I think it more probable it will be on the south side in the Lands lying between the Tanissee Ohio Missisippi and Carolina boundery. These Lands belong to the Chickasaw indians, who from intelligence which we think may be relied on, have entered into war with us.

The expenditures of the Ilinois, have been deemed from some expressions in the act establishing that county not subject to the examination of the board of Auditors. As the auditing these accounts is very foreign to the ordinary office of the Council of State, would employ much of that [time] and attention which at present [is] called to objects of [more] general importance and as their powers wou'd not enable them to take into consideration the Justice and expediency of indemnifying Colo. Todd for his losses and services as desired in the inclosed Letter from Him of the thirteenth instant they beg leave to submit the whole to the consideration of the General Assembly.

I have the honor to be with great respect & esteem Sir Your most obedient & most humble servt.,   TH: JEFFERSON

RC (Vi), in a clerk's hand, with complimentary close and signature in TJ's hand. Addressed by the clerk to Harrison as Speaker; endorsed by Beckley: "Governors Letter June 14th: 1780. inclosing others from Jno. Todd jr. Esq: Refd: to whole on Commonwealth." Enclosures: John Todd to TJ, 2 June (q.v.) and 13 June 1780 (missing).

TJ's earlier LETTER mentioned in the first sentence was doubtless that of 9? May 1780; see entry under that date. The present letter was read in the House and referred on the day sent to the committee of the whole on the state of the commonwealth (JHD, May 1780, 1827 edn., p. 46).

To Thomas Sim Lee

SIR   Richmond June 14th 1780

I lately received a resolution of Congress of the 5th instant requesting the establishment of a line of expresses from Cape Henry to Philadelphia. I had before on application from General

Washington formed such a Line from Cape Henry to this place in order to communicate such intelligence as I should receive to the gentleman entrusted by the General with the duty of keeping a Look out at that Cape: and that our intelligence from the south might be more perfect and speedy while the operations in that quarter continue so interesting I have sent a confidential person to the neighbourhood of the hostile army in Carolina, to convey to us information of their movements by a line of expresses stationed from him to this place. These circumstances determined me on receipt of the resolution of congress to execute their desire by employing three additional riders from hence to Alexandria which by availing them of what had been done before, will save expence, will give them the benefit of our southern communications, and will I think render the conveyance of dispatches more certain and expeditious than they would be were they to cross the bay to cape Charles, or to cross James river at Hampton; the incertainty of the former is well known to all, and the latter ferriage is of eighteen miles which very frequently employs a day in the passage. The riders being stationed at forty miles distance, with orders to ride by night and by day without regard to weather, will I hope transmit their dispatches at the rate of one Hundred and twenty miles every twenty four hours. I have ordered the third rider from this place who will be stationed at Alexandria to proceed and receive your Excellency's commands as to the Station at which you shall think proper to fix a person to receive dispatches from him, to which station he will hereafter convey whatever he shall receive. When the communication from cape Henry to this place shall be rendered unnecessary by the arrival of the french fleet it may still perhaps be thought expedient to continue for a time the riders from hence to Philadelphia as the conveyance of intelligence will be thereby so much expedited.

With every sentiment of esteem & respect I have the honor to be Your Excellency's most obedient & most humble servt.,

Th: Jefferson

P.S. I beg leave to trouble your Excellency with forwarding the inclosed.

RC (Andre deCoppet, New York City, 1949). Endorsed: "14 June 1780 Governor Jefferson." Addressee identified from internal evidence. See Gov. Lee to TJ, 10, 17 June 1780.

To Benjamin Harrison

[*Richmond, 15 June 1780*. JHD, May 1780, 1827 edn., p. 48: "The Speaker laid before the House a letter from the Governor, respecting the removal of the Convention troops in case of danger, and enclosing one from Col. Wood on the same subject." TJ's letter has not been found; James Wood's letter, enclosed, must have been that of this same day, delivered "By Light Dragoon" from Charlottesville.]

To Samuel Huntington

SIR   Richmond June 15. 1780.

I received your Excellency's letter inclosing a resolution of Congress of the 5th. inst. for the establishment of a line of expresses from Cape Henry to Philadelphia. I had before on the request of General Washington formed such a line from Cape Henry to this place. I therefore thought it better to execute your desire by continuing the line from this place Northwardly, as it would save expence by availing you of what had been done before, and will probably render the conveyances more certain and expeditious than they would be were they to cross the bay to Cape Charles, or to cross James river to Hampton. The incertainty of the former passage is well known to all; and the latter ferriage is of eighteen miles, which frequently employs a day in the passage. I am forming a like line from this place to the neighborhood of the enemy's army in Carolina, sending thither a confidential and judicious person to collect and to convey intelligence of their movements and to continue there so long as their operations shall be so very interesting as they are at present. I mention this latter circumstance to your Excellency because before the receipt of your letter I had made it the ground of a suggestion to General Washington whether it might not be proper (in order to give him the benefit of our Southern communications) to establish such a line from hence Northwardly. Congress having in the mean time desired the establishment of such a line, I am only to submit to them whether when the communication from cape Henry to this place shall be rendered unnecessary by the arrival of the French fleet, it may not still be expedient to continue for a time the riders from hence to Philadelphia. These riders being stationed at distances not too great for a horse to pass without rest, and being ordered to travel by night and by day without regard to weather, I shall hope will convey intelligence at the rate of 120 miles the twenty four hours, which is a much greater dispatch than can be expected from the post, should a post be established on this road.

With the highest sentiments of respect I have the honor to be Your Excellency's Most obedient & most humble servt.,

TH: JEFFERSON

RC (DLC: PCC, No. 71, 1). Endorsed by Charles Thomson: "Letter from Govr Jefferson June 15. 1780 Read 23. Referred to the comee on the post Office."

Huntington's LETTER here acknowledged was that of 5 June, q.v. TJ's letter was read 23 June and referred to the post-office committee, which reported on 29 June, and it was resolved "That Congress approve the line of communication which Governor Jefferson . . . is forming, by expresses, southward and northward, and that the same be continued until the further order of Congress" (JCC, XVII, 551, 574-5); see also Huntington to TJ, 30 June 1780.

From Philip Mazzei

Paris, 15 June 1780. Sends Leyden gazette of 6 June with accounts of "various insolent and ignominious actions of the British subjects at sea." The whole world now believes that "the sentiments contained in the enclosed Manuscript No. 1. may be considered as the Emperors"—an East India Company now forming at Trieste under his auspices. King of Naples goes on as fast as possible to form his marine. His minister of marine, and admiral at the same time, is "the brave and intelligent Mr. Acton, who directs and superintends the whole." Sends French gazette of 9 June and extracts from other papers. Refers to the "disorders and Crimes lately committed" in England "by fanatics and thieves."

RC (CtY); 2 p.; in a clerk's hand, signed by Mazzei; at head of text: "19 [i.e. dispatch No. 19]. 2d. Copy." The "3d Copy" of the same dispatch is in NN and has been printed in Marraro, *Mazzei,* p. 56. Enclosures missing.

To William Preston

SIR   Richmond June 15 1780

The present campaign promises our handsful of emploiment from every quarter. Of this you are likely to have your share. While we are threatned with a formidable attack from the northward on our Ohio settlements and from the southern indians on our frontiers convenient to them, our eastern country is exposed to invasion from the British army in Carolina. To the counties of Washington and Montgomery we must allot the operations against the southern indians. We are informed that the Carolinians are meditating an attack on the Chickamogges and will want aid. I am therefore to require that one hundred and fifty militia from Washington and one hundred from Montgomery be embodied in such time and manner as may cooperate with the Carolinians and strike a decisive and memorable blow against those hostile towns, taking great care that no injury be done to the friendly part of the nation. For this purpose you will of course open a proper correspondence with the county Lieutenants of Washington and the commanding officer of the Carolinians. With the county Lieutenant of Washington you will also concert measures for taking a post on proper grounds at or not far from Martins cabbin to be garrisoned by thirty militia from Washington and twenty from Montgomery to continue in service until relieved from their counties. I have no reason to suppose that the Carolinians woud propose to confound together the friendly and hostile parts of the Cherokee nation: it is my duty however to guard against possibilities, and to direct that our people do by no means cooperate against the friendly towns. They have our faith pledged for their protection and tho we cannot oppose force on their behalf in such an event, it is our desire that every thing short of that be exerted in their favour.

The settlements on the Ohio are without ammunition. I have therefore sent orders on Colo. Fleming and Colo. Lynch for powder and Lead to be delivered to the commanding officer of those souldiers who had been enlisted for the western service and who on the apprehension of a design against the Lead mines were stationed there till further orders. The time is now come when it is necessary for them to join their regiment and at the same time perform the useful service of escorting the powder and Lead to Kentucky. The inclosed Letter to the officer I must pray you to deliver. A guard of militia of Washington and Montgomery in proportion to their numbers must supply their place at the mines, which must be proportioned to what you shall think there is reason to apprehend. A small one at any rate will be necessary to guard against the mischief which might be done secretly by solitary or small combinations of disaffected persons.

Five hundred weight of powder will immediately be sent from hence for the Chickamogga expedition and other public uses of your two counties and I inclose an order on Colo. Lynch for one thousand pound of Lead. Mr. Baker the southwestern commissary and quarter master must furnish the aids of his departments.

Since writing the above we have concluded to put the men going against the Chuccamoggas under command of Colo. William Campbell now here, to whom therefore I have given the order for the lead, and who will superintend the sending from this place the necessary articles of other kinds.

I am Sir With great respect Your most humble servt,

TH: JEFFERSON

RC (WHi); in a clerk's hand except for last paragraph, complimentary close, and signature by TJ. Endorsed: "Governors Letter." Recipient's name as-signed from internal evidence and the fact that the original is in the Preston Papers.

See TJ to Preston, 28 June 1780.

From James Wood

SIR   Charlotteville 15th. June 1780.

I am Honour'd with your Letter of the 9th. Instant with the Several Inclosures, and shall think myself Happy if I am Able to Carry your Ideas into Execution. I have Issued Peremptory Orders for *all* the Officers without Distinction, to repair within five Days to the Barracks, and shall Certainly inforce them with Strictness; at the same time I must beg leave to Suggest it as my Opinion, that in Case it shou'd be Necessary to remove the Troops, it wou'd have Greatly Facilitated their march, for the Officers to have re-mained at their Quarters; they will Certainly when Confined to the Limits of the Barracks, Concieve themselves Discharged from their Paroles—will encourage Desertion among the Soldiery—and in Case of being Obliged to remove, will throw every Obstruction in the way. It will be altogether Impossible to Secure the Troops, and Prevent Desertion with the Guards I have; and the State of Pro-visions, and the Prospect of Securing Supplies, will not admit of my Calling in any of the Militia at Present. From the State of the Post which I have frequently made to your Excellency, you will Please to Observe, that the waggons which are employed, are not more than half sufficient to Transport Provision and Forage, and that unless my hands are strengthened by Government, it will be Morally impossible for me to remove such a Body of Men thro' a Country remarkably Scarce of Provision and Forage, without a Days Provision before hand, without Money to Purchase, and without Authority to empress either Provisions, Horses, or Car-riages.

I am well assured had the Assembly Entended their resolution no farther than to have restricted the Officers to the Limits of the County, and Called in all their Supernumerary Servants, it wou'd have answered a Much Better Purpose; I hope I shall be Excused for giving my Opinion thus freely, as your Excellency may be assured it Proceeds from my Zeal for the Service.

I shall immediately Order two Hundred Mil[itia] from each of the Counties of Albemarle, and Augusta, to be Appointed, Arm[ed] and held in the most Perfect readiness to march at the shortest Notice. At Present I am inclinable to think, in Case of the rapid Approach of the Enemy, it wou'd be better to march the Troops through Orange and Culpeper, and Cross the Blue Ridge at Chesters gap; my reason for this Opinion is, that if the Convention Troops shou'd be the Object of the Enemy, they will most Certainly Keep the upper Road as far as Possible above the Blue Ridge, and there will be a much better Prospect of my being Supplied that route than the Other. I shall be Extremely Glad to be informed by the return of the Dragoon, whether the Officers are to be Closely Confined to the Barrack[s;] whether some of them who have Built Huts within the Distance of four Miles are to be removed? And whether I am to Demand Other Paroles of them, and what the Tenor of the New Ones are to be? I must again repeat that without the Most Ample Supplies of Money to the Different Staff Departments, the Troops (when they are all Collected) cannot be supplied at the Barracks. I have been Closely Confined for five Days past with a violent Fever, it is with the Greatest Difficulty I set up to write, therefore hope you will Excuse the imperfections in this Letter. I have the Honor to be with the Greatest respect Yr. Excellency's Very Obt. Servt,   JAMES WOOD

P.S. General Hamilton requests to Know whether the General Officers, their Aids de camp Brigade Majors and Servants are Meant to be included. He says they will willingly give any Parole that may be thought Necessary.

RC (Vi). Addressed: "His Excellency Governor Jefferson. Richmond. By Light Dragoon." Endorsed: "15th June 1780. Col. Jas Wood to Govr Jefferson respectg Convention Troops." This letter reached Richmond in time to be transmitted by TJ to the Speaker of the House on the same day; see preceding entry and also TJ's letters to Wood of 9 and 16 June.

To Benjamin Harrison

[*Richmond, 16? June 1780.* JHD, May 1780, 1827 edn., p. 50 (16 June): "The Speaker laid before the House, a letter from the Governor, enclosing several letters and papers from a committee of Congress, on the present state of the army." Not located. Enclosures: presumably the Committee of Congress at Headquarters' two letters to TJ of 25 May

1780, q.v.; that of 2 June was apparently not transmitted until 19 June.]

From Samuel Huntington

Philadelphia, 16 June 1780. Acknowledges TJ's "Despatches" of 9 June. They have been referred to Board of War and Committee on the Post Office. Encloses resolutions of Congress of 14 June authorizing Gen. Gates to call on Virginia and other southern states for militia and supplies and recommending those states to give every assistance in their power to carry into execution "such Measures as Genl. Gates shall judge most proper."

RC (Vi); 2 p. FC (DLC: PCC, No. 15). Enclosure (Vi): copy of resolutions of Congress, 14 June 1780, attested by Charles Thomson; printed in JCC, XVII, 510-11, endorsed by a clerk as received in June. A fuller version of the enclosure (apparently sent later, for the endorsement states that it was "recd. July [17]80") is also in Vi; likewise attested by Thomson, it contains the "orders" as well as the "resolutions" adopted by Congress on Gates' assuming command in the South. The orders were for financing Gates' army; see JCC as cited above.

To James Monroe

SIR   Richmond June 16th. 1780

You will proceed with the riders provided for you, stationing one at every forty miles or thereabouts from hence to the vicinity of the British army in Carolina where you will continue yourself, observing their movements and when their importance requires it, communicating them to me. Instruct your riders to travel by night and day without regard to weather giving and taking way bills expressing the hour and minute of their delivering and receiving dispatches, also direct them to engage in the neighbourhood of their station, some able and trusty person to take their place in case of their becoming sick or otherwise unable to perform their duty. Important events also tho they should not be attended by any movement, which respects us, I would wish you to communicate. The state and resources of our friends, their force, the disposition of the people, the prospect of provisions, ammunition, arms, and other circumstances, the force and condition of the enemy, will also be proper articles of communication. Inform Governors Nash and Rutledge from time to time of your station, also the commander of the american force and of the particular troops of this commonwealth; that [they] may through you be enabled to correspond with me. I must leave to your own discretion tho to decide when the importance of their communications may render it proper for you to put your Line of riders into motion as it is of consequence for the quick conveyance of important Letters that the horses be kept fresh. I shall expect as soon as you shall have obtained knowledge of the present state of things that you communicate it to me and afterwards only from time to time as before directed. Indeed should a fortnight at anytime have intervened without any occurrence worth communicating it might not be amiss to write that that is the Case, as the Horses cannot be injured by performing their stage once in that interval of time.   Th Jefferson

Tr in Board of War Letter Book (MiU-C). At foot of text: "Colo Munroe." See TJ to Nash, 16 June, and Monroe to TJ, 26 June 1780.

To Abner Nash

Sir   Richmond June 16. 1780.

The tardiness and incertainty of intelligence from the Southern states, and the very interesting situation of things there at present have induced me to send Colo. Monroe, a sensible, judicious, and confidential person, to the neighborhood of the hostile army, for the purpose of collecting and communicating notice of their movements. He is attended by a sufficient number of expresses to station one at every forty miles distance from hence to the termination of his line, where he will keep with him a serjeant and single horseman. These having instructions to bring on his letters by night and by day, without regard to weather, intelligence will come to us at the rate of 120 miles in the 24. hours. I thought it proper to inform your Excellency of this measure, as well because it might afford you a ready and safe conveyance for any communications with which you may please to honour me, more especially if you should think proper to establish a similar line of communication with Colo. Monroe, as that I might recommend that gentleman to your patronage, aid and confidence, should any circumstance arise in which the general good would be thereby promoted. Colo. Monroe will inform your Excellency of the stations he shall take from time to time and will take pleasure in communicating to you any intelligence he shall obtain, if you have no better means already established. The same difficulties of correspondence with Genl. Washington have induced me to take the liberty of suggesting to the Genl. the expediency of his establishing a like communication with this place.

The situation of the Convention troops in our country, has rendered it necessary on every occasion to be watchful of every movement of the enemy which might terminate in an attempt to rescue them, which with large bodies of cavalry, and by rapid marches they might suppose practicable. I have therefore directed Colo. Wood to form a line of communication from the barracks to the enemy's army in the same manner I do from this place and to send a trusty officer to watch their motions. I do not know who this gentleman will be, but beg leave to recommend him also to your excellency's protection when he shall be made known to you.

Since writing so far, I have received a requisition of Congress in conjunction with Governor Lee to form a line of riders from Cape Henry to Philadelphia. This I have accordingly done, conducting the line thro' this place.

I have the honor to be with the greatest esteem Your Excellency's most obedient & most humble servt,   Th: Jefferson

RC (NcDAH). Addressed by TJ: "His Excellency Governor Nash. Newbern. by Colo. Monroe." Endorsed: "[Governor] Jeffersons Lett [June] 16th. 1780."

To James Wood

Sir   Richmond June 16. 1780. 2 H. P. M.

The assembly (on your letter being laid before them) having taken off the restraint of their resolution leaves us free to follow our own judgment which coincides with yours as to the inexpediency of calling the officers to the barracks. This measure may therefore be dispensed with, and the rather as no intelligence gives reason to apprehend that the enemy have ventured to make them an object of their contemplation. The supernumerary servants you will call in or not as you see best, and in general we must leave you to exercise your discretion; more especially as by now you will be in the way of receiving authentic intelligence. I think it a matter of some moment to avoid discovering to the Conventioners any symptoms of fear. It suggests to them that the attempt is thought practicable. Should any future information give reason to apprehend a necessity of removing them, you shall be furnished with money, powers of impressing &c. I am Sir Your very humble servt.,   Th: Jefferson

P.S. The letter to Divers is of consequence.

RC (Lloyd W. Smith, Madison, N.J., 1946). Endorsed: "Govr. Jefferson 16th. June 1780." Addressee identified from internal evidence.

Written in answer to Wood's letter of 15 June, which had objected to the Assembly's resolution of 9 June respecting the Convention troops. TJ laid Wood's letter before the House on the day it was written, and on the next day the governor was directed to take such measures as were eligible, regardless of the earlier resolution (JHD, May 1780, 1827 edn., p. 49). TJ now conveys this information to Wood on the same day as the legislature acted; this was remarkably prompt action all around.

From Thomas Sim Lee

SIR   In Council Annapolis 17th. June 1780

Before we were honored with your Excellency's Letter of the 14th. Inst., we had, in Pursuance of the Resolution of Congress 5th. established a Line of expresses extending from Young's Ferry on Patowmack to Philadelphia, and wrote immediately by Post, advising you of it, and that the Rider at Young's Ferry would be in constant Readiness to receive your Excellency's Commands. To keep up the Line of Communication already established by you, we have requested Colo. Hooe to procure a trusty Person and station him at Alexandria to receive your Dispatches and shall countermand the Orders, by which we had established a different Line. We shall take the first Opportunity of forwarding the Letter to the President of Congress.

We have the Honor &c.

FC (MdAA).   See Gov. Lee to TJ, 10 June; TJ to Lee, 14 June.

From John Walker

DEAR SIR   Philada. June 17th 1780

Your Favor of the 9th Ult: I received with pleasure, and shall always be glad to hear from you when leisure and Inclination occur.

For business I refer you to our public Letter. The propositions contained in yours to the President, will I doubt not, be immediately comply'd with. Business in Congress goes on better than I expected, each Member appearing willing to contribute all in his power to the good of the whole. This State is making Exertions worthy of imitation. The Merchants have lately subscribed a sum, which is thought sufficient to fill up their Continental Line, and have moreover advanced £200,000 Sterling upon Loan, to supply the Army with provision[s] in which they have lately been very deficient for want of Cash. This Patriotic fire 'tis to be hoped will spread both North and South.

My Family is perfectly recovered of the Small-pox, but we are all unwell perhaps occasioned by our change of Life and want of Exercise. Our affectionate wishes attend you all. Adieu.

JN. WALKER

Please present my respectful Compliments to the Gentlemen of your board.

RC (DLC). TJ's FAVOR OF THE 9TH ULT: and the Virginia Delegates' PUBLIC LETTER are both missing. TJ's letter TO THE PRESIDENT (Huntington) will be found above under 9 June 1780.

From the Committee of Congress at Headquarters

In Committee of Congress, Morris Town,
June 19th., 1780.

SIR

We inclose you a copy of General Washingtons letter to us of this day (see page 214). We have in our former letters dwelt so forcibly on the several matters contained in the generals letter, that it is now become almost unnecessary for us to say any thing more on *them*. But when we consider the season for operation wears fast away; the small force we now have in the field, being still fed in a scanty and uncertain manner, the hourly expectation of the fleet and Army of our ally, on our coast, and that the Commander in Chief, as well as ourselves, are as yet totally uninformed what are to be our expectations on the subject of our former letters; Be assured, Sir, we feel an anxiety congenial with his. You will there-fore, we are persuaded, pardon us for being thus solicitous, when we again intreat you in the most earnest, in the most urgent man-ner, to use every exertion in your power to engage your state, to a speedy and decisive complyance with our former requisitions. The two points we would wish to impress most forcibly on yours, and the minds of the legislature of your state, are immediately forward-ing your quota of troops, necessary to complete your batalions in the Continental Army, and of supplies of provision agreable to the estimates inclosed you in our letter of the 2d. Instant. At the same time, we would not wish you to consider *any part* of our former requisitions as become in the least degree unnecessary; on the contrary, we are more strongly convinced that they are already as small as the important objects in view, can possibly admit of; we only mention the two first as the most *immediately*, and *indispensibly* necessary, for *reinforced* as the enemy now are, by the return of their troops from the reduction of Charles Town, we momently expect an attack will be made on our weak and almost resistless Army; Should this event happen, whilst in this state, we seriously dread the result.

From the well known indefatigable attention of your state to the welfare of the United States, we cannot entertain a doubt of its exertions, at this interesting conjuncture, and we most earnestly intreat you to give us the earliest information of the final determination of your state, on the subject of this, and our former letters.

We are Sir, with the highest respect, Your most Obedt. Servants,

JNO. MATHEWS

NATHL. PEABODY

FC (DLC: PCC, No. 11); at head of text: "Circular, No. 5." Enclosure (missing): Washington to the Committee, 19 June; printed in *Writings*, ed. Fitzpatrick, XIX, 31-2 (the page reference in the present text is to a copy in the Committee's Proceedings, whence the present text derives). What may be the recipient's copy but is more likely a transcript of the present letter is in the Virginia Board of War Letter Book (MiU-C); it is addressed to TJ, but the text is incomplete and fragmentary.

To Benjamin Harrison

[*Richmond, 19? June 1780.* JHD, May 1780, 1827 edn., p. 51 (19 June): "The Speaker laid before House a letter from the Governor, enclosing a letter from the committee of co-operation appointed by Congress, calling for specific aids of men, provisions, forage, &c.; which were read, and ordered to be referred to the committee of the whole House on the state of the Commonwealth." TJ's letter not located; the committee's letter, enclosed, was apparently that of 2 June 1780, q.v.]

From Charles Thomson

[*Philadelphia*] *20 June 1780.* Circular letter to the state executives quoting Congress' resolutions of 2 May 1780 respecting the issuance of commissions to private vessels of war. Such commissions are hereafter to be obtained by application to the Board of Admiralty.

FC (DLC: PCC, No. 18A); 2 p. For text of resolutions of 2 May, see JCC, XVI, 408-9. This method of issuing commissions was altered by the resolve of Congress of 27 July; see circular letter from Charles Thomson, 28 July 1780.

From Samuel Huntington

SIR   Philadelphia June 21. 1780

I have the honour to transmit your Excellency the enclosed Acts of Congress of the 17th and 19th Instant pointing out the Measures they deem necessary to be taken, for the Support of the southern Army.

I make no Doubt the State of Virginia will avail itself of its numerous and spirited Militia, as well as great resources, at this important Crisis, when her own immediate Interest is so intimately connected with that of the Union.

I have the honor to be with the highest respect your Excelly's most hbble servt,   SAM HUNTINGTON   President

P.S. I have been honored with your Despatches of the 9th Instant.

RC (Vi). FC (DLC: PCC, No. 15). Enclosures (also Vi): (1) attested copy of resolutions of Congress of 17 June, calling (among other things) for the executive of Virginia to order 5,000 militia to join the southern army at once; endorsed: "resolve of Congress providg for the Southern defence rec'd July 80"; (2) attested copy of resolution of Congress recommending that Virginia and North Carolina recruit, mount, and equip Baylor's and White's regiments of light dragoons to the number of 150 rank and file per regiment, endorsed: "resolve of Congress for equiping remountg Dragoons. 1780 June 19th." The resolutions are printed in JCC, XVII, 523-4, 527-8. An order of Congress of 16 June (attested copy in Vi; printed JCC, XVII, 518-19), instructing Brig. Gen. Weedon and Col. Daniel Morgan to place themselves under Gates' command in the South, was transmitted to TJ in a letter (perhaps from the Virginia Delegates in Congress) of about this date which has not been found.

From Samuel Huntington

SIR   Philadelphia June 21. 1780

Congress have at different Periods recommended Measures which they deemed essentially necessary for the public Good.

They now request of those States which have not made returns of their Transactions in that respect, the most expeditious Information of the Measures they have taken in Consequence of the several resolutions, a list of which is annexed to the enclosed Act of Congress of the 17th Instant.

I have the honor to be with great respect your Excelly's most hbble servt,   SAM. HUNTINGTON   President

RC (Vi). Endorsed: "resolve of Congress calling on the States for information wth respect to what had been done in consequence of Sundry resolves." FC (DLC: PCC, No. 15), labeled "Circular." Enclosures (Vi): Copy, attested by

Charles Thomson, of resolve of Congress of 17 June 1780, to which is added a list of resolutions relating to men, money, and provisions, 9 Mch. 1779 to 20 May 1780, on which information as to state action is wanted; the resolution without the list is printed in JCC, XVII, 525. TJ annotated the MS list and incorporated the substance of the different resolves in his lengthy and carefully prepared answer, 27 July 1780, q.v.

To Benjamin Harrison

[*Richmond, 22? June 1780.* JHD, May 1780, 1827 edn., p. 58 (22 June): "The Speaker laid before the House a letter from the Governor, enclosing a memorial of the officers of the Virginia line in captivity at New York; also several letters from General Washington and the committee of co-operation [Committee of Congress at Headquarters]; which were read." TJ's letter does not survive, but the enclosed Officers' Memorial (printed above under 24 May 1780), with an address leaf and an endorsement, does survive. The endorsement reads: "Governors Letter inclosing Memorial from Officers of Virginia Line, who are prisoners in New York. June the 22d. 1780. Referred to [committee of] Trade. June the 23d. 1780. Reasonable. 5000 wt. of Tobacco allowed to each of the Officers, except those on Parole. The Governor [to] take proper measures for the immediate conveying the same to New York." The endorsement is not complete, since the resolution did not pass until 30 June after amendment by the Senate; see JHD, May 1780, 1827 edn., p. 58, 59, 62, 68. See also TJ to Washington, 4 July 1780. The other enclosures in TJ's letter cannot be certainly identified, though they are no doubt all printed or entered above.]

From Philip Mazzei

Sir   Paris, June 22d. 1780.

Bad news have long legs. I have just seen the Capitulation of Chs. Town in the London extraordinary gazette. I never was so afflicted in Virginia, by our bad events, as I am now. I thought I was singular in that, but our good Americans here tell me that it is the Same with them. We are really dejected, and we would be much more so, if all circumstances did not agree to make us hope that we shall soon be more than indemnified for our loss. It is amazing the impression such an event makes in Europe. The greater the distance, the more it will be magnified in men's own imagination, besides the effect of exaggerated accounts. There is here a number of valuable people So deeply attached to our cause, that the loss of the french Islands would not have affected them so much. Men of liberal sentiments consider all other causes as secondary, and of little moment, in comparison to the establishment of a free asylum for mankind. Want of information makes them apprehensive of consequences too bad, and very distant from probability. And the English, you may depend will not be idle in spreading everywhere as they have already begun, that it is all over with us. I should however be much mistaken if in less than 12 months it is not all over with them. This is the only and great comfort I find to compensate for the bitterness of the pill, with which I shall set out on my journey to Italy the 27th. Instant.

I could not finish this letter before, having been ever since I wrote the above, almost constantly Employed in public and private companies, to ease the minds of our friends about the loss of charlestown. That unlucky event, has brought me to the certain knowledge, that the number of our hearty friends is infinite, and I have been exceedingly affected by their feelings for our Just and glorious cause. I have been considered as an Angel descended from heaven among them (to make use of their expressions) for having assured them that such a loss would not materially affect our operations and that it is trifling in comparison to the unshaken constancy of the Americans. I have found Mr. Adams almost worn out in the same kind of business. This will appear very natural to you; but you will certainly be surprised to hear that that champion of firmness, as you represented him to me in our most critical and most alarming times, while a powerful body of enemies infested the place of his nativity, should now Want some body to comfort him, when no body can see better than he does the most promising prospect of our affairs, and the unavoidable approaching ruin of our Enemy. Our feelings for our friends and country must therefore be increased in proportion to the distance. Mr. Dana, his secretary of Embassy, says that if he knew french well, he would make a point of going to every Coffee house in Paris to clear up the point, and put a stop to the alarm. As it may be Injurious to our Credit, while it feeds the English pride and vanity, and may favour the schemes of the ministry; I am determined to clear up the matter in the Italian news papers, and will propose to Mr. Adams to write for other Countries, if he has not done it alredy. He has lately received the final resolution's of Congress relative to the new plan of our finances. He has been so kind as to shew me what he has written to Justify their measures; and having digested the matter with him in a long conversation, I think myself now qualified to Support my arguments, which is a most material point for encouraging adventurers to go and trade with us and for obtaining a loan of money in Europe. I have aquainted him with the nature of my business, as in letter 13 I hinted that I should probably do, and indeed after having discovered the goodness of his heart, Joined to the extraordinary abilities of the mind, I would have thought it prudent to solicit the favour of his advice and assistance, exclusive of other reasons, but considering besides his established great character, as mentioned in said letter, and the disapointment I have met with from the Gentleman to whom you directed me, I should have thought myself much to blame had I acted otherwise. Since I wrote said letter the 21th. of April, I think I have been about 15 times to the Doctor, I never failed whenever I found him to enter on the subject therein mentioned; and all I could get from him is, that he don't See why the states should individually want any money; that he don't know that Congress will now want any money in Europe, Since they have determined to call in the currency by taxation. That he finds that they intend to raise in the Country the money they will want hereafter, which will be better, as the interest will remain there, and that he dont think it possible for us to find money at 6 ⅌ cent, when the nations of Europe give much higher interest. I begged leave to observe that no European nation gives a higher interest, except the English, which must be considered in a state of bankruptcy, and to disagree in all other points, the reasons being too obvious to need being mentioned in this place. I turned myself to Mr. Adams by whom I have been favoured with all the informations I could wish, and he has promised me to write to you on the subject. I shall Set out immediately for Genoa and florence and do all my endeavours to pave the way for executing such orders as I may hereafter receive. As to my finances you have been sufficiently informed in my preceding letters, and you know already without them that I spend the money which I am able to raise on my own credit. I send you inclosed an account of those of my letters, which I know have been dispatched, and every now and then shall do the same, if my method gives satisfaction. I have the honour to be most respectfully, Sir, Your Excellency's most Obedt. & most Humble Servant,

Philip Mazzei

RC (CtY); in a clerk's hand, signed by Mazzei; at head of text: "20 [i.e., dispatch No. 20]. 2d. Copy"; endorsed: "Mr. Madzei Lr. Jany [81?] recd." The "3d Copy" of this dispatch, in the same clerk's hand, is in NN.

AN ACCOUNT OF THOSE OF MY LETTERS, WHICH I KNOW HAVE BEEN DISPATCHED: This is a 2-page list (CtY)

of Mazzei's dispatches numbered 1-15, with the names of the vessels by which the several copies of each were sent. Mazzei enclosed a continuation of this list in his letter to TJ, 5 Jan. 1781, q.v. Mr. Marraro (in his *Mazzei*, p. 11-12) has published a complete record of dispatches 1-22 from a similar MS memorandum in NN.

From the Committee of Congress at Headquarters

Morristown, 23 June 1780. Circular letter to the state executives, enclosing a copy of Gen. Washington's letter of same date, reporting the advance of the enemy beyond Springfield toward Morristown. The likelihood of an American defeat if these forces in New Jersey pursue their objective makes it imperative for the states to send on their quotas of men.

FC (DLC: PCC, No. 11), signed by the copyist with the names of Mathews and Peabody; 1 p. Enclosure (not found): Washington to Committee, 23 June 1780; printed in his *Writings*, ed. Fitzpatrick, XIX, 57-8.

From James Madison

DEAR SIR   Philadelphia June 23d 1780

Nothing material has taken place since my last. The fact is confirmed that Clinton has returned to N.Y. with part of the Southern army, and has joined Kniphausen. They are at present man[oeuvering] for purposes not absolutely known, but most probably in order to draw Genl. Washington to an action in which they suppose he may be disabled to give the necessary co-operation to the french armament. Could they succeed in drawing him from his strong position, the result indeed ought to be exceedingly feared. He is weak in numbers beyond all suspicion, and under as great apprehension from famine as from the Enemy. Unless very speedy and extensive reinforcements are received from the Eastern States which I believe are exerting themselves, the issue of the Campain must be equally disgraceful to our Councils and disgustful to our Allies. Our greatest hopes of being able [to] feed them are founded on a patriotic scheme of the opulent Merchants of this City who have already subscribed nearly £3,000,000 and will very soon complete that sum, the immediate object of which is to procure and transport to the Army 3,000,000,000 of rations and 300 Hhds of rum. Congress for the support of this bank and for the security and indemnification of the Subscribers, have pledged the faith of the United States and agreed to deposit Bills of Exchange in Europe to the Amount of £150,000 Sterling, which are not however to be made use of unless other means of discharging this debt [should] be inadequate. With sincere regard I am Yr. Obt Servt,   J. MADISON Junr

RC (DLC: Madison Papers).

A PATRIOTIC SCHEME: The plan of a private bank or "Merchants' Association" in Philadelphia to accumulate funds for provisioning the army; see Burnett, *Letters of Members*, v, index, under "Merchants' association." Burnett (v, No. 275, note 2) points out that Madison "evidently meant to write £300,000 and 3,000,000 rations."

From Edward Carrington

Richmond, 25 June 1780. Encloses "separate returns of the Officers of the Virginia, part of the first Regt. of Artillery, who are to be Actually in the Field the present Campaign—and of those who are to be otherwise situated, with notes signifying where they will be." TJ may now distribute them according to the plan mentioned by him to Carrington a few days ago.

RC (Vi); 3 p.; signed "Ed. Carrington." Addressed: "Public service. His Excellency Thos. Jefferson Governor of Virginia." Endorsed in a clerk's hand. Enclosures not further identified.

From Abner Nash

SIR   Cross Creek June 25. 1780.

I received your favor by Colo. Monroe, three days agoe at this place, where Genl. Caswell is posted with about 1500 Militia, and shall be very happy Sir in the Correspondence you propose: The Enemies Opperations in So. Carolina and their practices among the Country People on the Southern borders of this State are not a little alarming. Their nearest post to this place is at the Cheraw Hill on pedee River about 60 miles distant in a south west direction; from the best intelligence we have their Numbers are about 600 Regulars and a considerable Number of new recruits from amongst the Inhabitants; here they are collecting Magazines of Provisions; the river Lands affording Grain and forage and the barren Country between that River and this the greatest abundance of Cattle. Their party and ours at this Post are equally concerned in the important object of collecting Cattle, with this material difference however in their favor that pedee River is rich in grain for the support of their party and this quite the reverse; and that the Inhabitants between the Rivers [are] 9/10ths Highlanders and well affected to the British. In short they do all in their power to distress us by concealing all the Cattle and Horses that they do not drive into the Enemy's Camp. The Enemy's next Post and indeed by far the most dangerous to us is at Cambden on the Wateree River. This place lies still higher up the Country and points directly to Charlotte, the richest and finest part of our back Country; at this place the Enemy are said to have upwards of 4,000 regulars; at Charlotte about 60 or 70 miles from Cambden our Western Militia to the number of about eleven hundred are assembled under Brigadr. Genl. Rutherford; and the Baron de Kalb with his little Army is still no further advanced than to Hillsborough and is there exceedingly distressed for Provision and forage. An Express went off to him four days agoe advising that it would in our opinion be best for him to direct his course south westwardly towards Charlotte in order to support Genl. Rutherford and to prevent the Army of the British by all possible means from turning the right of our Armies, thereby cutting off from us the fertile hilly and thick settled back Country whose Inhabitants at present are well attached to us but who under circumstances so unfavorable 'tis to be feared would fall off. It appears to us of so much consequence to counteract and defeat what we conceive to be the Intention of the Enemy in penetrating so far into the interior part of the Country that I have determined that Genl. Caswell also shall march to the Westward tho' I must thereby expose the middle and lower Country to devastation, should the Enemy posted at Cheraws, Mars bluff, and still lower down pedee paralel with the County line think proper to invade us. The Injury in the Cattle case I conceive will be only temporary provided we can be successful to the Westward; but should we by endeavoring to guard the long and indeed indefensible line that parts us from So. Carolina, suffer the Enemy to posess themselves of the rich and thick settled back parts of our Country with the mountains in their rear such an Advantage in its consequences might prove fatal to us and indeed to the Neighbouring States. This however can never happen but from a want of firmness and public Virtue in these States: and the Enemy from the boldness of what seems to be their present enterprize must suppose either that we want those qualities, or adequate resources; or like desperate Gamesters they are putting their last stake in the wheel of fortune; for tis evident that ruin must attend a failure in the execution of such a project: in short it seems to me the Enemy are hurrying on the conquest to a Crisis and that our fate either favorable or unfavorable is at hand. I am doing all in my power for the general defence; I came here to visit the Armies and to enable me the better to judge of the designs of the Enemy; I did not intend to return untill the fate of the Campaign had been decided but finding that your Militia are not yet arrived nor even on their march that I know of I durst not depend any longer on their coming in time to check the Enemy; I have therefore determined yesterday to call out a further aid of 4000 Men, and have issued orders for this purpose; this Measure obliges me to return to Newbern to emit a Sum of Money adequate to so vast an expence as it will occasion. Before I conclude I am to acquaint your Excellency of the Intelligence we have from C. Town. I believe Sir it is to be depended on that an embarkation of about 5000 troops has taken place from thence, their destination only to be guessed at; if the arrival or expectation of a french Army and fleet in America don't controul the operations of the Enemy; I should suppose their destination to be for Virginia; in this case you too Sir will have some trouble, but the aid intended for us I make no doubt will still come on. I shall depend on you for such intelligence as you may obtain from the Northward; Your Letters directed to Newbern will come safe. I shall not fail on my part to advise you constantly of the occurrences this way: with the highest respect & regard I have the honor to be Sir Yr. Excellency's most obedt Serv[t],

A. NASH

Tr (DLC: PCC, No. 71, i); at head of text: "(Copy)." Enclosed in TJ's letter to Huntington, 28 June 1780. Also Tr (CSmH); a brief extract and summary only.

YOUR FAVOR BY COLO. MONROE: TJ's letter of 16 June 1780, q.v.

From James Monroe

SIR   Cross-Creek June 26. 1780.

Some few days since I arriv'd here and trust I have so arranged the line of communication between us, that whatever alteration the course of events may effect in my own situation, I shall have it in my power to make it subservient to my wishes. I expected I shou'd more effectually put in execution your Excellency's Orders by coming immediately here, the source from which Governor Nash at Newbern, or Baron de Kalb at Hillsborough get their intelligence, than by taking my rout to either of those posts, and I have had the good fortune in meeting Governor Nash here to approve my determination. The Governor was on his rout to Baron de Kalb and call'd upon General Caswell here with a view of making himself acquainted with his Force and Object, in order to concert some regular and connected plan of either offensive or defensive action, as circumstances might admit, for the protection of the Country. I have it not in my power to give your Excellency at present, information upon all the points you require, but an event we are informed has taken place of such importance in its probable consequences to the State of Virginia, as to make it necessary I shou'd immediately inform you of it. We have it from authority we cannot doubt, that an embarkation has taken place at Charles town and sail'd some days since under the Command of General Clinton, consisting of about 6,000 men, the remainder of their Army— supposed upwards of 4,000 with their Cavalry forming a corps of 600 under Col. Tarleton are left behind under Lord Cornwallis. General Caswell has repeatedly had information, they had embarked, but never 'til to day that they had sailed; and to day I examined myself two men of Woodfords Brigade, lately escaped from Charles-town, who confirm it. A Garrison of about 800 are said to be left at Charles-town; 2500 at Camden; the Cavalry are stationed about 40 miles above Camden; about 600 of the 71st. regiment on the river Peedee between long bluff and Ansons C. House. What may be the object of those who have sailed or of those who remain is incertain and must depend on the part the Court of France means to take this year in our favor; but if We may judge from the View which has hitherto evidently influenced their Councils (if no internal event has happen'd to their prejudice) provided they act on a consistent plan, we must conclude they mean to land somewhere in Virginia, and by directing their Armies to the same object endeavour to conquer all these Southern States. Upon this Principle I am inclin'd to think their operations have of late been taken and that upon this principle they will determine. What again wou'd induce this beleif and with me it is only an inferior circumstance (for upon Principles of expedience they shou'd act thus) is the universal scarcity of all kinds of provisions, except Meat, which prevails in this Country. Upon this account the Army under General de Kalb at Hillsboro, and that under General Caswell here, are no longer able to hold those Stations and are in that dilemma, that they have only the alternative of advancing shortly on the Enemy or retiring to Virginia. This however will in a great degree be remedied when the Harvest comes in. What plan General de Kalb may take to oppose them I cannot determine, but as that which the Enemy have adopted creates a division of their force, ours also must necessarily be divided and in that case rather than hang or temporize between them, I doubt not he will take a decided part against this Body. I mean I hope he will keep on their left Flank and harass and retard them in all their Movements as much as possible. Their forces have been pointedly directed against the Continental Troops, and to get the Country and throw them down on the Sea Coast would necessarily be a great object; a considerable advantage also arising from the position I have suggested would be that the troops who oppose this Army and those who oppose that which may land in Virginia might act on a common principle and when the Enemy effect a junction they might join also, still keeping the command of the Country. This plan has not the protection of any particular Spot but is on a larger Scale and has Independance for its Object. Acting on any other principle and taking particular positions for particular purposes may lead the respective Corps into danger and perhaps ruin. Genl. Clinton previous to his departure issued a Proclamation discharging all who had taken them from their paroles and requiring their immediate attendance to swear allegiance and bear Arms in favor of his Sovereign declaring that all who refuse to comply with these reasonable terms who shall be found in arms hereafter in favor of the rebellion shall not be treated as Soldiers and prisoners of War but as banditti and robbers. I have not seen the Proclamation but Govr. Nash who has tells me this is the purport of it; only 1500 Militia are collected here under Genl. Caswell and about 1100 under Brigr. Rutherford west of the Enemy, who hold the position I could wish B. de Kalb to take with the Continental Troops at least. At Charlotte, Salsbury or Chatham the country is better able to support an Army and when harvest comes in will be more so, while that near here or towards the coast is much exhausted. Between here and Halifax it is so much so (and I am told by the Inhabitants on the Road that want is not confined to them alone but extends considerably to the Right and left) that I could scarcely get provisions for myself and men and in many instances could not procure Corn for my Horses at any rate. The Governor of this State has extensive powers and except where it affects the Life the Advice of Council he knows no restraint on his will. He also seems well disposed to act with that firmness and decision in most instances which the unhappy State of his Country requires, without regard to any local or personal enmity which may arise against him in the discharge of the duties of so important a trust. He is constrained to emit money constantly, as occasion requires and has now ordered out 4,000 militia in addition to those I have mentioned as already in the field. At Govr. Nash's request I shall attend him tomorrow to where B. De Kalb may be, or if the Governor does not go himself, shall perhaps go upon the business I have referd to and in my next shall have it in my power to inform your Excellency of the plan B. de Kalb may take for his future operations, with the probability of Success, or what effect it may have on the movements of the Enemy. I have the honor to be with the greatest respect & Esteem Yr. Excellencys Very humbl. servt,

JAS. MONROE

P.S. I cannot inform you where Porterfield is but expect somewhere near the Baron. Colo. Armands Corps are here under command of Genl. Caswell. We have had reports a French fleet are off C. Town but not from such Authority as to gain assent.

Tr (DLC: PCC, No. 71, I); at head of text: "(Copy)"; enclosed in TJ to Huntington, 28 June 1780. Another Tr (CSmH). YOUR EXCELLENCY'S ORDERS: TJ to Monroe, 16 June 1780, q.v.

From Samuel McDowell

SIR   [Before 27 June 1780]

Please to Send me by the bearer the Revised Bill respecting the Vesterys and oblige your Humble Servt.,   SAML. McDOWELL

RC (DLC). At foot of text: "His Excellency Thos. Jefferson." On the verso TJ made the following notes taken apparently from some book and possibly made at a later date: "Christianing. Exorcising meat. hble. servt. Excy. honour. Funl. cerem. head facing east on opn. that earth like trencher. opn. that right founded on power. viz. women. slaves. not educate daughters. estates to sons. rifles."

The date of this letter cannot be determined except from the fact that it was directed to TJ as governor. It has been placed under the present date because Samuel McDowell, member of the House of Delegates from Rockbridge co. in the May 1780 session ("Register of Va. General Assembly," p. 12), was a member of the committee on religion which on 27 June 1780 brought in a bill "for the dissolution of vestries, and appointing overseers of the poor" as the result of petitions from Rockbridge and other counties requesting such a dissolution (JHD, May 1780, 1827 edn., p. 4, 16, 64). THE REVISED BILL RESPECTING THE VESTERYS probably refers to a general bill for the dissolution of vestries introduced in the May 1779 session by a committee of which TJ was a member but which was not passed (JHD, May 1779, 1827 edn., p. 11, 26, 27, 59). There is no evidence that TJ prepared the 1779 bill.

To Samuel Huntington

SIR   Richmond June 28. 1780. 9. o'clock P.M.

The want of intelligence of the Southern movements of the enemy, and the anxieties we have felt on that account, cannot have been less experienced by Congress. Having just now received a state of things as they are at present in that quarter, from Governor Nash, and from Colo. Monroe (the gentleman whom in a former letter I had informed Congress I had sent to hang as near as he could about the enemy's principal post and inform me of their movements by riders posted between us for that purpose) I take for granted Congress will be glad to have it communicated. I therefore have thought the occasion sufficient to set in motion the line of riders established from hence to Philadelphia, with orders to them however to return immediately to their fixt stations, that they may not be out of the way to receive the particular communications for the conveyance of which they have been established.

The embarkation spoken of by Govr. Nash and Colo. Monroe, cannot have been destined for this state, or they would have been here before this; had they reached our capes by yesterday, I must have known it at this hour.

Governor Nash, at the time of writing his letter, seems not to have heard of the motions of our militia. It is certain however that some of them were at Roanoke on the 20th. and that the whole have got that far by this time; being 2500 in number.

I have been greatly mortified at the detention of the important supply you had called for, so much longer than I had expected. I had every reason to beleive it might have been sent from hence by the 19th. It does not however go off, till tomorrow. It will I hope be nearly what I had given you reason to expect in my letter on that subject.

I have the honor to be with every sentiment of esteem & respect Your Excellency's most obedient & most humble servt.,

TH: JEFFERSON

P.S. The Quarter-master has provisions on board vessels ready to proceed to the Head of Elk, which however he dares not send into our bay, that having been for some time occupied by from seven to eleven privateers, the largest of 20 guns, who take whatever goes out of our rivers. Our provisions when collected, whether destined for the Northward or Southward will be effectually blocked up. Land-transportation cannot possibly be procured.

RC (DLC: PCC, No. 71, I); endorsed by Charles Thomson: "Letter from Govr Jefferson Richmond June 28. 1780. Read July 3." Enclosures: Nash to TJ, 25 June, and Monroe to TJ, 26 June 1780, qq.v. Tr (CSmH); lacks postscript.

Read in Congress 3 July; postscript referred to Board of Admiralty (JCC, XVII, 582, 584). TJ's date and hour on this letter give some clue to the effective-ness of the line of communications that he had ordered James Monroe to establish to the southward. Whereas it had taken precisely a week for TJ's letter of 16 June to reach Gov. Nash (see Nash to TJ, 25 June 1780), those sent by Nash and Monroe on 26 June arrived at Richmond in about forty-eight hours, perhaps less.

To William Preston

SIR   Richmond June 28. 1780.

Since my last letter to you we have concluded to send from hence fifty stand of arms for the regulars at the mines, which with a few at Colo. Fleming's and such as you have fit for service wi[ll] arm the regulars at the Leadmines so that they may escor[t] the ammunition to Kentucky and render an escort of militi[a] unnecessary. Such of the arms as you have, unfit to be de[liv]ered to them, be pleased to send to this place by the waggo[ns] gone up with Indian goods or by the one now going with new arms. We are at present so distressed by calls of men to the Northward and Southward that it is out of our power to send any to your quarter. I hope the prospect we have of doing something brilliant by the union of a large army collecting by Genl. Washington and that of our allies hourly expected, will more than balance our losses at Charlestown and keep the Tories in quiet, and that in the mean time the good peo[ple] with you will be particularly vigilant. I am Sir with great esteem Your very humble servt., TH: JEFFERSON

RC (WHi); mutilated slightly; endorsed: "Governours Letter June 28th. 1780 came to hand the 18th. July 1780." MY LAST LETTER TO YOU: dated 15 June 1780, q.v.

From John Adams

MY DEAR SIR   Paris June 29. 1778. [i.e., 1780]

Mr. Mazzei, called on me, last evening, to let me know that he was this morning at three to Sett off, on his Journey, for Italy. He desired me to write you, that he has communicated to me the Nature of his Errand: but that his Papers being lost, he waits for a Commission and Instructions from you. That being limited to five Per Cent, and more than that being given by the Powers of Europe, and indeed having been offered by other States and even by the Ministers of Congress, he has little hopes of succeeding at so low an Interest. That he shall however endeavour to prepare the way, in Italy for borrowing, and hopes to be usefull to Virginia and the United States.

I know nothing of this Gentleman, but what I have learned of him here. His great affection for you Mr. Wythe, Mr. Mason, and other choice Spirits in Virginia, recommended him to me. I know not in what Light he Stands in your Part: but here, as far as I have had opportunity to See and hear, he has been usefull to Us. He kept good Company and a good deal of it. He talks a great deal, and was a zealous defender of our Affairs. His Variety of Languages, and his Knowledge of American affairs, gave him advantages which he did not neglect.

What his Success will be in borrowing money, I know not. We are impatient to learn whether Virginia and the other States have adopted the Plan of Finances recommended by Congress on the 18 of March. I think We shall do no great Things at borrowing unless that System or some other, calculated to bring Things to some certain and Steady Standard, Succeeds.

Before this reaches you, you will have learned, the Circumstances of the Insurrections in England, which discover So deep and So general a discontent and distress, that no wonder the Nation Stands gazing at one another, in astonishment, and Horror. To what Extremities their Confusions will proceed, no Man can tell. They Seem unable to unite in any Principle and to have no Confidence in one another. Thus it is, when Truth and Virtue are lost: These Surely, are not the People who ought to have absolute authority over Us. In all Cases whatsoever, this is not the nation which is to bring us to unconditional Submission.

The Loss of Charlestown has given a rude Shock to our Feelings. I am distressed for our worthy Friends in that Quarter. But the Possession of that Town must weaken and perplex the Ennemy more than Us.

By this Time you know more than I do, of the Destination and the operations of French and Spanish armaments. May they have Success, and give Us Ease and Liberty, if the English will not give Us Peace.

I have the Honour to be with an affectionate Respect, Sir your Frnd & Servt.

FC (Adams Manuscript Trust, Boston); misdated 1778. THE INSURRECTIONS IN ENGLAND: The No-Popery or Gordon Riots that broke out in London early in June; see DNB under George Gordon, 1751-1793.

From George Washington

Dr Sir [Headquarters, Ramapo, N.Y., 29 June 1780]

I have been honored with two of your Excellency's favors both of the 11th inclosing an extract of a letter from Governor Rutlege.

I cannot but feel most sensibly affected by several parts of your

Excellency's letter. The successive misfortunes to the Southward—the progress of the enemy—and the great deficiency in military stores give rise to the most serious reflections, while our situation in this quarter precludes every hope of affording you further assistance. What from the system of short inlistments, and the unfortunate delays in filling up our battalions the army in this place, is reduced to a mere handful of men, and left as it were at the mercy of a formidable enemy, subject to see the honor and dignity of the States daily insulted without the power either to prevent it or to retaliate. Under these circumstances your Excellency will perceive how utterly impossible it is to go further in succours than what is already sent. To oppose our Southern misfortunes and surmount our difficulties our principal dependence must be on the means we have left us in your quarter. And it is some consolation amidst all our distresses that these are more than adequate to remove them; and to recover what we have lost that it is only necessary these be properly directed.

The steps your Excellency has taken to establish posts of communication with the Southern army are essential to facilitate your measures, the necessity of which I had urged in strong terms to Congress. I am apprehensive that Congress have it not in their power to furnish you with the Cartouch boxes.

I have the honor to be with Great respect,   G W

Dft (DLC: Washington Papers); in hand of James McHenry, with corrections by Washington. Endorsed (in part): "29th June 1780."

To Samuel Huntington

Sir   Richmond June 30. 1780.

By Mr. Foster Webb you will receive in part of the requisition of Congress of 1,953,200 Dollars, the following sums, to wit 650,000 Dollars in money, and bills for 780,239$\frac{8}{9}$ Dollars, making in the whole 1,430,239$\frac{8}{9}$ Dollars. There remains a deficiency of 522,960$\frac{1}{9}$ dollars which I hope to be able to send on within four weeks from this time. I should have been very happy to have been enabled to have sent on the *whole*, in *money*, and by the *day prescribed*: but be assured it was absolutely impossible. There is less *money* than our contracts had authorized us to expect, as you will perceive by comparing the sum sent with that I had mentioned to you in a former letter. This has been occasioned by a breach of contract in those to whom we had sold property to raise the money.

Instead of this they have given us bills, which are sent on, and I hope will be paid so as that no disappointment may happen.

I have the honor to be with the greatest respect Your Excellency's most obedt. humble servt., TH: JEFFERSON

RC (DLC: PCC, No. 71, I). Endorsed by Charles Thomson: "Letter from Govr Jefferson Richmond July 3 [corrected in another hand to:] June 30. 1780. Read 10."

From Samuel Huntington

SIR Philadelphia June 30. 1780

By the Act of Congress of the 29th. Instant herewith enclosed your Excellency will be informed they have approved of the Line of Communication which you have been forming by Expresses Southward and Northward and resolved that the same be continued until the further Order of Congress.

I have the honour to be with the highest respect your Excys most obedt servant, SAM. HUNTINGTON President

RC (Vi); in a clerk's hand, signed by Huntington; endorsed: "Governor of Virginia." FC (DLC: PCC, No. 15). Enclosure (Vi); endorsed: "resolve of Congress approving of the line of Communication"; this resolution is printed above in note to TJ's letter to Huntington, 15 June 1780.

From Joseph Jones

DEAR SR. Phila: 30th: June 1780

The Troops left by Sr. Henry Clinton in South Carolina amounting to about 3500 Men besides 1500 sent to Georgia cannot be sufficient unless increased by the accession of Tories, to overawe that State, especially when the Inhabitants shall find themselves supported by the Regulars and Militia going to their assistance. The 5000 Militia recommended by Congress to be raised by Virga. to join the Southern Army including the 2500 then or about to be raised and the additional Body to be kept in readiness, if your intelligence corresponds with the above state of the Enemies Strength cannot now be necessary the requisition being made upon a supposition a much greater Force would have continued in South Carolina. The alteration of circumstances will justify an alteration of measures and by lessening the Draughts of Militia increase the number of Recruits for the Regular Army upon [which] and not upon Militia is our great dependence. Besides the caling forth, if it can be safely avoided, such large Bodies of Militia lessens the productions of the Earth and generally produces great distress to a number of Families. Sr. Henry Clintons proclamation exempting the Inhabitants of S. Carolina not taken in the Town from their paroles, evinces his design and expectation of gaining the people to his side, and that they will take up arms in support of the British Government. It is not improbable his threats and promises may in their present unsupported situation induce many to do so, unless the approach of the american Troops shall afford them hopes of Protection, in which case I am inclined to think he will be disappointed as the people cannot but feel resentment at the sudden transition from assumed lenity to a demand of bearing Arms in manifestation of their loyalty, or being exposed to confiscation of property and punishment for supposed Crimes. We hear our assembly are about to reconsider their late determination respecting the scheme of Finance recommended by Congress, and that it was expected the Measure would yet be adopted. I am happy to hear it, being confident the rejection of the proposition and the emission of more paper money could not fail of producing the worst of consequences. Let us not depart from the determination not to increase the quantity. That resolution has already appreciated the money and a steady adherence to the measure will at length effectually do it. The present is the season for accomplishing the great work of Confederation. If we suffer it to pass away I fear it will never return. The example of New York is worthy of imitation. Could Virginia but think herself as she certainly is already full large for vigorous Government she too would moderate her desires, and cede to the united States upon certain conditions, her Territory beyond the Ohio. The Act of New York the Instructions of Maryland to their Delegates and the Declaration of that State upon the subject And the late remonstrance of Virga. are now before a Committee, and I expect they will report, that it be recommended to the States having extensive western unappropriated Claims to follow the example of New York and by Law authorise their Delegates to make the cession. I some time past sent Mr. Mason a Copy of the New York Act. Gloomy as the prospect of our affairs has been and in fact still is when compared with the Objects we have in view through the course of this Campaign I yet feel myself revived by the accounts lately received from our State that the people are at length awakened from their slumber and appear to act with becoming Spirit and ardor at this important conjuncture, especially as the States in general, for the present moment, seem to be roused and impressed with the necessity of great and immediate exertions and if the Spirit is kept up for a while we may reasonably hope for the happiest Consequences. I have been much and still am depressed to think that America should do so little for herself while France is preparing to do so much. That we should, contending for every thing dear and valuable to her, look on with folded arms and suffer other Powers almost unassisted by us, to work out our salvation and Independence. The Idea is humiliating. The Fact must be dishonorable and our Posterity will blush to read It in future story. Letters from Martinique so late as the 3d and 4th. of this month inform us of the arrival of a Spanish Frigate announcing that 12 Spanish Ships of the line, 4-50 Gunship[s] and six Frigates with about 10,000 Troops were about 200 leagues to windward when the Frigate left them, coming forward to join the French fleet and forces. The Ct. Guichen was going out with 16 sail of the line to meet them. Upon the junction of these Fleets, the superiority of the Combined Force will be decided and we may expect soon to hear of some important stroke made in that Quarter. It was conjectured their first attempt would be St. Lucie if the approach of the hurricane months did not discourage the enterprise [then] Jamaica and from thence come round and by uniting the whole Forces sweep the Coast of North America. The representa[tion] is grand and opens so pleasing a prospect to us, I will not lessen your pleasure by a doubt of it being verified. These letters further inform us that the Armament carrying on at Brest and which they expected was for the Wt. Indies is for North America and that it was expected to sail about the 15th. April. It is said to consist of ten ships of the line and a large Body of Troops—no doubt they will make it as large as they well can as it is evident the war will be principally here and in the Wt. Indies. Between the 12th and 15th. of last month Rodney and Guichen have had three engagements. The last a severe action in which the Count kept the Sea. For further particulars I refer you to the inclosed paper as well as for the account so far as we are yet informed of the action at springfield in the Jerseys between our Troops and Militia under Genl. Green and the British and Hessians under Kniphausen. The Jersey Militia acquired immortal Fame as indeed they do upon almost every occasion where they are engaged with the Enemy. With great respect I have the honor to be [Sir Your] most obedt. Servt.,   Jos: Jones

Congress have formed the Scale of Depreciation to apply to Loan office Certificates.

from the 1st. Sept. 1777 to 1st. March 1778   at 1.¾
Thence to Sept. 1st.   78 - - - - - 78 - - 4.
Thence to March 1st. [79] - - - - - 79 - - 10
Thence to Sept. 1st.   - - - - - 79 - - 18
Thence to Mar: 18th.   - - - - - 80 - - 40

The intermediate time of the respective periods to be calculated in Geometrical proportion. The Resolves will be immediately published. This will reduce the principal of Loans from 46.559.235 to 11.053.573.

RC (DLC). The postscript is on a separate slip of paper.
The more important parts of this letter are printed by Burnett, *Letters of Members*, v, No. 288, and are fully annotated there. See also Huntington to TJ, 10 Sep. 1780, on the problem of western land claims by the states.

From Francis Mallory

[*Elizabeth City County, 30? June 1780. Va. Council Jour.*, II, 264 (1 July): "The Govr. laid before the board a Letter from Colo. Mallery of Eliz City informing him of the appearance of a fleet supposed to be hostile in Chesapeake bay and hampton road. Whereupon they advise the Govr., to inform Genl. Nelson that if an actual invasion shall take place and a sufficient number of men be embodied to authorize them under the law to appoint a General Officer, they mean to ask his assistance in that Character; that in the mean time he be desired to repair to those parts threatened with invasion," &c. This letter has not been found, nor any communication from TJ to Thomas Nelson in consequence of it. "Colo. Mallery" is no doubt Francis Mallory, lt. col. of Elizabeth City militia, 1778, who was killed 8 Mch. 1781 in a skirmish with British raiders at Tompkins Bridge near his home (Gwathmey, *Hist. Reg. of Virginians in the Revolution*; VMHB, XIV [1907], 433-4). His letter was transmitted, as from "the county lieutenant of Elizabeth City," to Speaker Harrison on 1 July, following.]

To Benjamin Harrison

[*Richmond, 1? July 1780.* JHD, May 1780, 1827 edn., p. 71 (1 July): "The Speaker laid before the House a letter from the Governor, enclosing several others from the President of Congress, General Washington, and the committee of co-operation, together with several resolutions of Congress, respecting supplies of men and money. As also a letter from the county lieutenant of Elizabeth City, containing information of the arrival of an enemy's fleet." Read and referred to committee of the whole on the state of the commonwealth. TJ's letter not located. Only one of the enclosures is precisely identifiable, namely the letter from Francis Mallory of Elizabeth City to TJ, preceding.]

To the Committee of Congress
at Headquarters

GENTLEMEN   Richmond July 2. 1780.

I have received three several letters which you did me the honor of writing on the subject of supplies of men and provisions to the grand army. The compliance with these requisitions not lying within the extent of my powers, I immediately laid them before the General assembly then and still sitting. A bill is now passed by them enabling me to call into public use whatever provisions may be spared by our citizens; and this is put into a train of execution. I hope it will enable me to furnish the quantity of salted meat called for by Congress, and I think within a short time. Congress have left to us to determine whether we can spare any grain to the Northward. It will not be in my power to say whether we can or not until I shall receive a return from those commissioned with the execution of the act, which will not be till the last of this month. I can assure you of the strongest disposition to contribute every thing within our power to aid the Northern operations. But it is necessary to apprise you of one circumstance. Transportation by land has been little practised in this country. We have therefore few waggons, and a great part of these have been lately drawn to the Southward. Transportation by water has been cut off for some time by the privateers which have been constantly cruising in our bay. These have been from six to eleven in number; the largest carrying twenty guns. To them are added at present eight frigates; tho' I can scarcely beleive these mean to continue. In this situation nothing can venture out of our rivers. The Quartermaster has salted provisions for your army actually laden on board vessels, and a considerable supply of corn ready to send. But we see no prospect of getting it up the bay. The same causes will obstruct our supplies to the Southern army except from those parts of our country bordering on Carolina.

The assembly have before them a bill for supplying by draught 5000. regulars to serve eighteen months. This I have no doubt will pass. It's execution will probably take a month, counting till the general rendezvous of the levies in this country. Hence I fear that should Congress call them Northwardly they will not be ready to co-operate with the main army till late in August.

I have the honor to be with the greatest respect Gentlemen Your most obedient & most humble servt.,   TH: JEFFERSON

RC (DLC: PCC, No. 39, III); endorsed: "From Thomas Jefferson Govr. of the State of Virginia July. 2d. 1780. ansd. the 23 July." Tr in TJ's hand (DLC: PCC, No. 71, I), marked "(Copy)," enclosed in TJ's letter to Huntington, same date, q.v. Tr by the clerk of the Committee at Headquarters (DLC: PCC, No. 11).

A BILL IS NOW PASSED: This was an Act for procuring a supply of provisions and other necessaries for the use of the army, by which the governor, through commissioners appointed in such counties as were necessary, was empowered to purchase or impress provisions at stipulated prices, to hire or seize storehouses for the storage of such supplies, and to hire or impress wagons, teams, boats, &c. for their transportation; passed 21 June (JHD, May 1780, 1827 edn., p. 57; Hening, X, 233-7). A BILL FOR SUPPLYING . . . 5000. REGULARS: Passed as an Act for speedily recruiting the quota of Virginia for the Continental army, 12 July, but the number of troops had been reduced to 3,000 before enactment (JHD, May 1780, 1827 edn., p. 84; Hening, X, 257-62).

To Samuel Huntington

SIR   Richmond July 2. 1780.

I have received and shall duly comply with the recommendations of Congress for corresponding with their committee at Headquarters. It having been necessary to lay their and your requisitions before the General assembly, it has not been within my power to give any effectual answer till within these few days; and now only on the article of provisions. I beg leave to refer you to my letter to them of this date, a copy of which I inclose. The frigates now in our bay will probably retire. Were it possible for you to find means of clearing our bay of the privateers which have for some weeks infested it, we should be ready by the last of this month to send on our supplies. I think that Genl. Clinton having carried so considerable a part of the Southern army to the Northward, will leave it in our power, exercising the discretion you have been pleased to leave to us, to send a considerable proportion of the grain we shall have to the Northern army, unless a larger force should be embodied in the South than the present strength of the enemy seems to call for. I should conceive that to embody there more than double the number of the enemy would be a waste of exertion both as to men and provisions.

As it is expected our assembly will rise in the course of the present week. I shall then have it in my power to give an answer on the several subjects stated in a late letter from you, by informing you what is, and what is not done, and what also may be expected from the Executive in consequence of any powers the legislature may vest them with.

I have the honor to be with every sentiment of esteem & respect Your Excellency's most obedient & most humble servt.,

Th: Jefferson

RC (DLC: PCC, No. 71, I). Endorsed: "Letter from Gov Jefferson Richmond July 2. 1780. Read 10." Enclosure: copy of TJ's letter of this date to Committee of Congress at Headquarters, q.v.

A LATE LETTER FROM YOU: Dated 21 June (second letter from Huntington of that date) and answered by TJ, 27 July 1780.

To George Washington

Sir   Richmond July 2. 1780.

I have received from the Committee of Congress at Headquarters three letters calling for aids of men and provisions. I beg leave to refer you to my letter to them of this date on those subjects. I thought it necessary however to suggest to you the preparing an arrangement of officers for the men: for tho' they are to supply our battalions, yet as our whole line of officers almost are in captivity, I suppose some temporary provision must be made. We chearfully transfer to you every power which the executive might exercise on this occasion. As it is possible you may cast your eye on the unemployed officers now within the state, I write to Genl. Muhlenburg to send you a return of them. I think the men will be rendezvoused within the present month. The bill indeed for raising them is not actually passed but it is in it's last stage, and no opposition to any essential parts of it. I will take care to notify you of it's passage.

I have with great pain perceived your situation: and the more so as, being situated between two fires, a division of sentiment has arisen both in Congress and here, to which the resources of this country should be sent. The removal of Genl. Clinton to the Northward must of course have great influence on the determination of this question and I have no doubt but considerable aids may be drawn hence for your army, unless a larger one should be embodied in the South than the force of the enemy there seems to call for.

I have the honor to be with every sentiment of esteem & respect Your Excellency's most obedient & most humble servt.,

Th: Jefferson

RC (PHi). Tr (DLC).

TJ's letter to GENL. MUHLENBERG is missing; however, Washington received the returns from Muhlenberg requested of the latter by TJ and forthwith made the arrangement of officers that TJ proposed; see Washington to TJ, to Gates (or Muhlenberg), and to Muhlenberg, all dated 18 July 1780 (Writings, ed. Fitzpatrick, XIX, 194-6, 196-202, 203-5). Muhlenberg's returns of Virginia officers are in DLC: Washington Papers; see Cal. Wash. Corr. with Officers, II, 1387, 1395.

To William Campbell

SIR   Richmond July. 3d. 1780

I have received advice from Colo. Preston of a dangerous insurrection on new river. He thinks the Insurgents will attempt to destroy the works at the lead mines, and has called on the militia of Washington and Botetourt to oppose them. As this is an Object requiring more immediate attention than the one on which you were lately appointed I am to desire you will a second time take in hand these parricides, and if they have proceeded as we have heard to actual murder, to recommend that you take such effectual measures of punishment as may secure the future safety of that quarter. The Militia of Washington, Montgomery and Botetourt are already called on by Colo. Preston. You will therefore put yourself at their head and apply to this object the means and powers put into your hands for the Indian expedition. I am Sir Your very humble servt,   TH: JEFFERSON

RC (CtY); in a clerk's hand, with complimentary close and signature by TJ; addressed by TJ: "Colo. William Campbell Washington"; endorsed: "From Mr. Jefferson 1780. New River insurrection." Tr (Vi). In the present text some words are supplied from Tr for passages torn away in RC.

INSURRECTION ON NEW RIVER: On this extensive Tory uprising in the summer of 1780, see Wis. Hist. Soc., *Colls.*, XXIV, 23-8, 195ff.; its objective was Virginia's lead mines located on that river in Montgomery co., and its suppression required much of the skill and resources of the Virginia border captains throughout the summer. THE INDIAN EXPEDITION to which William Campbell had been lately assigned was a punitive attack on the Chickamaugas (i.e., the hostile Cherokees of the Chickamauga towns) in present Tennessee. The Council's orders for this expedition are missing, but see Memoranda concerning Western Defense, printed under date of ca. 8 June 1780; see also Campbell to TJ, July 1780, and TJ to Abner Nash, 12 Aug. 1780.

From Timothy Pickering

SIR   War-Office July 3d. 1780

We did ourselves the honour of writing to your Excellency on the 20th ulto. when we expected to be able to send you 2000 cartridge boxes: but we have been disappointed; and Major Peirce has received at present but between six and seven hundred: nor, are we certain how soon the rest can be furnished. But as the whole number will be incompetent to the demands of your state, we beg leave to suggest to your Excellency the expediency of getting a quantity made in Virginia; and as the time is pressing, a slighter kind may be provided. The British have for several years past furnished their new levies with cartridge boxes made of close wood (as maple or beech) with no other covering than a good leathern flap nailed at the back near the upper edge, and of sufficient breadth to cover the top and whole front of the box: they are fixed to the body by a waist belt which passes thro' two straps that are nailed to the front of the box. Cartouch boxes of this kind will answer very well, and may be made at small expence and with great dispatch.

An additional quantity of cartridge paper and a supply of pack thread are gone with the cartridge boxes now sent.

We are taking measures for establishing a continental laboratory for supplying the southern army with amunition. We propose also to send a fit person to take charge of the whole department of military stores, in which will be included the repairs of arms, and the repairing and making of carriages for field pieces, as well as the laboratory; and to furnish a few experienced workmen in these branches of business. As much dispatch as possible will be given to a matter so essential to the operations of the southern army.

We have honour to be with the greatest respect your Excellency's most obedient servants. In behalf & by order of the board,

TIM: PICKERING

RC (Vi). Addressed: "(On public service) His Excellency Governour Jefferson at Richmond Virginia (War-Office)." Endorsed: "Contl. Bd of War to the Governour July 3d 1780 respecting Cartouch boxes &c. Tim Pickering."
The Board's letter of 20 June 1780 has not been found.

To William Preston

SIR   Richmond July 3d. 1780.

The measures you have taken for the preservation of the Lead-mines by calling in the militia of Montgomery Washington and Botetourt are as wise as could have been advised, and as effectual as, in the present State of things, can be administered. The distress of the Western Frontier is much too general to confine Crocket's battalion to a single part. It is indispensably necessary that he proceed to aid in taking posts to cover the Western Country and occasionally to join Colo. Clarke. As little are we able to send any assistance from below the blue ridge as from that Country. 5000 Militia are marched and to be marched to Carolina. It is in our power therefore only to approve of your calling on the militia of the Counties before mentioned; and in order to enforce your calls I write to the Lieutenants of Washington and Botetourt. Colo. William Campbell [is] lately gone up to undertake an expedition of another kind. As it now appears more necessary to turn his arms against our internal enemies, I write to him to do so, former experience having proved him very equal to such a duty. In this as in other cases generally active offensive enterprizes are to be preferred. It will probably be better to seek the insurgents and suppress them in their own settlements than to await their coming, as time and Space to move in will perhaps increase their numbers. However at this distance we cannot pretend to give precise orders, but leave the direction of proper measures to the discretion of those who are [to] be in command. Should exigencies require it you will extend your call of Militia to such other Counties as may be necessary. I am Sir Your very humble servt,   TH: JEFFERSON

RC (WHi); in a clerk's hand, with complimentary close and signature by TJ; endorsed: "Governours Letter July 3d. 1780. came to hand the 18th. July."

Addressee assigned on the basis of internal evidence and the fact that the original is among the Preston Papers in the Draper Collection.

To George Washington

SIR   Richmond July 4. 1780.

The assembly have directed me to send a quantity of tobacco to the Virginia officers in captivity at New York and Long island, or if the enemy will not admit that, that it be sold for hard money and sent to them. I own I do not expect they will admit it. As you are a better judge of this, should you be of opinion they will suffer the officers to receive and dispose of the tobacco, I must trouble you to get permission for a flag to go hence by water with it. If you think they will not consent to it, and will be so good as to inform me of it, I will not give you the trouble of applying for a flag, but will proceed immediately to procure hard money according to the desire of the assembly.

I have the honor to be with the greatest esteem & respect Your Excellency's most obedient & most humble servt.,

TH: JEFFERSON

RC (MA). Addressee identified from internal evidence; see entry for TJ to Harrison, 22 June, and Washington's reply to the present letter, 29 Aug. 1780. Also, there is in DLC: Washington Papers, filed with TJ's letter to

Washington of 2 Aug. (see note there), what appears to be the endorsement for this letter: "Govr. Jefferson 4th July 1780—recd only the 26 Augt ansd 29 Augt."

To Benjamin Harrison

[*Richmond, 5? July* 1780. JHD, May 1780, 1827 edn., p. 75 (5 July): "The Speaker laid before the House a letter from the Governor, enclosing several others from General Washington, and the committees of co-operation, respecting the state of the army." Read and referred to committee of the whole on the state of the commonwealth. TJ's letter has not been located, and the letters it transmitted are not precisely identifiable.]

Affidavit of Benjamin Harrison's Oath as Speaker

VIRGINIA TO WIT   [7 July 1780]

The honble. Benjamin Harrison Speaker of the house of delegates this day took before me the oath prescribed by the joint resolution of both houses of assembly of the 6th. instant. Given under my hand this 7th. day of July 1780.   TH: JEFFERSON

MS (Vi); entirely in TJ's hand.

On 6 July the House and Senate unanimously adopted a resolution "That every member of the General Assembly shall give an unequivocal proof of his uniform and steady determination to support and maintain the cause of America and the independence of his country, by taking the following oath or affirmation, to wit: 'I, A. B. do solemnly and sincerely declare and swear, or affirm, that the State of Virginia is, and of right ought to be, a free, sovereign and independent State; and I do forever renounce and refuse all allegiance, subjection and obedience to the King or Crown of Great Britain. And I do further swear (or solemnly, sincerely and truly declare and affirm), that I never have, since the Declaration of Independence, directly or indirectly, aided, assisted, abetted, or in anywise countenanced the King of Great Britain, his generals, fleets or armies, or their adherents, in their claim upon these United States; and that I have ever since the Declaration of Independence thereof, demeaned myself as a faithful citizen and subject of this or some one of the United States, and that I will at all times maintain and support the freedom, sovereignty and independence thereof,'" &c. The resolution further stipulated that each speaker should take the oath before the governor; that, on the following day, the speakers should in turn administer the oath to each member in the presence of the other members of the respective houses; and that those members who happened to be out of town should, at the next meeting of the county court after the adoption of the resolution, take the oath before the court and, at the following session of the General Assembly, produce a certificate from the clerk of the county court to the effect that the oath had been taken. On 7 July Harrison laid TJ's affidavit before the House and proceeded to administer the oath to eighty-eight members; this, of course, was not the entire membership of the House, but it is uncertain whether those who did not take the oath on 7 July were absent or not (JHD, May 1780, 1827 edn., p. 76-7). It is obvious, however, that the suddenness of this move and the requirement that all members take an oath of allegiance reflected a suspicion that the loyalty of one or more representatives was open to question.

From Bernardo de Gálvez

New Orleans, 9 July 1780. Introducing Luis Toutan [Toutant] Beauregard, merchant of New Orleans, who comes to Virginia to obtain payment of sums due him for goods furnished to the troops quartered in the Illinois country. Gálvez desires to find occasions to be of service to TJ.

RC (Vi); 2 p.; in Spanish; in a clerk's hand, signed "Bdo. de Galvez." Also a translation of the same, attested by "Lacoste"; endorsed: "Lr: from Galves respecting Beaugard." The translation is printed in CVSP, I, 365-6.

On Beauregard's claims, see an opinion rendered by Attorney General Edmund Randolph in 1790, CVSP, V, 109-11, and other references in the same volume.

From the Committee of Congress at Headquarters

Preakness [N.J.], 10 July 1780. The forming of a magazine of short forage in the vicinity of the Hudson River is immediately necessary. The quantities earlier called for by the Committee should therefore be hastened forward. New Jersey's supply of forage is exhausted by the army's having wintered there.

FC (DLC: PCC, No. 11); signed by the copyist with the names Schuyler and Peabody. At foot of text: "Circular, to the States of Delaware, Pensylvania, Maryland & Virginia." A further note

explains that the copy of this letter sent to Virginia permitted that state to withhold such stocks of forage as were necessary "for the southern operations."

From Cyrus Griffin

Without place, 11 July 1780. Acknowledges a letter from Jefferson which "has given me the greatest pleasure I have felt since my entrance into public life." Hopes to continue to be of service in his new post on the Court of Appeals: "if I can preserve the friendship of a Jefferson and a very few others, I shall think myself perfectly happy and safe."

RC (DLC); 3 p. The letter is without salutation and perhaps lacks an initial page.

The letter acknowledged by Griffin

has not been found; it was evidently written by TJ on behalf of the Virginia Council and was in answer to Griffin's letter of 9 June 1780, q.v.

From John Walker

DEAR SIR   Philada. July 11th 1780

Your favor by the new line of Expresses I received, and should have answer'd it thro' the same channel, but the bearer was gone before it came to my hand.

I rejoice to hear of the late proceedings of our Assembly with respect to the new Scheme of Finance, the Pennsylva. Line &c; these I think are objects of vast Consequence. I wish the business of our back Lands was setled, that the Confederation might be compleated. Do you not think it would be advisable in Virginia to give up her exclusive Claims beyond the Ohio, to be guaranteed in all her Teritory on this side? From the present face of affairs here, I am doubtful whether these are not as good Terms as the Confederation could now be compleated on. The United States making us a Compensation for our extraordinary Expence incurred in the defence of that Country. I wished to have consulted you on this business before I came here, but had not the pleasure of seeing you. There is now a Committee of Congress deliberating on this Business and I suppose some steps will shortly be taken in it, but expect they will be merely recommendatory. In the mean time should be glad to know your Sentiments on the Subject.

With regard to the late vote, by which I was left out of the next year's Delegation, my Interest could not have been more effectually promoted, tho' certainly it had not the suaviter in modo. I now consider myself as fully absolved for the remainder of my Life, from all civil Employments, having been rejected both by my County and Country: possessd however of the Mens conscia recti and the Friendship of such as you, I envie no Man his Lot.

I am glad you kept the map sent me by my Father, it was intended chiefly for the use of your honble. Board. Part of his Letter too related to the Commonwea[lth] of Virginia. If you did not read it pray inform me, that I may send you such Extracts from it as may deserve your attention.

Perhaps you or Mrs. Jefferson may have some little Commissions here, if so I claim them as my right. Almost any thing may be had here for money *enough* a little will get nothing. Goods are generally about 50 Pr. Ct. above what they used to be in hard money and if paid in paper 60 for one on that. I rejoice to tell you, that in the Eastern States, where the new bills begin to circulate, there is no kind of difference between them and silver. A strong argument in favor of the Resolution of the 18th of March.

Inclosed you have the last paper to which I beg leave to refer you for news.

Offer our respectful Compts. to Mrs. Jefferson &c and believe me to be My Dear Sir Affectly. yours &c, Jn. Walker

Madison sends the News paper.

RC (DLC).
TJ's FAVOR to Walker is missing. THE MAP SENT ME BY MY FATHER: John Walker was a son of Dr. Thomas Walker of Castle Hill, Albemarle co.; the map has not been identified.

To John Page

The bill for draughting the militia of the several counties is not yet passed: however, from what I have heard of it's contents, it will not give the Executive a power to commute the demands for infantry into cavalry. Perhaps it would not be prudent to do so, because Genl. Washington (who knows best what he wants) has called for infantry, not cavalry, because it is very doubtful whether additional cavalry could be subsisted there—and because every county would have equal right to claim the commutation, in which case it might become a question whether a single man for the infantry would go. We have had offers from six or eight counties to raise each a troop of horse voluntarily to serve a twelvemonth, without desiring any credit in their draughts. These offers have been declined because we were informed that cavalry could not be subsisted at either camp. Genl. Gates is to let me know on his arrival in Carolina whether more horse are wanting there, and whether they can be fed. In the mean time it will be proposed in Council to have them ready raised to proceed if he calls for them. But even these cannot be taken in lieu of infantry under the law as I understand.

The council had determined not to allow more than three Commissioners of the provision law in any county. They have however on your request added Anderson and Seawell to the two they had before appointed.

We some time ago gave a Commodore's commission to James Barron; and understanding that one of the Eastern shore gallies was abandoned by officers and men, we directed him to bring her to the Western shore and keep her on duty there. We recommended (but did not expressly order) the other to be brought round and stationed on the bay side of the Eastern shore, because there she might co-operate in the defence of the bay, and be convenient to receive his orders. I suppose Barron will remove her. Without doubt it was great partiality to keep such a proportion of our small naval force to defend half the trade only of two counties.

I beg you not to suppose a multiplicity of letter writing would prevent my answering yours. Were duty out of the question I have other prevailing motives for taking every opportunity of corresponding with you. For the present I have little to offer you more than the preceding answer to the articles of your letter. I suppose you have heard that the French fleet actually sailed from Toulon on the 20th. of April. This is authentic. Report adds that they have 104. transports. Gates thinks they cannot be expected till the 20th. inst.

I am Dear Sir with sincere esteem Your friend & servt.,

TH: JEFFERSON

RC (CSmH). Addressed: "John Page esq. Rosewell." Page's LETTER to which this is an answer is missing.

To James Wood

SIR   Richmond July 14. 1780.

I inclose you a remission of the sentence against La Brune, also a letter to the Commissioners for carrying into execution the provision law in Albemarle directing them to send to the barracks their salt meats also. This with others to the six circumjacent counties of Amherst, Buckingham, Fluvanna, Louisa, Orange and Culpeper had been made out before the receipt of yours. The others are sent by other conveyances. Nothing having been yet sent to us from the assembly for extending the power of the Commissioners to live stock, we are unable to give directions on that head. Your waggons may still continue to come here for salted beef. I understand the assembly are passing a bill to supply the treasury with money to a certain extent by emission. We shall immediately (as soon as it can be struck) send a supply to your post to pay off the two regiments and to relieve the Quartermaster and Commissary as far as we can.

I am Sir Your very humble servt.,   TH: JEFFERSON

RC (Lloyd W. Smith, Madison, N.J., 1946). Endorsed: "Govr. Jefferson 14. July 1780." Addressee identified from internal evidence. Enclosures missing.

Notes on Certain Acts of Assembly

[After 14 July 1780]

Resoln Ass. June. 8. 1780. the certificates of the purchasers to be a discount for any future taxes, or paimt. in 6. months, or loan off. certificates Selden. the Claibornes. Randolph. this was extended by the Executive to waggons & teams. Elliott & Southall.

July. 14. 1780. ass. to make provision at next session for speedy paimt. & intt. the delegates &c.

May. 20. resoln. to impress waggons & teams to move Maryland troops. to be appraised & paid for as in other cases
of impress but by resoln. of the 20th. of June may pay
taxes, or take loan off. certif. or be paid in 6. months.
Act of assembly. sendg militia to So. Carola. power to impress. to
be pd. in tobo. provn. still to be made by ass.
Provision law. certif. pay next money tax, or specific tax
Law givg further powers. power to impress cattle, waggons, horses,
duck. Certif. pay as Provn. law.

N (DLC); in TJ's hand. A literal text is given here.

All of the listed Acts and resolutions of the legislature grant powers to the executive for raising and equipping troops. For the RESOLN ASS. JUNE. 8. 1780., see JHD, May 1780, 1827 edn., p. 39; of JULY. 14. 1780., same, p. 89; of MAY 20., same, p. 16; ACT . . . SO. CAROLA., passed in Oct. 1779 session "for re-enlisting the troops of this state in the continental army, and for other purposes" (Hening, X, 214-15); PROVISION LAW, passed in the May 1780 session "for procuring a supply of provisions and other necessaries for the use of the army" (same, p. 233-7); LAW GIVG FURTHER POWERS, passed in the May 1780 session "for giving farther powers to the governour and council" (same, p. 309-15).

To George Muter

In Council July 17th. 1780.

The Board are of opinion that Mrs. Burnley may be permitted to repair to and remain within the county of Hanover, subject to the future direction of the Executive and Colo. Muter is desired to take measures accordingly and for the dispatch of the flag. They wish Mrs. Burnley to be reminded that she must be conscious of the many circumstances which render her disposition towards this country suspicious and which may justly induce a belief that motives of interest and not of affection to the state must have brought her here; and therefore that she be admonished to conduct herself with the greatest circumspection, as a want of that added to the very unceremonious manner in which she has ventured to introduce herself and flag may dispose the executive to discontinue her residence here if they shall have any cause to believe she shall be conducting herself improperly. TH. JEFFERSON

Tr in Board of War Letter Book (MiU-C).
MRS. BURNLEY: Perhaps the wife of Hardin Burnley (CVSP, III, 12).

To George Muter

SIR   Richmond July 17th. 1780.

The Assembly having directed that the ship Dragon shall be repaired and manned for service, it becomes necessary to decline the sale of her, which they had formerly directed. You will therefore be pleased to take measures for stopping the sale.

Your mo: obt. servt.,   TH: JEFFERSON

Tr in Board of War Letter Book (MiU-C).

The DRAGON was to be recommissioned by the terms of the Act for putting the eastern frontier into a posture of defense; see Hening, x, 297. The Council on 26 June had ordered this vessel to be sold (*Va. Council Jour.*, II, 260).

To George Muter

SIR   Richmond July 17. 1780

The Council have thought it best that the several prisoners of war in this state, except Governour Hamilton and Major Hay, be given up to congress, according to their resolutions of January 13. 1780. You will therefore be pleased to give the necessary orders for this purpose. I am sensible a difficulty must occur as to the manner of guarding them on their march. Perhaps you'll be able to devise some better method than occurs to me. I shall be ready to confer with you on this subject whenever you please. Governour Hamilton and Major Hay are to be sent to a place of greater safety if you can find such a one. I am Sir Your very hble servt., TH: JEFFERSON

Tr in Board of War Letter Book (MiU-C).   For Congress' RESOLUTIONS OF JANUARY 13. 1780 relating to prisoners of war, see JCC, XVI, 48-52.

To Abner Nash

SIR   Richmond July 17th. 1780.

I have the honor of inclosing to you a resolution of the general assembly of Virginia on the claims to lands within the neighbourhood of the boundary lately run between our States and to ask the favor of you to transmit to the Speaker of the house of Delegates of your State the inclosed letter containing another copy of the same resolution.

I am with every sentiment of esteem & respect Your Excellency's mo: obedt. & most hble Servant,   TH: JEFFERSON

RC (NcDAH); in a clerk's hand, signed and addressed by TJ: "His Excellency Governor Nash North-Carolina." Endorsed (in part): "Recieved the 1st Aug." Enclosures missing; the Assembly's resolutions on land claims along the newly extended Virginia-North Carolina boundary were passed on 6 July and are printed in JHD, May 1780, 1827 edn., p. 74-5.

To Joseph Reed

[*Richmond, 17 July 1780*. From the Minutes of the Supreme Executive Council of Pennsylvania, *Penna. Colonial Records*, XII, 444 (7 Aug. 1780): "A letter from his Excellency Governor Jefferson, of Virginia, dated the 17th of July, enclosing a resolution of the Legislature, confirming the line agreed on by the Commissioners in August, 1779, between the two States, on certain conditions, was read; and *Ordered*, To be laid before the Assembly at their next meeting." Neither letter nor enclosure has been found. The Virginia Assembly's resolutions ratifying the agreement of Aug. 1779, but with provisos relative to settlers' title claims, are printed under date of 23 June 1780 in JHD, May 1780, 1827 edn., p. 60-1. See also TJ to Huntington, 9 Feb. 1780, and references there.]

From George Washington

SIR   Head Qrs. near Passaick Falls July 18. 1780

I had the honor a few days ago, to receive Your Excellency's Letter of the 2d Instant, and at the same time one from General Muhlenburg, inclosing the Return you had requested him to send me. I am exceedingly obliged to Your Excellency for your attention in this affair, and beg leave to refer You to the inclosed Copy of a Letter, addressed to Major General Gates if he should be at Fredericksburg or Richmond, and if not to General Muhlenburg, for the Arrangement I have made, with respect to the Levies in contemplation to be raised by the State when You wrote, and of the Officers to command them. It is the best that has occurred to me, under a consideration of all circumstances, and I shall be happy if it meets your approbation. It is to be wished there were more Officers, but any New appointments except to Insigncies, would be considered as injurious and would be the source of infinite complaints and confusion. I have entreated Genl. Muhlenburg to whom I have written and thro him, the Whole of the Officers, to use every possible exertion to collect and discipline the Men and reminded them, that the charge of fitting a New Army or at least the Troops of a whole State for the field, had devolved on them; and as these should act, so would be their reputation. I hope they will avail themselves of the occasion to distinguish themselves and will do all in their power to qualify the Men for service. How the force will be applied I can't determine at present; but whether it shall be directed to either Object, this or the Southern Army, or a part to both, the necessity for its being ready is equal and most pressing. It gives me great pleasure to find that the Men are to serve for Eighteen Months and it would have been still more fortunate and more to our interest if they could have been obtained for the War. Short inlistments have subjected Us to such distresses, to such enormous expences, have so intimately hazarded our liberties that I never reflect upon them, but with a degree of horror. The consideration is the more painful now, from the unhappy state of our finances, and as at the close of the present year, All the Levies now raising under the most extravagant bounties, will disband, except Yours and those of Maryland ⟨*who, convinced of this fatal policy, is exerting herself to engage hers on a permanent footing*⟩. At this period we shall be again reduced, and it may be within the compass of things for the States to suffer greater insults even, than those they experienced in the late incursions of the Enemy in Jersey.

I very sincerely congratulate Your Excellency on the arrival of the Armament from France. The fleet got into Rhode Island on the 11th. This very generous succour must fill every Friend to America with gratitude towards the Prince and Nation who have sent it, and I trust will be answered by correspondent exertions and the best of good Offices on our part. But I am also to inform Your Excellency that Adml. Greaves has since arrived (on the 13) off Sandy Hook, with Six Ships of the line. This is an unlucky incident and at present embarrassing, tho it may not eventually be injurious.

I have the Honor to be with very great respect & esteem Your Excellency's Most Obedt St., G W

Dft (DLC: Washington Papers); in hand of R. H. Harrison; endorsed.

See TJ's letter to Washington of 2 July 1780, and references there to Washington's several letters relative to staffing the Virginia recruits for the Continental Line.

Memorandum of Executive Agenda

[ca. 19 July 1780]

Resolution of assembly as to claims of land South of Carolina boundary.

√Another copy from clerk of assembly.

√One to be inclosed to Governor N. Carola.; √the other to assembly.

√Resolution on Pennsylva. boundary.
　　To be inclosed to President of Pennsylva.

Act for putting the Eastern frontier of this Commonwealth into posture of defence.
　　Write letter to County Lieutenants Prs. Anne, Norf., Nansemd., I. Wight, Southampt., Surry, Sussex, Pr. Geo. to hold 1/6 of militia in readiness.
　　Inclose extract of act.
　　Arm and accoutre 1/3 of said counties and send ammunition.
　　√Direct Commissioner of Navy to order Thetis, Tempest, Dragon, Jefferson to be immediately repaired, manned for bay and sea coast &c., and Henry Galley for Hampton.
　　√Appoint board of Commissioner of Navy and six captains to reform officers of navy.
　　√Instruct officers of navy to enlist seamen. 1000D. bounty to those enlisting for 3. years or war, 2. D. per day with former privileges of act concerning officers, souldiers, &c.
　　Appoint 5. Captains and 15. Lieutenants to enlist. Each Captain, 25 marines and each 1st. Lieutenant 15, 2d Lieutenant 12, 3d Lieutenant 8.

Act the more effectually to prevent and punish desertion.
　　√Have 1500 copies[1] printed and sent to counties.
　　Send copy of act to Genl. Washington and desire proclamation of pardon.
　　Send a copy to commanding officer of every Virginia regiment.
　　√Publish act in Gazette.
　　Send a copy to French Consul. And inform him that if he desires it a copy of the descriptive lists from masters of vessels shall be furnished him.

Act to repeal the acts establishing boards of war and trade and for appointing Commissioners of the Navy and War office and Commercial agent.
　　To demand and receive papers from Boards of war and trade.
　　Appoint Commissioners of √Navy, √War, and Trade.
　　Define their duties.

Act to enable Governor to provide laboratory and magazines.
　　Direct Commissioner of War office have magazines erected at Westham, Hoods.

Direct A. Q. D. [ad quod damnum] to be issued by clerks of Henrico, Pr. Geo.

Act for giving further powers to the Governor and Council.
√Have articles of war printed and copy sent to every county, Sep. 20. 1776. Art.4. §6.   18 and 19. Art. §13.
√Have them published three times in the Virga. gazette with copy of this act.
Direct Commissioners of Provision law to take live stock, linen for tents to be appraised.
Call for Volunteer cavalry, to serve till Dec. 1781.
√Employ a printer at public expence.
Appoint a Major of marines.
√Send to Genl. Stevens extract from the Ryder putting militia under martial law.
√Send printed copy of paragraphs for taking deserters and concerning Quakers to County Lieutenants.

√Act for laying off three new counties.
Sheriffs to be appointed.[2] Justices and Militia officers.

√Act for laying embargo.
Renew proclamation.

√Act for emitting money.[3]

√Act to suspend certain escheats of British property.
To allow G. Hamer maintenance upon application.

√Act to amend Continental loan office act.
Nothing to be done immediately.

√Act to amend Illinois act.
Nothing to be done immediately.

√Act to permit slaves from S. Carola. and Georgia.
Nothing to be done immediately.

√Act to amend tobacco law.
Nothing to be done.

Act for speedily recruiting the quota of this state for Continental army received July 18. 1780.
Send expresses to all the counties except Illinois, and the Pennsylva. counties with copies.
Appoint places of Rendezvous South of James river. Hillsborough.[4]
Send out 3600 tobacco loan office certificates viz. 1. for every 15 militia in every county.

Appoint officer to go to each place of rendezvous.

Give him power of taking waggons and provisions, which power may be endorsed on the back of the extract.

Furnish him with some money.

√Act for punishing crimes injurious to the Independance of America met with in the newspaper of July 19.

Nothing to be done.[5]

Act for calling in the money in circulation.

Appoint Commissioners and places to receive tobacco, hemp &c. in lieu of tax before Jan. 1. 1781.

Inclose a copy to Congress.

Appoint Commissioners for preparing and signing new money with Commissioners of Congress.

Write to delegates to send authentic information of the states which approve of and accede to the resolutions of Congress of March 18. 1780.

N (DLC); entirely in TJ's hand.

This highly interesting paper was written by TJ, probably at more than one sitting, soon after the Assembly had adjourned on 14 July 1780. It was not completed until 19 July or after; the ACT FOR PUNISHING CRIMES INJURIOUS TO THE INDEPENDANCE OF AMERICA was "met with" in Dixon & Nicolson's *Virginia Gazette* of that date. The items in the list checked by TJ are no doubt those he had taken care of; some were apparently dispatched as the list was being compiled. Curiously, TJ does not mention one Act in which he was specifically mentioned and in which he had great interest—the Act "for locating the publick squares, to enlarge the town of Richmond, and for other purposes," in which it was stipulated that "the ground to be appropriated to the purpose of building thereon a capitol, halls of justice, state house for the executive boards, and an house for the governour, shall be located on Shockoe hill; and those to be appropriated to the use of the publick market, shall be below the said hill, on the same side of Shockoe creek; which location shall be made immediately; and where the nature of the ground shall render other form more eligible for the said uses than a square, it shall be lawful for his excellency Thomas Jefferson, esquire, Archibald Cary, Robert Carter Nicholas, Richard Adams, Edmund Randolph, Turner Southall, Robert Goode, James Buchanan, and Samuel Du-Vall, directors . . . to lay off in such form, and of such dimensions as shall be convenient and requisite," &c. (Hening, x, 317-20). This Memorandum lists only sixteen of the thirty-seven Acts passed at the May 1780 session, however, and it is quite possible that TJ had not seen all of them when he drew up this list; in any case, the fact that the Governor first saw an Act of Assembly in a newspaper is probably a reflection of the urgent military situation existing at the time, though TJ's making note of the fact would seem to indicate some other explanation for this apparent lack of legislative-executive coordination. G. HAMER (i.e., George Harmer): See an Act for restoring certain slaves to George Harmer, same, x, 371; see also JHD, May 1780, 1827 edn., p. 65.

[1] The words "of 1st and last paragraph" were struck out at this point.

[2] The words "qu. when?" were here struck out.

[3] A line following this was struck out: "Inform treasurer we want immediately £100,000 to pay off army."

[4] This word substituted for "Petersbg. and New London," lined out.

[5] This line substituted for the following, lined out: "Print 1000 copies and send out for every captain."

Payments Made by Virginia for the United States, May 1779 to July 1780

Monies answered for the Continent from May 21. 1779. to July 19. 1780.

Quarter master's departmt.

1.	Charles Petitt	£294,000
2.	William Finnie	750,000
3.	George Elliot	735,000.13
4.	Stephen Southall	196,442
5.	Gressitt Davies	10,800
6.	Richard Young	10,000

Commissary's.

7.	Chaloner & White	705,000
8.	Robert Forsyth	173,200
9.	Ephraim Blaine	450,000

Other purposes.

10.	Ambrose Gordon to recruit Baylor's regiment	20,000
11.	John White & Joseph Gray by warrt. Feb. 12. for Georgia	90,000
12.	Joseph Carleton P. M. Board of war	80,000
13.	Jonathan Burrell Assist. P. M. Genl.	3,000
14.	Majr. Galvan in part of warrant B. Harrison	3,000
15.	do. by order on sheriff of Norfolk	3,000
16.	different officers to subsist militia on their march Southwd.	29,890
17.	Brig. Genl. Stevens for military chest to militia	125,000
18.	Daniel Call to purchase horses for Washington & White	28,808
19.	William Claiborne for do.	5,000
20.	Miles Selden for do.	32,300
21.	Commrs in the several counties for do. (not exactly known) about	662,000

	4,404,440.13
Amount of the requisitions of Congress	3,180,000

Overpaid   Dollars 4,081,368⅚ = £1,224,440.13

No. 1. this is made up of No. 4.5.9.15. of the Treasurer's certif.
    2. see No. 2.6.7.10.14.22. Treasurer's certif.
    3. made up of No. 19. Treas. certif. & Elliott's return of certificates issu[ed.]
    4. made up of No. 20. Treas. certif. & Southall's return of certif. issued.
    5. see No. 21. Treas's certif.
    6. see No. 16. Treas. certif.
    7. see No. 12. & 17. Treas. certif.
    8. see No. 1. 11. 13. 26. Treas. certif.
    9. see No. 23. Treas. certif.
  10. see No. 3. Treas. certif.
  11. see No. 8. Treas. certif. for £60,000. and the balas. £30,000 was paid by John [. . . .]
  12. see No. 24. Treas. certif.
  13. see No. 25. Treas. certif.
  14. see No. 17. Auditor's certif.   this was paid by the Treasurer on the Gov's orde[r.]
  15. this order was given by the Govr. & inclosed by T. Newton.
  16. see No. 18. Auditor's certif.
  17. the Treasurer can certify this to have been paid (to Majr. Mosby I think)
  18. see No. 16. Treasurer's certif.
  19. see Council books
  20. see Council books
  21. there are 60 horses still to be purchased by Call, Selden, & the Claibornes a[nd] 160 by commrs. in several counties, which will average probably £3[ ]

Tabular MS (DLC), entirely in TJ's hand.

This table, with its appended list of vouchers supporting the figures given, is Virginia's account against the United States drawn up in preparation for TJ's answer to Pres. Huntington's letter of 21 June 1780. The answer was sent on 27 July, q.v., and a copy of the present statement was enclosed therein.

From Horatio Gates

SIR   [Hillsborough, N.C., 19 July 1780]

When I had the honor of seeing your Excellency at Richmond I was taught to look forward to much difficulty and a perplexed department, yet I cannot but profess that, in the course of a long and often critical service, it has hitherto never fallen to my lot to witness a scene of such multiplied and increasing wants, as my present command exhibits. Of the Militia voted by your State only 1438 are now upon the Ground Commissioned and Non Commissioned Officers included and Those not so compleatly supplied as I either wish'd or expected. The arms were yesterday distributed among them, a few out of repair, but too many without cartouch-Boxes, and all destitute of bayonet Belts which I need scarcely tell your Excellency is the certain loss of the Bayonet. They are deficient also in hatchets or light axes. This article you will find in the list of Military stores and one which becomes doubly necessary from the face of the Country in which we shall act. These defects are however but trifling when compared to the weightier considerations of Arms, amunition and provision. This State is unhappily but too much at a loss for the first. The casualties of the campaign may render issues necessary to the regular Troops and such Volunteer Corps as I may find it expedient and practicable to embody; this leads me to press your Excellency that, not only such Arms and amunition, as you may allot us from the State Stores, but all supplies from the board of War may meet with as immediate a passage into this State as possible. Upon the subject of provisions my reports must be still less satisfactory. An officer just from the Baron's Head Quarters has assured me that, there are often intervals of 24 hours in which the army without distinction are obliged to feed upon such green vegetables as they can find, having neither animal food or Corn. So frequent and total a want, must eventually break up our Camp, should not the evil be hastily remedied, and has unfortunately arose from several causes, one of which can alone be corrected. The scarcity of Crops for the last year, the disaffection of many of the Inhabitants and a want of Economy, and management. The supplies have been precariously obtain'd by detachments from the Army whose misapplied violence in some instances must affect any future purchase. I have this day made a representation of our wants in this and other respects, to Governor Nash, and Gen. Huger has taken charge of my Dispatch and will personally urge such steps to be taken by the Council of this State —as in conjunction with those I cannot but hope for from your Excellency—may soon restore our affairs and enable me to prosecute my own wishes and the Intentions of Congress.

I cannot conclude this letter, without suggesting the necessity that the 1000 tents, for which I had your Excellency assurances, may be sent on without a moments delay, and that Mr. Finney, D. Q. Master Gen. may be ordered to repair to my Head Quarters immediately. A system of communication will be settled; at the establishment of which, he must necessarily be present. I have other reasons also for wishing him here.

I must also beg the liberty of adding the very defective State of Maherring Bridge, to the representation I have already made of Pamunkey and Petersburgh ferries. I hope these objects, as they need the redress, so they will meet with the attention of your Honble. Council.

I am, Sir, Your Most Obedt. Servant,   HG

Dft (NHi); endorsed: "Copy of a Letter to His Excy: Governour Jefferson dated Hillsborough 19th: July 1780. No. 9." Tr (DLC). The Dft is so heavily corrected as to be difficult to decipher, and some readings have necessarily been taken from Tr; on the genesis of this and other transcripts of Gates' letters now in the TJ Papers, see below. Another Tr is in DLC: PCC, No. 154, II (Gen. Gates' Letters to Congress); this contains a postscript not in either of the other MSS, reading as follows: "inclosed is a Copy of a Letter I have this Morning received from Baron De Kalb. 500 falling Axes are much wanted with the Army, I pray they may be procured and sent forward." (Kalb's letter has not been found.)

In DLC: TJ Papers, 5: 742-3, is a 3-page list of Gen. Gates' letters (187 in all) to 55 correspondents during the period 21 June 1780 to 7 Oct. 1781. These have page references but no dates and quite evidently enumerate the letters which were copied under TJ's supervision from Gates' own letter book, lent to TJ in 1793 for the purpose of filling the gaps in the files of the State of Virginia for the Revolutionary period. TJ's letter appealing for Gates' aid in this project is dated 12 Mch. 1793; see further his letter of 21 Mch., and Gates' replies of 15 and 19 Apr. 1793; also Gates to TJ, 5 Jan.; TJ to Gates, 3 Feb.; and Gates to TJ, 14 Mch. 1794. Gates acknowledged the return of his letter book by Madison in a letter to TJ of 9 May 1797. The result of this transaction is that a mass of transcripts of Gates' letters during and after his southern campaign are now in the TJ Papers; they are not very good transcripts, but they were carefully read and corrected by TJ himself. All are derived from originals in the Gates Papers now in the New-York Historical Society.

To Edward Stevens

Sir   Richmond July 19. 1780

I think it proper to inclose you a Paragraph from a late Act of Assembly putting the Militia with you under martial law. It is the only part of the Act which relates at all to the Militia, for which reason I do not send the whole Act, the Clearks being very busy. This Act having been made after the Militia went on duty may perhaps be thought by them to be in the nature of an ex post facto law; but as it is in your Power to restraint it's Penalties from all Acts previous to its promulgation by you and even if you please from all subsequent ones except desertion, and such others as you shall find necessary, they may perhaps think it less hard. I am Sir with the greatest respect Your most obt. & most hum. Serv,

Th Jefferson

FC (DLC); signature as well as text in clerk's hand. Endorsed: "Copy of a Letter from Governor Jefferson to Edward Stevens dated July 19. 1780."

A LATE ACT OF ASSEMBLY: An Act for vesting "the executive with extraordinary powers for a limitted time"; by this Act the executive was authorized to call into service any number of the militia not exceeding 20,000; to send them out of the state; to remove or to confine disaffected persons in case of invasion; to call into service volunteer companies of cavalry, &c. The Act also provided that, in case of insurrection or invasion, anyone who gave aid to the enemy, acted as a guide or spy, encouraged desertion from the army, &c., was "declared to be subject to the law martial as declared by congress" on 20 Sep. 1776; it further provided that the militia in actual service should also be subject to the Continental articles of war (Hening, x, 309-15). When this bill was before the House and had passed its second reading on 11 July, an effort was made to delete the clause "for enforcing martial law in case of an invasion," but this motion was defeated by a roll-call vote of 53 to 23 (JHD, May 1780, 1827 edn., p. 83).

Appointment of James Maxwell as Commissioner of the Navy

[*Richmond, before 21 July 1780.* A fragmentary MS (Vi) which has a caption in an unidentified later hand: "Remnants of Minutes of the Navy Board (James Maxwell Comr.)," and hereafter referred to as Journal of the Commissioner of the Navy, covering the period 21 July to 19 Dec. 1780, has the following as the first entry: "Monday the 21st of July. 1780. In pursuance of my Apointment as Commissioner of the Navy by his Excellency the Governor and Council held my Office at the State house in Richmond having previously taken the Oath of Fidelity to this Commonwealth and the Oath of Office before William Foushee Gen: A Magisterate thereof and proceeded to Business." Signed, at the foot of the page, "James Maxwell, Comr." Maxwell's commission has not been located, nor have any of the letters mentioned in the Journal except that of 7 Dec. 1780.]

From Horatio Gates

SIR   Hill's borough 21st. July 1780

I had the honor of addressing your Excellency yesterday upon a variety of important subjects. One has since arose which may properly fall within your Excellency's notice. The mark'd lines of the enclosed letter from Baron De Kalb have induced me to order the remains of Buford's, Gibson's, and Brent's Regiments, to join the army under my command, as early as possible. No objection can arise in complying with this order, if it be not a want of arms and cloathing—an objection which I hope the present state of your public stores will be as far from justifying, as I am persuaded it is distant from your Excellency's wishes to countenance.

In the already small and decreasing number of the Maryland division &c. I need not point out the necessity of gaining every accession of regular force.

With much esteem, I am Sir Your Excellency's Most Humble Servant, HORATIO GATES

The enclosed report was this moment put into my hands. It is so extraordinary in itself that your Excellency will be necessarily lead into an enquiry of the State in which they left Virginia and to whom entrusted, as it carries exceedingly the appearance of neglect, or fraud.

RC (Vi); endorsed: "Horatio Gates July 21. 1780." Dft (NHi), dated "20th July," but endorsed "21st July"; the letter was drafted on the 20th, the postscript added and the letter sent off on the 21st. Tr of Dft (DLC); see note on Gates to TJ, 19 July 1780. Enclosures: (1) copy of Kalb to Gates, Camp on Deep River, 16 July 1780, missing (printed in *N.C. State Records*, XIV, 503-4); (2) copy of Edward Stevens to Gates, Hillsborough, 21 July 1780 (DLC), reporting that the 300 cartouche boxes just arrived from Virginia "are not deserving of the Name" (printed in CVSP, I, 366-7).

From William Lee

Bruxelles. 21 July. 80.

As it is fair to judge of the future by the past I may venture to take it for granted that those whose particular duty it is, will not take the trouble of giving you the following intelligence for which I shall not make any apology for doing myself. Since the surrender of C. Town and the subsequent advices from G. Clinton from So. Carol: as late as the 5. of June last, the Br. Ministry do not think of any peace with [America] but on the terms of unconditional submission and about 10 daies ago orders were sent to Geo. Clint: and Cornwallis to bend their whole fo[rce] 1st. against N.C. and then against Virga., so to advance Northward as fast as they can. The Tories and discontented will no doubt slight this intelli[gence] in hopes that you may be taken unprepar'd, but I presume you will look upon it in a different light and act accordingly. The uncertainty of this letter getting safe to hand makes me conclude without adding farther than that I have the Honor &c.

FC (ViHi), in Lee's Letter Book. At head of text: "Excy. Thos. Jefferson Gov. of Virga." A nearly complete copy (Vi) of this letter was transmitted by TJ in a letter to Speaker Harrison, 11 Dec. 1780, q.v.

To Edward Stevens

[*Richmond*, *21 July 1780*. TJ's earliest, fragmentary Epistolary Record under this date contains an entry for this missing letter reading as follows: "arms furnd [furnished] to U.S.?" See also TJ to Stevens, 4 Aug. 1780.]

To the Committee of Congress
at Headquarters

GENTLEMEN   Richmond July 22. 1780

I do myself the honor of inclosing you an act of the assembly of this state for raising by draught three thousand regulars to serve to Dec. 31. 1781. These with 2500 militia before ordered to Carolina will it is hoped after all probable deductions make up the number called for from this state. We take for granted that they are to be ordered to the Southward under the resolutions of Congress of June 17th. Indeed we should have been led to the same supposition by reflecting that one fourth or fifth of the enemy's whole force being left in S. Carolina, a similar division of the strength of the United states should take place, in which Georgia and S. Carolina are not to be counted as any thing in their present state.

The Quarter master has for some time informed me that he has had vessels loaded with grain to send up the bay. But they cannot venture into it on account of the privateers formerly mentioned. It is not certain that all the ships of war have yet left us. Provisions of various kinds have been collecting at navigable ports in this state ever since the 1st. of this month. From what I hear I have no doubt we can furnish the salted meats required to be sent Northwardly. Probably also good quantities of short forage might be sent; of this however I cannot speak with precision till returns shall be made me of the quantities collected, which will not be till the last of this month. But nothing can move either Northwardly or Southwardly while the bay is possessed by the enemy: except indeed from our counties in the neighborhood of N. Carolina.

I have the honor to be with great respect Gentlemen Your most obedient & most humble servt.,   TH: JEFFERSON

RC (DLC: PCC, No. 39, III). Addressed by TJ: "The honble. The Committee of Congress at Preakness New-Jersey." Endorsed: "Gov. Jefferson. Richmond 22 July 1780. entd. & exd." FC (DLC: PCC, No. 11). Enclosure (Tr in Committee's Proceedings, DLC: PCC, No. 11): Act for speedily recruiting the quota of this state for the Continental army (Hening, x, 257-62).

From Horatio Gates

I sent your Excellency a large Packet Yesterday by Captain Pendleton of The Caroline County Militia. He was directed to deliver it to the Stationed Express on Roanoak near Taylors Ferry who had a Written Order from me to set out with it immediately for the next Stage. The Letter for The Congress, Board of War &c., I conclude Your Excellency will forward with the like dispatch. This morning Mr. Sam. Lewis appeared here, with a large drove of Cattle, going with Them to Charlotteville. The Troops here being intirely in want, I have detained Sixteen of them for your Militia under General Stevens. I perceive Mr. Lewis Contract is for 3000 Head, and he informs me They are all Designed to be sent into Virginia. I beg your Excellency will consider how enormous a Draught this is from a State already invaded, and where the Southern Army, Void of a Magazine, is to be supported. I exceedingly approve of Mr. Lewis Vigilance and Activity in procuring Cattle but cannot help requesting the produce of his Industry may be applied to the Maintainance of This Army, or at least so large a proportion thereof as to leave Us out of the reach of Want. I am happy to find by Your Excellencys Letter to Col. Monroe, that The Two Regiments of Cavalry, with Gibsons, Brents, and Bluefords [Buford's], Infantry are in a way to be pushed forward to Camp. The same Letter also acquaints me that Major Lee's infantry are also on the March to Join Us. I beseech Your Excellency to continue to leave all this Corps, without a reason for not Joining the Southern Army as soon as Their Zeal for the Public Service will prompt them to do it. I am told There is a Great deal of Tent Cloth in this State, I think at Willmington, Edenton, Hallifax, and Cross Creek. Your Excellency will doubtless by this information be induced instantly to provide Your Militia from thence. I despair of any Assistance from the Continental Board of War in this Article, and request Your Excellency not to think of it. I request the favour of Your Excellency to be particular in forwarding the inclosed [to] Mrs. Gates, by the first safe conveyance; her letters to me, will be sent addressed to Your care. With Great respect & esteem, I am Sir Yr. Excys. Most Obbdt Hble Servt,   HG

Dft (NHi); endorsed: "Copy of a Letter to Governor Jefferson from Genl. Gates Hillsborough 22 July 1780 No. 18." Tr of Dft (DLC).

The LARGE PACKET doubtless accompanied Gates' letter to TJ of 21 July; its contents are not precisely identifiable.

From George Washington

Headquarters [Preakness, N.J.] 22 July 1780. Has just received a letter from Gen. Muhlenberg of 11 July enclosing a list of officers in Col. Gist's regiment, omitted in his former return, and has written to Gen. Gates to incorporate these officers with the others or "to divide the Drafts into another Regiment as may appear most eligible from a view of all circumstances."

Dft (DLC: Washington Papers); 2 p.; in hand of R. H. Harrison; endorsed: "To Govr Jefferson July 22. 1780 Vid Letter 18 July. About Gist's Officers"; printed in Washington, *Writings*, ed. Fitzpatrick, XIX, 229. Also on verso is the list referred to (in Harrison's hand) of officers in Col. Nathaniel Gist's regiment. Muhlenberg's letter of 11 July is in DLC: Washington Papers; the list of officers is printed in Fitzpatrick's note.

From the Committee of Congress at Headquarters

SIR   In Com[mitte]e of Congress Preakness July 23d 1780

We were honored with Your Excellency's favor of the 2d Instant on the 21st.

The cantonments of the Army In this quarter added to the Extreme badness of the Crops last season has so totally exhausted the Country of grain for forrage that the army is in great distress on this Account. The transportation of the necessary stores delayed, and every Embarrasment Increased. We have therefore to Intreat that the moment the Impediments to the transportation from Your State to the head of Elk are removed, your Excellency will please to direct the proper Officers to lose no time in Expediting to the army as much grain as can possibly be spared together with the bacon, and any other provisions which you may have as a surplus of what is necessary for the Southern Army.

Whether all or any of the five thousand troops raising by your state will be ordered hence, will probably depend on the State in which our affairs may be to the Southward in the Course of next month. The Commander In chief will advise you on that subject.

We have the honor to be with Great respect Your Excellency's Most Obedient & most Huml servts,

PH: SCHUYLER

JNO. MATHEWS

N. PEABODY

FC (DLC: PCC, No. 39, III); endorsed: "To Thomas Jefferson Esqr. in answer to his letter of the 2d Inst. July 23. 1780. No. 13." Another FC (DLC: PCC, No. 11).

To the County Lieutenant of Botetourt

Sir   RICHMOND, July 24, 1780.

You will receive by this express an act to prevent dese[rtion]; an extract on the same subject from another act; an act for drafting your militia; and sixt[y]¹ tobacco loan office certificates. For the last mentioned act, and the certificates, be pleased to return your receipt by the bearer. You stand debited in the Auditors books with these tobacco certificates. You will be pleased therefore to take a receipt from every soldier for the certificate delivered him, which receipts, with the certificates not delivered but, being transmitted to the Auditors, they will pass them to your credit, and give you a quie[tu]s. To prevent danger from misapplication before they get to your hands, we are obliged to declare that none of these certificates shall be deemed to have been duly issued, or to oblige the state to payment, unless they are attested by the County Lieutenant or other Commanding Officer, on delivery to the soldier, which attestation you will, at the time you fill up the blank with the name of the soldier, enter in the lower left hand corner in some such form as this: "Witness *A.B.* County Lieutenant of   ." According to authority given the Executive by another act of Assembly: *Brunswick* and *Pittsylvania* courthouses are appointed additional places of rendezvous: And as it is almost certain that these troops are to join the southern army, I would recommend that you have regard to this in determining to which place of rendezvous you will send your recruits. To subsist them to the place of rendezvous, you are hereby authorized to call on the commissioners of the provision law for your county (if any were appointed therein) for a day's subsistence for every man and every twenty miles he has to march to the rendezvous, out of the stock they have on hand, or if they have none, or not enough, they must obtain it as directed in the act "For procuring a supply of provisions and other necessaries for the use of the army;" their powers are also hereby extended for this special purpose to live cattle, horses, waggons, boats, or other vessels and their crews; and for their guide herein, I send you the inclosed extract from the law authorizing this extention. If no such commissioners have been appointed in your county, you are hereby authorized to appoint one for the same special purpose of subsisting and carrying your recruits to the place of rendezvous, where provision will be made for their further subsistance and transportation.

I am Your hble Servt.,²   *Th: Jefferson*

P.S. Be pleased to make me an exact return of your M[ili]tia after your draughts shall be taken out.[3]

RC (International Business Machines Corporation, New York, 1948); a printed form letter (not recorded in Swem's "Va. Bibliog."), with handwritten additions (see textual notes below); signed by TJ. Addressed: "The County [Lieu]-tenant of Botetourt." The lieutenant of Botetourt co. was presumably still William Fleming, appointed in 1776.

This is apparently the sole surviving copy of a circular sent to many if not all of the county lieutenants. The Memorandum of Executive Agenda, printed under 19 July above, makes clear what the enclosures were: (1) an Act the more effectually to prevent and punish desertion (Hening, x, 263-7); (2) the paragraph providing for court-martialing deserters in an Act for giving further powers to the governor and Council (same, x, 314); and (3) an Act for speedily recruiting the quota of this state for the Continental army (same, x, 257-62). According to the memorandum of 19 July, 1,500 copies of enclosure No. 1 were to be printed (Sabin 100326 records a copy in DLC); No. 2 was likewise to be printed; and No. 3 is known to be printed, for a copy was sent in TJ's letter to Huntington, 27 July, and is preserved with that letter, q.v. AUTHORITY GIVEN THE EXECUTIVE BY ANOTHER ACT OF ASSEMBLY: After the fall of Charleston had become known to the General Assembly, an Act was passed authorizing the governor to designate some other place of rendezvous for the militia, since "it hath become inexpedient to rendezvous at Hillsborough" (Hening, x, 229). THE ACT "FOR SECURING A SUPPLY OF PROVISIONS . . ." is printed in same, x, 233-7; a contemporary printing was enclosed in TJ's letter to Huntington, 27 July.

[1] The word "sixty" is inserted in a clerk's hand.
[2] The complimentary close is in a clerk's hand.
[3] The postscript is in another clerk's hand.

From George Muter

SIR   War Office Richmond 25th July. [1780]

Permit me to lay before your Excellency, the great Necessity there is of appointing proper Officers, to have the immediate care of the Arms and Ammunition belonging to the State. Great inconveniencies, as well as heavy losses, have Arisen in consequence of the Want of such people. The Arms have been ruined in many places and the powder wasted; great quantitys of powder have been Obliged to be sent to the Powder Mill to be worked over, at a very considerable expence, a considerable quantity requires to be worked over now, and there is the whole of the powder at one Magazine, now in want of sifting, (besides a considerable quantity at each of the others in the same situation), before it can be fit for action. The State of the powder is really allarming, and the Consequences might be fatal to the State. All this I apprehend may be in some degree if not quite remeded, by appointing proper Officers, at Adequate Sallaries, to have the charge of the Arms and Powder, who could be compelled to do their duty in the care of them.

[504]

I beg leave to mention to your Excellency, the Officers and others it seems to be necessary to appoint—

A Commissary of Stores, to have the General Charge of all the Arms and Ammunition in the State: under him, Conductors, or Magazine keepers at the different posts and Magazines: A principal Armourer at this place (Mr. Anderson would execute this Office as well as any man) and one or more Armourers at every place where arms are Stored to keep them in constant good order: and one or more Assistants to Visit the different Posts and Magazines to see that every thing is kept in proper Order. Indeed the Commissary in my opinion should occasionally Visit them himself. This Arangement would at first site appear very expensive; but I am convinced when every circumstance is duly considered, it will be found more likely to produce a Considerable saving: besides, if every person does his duty, an immense Advantage would arise from the Arms and Ammunition being constantly in good order and fit for action. Permit me [to] add that I do not know of one Magazine in the State at present, fit in any degree for the purpose. There is another circumstance I wou'd wish to mention to your Excellency. From experience, I am convinced there is the most urgent Necessity for an Officer of proper Marks visiting the different Posts, to inspect into the State of the Amunition, the Arms in the hands of the Soldiers, their dicipline cloathing &c. and to examine on the Spot into the accounts of the Expenditure, of every Article of Military Stores &c, that is sent to the post. For want of such a regulation, great Inconveniences have arisen, and among them a dangerous relaxation of dicipline.

I have the honor to be, your Excellys, mo: hble Servt.

I do not know but the Establishing a Continental Laboratory in this Neighbourhood, may induce an Opinion, that one for the State may probably not be necessary. If it cou'd be depended on that the Troops of the State and its Malitia cou'd always be fully Supplyed with every Article of Military Stores from the Continental Laboratory; one for the State might be need less; but it is to be feared, that would hardly be the case, and that Laboratory wou'd certainly be liable to be removed at the pleasure of Congress. If I may venture to give an Opinion in this case, I should think that the fixing a Continental Laboratory, makes very little difference, as to the Necessity of Establishing a Laboratory for the State in this Neighbourhood.

FC in War Office Letter Book (Vi).

To James Wood

The multiplicity of business which happened to be on us when your express came has occasioned his being delayed. . . . I enclose you letters to the commissioners of the circumjacent counties extending their powers to live cattle. It has been always necessary for the State and continent to lend interchangeably such articles as the one has and the other wants. . . . You can readily conceive that in this friendly intercourse it must have happened much more frequently that the State could lend to the Continent than the reverse. If you think proper to order as much leather to Col. Crockett as will make his pouches and lapposus[1] his order on our quartermaster here for special prepayment shall be complied with.

MS not located. Text (extracts only) from American Art Association sale catalogue, 30 Nov. 1927 (Henry Goldsmith Sale), lot 7; a 1-page A.L.S. Enclosure not further identified. Addressee identified only from the fact that the letter was part of a collection of letters to James Wood dispersed at this sale.

YOUR EXPRESS: This letter not located.

[1] Thus in printed text, obviously a misreading of the MS. It is possible that the word in the original was "leggings" (or "leggins"); it may even have been "moccasins."

To James Madison

DEAR SIR   Richmond July 26. 1780.

With my letter to the President I inclose a copy of the bill for calling in the paper money now in circulation, being the only copy I have been able to get. In my letter to the delegates I ask the favor of them to furnish me with authentic advice when the resolutions of Congress shall have been adopted by five other states. In a private letter I may venture to urge great dispatch and to assign the reasons. The bill on every vote prevailed but by small majorities, and on one occasion it escaped by two voices only. It's friends are very apprehensive that those who disapprove of it will be active in the recess of assembly to produce a general repugnance to it, and to prevail on the assembly in October to repeal it. They therefore think it of the utmost consequence to get it into a course of execution before the assembly meets. I have stated in my public letter to you what we shall consider as *authentic advice* lest a failure in that article should increase the delay. If you cannot otherwise get copies of the bill, it would be worth while to be at some extraordinary expence to do it.

Some doubt has arisen here to which quarter our 3000 draughts are to go? As Congress directed 5000 militia to be raised and sent to the Southward including what were ordered there, and these 3000 (which I think will be 3500) draughts are raised in lieu of so many militia, the matter seems clear enough. When we consider that a fourth or fifth of the enemy's force are in S. Carolina, it could not be expected that N. Carolina, which contains but a tenth of the American militia should be left to support the Southern war alone; more especially when the regular force to the Northward and the expected aids are taken into the scale. I doubt more whether the balance of the 1,900,000 Doll. are meant by Congress to be sent Northwardly, because in a resolution of June 17. subsequent to the requisition of the sum before mentioned they seem to appropriate *all* the monies from Maryland Southward to the Southern military chest. We shall be getting ready the balance, in which great disappointments have arisen from an inability to sell our tobacco; and in the mean time wish I could be advised whether it is to go Northward or Southward. The aids of money from this state through the rest of the present year will be small, our taxes being effectually anticipated by certificates issued for want of money, and for which the sheriffs are glad to exchange their collections rather than bring them to the treasury. Congress desired N. Carolina and Virginia to recruit, remount, and equip Washington's and White's horse. The whole has been done by us except as to 200 saddles which the Q. M. expects to get from the Northward. This draws from us about six or seven hundred thousand pounds, the half of which I suppose is so much more than was expected from us. We took on us the whole, because we supposed N. Caroline would be considerably burthened with calls for occasional horse, in the present low state of our cavalry; and that the disabled horses would be principally to be exchanged there for fresh.

Our troops are in the utmost distress for clothing, as are also our officers. What we are to do with the 3000 draughts when they are raised I cannot foresee.

Our new institution at the college has had a success which has gained it universal applause. Wythe's school is numerous. They hold weekly courts and assemblies in the capitol. The professors join in it; and the young men dispute with elegance, method and learning. This single school by throwing from time to time new hands well principled and well informed into the legislature will be of infinite value.

I wish you every felicity & am Dr. Sir Your friend and servt.,

Th: Jefferson.

P.S. You have not lost sight of the map I hope.

RC (Munson-Williams-Proctor Institute, Utica, N.Y.); endorsed with date. MY LETTER TO THE PRESIDENT: Dated 27 July, q.v. THE BILL FOR CALLING IN THE PAPER MONEY: The Assembly had passed this bill on 12 July only after a protracted struggle and with a clause suspending its operation until after a majority of the states had agreed to Congress' proposal (see note on Huntington's letter to TJ, 20 Mch. 1780). MY LETTER TO THE DELEGATES: Perhaps of this date, but not located. OUR NEW INSTITUTION AT THE COLLEGE: i.e., the curricular reforms effected by TJ at the College of William and Mary while serving on its board of visitors in 1779, and particularly the "Professorship of Law and Police," of which the first incumbent was George Wythe (TJ, Autobiography, Ford, I, 69-70; DAB, article on Wythe; R. M. Hughes, "William and Mary, the First American Law School," WMQ, 2d ser., II [1922], 40-3).

From Samuel Huntington

SIR   Richmond July 27. 1780.

According to the desire of Congress expressed in their resolutions of the 17th Ult. I shall endeavor to inform them what has been done by this state in consequence of the several resolutions there referred to.

1779.[1]
  Mar. 9. Recommendation to the states to compleat their respective quotas of 80 battalions.
1780.
  Feb. 9. United states to furnish their respective deficiencies of 35,211 men on or before the 1st. of Apr.
  May 20. The United states to forward their quotas of troops to join the Continental army.

The assembly at their session in May 1779. (being the first after the recommendation of Mar. 9.) desirous not only of furnishing their quota of troops then wanting, but to provide permanent means for keeping up the same by voluntary enlistments, passed an act for appointing a recruiting officer to be resident in every county, whose occupation it should be constantly to endeavor to enlist within his county souldiers to serve during the war. That the officer might be industrious he was allowed a premium of 150. paper dollars, then worth 12½ hard dollars for every man he enlisted: that the people within the county might encourage the recruiting service, they were to have credit in any future draughts for all the men their recruiting officer should raise: and the souldier was to receive a bounty of 750. paper dollars, then equal to 62½ hard dollars, the advantage of laying out his pay in the public store, at the hard money prices, and the other usual donations of clothes and lands. These encouragements however did not fully answer our expectations. The assembly therefore at their next ses-

sion in Oct. 1779 took supplementary measures for raising their
quota by endeavoring to re-enlist, for the war, their souldiers whose
times of service would expire within the ensuing year. This essay
also failed to produce their quota of men even as settled in the resolutions of Feb. 9. 1780. The Executive therefore immediately
ordered nearly the whole of their troops which had been reserved
for the particular defence of the state, to join the Continental army
to the Southward. That some idea may be formed of the proportion of their quota which this addition effected, I beg leave to refer
to the inclosed state No. 1. made out from the returns therein
referred to which have been made to me, their dates being from
Oct. 13. 1779. to Mar. 5. 1780, except as to the state troops
ordered into service as above, whose numbers are entered as they
marched the 2d. of May following.[2] To these may be added something upwards of 300 new recruits then engaged for the war, of
whom no return having been regularly made they are not entered.[3]
The assembly which met in May of the present year passed one act
for sending 2500 militia into the feild, which has been carried into
execution: and another for raising by way of draught one fifteenth
of the whole number of our militia, which after all probable deductions they count upon as 3000. men. These are to serve as regulars
till Dec. 31. 1781. and will be rendezvoused about the last of the
ensuing month.

1779.
    May 21. United states called on for a tax of 45,000,000 D. in
addition to what was called for 2d. Jan. to be paid by 1st. Jan.
next.
    Sep. 13. Circular letter, among other things stating the necessity
of paying into the Continental treasury the monies called for and
of adopting measures to bring their respective quotas of troops
into the feild early next campaign and provide the supplies necessary in the course of it.

By the resolution of Jan. 2. and 5.[4] 1779. Virginia was to pay
             for the year 1779.   2,400,000. Doll. =   720,000.£
             for the year 1780.   1,000,000.   =   300,000.
By the resolution of May 21. we
were to pay between
Feb. 1. and Oct. 1.   7,200,000.   = 2,160,000.

making in the whole   10,600,000.   = 3,180,000.
I beg leave to refer you to the inclosed No. 2. a very imperfect
state of our disbursements for the Continent. Whenever the books

of our Auditors shall be put under a proper course of examination many other articles of expenditure for the Continent will doubtless be found which have escaped the present hasty examination. By this state it appears that we have answered for the Continent since May 21. 1779. £4,404,440-13 = 13,681,368⅚ Dollars. There are still very considerable warrants out, which we have assumed; some of them partly unpaid, some wholly so.

1779.
  Oct. 6. 7. United states to collect and pay into the Continental treasury their respective quotas of 15,000,000 D. monthly from Jan. inclusive to Octob.
    9. Circular letter urging necessity of a punctual paiment of the quotas.
1780.
  Mar. 18. Sundry resolutions for calling in the bills in circulation and emitting new bills on certain funds.

The assembly which was sitting when the resolutions of Oct. 6. 7. came to hand, passed acts for increasing the public taxes and for borrowing money in order to enable them to comply with the requisition of Congress. The subsequent resolutions however of Mar. 18. 1780. as to the same money having rendered it necessary for the assembly to make a corresponding change in their measures, they passed at their late session the inclosed act No. 3. to which I beg leave to refer Congress, and to assure them at the same time that the moment I can receive authentic advices that five other states shall have acceded to the resolutions of Mar. 18. this act shall be put into a course of execution.

1780.
  May 19. The states from N. Hampshire to Virginia inclusive to pay into the Continental treasury 10,000,000 dollars in thirty days.

This requisition could not be complied with in point of time for reasons explained in my letter to your Excellency of June 30. 1780. With that we sent on in money and bills 1,430,239$\frac{8}{9}$ Dollars. We are still to send on 522,960$\frac{1}{9}$ Dollars to make up our whole quota of 1,953,200 Doll. unless the resolution of June 17. was meant to appropriate this requisition to the supply of the military chest in the Southern department. There is no other balance due from this state whereon that resolution can operate, as will be perceived by my observations on the resolutions of May 21. On this head I pray instructions from Congress.

1779.

Dec. 11. Virginia, Maryland, Delaware, Pennsylvania, N. Jersey, and Connecticut certain quantities of flour and corn by 1st. of April.

1780.

Feb. 25. United states to furnish their respective quotas of specific supplies mentioned.

It is not in my power to state with accuracy what is done towards furnishing these supplies. Extensive orders have from time to time been given out, which have been carried, and still are carrying into execution; but no returns are made which enable me to say what is precisely done. On receipt of the resolution of Dec. 11. notice was given to the Continental Q. Master that we should be ready to give him orders for the grain which was then coming in under an act of assembly which had laid a specific tax in grain. What would be the amount of this, was not then known. We since find that what we allotted to Continental use amounted to about 80,000 bushels of short forage. Part of this has been received and the rest we are collecting for the Continental Quarter master and Commissary, to the posts recommended by Genl. Washington. This no doubt is counted in part of the subsequent requisitions of Feb. 25. Large orders are out for the purchase of beeves. Considerable quantities of specifics have been furnished to the troops marching to the Southward. Our endeavors indeed have been much disappointed by the insufficiency of our revenues to answer these, and the calls for money for other purposes. Our ultimate dependance for supplying deficiencies in the articles of meat, flour, salt, short forage, and rum, is on the act No. 4. herewith transmitted.

A specific tax in tobacco is paiable on the 31st. day of December next. Of this about 3725 hogsheads were appropriated as a fund whereon to borrow money under the calls of Congress of Oct. 6. and 7. 1779. But another provision for this call being made by the act No. 3. these tobaccos remain unappropriated and of course free to be applied by the assembly according to the requisitions of Feb. 25. They will have brought in under the same specific tax as much as would make up the residue required. Whether they may think proper to change the appropriation of it for this purpose, or how otherwise they will furnish it, is for them to determine.[5]

It would have given me great pleasure to have been able to shew Congress that their requisitions had all been complied with in this state accurately in time, quantity and every other circumstance. It will doubtless occur that some of these requisitions were difficult in their nature, that others were new in experiment, and all of them on as large a scale as the people think themselves equal to. In states more compact, experiments, tho' new, and difficult, are made with promptitude, their defects soon discovered and readily supplied. In those of greater extent they are carried into execution with less vigor and punctuality, and the time for complying with a requisition expires frequently before it is discovered that the means provided were defective. The time necessary for convening the legislature of such a state adds to the tardiness of the remedy, and the measure itself is so oppressive on the members as to discourage the attempting it, but on the last emergencies. These and other considerations will readily occur to Congress, and will refer to their true causes any inaccuracies which may have occurred in the execution of their desires.

I have the honor to be with all possible respect Your Excellency's Most obedient & Most humble servt.,   TH: JEFFERSON

RC (DLC: PCC, No. 71, I); endorsed by Charles Thomson: "Letter from Govr. Jefferson July 27. 1780 Read Aug. 4." Dft (DLC), without complimentary close or signature; heavily corrected in the course of composition; a few of the corrections are recorded in the textual notes below. FC (Vi, photostat from Brit. Mus.: Add. MSS 38,-650, Governor's Letter Book, July-Sep. 1780, captured during Arnold's raid on Richmond, Jan. 1781). Tr (ViU); extract only.

This letter, drafted by TJ with much thought and care and then copied in his neatest hand for transmittal to Pres. Huntington, is an answer to Huntington's letter of 21 June 1780, q.v., enclosing a list of RESOLUTIONS OF CONGRESS, 1779-1780, concerning which that body, on 17 June, resolved to request information as to the different states' action. There were five enclosures in TJ's letter. (1) THE INCLOSED STATE NO. 1: This is a paper or papers, now missing, containing returns of the Virginia troops in service based on the returns accumulated by TJ at the end of 1779 and beginning of 1780, some of which are included in the present volume; see also textual notes 2 and 3, below, which provide a summary of these returns. (2) AN ACT . . . FOR RAISING BY WAY OF DRAUGHT: A 2-page printed law, preserved with TJ's letter in PCC, No. 71, I, entitled "An Act for speedily Recruiting the Quota of this State for the continental army" (Sabin

100325). (3) A . . . STATE OF OUR DISBURSEMENTS FOR THE CONTINENT: Called "the inclosed No. 2" by TJ and now missing, this was a fair copy of TJ's paper printed above under date 19 July 1780, as Payments made by Virginia for the United States. (4) THE INCLOSED ACT NO. 3: A MS copy, now missing, of an Act for calling in and redeeming the money now in circulation &c. (Hening, x, 241-54); see note on Huntington to TJ, 20 Mch. 1780. (5) ACT NO. 4. HEREWITH TRANSMITTED: A 2-page printed law entitled "An Act for procuring a supply of Provisions and other necessaries for the use of the Army," preserved with the letter of transmittal in PCC, No. 71, I. TJ's letter was read in Congress on 4 Aug.; the first enclosure was referred to the Board of War, and the fourth to the Board of Treasury (JCC, XVII, 691-2).

[1] In all the MSS these headings of resolutions of Congress, which are here printed in smaller type, appear in the form of marginal glosses.

[2] In Dft there follows a passage, later deleted, reading as follows: "Our quota by the resolutions of Feb. 9. was 6090. By this state it appears we had in Continental service 2029. engaged for the war, 395 till Sep. 30. of the present year: 1781 whose terms of enlistment were not specified in the returns but they were principally Genl. Scott's brigade who were to serve to the end of this campaign, and cavalry who are still

as full as they then were, making in the whole 4205."

3 In Dft there follows a passage, later deleted, reading: "So that our force in the feild was about 4500 men, being three-fourths of our quota, without counting 1876 whose times of service were to be expiring from the date of the 1st. return till Sep. 30. a considerable number of whom are still in service and who it is supposed may be set against" (sentence unfinished).

4 "and 5" interlined in RC and not found in Dft.

5 In Dft there follows a passage, later deleted, reading as follows: "The provisions and forage necessary for the support of the post at the barracks where upwards of 5000 rations a day I beleive and forage in proportion are necessary, (which by the resolution of Mar. 30. are to be credited on our account of specifics) when compared with the total ⟨Continental⟩ demand, will probably be found to make a considerable impression on the quantities called for from us. I make no doubt but in their requisitions a proper allowance for this will always be made."

To the Continental Board of War

Richmond July 28. 1780.

General Gates has written to me most pressingly for 1000 Tents. We have not a single Tent, nor is there stuff to be got within the State to make one. What we had were formerly lent to Colo. Finnie and have not been replaced. Our Militia went without a single Tent; and Porterfield's Detachment carried but few. I think it my duty to state this matter to you as I am satisfied the Southern Army cannot be supplied with this article but from you. Some other articles as falling axes &c. we shall supply with all possible expedition.

Tr (DLC: PCC, No. 148, I); extract only, in a clerk's hand, transmitted to the President of Congress in a letter from the War Office, 14 Aug. 1780, which is signed "by ord Ben Stoddert Secy." (same location) and endorsed: "Letter from Board of War Read Aug 14., 1780 Referred to board of war to report."

The Board of War reported on this letter 28 Aug., and Congress ordered that 1,000 soldiers' tents be sent to the southern army; see JCC, XVII, 730, 787.

From Samuel Huntington

Philadelphia, 28 July 1780. Circular letter to the state executives enclosing a resolve of Congress of 25 July authorizing the states furnishing wagons for Continental service to make adequate allowances for wagon hire until deputy quartermasters are appointed for the states.

RC (Vi); 2 p.; endorsed. FC (DLC: PCC, No. 15). Enclosure (Vi): copy of Congress' resolution of 25 July 1780, attested by Charles Thomson; printed in JCC, XVII, 665.

To Daniel Morgan and Other Late Commanding Officers of the Virginia Line

SIR   Richmond July 28th. 1780.

It has become necessary on the Settlement of our Account of Arms furnished the Continent to produce Vouchers for the Numbers. When our Regiments went first into Continental Service Most of them were full Armed, no Receipts or Certificates however were taken at the time. It remains that we supply this Omission in the best Manner we can, which is by application to the feild Officers who had command in the Several Regiments to certify as nearly as they can by Memory at what time their Regiment was taken on the Continental establishment, whether they were Armed by the State and carried those Arms into the Continental Service and how many they carried. Duplicate Certificates will be necessary the one to Send to Congress, the other to retain here in case of accident happening to the one sent. As you had Command in one of those Regiments, give me leave to ask the favor of you to send Certificates of the nature above described as to your Regiment, as exactly as your Memory will enable you to do. As we are now preparing to Send on Such an Account to Congress I shall be Much Obliged to you to avail Yourself of the first Safe Conveyance of the Certificates to me.

I am Sir Your very humble Servant,   TH: JEFFERSON

RC (NN); in a clerk's hand, signed and addressed by TJ: "Colo. Daniel Morgan. [*In another hand:*] Frederick County"; endorsed: "from his excellency the governor Virga to colo Morgan. 28 July 1780." This is one copy of a circular, of which a file copy is found in the Governor's Letter Book, July-Sep. 1780 (Vi, photostat from Brit. Mus.: Add. MSS 38,650), bearing the caption "The late commanding officers of regiments in the V. Line in Cont: service," and, at foot of text, "32 copies made out and forwarded." Another signed RC, no doubt sent to George Weedon since it is from the Weedon Papers, is in PPAP; it has at head of text the number "32." Another RC, in a clerk's hand but signed and addressed by TJ to "Colo. Theodoric Bland Prince-George" and endorsed by Bland, is among the papers deposited by Mrs. Kirkland Ruffin in ViU. Still another RC, signed but apparently not sent and without indication of addressee, is in MHi. An endorsed Tr of the copy sent to Edward Stevens is in DLC.

To George Muter

In Council July 28 1780

The board are of opinion that the hospital at Wmsbg. be discontinued. Mr. Ferguson may have the use of the house and garden for the care of them till further orders. Hospitals are to be kept up at York, Hampton and Portsmouth on the smallest Scale practicable. The Surgeon of the Artillery regiment may attend York and Hampton and that of the State garrison regiment reside at Portsmouth. It is thought necessary that a sufficient guard be kept in Wmsburg. to keep a centinel constantly at the Palace and Capitol to take care of them; under a commissioned officer. If any of these be sick Dr. Galt must be called in occasionally. The allowance of 30/. the day to Mr. Ferguson, of 25 Dollars the week to the nurses and of 10/. the day to Dr. Galt to be paid as stated by Colo. Muter are approved. TH JEFFERSON

Tr in Board of War Letter Book (MiU-C).

MR. FERGUSON: Perhaps Robert Ferguson, a surgeon's mate in the state navy, which was largely ashore at this time (Gwathmey, *Hist. Reg. of Virginians in the Revolution*; VMHB, I [1893-1894], 68; XVI [1908], 43).

From Charles Thomson

[*Philadelphia*] *28 July 1780*. Circular letter to the state executives enclosing a resolve of Congress of 27 July declaring that commissions for private armed vessels are hereafter to issue from the office of the secretary of Congress. Also enclosed are blank commissions to be filled out and substituted for those now in effect; bonds for them, as soon as executed, are to be transmitted to the secretary's office.

FC (DLC: PCC, No. 18A). Enclosures missing; the resolve of Congress of 27 July relating to commissioning armed vessels is printed in JCC, XVII, 674. This supersedes the method of issuing commissions authorized by resolutions of Congress of 2 May 1780; see circular letter of Thomson 20 June 1780.

List of Loan Office Certificates Sent to the County Lieutenants

In Council, July 29. 1780

The Governor is advised to certify to the Aud[itor] the number of tobacco loan offices certificates [sent] to the Lieutenant of each county under the [. . . .][1]

[Ea]ch such County Lt. is to be debited [for certificates?] accordingly certified as follows viz:

	Certif.	acts		Certif.	acts
P. George	33	13	Brunswic.	94	28
Dinwiddie	59	19	Sussex	57	19
Lunenburg	49	17	Southampton	68	22
Mecklenburg	76	24	Nansemond	58	19

	Certif.	acts		Certif.	acts
Norfolk	70	23	Berkley	85	26
Princess Ann	47	16	Hampshire	80	25
I. Wight	50	17			
Surry	30	12	Hanover	78	24
			Caroline	74	24
Chesterfield	66	21	Spotsylvania	52	18
Amelia	87	27	K George	32	13
Pr. Edwd.	44	16	Stafford	57	19
Charlott.	50	18	P. William	60	20
Halifax	80	25	Fairfax	60	20
Pittsylvania	57	19	Loudoun	148	32
Henry	63	20	Fauquier	87	27
Montgomery	49	17	Culpepper	135	39
Washington	75	24	Orange	46	16
Kentuckey	230	64	Louisa	55	18
Powhatan	28	11	Chas City	24	11
Cumberland	38	14	New Kent	32	13
Buckingham	49	17	K. Wm.	37	14
Bedford	120	35	K. & Queen	45	16
Rockbridge	49	17	Essex	50	17
Bottetourt	60	20	Richmond	40	15
Greenbriar	43	15	Westmorld.	38	14
			Northumbd.	55	19
Goochland	43	15	Lancaster	18	9
Fluvanna	35	20	Middlesex	18	9
Albemarle	70	22	Gloster[2]	67	21
Amherst	46	16	York	18	9
Augusta	119	35	Jas. City	18	8
Rockingham	40	15	Warwick	10	7
Shenandoe	70	23	Eliz.	13	8
Frederick	80	25	N. Hampton	40	14
			Accomack	90	28
				4044	

Two certificates viz. No. 2555. & 2556. were returned to the Treasurer as being supernumerary.

Tabular MS (DLC). The names of the counties and first column of figures are in a clerk's hand. The second column of figures, under "acts," is in TJ's hand, and a vertical line has been run through the entire second column (see below). The memoranda preceding and following the list are also in TJ's hand.

This list was compiled as a record of the tobacco loan office certificates sent to the various counties for the purpose of drafting troops for the Continental army according to an Act passed at the May 1780 session; see Memorandum of Executive Agenda, 19 July 1780; also Hening, x, 257-62; and TJ to County Lieutenant of Botetourt, 24 July 1780;

the last fully explains the procedure for handling and using these certificates. The second column of figures, deleted in MS, undoubtedly tabulates the number of copies of the Act forwarded to each county with the certificates; this was a temporary memorandum, and the data were eliminated before TJ had the list of certificates copied off to be sent, with his certification, to the auditor.

[1] MS mutilated; two or three words missing.
[2] The entries for Gloucester and the next four counties were enclosed in rectangular lines, the significance of which is not known.

To William Armistead

SIR   In Council July 31. 1780.

Till the appointment and qualification of a Commercial agent, we are forced to put on you all the duties of that office. You will perceive by the inclosed letters that a compromise as to the recaptured vessel may perhaps be obtained if the master has proper authority to compromise. This would be more agreeable to us than to go into a court of admiralty. I inclose you the letters to undertake the compromise. Whatever you agree to you will of course keep open for the confirmation of the Executive.

It is said a considerable quantity of goods have lately come to this place. You know what is wanting and how extremely we want to make up the half year's allowance of clothing for the officers remaining in the country. We also shall be glad to take as much as can possibly be bought on reasonable terms, of whatever will do for souldiers. Blankets are most especially and immediately wanting. If as many as 400 at least of these can be got in stores or elsewhere we wish it to be done immediately. Paiment may be made in either money or tobacco. I am Sir Your very humble servt.,

TH: JEFFERSON

RC (Vi). Addressed by TJ: "Mr. William Armistead Commissary of stores." Endorsed: "Governors letter & the necessary Papers relative to the Compromise wth. the Recaptors of the N. Hampton." In another hand: "Letter to Commercial Agent." Enclosures not further identified.

From William Campbell

[July 1780]

Immediately after my coming home from Richmond, I applied to the Commanding officers of Washington and Sullivan counties in North Carolina, to know if they woud furnish any men to proceed with the Virginians against the Chickamoggas, which they appeared very willing to do and as many as are necessary. But upon enquiring if they woud put them under my command the commanding officer of Washington told me that the feild officers of his county were to meet upon the 11th of this month (July) at which time they would consult on that particular, and let me know their determination. I have since waited without hearing a word from them on the subject, and from some hints that were dropped to me, I believe if they join us at all, they wish to do it as a separate corps under the command of their own officers. The feild officers of Washington (N:C.) have had in contemplation the carrying an expedition against the friendly towns and I was told had actually engaged five or six hundred men for that purpose and I [am] well persuaded the people of that county at this time wish more to destroy the friendly towns than the Chickamoggas, tho in this they are opposed by the officers of Sullivan. Shoud the Carolinians in this service be altogether independent of the Virginians or without receiving particular orders from the executive of their state, I fear they might do something that woud bring on a war with those Indians who I think wish to live in friendship with us. In such a situation I shoud be very unhappy and tho I might do everything in my power to prevent acts that woud be disagreeable to government, yet I might not altogether avoid the censure of those who did not know my situation. If I have the command of men that will be governed I am willing to be answerable for the[ir] Conduct.

Tr (NcDAH); extract only, without date, enclosed in TJ's letter to Gov. Nash, 12 Aug. 1780, q.v.

Though the writer's first name is not given, it was undoubtedly William (rather than his cousin Arthur) Campbell;

see TJ to William Campbell, 3 July 1780. HOME FROM RICHMOND: William Campbell was a member of the House of Delegates from Washington co.; the Assembly had adjourned on 14 July, hence this letter was probably written very late in the month.

To the County Lieutenants

SIR   [Before 1 August 1780]

Understanding that there are dispersed through the several counties of the Commonwealth a considerable number of draughts or substitutes heretofore raised [blank for the name][1] is instructed to attend to receive them at[2] your court house and will give you notice of the day on which he will attend. Our Eastern garrisons being extremely weak, we are under an absolute necessity of [rein]forcing them, and as I am very anxious to keep every burthen of that kind from our militia, let me entreat you for their quiet as well as for the safeguard of your country to exert yourself in collecting these men and also any others which may have been raised for the Eastern service and in having them punctually delivered at the time he shall appoint.

I am Sir Your very humble servt.

Dft (Vi); entirely in TJ's hand, with numerous deletions and corrections, the more important of which are noted be-

low. On verso, also in TJ's hand: "75. copies to be printed"; endorsed in an unidentified (probably later) hand:

"Govr. Jefferson to County Lieuts. relative to dispersed drafts. 1781."

In spite of TJ's notation on verso, there is no evidence that this letter was printed or even sent. It is printed in *Official Letters* (II, 380), without date, in a note on TJ's letter to Nathaniel Burwell, 1 Mch. 1781, as possibly belonging to that period. It is printed at this point in the present edition because the dates in the deleted matter (see note 2, below) suggest July 1780 as the more probable date and because during that month the governor and council were concerned with building up the defense of the eastern frontier under an Act passed in the May 1780 session; see Memoranda of Executive Agenda, 19 July 1780.

[1] Brackets in MS. TJ first wrote: "Major Quarles"; he then deleted it and substituted the present text in brackets.

[2] Following this TJ first wrote: "Petersburg on the 1st. day of Aug. next, at New London on the 6th. of the same month, at Staunton on the 12th., at Winchester on the 18th. and at Fredsbg. on the 24th."; he then deleted this passage and substituted the matter from here to the end of the sentence.

To James Callaway

SIR   Richmond August 1st. 1780

Your proceedings in sending a party immediately to apprehend those who are concerned in the conspiracy you describe, were very proper as is your keeping a sufficient guard for their security. Such of them whose offence amounts to high treason had better be tried as soon as possible before the examining court and sent down if found guilty. I mean this of the ring leaders, those who have enlisted others into the conspiracy, or who have accepted of commissions. The more ignorant and insignificant who give proofs of sincere repentance and may be useful as witnesses to convict the others had better not be put under prosecution. The reason is that if they be prosecuted and convicted of treason the Executive have no power to pardon; by keeping them out of a course of law the executive will have in their power to recommend them to the Legislature at their meeting in October to be the subjects of an act of pardon, if their conduct in the mean time shall be such as shews they merit to be so recomended. They must however be disarmed till further orders. You will doubtless be assisted in your proceedings by the attorney for the commonwealth in your county. I can therefore add nothing but exhort you to a continuance of the vigilance and decision with which you have begun to spare no means of securing the offenders by guards, assured that in so doing you will meet the public approbation which you have merited. I send you forty one blank militia commissions and a copy of the act for punishing crimes of a treasonable nature, but not amounting to treason. We have not in any instance undertaken to remit the penalty of the law obliging the delinquents of the militia to serve eight months conceiving that the exercise of this power shou'd be left with Genl. Stevens to be put in use at the time of their attending on him if circumstances shall justify it. It is therefore best that those from your county shou'd proceed to him immediately carrying with them your recommendation, which will doubtless have its proper weight in their favor with the General.

I am sir, Your most obedient servt., TH: JEFFERSON

FC (Vi, photostat from Brit. Mus.: Add. MSS 38,650). At head of text: "Colo: James Calloway, Bedford." Enclosures not found.

Callaway was lieutenant of Bedford co.; his letter to which this is a reply has not been found. THE ACT FOR PUNISHING CRIMES OF A TREASONABLE NA-

TURE: This was an Act passed at the May 1780 session to provide less severe punishment for crimes "inferiour in malignity to treason . . . yet injurious to the independence of America" than was stipulated in the Act for the punishment of certain offences passed at the Oct. 1776 session (Hening, IX, 170-1; X, 268-70).

From John Dodge

SIR   Fort Jefferson 1st. August 1780.

I think it my indispensible duty to lay before you a true state of our situation in this Country since my arrival which probably may throw some lights on the various reports which may reach you through channels not so well acquainted with its real wants as I am.

On my arrival at the falls of ohio Colo. John Todd gave me instructions to proceed to Kaskaskies in order to take charge of the goods when arrived which were purchased by Mr. Lindsay for this department with farther orders to divide them into two parcels one of which for the troops, and the other to be disposed of to our friendly indian allies, considering it better to sell them on reasonable [terms] than dispose of them in gifts. Horses and ammunition being articles much wanted for the troops I contracted for and received a quantity of lead and some horses before the arrival of the goods and having discretionary powers was constrained to accept of orders drawn on me for provisions which could not otherwise be obtained. Since the goods came into my hands, the troops and Inhabitants at this place not having received the expected supplies from Government, and being well assured that without some timely releif the fort and settlement must be evacuated, I was also constrained at divers times to issue quantities of the goods intended to be disposed of to our indian allies in order to furnish them with the means of subsistance. The few troops that are now here are too inconsiderable to guard themselves nor are the inhabitants much

better, notwithstanding they remain in great spirits in expectation
of releif from Government and have with great bravery defeated a
very large party of savages who made a regular attack on the
village at day break on the morning of the 17th ulto. Colo. Clark
has divided his few men in the best manner possible so as to preserve the Country. The apprehension of a large body of the enemy
in motion from detroit towards the falls of ohio has called him
there with what men he could well spare from this country, before
he had well breathed after the fatigue of an expedition up the
Missisippi, and Colo Crockett not arriving with either men or provisions as was expected, has really involved both the troops and
settlers in much distress, and greatly damped the spirits of industry in the latter which till lately was so conspicuous. I see no
other alternative from the present appearance of our affairs but
that the few goods I have left after supplying the troops must all
go for the purchase of provisions to keep this settlement from breaking up, and how I shall ever support my credit, or acquit myself
of the obligations I have bound myself under to those of whom I
have made purchases for the troops before the arrival of the Goods
I know not. Our credit is become so weak among the French inhabitants our own and the spaniards on the opposite side of the
missisippi that one dollar's worth of provision or other supplies
cannot be had from them without prompt payment were it to save
the whole country. By which you will perceive that without a constant and full supply of Goods in this quarter to answer the exigencies of Government nothing can ever be well effected but in a very
contracted manner.

I observe that the distance the settlers who come in general to
this country have to travel impoverishes them in a great degree.
They come at the expence of their all in full hopes and expectations
of being assisted by Government. Were these hopes cherished and
supplies of necessaries of all kinds furnished them in the manner
of the neighboring spaniards to be paid in produce such as might
answer for the troops or for exportation many good consequences
would be attendant. Emigrants on such encouragement would flock
to us in numbers instead of submitting to the spanish yoke. The
principal part of their new settlements would join us. All those
from the Natchez in particular only wait the encouraging invitation to remove themselves and their properties to our settlement,
preferring the mildness of our laws to the rigours of the [Spanish]
which they detest notwithstanding their great offers. Such encouragement would be a spur to industry which would never die. The

troops in a little time would be solely furnished in provisions by our settlers and in process of time a valuable trade might be opened with the overplus. These hints I beg leave to offer to your own better judgment conscious that if they are worthy of notice you will direct their proper uses.[1]

I have got a party of the friendly savages of the Kaskaskie tribe to hunt and scout for us. They are of singular service as the provisions in store are totally exhausted, and indeed their hunting tho' it may afford an useful yet is a very precarious supply.

As to the general disposition of those indians in alliance with us, it appears at present to be very peaceable, but as poverty is always subject to temptation, I fear their good intentions may be seduced by those who have it more in their power to supply their wants being well convinced of the necessity of having proper supplys for them which will not only keep them in our interest, but even afford us a very beneficial traffic.

The bearer of this travels to the falls of ohio thro' the wood. I am uncertain what the fate of my letter will be as I know he has a dangerous and tedious journey before him. However by the next opportunity I shall do myself the honor of writing your Excellency a few more of my observations, begging leave once more to remark the necessity of keeping at all [times] full supplies of goods in this remote quarter in order to forward the service of Government, encourage the settlement of the frontiers, supply our troops with necessaries, provision &c. and finally open a very profitable and extensive trade in little time.

Forgive the freedom of my remarks which you will please to do me the honor to correct.

I have the honor to be Your excellency's Most obedient and most humble Ser[vant],   JOHN DODGE

* Should your Excellency concur with me in [this] opinion I think some person who understood the circumstances of this country and the goods [necessary?] for this purpose ought to be sent on the occasion to purchase them. And as I purpose attending on Government as soon as the Goods on hand are disposed of which will be very soon, I shall be very happy in rendering any services in my power which your Excellency may think proper to entrust to my management.

RC (Vi); endorsed: "Mr. Dodge Augt. 1st 1780."

[1] The passage marked by an asterisk, for which there is no corresponding asterisk in the text, may have been intended as a postscript pertaining to the foregoing paragraph.

To Charles Lynch

Sir   Richmond August 1. [1780]

It gives me real concern to find that there is any one citizen in the [common]wealth so insensible of the advantages which himself and his posterity must [derive] from the present form of Governm[ent compared with what?] they can expect on a [return to] dominion under a foreign State, as to wish to return to it. I supp[ose] that [they have] maturely considered the matter before they took the dangerous step [they have ventured] on, that they have made up their minds and reasoning on the subject is vain. It remains to determine what shall be done. The most vigorous, decisive measures shou'd be continued for seizing every one on whom probable proof of guilt shall appear. Those who have been the leaders of the combination, who have enlisted others into it, or who have accepted of commissions from the enemy, shou'd be tried before an examining court for high treason, and if found guilty sent here for further trial. Those smaller offenders, who have barely assented to it, whose unequivocal proofs of repentance give assurance of a real change of opinion and who may be useful as witnesses to discover the whole plot, and convict the offenders it wou'd perhaps be better to disarm but not to put into a course of legal prosecution. A pardon is what in any other case might be granted them to qualify them as witnesses, but in the case of high treason the executive have no power of pardon: that rests with the Legislature who will not meet you know till october. Your activity on this occasion, deserves great commendation, and meets it from the Executive. The method of seizing them at once which you have adopted is much the best. You have only to take care that they be regularly tried after[wards. No expense of guards must be spared as far as] they shall be found neces[sary, and the] sooner those found guilty can [be s]ent down the better. The attorn[ey for the Common]wealth in your county will doubtless advise you in yo[ur proceedings to which I] can add nothing but an exhortation to continue the [energy with which you have] begun [to sup]press [these] parricides of their cou[ntry before they shall have] further Leisure to draw other innocent men into the same danger.

I am sir, with great respect, Your mo obedient servant,

TH: JEFFERSON

FC (Vi, photostat from Brit. Mus.: Add. MSS 38,650). At head of text: "Colo: Charles Lynch, Bedford." MS mutilated; passages in square brackets have largely been supplied from text printed in *Official Letters*, II, 147-8.

To George Washington

SIR   Richmond Aug. 2. 1780.

In obedience to the act of our assembly, a copy of which I now do myself the honor of inclosing you, I am, in the name of the General assembly, 'to request you to proclaim pardon to all deserters from the Virginia line of the continental army, who shall within two months after the publication of the act' (which took place about a week ago) 'return to their several companies, if on land, and if at sea, within two months after their return, and serve during the war, if so engaged, and if otherwise, shall serve two years over and above the time for which he or they engaged.' The capture of the Virginia line took place during the session of the assembly, and probably was not known when this act passed. This will account to your Excellency for the requisition to deserters to join *their companies*; and will no doubt point out to you the necessity of changing it in that part. Your Excellency having had experience of the efficacy of Proclamations can better judge what expectations may be formed from the one now asked: from that part of the act which makes it the duty of the militia captains to seek for deserters I do hope that very good effects will proceed.

I have the honor to be with every possible sentiment of esteem & respect Your Excellency's Most obedient & most humble servt.,

TH: JEFFERSON

RC (DLC: Washington Papers); endorsed: "Govr. Jefferson Augt 2. 1780 recd 26   ansd 29.—& 4 July—recd 26 Augt.   ansd 29." FC (Vi, photostat from Brit. Mus.: Add. MSS 38,650). Enclosure: printed copy of an Act the more effectually to prevent and punish desertion (Sabin 100326, in Washington Papers).

See Washington to TJ, 14 and 29 Aug. 1780.

From Horatio Gates

                              Camp at Mask Ferry, on the West Bank of
SIR   Pee-dee, 3d. August 1780

I have not received any Answer to the Letters I had the Honour to write Your Excellency from Hillsborough. Since I Joined the Army upon Deep River my Distress has been inconceivable of which, The inclosed Copy of a Letter of this days Date to Governour Nash will convince Your Excellency. I wish I could say the Supplies from Virginia, had been a reprovall to North Carolina. I am ashamed to say, their backwardness, rather Countenances, than disgraces, their Sister State. What can the Executive Councils of Both States believe will be the consequences, of such unpardonable Neglect? I will Yet hope Your Excellency is doing all in Your power to supply your half Starved Fellow Citizens. Flour, Rum, and Droves of Bullocks, should without Delay be forwarded to this Army or the Southern Department will soon want one to defend it; it has rained Furiously for several days and your Militia are still without Tents. Therefore I expect Desertion, and The Hospital will speedily leave General Stevens without any to Command. I wish I could present Your Excellency with a more pleasing Account of The Public Affairs this Way, but The Duty I owe the US, obliges me to represent Things truly as they are. Col. Harrison of the Artillery, has been severely Wounded in the Leg by a Kick from a Horse, which Splintered the Bone. He was left at Buffalo Ford, on Deep River, and I am this day inform'd is Worse than when I parted from him. As the Time of His Recovery is Uncertain, I beg the Favour of Your Excellency to acquaint Lt. Col. Carrington that it is my Orders he forthwith Join this Army. I must also request Your Excellency to Order, one Hundred Copies of the inclosed Proclamation, to be immediately Struck off, and sent me by The return of This Express.

I am Sir,   H G.

Dft (NHi); endorsed. Tr (DLC), with two minor corrections in TJ's hand. Enclosures: (1) copy of Gates' letter to Gov. Nash, same date, detailing the privations of his army (Tr in DLC); (2) draft of a proclamation by Gates to the inhabitants of South Carolina, dated at his headquarters on the Peedee River, 4 Aug. 1780 (printed in *Va. Gaz.* [D & N], 23 Aug.).

From Thomas Sim Lee

Annapolis, 3 Aug. 1780. Is informed that Stephen Mister, under indictment for high treason in Maryland, has escaped to Virginia, where he is confined to stand trial for treason against Virginia. Should the prisoner be acquitted in Virginia, it is requested that he be delivered for trial in Maryland. A transcript of the record is enclosed under seal.

FC (MdAA); 2 p. Enclosure not found, but see TJ's reply, 15 Aug. 1780.

To Benjamin Day

[SIR]   Richmond Aug. 4. 1780.

Being daily [called on] for tobacco, as well to pay debts as to make purchases, one of Mr. Armisteads assistants is sent to receive from you whatever tobacco notes are in your hands of public property, and for a *List* of whatever tobaccoes we have where the notes are not in your possession. Shoud the tobaccoes have been shipped or parted with in any instance and the notes retained be so good as to send a memorandum of it. The bearers receipt at the foot of a List of the notes you shall deliver him will be a sufficient voucher for you on settlement of your accounts. Be so good as to inclose to me at the same time a List of what you deliver him.

I am sir, Your very [humb]le servt.,   TH: JEFFERSON

FC (Vi, photostat from Brit. Mus.: Add. MSS 38,650).

To Horatio Gates

SIR   Richmond August 4. 1780.

Your several favors of July 19. 21. and 22. are now before me. I have enquired into the state of the Cartouch boxes which were sent from our magazine. The Quarter master assures me they were in very good order. I must therefore conclude that the 300 complained of by Genl. Stevens were some sent from Petersburg by the Continental Quarter master or that they were pillaged of the leather on the way, to mend shoes &c. We had hopes of getting 2000 from the Board of War, but we got only about 600 and they are said to be unfit for use. We are engaged in making bayonet-belts, which shall be forwarded. But it is extremely difficult to procure leather. The consumption of beef by your army will, I hope, remove the want of this article another year. I have ordered the 500 axes you desired with some tomahawks to be made. They turn out about 20 a day. About 100 will go on by the waggons Genl. Stevens sent us, which are now loading at this place. These waggons will carry some ammunition and spirit. A vessel with about 3000 stand of arms coming down the bay for the use of your army, was driven by privateers into Wicomico. We are endeavouring to get them forwarded either by land or water. The want of waggons will greatly retard them. What is to be done for tents, I know not. I am assured that very little duck can be got in this country. Whatever there is however will be produced under a commission gone out for that purpose. The duck you speak of as being in North Carolina cannot be procured by that state on continental account for the use of the army.[1] I communicated your orders to Colo. Finnie and to Colo. Buford and have directed proper applications for the repairs of the bridges &c. you mention. Arms are ready for Bufords, Daviess and Gibsons men. Gibson's are cloathed and wait only to be paid, which will be done within the course of a week. Clothing has been issued some time for the others, which is making up under the superintendance of Colo. Davies. They are utterly destitute of blankets, and I fear we shall be unable to get any. Brents infantry are but 30. and cannot be sent on without bringing on disagreeable disputes about rank between his officers and Gibsons. To silence these, the march of his men has been countermanded. Colo. Finnie informs me that Major Lees infantry has been sent back by special orders. We have ordered 243 horses to be purchased for Colos. White and Washington. The orders to Mr. Lewis to purchase beef in Carolina were given by the Continental commissary so long ago as last winter when it was not foreseen there woud be such a call for it in that country. Having no other means of conveying a Letter to him, I take the liberty of putting one under cover to you with instructions to him to discontinue his purchases in North Carolina and to furnish you with so much of the beef he has as you may think necessary. It wou'd be expedient for you to leave in his hands whatever quantity is not absolutely necessary for your army: as, depending on that, no other provision has been made for the post at Charlottesville and you know our country so well as to foresee that a post at which 5000 rations a day are issued cannot be fed by the purchase of the day.

We have reason to believe the French fleet arrived at Newport the 10th ult. but it is not certain. Admiral Graves with six sail of the Line is certainly arrived at New york.

I have the honor to be with the greatest respect Sir Your most obedt. & most humble servt.,   TH: JEFFERSON

RC (DLC); in clerk's hand, with complimentary close and signature in TJ's hand; endorsed: "Richmond 4th. Augst. 1780 Governr. Jefferson recd 28th. Augst." FC (Vi, photostat from Brit. Mus.: Add. MSS 38,650); at head of text: "General Gates."

1 FC reads correctly: "Cannot the duck you speak of . . . be purchased by that state"; see TJ to Edward Stevens, 4 Aug. 1780.

From Samuel Huntington

SIR   Philada August 4. 1780

By return of the Express who has just handed me your Despatches of the 27. Ulto I have the Honor to inform your Excellency that the several States of New Hampshire, Massachusetts, Connecticut, New York, New Jersey, Pennsylvania and Maryland have adopted the Act of Congress of the 18. of March and transmitted their Laws on that Subject to Congress some time since. These are all absolute except Pennsylvania, which contains a Proviso similar to that of Virginia now received.

The new Bills have been already forwarded to several of the States at their request, and a Letter from the Governor of Rhode Island informs me the Act of that State on the same Subject will probably pass and soon be forwarded to Congress.

I have the Honor &c.,   S. H.

FC (DLC: PCC, No. 15).
THE ACT OF CONGRESS OF THE 18. OF MARCH was that recommending the redemption of the old Continental currency at 40 to 1 and the funding of a new emission by state taxes; see Huntington to TJ, 20 Mch.; also TJ to Huntington, 27 July; TJ's Proclamation, 28 Aug.; and Charles Lee to TJ, 7 Aug. 1780.

To Samuel Lewis

SIR   Richmond August 4. 1780.

The great demand which has arisen for Beef in the western parts of North Carolina for the army there, has rendered it proper to discontinue your purchases in that state: as also to supply General Gates's army with so much of what you have as he shall call for. I am in hopes he will not find the whole necessary as the post in Albemarle, depending on your supply, is not otherwise provided for and it will take time to renew the purchases in another quarter. You will of course take proper receipts for all you deliver for either purpose, stating the weight precisely.

I am sir, Your very humble servant,   TH: JEFFERSON

FC (Vi, photostat from Brit. Mus.: Add. MSS 38,650).
This order was in compliance with Gen. Gates' request in his letter of 22 July, q.v.

To Edward Stevens

SIR   Richmond August 4th 1780.

Your several favors of July 16. 21. and 22. are now before us. Our Smiths are engaged making 500 axes and some tomahawks for General Gates. About 100 of these will go by the waggons now taking in their Loads. As these are for the army in general, no doubt you will participate of them. A chest of medicine was made up for you in Williamsburg, and by a strange kind of forgetfulness the vessel ordered to bring that, left it, and brought the rest of his shop. It is sent for again and I am not without hopes will be here in time to go by the present waggons. They will carry some ammunition and the axes and will make up their load with spirit. Tents I fear cannot be got in this country. We have however sent out powers to all trading-towns here to take it wherever it can be found. I write to General Gates to try whether the duck in north Carolina cannot be procured by the executive of that state on continental account; for surely the whole army as well our militia as the rest is continental. The arms you have to spare may be delivered to General Gates's order, taking and furnishing us with proper vouchers. We shall endeavour to send our draughts armed. I cannot conceive how the arms before sent coud have got into so very bad order; they certainly went from hence in good condition. You wish to know how far the property of this state in your hands is meant to be subject to the orders of the Commander in chief. Arms and military stores we mean to be perfectly subject to him. The provisions going from this country will be for the whole army. If we can get any tents they must be appropriated to our own troops. Medicine, sick stores, spirits and such other things we expect shall be on the same footing as with the northern army. There you know each state furnishes its own troops with these articles and of course has an exclusive right to what is furnished. The money put into your hands was meant as a particular resource for any extra wants of our own troops: yet in case of great distress you wou'd probably not see the others suffer without communicating part of it for their use. We debit Congress with this whole sum. There can be nothing but what is right in your paying Major Mazaret's troops out of it. I wish the plan you have adopted for securing a return of the arms from the militia may answer. I apprehend any man who has a good gun on his shoulder, wou'd agree to keep it and have the worth of it deducted out of his pay[, more] especially when the receipt of the pay is at some distance. What wou'd you think of notifying to them further that a proper certificate that they are discharged and have returned their arms will be required before any pay is issued to them? A roll kept and forwarded of those so discharged and delivering up their arms wou'd supply accidental losses of their certificates. We [are] endeavouring to get bayonet belts made. The state quarter master affirms the cartouch boxes sent from this place (959. in number) were all in good condition. I therefore suppose the 300 you received in such very bad order must have gone from the continental quarter master at Petersburg: or perhaps have been pillaged on the road of their flaps to mend shoes &c. I must still press the return of as many waggons as possible. All you will send shall be loaded with spirits, or something else for the army. By their next return we shall have a good deal of bacon collected. The inclosed is a copy of what was reported to me as heretofore sent by the waggons.

I am sir, Your very humble servant,   TH: JEFFERSON

FC (Vi, photostat from Brit. Mus.: Add. MSS 38,650). Another FC (or Tr) is in DLC, varying slightly in text. Enclosure not identified.

Stevens' SEVERAL FAVORS OF JULY 16. 21. AND 22. are all missing, unless that of the 21st is Stevens' letter to Gates; see Gates to TJ, 21 July.

From Samuel Huntington

Philadelphia, 5 Aug. 1780. The enclosed resolve of Congress of this date will inform TJ "that the recruits now raising in Virginia for filling their quota of Continental Troops are ordered to join the Southern Army as soon as possible."

RC (Vi); 2 p. FC (DLC: PCC, No. 15). Enclosure (Vi): copy attested by Charles Thomson, endorsed: "resol. of

Congress for sendg forces to the Southward"; printed in JCC, XVII, 699.

To James Maxwell

SIR   Richmond August 5. 1780.

You will be pleased to advertise the Tartar for sale at some future day as you propose, as also the Safeguard galley. The Council agrees to suspend the sale of the Lewis Galley till the Assembly shall declare their sense of the matter. We shall be very glad to purchase the ground you speak of above Hoods proper for making a wharf for public use, if the owner shall be willing to sell it for a reasonable price. You will be pleased to treat with him on that subject.

I am sir, Your very humble servt.,   TH: JEFFERSON

FC (Vi, photostat from Brit. Mus.: Add. MSS 38,650).

To John Mazaret

SIR   Richmond August 6th. 1780.

I am sorry to hear that so many muskets have got injured in their transportation. They certainly went from hence in good order.

As to the sending artificers from this place to repair them it is impracticable as we have them not to spare. Those we have, are employed daily in repairing arms, preparing tools and necessaries for the southern army, so that were we to send them away, you wou'd lose the fountain from whence your supplies are to come. I make no doubt but General Gates will find it necessary to order the establishment of an armourers shop in North Carolina for the repair of the arms of his troops which must be daily getting out of repair. Whether this shoud be at Hillsborough or where else he is best judge. This is the only method which occurs to me of having those repaired which are now in your possession. If no prospect of this should arise you may return them to us by some of the empty waggons and we will have them repaired and sent back if we can get waggons. But the waste of waggonage in this mode is so evident at a time too when there are so many other articles to transport in that way, that I cannot but suppose it will be thought better to establish a continental shop on the spot, or some where else convenient to the army. I wish to be informed from the proper officer whether any more musket cartridges will be wanting after the arrival of the present supplies, and how much more.

I am sir, Your very humble servant,   Th: Jefferson

FC (Vi, photostat from Brit. Mus.: Add. MSS 38,650).

From Charles Lee

Sir   Treasury Office August 7th. 1780

The Act of the Commonwealth of Virginia "for calling in and redeeming the Money now in circulation, and for emitting and funding new bills of Credit according to the resolution of Congress of the 18th. of March last," has been submitted to the consideration of the Board, and is ordered to remain in this Office for their Direction.

They are happy in informing you that the States of New Hampshire, Massachusetts Bay, Connecticut, New York, New Jersey and Maryland have actually and unconditionally approved of and acceded to the resolution of Congress of the 18th. March last. In consequence of which, Bills of Credit have been prepared and transmitted to each of those States, except Maryland which will receive a supply in a short time. The Acts of the several States are here and dated in the manner following—Connecticut 13th. April,

New Hampshire 29th. of April, Massachusetts bay 5th. May, New Jersey 9th. June, New York 15th. June and Maryland 28th. June.

I have the honor to be &c., CHA LEE Secy.

RC? (Vi); at head of text: "Copy"; endorsed: "Congress Papers respecting Loan of Money, &c. Oct. 1780." Presumably addressed to TJ in consequence of a request by the Virginia Delegates for official information of state action on the "new plan of finance" of 18 Mch. 1780. Accompanying the letter in Vi is a 2-page certificate, dated Philadelphia, 5 Sep. 1780, in James Madison's hand and signed by Joseph Jones, Madison, and John Walker, stating that Congress had received "authenticated Copies of Acts of the Legislatures of the following States, complying with their reso-lutions of the 18th. of March last relative to the public finances, viz." Maryland, New Jersey, New York, Massachusetts, New Hampshire; and "a Conditional Act of the Legislature of Pennsylvania." This document is printed in full in Burnett, *Letters of Members*, V, No. 418; see references there, especially to same, No. 314, where a dated list of state compliances is given from JCC.

See above: Huntington to TJ, 20 Mch.; TJ to Madison, 26 July; TJ to Huntington, 27 July; Huntington to TJ, 4 Aug. 1780.

Martha Wayles Skelton Jefferson to Eleanor Conway Madison

MADAM Richmond August 8th 1780

Mrs. Washington has done me the honor of communicating the inclosed proposition of our sisters of Pennsylvania and of informing me that the same grateful sentiments are displaying themselves in Maryland. Justified by the sanction of her letter in handing forward the scheme I undertake with chearfulness the duty of furnishing to my country women an opportunity of proving that they also partici-pate of those virtuous feelings which gave birth to it. I cannot do more for its promotion than by inclosing to you some of the papers to be disposed of as you think proper.

I am with the greatest respect Madam Your most humble serv-ant, MARTHA JEFFERSON

RC (NcDAH). At foot of text: "To Mrs James Madison." Enclosure missing. The original is one of the very few surviving examples of Mrs. Jefferson's handwriting, for after her death in 1782 her husband evidently destroyed all records of the brief but very happy period of his married life with her. These are the only MS records that, so far as the editors know, he ever did destroy, and he seems never to have alluded to the fact that he had done so.

The letter pertains to a colorful but little-noticed incident of the Revolution —the organization of "ladies' associa-tions" in the states from New Jersey to Virginia to collect money and make clothing for the ill-provided Continental soldiers. The movement began in Philadelphia under the leadership of Esther DeBerdt Reed, wife of Joseph Reed, president of Pennsylvania; correspond-ence between the Reeds, Washington, Lafayette, and others relating to it, to-gether with full records of the cam-paign for donations in Philadelphia, is printed in William B. Reed's *Life and Correspondence of Joseph Reed*, Phila., 1847, II, 260-71, 428-49; see also Wash-ington, *Writings*, ed. Fitzpatrick, XIX-

XXI, *passim*; Frank Moore, *Diary of the American Revolution*, N.Y. and Lond., 1860, II, *passim* (newspaper extracts). In Virginia, at Mrs. Washington's suggestion, Mrs. Jefferson was placed at the head of what would now be called the "drive" for funds. A public announcement of the plan, perhaps written by her with her husband's collaboration, is in *Va. Gaz.* (D & N), 9 Aug. 1780; it proposes that the collections be made at the churches throughout the state,

"at which sermons suited to the occasion will doubtless be preached by the several Ministers of the Gospel." At one time there was among TJ's papers an undated and very fragmentary return of the Virginia ladies' donations. It is printed in TJR, I, 459-60 (Appendix, Note D), where it is said to have been "inserted" among TJ's papers following his letter to George Washington, 2 July 1780. The original has not been found.

From George Muter

SIR [8 August 1780]

Inclosed is a Letter I send to the County of Gloster, with the Arms and Ammunition, if it meets with your E[xcellency's] approbation. The whole case Shipped on board the Dasher and she is ready to go down the river.

I have the honor to be &c.

Tr of letter and enclosure in War Office Letter Book (Vi); 1 p.

From William Preston

SIR Montgomery Augt. 8th. 1780

A most horrid Conspiracy amongst the Tories in this Country being providentialy discovered about ten Days ago obliged me Not only to raise the militia of the County but to ca[ll] for so large a Number from the Counties of Washington and Botetourt that there are upwards of four hundred men now on Duty exclusive of a Party which I hear Col. Lynch marched from Bedford towards the Mines yesterday. Colo. Hugh Crocket had Sent two young men amongst the Tories as tory Officers, with whom they agreed to Embody to a very great Number near the Lead Mines the 25th. Instant, and after securing that Place to over run the Country with the Assistance of the british Troops, who they were made to believe would meet them, and to relieve the Convention Prisoners. These they were to Arm and then subdue the whole State. A List of a Number of Officers was given to our Spies. This Deception gave our Militia an Opportunity of fixing on many of them who have been taken and I believe there are near sixty now in confinement. A number of Magistrates were called together from this County and Botetourt to examine Witnesses and enquire fully into the Conduct of those deluded Wretches In which we have been Engaged three Days; and I am convinced the Enquiry will continue at least a fortnight, as there are Prisoners brought in every hour and new Discoveries making. One has been enlarged on giving Security in £100,000 to appear when called for, some have been whipped and others, against whom little can be made appear, have enlisted to serve in the Continental Army. There is yet another Class who comes fully within the Treason Law, that we cannot Punish otherwise than by sending to the best Prisons in the Neighbouring Counties, untill they can be legally tried according to an Act of the last Session of Assembly, to which however we are Strangers, as we have not been able to procure a Copy of the Act and have only heard of it.

Some of the Capital offenders have dissappeared whose personal Property has been removed by the Soldiers and which they insist on being sold and divided as Plunder to which the Officers have submitted, otherwise it would be almost impossible to get men on these pressing Occasions. I would beg your Excellency's Opinion on this head; as also what steps you Judge necessary to be taken by the Officers and Magistrates with the Prisoners, other than what I have mentioned.

I am your Excellency's most obedt. Servt.

Dft (WHi); endorsed by Lyman C. Draper. The writer is identified by the provenance of the letter (Preston Papers) and by Digges' acknowledgment (see below).

Preston's letter was acknowledged by Lt. Gov. Dudley Digges, 17 Aug. 1780 (FC: Vi, photostat from Brit. Mus.: Add. MSS, 38,650). The letter arrived, says Digges, as TJ was about to "set out on a Journey home to take some little recess from Business after a very long and laborious confinement"; Preston's measures against the Tories are approved and commended. (Full text of Digges' letter is printed in *Official Letters*, II, 168.)

To Arthur Campbell

Sir   Richmond August 9. 1780.

Your Letter of July the 13th came to hand two days ago; we are well pleased with the spirited manner in which the insurrection of the tories has been suppressed. As to the appropriation of the plunder of the insurgents among the militia, who were engaged in the expedition, you are too well acquainted with our government not to know that no power of doing that is lodged with the executive. You can also judge whether if the appropriation is made by the people themselves and nothing said about it, there will be any danger of the former proprietors troubling them with actions. It would seem probable they will hardly ever hazard their lives by stirring such a question, unless they were really innocent, in which case it ought to be restored to them. This is all I think myself at liberty to say on this question. I am sir Your mo obedient servt.,

Th: Jefferson

FC (Vi, photostat from Brit. Mus.: Add. MSS 38,650).

Campbell's LETTER OF JULY THE 13TH has not been found. See William Preston's letter of 8 Aug. for another instance of officers permitting militiamen to plunder personal property of loyalists.

To the Clerk of Henrico County

Sir   In Council August 9th. 1780.

The Executive having thought it expedient to erect a magazine and Laboratory on certain Lands within your county of the property of Thomas Booth and Jno. Ballendine, lying near to the foundery, and having for that purpose had laid off and described by certain metes and bounds by the surveyor of the said county two acres and three quarters of the said lands of Thomas Booth, and three acres and one quarter of the said Lands of Jno. Ballendine. You are hereby required to issue a writ of ad quod damnum to be directed to the sheriff of the said county, commanding him to summon and empannell twelve able discreet free holders of the vicinage, no ways concerned in interest in the said Lands nor related to the owners or proprietors thereof, to meet on the said Lands respectively on a certain day to be mentioned in the said writ, not under five, nor more than ten days from the date hereof, of which notice shall be given to the respective proprietors of the said Lands, if they be found within the county and if not, then to their respective agents if any there be, which freeholders are to value the said lands so laid off as directed by an act of the late session of assembly intituled an act to enable the Governour to provide a laboratory and proper magazines for the reception of arms ammunition and other public stores. To prevent all mistakes be pleased to notify that the high sherif must attend in person at the execution of a writ of ad quod damnum, being of a judicial nature, cannot be done by a deputy. I am sir, Your very humble servant,   Th: Jefferson

FC (Vi, photostat from Brit. Mus.: Add. MSS 38,650).

To William Davies

SIR   In Council August 9. 1780.

Mr. Robertson receives a warrant for £2500, and an order for a tierce of rice from our stock. We have none of the other articles desired, but am in hopes he may be able to purchase them. As to the soap from the Barracks I imagine the requisition to the commissary general of issues would go more properly from yourself, as it is continental property. Shoud any difficulty occur in this, Genl. Muhlenburg will be here in a Day or two, to make this his head quarters, and will be able to remove the difficulty. Stuff for knapsacks shall be delivered you on demand. If there be as many blankets to be had in the state, they shall be got. We have taken measures to get them in most of the principal towns. For waggons you will of course make your requisitions to Colo. Finnie.

I am Sir with great respect your most obedient servant,

THO. JEFFERSON

P.S. I have also given Mr. Robertson an order for a barrel of molasses, if there be any in the country store.

FC (Vi, photostat from Brit. Mus.: Add. MSS 38,650).
MR. ROBERTSON: Presumably John Robertson, mentioned as assistant commissary of purchases in Jan. 1781 (*Va. Council Jour.*, II, 275).

To William Finnie

SIR   Richmond August 9th. 1780.

Congress having taken upon themselves the expresses established by this State from hence to the southern army, you will be pleased to undertake their superintendance. I suppose the expence is to be theirs from the 29th day of June when their vote was passed. If you find the horses already employed necessary to be continued you will be pleased to receive them from our quarter master at the prices they cost him, and to settle with him also for any monies he may have disbursed for services done by those expresses since that date. I am sir Your very humble servt.,

TH: JEFFERSON

FC (Vi, photostat from Brit. Mus.: Add. MSS 38,650).
For Congress' resolve of 29 June concerning the EXPRESSES, see JCC, XVII, 574-5; see also Huntington to TJ, 5 June 1780.

To Robert Forsyth

Richmond August 9th. 1780.

It being once settled that you are the person to receive the provisions from the commissioners of the provision law, I am perfectly satisfied on that head. I inclose you a List of the posts at which these provisions have been directed to be stored, and the counties which are at liberty to send to each post, as also twenty copies of orders on the several commissioners to make the delivery to you. I supposed one might be necessary to be kept at every post to be shewn to the commissioners or their agents who bring provisions. To have had the whole of these provisions brought to the few posts you mention woud have been too great a burden on the commissioners; who have, even under our arrangement a sufficiency of the commissarys and quarter masters duties put on them. I think that two or three posts on each of the great navigable waters cannot be complain'd of. The provisions received on the southern road, leading from Petersburg to Carolina, are to be carried to the southern army. Those at the barracks are for that post. Those at Staunton the warm springs, and Botetourt court house are for state purposes, and all the rest are to be sent to the northern army, except that we shall take some little for our garrisons at Richmond, York, Hampton, and Portsmouth from the posts convenient to those garrisons and for vessels fitting out. We will furnish you with such moderate sums of money as may be necessary for coopers, packers &c for these provisions. We have empowered the Commissioners in the neighbourhood of the barracks to take live cattle for that post. Colo. Lewiss beaves are some of them come in, but we are apprehensive not many more will come from him as General Gates has authority to take what he thinks proper of them for the use of his army. I agree with you that a sufficient means of transportation would have kept that post from suffering and that the Quarter master is blameable for not having a sufficiency; but I think also that if you had communicated a just share of the monies you have received to your deputy there much provisions might have been purchased in that part of the country and great transportation been thereby saved and that in this way also the post might have been kept from sufferance. I am sir, Your very humble servant,

TH: JEFFERSON

ENCLOSURE

In Council August 9. 1780.

Since the directions to the commissioners of the provision Law for delivering the provisions they shoud obtain to the continental quarter master or order, it having been made the duty of the Continental purchasing commisary to receive the same, the commissioners for the several counties are hereby authorized and desir'd to deliver their several articles of provision to the continental commissary of purchases or order, excepting always the commissioners of those counties who were to store their provisions at the Barracks in Albemarle, or who were directed to deliver them to the state commissary or quarter master. (20 copies delivered.)

FC (Vi, photostat from Brit. Mus.: Add. MSS 38,650). A copy of one enclosure (also Vi) is printed herewith; no copy of the other has been found.

To George Gilmer

SIR   Richmond august 9th 1780

I have spoken to Dr. Rickman on the subject of your Letter. He sais his medicines are just come to Petersburg and that as soon as they are opened, he will send a proper supply for you to this place, from whence it shall be forwarded by the first waggons from your post. Money he cannot furnish you because he has it not. I therefore send £2000 to the commissary to procure for the use of the hospital such meats &c as you shall direct out of the ordinary course of purchases. I also send you a tierce of rice for the use of the hospital.

I am Sir, Your very humble servt.,   TH: JEFFERSON

FC (Vi, photostat from Brit. Mus.: Add. MSS 38,650). At head of text: "Dr.   Gilmour"; the letter was obviously intended for TJ's old friend George Gilmer, serving at this time as a military surgeon (Blanton, *Medicine in Va. in the 18 Cent.*, p. 282, 404, &c.).

Gilmer's LETTER to which this is a reply is missing.

To Joseph Holmes

SIR   Richmond August 9th 1780.

I laid before Council your Letter, desiring that barracks might be provided for the Continental prisoners in your charge. Tho it seems highly necessary, and that they might probably be built of logs in the manner of those in Albemarle at no great expence, yet it is to Congress or to the Continental Board of war, to whom your application must be made, and from whom the order must come. Perhaps if their suit against Hobday for his breach of contract, is likely soon to bring them in money to answer this expence, it might be an inducement to them to order barracks on the cheap plan proposed.

I am Sir, Your very humble servt., TH: JEFFERSON

FC (Vi, photostat from Brit. Mus.: Add. MSS 38,650). At head of text: "Mr Jo: Holmes D. C. G. [Deputy Commissary General] Prisoners at Winchester." Holmes' LETTER to which this is an answer is missing.

From Samuel Huntington

Philadelphia, 9 Aug. 1780. Encloses a resolve of Congress of 7 Aug. "giving certain Encouragements to Officers and Privates that shall incline to serve as Volunteer Horsemen in the Southern Department, in the Army under General Gates."

RC (Vi); 2 p.; in a clerk's hand, signed by Huntington. FC (DLC: PCC, No. 15); at foot of text: "N.B. The like verbatim to N. Carolina, S. Carolina & Georgia." Enclosures (Vi): attested copies of (1) resolve of Congress, 7 Aug., concerning volunteer horse for Southern army; (2) resolve of Congress, 7 Aug., assigning balance of Virginia's $10,000,000 quota to the support of the southern army; both printed in JCC, XVII, 706-7.

To Richard Kenny

SIR   Richmond August 9. 1780.

We approve of your selling the corn wherever you find it will be most to the public interest to do so, but it is necessary that the money arising from the sale, or so much at least as is not requisite for expences, be laid out again in corn at the post, to be delivered for the use of the continent, as Congress, Genl. Washington, and the act of Assembly all concur in this direction. The Commissioner of King and Queen as well as all the commissioners is to apply to the court of his county, who are authorized by law to make him such allowance for his trouble as they think reasonable. This precise mode is pointed out by the act of assembly.

I am Sir Your most obedient servant, TH: JEFFERSON

FC (Vi, photostat from Brit. Mus.: Add. MSS 38,650); at head of text: "mr Richard Kenny fred:burg."

To the Officers of Joseph Crockett's Battalion

SIR   Richmond august 9th. 1780.

At the time the legislature past the act for raising four battalions for the defence of this commonwealth, and giving to the executive a power of appointing officers, it was foreseen that nothing like that number woud be raised. The executive has also seen the state by a hasty appointment of officers before their men were actually raised, run to the expence of paying regiments of officers which had no men. They have therefore on all late occasions, thought it their duty to avoid commissioning officers, till they shou'd have actual commands in being. Had they not pursued this plan in the instance now under consideration the state woud have had the officers of four regiments on pay, when there have never been men enough for half a regiment raised; the nomination of officers by the gentlemen, who were desired to nominate, was merely recommendatory and subject to be approved or rejected by the executive, and expressly said to be so in the letter to the county Lieutenant to preclude every claim of pay and other emoluments, which a final appointment might have given rise to. Where half the quota of men was never raised at all, the recommendation became a mere nullity and as if it had been never made; where the half quota was raised, that recommendation was brought into effect on the day the half quota was compleated, according to precise stipulation in the Letter. The executive used every precaution they cou'd to guard against what they thought would be improper, that is, the paying officers before they had men. Their Letter, under which the officers were recommended, was explicit in this point, and the gentlemen accepted of their appointments under this Letter. It is believed therefore they cannot now think it a hardship not to receive that which it had always been declared, was not to be received. These are the reasons which induced the council originally to determine against pay or other emoluments accruing before the half quota raised, and which still induce them to think the claim not founded in right. I cannot but flatter myself it will appear so to the gentlemen themselves, taking a view of the subject on a large scale and forming a general rule to be applied to all cases equally. I am with great respect, Gentlemen, Your most obedient servant,

TH: JEFFERSON

FC (Vi, photostat from Brit. Mus.: Add. MSS 38,650); at head of text: "The officers of colo Crockets Battalion." This was Joseph Crockett's detachment of frontier troops, who had been ordered in June to occupy posts on Sandy Creek and Licking Creek (Proceedings of Council concerning Western Defense, 8 June 1780).

THE ACT FOR RAISING FOUR BATTALIONS: Passed 26 June 1779 (Hening,

x, 32-4); see Orders for Defense of the Western Frontier, 23 July 1779. The Officers' protest to which TJ is replying has not been found; nor has the executive LETTER here referred to.

To William Rose

SIR   Richmond August 9. 1780.

Congress having taken upon themselves the expresses established by this state from hence to the southern army you will be pleased to turn them over to Colo. Finnie. All expences incurred since the 29th day of June are to be continental. If Colo. Finnie requires the same horses to be continued you will settle with him for them at the price they cost us, otherwise call them in. Whatever sum you debit Colo. Finnie with, you will be pleased to take a proper voucher from him, and deliver it to the executive. I am Sir Your very humble servt.,   TH: JEFFERSON

FC (Vi, photostat from Brit. Mus.: Add. MSS 38,650).
See TJ's letter to Finnie of this date.

To George Washington

SIR   Richmond August 9th 1780.

Agreeable to the resolutions of Congress of January 13. 1780, we have turned over to the Continental Commissary of Prisoners at Winchester forty prisoners of war, a roll of whom I now take the liberty of inclosing to your Excellency.

I have the Honor to be with all possible respect & esteem Your Excellency's most obedient and most humble servt.,

TH: JEFFERSON

RC (DLC: Washington Papers); in a clerk's hand, signed and addressed by TJ: "His Excellency General Washington Head-Quarters"; endorsed. FC (Vi, photostat from Brit. Mus.: Add. MSS 38,650). Tr (DLC). RC and Tr are accompanied by "A list of the Prisoners of War, sent from Williamsburg, and other places in Virginia by order of the Supreme Executive of that State, under the care of Lt. Thomas Bryant of the State Garrison Regiment, to Winchester, there to be delivered to the Continental Commissary of Prisoners [Joseph Holmes] at that place, agreeable to the

resolution of Congress of the 13th. of January 1780." The list is signed by George Muter, "C. W." (Commissioner of War), dated at Richmond 8 Aug. 1780, and was prepared with meticulous care, giving the forty prisoners' names, their type of service (land or sea), rank, corps, where taken, and when taken. (Most were taken at Vincennes, Feb. 1779, or "at Sea.") The names are as follows: William La Mothe (Captain of Volunteers), John McBeath, Antoine Bellfuille, Wm. Boulton St. Clair, Benjamin Woodhouse, Michl. Gordon, Daniel Potts, Henry Wair, Robert Cummins,

John Knowler, John Burgess, John Tunkins, Thomas Nugent, William Jackson, James Rule, Thomas Prus, Dugal Kennedy, John Collins, James Givins ("Governor Hamilton's Servant"), Timothy Kelly, David Martin, James Parkeson, Abel Langley, Reidan Vessey, Robert Briant, Benjamin Pickering, Christo: McGra, John Baiban, William Taylor, John Southerland, John Fraser, John Horn, George Spittall, Thomas Kipple, William Perra, Richard Welch, Thomas Egglestone, James Share, Luke Young, John Thomson.

To Charles Yates

Sir   Richmond August 9. 1780

We are much obliged by the attention you pay to the sale of public tobacco put into your hands. The sale was directed in order to raise a large sum of money for which Congress called on us, and which indeed ought to have been in Philadelphia some time ago. If you think the person offering to pay for the tobacco at the continental treasury in 35 days from last Tuesday will make his payment punctually in cash, and not by proposing discounts we woud approve of the sale you mention. Otherwise we wish you to sell in parcels or in any other way you think proper which may raise the money most expeditiously. No part of this money is to be paid to Colo. Finnie or Major Foresythe unless Congress in any future order shoud direct it explicitly, as they desired it for a very particular purpose. I am sir Your mo obedient servant,

T. JEFFERSON

FC (Vi, photostat from Brit. Mus.: Add. MSS 38,650). Enclosed in TJ's letter to Yates of 10 Aug. 1780, q.v.

To William Greene Munford

Sir   In Council august 10th. 1780.

I received your Letter, inclosing a state of the issues. As soon as you send the residue I will have it settled. Since my writing to you to receive the provisions collecting under the provision law, when I think I mentioned to you that I directed my Letter to you because Colo. Finnie and Major Foresyth told me the duty was within your line, it has been settled by proper authority to be Major Foresyth's duty, who accordingly writes me he shall be ready to receive the provisions. I have sent him proper orders for this purpose which relieves you from the burthen. I am sir, Your very humble servt.,   TH: JEFFERSON

FC (Vi, photostat from Brit. Mus.: Add. MSS 38,650). At head of text: "colo Green Munford"; this was William Greene Munford, Sr., of Charles City co., colonel and deputy commissary of issues (WMQ, 1st ser., XI [1902-1903], 260-1; *Tyler's Quart.*, III [1921-1922], 179-80; Heitman).

Neither of the earlier letters exchanged by TJ and Munford, here referred to, has been found.

To Charles Yates

SIR   Richmond august 10th. 1780.

Since writing the within, I receive information that Congress think to order the money which our tobacco is selling to raise, to be sent on southwardly. It becomes therefore necessary that the paiment offered for the tobacco in your hands should not be made in Philadelphia, but in Fredericksburg, or at our own treasury. I am sir Your mo obedient servant,   TH: JEFFERSON

FC (Vi, photostat from Brit. Mus.: Add. MSS 38,650). Enclosure: TJ to Yates, 9 Aug. 1780, q.v.

To Charles Alexander

SIR   Richmond august 11. 1780.

I inclose you the attorney general's opinion on the subject of importations from Maryland. We have lately appointed a commercial agent within whose particular line of duty it will be to provide spirit for the army. To him we shall refer the proposition of General Roberdeau to furnish whiskey. Since our Letter directing the delivery of your provisions to the continental quarter master, it has been made the duty of the purchasing commissary, to receive them on behalf of the Continent. We have accordingly furnished him with orders to receive. I am obliged to you for the information as to the flour in Loudon. The country below the blue ridge was divided into four districts and an agent, appointed to each to bring the grain to a particular post in it, or to make sale of it and buy more convenient. The grain of Loudon was to be brought to Alexandria, where such an agent was appointed. I hope he has notice of the situation of the flour in Loudon, and is taking proper measures to save it. I am Sir, Your very humble servant,   TH JEFFERSON

P.S. The necessity of taking the attorney General's opinion put it out of my power to send this by the return of post.

FC (Vi, photostat from Brit. Mus.: Add. MSS 38,650). Enclosure not found. OUR LETTER DIRECTING THE DELIVERY: Missing.

To William Finnie

SIR   Richmond august 12th 1780.

The inclosed extract of a Letter from Colo. Corbin of the eastern shore, will inform you of the danger, in which the corn there lies for which you had an order. The presumption that you would immediately remove it on receiving the order prevented us from taking measures for that purpose. This gives me occasion to observe to you that in all such cases we consider the grain as lying at your risk. I am Sir, Your very humble servant,   TH: JEFFERSON

FC (Vi, photostat from Brit. Mus.: Add. MSS 38,650). Enclosure not found. COLO. CORBIN: George Corbin, colonel of Accomac co. militia (Gwathmey, *Hist. Reg. of Virginians in the Revolution*).

To James Maxwell

SIR   Richmond August 12th. 1780

The enclosed Letter, giving a very unfavorable account of the situation of [the] Diligence and Accomack gallies, and pointing out the immediate necessity of interposition; I take the liberty of transmitting to you. If it shall be found that both gallies are deserted by the men, it may be worthy consideration whether it woud not be better to bring both to the western shore. I am sir, your very humble servant,   TH: JEFFERSON

FC (Vi, photostat from Brit. Mus.: Add. MSS 38,650). Enclosure not found.

To Abner Nash

SIR   Richmond August 12th 1780.

Frequent murders having been committed by the Cherokee Indians of the Chickamogga towns and some others who have associated with them, and seceded from the main body of the nation, we directed Colo. Campbell in the month of June[1] to raise 500 men from our counties of Washington and Montgomery in order to destroy those towns. He was instructed to use the utmost attention in distinguishing the friendly from the hostile part of the nation, and while he should chastise the latter to spare no assurance of friendship and protection to the former. Being informed at the same time that a similar expedition was meditated from your frontiers either under your authority or by the inhabitants themselves, we instructed Colo. Campbell to open a correspondence for the purpose of producing a cooperation against the common enemy. The inclosed is an extract of a Letter I received from him lately, which I take the liberty of transmitting to your Excellency, because if Colo. Campbell's information has been true, it discovers a disposition in the inhabitants of Washington county of your state to bring on a war with the friendly Cherokees. Without animadverting on the injustice of such a measure, it woud so much increase the difficulties with which our two states have at present to contend, that I thought it my duty to communicate this to your Excellency, as, shoud it wear any appearance of probability with you, it might suggest measures for further enquiry and for preventing an aggression if one shoud have been meditated. Our frontier counties being jointly and intimately interested in the transactions with the Cherokees, I hope I shall meet your Excellency's pardon for imparting to you any intelligence, coming to my ear, which may appear to threaten their peace: and I do it the more freely as I shoud myself most thankfully receive similar communications from you, of any thing on our side the line which might require the vigilance of our government.

I have the honor to be with every sentiment of esteem and respect, Your Excellency's most obedient and most humble servt.,

Th: Jefferson

RC (NcDAH); in a clerk's hand, signed by TJ. FC (Vi, photostat from Brit. Mus.: Add. MSS 38,650). Enclosure: extract of William Campbell's letter to TJ of uncertain date, printed above at end of July 1780.

1 "June" is written in TJ's hand.

To George Gibson

Sir   In Council August 14th 1780.

Your regiment having now received their pay and equippments for marching are put under General Muhlenburgs direction by an order of this day so that they will be considered as in continental service from this time: from him therefore you will be pleased to receive your future orders. I am Sir, Your most obedient servt.,

Th: Jefferson

FC (Vi, photostat from Brit. Mus.: Add. MSS 38,650). At head of text: "Colo Gibson"; this was no doubt George Gibson; see TJ to George Gibson, 11 June; to Muhlenberg, 14 Aug. 1780; also note in Official Letters, II, 164.

To Henry Lee

SIR   Richmond August 14th. 1780.

I this day received your favor of the 20th ult. It woud give us great pleasure to concur in any measure for consolidating into bodies[1] the several fractions of corps which we have in continental service, and we shoud be particularly pleased to have your corps made of our Line if it coud be done either by a transfer of individuals from other corps to that or by any other operation. The new Levies of which you desire that 30 may be alloted to you, are by the act of Assembly to be organized by General Washington. If you will be pleased to apply to him [for] any appropriation of that kind, which he shall direct, [it] shall be made as convenient to you as possible.

I am with great respect, sir, your most obedient and most humble servant,   TH: JEFFERSON

FC (Vi, photostat from Brit. Mus.: Add. MSS 38,650). The words in square brackets are conjectures for omissions by a careless copyist.

Lee's FAVOR of 20 July has not been found.

[1] The blank is in the MS.

To J. P. G. Muhlenberg

SIR   In Council August 14th: 1780.

Colo. Gibsons regiment being now equipped for service, I take the liberty of putting them under your orders. I understand many of them are sick. You will be pleased to judge whether it will be better to bring them to the hospital in Chesterfield or not. I am sir Your most obedient servant,   TH: JEFFERSON

FC (Vi, photostat from Brit. Mus.: Add. MSS 38,650).

To William Rickman

SIR   Richmond aug. 14. 1780

If you will be pleased to transmit me an account of the medicines furnished from the stores under your direction to the Fendant, while at York, with an acknowledgment thereon of satisfaction received from this state, I will see that you have credit for the same in your account with us. We wish this to be done, in order to put it in our power by paying off this account to idemnify them for an improper article of debit, which having been entered and paid before it came to our notice, we have no other means left of correcting. I am sir with great esteem, Your most obedient servt.,

Th: Jefferson

FC (Vi, photostat from Brit. Mus.: Add. MSS 38,650); at head of text: "Dr Wm Rickman Director General of the Contl shop."

To Benjamin Temple

Sir   Richmond August 14th. 1780

I this Day received from Mr. Walker of Congress your Letter on the Subject of Rum and other Refreshments for our Officers in the northern Service. As we could not justify the Expence of employing an Agent to the northward to furnish those Articles to the few Officers of ours remaining there, we have come to the Resolution of which I inclose you a Copy. It becomes necessary that we be furnished with a Return of those who will be entitled to these Articles. As we are altogether uninformed of them, I must ask the favour of you to make me this Return. It will also be necessary that some one should undertake to draw for and pay the refreshment Money to the whole. It will be very agreeable if you will undertake this Office and your Bills shall be duly honoured. Through the same Channel, I have also received a Letter from a Mr. Overton, with a State of Deficiencies of Cloathing founded on our Act of Assembly. No Funds that have ever yet been provided by the Assembly have enabled us to comply with that Act. All that these put in our power to do is to furnish a moderate Supply of Cloathing to the Officers. This was done generally to all those to the Northward in the Course of the last Winter, and it will not be in our Power to furnish another Supply till the next Winter.

I am Sir Your very hmble. Servt.,   Th: Jefferson

Tr (PHi) of missing RC. Addressed: "Colo. Benjamin Temple of Moylan's Dragoons." Endorsed: "Copy of a letter from Tho. Jefferson." FC (Vi, photo-stat from Brit. Mus.: Add. MSS 38,650). The letters mentioned in the text have not been found.

From George Washington

Sir   Head Qrs. Orange Town Augt 14 1780

I have been honoured with Your Excellency's favor of the 22 of July and with it's inclosure. With respect to appointing Officers for the Levies, Your Excellency I presume will have received before this, my Letters of the 18 and 22 Ulto, and by which You would find that I had arranged the matter, as far as the circumstances I was possessed of would admit, in consequence of your former application. But as the Officers of the 1 and 2 State Regiments were not included and they are complete, or nearly so, in their number, and your Excellency has determined that these Corps shall march to the Southward, I see no objection to their receiving a proportion of the Levies, and the less so, as it will make the officers of the Other Regiments, who are too few, more competent to their commands. I shall write a line to this effect to Genl. Muhlenburg today. The Levies I find by a Copy of a Resolution of Congress of the 5th Inst. are to join the Southern Army. It is certainly much more for the public interest that these Men are to serve till Dec. 1781 than for any shorter term, and I most earnestly wish, because I am certain the interest, if not the absolute safety and existence, of America demands it that the States would at once attempt to raise a sufficient number of Levies for the War. The expence in the first instance would be very little greater than the enormous bounties now paid for a five months service and in the end it would be found to be by far the most œconomical plan, both as to money and as to Men. To our Army's being levied on a short and temporary footing, the War has been protracted already to a period to which I am doubtful whether it would ever have otherwise extended; to this we may ascribe near all our other misfortunes and present embarrassments, and to this the loss of our liberties and Independence, if the fatal event should take place. This system of politics has brought us very low indeed and had we not been held up by Providence and a Powerful Ally, we must have submitted before this to the Yoke of bondage. A perseverance in the system may yet effect it. I beg Your Excellency to pardon this digression which the misfortunes we have suffered and the difficulties that now surround us have led me as it were to make involuntarily. I am happy to learn by Genl. Muhlenberg that several of our Troops have escaped from Charles Town, both as it releases them from captivity and as it adds Men of service and tried courage, without giving an equivalent for them, to our remaining force. The General mentions that he has heard 200 have returned, which I consider as a valuable acquisition; but he adds, that Many of them tho they were engaged for the War, conceive themselves discharged by reason of their captivity and escape and have gone to their homes. It is astonishing that they should have taken up such an idea, and I have directed him to pursue the most effectual measures to collect them. It is very unfortunate that the navigation of the Bay should be so interrupted and destroyed, and as I imagine that the Enemy's frigates are now drawn from thence, I would hope that means will have been found to drive away the smaller, pickerooning craft. Their continuing must be attended with great public inconvenience at least, and be highly prejudicial to the trade of Virginia and Maryland.

I informed Your Excellency of the arrival of the Armaments from France and also of Admiral Greaves's with Six Ships of the line on the part of the British. These added to the Ships the Enemy had before, give them a decided superiority at present over the French Squadron under the Chevr. de Ternay, and keep it blocked up at Rhode Island. We expect a reinforcement to the latter and hope it will be such as to turn the scale of superiority and that it will arrive before it is long and effect a junction, as upon the event our prospects and extensive operations must depend, should we be even so fortunate as to get matters in good train on our own part.

I have the Honor to be with very sincere respect & esteem Yr Excellency's most Obedt St.,   G W

P.S. From the information I have received that there are many Deserters in the State and also that many Soldiers who have been captured in the course of the War, and escaped from the Enemy, have gone to their homes and consider themselves as discharged from service, I have been induced to issue the inclosed Proclamation, which I request the favor of Your Excellency to have published in the News Papers.

Dft (DLC: Washington Papers); in hand of R. H. Harrison; endorsed. Tr (Vi), extract in clerk's hand of about the first half of the letter, with caption in TJ's hand. Enclosure (missing): Proclamation by Washington of pardon to deserters from the Virginia Line, dated from Headquarters at "Orange town," N.Y., 15 Aug. 1780; printed in *Va. Gaz.* (D & N), 6 Sep. and following issues; not in Fitzpatrick's edition of Washington's *Writings*. A revised form of this Proclamation was sent to TJ in a letter from Washington dated 29 Aug. 1780, q.v.

TJ's letter to Washington of THE 22 OF JULY AND . . . ITS INCLOSURE have not been located.

To Horatio Gates

SIR   Richmond Aug. 15. 1780

Your favor of Aug. 3. is just now put into my hands. Those formerly received have been duly answered and will no doubt have reached you before this date. My last letter to you was by Colo. Drayton.

I spoke fully with you on the difficulty of procuring waggons here when I had the pleasure of seeing you, and for that reason pressed the sending back as many as possible. One brigade of twelve has since returned and is again on it's way with medicine, military stores, and spirit. Any others which come, and as fast as they come, shall be returned to you with spirit and bacon. I have ever been informed that the very plentiful harvests of N. Carolina would render the transportation of flour from this state as unnecessary as it would be tedious, and that in this point of view the waggons should carry hence only the articles beforementioned, which are equally wanting with you. Finding that no great number of waggons are likely to return to us we will immediately order as many more to be bought and sent on as we possibly can. But to prevent too great expectations, I must again repeat that I fear no great number can be got. I do assure you how ever that neither attention nor expence shall be spared to forward to you every support for which we can obtain means of transportation. You have probably received our order on Colo. Lewis to deliver you any of the beeves he may have purchased. Tents I fear it is vain to expect because there is not in this country stuff to make them. We have agents and commissioners in constant pursuit of stuff, but hitherto their researches have been fruitless. Your order to Colo. Carrington shall be immediately communicated. A hundred copies of the proclamation shall also be immediately printed and forwarded to you. Genl. Muhlenburg is come to this place which he will now make his head quarters. I think he will be able to set into motion within a very few days five hundred regulars, who are now equipped for their march, except some blankets still wanting, but I hope nearly procured and ready to be delivered.

I sincerely congratulate you on your succesful advances on the enemy, and wish to do every thing to second your enterprizes, which the situation of this country and means and powers put into my hands enable me to do. I am Sir with sincere respect & esteem Your most obedt. & most humble servt., TH: JEFFERSON

RC (DLC). FC (Vi, photostat from Brit. Mus.: Add. MSS 38,650). MY LAST LETTER TO YOU: The last on record is that dated 4 Aug. 1780. On Gates' PROCLAMATIONS, see Gates' letter to TJ of 3 Aug.

To Thomas Sim Lee

SIR   Richmond August 15. 1780

On receipt of your Letter yesterday on the subject of Stephen Mister, I enquired of the Jailer and had from him information that such a person was Sent here from Accomack in June last, charged with high treason: that the Judges at the last court admitted him to bail, (the testimony probably appearing slight) binding him in a penalty of £100,000 himself and two sureties in £50,000 each for his appearance at the court in october next. Shoud he be cleared on trial I will see that due attention be paid to your Letter. In the mean time it will perhaps be best to say nothing as it might prevent his coming in.

I have the honor to be with every sentiment of esteem and respect, your Excellency's most obedient servant,

TH: JEFFERSON

FC (Vi, photostat from Brit. Mus.: Add. MSS 38,650).
YOUR LETTER: Lee to TJ, 3 Aug. 1780, q.v.

From William Lee

Paris, 15 Aug. 1780. Has repeatedly advised TJ of orders sent British officers in America to carry campaign into North Carolina and Virginia during coming months. If French squadron winters in Chesapeake Bay this will be prevented. In 1778 Lee was appointed by Gov. Henry commercial agent for Virginia in France. His mission for Congress in Germany prevented his serving Virginia effectively, but he authorized his brother [Arthur Lee] to act for him. A contract was made with Penet, D'Acosta Frères at Nantes to ship certain articles, but it was not complied with. "Some Cannon and other Articles were obtain'd *on the credit of the State for a considerable amount*, and were ship'd onboard the Ships Govr. Livingston, Mary Fearon and the Hunter, all three belonging to the house of Bondfield Haywood & Co. . . . who were the only people to be found in France that would charter their ships on the credit of the State." Two of the ships arrived safely in Virginia, "but to the great surprise of everybody" they returned with 300 hhd. of tobacco consigned to Penet, D'Acosta Frères & Cie. Another ship arrived in Bordeaux with 100 hhd. of tobacco for that firm, but still no orders have come to pay for the goods sent out last year by the Bondfield firm. Asks therefore that prompt payment be made. A debt is also due to the French ministry. The rising naval power of the northern states of Europe will force Great Britain to accept a different maritime code from that which she has tried to enforce on all Europe.

FC (ViHi); 2 p.; in Lee's Letter Book. At head of text: "Excy Govr. Jefferson. encd. to Bondfd. & Co. to forwd." MS dampstained, worn, and partly illegible.

From the Committee of Congress
at Headquarters

SIR   In Committee of Congress, Tapan, August 16., 1780

Inclosed you will receive copy of a letter of the 15th. Instant from the Commissary General, (see page 325).

Circumstanced as our Army at present is, the information contained in this letter becomes truely alarming. It requires the utmost attention of the Officers, together with all the necessaries, and even comforts of life, to render the service acceptable to recruits, and as the greatest part of the Army, at present consist of that class of men, if the time should unhappily arrive when we will be reduced to the necessity of putting them on half allowance of provisions, or probably have none to give them, the consequence must be, that those men unaccustomed to endure this species of distress, and not brought to that state of discipline, which can give their Officers that controul over them, they have acquired over the old soldiers, must revolt at the Idea of tamely submitting to a service, when divested as they are, of every other privilege the soldiers of all armies are entitled to, and are furnished with, they cannot receive even the means of subsistence—if reduced to the extremity I have just mentioned, and an irreconciliable disgust should once take place among these men, and desertions (or perhaps something worse) begin, the contagion, will beyond a doubt, pervade the whole Army: For it is not to be expected that the few old soldiers now remaining will be disposed to go on enduring the calamities they have so often experienced, when they find others equally bound with themselves and who have as yet had none of those difficulties to encounter manifesting so refactory a spirit, at what, they will conceive to be, trifles compared with their own sufferings.

Should such an event take place, the train of ruinous consequences that will inevitably ensue, must at once strike you so obviously, as to render unnecessary my entering into a detail of them. We do therefore earnestly request of you, Sir; that the Officers of your state, appointed to procure and forward the supplies, may be called on, in the most urgent manner, to give their utmost attention to the important business of keeping the Army regularly supplied with your quota of the articles that has been assigned to your state. As you must plainly perceive what embarrassments the least remission on the part of the States, or any of them, must

throw us into: For it must be remembered, that the monthly supplies, are no more, than what is barely necessary for the consumption of the Army in that time.

It is true that the Army does not at present amount to the numbers, on which the estimate was made, but as the men are daily
coming in, we are to suppose that the compliment of men will be
made up by the end of this month. But at all events it is incumbent
on us, to be provided to answer the largest demands that can be
made on us.

It is not only the immediate supply of the Army, that the Committee would wish to call your attention to, but likewise, the necessity there is, of the greatest punctuality in furnishing the supplies
agreable to the requisitions that have been heretofore made, to
prevent in future alarms, of this nature, and our giving you further
trouble on the subject.

I have the honor to be, with the highest respect Your Excellency's, Most Obt. Servant, In behalf of the Committee,

JNO. MATHEWS

FC (DLC: PCC, No. 11). At foot of text: "To the States from, New Hamp-shire, to Virginia—(Pensylvania except-ed.)." Enclosure: Ephraim Blaine to Committee at Headquarters, Tappan, 15 Aug. 1780 (FC in DLC: PCC, No. 11, to which the page citation in paragraph one of the present letter refers).

COMMISSARY GENERAL Blaine's let-ter reports the exhaustion of the Con-tinental magazines "in every part of the United States and no other method of procuring provisions [remains] but through the respective states."

Dudley Digges to Charles Magill

[*Richmond*] *16 Aug. 1780.* The governor being absent, Lt. Gov.
Digges acknowledges a letter addressed to TJ by Magill on 8 Aug. with
intelligence of "some successful advances on the enemy" by "our troops"
with the southern army. Is anxious to have further news of "their
progress and maneuvres."

FC (Vi, photostat from Brit. Mus.: Add. MSS 38,650); 1 p. Printed in *Of-ficial Letters*, II, 166-7.

Magill's letter here acknowledged has not been found.

Dudley Digges to Edward Stevens

Richmond, 16 Aug. 1780. The governor was yesterday just setting
out on a recess "for about 10 days," when dispatches from Stevens and
Gates arrived; that of Gates was acknowledged, and Stevens is referred
thereto for more detail. A brigade of wagons is on its way to Stevens
with medicines and military stores; when it returns it will be dispatched

again with bacon and spirits; flour, it is supposed, can be obtained in North Carolina, where a plentiful harvest is reported. Is pleased by news of advances on the enemy.

Tr (DLC); 3 p.; endorsed: "Copy of a Letter from Governor Jefferson [*sic*] to Edward Stevens dated August 16. 1780." FC (Vi, photostat from Brit. Mus.: Add. MSS 38,650); printed in *Official Letters*, II, 167.

Dudley Digges to Robert Forsyth

Richmond, 17 Aug. 1780. Acknowledges a letter to TJ (now absent) brought by Mr. Tate from Fredericksburg, 9 Aug. A warrant for £50,000 will be issued to Tate to enable him to confirm his contracts for meat for the Convention army. This is the last money that can be supplied for that army, at least until after the Assembly meets, because of the exhausting requisitions of the southern army.

FC (Vi, photostat from Brit. Mus.: Add. MSS, 38,650); 2 p.; printed in *Official Letters*, II, 168-9.

Forsyth's letter of 9 Aug. has not been found.

From the Committee of Congress at Headquarters

SIR   In Committee of Congress. Camp Tapan, Augt. 19th. 1780

When America stood alone against one of the most powerful nations of the earth, the spirit of liberty seemed to annimate her sons to the noblest exertions, and each man chearfully contributed his aid in support of her dearest rights. When the hand of tyranny seemed to bear its greatest weight on this devoted country, their virtue and perseverence appeared most conspicuous, and rose superior to every difficulty. If then, such patriotism manifested itself throughout all ranks, and orders of men among us, shall it be said at this day, this early day of our enfranchisement, and independence, that America, has grown tired of being free? Let us, Sir, for a moment take a retrospective view of our then situation, and compare it with the present, and draw such deductions from the premises, as every reasonable man, or set of men, ought to do. In the early stage of this glorious revolution, we stood alone. We had neither Army, military Stores, money, or in short any of those means which were requisite to authorize a resistance. The undertaking was physically against us. But Americans abhorred the very Idea of slavery! Therefore, reposing the righteousness of their cause in the hands of the supreme disposer of all human events, they boldly ventured to defy the vengeance of a tyrant, and either preserve their freedom, inviolate to themselves, and posterity, or perish in the attempt. This was the situation, and temper of the people of this Country, in the beginning of this controversy. At this day America is in strict alliance with one of the first nations of the earth, for magnimity, power, and wealth, and whose affairs are conducted by the ablest statesmen, with a prince at their head, who hath justly acquired the title, of the protector of the rights of mankind. A respectable fleet and Army of our ally, are already arrived among us, and a considerable reinforcement is hourly expected, which, when arrived, will give us a decided superiority in these Seas; the whole to co-operate with the force of this Country, against the common enemy. Another powerful nation (Spain) though not immediately allied with us, yet in fighting her own, she is daily fighting the battles of America, from whence, almost every advantage is derived to us, that could be produced in a state of alliance. An Army we now have in the field, part of whom, are veterans, equal to any the oldest established nations can boast. Our Militia from a five years War, are become enured to Arms. You have at the head of your Army a General, whose abilities as a soldier, and worth as a Citizen, stand confessed, even by the enemies of his country. Our officers of all ranks, are fully equal to the duties of their respective stations. Military stores are within our reach. Our money though not so reputable as that of other nations, with proper attention, we have reason to expect, will shortly emerge from its present embarressed state, and become as useful as ever.

Now, Sir, from a comparative view of our circumstances at the beginning, and at this day, how much more eligible, how much more pleasing, and important, must the latter appear, than the former, to every dispassionate man? Then, shall we leave to future generations to say, shall we at present commit ourselves to the world to exclaim, that, when Providence had benignly put into our hands the most essential means of obtaining by one decisive blow, the inestimable prize we had been contending for, it was lost; disgracefully lost; for want of proper exertions on our part? That avarice, luxury, and disipation, had so enervated the boasted sons of American freedom, that rather than forego their present ease, and wanton pleasures, they would tamely, cowardly submit to the loss of their Country, and their liberty, and become those abject slaves, which their generous natures, but a few, very few years before, would have revolted at the bear Idea of?

These reflections arise, Sir, from the extraordinary backwardness of some states, and great deficiencies of others, in sending the men into the field, that was required of them, near three months ago, and ought to have joined the Army fifty days past; and an apprehension that, from this torpitude, America has forgot she is contending for liberty, and independence, and the good intentions of our generous ally will be totally frustrated by our unpardonable remissness. Our former letters to the states, have been full on this very important subject, and we are concerned to be driven to the necessity of reiteration; but our duty to our Country, our respect for the reputation of the Commander in Chief of our Army, impel us to it: For a knowlege of the force that has been required of the states for the Campaign, and which was allowed to be adequate to an important enterprize, will induce a belief in our Countrymen, in the world, that it has been furnished, and they must stand amazed to see our Army inactive, and things not in that train for operation, which ought, in such a case, to be expected, especially at this advanced season of the year.

Again;—The force of our ally, now with us, and the shortly expected arrival of its second division, must clearly evince the utility of our Army's being put in a condition to undertake an enterprize, which if successful, must give a deadly wound to our unrelenting and ambitious foe. But what apology can be made, if, when the Commander in Chief of our Army, should be called on by the Commander of the forces of our generous ally, and informed, he is ready to undertake with him, whatever measures he shall think proper to point out, he shall be reduced to the cruel necessity of acknowledging his inability to engage in any enterprise, that can possibly redound to the honor, or reputation of the Arms of either nation? Sir, the reflection is too humiliating to be dwelt on, without the extremest pain; nay horror!

You must pardon us, worthy Sir, for the freedom with which we have now delivered our sentiments on this truly interesting subject. We flatter ourselves, great allowances will be made for our situation, when we daily have before our eyes specimens, of that want of energy in conducting our affairs, which must shortly, so far embarrass us, as to render all future exertions inadequate to the attainment of those great purposes, at which we aim. America wants not resources; we have men (independent of those necessary for domestic purposes) more than sufficient to compose an Army capable of answering our most sanguine expectations: And our Country teems with provisions of every kind necessary to support them. It requires nothing more than a proper degree of energy

[556]

to bring them forth, to make us a happy people. This we trust, Sir, the state over which you preside, will shew no reluctance in contributing her aid to, by taking such decisive measures, as will, without loss of time, bring into the field, the remainder of your quota of men, that have been required for the campaign.

The articles of provisions, forage, and teams, are no less important than men; but as the Committee had the honor of addressing you but a few days ago, on the subject of provisions, and the other articles, being so nearly allied with that, we will not intrude it on you, at this time.

Inclosed is copy of a letter from the Commander in Chief, of the 17th. Instant to the Committee; (see page 218). It will fully shew you the state of the Army, at this time, and how great a deficiency of men there is, to what their ought to have been before this day. However we hope, Sir, it will be no discouragement to your state, to using their utmost exertions, for furnishing the remainder of their troops, to join the Army as soon as possible; and that the idea of its being probably too late, before a sufficient force can be collected to promise a successful Campaign, will be totally banished; for policy, as well as interest, dictate to us, to be always prepared to take advantage of every favourable conjuncture, and it is impossible to say how soon such a one will present itself.

The Generals letter treats this subject in every other respect so fully, as renders it unnecessary to add more, than that, we have the honor to be, With the greatest respect, Your Excellency's, Most Obedt. Hble Servts., In behalf of the Committee,

JNO. MATHEWS

FC (DLC: PCC, No. 11). At foot of text: "To The States from New Hampshire, to Virginia—(Pensylvania excepted)." Enclosure: Washington to Committee, 17 Aug. 1780 (FC in the Committee's journal of proceedings, to which the page citation in the present letter refers; printed in Washington, *Writings*, ed. Fitzpatrick, XIX, 391-4).

From Philip Mazzei

[*Genoa, 19 Aug. 1780.* Mazzei's "Representation," written in 1784, states that he wrote in his dispatch No. 21, of this date, "that some money might be obtained there [Genoa] at 5 P. Cent. Interest, allowing three or four P. Cent for all charges, once for ever, which rendered the loan much cheaper to the borrower than one P. Cent Annually, as it had been offered for charges by Doctor Franklin" (Marraro, *Mazzei*, p. 91). No copy of this dispatch has been found.]

From Edward Stevens

SIR   Carolina Spinkes. August 20. 1780.

This is the first Opportunity that I have had since our unfortunate affair of the 16th Instant between Rugeleys Mill and Camdon to advise you of it. But as I am told Genl. Gates has got to Hillsborough presume he has done it before now.

Our Army moved from Rugeleys on the Night of the 15th Inst. at about Ten OClock with an intention to take post on a Creek about 6 Miles from Camdon, where the Enemy had collected all their force. They under the Command of Lord Cornwallas moved out of Camdon about 9 OClock and our advanced party's of Cavelry and Infantry fell in with each other about five Miles from Rugesleys between 10 and 12 OClock. This occasioned a halt of Both Armeys, as our meeting at this time was unexpected to both Parties; for from some Prisoners that was taken I am informed they moved out with an intention to attack us in our Encampment at Rugesleys and if what they say with respect to their numbers be true, General Gates has been greatly deceived. We formed and remained on the ground till about day Break when we advanced a few Hundred Yards and fell in with each other. I was flushed with all the hopes Possible of Success as our left where I was had gained such an Advantage over the Enemy in outflanking their Right; but alas on the first Fire or two they Charged and the Militia gave way, and it was out of the power of Man to rally them or even small Parties. This gave the Enemy an Opportunity of pushing their whole force against the Maryland line, who was not able to stand them long, and in a very little time the whole was in the utmost Confusion, and the greatest Panick prevailed that ever I had an Opportunity of seeing before; a more compleat Defeat could not possible have taken place without a General loss. All the Artillery which amounted to Eight or Ten Peices all the Ammunition the Military Chests, all the Waggons and Baggage of the whole Army is taken, in short picture it as bad as you possible can and it will not be as bad as it really is. We had to retreat through a Country of upward of a 100 Miles which may be truly said to be Inhabited by our Enemies and before any large party of ours could be Collected the Inhabitants rose in numbers, took and disarmed the cheif of our men. I am now where scarce a Friend is to be found. We are still in such a dispersed situation, that I cant pretend to say, what may be the loss of our men but with respect to the Militia, themselves, it matters not, for from their Rascally Behaviour they deserve no pity. Their Cowardly Behaviour has indeed given a Mortal Wound to my Feelings. I expect that near one half of the Militia will never halt till they get Home. And from what I have already seen I think I may venture to say that out of those who may be Collected, there will not be more than one fourth of them that will have their Arms, many of them you [may] depend have thrown away their Arms with an expectation of getting Home by it. I am doubtfull it will be a very difficult matter to Collect any number of the Militia of this State together again, tho' if any thing else could be done it had better, for Militia I plainly see wont do. If Virginia dont exert herself, I fear this State will be in the same Predicament as the South which I think is for a time firmly fixed to the British Government, and through Choise of a very great part of the Back Inhabitants. I am Just told that Col. Sumpter who was detached with 800 or 1000 men upon the Waterree the Evening of our defeat met with the same fate as we did. I am &c.

Tr (DLC); endorsed: "Copy of a Letter from Edward Stevens to Governor Jefferson dated August 20th. 1780."

From Timothy Pickering

Philadelphia, *21 Aug. 1780*. Having been appointed by Congress to "an important and at this time a most difficult and ungratefull office," that of quartermaster general, Pickering is obliged to request the governor and Council of Virginia to appoint a deputy quartermaster general for Virginia. Has consulted the Virginia delegates in Congress and requested them to recommend a proper person, but they could not; hence is obliged to call on TJ. Explains duties and importance of the office: "The Congress and the people at large expect a reformation of Abuses and retrenchment of expences. The deputy quarter master therefore should be an œconomist, and possess'd of a good Share of firmness." Encloses a warrant and instructions for the deputy appointed, and requests notification of action taken.

FC in Pickering's Letter Book (DNA: RG93). Enclosures not found.

Pickering had been elected to the office of quartermaster general to succeed Gen. Nathanael Greene on 5 Aug. 1780

(JCC, XVII, 698). He was expected to put into effect a new plan for conducting that sadly disordered department, which had been set forth in a lengthy report adopted by Congress on 15 July (same, p. 615-35). See TJ's reply, 6 Sep. 1780.

From George Rogers Clark

Louisville, August 22, 1780

By every possible exertion, and the aid of Colonel Slaughter's corps, we completed the number of 1000, with which we crossed the river at the mouth of Licking on the 1st day of August, and began our march the 2d. Having a road to cut for the artillery to pass for seventy miles, it was the 6th before we reached the first town, which we found vacated and the greatest part of their effects carried off. The general conduct of the Indians on our march, and many other corroborating circumstances, proved their design of leading us on to their own ground and time of action. After destroying the crops and buildings of Chelecauthy, we began our march for the Picawey settlements on the waters of the big Miame, the Indians keeping runners continually before our advanced guards. At half past two in the evening of the 8th, we arrived in sight of the town and forts, a plain of half a mile in width laying between us. I had an opportunity of viewing the situation and motion of the enemy, near their works.

I had scarcely time to make those dispositions necessary, before the action commenced on our left wing, and in a few minutes became almost general, with a savage fierceness on both sides. The confidence the enemy had of their own strength and certain victory, or the want of generalship, occasioned several neglects, by which those advantages were taken that proved the ruin of their army, being flanked two or three different times, drove from hill to hill in a circuitous direction for upwards of a mile and a half; at last took shelter in their strong holds and woods adjacent, when the firing ceased, for about half an hour, until necessary preparations were made for dislodging them. A heavy firing again commenced, and continued severe until dark, by which time the enemy were totally routed. The cannon playing too briskly on their works, they could afford them no shelter. Our loss was about 14 killed and thirteen wounded, theirs at least tripple that number. They carried off their dead during the night, except 12 or 14 that lay too near our lines for them to venture. This would have been a most decisive stroke to the Indians if unfortunately the right wing of our army had not been rendered useless for some time by an uncommon chain of rocks, that they could not pass, by which means part of the enemy escaped through the ground they were ordered to occupy.

By a French prisoner we got the next morning we learn, that the

[560]

Indians had been preparing for our reception ten days; moving their families and effects. That the morning before our arrival, they were 300 warriors, Shawanese, Mingoes, Wiandatts, and Delawares. Several reinforcements coming that day, he did not know their numbers; that they were sure of destroying the whole of us; that the greatest part of the prisoners taken by Byrd, were carried to Detroit, where there were only 200 regulars; having no provisions except green corn and vegetables. Our whole store at first setting out, being only 300 bushels of corn, and 1500 lb. of flour; having done the Shawanese all the mischief in our power; after destroying Picawey settlements, I returned to this post, having marched in the whole, 480 miles in 31 days. We destroyed upwards of 800 acres of corn, besides great quantities of vegetables, a considerable proportion of which appear to have been cultivated by white men, I suppose for the purpose of supporting war parties from Detroit. I could wish to have had a small store of provisions to have enabled us to have laid waist part of the Delaware settlements, and falling in at Pittsburg, but the excessive heat and weak diet shew the impropriety of such a step. Nothing could excel the few regulars and Kentuckyans that composed this little army in bravery and implicit obedience to orders. Each company vying with the other, who should be the most subordinate.

MS not located. Text from *Virginia Gazette* (Dixon & Nicolson), 4 Oct. 1780, with caption "Extract of a letter from Col. George Rogers Clarke, to his Excellency the Governour."

The chastisement of the Shawnee Indians in the vicinity of CHELECAUTHY (Chillicothe, Ohio) was an object TJ had long had in view; see his letters to Clark of 1 and 29 Jan. 1780. For a fuller account of this expedition, see Henry Wilson's narrative in *George Rogers Clark Papers, 1771-1781*, p. 476-84. PRISONERS TAKEN BY BYRD: Capt. Henry Bird, of the 8th or King's Royal Regiment, led a detachment of "green coat Rangers," with assorted Tory and Indian allies, on a successful expedition from Detroit against frontier posts in Kentucky in the early summer of 1780 (Wis. Hist. Soc., *Colls.*, XXIII, 252, note; XXIV, 185 and note).

From Johann Friedrich Specht

Irvin's House [i.e., Colle, Albemarle co., Va.], *23 Aug. 1780*. Acknowledges TJ's letter of 12 Apr., received 14 May. TJ's previous kindness in forwarding letters to Generals Phillips and Riedesel emboldens him to ask once more that the enclosed letters be sent. Names of addressees and nature of enclosures not identified.

RC (DLC); 1 p.; in a clerk's hand, signed "JF Specht Brig: Gener." TJ's letter to Specht, here acknowledged, has not been found.

To James Wood

Sir   Monticello Aug. 23. 1780.

I am satisfied that in the midst of a campaign and while N. York may perhaps be the object, Genl. Washington would not permit a convention officer to pass from his camp to N. York; nor can I suppose it proper such a one should see his camp as he might find means of communicating with the enemy: but in this you will do as you please. I see no objection to General Hamilton's sending an express, a citizen of the state. In such case I think he should go by Richmond to take letters from the Executive on the same subject with the General's. I enclose you my letter to him open, which please to seal when you shall have read it.

I know but three things in your power for the relief of the post: 1. to send an express to Colo. S. Lewis to hasten what beeves he can: 2. to quicken the contributions from the circumjacent counties: 3. to have the number of waggons increased so as to bring greater quantities of salted meats from below. To these we can add two others 1. to extend the powers for taking live cattle to such other counties as you shall desire: 2. to instruct Mr. Baker to send to you part of a purchase of beeves he has made. The latter I will propose to the council on my return; the former will await your application. If those who have contracted to sell meal to Mr. Tate should have so little concern at the public distress as to refuse performance for want of paiment on the precise day stipulated, I know of no remedy but to apprise the Commissioners of the provision law of their having the corn or meal to spare, and getting them to make seizure. Information since I came here from some individuals that the beeves they have furnished to the barracks have immediately returned home, suggest that an enquiry would be proper for you whether carelessness in the commissaries may have no share in producing the present distress; and whether due care is taken to fix on them the losses of this kind. I shall be obliged to you to inform me hereafter if any bad provisions shall come from below after I shall have had time on my return to notify the Commissaries at those posts.

I am Sir with great esteem Your most obedt. humble servt.,

Th: Jefferson

RC (Lloyd W. Smith, Madison, N.J., 1946); endorsed. Addressee identified from internal evidence. Enclosure: TJ to Brig. Gen. James Hamilton of the Convention army (no date indicated), not found.

From Edward Stevens

Sir   North Carolina Hillsborough August 27th. 1780

Agreeable to orders I am Just arrived here with all the Men that was Collected about Peadee. I wrote you from Spinkes about 70 Miles from this giving you an Account of our unfortunate affair of the 16th. It is not in my power to give you a more Satisfactory Account of the Disaster now than I did then, and as you have had an Opportunity of seeing Majr. McGill presume he has given you every Information that I could do. Great Numbers of the Militia has certainly gone home, it is not Possible to say what numbers of them was lost; I now furnish you with a Return of those we have Collected, having lost every Paper I cannot inform you of the Situation of the Brigade before the Action.

The total loss of my Papers renders every thing more confused than it otherwise would have been. All the Publick Money which was in the care of the Q. M. is lost except about   which was all that he could get off. We had expended little, or none of it, in any thing else but the payment of the £50 a man. By a return I now furnish you with you'll see that the Militia have lost nearly all their arms and Accoutrements. I am determined unless ordered to the Contrary that those who have lost them shall pay for them out of their Wages. This has been notified to them and is what they expect, tho' then it will by no means be adequate to the loss of the Arms. How they are to be again furnished or what is to be done with them must rest with you, And the sooner I can hear from you on the Subject the better. I believe it is Genl. Gate's Intention as soon as the Virginia Militia can be armed to send them forward to Guilford.

The Assembly of this State was to have set at this Place the 20th of this Month but they cannot yet make a House. What may be their Intentions with respect to their present situation of affairs I am a Stranger to. But make no doubt the Governor of the State has wrote you since our disaster. All the spare Arms that I left here in the care of Major Mazarett, by order of Genl. Gates, was delivered out to the Militia of this State. They have all lost their arms as Well as the V. Militia.

The Men under me are in a very distressed situation on Account of the loss of their Cloths, and if they are Continued in Service untill cold Weather they will be much more so. It is true from their Rascally Behaviour they deserve very little attention to be paid to their distresses but if no attempt is made to alleviate them, Bad Consequences may result from it, for when they return Home, they will make such imp[res]sions on the Minds of others that whenever there is a necessity of calling on the Militia again it may add greatly to the Difficulty of getting them out. Indeed Humanity requires that something should be attempted for their relief. From these Considerations I have obtained Genl. Gates approbation to send an Officer to every County with a list of the Mens Names to Collect from their Friends Cloaths and other necessaries for them, and as numbers of Waggons must be sent on from Virginia for the use of the Southern Army they can be handily sent out and if it meets your Sanction the business will go on, if not you'll Countermand it.

The Report of Colo. Sumpters Defeat has turned out to be too true. He had got near 60 Miles from Camdon with a Number of the Enemies Waggons but was persued by a Body of Horse and was Surprised while his Men were getting some refreshment.

Lord Cornwalles had his Baggage taken by a party of Militia as it was going from Charles Town to Camdon.

I am &c.

Tr (DLC). Endorsed: "Copy of a Letter from Edward Stevens to Governor Jefferson dated August 27. 1780." The enclosed return of troops has not been found.

To Dudley Digges, Joseph Prentis, and Meriwether Smith

GENTLEMEN   In Council August 28. 1780

The disaster which has lately befallen our Army under the command of Major General Gates calls on me for an immediate and great exertion to stop the progress of the enemy, if nothing can be done.[1] The measures most likely to effect this are difficult both in choice and execution. I wish therefore to have the advice of as full a board as can be collected before any thing is finally determined; and for this purpose must beg the favor of your attendance at the board on Friday next, when I propose to take the advice of Council on this subject.

I am Gent. Your most obedient servant,   TH: JEFFERSON

FC (Vi, photostat from Brit. Mus.: Add. MSS 38,650).
FRIDAY NEXT: 1 Sep. 1780.

[1] It is likely that the clerk, in making the FC of this circular letter, omitted a line or otherwise garbled what appears

here as the initial sentence, since it seems more probable that TJ would have written ". . . General Gates calls on me" than "The disaster . . . calls on me." If this assumption is correct, a conjectural reading of the beginning of the letter would be: "The disaster which has lately befallen our Army under the command of Major General Gates [is . . . . General Gates now] calls on me for an immediate and great exertion to stop the progress of the enemy, [and asks] if nothing can be done." The final clause in this passage ("if nothing can be done") is both ungrammatical and meaningless unless it is assumed that something has been omitted.

From Thomas Sim Lee

Sir   In Council Annapolis 28th. Augt. 1780

The alarming State of the Trade of Virginia and Maryland in the Chesapeake and above all, the extreme Difficulty and Hazard of supplying the Northern Army with Provisions from Virginia and the Southern Parts of this State, occasioned by the continued and encreasing Depredations of the Enemy have rendered the immediate Expulsion of them from the Bay, an Object of Magnitude to this Board. The Merchants of Baltimore have, on this Occasion, undertaken to second us with two armed Brigs and three large Barges, every of which we shall furnish sufficiently with Men, Arms and Ammunition. This Force will be accompanied by two fast sailing State Boats, to act as Tenders. We most earnestly solicit your Excellency to aid us in this service, so beneficial to the States in General and to Virginia and Maryland in particular. Only such Vessels of War which can be immediately equipped, can be serviceable, as the Success of this Attempt will depend in a great Measure upon the Secrecy and Expedition with which it is executed. We expect our Vessels will be ready to proceed down the Bay the 6th.[1] of next Month.

We are &ca.

FC (MdAA). The original was transmitted to TJ by Col. Robert Hooe of Alexandria (*Md. Archives*, XLIII, 267).

On the project of sweeping Chesapeake Bay free of loyalist privateers, see TJ to James Maxwell, 31 Aug. (in which a copy of Lee's letter was enclosed); TJ to Lee, 3 Sep. 1780; and several pertinent letters in *Md. Archives*, XLIII, 267, 269, 277, 283, 284, 290, 295-6, 311, 313.

[1] But both TJ's orders to Maxwell, 31 Aug., and his reply to Gov. Lee, 3 Sep., give this date as Sep. 9.

Proclamation of the Act concerning Redemption of Continental Money

[28 August 1780]

Whereas the General Assembly at their last session, passed an act intituled 'an act for calling in and redeeming the money now in circulation and for emitting and funding new Bills of credit according to the resolutions of Congress of the 18 of march last,' to which act they annexed a Proviso that the execution thereof shou'd be suspended until the Governor shou'd receive authentic advices that a majority of the united States of America therein described shall have actually or conditionally approved of, and acceded to the said resolutions of Congress of the 18th of march last; And whereas I have received authentic advice that a majority of the states so described have approved of and acceded to the said resolutions of Congress, I have therefore thought fit by and with the advice of the Council of state to issue this my proclamation hereby apprizing the good people of this Common wealth of the premises, and declaring that the suspension of the said act of the General Assembly of this Commonwealth, intituled 'an act for calling in and redeeming the money now in circulation and for emitting and funding new bills of credit according to the resolutions of Congress of the 18th of March last,' is removed, and the said act become absolute and of full force. Given under my hand and the seal of the Commonwealth at Richmond this 28th day of August in the year of our Lord 1780: and of the Commonwealth the fifth. THO: JEFFERSON.

Tr in Board of War Letter Book (MiU-C); copy of seal opposite signature. Printed in *Va. Gaz.* (D & N), 6 and 13 Sep., under date of 29 Aug.

This Proclamation was issued in consequence of the information received from Pres. Huntington that a majority of the states had agreed to Congress' "new plan of finance"; see Huntington to TJ, 20 Mch.; TJ to Madison, 26 July; to Huntington, 27 July; and Huntington to TJ, 4 Aug.; Charles Lee to TJ, 7 Aug. 1780; and the suspending clause in the Act as adopted, Hening, x, 254.

To James Adam

SIR   Richmond August 29. 1780.

Your Letter of the 18th instant came to hand yesterday. You seem in that to decline meddling with the grain in the counties of Westmoreland, Northumberland because the quantity is small and the commissions too trifling to be worth your attention; while you undertake the care of the grain in those counties, where the quantity is considerable. You will please to recollect that the charge we offered you, was an entire charge, and it was no part of our proposition that you shoud accept such parts of it as were beneficial and decline what was not so. You were to undertake or reject the whole. Your having begun the exercise of your office in a part, is therefore deemed as undertaking the whole: and we shall expect from you an account of the specific articles in all the counties put under your care. At the same time it is perfectly consistant with your instructions to transact any part of the business, whether distant or near by any other person whom you may think proper to employ at your own charge or without charge. Any grain which shall have been delivered to any continental quarter master or commissary will be considered as properly disposed of. The nett proceeds of your corn are to be invested in the same article at your post and delivered as mentioned in your instructions. If you will recur to the advice of council of may 29. you will find that all the enumerated articles except tobacco are to be collected at your post and there delivered to a continental quarter master or commissary; and as the wheat of which the flour is made is an enumerated article it is of course comprehended in the general order.

I am Sir, Your mo. obedient servant,   TH: JEFFERSON

FC (Vi, photostat from Brit. Mus.: Add. MSS 38,650). At head of text: "Mr. James Adam agent of the grain tax Alexandria."
Adam's LETTER of 18 July is missing.

To Evan Baker

SIR   Richmond August 29. 1780.

The distress of the post at the Barracks in Albemarle, for want of animal food being very great, you are desired after reserving 200 of the beeves you have purchased to go with Colo. Crocket, and 600 others to be sent when he shall furnish you with a proper escort, to send all the rest to the barracks in Albemarle. The two hundred it is supposed must be of the first you purchase; but that the 600 need only be ready when called for by Colo. Crocket, so that in the mean time it is hoped you may throw in a considerable number to the barracks. The necessities of that post require all the expedition you possibly can use. You are desired also to give notice to the commissary there from time to time of the supplies which he may expect from you and when they will be delivered.

I am Sir, Your mo. obt. servant,   TH: JEFFERSON

FC (Vi, photostat from Brit. Mus.: Add. MSS 38,650). A duplicate of this letter was enclosed in TJ's letter to Col. Wood of this date.

To the Commissioners of the Provision Law for Albemarle and Certain Other Counties

GENTLEMEN   In Council August 29. 1780.

As we understand that the post at the barracks in Albemarle is distress'd for meal, we hereby extend your powers as commissioners of the provision Law to wheat of the present crop, and desire that you will by virtue of your commission endeavour to furnish as speedily as possible such quantities of wheat or flour of the present crop as Colo. Wood shall apply to you for. We repeat our entreaties that you be very exact in taking vouchers. I have the honour to be with great respect Gentlemen Your most obedient servant,

TH: JEFFERSON

FC (Vi, photostat from Brit. Mus.: Add. MSS 38,650). At head of text: "The Commissioners of the provision Law for Albemarle, Orange, Culpeper, Louisa, Fluvanna, Rockingham [error for "Buckingham"; see TJ to Wood, and TJ to Commissioners . . . for Bedford, &c., both of the present date], and Amherst."

To the Commissioners of the Provision Law for Bedford and Certain Other Counties

GENTLEMEN   In Council August 29. 1780

As we have received information that the post at the Barracks in Albemarle is greatly distressed for provisions we hereby extend your powers as commissioners of the provision Law to live cattle, and wheat or flour of the present crop, and desire that you will by virtue of your commission furnish as speedily as possible such numbers of beeves and quantities of wheat or flour of the present year as Colo. Wood shall apply to you for. I inclose you for information as to the manner in which you are to proceed with respect to the beeves an extract from the act of assembly passed for that purpose. I repeat my entreaties that you be very exact in taking vouchers.

I have the honor to be with great respect gentlemen Your most obedient servant,   TH: JEFFERSON

FC (Vi, photostat from Brit. Mus.: Add. MSS 38,650); at head of text: "The Commissioners of the Provision Law of Bedford, Cumberland, Goochland, Shenandoah, Rockingham, and Augusta." The copy actually sent to the Goochland Commissioners survives (Vi); in a clerk's hand, signed and addressed by TJ: "The Commissioners of the Pro- vision law Goochland"; endorsed: "Augt. 29. 1780. His Excy Govr. Jefferson To Coms. Prov Law." Enclosure: extract of Act enlarging the powers of the Governor and Council (see TJ to Commissioners to Be Appointed by General Muhlenberg, this date). A duplicate of the present letter was enclosed in TJ's letter to James Wood of this date.

To the Commissioners of the Provision Law for Hanover and Certain Other Counties

GENTLEMEN   In Council august 29. 1780.

The garrison at   being likely to want provisions, we hereby extend your powers as commissioners of the provision Law to live Cattle, and desire that you will by virtue of your commission furnish such number of beeves as the state commissary shall apply to you for, taking proper vouchers for their delivery and transmitting them to me. I inclose you for information as to the manner in which you are to proceed, an extract from the act of assembly passed for that purpose. I have the honor to be with great respect Your most obedient servant,   THO: JEFFERSON

FC (Vi, photostat from Brit. Mus.: Add. MSS 38,650). At head of text: "The Commissioners of the Provision Law, of Hanover, York, Eliza City, Norfolk, Pr: Anne, Chesterfield and James City." At foot of text: "In the Lre to James City insert 'artificers and labourers at the shipyard' instead of the word garrison." In the margin: "Similar Lres written 26. octo: 80. to the comrs. of Caroline, N. Kent, C. City." Enclosure: extract of Act enlarging the powers of the Governor and Council (see TJ to Commissioners to Be Appointed by General Muhlenberg, this date).

To the Commissioners to Be Appointed by General Muhlenberg

SIR   Virginia In Council August 29. 1780.

You are hereby appointed a Commissioner under the 'act for procuring a supply of provisions and other necessaries for the use of the army,' but restrained specially to the procuring the articles enumerated in the said act, and live cattle, horses, waggons, and their gear, for their subsistance and transporting the baggage of the recruits raised under an act of the last session of Assembly. You are in the first instance if it can be done with any convenience to call on the continental commissaries or on the commissioners of the same provision law appointed in each county, in which you may be with the said recruits to furnish provisions for their subsistance during their stay at any place within this state, or their march through the same. Your receipt to such commissioners shall be to them a good voucher for the delivery of any articles you shall call on them for, notwithstanding any former orders we may have given, to deliver them otherwise. If neither the said commissioners, nor commissaries can furnish you with subsistance you are in that case, and in that case only to exercise the powers hereby given you within the counties before described. When you shall have passed with the recruits out of the limits of this state, or your attendance on them for the purposes of this commission, shall be dispensed with by any continental officer having authority so to do, this commission is to determine, and you are to transmit to me by safe conveyances duplicate Lists of all the Certificates or receipts you shall have given for articles hereby submitted to your seizure, specifying the name of the owner, the article seized, the price to be paid and time of seizure. That you may be informed of the manner in which you are to proceed in the execution of this commission you will receive herewith a copy of the provision Law, and an extract from another act relative to the particular articles of live stock, horses, waggons, and their gear, this last being the only article to which under the term 'necessaries' used in the act, we mean that your power should extend.

I am Sir, Your very humble servant,   TH: JEFFERSON

FC (Vi, photostat from Brit. Mus.: Add. MSS 38,650). At head of text: "To such Persons as General Muhlenburg shall appoint to act as Commissioners to supply the — — — new Corps." Enclosures: printed copy of Act for procuring a supply of provisions and other necessaries for the army (Hening, x, 233-7); extract of Act for giving further powers to the Governor and Council, section giving the executive power to seize cattle, horses, wagons, &c. (Hening, x, 311-12).

See similar appointments under dates of 8 Oct. and 2 Nov. 1780; all of them vary in important particulars.

To George Muter

In Council august 29. 1780.

The Board are of opinion that Lieutenant Bryant shoud be allowed ten dollars a day for performing the duty of a Provost Marshall.   TH JEFFERSON

Tr in Board of War Letter Book (MiU-C). The following words appear at the head of text: "The following returned to Colo. Muter commissioner of the War office, in answer to his Letter of August 28. 1780" (not found).

From George Washington

SIR   HeadQrs. in the vicinity of Fort Lee, August 29. 1780

I had not the honor till Three days ago to receive Your Excellency's Letters of the 4th Ulto. and 2d Instant.

With respect to your enquiry about sending Tobacco to New

York and Long Island for the Prisoners, it is not in my power to give You a decisive answer, but I am much inclined to think that it would not be permitted by the Enemy. I have heard by report that the matter has been mentioned, on some occasion, and it was said not to be admissible; and also that they would not allow a quantity of *Iron* or lumber to be sent from Maryland for their Prisoners. The more eligible way I believe will be for Your Excellency to pursue the Alternative You proposed, and to transmit the Money.

The good effects arising from Proclamations to bring in Deserters have not hitherto been very extensive; however I was induced from the reports I had received that there were many in Virginia, who would probably surrender themselves on a promise of pardon, to issue One, which I took the liberty of transmitting to Your Excellency in a Letter of the 14th Inst., which I presume will have come to hand before this time. I now inclose Your Excellency Another founded on the Act of Assembly transmitted in your Letter of the 2d, with an additional clause respecting Prisoners who have escaped from the Enemy and returned to their Homes. Your Excellency it is probable, will have witheld the former proclamation, if You have You will be so obliging, after filling up the blank left for inserting the date and manner of publishing the Act to which the present one refers, as to commit it to the Printer.

Our prospects of an operation against New York this Campaign have become very precarious and contingent. The Alliance Frigate has just arrived at Boston from L'orient, which she left the 9th of July, and we learn by her that the Harbour of Brest from whence the Second division intended to cooperate with us was to come was then blocked up by 32 British Ships of the line, and that the division had not sailed. We also hear through the same channel, that the combined fleet consisting of 36 or 38 ships of the line had sailed from Cadiz to open the Harbour and form a junction with several Other Ships of War, which were shut in. From this intelligence it is probable we shall soon be informed that a great naval combat has taken place between the Two fleets. I sincerely wish success to our Allies and I will not doubt it, but if it should be the case the arrival of the 2d division, making a reasonable allowance for their passage and delay afterwards for refreshing the Troops and Seamen will hardly be in time for us to commence so extensive an Operation as the one against New York, with a reasonable hope of carrying it through before winter sets in with severity. But this is not the only objection. The States remain most amazingly deficient in their Quotas of Troops and I have too much reason to fear it would be the case, if the remainder of the french force was here. This must be the consequence of our fatal system of short inlistments by which we have Armies to raise on the spur of the occasion and by the repetition of which the Patriotism and purses of the people have been so often and so far extended, that they are discouraged and go about to comply with any requisitions with an infinite indifference. And besides this failure on our part, I have the mortification to inform Your Excellency that for several days past, the Army has been almost entirely destitute of meat, on some days without a mouthful, and has drawn the chief part it has had from the scanty supplies in the hands of the Inhabitants in the vicinity of it, who had been impoverished before. These failures and these wants on our part blast almost every hope of successful operations in any case, and the latter produce a most licentious spirit in the soldiery. An Army should be well fed, well cloathed and paid and then You may expect almost any thing from it. This is a universally receivd maxim among military Men founded in the most obvious *reason*, but with respect to Our Army it does not operate in any one of these instances.

I have the Honor to be with very great respect & regard Yr Excellency's Most Obed St,   GW

P.S. If Your Excellency, when this comes to hand, should have published the Proclamation transmitted in my Letter of the 14th. and should still chuse to publish the Present One as being conformable to the wishes of the Legislature, You will be pleased to erase the last Paragraph respecting Soldiers who have been Prisoners and escaped, before it goes to the Press, as the former contained one nearly similar.   Yrs.

Dft (DLC: Washington Papers); in hand of R. H. Harrison; endorsed. Enclosure (not found): Washington's proclamation of pardon to deserters from the Virginia Line, issued in conformity with the Act the more effectually to prevent and punish desertion (printed in Washington, *Writings*, ed. Fitzpatrick, xix, 471-2, from a draft in the Washington Papers); for some reason, however, the revised form of the proclamation was not substituted for the earlier form sent by Washington to TJ on 14 Aug. (see under that date and also TJ to Washington, 2 Aug. 1780).

To James Wood

SIR   Richmond August 29. 1780.

I inclose you a duplicate of a Letter to Evan Baker to furnish supplies to your post, which perhaps you have an opportunity of forwarding, also Letters extending the powers of the commissioners of the provision law for the counties of Albemarle, Orange, Culpepper, Louisa, Fluvanna, Buckingham, and Amherst to wheat and flour of the present crop, and of those for the counties of Bedford, Cumberland, Goochland, Shenandoah, Rockingham, and Augusta, to wheat and flour of the present crop and to live cattle. You will see by them that it is left to yourself what use to make of them. These are the only measures, which occur to us as within our power to adopt for the relief of your post. The[y] consent if Cornet Brent should find it necessary to his private affairs to resign his commission that you should receive it, giving immediate notice that his place may be supplied.

I am sir, with great respect, Your mo. obedient servant,

TH: JEFFERSON

FC (Vi, photostat from Brit. Mus.: Add. MSS 38,650). RC (A.L.S., 1 p.) sold at American Art Association, 30 Nov. 1927 (Henry Goldsmith Sale), item 9; bought by F. W. Best; present location unknown. Enclosures: duplicates of TJ's letters to Baker, to Commissioners of Albemarle, &c., and to Commissioners of Bedford, &c., all of same date and all printed above.

To Charles Yates

SIR   Richmond August 29. 1780.

I received yesterday your favor of the 23rd instant. Your several proceedings therein mentioned are such as meet our approbation, and we will ask the favor of you, when you have received the money to avail yourself of any safe opportunity, which may occur of transmitting it here. The Council think the offer made by Mr. Maury not an equal one, and have therefore declined it, hoping you will be able to do better with the tobacco remaining. I am sir, with great respect, your most obt. servt.,   TH: JEFFERSON

FC (Vi, photostat from Brit. Mus.: Add. MSS 38,650).
Yates' FAVOR OF THE 23RD INSTANT has not been found.

From Horatio Gates

SIR   Hillsboro 30th. August 1780

The inclosed Pacquets for Congress and General Washington I send with flying Seals that you may peruse them; but I must request they may not be delayed; but sent forward with the utmost Dispatch to Philadelphia. Your Excellency will please to be careful to put the proper papers to each; in the right Cover, and Seal only the Cover you send them in to Congress. The Requisition addressed to Your State, I cannot but beleive will as soon as possible be furnished. This State Governor Nash assures me, will not hessitate a[n] Instant in supplying there Part. General Stevens informs me he has wrote frequently since our u[n]fortunate Defeat to Your Excellan[c]y. He marched from hence Yesterday, with what remained of your Militia (about 400). They are to be stationed for a Time at Guilford Court House. Four Hundred deserted in the last [two?] Days they were here. And the General is apprehensive, he shall very soon be left by many of those that went with him from hence. In Your Letter of the 12th Instant you mention 500 Regulars, being just fitted, and ready to march from Petersburgh. I wish they were here; but as yet I have no intelligence of their being upon the March. I beg Sir they may be expedited to this Place. I shall do my Utmost to procure the best Intilligence of the Motions of the Enemy of which Sir, you may depend upon my giving You the earliest Information in my power. I am &c,   HG

Tr (DLC); in a copyist's hand, with corrections by TJ (see note on Gates to TJ, 19 July 1780). Enclosures: Gates to Huntington and to Washington, 30 Aug.; transcripts of these letters are also in DLC; the originals were forwarded by TJ to Huntington on 3 or 6 Sep.

THE REQUISITION ADDRESSED TO YOUR STATE: Very likely the document printed below, Aug. 1780, under the title Supplies Required for Gates' Army, q.v. YOUR LETTER OF THE 12TH INSTANT: Not found.

To William Grayson

Sir   Richmond August 30th 1780

I happened to be absent from this place when Captain Joy brought your Letter of July 28. He saw some of the articles of military stores which we have and others he did not see but what he concluded to take or how to convey them I cannot find by any enquiry I have been able to make. I therefore take the liberty of inclosing you as good a state as I can at this time get of what we are able to furnish you with of the articles enumerated in your Letter, which if you chuse them shall be delivered to your order. I also take the liberty of offering you some military stores landed for us at Boston last summer of which an invoice is inclosed. We should expect to be allowed for them their cost in France (which is stated in the invoice) common freight and a reasonable insurance and that a credit to the amount should be allowed to your agent

Mr. Lee in the settlement of his account with you, who in order to furnish some stores on our application ventured to advance some continental monies in his hands, which no endeavours of ours have yet enabled us to replace in France. We have reason to believe the articles were well bought as we sent a special agent for the purpose and have found as to such articles as were brought here that his commission was faithfully executed.

I have the Honour to be Sir Your most obedient

TH: JEFFERSON

FC (Vi, photostat from Brit. Mus.: Add. MSS 38,650). At head of text: "The Honourable William Grayson, Board of War" (i.e., Continental Board of War). Enclosures not found. YOUR LETTER OF JULY 28: Not found.

From John Page

DEAR SIR   Rosewell Augt. the 30th. 1780.

I had not the Pleasure of receiving your Letter till I was setting out on my Journey to Mannsfield, which I did not finish in less than 4. Weeks. Had not this been the case, you should before this have received my Acknowledgement of the Receipt of [that] Letter, with many Thanks for the friendly Sentiments it contained; and of the [obli]gations I think myself under to the executive for the particular Attention they paid to my Recommendation of Messrs. Anderson and [Seawell.] I have not yet learned what Success they have met with in the Execution of their Office but from the Zeal and Alacrity with which they set out, I make no Doubt they will do ample Justice to my Recommend[ation.]

I was informed today that the Grain which had been collected and stored in this County under the Specific Tax was lying wasting and exposed in such a Manner that several Persons had made that a Pretence for not sending in their Grain and others had declared they [never?] would send in any and it is not long Since I heard a similar Complaint respecting Tobacco, which has been evinced to the [Commissioners?] under the same Act, but particularly that it had not been cropped as they [Favor?] it, so as to be fit for Market. I mention these Things Sir as possibly through [the inattention?] of the Commissioners, or from Some other Cause, this may have been the Case in some other Counties to the great Injury of the Commonwealth. [It] may be in your Power to give such Instructions to the Commissioners as may remove the Inconveniencies now complained of and may prevent a Repetition of them.

I most heartily condole with you on the Defeat of our Troops under General Gates. Did not the General venture on too boldly, relying too much on a Continuance of his former good Fortune? I had no idea of his pushing on so rapidly towards Chas. Town. I conceived that no Operations would have been commenced in So. Carolina till Novr. However, Gates certainly knew better than I can pretend to know, what was best to be done, and may have only failed, by relying too much on Militia. May not this Affair at last turn out to our Advantage? May it not rouse up our Northern States to exert themselves more vigorously and bring about the Reduction of N. York? You see I have presumed upon the Liberty you gave me, and should you think yourself bound to answer this Letter you must thank yourself for it. Our Compts. & best Wishes to you your Lady & Family. I am dr. Sir Yrs. sincerely,

JOHN PAGE

RC (DLC).   YOUR LETTER: Dated 12 July 1780, q.v.

From Edward Stevens

SIR   Hillsborough August 30th. 1780

Your Favours of the 19th. and 28th July and 4th August was all put into my hands the day before Yesterday. Where they have been all this Time I cant Account for. I also received the Lieutenant Governours Favour of the 16th Instant. The Ammunition Medicine Rum &c. arrived the same day and very timely. As there was neither Medicines nor Rum in the whole Army some of the first I have lent to the General Hospital who was suffering greatly for the want of it, and a part of the Rum I have lent to the Maryland Troops who deserve it more than the Militia. As this was done by request of Genl. Gates and the Consent of the Commanding Officers of the deferent Corps of the Virginians, I hant the least doubt but it will meet with your approbation.

As there is scarce a Waggon left with the Army, Those that brought on the Supplies I have permitted to be sent to Cross Crick for arms.

Your request with respect to furnishing you with Certificates of the Arms that the State furnished the Regiment I had the Honour to Command in the Continental Service I can easily Comply with. They did not Carry a single Muskett out of the State but were Armed in Philadelphia. Since my last of the 27 Instant, and by the

Inclosed return you'll see the whole Militia, Great Desertions has taken place. This has been in consequence of their being Armed and ordered forward again and this fully proves they never had any intention of rendering their Country Service. Judge what my Situation must be. My Pen cannot describe the trouble and Feelings I have had since I first took Charge of them. Such disgracefull behaviour I believe was never Instanced before. In these Cases the Innocent are generally involved with the Guilty. I must now rub through it the best way I can. I have sent Colo. Richardson on to lay matters properly before you. If every Man Deserts me I will remain till I hear from you on the Subject. With great respect I have the Honour to be Sir your most Obt Huml. &c.

Tr (DLC). Endorsed: "Copy of a Letter from Edward Stevens to Governor Jefferson dated August 30th. 1780." Enclosure not found.

To La Luzerne

SIR   Richmond August 31. 1780.

Your Excellency's Letter of the 27th of July should not have been so long unanswered, but that I have been for sometime past absent in the country. The generous aid from your Sovereign, the arrival of which is announced in your Letter, must have filled up the measure of gratitude felt by every American if there was room still left for an increase of grateful sentiment. With me there was none. I think these essential succours must impress the minds of all our people to the latest time, and that which affects the minds of all must forever influence the public councils and conduct, notwithstanding the too general prevalence of the interest of the day on the measures of nations. The interest of this State is intimately blended so perfectly the same with that of the others of the confederacy that the most effectual aid it can at any time receive is where the general cause most needs it. Of this yourself, Congress, and General Washington are so perfect judges that it is not for me to point it out. You can as well, and will as impartially judge whether the late disasters in the south call for any of those future aids so generously tendered in your Excellency's Letter. If their action in the north will have more powerful influence towards establishing our Independence, they ought not to be wished for in the south be the temporary misfortunes there what they will. Upon this head we resign ourselves to the care of your gracious sovereign and good offices of your Excellency, who sees us all with an equal eye.

Were it possible for this state to have an interest distinct from its confederates in any point, it would be in the bay of Chesapeake, the unavoidable channel of all our commerce. Our own attempts to establish a force on the water have been very unsuccessful; and our trade has been almost annihilated by the most contemptible part of the enemy's force on that element. I will acknowledge to you that I have thought (as I have also said to Congress) that their cares were not equally extended to us in this particular; and I should think myself justifiable in applying to the friendship of other powers for any naval aid, which could be given us separately. But I am far from asking it of you, who have done for us more than we could have asked before, unless to protect the Commerce of your own state with us might be an object worthy a stationary force of some sort. What is best for your nation, is best for us also, who so effectually participate of the benefits of all their successes. I shall avail myself of every opportunity of manifesting my sense of the obligations we are under to them in general, and particularly for the friendly disposition your Excellency has been pleased to show this state, and am with every sentiment of esteem and respect, Your Excellency's most obedient & mo. hble. servt.,

Th: Jefferson

FC (Vi, photostat from Brit. Mus.: Add. MSS 38,650).
La Luzerne's LETTER OF THE 27TH OF JULY has not been found.

To James Maxwell

Sir   In Council august 31. 1780.

I inclose you a copy of a Letter from Governour Lee. We are very desirous to afford all the cooperation in our power. The brig and such of the boats and two eastern shore gallies as can be equipped we wish to have sent. We therefore think it will be adviseable in you, laying aside all other business, to proceed immediately to hampton or what ever other place you can act from with most energy, and put every thing in motion to prepare for this expedition. Knowing the design of the state, of our bay, the force we can set on foot, and that prepared by maryland, you are desired to make your orders as to our part final and not to await my countersignature. Be pleased to inform me by the return of the express what aid we can yield, and what time, place, and other circumstances of rendezvous you think most practicable, in short what plan you mean to pursue that I may communicate the same to Governor Lee.

I am with great respect, sir, your mo. obedient servant,

TH: JEFFERSON

P.S. To Captain Maxwells Letter of Sepr. 2d. to Commo. Barron. That Commodore Barron may clearly understand our intentions I woud observe to him that the Maryland force is to sail from Baltimore on the 9th instant. If the vessels sail that day the Commodore will convoy them as he now intends, and if on his way up he shou'd meet the Maryland force he is to leave the provision vessels, and join the Marylanders; but if he should not meet them, he is when he has attended the provision vessels as far as is necessary to proceed to Baltimore, and there join the Marylanders. If the provision vessels should not sail before the 9th Commo. Barron is to go round to york and there lie ready either to join the provision vessels or the Marylanders which ever shall first appear. If the provision vessels first appear he will join them, and conduct himself as in the case first supposed. The object of this joint cruize is to clear the bay. Whether the cruize of our vessels is to be extended out of the capes, must be left to the discretion of the Commodore. If any future cruizes can be established in concert, we shall be pleased to cooperate in them so far as they shall have for their object the clearing Chesapeake bay or the vicinities of the Capes.

TH: JEFFERSON

FC (Vi, photostat from Brit. Mus.: Add. MSS 38,560). Enclosure: copy of Thomas Sim Lee's letter to TJ of 28 Aug., q.v.; see also TJ to Lee, 3 Sep. 1780.

To the Virginia Delegates in Congress

GENTLEMEN   Richmond August 31. 1780.

We agree to employ Mr. Dunlap according to his proposals inclosed in your Letter of the 15th instant except that we must adhere to our requisition that a complete sheet of his weekly paper shall be kept clear of advertisements, and reserved for intelligence, essays, &c., except that advertisements from the Legislature or Executive shall be put into the same sheet with the intelligence. The standing salary is to be fixed by the assembly, not by the executive, and we will recommend to them in settling it to consider the utility of the weekly paper and make liberal allowance for that over and above Mr. Dunlaps services in printing the public acts,

Journals, proclamations, advertisements, &c. and this we can venture to undertake will be done. As to money which you say Mr. Dunlap will want as soon as he comes we are not in a condition to make him any advances between this and the meeting of assembly but immediately after their meeting we have no doubt it will be in our power. I hope his press will be got to work before they meet. We will give him any aid in our power in procuring a house here, and if we should have any vessels coming from the head of Elk down the bay they shall take in any thing he pleases to have lodged here without charge. I wou'd recommend strongly to Mr. Dunlap that his manager here obtain the postmaster's office of the place. Besides that it will carry custom to his shop it will give him an exemption from militia duties which may otherwise be a considerable interruption. I have the honor to be with every sentiment of respect Gent., Your mo. obedient servant,   TH: JEFFERSON

FC (Vi, photostat from Brit. Mus.: Add. MSS 38,650).

The Delegates' LETTER OF THE 15TH INSTANT, with its PROPOSALS from MR. DUNLAP enclosed, has not been found. Obviously, however, they were made by John Dunlap (publisher of the *Pennsylvania Packet* at Philadelphia and until lately of *Dunlap's Maryland Gazette* at Baltimore) in reply to proposals from TJ transmitted by the Virginia delegates. In their recent session the General Assembly had authorized the executive "to engage with, and employ, at the publick expense, and for the publick service, a good and able printer, of firm and known attachment to the independence of the United States, who may be willing to bring a good and well provided press into this commonwealth" (Hening, x, 313). TJ very likely opened negotiations in his missing letter to the delegates of ca. 26 July 1780 (see TJ to Madison of that date). What happened afterward may be traced in a series of documents printed in Swem, "Va. Bibliog." pt. II, App. J. An agreement was quickly reached with John Dunlap and James Hayes (until recently the publisher of the *Maryland Gazette* at Baltimore and Annapolis, part of the time in partnership with Dunlap), who "shipped a costly printing apparatus with materials of great worth, on board the Bachelor, a ship belonging to Philadelphia, in order to begin a business in this commonwealth"; the ship was driven ashore by bad weather in Chesapeake Bay and taken by the enemy; and in November Dunlap and Hayes petitioned for compensation (JHD, Oct. 1780, 1827 edn., p. 28). On 14 Dec. the Assembly agreed to compensate the partners for their loss and to encourage them to try again (same, p. 49). Their equipment was this time sent by land (see Joseph Jones' letter to the Auditors, 16 Mch. 1781, and references there), and at length in Dec. 1781 the *Virginia Gazette or Weekly Advertiser* was established by James Hayes at Richmond (Brigham, *Amer. Newspapers, 1690-1820*). Dunlap petitioned for payment for his captured press as late as Mch. 1788 (Swem, as cited above).

To Timothy Pickering

SIR   Richmond August 1780.

At the request of General Hamilton I inclose you his state of the deficien[cies] of provisions furnished to the Barracks. I have no reason to doubt the truth of the state so far as it may be understood of animal food, for of meal they have [had] always enough; but in Justice &c. (precisely as the above letter to General Washington only leaving out your Excellency in inserting your board).

I have the honor to be with every sentiment of respect Your most obedient servant, TH: JEFFERSON

FC (Vi, photostat from Brit. Mus.: Add. MSS 38,650). At head of text: "Timothy Pickering esquire of the Board of war." Enclosure not found.

THE ABOVE LETTER TO GENERAL WASHINGTON: I.e., the letter immediately following the present one.

To George Washington

SIR   Richmond august. 1780.

At the request of General Hamilton I transmit you Letters from General Specht and himself, to Generals Philips and Reidesal, and a state of the deficiencies of provisions furnished to the barracks. I have no reason to doubt the truth of the state they send, so far as it may be understood of animal food, for of meal they have had always enough, but in justice to ourselves must assure you that the deficiencies have not been produced by any want of attention in the executive of this state. We have furnished to Major Foresythe the Continental deputy commissary in this department in money and credit near four million of dollars, since the first of November—£361,279.5.9. only. How much of this was between these two dates I am not informed. Had he furnished a sufficient proportion to his deputy there (instead of laying it out himself in the lower and distant parts of the country from whence the waggonage was difficult) the post might have been supplied from the neighbouring counties as has appeared by the plenty carried to their daily market, and on which they have been actually subsisted tho' at their private expence, to the continental deputy quartermaster of this department. We have paid since the first of January about five millions of dollars of which he has transmitted to his deputy at the barracks £130,000. only, with which sum he has not been able to transport provisions enough from the distant stations at which they were stored. Besides the above means provided by the executive of this state for the support of the convention troops and guards we employed persons to purchase a large number of beeves in the western parts of this state and north carolina. Unfortunately for the Albemarle post, the gentleman from whom the first supplies were expected had made his purchases about Charlotte in north Carolina, and we apprehend they have been most appropriated by the two contending armies lately in that quarter. We have now empowered the commissioners of the provision law in the several counties round about the barracks to take under that law provisions for the support of the post. This and the purchases of beeves before-mentioned will be our principal dependence for some time to come and I hope they will be sufficient. I thought it necessary to mention to your Excellency these circumstances that you might be able to form a judgment of the causes from which these deficiencies have arisen. We shall omit nothing in our power for the support of the troops, but I must apprise you that our means of supply are not at present what they have been; so that they may perhaps suffer, tho they shall not if we can prevent it. It may be proper to observe that the Convention troops fare precisely as our own regiments of guards there the same deficiencies being due to these. I have the honor to be with all possible respect & esteem Your Excellency's most obedient & hble servant, TH: JEFFERSON

FC (Vi, photostat from Brit. Mus.: Add. MSS 38,650), dated as above. On 11 Sep. 1780 Washington acknowledged this letter as one "without date"; it was undoubtedly written after 23 Aug., the date of Specht's letter, q.v., transmitting letters here forwarded by TJ. Enclosures not further identified.

Supplies Required for Gates' Army

State of North Carolina   August 1780.

500 Tents Compleat	Intrenching Tools
2000 Barrels Flour	* 500 Spades
4000 do. Corn	*200 Grubbing Hoes
250 do. Rice	*100 Common Hoes
50 Hogsheads Rum	*200 Felling Axes
10 Hogsheads Sugar	
10 Barrels Coffee	
*10 Barrels Vinegar	
1000 Bushels Salt	

Forage

To be stored at the Magazines and at the Halting places in approach to the Magazines.

The Ferries to be put upon the best Footing; the Boats well repaired, and well caulk'd. The Roads and Bridges, to be thoroughly and substantially repair'd—The Bridge at Meherrin River particularly—Virginia to be applied to for this.

General Hospital at Hillsborough

NB. If One Hundred Waggons are too great a Proportion for this State to furnish, might not each County be rated at one; or in Proportion to its ability to supply Waggons and Horses. Those Counties that are defficient in Waggons and Horses to furnish Something Equivalent, to those who are more able to supply the Army. HORATIO GATES

Tr (Vi). Caption at head largely torn away along vertical folds and omitted in the present text.

This is evidently a copy of a list sent by Gates to Congress very soon after 30 Aug. Gates wrote that day to TJ concerning supplies wanted from Virginia, and in his acknowledgment of

3 Sep. TJ asked Gates to specify the articles and quantities wanted. On 6 Sep., however, TJ told Huntington that he had now seen such a specific list accompanying Gates' recent dispatches to Congress, left open for TJ's perusal. See also TJ to Muter, 13 Sep.

From George Muter

[Richmond] 1 Sep. 1780. A new regulation respecting the pay of wagonmasters, foragemasters, &c., being absolutely necessary, a memorandum on that subject from Mr. Rose is enclosed for TJ's consideration.

RC (Vi). Endorsed in clerk's hand: "Septr. 1st. 1780. From Colo. Muter to Governor Jefferson, informing that an

arrangement in the QMr's. department must be made." Enclosure not found.

From Samuel Huntington

SIR   Philada September 2. 1780

Your Excellency will receive herewith enclosed an Act of Congress of the 26. Ulto., earnestly recommending to the several States to take the most speedy and effectual Means in their Power for drawing in their respective Quotas of the Continental Bills of Credit to be destroyed either by Tax or by exchanging for them new Bills emitted pursuant to the resolution of the 18. of March last at a rate not less than forty for one, that the whole of the new Bills may be issued.

Also recommending to the several States to raise by Taxes payable in the new Bills above mentioned or Specie their respective Quotas of three Million of Dollars agreeable to the Apportionment of the 7. of October 1779 and pay the same into the Treasury of the United States as soon as possible, the Payment to be fully completed by the last Day of December next, each State to be allowed Interest from the Time it is paid; to be hereafter adjusted according to a resolution of the 6. of October 1779.

You will also observe by this Act Provision is made for Payment of the public Debts due in any of the States in the Departments of the late Quarter Master Greene and Commissary Wadsworth, as also the present Commissary General of Purchases.

And in Order to prevent the Possibility of a Depreciation in the new Bills it is earnestly recommended to the several States not to issue Bills of Credit for a Currency on any Account whatever in such Manner as to have in Circulation a greater Amount than their respective Quotas of the new Bills.

And in Order that Justice be done to the Creditors of the United States for Supplies furnished the Army or Transportation thereof, Provision is made by this Act that such Creditors be paid the just Value of their Debts, to be ascertained in the Manner expressed in the Act, and all Debts due to the United States are to be justly paid in like Manner.

I have the Honor to be with the highest respect your Excellencys most obedient & most humble servant, S. H.

FC (DLC: PCC, No. 15). At head of text: "Circular." Enclosure (missing): resolve of Congress, 26 Aug. 1780; printed in jcc, xvii, 782-4.

To John Mathews

Sir   Richmond September 2nd. 1780.

I have been honoured with your Letters of the 13 and 19 ult. No person can feel more poignantly than I do for the distresses of our army to the north nor the idea of blasting well grounded hopes of decisive operations there for want of those supplies which constitute the force of war. That something brilliant there shou'd take place is the more necessary to keep up the spirits of our people since the repeated calamities which have befallen us in the south. By the resolutions of Congress of June the 17. we are desired to send 5000 militia to reinforce the southern army and they determine that no supplies of men or provisions (except bacon [and so] much grain as the executive of the state conceive may be spared from the southern army) be removed to the northward of the state, and that all monies raised within the state be appropriated to the southern department. The Assembly having determined instead of so many of the militia to raise 3000 or 3500 regulars for 18 months, Congress by their resolutions of August 5, direct that they shall join the southern army. From these several resolutions we did not conceive that men, money or provisions, were now expected from us to the northward, except the bacon called for (60000 wt.) and so much corn as we can spare. I have returns of bacon collected for this purpose to the amount of 58,790 ℔ and there are several counties from which no returns are yet made. I have therefore hopes that the whole quantity is ready. Of the collection of corn which has been returned to me between 13 and 14000 bushels lying in our northern counties will go to the northward under the orders we have given, besides other quantities and not returned and therefore unknown and part of a former collection, for which the Q. M. had orders early in the spring which is not yet all sent. A prospect now opens to us of clearing our bay which will admit the safe transportation of these articles for which they have long waited. If any later resolutions of congress have directed men to go hence northwardly or other supplies of provision, they have not been communicated to me, nor can I suppose such to have been formed as the calling northwardly the supplies of men and provisions from this state would be to leave a fourth of the enemy's force on the Continent to be opposed by the state of north Carolina alone, a state whose militia are not more than a 10th of those of the whole confederacy and these extremely divided in affection among themselves. To shew you how little equal that state is to such a contest, and how largely and cogently we are called on to aid them, I take the liberty of inclosing you extracts of a Letter from Governor Nash and of another from General Gates, calls indeed which we are in no condition to answer fully or tolerably and I wish that with the aid of our sister state of Maryland which seems also to have been put into in the southern department, the late losses may be supplied. I have the honor to be Your most ob: servant,   THO: JEFFERSON

FC (Vi, photostat from Brit. Mus.: Add. MSS 38,650); at head of text: "The honorable Jno. Matthews of the Committee of Congress at Head Quarters." Enclosures not precisely identifiable.

YOUR LETTERS OF THE 13 [*error for 16*] AND 19 ULT. were written by Mathews in behalf of the Committee of Congress at Headquarters; see under those dates, above.

From James Maxwell

[*Richmond*, 2 Sep. 1780. Minute in Journal of the Commissioner of the Navy (Vi) under this date: "Wrote a letter to his Excellency the Governor." Not located.]

To Timothy Pickering

SIR   Richmond Septemr. 2nd. 1780.

Your Letter of August the second has come duly to hand. We agree with you that the post at fort Pitt may be supplied much more œconomically from the settlements round about it, and these settlements have such a sufficiency of provision for the subsistance of the post that it is a waste of effort and of the public treasure to purchase and remove them from the east side of the Allegany. The committee of congress at camp did not call on us for any supplies of provisions for that post. They required from us 60,000 wt. of bacon to be sent northwardly which we are preparing to send. On the contrary, Congress desired [by] their resolution of June 17. that no supplies of provisions except bacon and so much corn as we can spare shou'd be sent from this State northwardly. Indeed we have now no means of procuring a single article of provision, but by seizing them under an act of Assembly made for that purpose and giving certificates receiveable from the holder in paiment of his taxes. This act of power we cannot exercise in that country, as the late Line proposed between Pensylvania and us cedes the whole of it to them except a narrow slip to the westward of it, the precise location of which is not yet known. Had the resolutions of congress required us to have furnished provisions to that post they must have gone from our counties between the blue ridge and Allegany, from which I fear we shou'd have found it impracticable to have transported them at the time; as the small efforts which we can spare from the southern calls are insufficient for the supply of our posts down the Ohio at which we are obliged shortly to have about 800 men stationed for the defence of our own inhabitants. Thus unauthorized to take by force in the fort Pitt settlements, and unpossessed of money to purchase these,[1] or to transport thither from our own country, any undertaking to supply the post wou'd only add to its distress by disappointments which necessities felt and foreseen wou'd render unavoidable, and which by timely turning your attention else where may perhaps be provided against. I have the honor to be your most obedient servant,   THO. JEFFERSON

FC (Vi, photostat from Brit. Mus.: Add. MSS 38,650).
Pickering's LETTER OF AUGUST THE SECOND has not been found.
[1] FC is clearly "these," but this may have been a clerk's error for "there."

To Charles Washington

SIR   Richmond Sepr. 2d. 1780.

I have received your Letter of August 23. and in answer thereto am to inform you that I should not myself question but that auditors warrants, would be received in paiment for British escheated property; but I think certificates wou'd not be so received as the law has only made them paiable in taxes. However it is not within the line of my authority to give any answer on this subject which wou'd oblige the officers who have the direction of the treasury. I am with great respect, Your most obedt. servant,   THO: JEFFERSON

FC (Vi, photostat from Brit. Mus.: Add. MSS 33,650). At head of text: "Mr Charles Washington fredericksburg."

Charles, brother of George Washington, was an officer of the Spotsylvania militia (Gwathmey, *Hist. Reg. of Virginians in the Revolution*). HIS LETTER OF AUGUST 23 to TJ has not been found.

From Anthony Walton White

[*Place not known, 2 Sep. 1780*. In his letter to Samuel Huntington, 8 Sep. 1780, TJ enclosed a letter "from Colo. White complaining of (a) limitation of price" for horses purchased to remount White's cavalry. White's letter was read in Congress, and a committee reporting on it declared "That the Style of Lt. Colo. White's letter of Septr. 2d. 1780, which was addressed to the Governor of Virginia, is improper and inconsistent with the confidence which ought to be reposed in the Executive of a State, exerting itself for the advancement of the common good, by every means in its power" (JCC, XVIII, 850). Not located. See, however, TJ to the Persons Appointed to Purchase Horses, 6 Sep., and note on TJ to Huntington, 8 Sep. 1780.]

To William Davies

SIR   Richmond Sepr 3d. 1780.

The Bearers of your Letters have unfortunately called on me generally in the afternoon when it is impossible to consult the Council, and of course to answer you, which occasions a delay of answer. This was the case with Dr. Munro. I now inclose you an order for the medicine. We can furnish you with about 400 yds. of a coarse woolen which may be made to answer the purpose of blankets in the hospital. I am sorry it is not in my power to order a particular issue of cloathing to you as requested. The council have fixed by their rules the manner of issuing, and determined it shall be general, that all may fare alike. Tho the stock procured is likely to be small it is impossible probable[1] that whatever it be will be provided before the Officers go on with the new recruits. I am sir with great respect, Your most obedient humble servant, [TH: JEFFERSON][2]

FC (Vi, photostat from Brit. Mus.: Add. MSS 38,650).

Davies' LETTERS here acknowledged have not been identified.

[1] Thus in FC; the carelessness of the clerk has made it impossible to tell

whether TJ meant to assure Davies that the stock would probably be provided before the officers went on with the recruits or to inform him that it would be impossible for this to be done.

[2] The clerk was so careless as to sign the name "Tho: Davies" to FC.

To Horatio Gates

SIR   Richmond Sepr. 3. 1780.

I am extremely mortifyed at the Misfortune incurred in the South and the more so as the Militia of our State concurred so eminently in producing it. We have sent from Chesterfield a week ago 350 regulars, 50 more march tomorrow, and there will be 100, or 150 still to go thence as fast as they come out of the Hospital. Our new recruits begin to rendezvous about the 10th: inst. and may all be expected to be in by the 25th. We call on 2000 more Militia, who are required to be at Hillsborough by the 25th. of Octo. but we have not Arms to put into the Hands of these men. There are here going on to you 3000 stand from Congress. We have about the same number in our magazine. I trust Congress will aid us. We are desired in general to send you all kinds of Military Stores, but I wish you would be so good as to send me a specification of the Articles and quantities you most want, because our means of transportation being very limited we may otherwise misemploy even these. Powder, flints, Cannon, Cannon-ball are the only Articles I think we can send. Lead I hope you will get immediately from the Mines, which will save a vast deal of transportation. Our treasury is utterly exhausted and cannot again be replenished till the Assembly meets in October. We might however furnish considerable Quantities of Provision were it possible to convey it to you. We shall immediately send out an Agent into the Southern Counties to collect and forward all he can. Will Militia volunteer Horse be of service to you and how many? I am with the greatest esteem & respect Sir Your most obedt. humble sert.,

TH: JEFFERSON

RC (DLC); in a clerk's hand, with complimentary close and signature in TJ's hand; endorsed: "From Governour Jefferson 3d: Sepr: 1780." FC (Vi,

photostat from Brit. Mus.: Add. MSS 38,650).
A SPECIFICATION OF THE ARTICLES AND QUANTITIES YOU MOST WANT: See Supplies Required for Gates' Army, Aug. 1780; also TJ to Huntington, 6 Sep. 1780.

To Samuel Huntington

SIR   Richmond Sep. 3. 1780.

It is not in my power to add any circumstance of consequence to those communicated to you by Genl. Gates, and as I suppose to the delegates of N. Carolina by Gover. Nash a letter from whom accompanies this, and I take for granted communicates the later intelligence which he was so kind as to transmit me at the same time. A force is again collected of between four and five thousand men consisting of the remains of the Maryland brigade, of Porter-feild's corps of regulars, Armand's legion, such of the fugitive militia as are a little recovered of their fright, and new corps of N. Carolina militia who have readily embodied themselves. 300. regulars of this state marched from Chesterfeild a week ago; about 50 march tomorrow, and there may be 100 or 150 more to go from the same post as soon as they get out of the hospital. Our 3000 new recruits will begin to rendezvous about the 10th. inst. and may all be expected to be rendezvoused by the 25th. We have determined to call out also 2000 militia who however cannot be got to Hillsborough sooner than the 25th. of October. This is as exact a state of the force we expect to oppose to the enemy as I am able to give. Almost the whole of the small arms having been unfortunately lost in the last defeat, the men proposed for the feild will be unarmed, unless it is in your power to furnish arms. Indeed not only a sufficient number is wanting to arm the men now raising, but, as our stores will be exhausted in effecting that as far as they will go towards it, it seems indispensible that Congress should form a plentiful magazine of small arms, and other military stores that we may not be left an unarmed prey to the enemy, should our Southern misfortunes be not yet ended. Should any disaster like the late one, befal that army which is now collecting, and which will be so much weaker in regulars as that brave corps is lessened in the unequal conflict which was put upon them, the consequences will be really tremendous if we be found without arms. With a sufficiency of these, there can be no danger in the end. The losses of our brethren in the mean time may be great, the distresses of individuals in the neighborhood of the war will be cruel, but there can be no doubt of an ultimate recovery of the country. The scene of military operations has been hitherto so distant from these states, that their militia are strangers to the actual presence of danger. Habit alone will enable them to view this with familiarity, to face it without dismay; a habit which must be purchased by calamity, but cannot be purchased too dear. In the acquisition of this, other misfortunes may yet be to be incurred, for which we should be prepared. I am earnestly therefore to sollicit Congress for plentiful supplies of small arms, powder, flints, cartridge boxes and paper; and to pray that no moment may be lost in forwarding them. Not doubting that the importance of this will be seen in the extent it deserves, I beg leave to subscribe myself with every sentiment of respect & esteem, Your Excellency's most obedient & most humble servt.,   TH: JEFFERSON

RC (DLC: PCC, No. 71, I); endorsed by Charles Thomson: "Letter from Govr Jefferson Septr. 3. 1780 Read 7. Referred to Mr Henry Mr Adams Mr Walker Mr Bee Mr W Jones." FC (Vi, photostat from Brit. Mus.: Add. MSS 38,650). Enclosures: dispatches from Gates; see Gates to TJ, 30 Aug.

The letter from Gov. NASH to THE DELEGATES OF N. CAROLINA, dated 23 Aug. 1780, is in DLC: PCC, No. 72, and is partially printed in *N.C. State Records*, xv, 60; that from Nash to TJ of the same date (see TJ to Nash, 3 Sep.) has not been found. For the action of Congress on the present letter, see JCC, XVIII, 809, 813, 818 (7, 8, and 11 Sep.).

From Samuel Huntington

Philadelphia, 3 Sep. 1780. Circular letter to state executives enclosing resolve of Congress of 25 Aug. establishing as a general rule a policy theretofore employed in particular cases concerning "the rank of the Governors or Presidents of the several States whenever they shall act in the Field together, or in Conjunction with the Continental Army."

RC (Vi); 2 p.; in a clerk's hand, signed "Sam. Huntington President"; endorsed. FC (DLC: PCC, No. 15). Enclosure (Vi): copy attested by Charles Thomson of resolution of 25 Aug. 1780 (printed in JCC, XVII, 777).

To Thomas Sim Lee,
enclosing Signals of Recognition for Maryland and Virginia Vessels

SIR   Richmond Sep. 3d. 1780.

I received your Excellency's favor of the 28th. of August on the 30th of the same month, and should have answered it immediately but that a previous enquiry was necessary what force we could certainly contribute to the enterprize proposed. I have it now in my power to inform you that a brig carrying 14. Guns, 4. pounders and two swift sailing armed boats shall be ready to join the force from your State; being the only vessels we have manned. They are just now returned from a cruize up the bay where they took five schooners and rowboats, and are now waiting at Hampton to convoy some provision boats up the bay. I have given notice to the Commanding Officer that your vessels will be ready to sail on the 9th and directed him 'if the provision vessels sail before that day, to convoy them as before intended, and if on his way up he should meet the Maryland force, he is then to leave the provision vessels and join that force; but if he should not meet them, he is, when he has attended the provision vessels as far as is necessary, to proceed to Baltimore and there join your vessels. If the provision vessels should not sail before the 9th. he is to go round to York and there be ready either to join the provision vessels or those of Maryland whichever shall first appear. If the former, he is on joining them to conduct himself as in the case first supposed. He is informed that the object of this joint cruize is to clear the bay, and whether it shall be extended, as to our vessels out of the capes is left to his discretion. And also that if any future cruizes can be established in concert we shall be pleased to co-operate in them so far as they shall have for their object the clearing Chesapeake bay or the vicinities of it's capes.' It was also thought necessary that signals should be agreed on whereby they might know each other on meeting; the inclosed have been sent for that purpose to our Commanding officer, and are submitted to Your Excellency for communication to yours, if you think proper.

I have the honor to be with the greatest respect Your Excellency's Most obedient & most humble Servant, TH: JEFFERSON

ENCLOSURE

Signals whereby to know each other in case of meeting in the bay.

He who first makes the signal is to take in his foretop-gallant sail and hoist the Continental ensign at the foretop-gallant mast head.

The other to answer by letting fly his main-topgallant Sheets, and hoisting a Continental Jack at the main-top-gallant mast head.

RC (MdAA); in a clerk's hand, signed by TJ. FC (Vi, photostat from Brit. Mus.: Add. MSS 38,650). Enclosure (MdAA); in a different clerk's hand.

The COMMANDING OFFICER to whom TJ's instructions had been sent was Commodore James Barron; the instructions will be found in a fuller form as a postscript (of 2 Sep.) to TJ's letter to James Maxwell, 31 Aug. 1780, q.v.

To Abner Nash

Richmond Sepr. 3rd. 1780.

I am much obliged by your Excellency's favor of the 23rd ult. It contained much information, which I had not before received. The misfortune we have met with is indeed matter of great grief to me, and the more so as the militia of this state bore so eminent a share in producing it. It remains however that we look forward, and consider what is to be done to re-establish our affairs. I am happy to find that the militia of your state have turned out with such alacrity. We sent off from Chesterfield a week ago 350 regulars. 50 more will march tomorrow, and there will be 100. or 150. more from the same post as fast as they come out of the hospital. Our new recruits about 3000 in number, who are to serve till Christmas twelvemonth will repair to the several places of rendezvous between the 10th and 25th instant, and we are calling in 2000 militia who I think cannot be at Hillsborough till the 25th of October. The 3000 stand of arms from Congress are at this place, and will be forwarded as soon as waggons can be procured. We have about 3000 stand of our own, but these will not suffice for our men, and we shall then be left utterly destitute. I have written most pressingly to Congress to send on small arms, powder, flints, cartridge boxes and paper. In the mean time we will endeavour to forward to you powder and flints. The distance is so much less from our lead mines to Hillsborough, that I hope you will find means to bring the lead from thence. The manager had orders to furnish Genl. Gates. We too are utterly destitute of money, nor can [we] have a shilling more till our Assembly meets in the middle of October. Yet we cou'd procure provisions had we means of transporting them to you, but the difficulty of procuring waggons is next to insuperable. We shall however immediately send an Agent to do in this matter whatever is practicable. Your draft in favor of Mr. Ross shall be answered by some means or other. I am with every sentiment of respect, Your Excellency's most ob: servt.,

                                                    THO. JEFFERSON

FC (Vi, photostat from Brit. Mus.: Add. MSS 38,650).
Nash's FAVOR OF THE 23RD ULT. has not been found.

To Edward Stevens

Dear Sir   Richmond Septemr. 3rd. 1780

I sincerely condole with you on our late Misfortune which sits the heavier on my mind as being produced by my own Country Men. Instead of considering what is past, however, we are to look forward and prepare for the future. I write Genl. Gates and Governor Nash as to Supplies and reinforcements. A New Body of 2000 Militia are ordered to you to rendevous at Hillsborough on the 25th October. They come from the middle and North Counties beyond and adjoining the blue Ridge. I am told, also, that a Spirit of raising Volunteers is springing up. The Truth of this however is not Certainly known, nor can its Success be depended on. Governor Nash writes me that 400 Waggons were lost. An officer here however thinks they are not. This indeed would be a heavey loss, as well as that of the small Arms. We shall exert every Nerve to assist you in every way in our Power, being as we are, without any Money in the Treasury, or any prospect of more till the Assembly meets in Octr. I am with great esteem your most Obt & most hum Servt.,

TH: JEFFERSON

Tr (DLC); endorsed: "Copy of a Letter from Governor Jefferson to Edward Stevens dated Septr 3rd. 1780." FC (Vi, photostat from Brit. Mus.: Add. MSS 38,650).

To George Washington,
with a Narrative of the Battle of Camden

Sir   Richmond Sep. 3. 1780.

As I know the anxieties you must have felt since the late misfortune to the South, and our later accounts have not been quite so unfavorable as the first, I take the liberty of inclosing you a state of this unlucky affair extracted from letters from General Gates, Gen. Stevens, and Govr. Nash, and taken as to some circumstances from an officer who was in the action. Another army is collecting. This amounted on the 23d. Ult. to between four and five thousand men consisting of about 500 Maryland regulars, a few of Harrison's artillery and Porterfeild's corps, Armand's legion, such of the fugitive militia as had been reclaimed, and about 3000 N. Carolina militia newly embodied. We are told they will increase these to 8000. Our new recruits will rendezvous in this state between the 10th. and 25th. inst. We are calling out 2000 militia who I think however will not be got to Hillsborough till the 25th. of October. About 350 regulars marched from Chesterfeild a week ago; 50 march tomorrow and there will be 100, or 150 more from that post when they can be cleared of the hospital. This is as good a view as I can give you of the force we are endeavoring to collect. But they are unarmed. Almost the whole small arms seem to have been lost in the late rout. There are here on their way Southward 3000 stand of arms sent by Congress, and we have a few still remaining in our magazine. I have written pressingly, as the subject well deserves, to Congress, to send us immediate supplies, and to think of forming a magazine here that in case of another disaster we may not be left without all means of opposition.

I inclosed to your Excellency some time ago a resolution of assembly instructing us to send a quantity of tobacco to N. York for the relief of our officers there, and asking the favor of you to obtain permission. Having received no answer I fear my letter or your answer has miscarried. I therefore now take the liberty of repeating my application to you. I have the honor to be with the most profound respect & esteem Your Excellency's most Obedt. & most humble servt.,   TH: JEFFERSON

ENCLOSURE

A Narrative of the late disaster in South Carolinia Collected from the Most authentic Accounts which have been Received.

On the 13th. of August Genl. Gates with the Maryland line the Artillery and North Carolina Militia arrived at Ridgeley thirteen miles from Cambden and took post there and was the Next day joind by Genl. Stevens with Seven hundred of the Virginia Militia. Col. Sumpter was then at the Waxsaws with four hundred South Carolinia Militia, and had on the Sunday before killed and taken near three hundred of the enemy who were posted at the hanging rock. This and other strokes on their advanced post Occasioned their Calling in all their out post to Cambden. The 15th. at day light Genl. Gates reinforced Col. Sumpter with three hundred North Carolinia Militia one hundred of the Maryland line and two three pounders. Col. Sumpter took possession of all the passes on the Wateree from Elkins's ford to Whiticars farm five Miles below Campden. At one of these he supprised the enemy's Guard killed Seven and took about thirty a mong which was Colo. Cary their Commanding officer with thirty eight waggons loaded with Corn rum &c. also a Number of horses; and afterwards on the Same day he took about Seventy prisoners, British, Six waggons, baggage

&c. on their way from Ninety Six. At ten OClock Genl. Gates's Army Marched intending to take post on an advantageous Situation where was a deep Creek in front about seven Miles from Cambden, the heavy baggage being ordered to proceed by the waxaw road; the March was in the following order, Col. Armand's legion in front supported on both flanks by Colo. Porterfield Commanding officer of Virginia regulars and the light infantry of the Militia, the advanced Guard of infantry, the Maryland line with their Artillery in front of the brigades, the N. C. Militia, the Virga. Militia, the Artillery &c. and the rear guard. Between 12. and 1 oClock after Marching About Five Miles they Met with the enemy, under the Command of Lord Cornwallis who had Marched out from Cambden about Nine OClock of the Same Night intending to attack our Camp by supprise about day break. This Meeting was equally unexpected on both Sides and Occationed a halt of both Armies. The enemy's Cavalry then charged Col. Armands legion which was well supported on the flanks by Col. Porterfield's Corps who repulsed the Assailants, but Unfortunately Col. Porterfield himself had his leg broke in the first fire. The enemy's infantry then advancing with a heavy fire, the troops in front gave way to the front of the 1st. Maryland brigade and a Confusion ensued which took Some time to regulate. At length the Army was ranged in line of battle in the following order, General Gist's brigade on the right with his right close to a swamp, the N. C. Militia in Close Order two deep in the Center, and the Virginia Militia in like order with the Light infantry and Porterfield's Corps on the left, the Artillery divided to the brigades and the first Maryland brigade as a Corps de reserve and to Cover the Cannon in the road at a proper distance in the rear. Col. Armands Corps was ordered to the left to Support the left flank and oppose the enemy's Cavalry. Their infantry from a defect in Numbers were only a Single file five feet apart. In this Situation they remained till day break of the 16th. when our troops advanced in a line a few hundred yards. The enemy attacked and drove in our light party in front; and after the first fire charged the Militia with bayonets where upon the whole gave way, except Col. Dixon's regiment of N C. Militia, and their cavalry continuing to harrass the rear. Such was the panic diffused through the whole that the utmost and unremitting exertions of the Generals Gates Stevens Caswell and others assisted by a Number of Officers to rally them even in small parties, at the several advantageous posts at which it was Occasionally attempted, proved ineffectual. They ran like a torrent and bore all before them. This shamefull d[e]sertion of the Militia gave the enemy an opportunity of bending their whole force against the Maryland troops and Dixons Regiment of N C. Militia. The Conflict was obstinate and bloody and lasted fifteen Minutes, Dixons Militia standing firm with their regular brethren and pushing bayonets to the last. Superior bravery was at length obliged to give way to superior Numbers, and this gallant Corps Compelled to retreat from the ground. They were then furisly charged by a party of British horse (their Numbers Not known) whom they Compleatly Vanquished, insomuch that not more than two of the party are said to have got off. These brave men suffered greatly, having lost as is believed one half of their number, and to their immortal honour made their retreat good. The waggons were some distance behind. The Waggoners cut loose the horses on which they were, the flying militia the rest, and left the waggons. How many they were is not yet known nor what numbers of them were lost. An account of no light authority sais they were all taken to the number of 400; an officer in the engagement sais that not more than 20 were taken, that the enemy never pursued so far as to the place where the waggons were posted; that the cavalry indeed did pursue beyond them, but as the waggons stood without horses, they were unable to carry them off; and that teams were afterwards collected at Charlotte which were sent and brought them away safely. We lost 8 pieces of cannon, all the ammunition which was with the army, tents, baggage, military chests papers and nearly the whole muskets which were in the hands of the militia who basely threw them away. The numbers of the enemy are not certainly known; prisoners say they were 3500 regulars; Colo. Sumpter's intelligence on the 15th. made them 1200 regulars 1000 militia and a reinforcement of 500 regulars on their way, but whether these had joined or not is unknown. It is believed their loss was full 500 killed and wounded. They retreated immediately to campden; but sent a party of horse against Colo. Sumpter, who after he had withdrawn up the Wateree 40 miles came on him by surprize, cut him off from his arms which they took retook the prisoners waggons and other things he had captured. Few of his men were lost as they flew to the woods. Generals Gates, Gist, Smallwood, Huger, Stevens, Butler and Gregory are safe. Generals DeKalb and Rutherford are missing, the latter a prisoner certainly, the former a prisoner and some accounts say mortally wounded, others that he is unhurt. Colo. Porterfield an inestimable officer, is said, we fear too truly to be dead of his wounds. About one third of his corps was lost. On this defeat the yeomanry of N. Carolina immediately turned out unsollicited. An army is collecting which when our last advices came away, viz August 23d. already consisted of between four and 5000 men.

RC (DLC: Washington Papers). Tr (DLC: TJ Papers); text defective. Enclosures: (1) "Narrative of the late disaster in South Carolinia . . ." (DLC: Washington Papers; a defective Tr is in DLC: TJ Papers), in an unidentified hand; (2) copy of resolve of Virginia Assembly respecting tobacco for captive officers of the Virginia Line (missing, but see TJ to Harrison, 22 June; TJ to Washington, 4 July; and Washington to TJ, 29 Aug. 1780).

The OFFICER WHO WAS IN THE ACTION and reported (orally?) on the battle of Camden to TJ has not been identified. A FEW STILL REMAINING IN OUR MAGAZINE: The "few" were approximately 3,000 stand of arms (see TJ to Abner Nash, 3 Sep. 1780). In DLC: TJ Papers (5: 873 and 870) are two other memoranda relating to this action. The first is a list, signed by A. Hoops (Adam Hoops, capt., 4th Md. Line, captured at Camden), of the British forces engaged and an estimate of their fatalities (2,852 engaged, 240 known killed). The second paper is in TJ's

hand and reads as follows:
"List of the British force engaged Aug. 16. 1780

23d. British regimt.	400
33d. do.	300
71st.	300
Ld. Rawdon's corps	350
Tarleton's legion	420
Reinforcemt. from Charles T. under Ld. Cornwallis of the 63d. regimt. of Hessn. corps	700
Bryant's and Harrison's new levies	600
	3070.

Tories incorporated, number unknown but did no damage, having run away the first fire of artillery

American force.

Maryland division reducd by detamt	800
Armand's Porterfeild's & Armstrong's corps	200
Caswell's N. Carola militia	1000
Stevens's Virginia militia	800
	2800."

Advice of Council respecting Reinforcements of Militia

[ca. 4 September 1780]

The board advise that 2041 militia be called into service to relieve those now on duty to the Southward to be made up by requiring so many men from the counties last called on for the Southern service as they failed to March from their county viz. Pittsylva. 45. &c.   notifying to the commanding officers of the said counties that every man to whose lot it now falls to go shall be excused by producing and delivering before the time of rendezvous to the jail of their county on warrant from the said commanding officer one of the delinquents or deserters of the militia so before called from their county and also that he may deduct from the number now required from his county so many as he shall have actually heretofore delivered of the said delinquents to any Continental officer. That the remaining number be made up from the following counties viz. Frederick 82. Berkeley 73. Hampshire 66. Shenand. 40. Rockingh. 52. Augusta 107. Rockbr. 40. Loudon 177. Fauqr. 105. Culpeper 161. Pr. Wm. 73. Fairfx 75. That the said militia rendezvous at Hillsborough in N. Carolina on or before the 20th. of Oct. next and serve the delinquents as provided by law, and the residue of the said militia 3. months from the time of their getting to the head quarters of the Commanding officer to the Southward. That a power be sent to each of the Commanding officers of the said counties to impress waggons, provisions and other necessaries for the subsistence and transportation of their men on their march; that they go under the command of captains and subalterns from their counties, be regimented by Genl. Stevens, and commanded by him and the feild officers under him.[1]

That instructions be given to one of the assistant Quartermasters to proceed to the Westward for the purpose of purchasing 100 waggons teams and geer to be paid for with certificates discountable for taxes or for land warrants, that he be also furnished with a power of seising so many waggons under the laws made for that purpose if his endeavors to purchase shall not be attended with full success.

Dft (Vi), in TJ's hand, with numerous deletions and corrections; the principal deletion is noted below. Without caption but endorsed: "Advice of Council 1779." The endorsement was presumably added later, for the date is not merely vague but mistaken; these instructions to the governor, prepared by the governor himself, were certainly written after Gates' defeat at Camden and were carried into effect by the circular letters to the county lieutenants of 4 Sep. 1780, below. These circulars, it will be noted, fall into two groups: (1) those to Frederick and certain other counties (here enumerated) which had *not* heretofore furnished militia for the southern army; and (2) those to Pittsylvania and certain other counties (the names being left blank, except for the first, in the draft Advice), which *had* furnished militia but less than the number required of them.

[1] Following this a whole paragraph was crossed out in Dft: "That two troops of volunteer militia cavalry be raised and annexed to Majr. Nelson's command to find their own horses and accoutrements (pistols and swords excepted) but these to be paid for by the public if lost or disabled in the service not through the default of the owner; to continue in service till the 1st. day of Dec. 1781, if so long wanted in the opinion of the Executive, to draw pay rations and forage, be exempted from the present call of militia from their county and be commanded by Captns. and subalterns of their own chusing; and as offers of troops have been made from the counties of Goochld. and Halifx. that this proposition be notified to the commanding officers of those counties."

Estimate of Militia Strength

[ca. 4 September 1780]

before called on	No. of Militia	No. called for	Delinquents
Pittsylva.	725	97	45
Bedford	1535	202	137
Halifx.	1139	141	31
Charlotte	656	89	30
Mecklbg.	975	128	45
Pr. Edwd.	560	75	19
Amelia	1125	154	21
Lunbg.	620	83	30
Dinwiddie	750	100	39
Brunsw.	1200	161	118
Buckingh.	625	84	37
Amherst	600	135	84
Powhatan	350	47	
Cumbld.	486	61	0
Chestfd.	850	114	17
Goochld.	550	75	22
Louisa	700	94	37
Henrico	624	83	14
Hanover	1000	135	13
Fluvanna	296	40	17
Caroline	957	128	27
Spotsylva.	675	92	9
Orange	600	80	35
Henry	800	108	54
	18398	2506	881

Counties betw. Allegany & Bl. R.	No. of Militia	$\dfrac{1}{15}$	No. called for
Frederick	1196	1116	112
			−30
Berkeley	1100	1027	103
			−30
Hampshire	1031	962	96
			−30
Shenandoah	925	863	86
			−26
Rockingh.	800	747	75
			−23
Augusta	1525	1423	142
			−35
Gr. Briar	550	514	51
			−16

Counties betw. Allegany & Bl. R.	No. of Militia	$\frac{1}{15}$	No. called for
Rockbridge	625	583	58
			−18
Botett.	781	729	73
Montgom.	625	583	58
Washington	965	900	90
			944
Counties between Bl. ridge & ti. waters.[1]			
Loudon	1900	1774	177
Fauquier	1125	1050	105
Culpeper	1728	1613	161
			443
On tide waters not exposed			
K. George	416	388	39
Stafford	725	677	68
Pr. William	781	728	73
Fairfax	800	747	75
			255
where Conventioners			
Albemarle	900	840	84
Counties on tidewaters, exposed			
Accomack	1200	1120	112
Northampt.	500	467	47
			159
Lancaster	232	217	21
Northumbld.	703	656	66
Westmoreld.	481	449	45
Richmond	520	485	48
			180
Gloster	850	794	79
Middlesx.	220	205	20
Essex	630	588	59
K. & Queen	575	537	54
K. Wm.	475	443	44
			256
Eliz. City	162	151	15
Warwick	121	113	11
York	225	210	21
Wmsbgh.	150	140	14
Jas. city	188	176	18

Counties on tidewaters, exposed	No. of Militia	$\frac{1}{15}$	No. called for
Chas. City	310	290	29
New Kent	410	383	38
			146
Pr. George	420	392	39
Sussex	682	637	64
Southampt.	842	786	79
Surry	390	364	36
I. of Wight	650	607	61
Nansemond	750	700	70
Norfolk	905	845	84
Princss. Ann	600	560	56
			489

Delinquents	990
Between Allegany & Bl. ridge	944
Between Bl. ridge and tide wat.	443
On tide waters, not exposed	255
County where Conventioners are	840
On tide waters exposed. East. shore	159
betw. Patowm. & Rappahan.	180
betw. Rappahan. & York	256
betw. York & James river	146
betw. Jas. riv. & Carolina	489

Tabular MS (DLC); entirely in TJ's hand. Without date.

These calculations of Virginia's militia strength were obviously drawn up in preparation for the Advice of Council assigned to this date (preceding) and the letters to the County Lieutenants (following), for the data in all these documents closely correspond where they overlap. In DLC: TJ Papers, 6: 1069-70, are two other lists of the Virginia counties in TJ's hand, apparently preliminary to the present paper, with the total militia strength of each county entered and containing numerous corrections; one of these tabulates the counties alphabetically and the other classifies them by location.

[1] The following (and also Albemarle, below) are merely the counties between Tidewater and the Blue Ridge *not previously called on* for militia in the southern campaign. In the second (or classified) preliminary list referred to above, Loudoun, Fauquier, Culpeper, and Albemarle are listed, together with all the counties from Pittsylvania to Henry in the list here printed, as "Between the Blue-ridge and Tide-waters."

To the County Lieutenants of Frederick and Certain Other Counties

SIR   In Council Sepr. 4. 1780.

The late misfortune to the southward renders it necessary that we send a reinforcement of militia from this State to assist in stopping the progress of the enemy should they be able to do no more.

I have in the first place required the counties which lately sent militia to the southward, to furnish now so many as failed to march then of the quota called on, but to make up a substantial aid other counties must contribute. I am therefore to require eighty two of your militia to proceed as soon as possible under [the] command of such officers below the [rank] of field officers as you shall find proper to send with them to Hillsborough, in North Carolina, at which place they must be by the 25th of October or as much sooner as may be, because by the last day of that month the time of service of the militia now in Carolina will be expir'd. They are to continue in service three months from the time of their getting to the head quarters of the commanding officer to the southward. [In] requiring this quota from you we have been governed by the prop[ortion] called for by the General assembly on the late occasion from the other counties, and have endeavoured to make allowance for the numbers withdrawn from you by the late draught and also for those sent, or to be sent to the western country.[1] You will be pleased to make return to me of the names of those who shall be ordered to march, and of those who shall fail; and as to the latter to spare no endeavors to take and send them on to duty, as justice to the counties on whom we shall be obliged to call hereafter in the course of rotation requires that we repeat our calls on the counties to whose turn it falls previously, until they shall have actually sent their full number into the field. I inclose you a power of taking provisions, waggons and other necessaries for the men on their march, with an extract of the act of assembly authorizing it, which I wou'd recommend to you to put into the hands of some discreet person of the party capable of doing the duties of quarter master and commissary. Arms will be provided at Hillsborough. I am Your very humb Servt., TH: JEFFERSON

The State being unprovided with Blankets for the 18 Months Men I am to desire you earnestly to recommend to them to carry their own Blankets the value of which they shall be immediately paid.[2]

RC (Vi); in a clerk's hand, signed by TJ; addressed: "The County Lieutenant of Frederick"; endorsed: "Governor Jefferson. Cy Lt. March under Capt John Smith. J. Smith Cy. Lt." FC (Vi, photostat from Brit. Mus.: Add. MSS 38,-650). Enclosures missing; the Act authorizing the Governor to seize provisions, &c., is in Hening, x; see specifically p. 312.

Copies of this circular letter were addressed to counties which had not hitherto furnished militia to the southern army; see the two preceding documents.

[1] The words "and also for those sent" to this point are enclosed in square brackets in the FC; a notation at the

To the County Lieutenants of Pittsylvania and Certain Other Counties

SIR   In Council Sepr. 4. 1780.

The late misfortune to the southward renders it necessary that we send on a reinforcement of militia from this state to assist in stopping the progress of the enemy shoud they be able to do no more. Other counties are therefore applied to for quotas of militia proportioned to those which were required by the General assembly from the counties first called on, of which yours was one. Justice to those now summoned to duty as well as those on whom the call will come hereafter in the course of rotation, requires that full quotas being expected from them full quotas shall also be afforded by the counties called on before them. I am therefore to require from your county   men under the command of such officers below the rank of field officers as you shall find proper to send with them, being the number which failed to march when formerly ordered. I am to inform you that any man on whom the lot now falls [to] make up for the delinquency of those who failed to march on the former occasion shall be excused on delivering to the jail of your county on warrant from you, one of those delinquents if able bodied or any other of your militia who shall have actually marched and since deserted. And also that you shall have credit on the number now required for any such delinquents who shall have joined General Stevens, or whom you shall have taken and sent into duty before you receive this. The men now called for, and the delinquents and deserters who may be delivered to you are to proceed as soon as possible to Hillsborough in N. Carolina at which place they must be by the 25th of Octo: or as much sooner as may be, because by the last day of that month the time of service of the militia now in Carolina will be expired. You are desired to make an exact return to me distinguishing how many of those you send are new militia, how many delinquents and how many deserters, as the two latter classes are made regular soldiers for eight months as a punishment of their offence whereas those newly called are to serve three months only from the time of their getting to the head quarters of the commanding officer to the southward. I inclose you a power of taking provisions waggons and other necessaries for the men on their march with an extract of the act of assembly authorizing it, which I woud recommend you to put into the hands of some discreet person of the party capable of doing duties of quarter master and commissary. I am to desire you to be very attentive to the taking and sending back all deserters and delinquents hereafter as we shall repeat our calls on every county till they shall have actually sent their full number into the field. And in doing this let me point your attention particularly to those dastardly fugitives from the late rout in Carolina, who have so much disgraced their country and who by such flight come within description of deserters. I am your most obedient servant,

THO. JEFFERSON[1]

FC (Vi, photostat from Brit. Mus.: Add. MSS 38,650). None of the counties is named in the caption of this form letter, but it was directed to those counties that had furnished at least partial quotas of men to Gates' army, and the first of these (Pittsylvania) is named in the Advice of Council printed above under the present date; see also Estimate of Militia Strength of this date. Enclosures: same as in preceding circular letter (to Frederick, &c.), q.v.

[1] In FC following the present letter there is a separate letter headed "In Council Sepr. 4. 1780." and addressed "To ditto"; this letter is identical with the marginal addendum to the preceding circular letter (to Frederick, &c.).

From James Maxwell

[*Richmond, 4 Sep. 1780.* Minute in Journal of the Commissioner of the Navy (Vi) under this date: "Letter written to the Governour relative to Capt: Dawsey." Not located.]

From Horatio Gates

SIR   Hillsborough 5th. Sepr. 1780

I have been under the Necessity of drawing on your State Payable to Col: Thomas Polk for the Purpose of purchasing Provisions for the Army in the District of Mecklenberg and Roan [Rowan] Counties, for One Hundred Thousand Pounds Lawful Money of your State in one Bill Dated the 14th Ultimo, and also on the 11th. of same Month I drew on you for 150,000 in two Bills, one for 54,712. Pounds the Other for £95,288. payable to Peter Mallett Esqr., and on the 31st. of August Mr. Clay Deputy Paymaster General drew on Your Excellency two Bills Payable to Morgan

Brown 32,500 Dollars each and, on the 2d Sepr. one Bill in favour of James Clay for 16,000 Dollars, and on the 4th September in favor of Peter Mallet Esqr. for 250,000 Dollars. All which Bills I hope will be regularly discharged, as they are drawn for payment of Goods already supplied, and without these Gentlemen are enabled to comply with their Contracts, the Business of Supply will go heavily on. I have in giving and ordering Draughts to be given, divided my Demands in due proportion, between Your State, and those of Maryland and North Carolina. I shall this Day do myself the Honor of writing to you again by Lt. Col: Dubuysson, and remain with Sentiments of Regard and Esteem Your Excellency's Obedt Hble Servt.

Dft (NHi); endorsed: "Copy to Govr. Jefferson 5th. Sepr. 1780." Tr (DLC).

From George Washington

Sir   Head Quarters Bergen County 5h: Sept. 1780

I was yesterday honored with your Excellency's favor of the 9h: ulto. inclosing a return of 40 prisoners of War delivered to the Continental Commissary at Winchester, for which the State will have the proper credit. Now I am upon the subject of prisoners, I would wish to be informed in what light I am to consider Governor Hamilton, as I do not observe him included in the list. That Gentleman has already been the subject of several propositions on the part of the enemy, and should others be made before I hear again from your Excellency, I shall be embarrassed, as I shall not know on what footing to place him. Indeed there will shortly be an interview on the subject of exchange, at which it is more than probable he will be again mentioned. From what I have heard, I have reason to beleive that the enemy will exchange him for a Lieut. Colonel.

Should there be any other Officers in Virginia who are considered as prisoners belonging to the State, I shall be glad to be informed of their names and Ranks, and whether I may include them should opportunities offer of making either a partial or general exchange.

I have the honor to be &c.

Dft (DLC: Washington Papers); in hand of Tench Tilghman; endorsed. On the disposition of Henry HAMILTON, see a communication from the Virginia Board of War to the commanding officer at Chesterfield Court House, 7 Aug. 1780: "Governor Hamilton and Major Hay are Ordered by the supreme Executive of this State, to Chesterfield Courthouse; there to be closely confined till they are exchanged, or till they consent to give their parole on the terms proposed to them. As we are extreamly weak at this place at present . . . it will be doing a very essential Service to the State, if you will order a Guard from the Troops under your command, to have the immediate charge of Governor Hamilton & Major Hay" (Vi: War Office Letter Book). See also TJ's reply to the present letter, 26 Sep. 1780, and James Maxwell to TJ of same date. On the Hamilton case generally, see TJ to Theodorick Bland, 8 June 1779, and references there.

To the Commissioners of the Specific Tax for Essex County

GENTLEMEN   In Council September 6 1780.

Be pleased to send us by the Bearer the Tobacco Notes still in your Hands of the Specific Tax. Should any Accident prevent your sending them by this opportunity, I am to urge your availing yourself of some other safe and early Conveyance. We do not receive any Notes older than January 1779, And suppose that Transfer Notes not returned to us in Time to have them converted into Crop, you have had so converted yourselves. Yr. very hble. servt.,

TH: JEFFERSON

RC (Vi); in a clerk's hand, signed by TJ; addressed: "Commissioners of Specific Tax Essex." Written in a clerk's hand on the face of the letter is a memorandum reading as follows:

"Thos. Bowler   21,054
 Robt. Mann   16,828
 Wm. Gatewood   10,663
                 ───────
                 48,545
 deduct 6 ℔ Ct.   2,913
                 ───────
                 45,632
                  1,350 for Casks
                 44,282 Nett Tobo"

A letter virtually identical in form and text, addressed to the Commissioners of the Specific Tax in King William co., is also in Vi; on its blank pages it bears numerous memoranda and calculations relating to the collection of tobacco, including a memorandum of a receipt issued to "Colo. Fras. West" for various notes and weights of tobacco, dated "Sept. 1780" and specifying the tobacco marks.

See the Essex Commissioners' reply, printed under 16 Oct. 1780.

To Samuel Huntington

SIR   Richmond Sep. 6. 1780.

Since the dispatches forwarded three days ago I have received others from Genl. Gates which he was pleased to leave open for my perusal and desired they might then be sent on by the line of expresses. He has therein informed you of the articles he has called on us for, and it may be important that you should know as well what we cannot as what we can do. Of the tents desired we cannot procure a single one, because the stuff is not in our country, and we have not money to procure them elsewhere, our treasury being entirely exhausted and no possibility of it's being replenished until the meeting of assembly. The articles of sugar and coffee I do not expect to be able to procure. The residue of his requisitions I have hopes may be complied with. I observe he desires provisions from Maryland and I make no doubt they will be necessary. I am only at a loss how they are to be transported; for despairing of our being able to transport to the southward any of our provisions collected on the north side of James river, I have given orders for sending them to the Northward. I am now apprehensive that this may be wrong, and should really be glad to be advised by Congress what to have done. It will seem inconsistent for our provisions to be going Northward while those of Maryland are passing to the Southward.

RC (DLC: PCC, No. 71, 1); endorsed by Charles Thomson: "Letter from Govr Jefferson Sept 6. 1780 Read 11th." The letter has neither complimentary close nor signature, probably because TJ thought he might add something to the text, did not do so, and had the letter dispatched without formally concluding it. FC (Vi, photostat from Brit. Mus.: Add. MSS 38,650); the copyist has concluded the letter as follows: "I have the honor to be with the most perfect respect and esteem your Excellency's most obedient and most hble servant T. Jefferson." Enclosures: further dispatches from Gates, including the list of Supplies Required for Gates' Army, printed above under date of 30 Aug.

To the Persons Appointed to Purchase Horses under the Resolution of July 14th, 1780.

In Council Sepr. 6th. 1780.

As we have reason to believe the number of horses desired is not yet purchased, we think it necessary to extend the time of delivery further to the 15th of October, only desiring you to forward what you have and praying your greatest exertions to make up the number desired as they are extremely wanted to the southward. I am, sir, Your very humble servant, THO: JEFFERSON

FC (Vi, photostat from Brit. Mus.: Add. MSS 38,650). At head of text: caption as printed above, except that "June" is given in error for July.

For the resolution of 14 July concerning purchase of horses, see JHD, May 1780, 1827 edn., p. 89; also TJ to Huntington, 8 Sep.; Huntington to TJ, 3 Oct. 1780 (second letter of that date from Huntington).

To Timothy Pickering

SIR   Richmond Sep. 6. 1780.

Your favor of Aug. 21. came to hand two days ago, and has been laid before Council. The appointment of a person really proper for the deputy Q. M's place is not very easy. The conduct of Colo. Finnie who has hitherto acted in that office has been certainly reprehensible at times, and he seldom I think pursues an object with that steadiness and attention which is so peculiarly necessary in that department. An indifferent measure carried through with perseverance is better than a good one taken up only at intervals. Colo. Finnie wants neither activity nor integrity. Had he been as able to comprehend more objects than one at a time, to see them all carried on together, or where that could not be done, to decide between the more and less important, he would have avoided complaint. On the other hand he is in possession of the office and without substantial misconduct might think himself injured if discontinued; he is master of the detail of the business and of the means in hand for executing it: we are now in the midst of a campaign, and in a crisis where his exertions to the Southward are peculiarly called for since our late total loss of waggons. In such a situation we might suffer much before a stranger would become acquainted with his duties. These various considerations have induced the council to suppose it might be better to continue him. However as by his last information we have reason to believe he is now gone to Philadelphia where you will have it in your power to settle the matter with himself, we wish to leave it to yourself, being ready to confirm that or any other choice you shall make, and to aid them as far as is in our power in the execution of their office. I shall therefore retain the papers you sent me and insert whatever name in them you shall be pleased to desire. If Colo. Finnie be appointed it is no matter how soon he return, as the present seems to be almost as ill-timed as his former journey to Philadelphia.

I have the honor to be with the greatest respect Sir Your most obedient & most humble servt,   TH: JEFFERSON

RC (DNA: RG 93). Addressed by TJ: "Timothy Pickering esq Q. M. General Philadelphia." Endorsed (in part): "About a deputy for Virginia Answd."

Richard Claiborne was eventually appointed deputy quartermaster for Virginia; see Pickering to TJ, 15 Dec. 1780; TJ to Pickering, 15 Jan. 1781.

To the Commissioners of the Provision Law

Sᴵʀ   In Council Sepr. 7th 1780

As it appears by the returns made to us that the spirits already procured under the provision Law are sufficient to answer the public purposes for a considerable time, and that the quantities of rum imported, and of brandy and corn spirits likely to be made is such as shoud justly reduce the price of these articles far below what has been allowed by the act of assembly; you are therefore desired to make an immediate return of the quantities you have and to discontinue from the time of receiving this, the taking any more than is already actually seized. [As soon as the season is such as that wheat of the late crop will keep either in bulk or manufacture, you will be pleased to procure as much as will make
pounds of flour, and have the same manufactured, barrelled and stored at the places pointed out in your first instructions. The seconds shoud be made into biscuits if you can have it done; otherwise have it barrelled and stored as before directed with respect to the flour. The cleanings and bran may serve as forage for the horses you use in transportation or may be bartered for any other article you are directed to procure or given in payment for manufacturing or other service.] Corn of the present years growth is not to be taken till further orders, and your powers as to salt have been discontinued by the act of Assembly, since the first of last month. In all other respects you will continue to pursue the instructions heretofore given, making your returns regularly once a month. You are also desired to transmit to me a list of the certificates you have given, specifying the persons name, the sum due him, and the date of the certificate, that it may be lodged with the auditors as a check on counterfeit certificates, and hereafter let such a list accompany every return. I am Gentlemen, Your most ob: humble servt,

Tʜᴏ: Jᴇꜰꜰᴇʀsᴏɴ

FC (Vi, photostat from Brit. Mus.: Add. MSS 38,650). Another FC, identical in substance and differing only in negligible points of phrasing, occurs a few pages earlier in the Governor's Letter Book with the date "sepr. 1780." The latter text contains no indication of the counties to which it was sent, but the former lists the counties both in the caption and in a table appended to the text which also lists the several flour quotas in pounds as follows: Dinwiddie 180,000, Chesterfield 180,000, Amelia 300,000, Cumberland 300,000, Pow-

hatan 180,000, Prince Edward 120,000, Goochland 240,000, Hanover 150,000, Henrico 150,000, Spotsylvania 150,000. There is also, just preceding the present letter in the Governor's Letter Book, a copy of a letter to the Commissioners of the Provision Law in most of the *other* counties in the state; this has the same text except for the omission of the passage relating to flour enclosed in square brackets (supplied) in our text. Its caption indicates that it was sent to Northampton, Accomack, Hampshire, Frederick, Berkeley, Loudoun, Fauquier,

Prince William, Fairfax, Westmoreland, Northumberland, Orange, Culpeper, Stafford, Caroline, King George, Richmond, Essex, Middlesex, Lancaster, Gloucester, New Kent, King William, King and Queen, York, Warwick, Bedford, Buckingham, Amherst, Albemarle, Fluvanna, Louisa, Prince George, Charles City, Surry, James City, Williamsburg, Isle of Wight, Nansemond, Norfolk, Princess Anne, Elizabeth City, Halifax, Charlotte, Lunenburg, Mecklenburg, Brunswick, Sussex, Southampton, Augusta, and Botetourt.

The duties and powers of the Commissioners of the Provision Law are enumerated in the Act for procuring a supply of provisions and other necessaries for the use of the army (Hening, x, 233-7). For all articles taken the Commissioners were to give receipts at certain rates fixed and enumerated in the Act, and "All such receipts or cer-

tificates shall be payable at the treasury within six months from the date, with an interest at the rate of six per centum thereon; allowing always for the difference of value between the time of payment and the delivery of the articles; . . . or otherwise any person holding such receipt or certificate, may pay them to the collector in discharge of his or her next money tax, or his or her next specifick tax, in like kind and quantity." Among TJ's papers survives an interesting tabulation of the results of the collection of supplies made under the Provision Law of 1780 (3 pages, in a clerk's hand, without date; DLC: TJ Papers, 235: 42248-42249). It lists in four columns the places of storage, the counties, the articles, and the names of the commissioners (some gaps occur here); appended is a separate table listing the return of the "Flour called for September 7th. 1780" by counties.

To William Eaton

SIR   In Council september [7,] 1780.

The distress of the southern army calling for our greatest exertions, it becomes necessary that we avail ourselves of the provision law to supply them; and as a call on the counties generally woud produce a glut for a short time, which woud exhaust them at once, and leave the army again in distress, we find it necessary to put it into the hands of some one person who shall call on so many counties at a time and so on successively as may furnish uniform and constant supplies. This duty we expect from you. You will receive herewith blank warrants of appointments which you will fill up with the names of two or three of the most honest and discreet persons in the counties of Pr. Anne, Norfolk, Nansemond, Isle of Wight, So.hampton and Surry, whereby they will be empowered to take live cattle for the use of the army. The acts of assembly made on the subjects and the warrants of appointment herewith transmitted will inform them in what manner they are to conduct themselves. It will be proper for you to withdraw first the beef to be spared from those counties most exposed to the enemy and to draw them off the closest and so proceed to the other counties in order as they stand exposed: it will be necessary for you to provide pastures, drovers &c. for the rent and hire of which you must draw on me. Keep up a punctual correspondence with the commissary attending the southern army that there may be a proper concert in your proceedings for its support. There is at present corn collected in those counties by commissioners of the provision law formerly appointed therein: and as soon as the corn of the present year is fit for use and will keep we shall take measures for procuring that also. The transportation of this is put on you likewise. You know the great scarcity of carts and waggons. We give you a power of impressing them, but are assured they cannot avail you much. Turn your attention therefore to transportation by water and south quay seems the proper point from which to set out. Three routs present themselves for carrying thence either wholly or in part by water to Halifax. 1. down the black water, and up Meherrin creek or Weecaunsee creek both of which point far towards Halifax. Want of information prevents my knowing whether they are navigable. I fear they are not. 2. down blackwater and up Meherrin river to the nearest landing to Halifax. This will leave a considerable portage. 3. down black water and Chowan and up Roanoke. This is very long and subject to great delays from freshes. You will judge from enquiring [the] means of transportation either by land or water of which you shall be possess[ed] which of these is most practicable. Inform me once a month what supplies [you] shall [have] furnished, what prospects you have, and what [counties you are engaged] in [at] the time; and before you shall have fully [executed your commission in all] those for which you have now warrants, apply to me for others. Your trouble in this undertaking shall be duly rewarded.

I am sir Your very hble servant,   TH: JEFFERSON

FC (Vi, photostat from Brit. Mus.: Add. MSS 38,650). Enclosures: letter of appointment to Eaton, same date, following, and blank appointments for commissioners under Eaton (printed as an enclosure under the following letter); also, presumably, copies of the Act for procuring provisions for the army (Hening, X, 233-7) and of that part of the Act empowering the Governor and Council to impress livestock, &c. (same, p. 312).

Entered in Governor's Letter Book (now in Brit. Mus.) under "September 1780," this letter obviously covered the following one, which is precisely dated.

To William Eaton,
enclosing Warrants for Impressing Cattle

SIR   In Council September 7th 1780

You are hereby appointed a Commissioner of the provision Law in all the counties on the south side of James river, but restrained specially to the procuring houses for storing them, waggons, carts, horses, gear, drivers, boats and other vessels and their crew for transporting provisions, materials for making such barrels or other proper casks or boxes for containing the same, and pastures for the live cattle. You are to transmit to me monthly by safe conveyances duplicate Lists of all the certificates or receipts you shall have given in pursuance of this power; specifying the name of the person the article seized or service performed the price to be paid and the date of the certificate to be lodged as a check against counterfeit certificates. In the execution of this power we trust to your discretion to make it as light and equal as you can on the people; and pay attention also to any particular circumstances which may distinguish special cases. I am sir, Your most obedient servant,

T: JEFFERSON

ENCLOSURE

Form of the blank warrants given Mr. Eaton for the appointment of Commissioners of live cattle in P. Anne, Norfolk, Nansemd., Isle of Wight, So.hampton and Surry.

In Council sepr. 7th. 1780.

You are hereby appointed a commissioner under the act for procuring a supply of provisions and other necessaries for the use of the army within the county of   but restrained specially to the procuring live cattle fit for beef and pastures to confine them in. As to the number of live cattle to be collected by you, not exceeding the proportion allowed by law, you will govern yourself by such instructions as you will receive from Mr. Eaton, appointed specially to receive these beeves from you at such place as he shall point out, from whence he is to convey them to the southern army. You are to transmit monthly to me a return of the amount of the beef you seize, and lists of all the certificates or receipts you shall have given, specifying the name of the owner, the price to be paid and the date of the certificate. Duplicates of these shoud come by different safe conveyances as they will be the only checks on counterfeits. That you may be informed of the manner in which you are to proceed you will receive herewith an extract from the act of Assembly. I am, Sir, Your most obed: servant,

TH: JEFFERSON

FC (Vi, photostat from Brit. Mus.: Add. MSS 38,650). Several copies of the enclosure (FC, same location; printed herewith) were originally enclosed, together with the original of the present letter, in TJ's other letter of this date to William Eaton, preceding.

To George Rogers Clark

SIR   Richmond Sepr. 8th. 1780.

Your Letters of July by Mr. Randolph came safe to hand. In a former letter to you on the Subject of this summer's operations (which I hear you never received) I informed you that the County Lieutenants to whom I had referred to determine on a plan of co-operating with their militia had estimated the expence at 1,995,-000 pounds, a greater sum than we had in our treasury, could every other demand of money for government have been suspended. This of course negatived the attempt on a large scale for this season: and indeed no wealth of which we have a prospect will enable us to undertake an expedition on their estimate, while the war continues to the Eastward. I have no doubt however but this estimate might by a judicious hand be greatly abridged. Thus disappointed of our first wish, we determine to order 280 militia out with Colo. Crockets men, who tho' principally intended to be stationed at posts, were yet made subject to your orders and expected to be employed by you in active enterprizes as long as the season would admit. Colo. Crocket will now march within a few days. In order that you might be supplied with provisions from the inhabited country between the blue ridge and Ohio, a Commissary and Quartermaster (Mr. Boush) was appointed at Winchester and another (Evan Baker) in Washington with orders to forward their provision to you. From the former I have heard nothing. The latter is preparing necessaries for Colo. Crocketts march. Our late misfortunes to the Southward will be related to you by Mr. Randolph. They occasion great calls on our militia and will compleatly disable us from further strengthening you this season. I am to ask the favor of you to countersign all demands for money which arise under you. We have been obliged to decline many, which very possibly might be just, because they were drawn by persons unknown to us, and for services perhaps not authorized by you. The Militia accounts incurred in the expedition you are now engaged in must come to the auditors authenticated in the same way. Some Draughts brought by Mr. Randolph have been rejected for this reason. Yours and Major Slaughters are duly honoured. There happened an unlucky circumstance for the owners of the latter. The assembly had raised the price of land by a law which was not to take place but on my receiving a certain matter of information and then proclaiming it. I happened to be from this place a fortnight. During my absence this information came, as did Mr. Randolph. He had occasion to leave town. I returned and witheld the proclamation two days waiting for his return that the peoples orders might be paid off and their money laid out as they had directed in lands at the old price. Unluckily he did not come for several days, and we were obliged to proclaim the law, which put it out of our own power to relieve them.

As to the choice of the situation on the Missisippi we leave it still, as before, to yourself altogether. I wish it were possible to engage the Piankishaws in war against the British Indians. Should the ammunition sent and to be sent this year to the Westward be insufficient, we will send a further quantity if desired by you. I am Sir with great esteem & respect Your most obedt. hble Servant,

TH: JEFFERSON

RC (WHi); in a clerk's hand, signed by TJ; endorsed in two different hands: "Govr. Jefferson Sept. 8th 1780. Operations against Detroit Fort Jefferson Piankishaws." FC (Vi, photostat from Brit. Mus.: Add. MSS 38,650).

Clark's LETTERS OF JULY have not been found; nor has the particular FORMER LETTER from TJ to Clark here mentioned, though see TJ to Clark, 19 Mch. 1780.

To Samuel Griffin

SIR   Richmond Sep. 8. 1780.

On the receipt of your first Letter on the subject of the public prison we desired Colo. Muter as Commissioner of the war office, to take order for making the necessary repairs. We knew that Mr. Brian was then returning, who executes provost duties there. I hope therefore that that business is in a proper train. It is not intended that any prisoners shall ever be kept there longer than till a guard can attend to bring them to the prison ship or carry them to Winchester. It was utterly unknown to me that a single prisoner was there at this time, having never been informed that any were sent there since we had the jail cleared of them. I must take for granted that the commanding officer there has by this time seen to their safe custody or to their being forwarded here. I shall always be obliged to you for any information of pretermissions of this kind that I may have it in my power to take order in them.

I am authorized to assure you that the bills drawn on us by Mr. Pollard and formerly presented by you shall be discharged at the current exchange at the time of actual paiment. I am Sir with the greatest esteem & respect Your most obedt. humble servt.,

TH: JEFFERSON

RC (Joseph E. Fields, Joliet, Illinois, 1948). FC (Vi, photostat from Brit. Mus.: Add. MSS 38,650).

Griffin's letters ON THE SUBJECT OF THE PUBLIC PRISON have not been found.

To Samuel Huntington

SIR   Richmond Septr. 8. 1780.

On receipt of the resolutions of Congress of June 19, for procuring Horses to remount Whites and Washingtons cavalry we laid the same before the assembly and were authorized by them to engage the state for payment. We thereon sent out powers to the different counties to purchase 160 Horses which were properly described in addition to 83, the purchase of which we had before authorized.

That some regard might be paid to œconomy we at first restrained the prices to average not more than £2500, and afterwards £3000 exclusive of incidental expences. The purchases have not been so soon made as we expected tho' a considerable number have been made and the gentlemen employed are still going on. The inclosed Letter from Colo. White complaining of this limitation of price, was not calculated either in its matter or stile to move us to an alteration of our instructions; conscious that our endeavours to reconcile œconomy and the public wants must meet with the approbation of every person who attends at all to the dangers impending over us from circumscribed finances. Your resolution[s] of August 7. which came to hand two or three Days ago and which restrain the allowance for horses in another instance tho to be used in a similar way to 100 Dolls. hard Money equal only to about £2000 at the present exchange have induced a doubt in us whether you may chuse that any future purchases for Whites and Washingtons Cavalry should be made at so high a price as we had authorized and ha[ve] caused me to trouble you with a Letter desiring your advice on that head. From the tardy progress made in purchasing at £3000 I must suppose that any considerable reduction would put a stop to them altogether. While it shews that our allowance was not extravagant, the numbers purchased also prove that it was not so frugal as to defeat the purpose.

Your instructions shall be implicitly followed, and will I hope be communicated to me. I have the honor to be with all possible Respect Your Excellency's Most Obed. & most hble. Servt.,

TH: JEFFERSON

P.S. I beg leave to add that measures are taken for cloathing and furnishing twelve horses to Major Nelson's two troops, which are what is wanting to equip them for service. It will be impossible to permit Capt. Read's troop to leave the barracks without giving up all the fugitives from the Convention troops.

RC (DLC: PCC, No. 71, I); in a clerk's hand, signed by TJ; endorsed by Charles Thomson: "Letter from Govr. Jefferson Sept 8. 1780 Read 14 Enclosed letter from Col White Sept. 2. Referred to Mr Bland Mr Henry Mr Hill." FC (Vi, photostat from Brit. Mus.: Add. MSS 38,650). Enclosure missing, but see entry for White to TJ, 2 Sep. 1780.

For Congress' RESOLUTIONS of 19 June and 7 Aug. relating to purchase of horses for the southern cavalry, see JCC, XVII, 527-8, 707-8; see also TJ to the Persons Appointed to Purchase Horses, 6 Sep. 1780. For Congress' action on the present letter, see JCC, XVIII, 824, 850-1, 874, 889 (14, 22, 29 Sep., 2 Oct.), and Huntington to TJ, 3 Oct. 1780.

From George Muter

SIR   Septr. 8. 1780.

I have the honour of inclosing to your Excellency, Mr. Ginters letter to Mr. Jamieson (with the papers it incloses) and a letter from Mr. Walter Peter to me.

Permitt me to observe Sir, that the whole of Mr. Fornier's pay added to the ration he drew, wou'd not have been sufficient to pay for his board at Mr. Ginters, unless he had thrown in along with his ration, his priveleges of drawing rum &c at the reduced prices. This I know to have been actually the case, with many officers at York last fall, when I had the command there, and on these terms they were boarded. I cannot certainly say that such were the terms on which Mr. Fournier boarded with Mr. Ginter. But, I am of opinion, if such were the terms (which is probable) and Majr. Fornier has received no compensation in lieu of drawing his rum &c at the reduced prices, that Mr. Ginter is entittled to draw those articles at the reduced prices, or ought to be allowed a reasonable compensation in lieu of them.

I beg leave to refer your Excellency, principally to Mr. Peter's letter; and wou'd only observe, that I cou'd fall on no other method of getting the necessary work done at Hoods, than getting the favour of Mr. Peter to hire labourers on the cheapest terms he possibly cou'd. I am much affraid I shall find it very difficult to get the bricks wanted. I have written to Mr. Harrison of Brandon (who has a large quantity he will not probably use soon) to purchase what are wanted from him; but when my letter got to his house, he was from home and expected to be so for some weeks, and his father cou'd not say whether he wou'd dispose of any of his bricks or not. The State is indebted a chimney to Mr. Peter, besides what are wanted for the barracks. I have the honour to be Your Excellency's Most humble servant, GEORGE MUTER

RC (Vi); addressed: "His Excellency the Governour"; docketed. Enclosures not found.

To George Muter

In Council Sep. 8. 1780.

A ton of lead should be sent to Fredericksburg in waggons returning empty to Mr. Washington who has the care of the powder. An order may be drawn on him also for 30 bushels of salt.

TH: JEFFERSON

RC (Vi); written below a letter of Charles Dick to George Muter, 5 Sep. 1780; see below. Addressed (twice) to Muter and docketed. The letter from Dick to Muter (printed in full in CVSP, I, 372-3), requesting lead and salt for use at the gun factory at Fredericksburg, was evidently transmitted to TJ for authorization, although there is no notation by Muter to that effect.

To John Nelson

SIR   Richmond sepr. 8. 1780.

On receipt of your Letter I have directed cloathing to be got ready for your men. Lieutenant Armistead is authorized to purchase twelve [horses] for you. He informs me that six saddles are still wanting. These we [shall] find it difficult to procure, because they are only in the hands of merchants who will let us have nothing, but for ready money which we have not, nor can have till the meeting of the assembly. We shall direct every endeavour to be used for procuring them. With respect to your officers going into continental service, we can have no objections to putting two of the troops altoge[ther] on the continental establishment, but that it transcends our power. The assembly alone can do this with the consent of Congress. If the officers chuse it I will propose it. The third troop must be reserved for the post in Albemarle where their services in retaking deserters are indispensable. You desire blank commissions to be sent you, but do not explain what kind of commissions or for what purpose. I am sir, with great respect Your most ob: and hble servant, TH: JEFFERSON

P.S. The troop at the barracks was lent to the Continent for the use of that particular post. They are not subject to their orders for any other purpose.

FC (Vi, photostat from Brit. Mus.: Add. MSS 38,650); at head of text: "Major John Nelson." Nelson's LETTER has not been found.

To D'Anmours

SIR   Richmond sepr. 9th 1780.

Your favour of the 3rd instant came to hand last night by Captain Laport. It is unfortunate for you that Major Galvan had left the station. It happened thus. The sailing of the french fleet in two divisions was a circumstance equally unknown to Major Galvan and my self. I received a Letter from General Washington congratulating me on the arrival of the french fleet in general terms, and no idea held out that it was only one division and that a second was still to come. I sent to Major Galvan an extract of that Letter who thinking I suppose that the purpose of his mission was over and that the Letter which shoud have conveyed him orders to withdraw must have miscarried, returned for Philadelphia, and sent in the line of expresses. So much in justice to him and myself. It happened unfortunately for the purpose now in contemplation that Commodore Barron with our brig and two armed boats sail this day up the bay to form a junction with some vessels of the state of Maryland for the purpose of a joint cruize to clear the bay and the vicinities of its capes of the little hostile vessels which have so long infested it. This leaves us without a single vessel which coud answer [your] purpose and in actual readiness. We have one which requires some alterations in her sails and cleaning which we are assured shall be compleated in a week. Having no earlier resource, she is ordered to be made ready with all possible dispatch and I think you may be assured of her going to you within that time. An officer will be put into her with orders to follow your directions implicitly. I enclose you a Letter to Colo. Wishart for a guard of 12 men the number Major Galvan had, desiring him if possible to raise six or eight militia horse to attend you. I also enclose you an order authorizing any commissary, quarter master, commissioners of the grain tax or the provision law or other persons[1] having public provisions in their hands or authority to procure them to furnish to yourself guard and horsemen whatever provisions and forage may be necessary. The expresses one of whom will carry this set out this evening or tomorrow morning to form a line between us. One of these is stationed at Sandy point another at Sleepy hole, which divides the whole distance into three, of from 40 to 45 miles. Their orders are to travel by night and by day without regard to weather noting on their dispatches the hour and minute at which each man receives and delivers them, that we may immediately know in what hands any delay happens. In this way if they do their duty intelligence shoud pass between us in 24 hours. I was setting in motion this morning the line of expresses from hence to Phila. Your Letter to the French Minister therefore went by this channel and saves Mr. Laport the Journey. The minister will receive it probably in three days. I shall be glad to use any means in my power to make your situation as safe and comfortable as possible and am with the greatest esteem & respect your most obedient and mo: hble servant,   TH: JEFFERSON

FC (Vi, photostat from Brit. Mus.: Add. MSS 38,650). Enclosures: TJ to Wishart, same date (below); order to commissaries, &c., to supply D'Anmours (missing).

D'Anmours' FAVOUR of 3 Sep. is missing, but see TJ to Wishart of the present date.

1 FC reads "purpose."

To William Davies

SIR   Richmond September 9th. 1780.

The Sentence of the court martial however inadequate the punishment is to the offence, seems to be such as the law has authorized, except as to the musket lost. For this indemnification we shall take more effectual measures by stopping the full worth out of the pay of the deserter. The Act of assembly named six places of rendezvous for the new recruits and authorized us to name two more and to appoint an officer to attend at each place to review and receive them. This power we delegated to Genl. Muhlenburg who has accordingly sent out orders [to] officers. We are endeavoring to get blankets from Baltimore. Besides this we expect some by importation. How ever apprehensive that neither of these resources might be timely enough, the measure you recommended was adopted, and an assurance given that such of the new recruits as woud bring their blankets into the service shoud be paid for them. Dr. Foushe on receiving my Letter to deliver you the medicine written for, called on me and informed me there were not in our stores more than two or three articles wanted, and that the house not being yet ready to receive them they still remained in such a state that he coud not get at any particular article. I think that he coud do it within a few days. I am with great respect sir Your most obt humble servt,

TH: JEFFERSON

FC (Vi, photostat from Brit. Mus.: Add. MSS 38,650).

Davies' letter to which this is an answer has not been found; nor has any

letter from TJ to DR. FOUSHE (doubtless William Foushee, director of the military hospital at Richmond; Gwathmey, *Hist. Reg. of Virginians in the Revolution*) on the subject of medicines.

From Horatio Gates

SIR   Hillsborough 9th: Sept: 1780

Intelligence of a very particular sort is Just arrived from Camden, by a person in whom we can confide; and no doubt remains, but that he may have been imposed upon by a Finesse of the Enemy. Since then, Two Deserters from the Enemys 23 Regiment, came in, in a manner confirm the Intelligence. It is as Follows. That Lord Cornwallis is going immediately to Embarque his Main Force at George Town for Cape Fear; and has wrote to Sr. Harry Clinton, to send a reinforcement to take immediate possession of Portsmouth, in Your State; That Two Regiments of Hessians only, are to remain in Garrison at Charles T., and the Seventh Regiment at Savanah. That a Guard would be left at Camden to Cover the General Hospital, and send the Sick, and Wounded, as they recover to Charles T. The 63d. Regiment had already march'd down with the prisoners and Brian[1] Corps. Tarleton with the Legion, was gone to the Waxhaws, to Collect Horses for the Waggons, to take the Baggage down the Country. The Council of Officers who assembled Yesterday at my Quarters, were of Opinion, that I should immediately Transmit this Intelligence to Your Excellency, that The Executive of Your State might be preparing to Defeat the Enemys Designs. Since I wrote to Your Excellency on the 5th. Colo. Marian [Marion] of So: Carolina has Surprized a party of the Enemy, near Santee River, escorting 150 prisoners of the Maryland Division, he took the Party, and released the Prisoners, who are now upon their March to Cross Creek, where I sent Lieut. Col. Ford, and proper Officers to Conduct them Hither. When these Join, Our loss in Continentals will be Few, in Comparison of what, from their once hopeless Situation, might have been expected. Certain persons here have been extreamly Anxious that I should remove the whole Force, and take post with them immediately in Mecklingbourg, an[d] Roan [Rowan] Countys, on the Western Border of this State. As this does not Correspond with my Own Judgement, nor with that of many Others whom I esteem very good Officers I shall defer doing it until I am convinced by some movement of The Enemy which way they Point, and what is the real Object they have in View. Should Willmington in this State, and Portsmo: in Yours, be the posts they intend to take, I conceive the Southern Army would be intirely misplaced at Charlotte Salisbury and the Ford upon the Yadkin. Consequently I shall Halt all The Continental Troops here until the designs of The Enemy become so apparent there can be no mistaking them. General Stevens, who is posted near Guilford Court House, acquaints me in his Letter the 6th: Inst. that his Command, is by Desertion, reduced to 130 Men, I have directed Him to Officer that Number in a proper Manner and come Himself with the Supernumerary Officers, to Hillsboro: in his Way to Richmond, where he can receive the Orders of The Executive for his Future Conduct. I am astonish'd at Col. Bluefords[2] Command arriving here this day without Tents; Sickness Death, and Desertion, must certainly be the dire result of sending Troops into the Field at the Autumnal Equinox unfurnish'd with so Essential an Article; Cost what they will, or get them how we may, they must be Supplied [or] ruin will ensue. I request Your Excellency to send an Exact Copy of this Letter, with your First Dispatch to Congress; and desire the President to order one to be sent immediately to His Excellency General Washington.

I am Sir, your Excellency's Most obedient servt.,

HORATIO GATES

Dft (NHi); endorsed. Tr (DLC) of Dft. Tr (DLC: PCC, No. 71, 1) of missing RC forwarded to Congress in TJ's letter to Huntington, 14 Sep. 1780, q.v. Other transcripts are in DLC: Washington Papers, in MdAA, and in CSmH. Complimentary close supplied from another text.

[1] Other texts read "Bryant's."
[2] Other texts read "Buford's."

From James Monroe

DEAR SIR   Richmond Sepr. 9. 1780.

Your kindness and attention to me in this and a variety of other instances has realy put me under such obligations to you that I fear I shall hardly ever have it in my power to repay them. But believe me in what ever situation of life the chance of fortune may place me, no circumstance can happen which will give me such pleasure or make me so happy, at present or during my progress thro' life, as to have it in my power to convince you of the proper impressions they have made on me. A variety of disappointments with respect to the prospects of my private fortune previous to my acquaintance with your Excellency, upon which I had built as on ground which could not decieve me and which fail'd in a manner which could not have been expected, perplex'd my plan of life and expos'd me to inconveniences which had nearly destroy'd me. In this situation had I not form'd a connection with you I should most certainly have retir'd from society with a resolution never to have enter'd on the stage again. I could never have prevail'd on myself to have taken an introduction to the Country or to have deriv'd any advantages or even to have remain'd in connection with one, by whom I felt myself injur'd but whose near relationship and situation in life put it in his power to serve me. In this situation you became acquainted with me and undertook the direction of my studies and believe me I feel that whatever I am at present in the opinion of others or whatever I may be in future has greatly arose from your friendship. My plan of life is now fix'd, has a certain object for its view and does not depend on other chance or circumstance further than the same events may affect the publick at large. In the late instance when we were threatned by an invasion from the south our prospects were so gloomy and the danger so eminent that I thought it the duty of every citizen to turn out and bear a part in repelling the invasion. The attention your Excellency and Council paid me in calling on me to perform the duties of so important a trust at so critical a time if it had went no further than intimating the good opinion you severally entertain'd of me, I knew did me honor and gave me more pleasure than any pecuneary compensation I could possibly derive from it. I was happy in undertaking the charge with a view of performing some service to the country and also of assuring you that even in an affair which had so distant a relation to you, how effectually you might command my small services. My plan of taking nothing for any little service I might do the publick in this cause did not commence with my late employment. During the greater part of my service in the army I had not my expences borne and as in this instance I have only acted the part which the opinion of the duty I owe to the publick dictated and which many worthy Republicans are now acting without even a similar compensation, it is my wish not to deviate from it. Under the present direction my prospects are fix'd and altho my private fortune is but small still it is sufficient for my maintenance in the pursuit of them. Colo. Lawson waited on me the other day and propos'd my bearing part with him in his present undertaking. I excus'd myself by every argument which my situation and the nature of his plan would admit of and had been happy to have evaded it altogether. I represented to him the nature of things in that country and that the ultimate advantage which the success of his plan could effect would be the driving the enemy into Chas. town from which they might advance so soon as the militia moulder'd away. I wish'd him, as Council are making every exertion in their power, for the defence of that Country, to change his view and rather form a corps within the state or one more immediately for its defence than to go in search of adventure more remote which promises at best but little advantage to our towns while it exhausts and weakens ourselves, but promis'd if he could get no one more capable or whose private circumstances would better dispence with their absence than myself, if his plan succeeded I would bear a part. If I can possibly avoid it I mean not to leave my studies a day, but if in the progress of things I should be so circumstanc'd as in your opinion I ow'd it to myself or the publick to bear a part, so far as the publick interest will be forwarded by furnishing myself or the troops I command with necessaries so far I shall be happy to receive them. You will forgive the liberty I have taken in writing you a letter of this kind. Your kindness has realy led me into it and at the same time it enables me to explain some part of my conduct. I am happy that it gives me an opportunity of assuring you how just a sense I have of your good offices.

I have the honor to be Dear Sir with great respect & esteem yr. sincere friend & very humble servt.,   JAS. MONROE

RC (DLC).

To John Smith

SIR   Richmond Sep. 9. 1780.

Your favor of the 31st. came to hand yesterday. We had been apprised of the destruction of Fort Randolph soon after it happened. But it was thought that the importance of the post required that it should be rebuilt, and we have no means of doing this without the aid of militia. Besides reestablishing this post and establishing others, we expect the militia will be engaged ranging on active enterprizes against the Indians. Colo. Crocket will be ready to march in a few days. We suppose he has taken measures for rendezvousing and marching all the militia from the several counties; this business having been confided to him.

We shall be glad if you can engage a guard for the prisoners at Winchester for a twelvemonth. We however have no authority to engage them but as militia, which you know precludes clothing. It will be a proper subject of application to the assembly who I am satisfied would give a pay equal to what it should be. There is the greater need for this as the prisoners there are likely to multiply since we have concluded to turn over all we get to the Continent. There are 50 here now to be sent there, and as many more coming from Carolina.

I am with great respect Sir Your most obedt. humble servt.,

TH: JEFFERSON

RC (Vi). FC (Vi, photostat from Brit. Mus.: Add. MSS 38,650); at head of text: "Colo: Jno. Smith, Frederic." The following is docketed on FC in the hand of Smith: "There was a company of militia marched on the rect. of this letter commd. by Capt. Aaron Mercer. J. Smith Cy. Lt Fk."

Smith's FAVOR OF THE 31ST. has not been found. FORT RANDOLPH, at the junction of the Great Kanawha and Ohio, had been named for Peyton Randolph (*Official Letters*, II, 200, note; 201, note). A GUARD FOR THE PRISONERS AT WINCHESTER: See John Smith to Isaac Zane, 16 Nov. 1780.

To William Wishart

SIR   Richmond Sepr. 9. 1780.

The french Consul the Chevalier D'Anmours goes to take the post lately occupied by Major Galvan. He will require the same attention, which I prayed you to shew the former gentleman. You will be pleased to furnish him with a guard of twelve men with proper officers from your militia or the ranging company as you find best. I must also desire you to use your utmost endeavours to raise six or eight men to furnish their own horses and do the duty of lookouts, the whole to be subject to the orders of the Council. I furnish him with authority to call on any person having public provisions to furnish himself, guard and horsemen with provisions and forage. The distance between us rendering it difficult to give new directions on any particular emergency I must beg the favor of you to consider it as [an] intention that every aid shall be furnished which the Cheva: D'Anmours shall desire and that you would use those diligent exertions in furnishing them, a confidence in which occasions the present reliance on you. I am sir with great respect, Your most ob: & mo: hble servant,   T. JEFFERSON

FC (Vi, photostat from Brit. Mus.: Add. MSS 38,650). At head of text: "Colo William Wishart of Princess [Anne] County." The original was enclosed in TJ to D'Anmours, same date, q.v.

From Samuel Huntington,
enclosing Papers Relating to Western Claims by the States

SIR   Philadelphia September 10. 1780

Your Excellency will receive herewith enclosed an Act of Congress of the 6. Instant, adopting the report of a Committee, together with Copies of the several Papers referred to in the report.

I am directed to transmit Copies of this report and the several Papers therein mentioned to the Legislatures of the several States, that they all may be informed of the Desires and Endeavours of Congress on so important a Subject, and those particular States which have Claims to the western Territory and the State of Maryland may adopt the Measures recommended by Congress in Order to obtain a final ratification of the Articles of Confederation.

Congress, impressed with a Sense of the vast Importance of the Subject have maturely considered the same, and the result of their Deliberation is contained in the enclosed report, which being full and expressive of their Sentiments upon the Subject: without any additional Observations; it is to be hoped and most earnestly desired that the Wisdom, Generosity and Candour of the Legislatures of the several States which have it in their Power, on the one Hand to remove the Obstacles, and on the other to complete the Confederation, may direct them to such Measures in Compliance with the earnest recommendations of Congress as shall speedily accomplish an Event so important and desirable as the ratification of the Confederation by all the States. I have the Honor to be with the highest respect & Consideration your Excellency's most obedient Servant,   SAM. HUNTINGTON   President

ENCLOSURE   I

By the State of Maryland
A Declaration

Whereas the General Assembly of Maryland hath heretofore Resolved "That the Delegates from this State should be instructed to remonstrate to the Congress that this State esteem it essentially necessary for rendering the Union lasting that the United States in Congress assembled should have full Power to ascertain and fix the western Limits of those States that claim to the Mississipi or South Sea."

"That this State considered themselves justly entitled to a Right in

Common with the other Members of the Union to that extensive Tract of Country which lies to the Westward of the Frontiers of the united States, the property of which was not vested in, or granted to Individuals at the Commencement of the present War; That the same had been or might thereafter be gained from the King of Great Britain, or the native Indians by the Blood and Treasure of all, and ought therefore to be a common Estate to be granted out on Terms beneficial to all the united States, And that they should Use their utmost Endeavours that an Article to that Effect be made part of the Confederation.

That this State wou'd contribute their Quota of Men and Money towards carrying on the present War with Great Britain for the Purpose of establishing the freedom and Independence of the United States according to such Rule of Proportion as should be determined by the united States in Congress assembled, and would pay their proportion of all Money issued or borrowed by Congress or which might thereafter be issued or borrowed for the purpose aforesaid. And that this State would accede to and faith[fully] execute all Treaties which had been or should be made by Authority of Congress, and would be bound and governed by the Determination of the United States in Congress assembled, relative to Peace or War.

That this State hath upon all Occasions shewn her Zeal to promote and maintain the general Welfare of the United States of America: That upon the same principle they are of Opinion a Confederation of perpetual Friendship and Union between the united States is highly necessary for the Benefit of the whole; and that they are most willing and desirous to enter into a Confederation and Union, but at the same time such Confederation should in their Opinion be formed on the Principles of Justice and Equity.["]

Which Resolves, Remonstrances, and Instructions were by our Delegates laid before Congress and the Objections therein made to the Confederation were submitted in Writing to their Consideration, and the several Points fully discussed and debated, And the Alterations and Amendments proposed by our Delegates to the Confederation in Consequence of the aforesaid Instructions by us to them given, were rejected, and no satisfactory Reasons assigned for the Rejection thereof.

We do therefore declare that we esteem it fundamentally wrong and repugnant to every principle of Equity and good Policy, on which a Confederation between free, Sovereign and independent States ought to be founded, That this or any other State entering into such Confederation, should be burthened with heavy Expences for the subduing and Guarranteeing immense Tracts of Country, if they are not to share any part of the Monies arising from the Sales of the Lands within those Tracts, or be otherwise benefited thereby. In Conformity to this our Opinion, the Sentiments of our Constituents, in Justice to them and Ourselves,—And least such Construction, should hereafter be put on the undefined Expressions contained in the third Article of the Confederation, and the proviso to the ninth (according to which no State is to be deprived of Territory for the Benefit of the United States) as may subject all to such Guarranty as aforesaid, and deprive Some of the said States of their Right in Common to the Lands aforesaid.

We declare that we mean not to subject ourselves to such Guaranty nor will we be responsible for any part of such Expences, unless the third Article and Proviso aforesaid, be explained so as to prevent their being hereafter construed in a Manner injurious to this State. Willing however to remove as far as we can consistently with the trust conferred upon us every other Objection on our part to the Confederation, and anxiously desirous to cement by the most indisoluble Ties, that Union, which has hitherto enabled us to resist the Artifices and the Power of Great Britain and concieving ourselves, as we have heretofore declared, justly entitled to a right in Common with the other Members of the Union to that extensive Country lying to the Westward of the Frontiers of the united States, the Property of which was not vested in or granted to Individualy at the Commencement of the present War.

We declare that we will accede to the Confederation, provided an Article or Articles be added thereto, giving full power to the united States in Congress assembled to ascertain and fix the Western Limits of the States claiming to extend to the Mississipi, or South Sea, and expressly reserving and securing to the united States a Right in Common in, and to all the Lands lying to the Westward of the Frontiers as aforesaid, not granted to, surveyed for, or purchased by Individuals at the Commencement of the present War, in such Manner that the said Lands be sold out, or otherwise disposed of for the Common Benefit of all the States, and that the Money ariseing from the Sale of these Lands, or the Quit Rents reserved thereon, may be deemed and taken as part of the Monies belonging to the United States, and as such be appropriated by Congress towards defraying the Expences of the War, and the payment of Interest on Monies borrowed or to be borrowed on the Credit of the United States from France or any other European Power, or for any other joint Benefit of the United States.

We do further declare that the exclusive Claim set up by some States to the whole western Country by extending their Limits to the Mississipi or South Sea, is in our Judgment without any solid Foundation, and we religiously believe, will if submitted to, prove ruinous to this State, and to other States similary circumstanced, and in process of Time be the Means of subverting the Confederation, if it be not explained by the additional Article or Articles proposed, so as to obviate all Misconstruction and Misinterpretation of those parts thereof that are hereinbefore specified.

We entered into this just and necessary War, to defend our Rights against the Attacks of Avarice and Ambition; We have made the most strenuos Efforts during the Prosecution of it; And we are resolved to continue them until our Independence is firmly established: Hitherto we have successfully resisted, and we hope, with the Blessing of Providence, for final Success. If the Enemy encouraged by the Appearance of Divisions among us, and the Hope of our not confederating, should carry on Hostilities longer than they otherwise would have done, let those be responsible for the Prolongation of the War, and all it's consequent Calamities, who by refusing to comply with Requisitions so just and reasonable, have hitherto prevented the Confederation from taking

Place and are therefore justly chargeable with every Evil, which hath flowed and may flow from such Procrastination.

By the House of Delegates

  Decr. 15. 1778

Read and assented to

By Order

  J Duckett   Clk H.D.

By the Senate Decr. 15. 1778.

Read and assented to

By Order R. Ridgly   Clk S

ENCLOSURE II

Instructions *of the General Assembly of Maryland to George Plater, William Paca, William Carmichael, John Henry, James Forbes, and Daniel of St. Thomas Jenifer, Esquires.*

Gentlemen,

Having conferred upon you a trust of the highest nature, it is evident, we place great confidence in your integrity abilities and zeal to promote the general welfare of the United States, and the particular interest of this State where the latter is not incompatible with the former. But to add greater weight to your proceedings in Congress and to take away all suspicion that the opinions you there deliver and the votes you give may be the mere opinions of Individuals, and not resulting from your knowledge of the sense and deliberate judgement of the State you represent, we think it our duty to instruct you as followeth on the subject in which unfortunately a supposed difference of interest has produced an almost equal division of sentiments among the several states composing the union. We say a supposed difference of interests: for if local attachments, and prejudices, and the avarice and ambition of Individuals would give way to the dictates of a sound policy founded on the principles of justice (and no other policy but what is founded on these immutable principles deserves to be called sound) we flatter ourselves this apparent diversity of Interests would soon vanish and all the States would confederate on terms mutually advantageous to all, for they would then perceive that no other confederation than one so formed can be lasting. Altho' the pressure of immediate calamities, the dread of their continuance from the appearance of disunion, and some other peculiar circumstances may have induced some States to accede to the present confederation contrary to their own interests and Judgments, it requires no great share of Foresight to predict, that when these causes cease to operate, the States which have thus acceded to the confederation, will consider it as no longer binding, and will eagerly embrace the first Occasion of asserting their just rights and securing their Independence. Is it possible that those States, who are ambitiously grasping for territories, to which in our judgement they have not the least shadow of exclusive right, will use with greater moderation the increase of Wealth and power derived from those territories, when acquired, than what they have displayed in their endeavours to acquire them? We think not. We are convinced the same spirit which hath prompted them to insist on a claim so extravagant, so repugnant to every principle of justice, so incompatible with the general welfare of all the States, will urge them on to add oppression to injustice. If they should not be incited by a superiority of Wealth and strength to oppose by open force their less wealthy and less powerful neighbours, yet the depopulation, and consequently the impoverishment of those States will necessarily follow, which by an unfair construction of the confederation may be strip'd of a common interest in and the common benefits derivable from the western country. Supposed, for instance, Virginia indisputably possessed of the extensive and fertile country, to which she has set up a claim, what would be the probable consequences to Maryland of such an undisturbed and undisputed possession? They cannot escape the least discerning—Virginia, by selling on the most moderate terms a small proportion of the lands in question, would draw into her treasury, vast sums of money and in proportion to the sums arising from such sales, would be enabled to lessen her taxes. Lands comparatively cheap and taxes comparatively low with the Lands and taxes of an adjacent State, would quickly drain the State thus disadvantageously circumstanced of its most useful inhabitants; its wealth and its consequence in the scale of the confederated States would sink of course.

A claim so injurious to more than one half, if not to the whole of the United States, ought to be supported by the clearest evidence of the right. Yet what evidences of that right have been produced? What arguments alledged in support either of the evidence or the right? None that we have heard of deserving a serious reputation.

It has been said that some of the delegates of a neighbouring State have declared their opinion of the impracticability of governing the extensive dominion claimed by that State; hence also the necessity was admitted of dividing its territory and erecting a new State under the auspices and direction of the elder from whom no doubt it would receive its form of government, to whom it would be bound by some alliance, or confederacy, and by whose councils it would be influenced. Such a measure, if ever attempted would certainly be opposed by the other States as inconsistent with the letter and spirit of the proposed confederation, should it take place, by establishing a Sub-confederacy Imperium in Imperio. The State possessed of this extensive dominion must then either submit to all the inconveniences of an overgrown and unwieldy Government, or suffer the authority of Congress to interpose at a future time, and to lop off a part of its territory to be erected into a new and free State and admitted into the confederation on such conditions as shall be settled by nine States. If it is necessary for the happiness and tranquillity of a State thus overgrown, that Congress should hereafter interfere, and divide its territory, why is the claim to that territory now made and so pertinaciously insisted on? We can suggest to ourselves but two motives; either the declaration of relinquishing at some future period a portion of the country, now contended for was made to lull suspicion asleep, and to cover the designs of a secret ambition, or if the thought was seriously entertained, the lands are now claimed to reap an immediate profit from the sale. We are convinced, Policy and Justice require that a country unsettled at the commencement of this war claimed by the British crown, and ceded to it by the treaty of Paris, if wrested from the common enemy by the blood and treasure of the thirteen States, should be considered as a common property subject to be parcelled out by Congress into free convenient and Independent governments in such manner, and at such times as the wisdom of that Assembly shall hereafter direct. Thus convinced, we should betray the trust reposed in us by our constituents, were we to authorize you to ratify on their behalf the confederation unless it be farther explained. We have cooly and dispassionately considered the subject, we have weighed probable inconveniences and hardships against the sacrifice of just and essential rights; and do instruct you not to agree to the confederation unless an article or articles be added thereto in conformity with our declaration: Should we succeed in obtaining such article or articles then you are hereby fully empowered to accede to the confederation.

That these our sentiments respecting the confederation may be more publickly known and more explicitly and concisely declared, we have drawn up the annexed declaration, which we instruct you to lay before congress, to have it printed, and to deliver to each of the delegates of the other States in Congress assembled, copies thereof signed by your-selves or by such of you as may be present at the time of the delivery to the intent and purpose that the copies aforesaid may be communicated to our brethren of the United States, and the contents of the said declaration taken into their serious and candid consideration. Also we desire and instruct you to move at a proper time that these instructions be read to Congress by their Secretary and entered on the Journals of Congress. We have spoken with freedom, as becomes Freemen, and we sincerely wish, that these our representations may make such an impression on that assembly as to induce them to make such addition to the articles of confederation as may bring about a permanent union.

True copy for the proceedings of December 15th. 1778.

Test   J Duckett   Cl. H.D.

ENCLOSURE III

Virginia to Wit. In General Assembly the 14th. December 1779. *The Remonstrance of the General Assembly of Virginia to the delegates of the United American States in Congress Assembled.*

The General Assembly of Virginia ever attentive to the recommendations of Congress, and desirous to give the great Council of the United States every Satisfaction in their power, consistent with the rights and Constitution of their own Commonwealth, have enacted a Law to prevent present Settlements on the North West Side of the Ohio River, and will on all occasions endeavour to Manifest their attachment to the Common interest of America, and their earnest wishes to remove every cause of Jealousy and promote that mutual confidence and harmony between the different States so essential to their true Interest and Safety.

Strongly impressed with these Sentiments, the General Assembly of Virginia cannot avoid expressing their Surprize and concern upon the information that Congress had received and countenanced petitions from certain persons stiling themselves the Vandalia and Indiana Company's, asserting claims to lands in defiance of the Civil Authority, jurisdiction and Laws of this Commonwealth, and offering to erect a separate government within the Territory thereof. Should Congress assume a Jurisdiction, and arrogate to themselves a right of adjudication not only unwarranted by, but expressly contrary to the fundamental principles of the Confederation; superseding or controuling the internal policy, Civil regulations, and Municipal Laws of this or any other State, it would be a violation of public faith, introduce a most dangerous precedent which might hereafter be urged to deprive of Territory or Subvert the Sovereignty and Government of any one or more of the United States; and establish in Congress a power which in process of time must degenerate into an intolerable despotism.

It is notorious that the Vandalia and Indiana Company's are not the only Claimers of large tracts of Land under titles repugnant to our Laws; that Several Men of great influence in some of the neighbouring States, are concerned in partnerships with the Earl of Dunmore, and other Subjects of the British Kind, who under purchases from the Indians, claim extensive tracts of Country between the Ohio and Mississipi Rivers; and that propositions have been made to Congress evidently calculated to secure and guarranty such purchases; so that under colour of creating a common fund, had those propositions been adopted, the public would have been duped by the Arts of Individuals, and great part of the value of the unappropriated Lands converted to private purposes.

Congress have lately described and ascertained the Boundaries of these United States, as an ultimatum in their terms of peace. The united States hold no territory but in right of some one individual State in the Union: the territory of each State from time immemorial, hath been fixed and determined by their respective Charters. There being no other rule or criterion to judge by, should these in any instance (when there is no disputed territory between particular States) be abridged without the consent of the States affected by it, general confusion must ensue; each State would be Subjected, in its turn to the incroachments of the others, and a field opened for future Wars of bloodshed; nor can any arguments be fairly urged to prove that any particular tract of Country, within the limits claimed by Congress on behalf of the United States, is not part of the chartered territory of some one of them, but must militate with equal force against the right of the United States in general; and tend to prove such tract of country (if North West of the Ohio river) part of the British province of Canada.

When Virginia acceded to the Articles of Confederation, her rights of Sovereignty and jurisdiction within her own territory were reserved and secured to her, and cannot now be infringed or altered without her consent. She could have no latent views of extending that territory; because it had long before been expressly and clearly defined in the Act which formed her new Government.

The General Assembly of Virginia have heretofore offered Congress to furnish lands out of their territory on the North West side of the Ohio river without purchase Money, to the troops on Continental establishment of such of the Confederated States as had not unappropriated Lands for that purpose; in conjunction with the other States holding unappropriated Lands, and in such proportion as should be adjusted and

settled by Congress; which offer when accepted they will most chearfully make good to the same extent, with the provision made by Law
for their own troops; if Congress shall think fit to allow the like quantities of Land to the other troops on Continental establishment. But
altho the General Assembly of Virginia would make great sacrifices
to the common interest of America, (as they have already done on the
subject of representation) and will be ready to listen to any just and
reasonable propositions for removing the *ostensible* causes of delay to
the complete ratification of the Confederation; they find themselves
impelled by the duties which they owe to their Constituents, to their
posterity, to their Country and to the United States in general, to
remonstrate and protest; and they do hereby, in the name and on behalf
of the Commonwealth of Virginia expressly protest against any jurisdiction, or right of adjudication in Congress, upon the petitions of the
Vandalia or Indiana Company's or on any other matter or thing Subversive of the internal policy, civil government or Sovereignty of this
or any other of the United American States; or unwarranted by the
Articles of the Confederation.

NATHAL. HARRISON   S.S.
BENJ. HARRISON   Sp. H.D.

Attest: JOHN BECKLEY C.h.d.

*An Act to facilitate the completion of the articles of confederation and
perpetual union, among the United States of America.*

Whereas nothing under divine providence, can more effectually contribute to the tranquillity and safety of the United States of America,
than a fœderal alliance on such liberal principles, as will give satisfaction to its respective members; and whereas the articles of confederation, and perpetual Union, recommended by the Honorable Congress
of the United States of America, have not proved acceptable to all the
States; it having been conceived that a portion of the waste and unculti-
vated territory, within the limits and claims of certain States, ought to
be appropriated, as a common fund for the expences of the war. And
the people of the State of New York being on all occasions, disposed to
manifest their regard for their sister States; and their earnest desire to
promote the general interest and security; and more especially to accelerate the fœderal alliance; by removing, as far as it depends upon them,
the before mentioned impediment to its final accomplishment.

Be it therefore enacted by the people of the State of New York represented in senate and assembly, and it is hereby enacted by the authority
of the same; that it shall and may be lawful to and for the Delegates
of this State in the Honble. Congress of the United States of America,
or the major part of such of them, as shall be assembled in Congress,
and they the said delegates or the major part of them, as assembled, are
hereby fully authorised and empowered, for and on behalf of this State,
and by proper and authentic acts or instruments to limit and restrict the
boundaries of this State, in the western parts thereof by such line or
lines, and in such measures and form as they shall judge to be expedi-

ent; either with respect to the jurisdiction as well as the right, or pre-emption of Soil; or reserving the jurisdiction, in part, or in the whole over the lands which may be ceded or relinquished, with respect only to the right or pre-emption of the Soil.

And be it further enacted by the authority aforesaid: That the territory which may be ceded or relinquished by virtue of this act, either with respect to jurisdiction, as well as the right or pre-emption of Soil; or the right or pre-emption of soil only; shall be and enure for the use and benefit of such of the United States, as shall become members of the fœderal alliance of the said States, and for no other use or purpose whatsoever.

And be it further enacted by the authority aforesaid: That all the lands to be ceded and relinquished by virtue of this act for the benefit of the united States, with aspect to property; but which shall nevertheless remain under the jurisdiction of this State, shall be disposed of and appropriated, in such manner only, as the Congress of the said States shall direct and that a warrant, under the authority of Congress, for surveying and laying out any part thereof, shall entitle the party in whose favour it shall issue, to cause the same to be surveyed, and laid out and returned, according to the directions of such warrant; and thereupon letters patent, under the great seal of this State shall pass to the grantee for the estate specified in the said warrant; for which no other fee or reward shall be demanded or received, than such as shall be allowed by Congress.

Provided always, and be it further enacted by the authority aforesaid: That the trust reposed by virtue of this act, shall not be executed by the Delegates of this State, unless at least three of the said Delegates shall be present in Congress.

State of New York ss:

I do hereby certify, that the aforegoing is a true copy of the original act passed the 19th. of February 1780. and lodged in the Secretary's Office. ROBT. HARPUR Dy. Secry. State.

ENCLOSURE V

In Congress Septr. 6th. 1780.

Congress took into Consideration the Report of the Commit[tee] to whom were referred the Instructions of the General Assembly of Maryland to their Delegates in Congress respecting the Articles of Confederation, and the Declaration therein referred to; the Act of the Legislature of New York on the same Subject, and the remonstrance of the General Assembly of Virginia which Report was agreed [to] and is in the Words foll[owing,] to wit,

"That having duly considered the several Matters to them submitted they conceive it unnecessary to examine into the Merits or the Policy of the Instructions or Declaration of the General Assembly of Maryland, Or of the Remonstrance of the General Assembly of Virginia, as they involve Questions, a Discussion of which was declined on mature Consideration when the Articles of Confederation were debated: Nor in the opinion of the Committee can such Questions be now revived with any Prospect of Conciliation: That it appears more adviseable to press upon those States which can remove the Embarrassment respecting the Western Country, a liberal Surrender of a Portion of their territorial Claims, since they cannot be preserved entire without endangering the Stability of the general Confederacy to remind them how indispensibly necessary it is to establish the fœderal Union on a fixed and permanent Basis, and on Principles acceptable to all its' respective Members, how essential to public Credit and Confidences, to the support of our Army, to the Vigour of our Councils and the Success of our Measures, to our tranquillity at home and our Reputation abroad, to our present Safety and our future Prosperity, to our very existence as a free sovereign and independent People.—That they are fully persuaded, the Wisdom of the respective Legislatures will lead them to a full and impartial Consideration of a Subject so interesting to the united States and so necessary to the happy Establishment of the fœderal Union. That they are confirmed in these Expectations by a review of the before mentioned Act of the Legislature of New York submitted to their Consideration. That this Act is expressly calculated to accel[er]ate the fœderal Alliance by removing as far as it depends on that State the Impediment arising from the western Country, and for that purpose to yield up a portion of territorial Claim for the general Benefit," Whereupon,

Resolved that Copies of the several Papers referred to the Committee be transmitted with a copy of the Report, to the Legislatures of the several states: And that it be earnestly recommend[ed] to those States, who have Claims to the Western Country, to pass such Laws and give their Delegates in Congress such powers as may effectually remove the only obstacle to a final Ratification of the Articles of Confederation. And that the Legislature of Maryland be earnestly requested to authorize their Delegates in Congress to subscribe the said Articles.

Extract from the Minutes
CHAS THOMSON   Secry.

RC (Vi); in a clerk's hand, signed by Huntington; at head of text: "Circular." FC (DLC: PCC, No. 15). Enclosures: (I) Tr (Vi); the draft of the Declaration that was submitted to Congress is in DLC: PCC, No. 70. (II) Tr (Vi). (III) Tr (Vi); endorsed: "Remonstrance of the General Assembly of the State of Virginia to Congress—read April 28th. 1780. (Copy)." (IV) Tr (Vi); endorsed: "Copy of An Act of the Legislature of New York 'to facilitate the completion of the articles of confederation & perpetual Union among the United States of America.'" (V) Tr (Vi); signed by Thomson.

This communication, together with its several enclosures which are printed in full here because of the "vast Importance of the Subject," unfolds the complex history, up to this point, of the controversy between those states claiming extensive territories in the West under 17th-century charters and those other states, such as Maryland, whose boundaries were limited. The issue that was here joined in one of the darkest periods of the war, just after Gates' defeat and just prior to Arnold's treason, was in part a legacy of an earlier century's ignorance of geography: charter-limits that ran to the "South Sea" (Pacific Ocean) in the 17th century were legally recognizable if impracticable claims that had assumed an increasing importance as the frontier moved westward toward the Alleghenies. Such conflicting charter claims as those between Connecticut and Pennsylvania and Pennsylvania and Virginia had, by the opening of the Revolution, produced animosities that came near wrecking the new confederacy, and the great land companies that had maneuvered in London to obtain support of the government for their ambitious schemes involving millions of acres of western lands now transferred their activities to state legislatures and to the Continental Congress. The Declaration of Maryland, the Act of Cession of New York, and the Remonstrance of Virginia—all have the lofty expressions proper to freemen engaged in defending their rights under principles of equity and justice; yet the researches of Alvord, Abernethy, and others have proved beyond doubt that land companies and individual speculators in land were far from disinterested spectators of this great drama concerning the American West. The Maryland Declaration—"ultimatum" would be a more precise term—avowing that she would never ratify the Articles of Confederation unless Congress were given power to fix the bounds of all states claiming to the Mississippi, and to secure to the several states a right in common to all lands westward of the bounds thus fixed, made a significant exception of lands that had been granted to or surveyed for individuals at the beginning of the war—an exception which protected the claims of the great land companies, with some of which, as the Virginia Remonstrance pointedly hinted, several of the political leaders of Maryland were associated. The author of the Virginia Remonstrance, George Mason, was himself interested in one of the land companies. New York's step was more magnanimous in appearance than in fact; its Act ceding its western lands —lands likewise claimed by Virginia and over which New York had extended scarcely a shadow of control—was expressly for the purpose of creating "a common fund for the expences of the war," but those who instigated it were also seeking support from states without western lands for New York's case in her current dispute with New Hampshire over Vermont.

Yet, admitting the full force of economic interpretations of the acts reflected in these significant documents, the uncompromising stand taken by Maryland in her eloquent Declaration cannot be explained solely in such terms. The Declaration upon western land claims was also a declaration upon the nature of the Union. Political leaders who were identified with land companies might have found private interest coinciding with public policy as they viewed Maryland's insistence upon the "general welfare" and upon principles of equity and justice, though there were some who advocated adoption of the Articles of Confederation when it appeared to be contrary to their private interest to do so (see St. George L. Sioussat, "The Chevalier de La Luzerne and the Ratification of the Articles of Confederation by Maryland, 1780-1781," PMHB, LX [1936] 391-418, especially the note at p. 406). There were also, undoubtedly, many disinterested persons who viewed with concern the threat of increasing power of a state like Virginia that might, in time, admit the necessity "of dividing its territory and erecting a new State under the auspices and direction of the elder . . . [thus] establishing a Sub-confederacy Imperium in Imperio." Indeed, TJ's proposed Constitution for Virginia of 1776 had made specific provision for what Maryland now prophesied by stating that Virginia's charter limits should stand until the General Assembly should lay off one or more territories west of the Alleghenies, to be "established on the same fundamental laws contained in this instrument, and . . . be free and independant of this colony and of all the world." Such a proviso, had it been adopted, would have confused the nature of the confederacy and have interfered with the constructive measures pertaining to the West, concerning which TJ later had so much to do. Maryland's ultimatum, whatever motives inspired it, forced one of the first and greatest of America's constitutional compromises and laid the groundwork for the Ordinances of 1784 and 1787. The significant fact is not that private and personal motives were present in the complex issue, but that, when Congress wisely refrained from investigating the charges and countercharges by which one state was impugning another's motives, statesmanship triumphed.

Both the Maryland Declaration (Enclosure I) and the Maryland Instructions (Enclosure II), passed together by the Maryland General Assembly on 15 Dec. 1778, were the product of committee authorship. The Declaration was laid before Congress on 6 Jan. 1779 and prudently deferred (JCC, XIII, 29-30). The Instructions, however, were withheld by the Maryland delegates until the Virginia delegates had taken the step, authorized by their Assembly on 19 Dec. 1778, of proposing the adoption of the Articles with less than thirteen states as signatories (see JHD, Oct. 1778, 1827 edn., p. 124-5; JCC, XIV, 617-18). A motion to this effect was introduced on 20 May 1778, and the next day the Maryland delegation drew forth its Instructions, which were spread upon the Journals. Maryland took the next step by instigating a resolution of Congress of 30 Oct. 1779 (see Huntington's letter to TJ of that date) calling upon Virginia to close its newly reopened land office (see the Act printed above under 8 Jan. 1778), and upon all the states with western claims to yield them only to the general government (JCC, XV, 1226-30). Virginia's rejoinder to this was the Remonstrance (Enclosure III), which was drawn by George Mason. This Remonstrance was laid before Congress on 28 Apr. 1780, but no action was taken upon it (same, XVI, 398). Meanwhile, New York, alarmed by Congress' resolve of 30 Oct. 1779 pointing toward nationalization of the West, adopted her Act of Cession (Enclosure IV), which was read in Congress on 7 Mch.; again no action was taken (JCC, XVI, 236). At last, on 26 June, Congress appointed a committee to consider the Maryland Declaration and Instructions, the Virginia Remonstrance, and the New York Act of Cession. The members chosen were Duane of New York (who had moved

that the committee be formed), John Henry of Maryland, Joseph Jones of Virginia, Sherman of Connecticut, and Willie Jones of North Carolina (same, XVII, 559-60). The result of this was the Report (Enclosure V) which was submitted 30 June, debated on 2 Sep., and adopted on 6 Sep. (same, XVII, 580, 802). It should be noted that on 30 June Joseph Jones, a member of the committee, wrote to TJ making observations to the same effect as the report —that states with western claims should, in brief, follow the example of New York in accelerating "the federal alliance."

In consequence of this appeal, Virginia ceded her western claims, with certain provisos, on 2 Jan. 1781 (see TJ to Huntington, 17 Jan. 1781), and Maryland ratified the Articles of Confederation exactly a month later; but this was far from the end of the problem of western claims by the states or of TJ's involvement in that problem. See Merrill Jensen, *The Articles of Confederation* [Madison], 1940, chs. X-XII; Burnett, *Continental Congress*, p. 493-501; Brant, *Madison*, II, ch. VII; Abernethy, *Western Lands*, p. 238-9, 242-5.

From William Smallwood

SIR   Hillsborough 10th. September 1780.

Colo: Harrison will address this, who commands the first Continental Regiment of Artillery, composed of Men from the States of Virginia and Maryland, to him I would beg leave to refer you for a true State of the Regiment, which is now much reduced.

I need not mention to you the Merit of a Corps which has so often distinguished itself, nor the Expediency of filling it up, to which purport I have addressed the State of Maryland and flatter myself their Companies will be compleated without delay.

The Sufferings of this Corps in the late unfortunate Defeat on the Morning of the 16th. Ult: by the entire loss of their Baggage, and their hardships on their Retreat has induced me in the strongest terms to request our State to foward immediately Supplies of Clothing, and Necessaries for the relief of their Companies. I would also beg leave to recommend a similar Step to your Consideration.

The extraordinary Exertions of that part of this Corps attached to my command in the late Action demand the highest Applause; and I should be wanting in Justice did I not acknowledge the Gallantry of Capt. Singleton, Capt. Lieut. Gaines and Lieut. Mosebey, the Officers who commanded and served my Artillery. The Conduct of Capt. Singleton in particular during the Action and on the Retreat was marked by that firmness and Fortitude, that justly excited my Admiration and will ever command my Esteem. This merits your Notice, and induces me to recommend to the Attention of the State the losses this Gallant Officer sustained by the Action, which will be more properly communicated by Col. Harrison to whom I would beg leave to refer you on this head. With the highest Esteem and Regard, I have the honor to be Your Excellency's most ob. and very humble servant, W. SMALLWOOD

RC (CSmH); in a clerk's hand, with this note in TJ's hand at head of text: "Letter from Genl. Smallwood to the Governor."

To Horatio Gates

SIR Richmond Sep. 11. 1780.

Your bill for £54,712 in favor of Mallett has been duly honoured. That for £95,288 we shall also discharge. Another bill (which being delivered back to be presented at the end of the ten days, I cannot recollect either the name of the holder or the sum) has been accepted. We are now without one shilling in the treasury or a possibility of having it recruited till the meeting of the Assembly which takes place on the 15th. of the next month. In this condition Mr. Duncan Ochiltree found us when he delivered your letter of the 5th inst., and draught for £100,000 in favor of Colo. Polk. The only thing in our power, after stating to him our situation, was to assure him that it should be paid as soon as we should be enabled to do it by the assembly, which, I flatter myself, will be as soon as they meet. Of this I am to notify him that he may know when to call for paiment. I shall be very glad if you can accomodate to the same circumstance any other draughts you may find it necessary to make on me.

We have sent a Mr. Eaton, Commissary for the state, to collect beeves in our Southern counties and forward them to your army. He has orders to keep up a proper correspondence with your Commissary. I have the honor to be with the greatest esteem & respect Sir Your most obedient & most humble servt., TH: JEFFERSON

Dft (DLC); in TJ's hand and addressed by him as follows: "The honble. Majr. Genl. Gates Hilsborough by Mr Ochiltree." This has the appearance of being an RC, since it has an address leaf and since it bears the following endorsement: "Richmond 11th Septr. 80 Governr. Jefferson." But its presence in TJ Papers is evidence that another copy was sent to Gates; the endorsement is clearly in the hand of some clerk who was in the Governor's office at this time. FC (Vi, photostat from Brit. Mus.: Add. MSS 38,650).

To Thomas Pleasants

SIR   Richmond September 11th. 1780

I have [been] waiting hoping to see Mr. Ross. I suppose his indisposition detains him. In the mean time a matter of pressing emergency will not admit a longer delay. It is the sending cloathing or something which may procure it, to our officers in Charlestown. An idea on this subject which you dropt in conversation with me has made impression and led me to enquiries which have proved it was just. I mean the converting tobacco which cannot be sent to Charles Town into hard money or good bills and forwarding that to them. [From] your assurances that this operation was practicable I was led to suppose you might yourself be willing to give hard money or good bills for tobacco, or at least that you coud inform me who woud. We have in our possession notes for two or three hundred hhds. and belonging to us (the notes for which may be got by sending expresses) eight or nine hundred hhds. more. Of this we woud gladly convert six hundred hogsheads into hard money or good bills. Very little of this tobacco is on James river, nearly the whole on Potowmack and Rappahanock. Some of this is old, and some light. We will bear the expence of reinspecting, and reweighing to make them agreeable to the purchaser. Will it suit you to purchase, or can you tell me who woud probably purchase on these terms? If you can do nothing in this matter, be so good as to advise me as a friend what I can best do for I am no merchant nor have as yet any public officer on whom I can put this business. I send the Bearer express to you and shall hope [to receive] your answer by him, and am with great esteem, your friend and servant,   TH: JEFFERSON

FC (Vi, photostat from Brit. Mus.: Add. MSS 38,650).

From George Washington

SIR   Head Quarters Bergen County 11h. Sept. 1780

I am exceedingly obliged by your Excellency's favor of the 3d. It has indeed relieved me from much anxiety as, from Genl. Gates's letter of the 20h. Augt. from Hillsborough, there was the greatest reason to apprehend that the whole of the Maryland line and the troops which made a stand with them had been cut off. The stroke, as it is, is severe; but the total loss of the regular troops would have rendered the speedy assemblage of another Army extremely difficult.

The loss of the Arms, which were thrown away by the Militia, is a most disagreeable circumstance at this time, as we are much disappointed in the quantity expected in the Alliance Frigate lately arrived at Boston, she having brought two thousand stand only. I am however happy to hear that three thousand stand sent from Philada. were yet on their way to Virginia, as they will be nearly if not quite sufficient to arm the Levies for 18 Months and the old soldiers who may be collected.[1]

The Cloathing by the Alliance was as deficient of the expected quantity as that of the Arms. I mention this circumstance, lest the Legislature, depending upon public importations, should relax in their endeavours to procure it by their own means. Indeed should the whole of what has been spoken of arrive, it will be inadequate to our wants.

In my letter of the 29h. Augt. which had not reached you, I informed you of the objection which would be made to shipping Tobacco to New York to supply the wants of our prisoners.

Your Excellency's favor without date, accompanied by letters from the General officers at Charlotteville came safely to hand. I am sorry that they have so good ground to complain of deficiency of provisions, but while they make those representations, they ought to consider that we are upwards of one hundred thousand pounds Sterling in advance upon that score, and that they either cannot or will not pay us one farthing.

Immediately upon hearing of the disaster near Campden I directed the additional Regiment of Maryland which was on the march to join this Army to return and proceed to the southward. This Regiment is raised for the War and by the last returns amounted to above 400 Men.

I have accounts thro' a variety of channels that an embarkation is preparing at New York. They differ materially as to numbers, but the prevailing opinion is that they are either bound to Virginia or Carolina. The moment I am more particularly informed, I will communicate the intelligence to your Excellency. In the mean time I think it would be prudent to direct the removal of any public stores which may be upon navigable waters, and to make the arrangements which may be necessary for defence in case such an event should take place.

There has been no alteration in the situation of things in this quarter or with the Fleet and Army of our Ally since I had the honor of addressing you last.

Dft (DLC: Washington Papers); in hand of Tench Tilghman; endorsed.

TJ's FAVOR WITHOUT DATE is that printed above at the end of Aug. 1780, q.v.

¹ The following is deleted in Dft at this point: "and I would take the liberty of earnestly recommending to your Excellency that these Arms may be appropriated to those purposes and not delivered to the Militia—except you find the other troops cannot be raised."

From Samuel Huntington

Philadelphia, *12 Sep. 1780.* Enclosing resolves of Congress of 8 and 11 Sep. P.S., 14 Sep.: acknowledges receipt of TJ's letters of 6 and 8 Sep. Latter was today laid before Congress; proceedings thereon will be forwarded as soon as completed.

FC (DLC: PCC, No. 15). Enclosures (Vi): printed in JCC, XVIII, 812-13.

The resolve of 8 Sep. 1780 called for the immediate establishment of magazines for provision and forage for 15,-000 men for six months; for North Carolina to furnish "magazines of forage, flour and salted provisions to the utmost of their ability" and "to use every exertion possible to fill up her quota of continental troops"; and for "the executive authority of Virginia . . . to equip and hasten forward the troops raised and now raising in that State as mentioned in Governor Jefferson's letter to Congress of the 3d. instant" (MS: Vi). Resolve of 11 Sep. called upon Virginia "to furnish her Quota of Supplies as speedily as may be agreeably to the requisition of Congress of the 25th of February last, with an Addition of Five Thousand Barrels of Flour to be deposited in Magazines at such place or places as the Commanding Officer in the Southern Department shall direct" (MS: Vi).

To Edward Stevens

SIR   Richmond Sep. 12. 1780.

Your letters of Aug. 27 and 30th. are now before me. The subsequent desertions of your militia have taken away the necessity of answering the question how they shall be armed? On the contrary as there must now be a surplus of arms I am in hopes you will endeavor to reserve them as we have not here a sufficient number by 1500, or 2000 for the men who will march hence, if they march in numbers equal to our expectations. I have sent expresses to all the counties from which those militia went requiring the County Lieutenants to exert themselves in taking them; and such is the detestation with which they have been received that I have heard from many counties they were going back of themselves. You will of course hold courts martial on them and make them souldiers for eight months. If you will be so good as to inform me from time to time how many you have we may perhaps get the supernumerary officers in the state to take command of them. By the same opportunities I desired notice to be given to the friends of the few remaining with you that they had lost their clothes and blankets and recommended that they should avail themselves of any good opportunity to send to them.

We approve of your accomodating the hospital with medecines and the Maryland troops with spirits. They really deserve the whole, and I wish we had means of transportation for much greater quantities which we have on hand and cannot convey. This article we could furnish plentifully to you and them. What is to be done for waggons I do not know. We have not now one shilling in the treasury to purchase. We have ordered an active quartermaster to go to the Westward and endeavor to purchase on credit, or to impress a hundred waggons and teams. But I really see no prospect of sending you additional supplies till the same waggons return from you which we sent on with the last. I informed you in my last letter we had ordered 2000 militia more to rendezvous at Hilsborough on the 25th. of Octob. You will judge yourself whether in the mean time you can be more useful by remaining where you are with the few militia left and coming in, or by returning home where, besides again accomodating yourself after your losses, you may also aid us in getting those men into motion, and in pointing out such things as are within our power and may be useful to the service: and you will act accordingly. I am with great friendship & esteem Dr. Sir Your most obedt humble servt., TH: JEFFERSON

RC (DLC). FC (Vi, photostat from Brit. Mus.: Add. MSS 38,650).

To Charles Harrison

SIR   Richmond Sepr. 13. 1780.

I have received a Letter from Genl. Gates mentioning your desire to have your regiment of artillery filled up from the 18 mo. recruits now raised. The act of assembly left to Genl. Washington the officering and regimenting of these men. He has disposed of them into 8 new battalions and appointed officers to six of them: the remaining two battalions to be under Colo. Gibson and Brent and their officers. It is therefore not in the power of the executive to interfere in this matter. I am not without hopes that the assembly at their ensuing session will think it prudent to begin without delay on some effectual plan for providing their whole quota of troops to serve for the war, in which case I shoud expect you woud come in for a more permanent reinforcement than the present levies woud give you. This however rests altogether with the Legislature.

I am, sir, with great respect Your most ob: servant,

TH: JEFFERSON

FC (Vi, photostat from Brit. Mus.: Add. MSS 38,650). The LETTER FROM GENL. GATES has not been identified; see William Smallwood's letter to TJ, 10 Sep. 1780, concerning Harrison's regiment.

To Richard Henry Lee

DEAR SIR   Richmond Sep. 13. 1780.

The clearing the bay of the pickeroons which infested it was attended to the moment the brig Jefferson was in tolerable readiness. About the 3d or 4th week of the last month Commod. Barron cruized up the bay as far as the Tangier islands and took five of those vessels which being as many as he could man he returned. About the 1st. inst. I received a letter from Govr. Lee desiring we would join two brigs &c fitting out at Baltimore and to sail the 9th. inst. for clearing the bay. We accordingly ordered the Jefferson and the boats Liberty and Patriot to join the Marylanders. They sailed from York for that purpose on the 12th. inst. Since this I have heard nothing from them, but their instructions were to sweep the bay and it's waters clear of this trash; and I have no doubt it is done and the vessels properly taken care of which have insulted your neighborhood. Our difficulty, nay impossibility, is to get men. The terms of the assembly were proposed; not a single man could be engaged. We then calculated what the bounty (converted into a daily pay of three years) the cloathing allowed by law converted into a daily sum and both added to the daily pay would do. These amounting to about 10. dollars per day, a few men were raised for the cruise and on these terms, aided by volunteers (mere landsmen) engaged for the special purpose of going up the bay. We have been able to send the brig and boats on these two small expeditions: but the Commodore assures me that with such a crew the brig is in danger of being taken by very inferior vessels. The Thetis is getting into readiness, the two Eastern shore gallies are to be brought over, but we have no prospect of men for them. I see no remedy but for the legislature to measure purses with the merchants and give what they give.

We sent expresses to every county in the state about a fortnight ago to put a stop to the purchase of spirits. Indeed the prudence of the Commissioners in most of the counties had stopped it before, finding the quantity so much beyond what the legislature or Executive could be supposed to have expected. Our two millions are all exhausted. Large debts are contracted for the horses purchased for the cavalry, and waggons which were sent on with the Maryland troops and our militia. These waggons which with those belonging to N. Carola. were 400 in number, being all lost, we are now obliged to get 200 more with teams and geer, till which we have it not in our power to send any thing to the Southern army, who are suffering greatly. The loss of every tent has been a circumstance of great distress. The loss of all the small arms not less so. The new recruits are now collecting. To these will be added the delinquents and fugitives of the late militia now become 8 months men, and 1000 good Western militia from the counties of Fauquier, Loudon, Frederic, Berkeley, Hampshire, Shenandoah, Rockingham, Augusta, Rockbridge. This I think will be a reinforcement of about 4000 men besides the delinquents and fugitives who, I apprehend can never be got to fight. But without aid from Congress they cannot be armed.

Your intelligence from Philadelphia is so much more direct, and punctual than mine, that I do not attempt to give you news from that quarter. We have nothing from the Southward since what was published in the last week's paper. Colo. Morgan goes hence this morning for the Southern camp.

The application requisite to the duties of the office I hold is so excessive, and the execution of them after all so imperfect, that I have determined to retire from it at the close of the present campaign. I wish a successor to be thought of in time who to sound whiggism can join perseverance in business, and an extensive knowlege of the various subjects he must superintend. Such a one may keep us above water even in our present moneyless situation. I am with great respect & esteem Dr Sir Your most obedt. humble servt.,   TH: JEFFERSON

RC (ViHi); endorsed. Addressee identified from the provenance (Lee Papers).
THEY SAILED . . . ON THE 12TH. INST.: This obviously is an error by TJ; see TJ to D'Anmours, 9 Sep., in which it is stated that "the boats sail this day up the bay."

From Thomas Sim Lee

SIR   In Council Annapolis 13th. Septr. 1780

We have received Information that a certain James Anderson, a Subject of this State, was captured in one of the Barges or Gallies which have, for some Time past, infested our Bay and interrupted our Trade, by Capts. Yellatt and Folger and carried into the State of Virginia, and is now confined at Richmond. Anderson, before and since our Government was formed, lived on Fell's Point in Baltimore Town, took the Oath of Allegiance and Fidelity to the State prescribed by Law, was appointed and commissioned a Lieutenant in one of our Gallies, and from his Activity and apparant Zeal, was always reputed a Friend to America and entrusted with the Command of a Vessel owned by some Gentlemen in Baltimore which he carried to New York; he is well acquainted with our Bay and has committed great Depredations on the Property of our Inhabitants. The above Recapitulation of Facts renders it unnecessary to suggest to your Excellency that the said Anderson cannot be deemed a Prisoner of War and exchangeable, though he may hold a Commission from the Enemy and was taken in one of their Vessels, because he was a Subject of this State, took the Oath of Allegiance as such, and no subsequent Act by him can dissolve the Obligation he was under to the State, and therefore was, at the Time he received his Commission and must now be considered a Subject of this State and amenable to its Laws for any Offence committed against the Peace and Government thereof. We do charge the said Anderson with High Treason against the State and solicit you to cause him to be sent to us under a sufficient Guard in Order to take his Trial at our General Court, which will be held on the second Tuesday in October next, and to transmit what Testimony you may have against him. We shall take Care that every Expence incurred thereby shall be reimbursed, as soon as it is ascertained. We are &c.

FC (MdAA).

To George Muter

SIR   In Council Sep. 13. 1780.

The following articles being called for from us by Genl. Gates you will be pleased to give orders to the proper persons to have them in readiness as soon as possible. I am Sir with great respect Your most obedt. servt., TH: JEFFERSON

10. barrels of Vinegar
500 spades.
200 grubbing hoes.
100 Common hoes.
200 Felling axes.

P.S. I have been informed there are at Petersburg belonging to the Continent a number of spades. Be so good as to enquire into it that they may be ordered on in part of the above. Perhaps there may be other articles in possession of the Continentl. Q. Mr. A return is wanting from our Commissaries and from Mr. Day and Mr. Armistead what quantities of salt we have and where.

RC (DeHi). Tr in Board of War Letter Book (MiU-C). On a blank page of RC are memoranda (by Muter?), omitted here, giving the number of spades, hoes, axes, &c. wanted that are "Ready," "Ordered," or "Engaged."

See Supplies Required for Gates' Army, Aug. 1780.

To Abner Nash

SIR   Richmond 13th Septr. 1780.

I have received with much concern your Excellencys information of the irregularities committed by the two troops of Cavalry sent from this State.

I cannot but wish that the result of a further investigation may prove more favourable to them; but be this as it will, it is far from our desire to stand between them and justice. It is for the good of the general service that it should be fully enquired into, and it concerns the reputation of those of them who have not swerved from Duty, to be separated by trial from their guilty Brethren, and not involved in an indescriminate censure.

Having received information that they wanted Cloathing, twelve Horses and about thirty Saddles to refit them for Service, Orders were given ten days ago to supply them. The materials for their Clothing are in hand their Saddles are provided except about half a dozen. What progress is made in purchasing the deficient Horses I am not informed. I think however on the whole they will be very shortly ready to obey the Generals call into Service. In the mean time should your Excellency think proper they can be ordered to Brunswick Court House within this State.

I have the honor to be with the greatest esteem & respect Your Excellency's Most obedient & most humble servt.,

TH: JEFFERSON

RC (NcDAH); in a clerk's hand except for complimentary close and signature by TJ. FC (Vi, photostat from Brit. Mus.: Add. MSS 38,650).

Nash's letter to which this is an answer has not been found.

To —— Patton

SIR   Richd. Sepr. 13th 1780

Colo. Finnie being about to send some provision vessels to the head of Elk, I have desired him to order one into Baltimore, to the master of which I shall be obliged to you to have delivered what ever cartouch boxes you have in readiness for us as we are in immediate want of them.

I am sir, Your very humble servant,   TH: JEFFERSON

FC (Vi, from photostat of Brit. Mus.: Add. MSS 38,650). At head of text: "Mr.   Patton." Elsewhere this name is spelled "Patoun"; he was a Virginia state commissary at Baltimore but has not been further identified.

From Horatio Gates

SIR   Hillsboro. 14 Sept. 1780

I am Honored with the receipt of Your Excellencys Letter Dated the 3d: Inst: and pleased to find from thence that Virginia is so Zealous, and Spirited, in Her Exertions against the Common Enemy. In my Letter to Congress of the 20th: Ult: I acquainted them with the necessity of sending a very Considerable Supply of Arms to this Department, as all the Militia had been Furnished with were thrown away, and Lost. There is no Doubt, but they will comply with the Requisition. Enclosed I send Your Excellency a Copy of the Letter that goes by this conveyance to Col. Carrington; I believe from the Tenor of your letter to me, You will approve of the Orders I have Given the Colonel. A Prize is Just Brought into Newburn from Glasgow, full of the best Assortment of Goods for the Army. Amongst the rest their is a very large Quantity of Tent Cloath. I have requested the whole may be taken for the Troops. I expect to know in a few days how far the Owners will agree to my proposals. Virginia will with readyness pay Her share of the Bargain I may be Obliged to make in her behalf: Blankets, and Shoes, to a considerable Ammount are in the Prize. These I have also Demanded: indeed it matters little what purse it comes out of, as in the End all must pay their Share of The Great Bill. I can neither confirm, nor refute, the intelligence I sent your Excellency in my Letter of the 9th. Instant: as I have not since then, been able to Learn with any Certainty the real Designs of the Enemy. Good Spies are difficult to be had without Gold; There I have most Sensibly Felt, the Advantage Lord Cornwallis has Over me. A Special Express will set out instantly, the moment I am convinced of the Route the Enemy are taking. I am much Obliged to Your Excellency for Supplying Col. Kosciuszco with Money for His Journey. Inclosed is Mr. Clay, the Paymaster Generals Draught for the Sum You advanced the Col. which will Liquidate that Demand.

Dft or FC (NHi); endorsed: "Copy to Govr. Jefferson 14th. Sepr. 1780." Tr (DLC). Enclosures missing; a transcript of one of them (Gates to Edward Carrington, same date) is in DLC.

To Samuel Huntington

Sir   Richmond Sep. 14. 1780

According to Genl. Gates's request I transmit to your Excellency the inclosed copy of a letter I received from him this morning. That the enemy should meditate taking possession of Portsmouth in the manner they give out does not seem probable, as Sr. Henry Clinton under the present appearances would scarcely consent to spare men from New York; and that they should think of taking possession of it at all seems equally unlikely while it is in the power of our allies to send a superior fleet into Chesapeake bay to which theirs would fall a certain prey. Nevertheless should they in this, as in so many other instances, go directly contrary to obvious principles of reason, they would find us in a condition incapable of resistance for want of small arms. Our militia have been long ago disfurnished of their arms for the use of the regulars; and when we shall have armed the 3000 new levies now rendezvousing we shall not have a single musket left in our magazine except a few which have been disabled. I must therefore intreat Congress in the most earnest manner to send all the aid in small arms which can be spared. We are also without a tent for the men who are now rendezvousing, nor does tent-stuff exist in this country. For this article therefore we must also throw ourselves on Congress. I have hopes that by this time the navigation of Chesapeake is made safe by a joint effort of this and the state of Maryland so that any necessaries may be transported through that channel and up James river to this place.

Another circumstance should be previously determined on supposition that an invasion of this state should take place. A spirit of disaffection which had never been suspected, has lately discovered itself in the counties of Washington, Montgomery, Henry, and Bedford, and had extended so far as that many hundreds had actually enlisted to serve his Britannic majesty, had taken oaths of allegiance to him, and had concerted the time of insurrection. The last of the counties abovenamed is within 60. or 70 miles of the Barracks in Albemarle and had always been considered as a barrier to any enterprize on them from the Southward. Other counties equally relied on may fail us in the hour of trial. Should an invasion of this state take place, and the progress of the enemy, or other circumstances render a removal of the Convention troops necessary, to what place should they be removed? I would beg the instructions of Congress on this head and at this time that we may at no future time be at a loss when such a measure shall be rendered necessary.

I have the honor to be with the greatest respect Your Excellency's Most obedient & most humble servt.,   TH: JEFFERSON

RC (DLC: PCC, No. 71, 1); endorsed by Charles Thomson: "Letter from Govr Jefferson Sept 14. 1780 Read 19. Referred to the board of war," followed by notation in another hand:

"Business done by a Comittee of Congress in Conference with the Board." Enclosure (same location): Gates to TJ, 9 Sep. 1780, printed above.

To Thomas Sim Lee

[*Richmond, 14 Sep. 1780.* Anderson Galleries, sale catalogue, 19-20 Jan. 1926 (James H. Manning Sale), lot 861, lists a 1-page A.L.S. from TJ to Gov. Lee of this date announcing recapture of 150 Maryland troops from the British and expressing doubt that the enemy will "risque any naval force at Portsmouth while the superiority of the combined naval power in the American seas is so decided." Copy of a letter from Gen. Gates is enclosed. The covering letter has not been located. The enclosure must have been Gates' letter to TJ of 9 Sep. 1780, q.v.]

To James Wood

[Richmond 14 September 1780]

Mr. Tate informs me you are now in condition to pay up the arrearages of animal food due the convention troops, but that he supposed they would not receive them. If you be really in such condition I should be glad to have the arrearages tendered, and if refused a proper certificate of the fact, that I may transmit it to General Washington and prevent any disagreable consequences from the representations already forwarded to him.

MS not located. Text (extract only) from American Art Association, sale catalogue, 30 Nov. 1927 (Henry Goldsmith Sale), lot 10. This is one of numerous letters and documents in the Goldsmith Sale deriving from the papers of James Wood and was undoubtedly addressed to him (see TJ to Wood, 23 Sep. 1780; also TJ to Washington, same date).

To Edward Stevens

SIR   Richmond Septr. 15th. 1780

I beg leave to trouble you with a private letter on a little matter of my own, having no acquaintance at Camp with whom I can take that Liberty. Among the Waggons impressed for the use of your Militia were two of mine. One of these I know is safe having been on its way from hence to Hillsborough at the time of the late Engagement. The other I have reason to believe was on the field. A Waggon Master who sais he was near her, informs me the Brigade quarter Master cut out one of my best Horses and made his Escape on him, and that he saw my Waggone[r] loosening his own Horse to Come off, but the Enemy's Horse were then Coming up and he knows nothing further. He was a Negroe man named Phill lame in one Arm and Legg. If you will do me the favour to enquire what is become of him, what Horses are saved, and to send them to me, I shall be much obliged to you. The Horses &c. were not public Property, as they were only impressed and not sold. Perhaps your Certificate of what is lost may be necessary for me. The Waggon Master told me that the Publick money was in my Waggon, a Circumstance which perhaps may aid your enquiries. After apologizing for the trouble I beg leave to assure you that I am with great sincerity Your Friend & Servt.,   TH: JEFFERSON

Tr (DLC); endorsed: "Copy of a Letter from Governor Jefferson to Edward Stevens dated Septemr 15th. 1780."

From James Maxwell

[*Richmond, 17 Sep. 1780.* Minute in Journal of the Commissioner of the Navy (Vi) under this date: "Letter written to the Governour informing him of the Boat Nicholson's leaving the Yard under the Command of Lieut. Steele to take her station." Not located.]

From Horatio Gates

SIR   Hillsborough 20th: September 1780

The inclosed Examination of one of Your Militia, who was wounded, and Taken, in the Action of the 16th. Ulto.; and the Copy of a Letter from Colonel Marian, of So. Carolina, also under Cover of this Letter, will partly certainly acquaint Your Excellency, with the Circumstances of the Enemys Force in and about Camden. Had I now Fifteen Hundred Continental Troops, with Shoes, Blankets, and Tents, sufficient for them, I would tomorrow begin my march for Charlotte; but until we are supplied with these Articles, and this State will furnish Carriages, and Provisions, it is in Vain to think of acting Ofensively against Lord Cornwallis. I will not risque a Second Defeat, by marching through Famine, and encountring every distress; and want of almost every thing an Army ought to be provided with. Slow, and I hope sure, will be our next attempt. With every Sentiment of respect for You and every wish for the Freedom and Independence of the U S I am Sir Yr. &c.

Dft (NHi); endorsed. Tr (DLC). Tr (MdAA), headed "(Copy)"; it may have been enclosed in a letter from TJ to Gov. Lee of Maryland, as was another of Gates' letters (see TJ to Thomas Sim Lee, 14 Sep. 1780). Enclosures not found.

ONE OF YOUR MILITIA: This was probably one William Allmond (see Gates to TJ, 24 Sep. 1780).

From Samuel Huntington

Philadelphia, 20 Sep. 1780. Encloses copy of a letter just received from Gen. Greene containing intelligence "something similar to what you have lately received from Genl. Gates."

FC (DLC: PCC, No. 15); 1 p. Enclosure (missing; original in PCC, No. 155, I): Nathanael Greene to Congress, 18 Sep. 1780 (see JCC, XVIII, 841).

From Samuel Huntington

SIR   Philada September 20. 1780

By the Act of Congress of this Day herewith enclosed your Excellency will be informed of the Measures they have adopted upon an Invasion of the State of Virginia, in Case the Conjuncture of Affairs should render the Measure necessary for removal of the Convention Troops to Fort Frederick in Maryland, and also to provide Magazines to supply them in Case of removal, although at the same Time it is to be hoped that Circumstances will not render their removal necessary; but that must be left to your Wisdom in Council to determine in Case of an Invasion.

Should you find the Measure necessary you will give seasonable Information thereof to Gover. Lee to whom I have transmitted a Duplicate of the Act enclosed. Should the report of the reinforcement of a french Fleet on this Coast prove true, there cannot be any Fear of an Invasion of Virginia.

Your Excellency may be assured Congress will use every Exertion to supply Tents and Arms for the Militia of Virginia and Maryland, and at the same Time recommend to those States to leave no Steps untried to furnish those necessary and important Articles.

I have the Honor to be &c,   S. H.

FC (DLC: PCC, No. 15). Enclosure (Vi): attested copy of resolve of Congress, same date, recommending among other things that the Convention troops be marched from Albemarle by way of Winchester to Fort Frederick, Md., if Virginia is invaded; resolution printed in JCC, XVIII, 842-3.

Petition of Captured Officers
of the Virginia Line
in Favor of General McIntosh

SIR   Haddrels Point. 20th. Septr. 1780.

The General and Field Officers whose Names are subscribed in behalf of ourselves and the other Officers of the Virginia Line, take the liberty (through your Excellency) to recommend Brigdr. Genl. McIntosh of the Continental army to the particular notice of our State, and we request that himself and his family may be entitled to Lands, and every other Emolument and advantage given for the encouragement of Officers, agreeable to the respective Ranks that each of them hold in the Service, in the same manner as if he belonged to the line of our State of Virginia.

We further request of your Excellency that you would use your Influence with the assembly to make some immediate provision for the Lady and Famely of this unfortunate Officer, who driven from the greatest Affluence in the State of Georgia, have experienced uncommon dificulties and hardships, and are now (as he is informed) wandering in some part of the State of Virginia, Friendless and unknown, while his situation as a prisoner deprives him of giving them even the assistance of his advice.

We are induced to make this application in behalf of Genl. McIntosh, to shew our esteem for him, as well as on account of his uncommon sufferings and the sacrifices he made in the service of his Country, which deserve particular attention, and we flatter ourselves that our State will not be backward in assisting distress'd Virtue.

This Gentleman has moreover upon many Occasions commanded part of our Line with approbation, and the Western department in our State for a considerable time, the good effects of which is still felt and acknowledged by our back Inhabitants, and we are happy to know, and have undoubted authority for saying, that his conduct as an Officer and a Gentleman, has given satisfaction in the Army, and gained the esteem and confidence of His Excellency Genl. Washington, and every other person whom he served under, alltho he met with some ungreatful returns for his Integrity from another quarter. We have the Honor to be, with the greatest Respect, Your Excellencies Most Obedt. humble Servants,

Wm Woodford Brigdr: Genl.
Chs. Scott. Br. Genl.
W Russell Colo. 5th. V. R.
N Gist Colo.
John Nevill Colo. 4th. V. R.
Will Heth, Colo. 3. V. Regt
B. Ball Lt. Colo. 1st: V: Regt.
Saml. Hopkins Lt. Colo. Commg.
    1st. Va. Br. Levies
Sam: J: Cabell Lt. Col. 4h. Virg:
    Regt. & Depy. Adj: Genl.
Jonath: Clark Lt. Col. 8. Regt

Gust. B. Wallace Lt. Colo. 11th.
    V R
Richard Anderson Major 1st.
    Virginia Regiment
A Waggener Maj 8th Virg Regt
D Stephenson Major 11th. Virginia Regt
W: Croghan Major 4th. V. Regt.
Will. Lewis Majr. 10th. Virga. Rt.
Cha: Pelham Majr. 2nd. V: Regt.
Presley Nevill Lieut. Colo. by
    Brevet.

MS (CSmH); in a clerk's hand, with signatures of the officers. At foot of text: "His Excellency Thomas Jefferson Esqr. Govr. of Virginia."

The signers of this petition were officers of the Virginia Line who had been captured at the surrender of Charleston and were being held at Haddrel's Point, S.C. They were petitioning in behalf of Lachlan McIntosh, a stormy figure in Georgia Revolutionary history, who held the rank of brigadier general in the Continental service and was their fellow captive. TJ laid the present paper before the Assembly on the opening of its session in Mch. 1781 (TJ to R. H. Lee, 1 Mch. 1781); that body resolved on 21 Mch. to authorize the executive to relieve the distress of McIntosh's family; and TJ promptly wrote Mrs. McIntosh (23 Mch.) that £10,000 had been ordered paid to Col. Russell for her benefit, see the letters referred to and also JHD, Mch. 1781, Va. State Libr., Bull., 1928, p. 46, 48.

Order of Council respecting Volunteers for the Southern Army

In Council Sep. 21. 1780.

The Governor laid before the board a proposition from Colo. William Preston to raise a body of volunteers to march to the Southward whereon the board are of opinion that the services of such a Corps be accepted on the following conditions. They shall serve three months from the time of their rendezvousing at the head quarters of the Sothern commander in chief or such other place as he shall appoint. They shall be subject to the Continental rules of war: two companies of them shall carry their own rifles and accoutrements, the rest shall be furnished with muskets bayonets and cartouch boxes: and the whole with medicine, rations, forage and such pay as is allowed to the militia lately sent to Carolina. They shall be formed into Companies of not less than 50. and regiments of not less than 400 men to be commanded by Colonels William Christian and Wm. Campbell if there be two regiments, and if but one, then that one to be commanded by Colo. Christian, and Colo. Campbell to have command of a regiment of the militia called from the neighbouring counties. The Counties from which any of these Volunteers shall go shall be allowed a credit of so many as shall go from each out of the late call for militia to go to Carolina, and the individuals going and actually performing this duty shall be entitled to have it considered as their tour of duty whenever the militia division of which they happen to be shall be hereafter called into service. They are to be at the head Quarters of the Southern commander in chief or such other place as he shall appoint by the 20th. Day of October. Their rations and forage shall commence when they march from their County. The arms and accoutrements put into their hands are to be delivered up to the Commander in chief before their discharge. They shall be Subject to the orders of the Commander in chief of the Southern army and of such Officer as he shall appoint especially to command their corps.

ARCH: BLAIR　C.C.

MS (Vi); in a clerk's hand, signed by Blair; endorsed: "Order of Council about Volunteers Sept. 21. 1780."

From Tench Tilghman

SIR   Head Quarters Orange Town 21st. Sept. 1780

The Commander in Chief set out last Sunday for Harford [Hartford] to meet the French Admiral and General at that place. More circumstantial accounts having been received since his departure of the embarkation mentioned in his letter of the 11th: instant, I have thought it my duty to communicate them to Your Excellency. One object of the expedition is said, in New York, to be the release of the Convention troops. A well informed Agent mentions that Sir Henry Clinton had invited the Refugees and their families from Virginia and Maryland to go with the Fleet, which it was generally beleived was to sail about the 25h. of this Month. The best accounts fix the number of troops at eight Regiments. The arrival of Sir Geo: Rodney at New York with ten sail of the line and a ship of 42 Guns may possibly occasion some alteration in Affairs. His intention in coming over to this Coast is yet a secret. No persons have been admitted to go into or come out of New York for some days past. No accounts have been received of the arrival of the French fleet upon any part of the Coast, tho' from the advices brought by a variety of Vessels which left them, some as far Northward as the Capes of Chesapeak, we have good reason to expect them. The General will probably be with the Army again the beginning of next Week.

I have the honor to be with the greatest Respect Yr. Excellency's Most obt. Servt.,   T. TILGHMAN

Dft (DLC: Washington Papers); endorsed.

To William Campbell?

SIR   Richmond Sep. 22d. 1780.

Having written very fully to Colo. Preston on the measures necessary to be pursued in your part of the Country, and being much thronged, I must beg leave to refer you to him. We shall be exceedingly glad if two battalions of volunteers can be raised, as we are very desirous of availing ourselves of your personal service. Where the Council speak of their being subject to the Commander in chief and such Officer as he shall appoint, I am to inform you they have in their eye Colo. Morgan who is gone on to the Southward and it is supposed will have a separate corps of woodsmen. He advised the proportion of rifles mentioned in the order; but as it is not absolutely certain that Muskets and bayonets for the Soldiers going on and for the Volunteers also will be ready, if your men were all to carry rifles they could only Store them a way under guard till their Discharge if there should be muskets to put into their hands. I am Sir Your most obedt. servt., TH: JEFFERSON

RC (NN); in a clerk's hand, signed by TJ; on second page are memoranda of purchases ("1 Doz plats half Doz Deep 2 Mugs 2 bools," &c.) in an unidentified and probably much later hand. There is no indication of the addressee of this letter, but William Campbell worked closely with William Preston, and it was he who was to command the second regiment of volunteers in the southern army if two were raised; see Order of Council, 21 Sep. 1780.

TJ's recent letter to Preston is missing.

To Charles Lynch?

SIR   Richmond Sep 22. 1780.

Be pleased to deliver to the order of Governor Nash two thousand weight of lead, for which this shall be your warrant.

TH: JEFFERSON

RC (Vi). On verso is a receipt, signed "A. Nash" and dated 1 Oct. 1780, for 2,000 pounds of lead received of Charles Lynch. Also in Vi is a letter from Isaac Shelby, Sullivan County [N.C.], 24 Sep. 1780, addressed "To Col. Charles Linch Lead Mines favr. Mr. E. Baker," enclosing a resolution of the North Carolina Senate, 5 May 1780, requesting Gov. Nash to obtain the lead from Gov. Jefferson; Shelby desires the lead to be immediately delivered to Evan Baker, "as the emergency is great."

From John Page

DEAR SIR   Rosewell Sepr. the 22d. 1780.

The particular Attention paid by the Executive to my Recommendations, and Informations could not but be flattering to me, but the Manner in which you expressed your Approbation of them, in your last Letter, greatly abated the Satisfaction I should have felt. But, should I tell you what I felt and thought on reading your Letter, you might think me either captious or Hypocritical for I must confess, I was much disposed to qua[rrel] with you, for one of your Expressions, and to say in general, what might appear like Flattery, to you, and like mere Affectation of Modesty, of myself. I therefore think it best to suppress in a great Measure my Sentiments on that Occasion and shall only venture to say, that should you resign, you will give me great Uneasiness, and will greatly distress your Country. As to my succeeding you, if my Abilities were ten times greater than my utmost Vanity can ever prompt me to suppose them, I could not think of it in the present Situation of my Affairs. Nearly 4½ Years total Neglect of my Affairs has rendered my Attention to them so indispensably necessary that my Patriotism can scarcely lead me to neglect them again even during the short Term of a Session of Assembly. I have however agreed to make this Sacrifice of my private Interest to the public Service and mean to serve my County in the next Assembly.

I find I was two or three Weeks too late in lodging my Information with you against our tardy Commissioners and Q. Masters; at least with Respect to the Grain Tax, for the grain, it seems, except a few Bushs. of Oats was delivered about 3 Weeks before the Date of my Letter. I wish I may have been a little more out with Respect to other Counties.

I really do believe that General Gates's Conduct will not be judged of, in general, so impartially as could be wished; but I cannot conceive that it was prudent to push forward in quest of Provisions, unless he had an Army capable of holding the Country he was marching into against the Enemy, and of laying it under Contributions. For without a Defeat he might be reduced to the greatest Extremity, by only being prevented from getting Provisions and in Case of a Defeat, he must have been compelled to retreat to that very Country which he had quitted through Want of Provisions.

I sincerely wish the General may soon repair his late Losses, make amends for his Miscariage and reap all the Glory his utmost Ambition can desire. I am my dear Jefferson your sincere Friend and most obedt.   JOHN PAGE

RC (DLC). Addressed: "To His Excellency Thos. Jefferson Govr. of Virginia Richmond"; endorsed: "Page John."

YOUR LAST LETTER: A missing letter from TJ in answer to Page's letter of 30 Aug. 1781.

To the Virginia Delegates in Congress

[*Richmond, 22 Sep. 1780.* JCC, XVIII, 899 (4 Oct. 1780): "The delegates for Virginia laid before Congress a letter of 22 September, from Governor Jefferson, which was read; Whereupon, *Resolved,* That the same be referred to the Board of War, and that so much of the 20,000 pounds sterling directed by a resolution of 2 instant, to be drawn on the honorable J. Jay and the honorable H. Laurens, as shall remain after discharging the debts due to Messrs. Tracey and Company, and advancing seven thousand pounds sterling to Mr. W. Bingham, be appropriated to the providing and transporting arms for the troops raising in Virginia for continental service." TJ's letter has not been found.]

From William Woodford

Charleston, 22 Sep. 1780. Introducing Master Alexander Frazier Grigorie, whose father, James Grigorie, "late of Urbanna [Va.]," had shown Woodford kindness in Charleston.

RC (NN); mounted in an extra-illustrated volume and assigned to TJ as recipient by a previous owner, probably being done at the time the address-leaf was removed so that the letter could be mounted. However, even if this assignment were conjectural, internal evidence would seem to support it.

From Daniel Brodhead

SIR   Fort Pitt, Sep'r 23rd, 1780.

The Troops under my command having suffered for want of provisions I applied to the hon'ble. Board of war at Philad'a, for information respecting supplies. They have instructed me to apply to the Commissioners of Virg'a and Pen'a, on this side the mountains who they alledge have received orders to make ample provision. I have heard of one County Commissioner appointed for Pen'a, but I cannot learn that any have been appointed by the State of Virg'a, and as the Pen'a Commissioner has not as yet procured any supplies I have been under the disagreeable necessity of using Compulsary means to prevent the Troops from starving. I shall therefore be greatly obligded to your Excellency for giving the necessary orders to have the expectations of the Board of War in this respect complied with.

I have received intelligence that a Thousand British Regulars and a great number of Indians are on their March towards this Frontier. I believe it wants Confirmation, but should it prove true, there is the greater necessity to enable us to face them before they reach the settlements or hold out at the respective posts which are erected to cover them.

The Officers of the 9th Virg'a Regt., well acquainted in this Country, inform me, that it is their opinion, should the Enemy reach the Frontier in force, a very considerable part of the Inhabitants would join them, provided they have a promise of protection.

I should have been happy in a compliance with your request of the 16th of June, could I have been honored with it in convenient time and furnished with necessary resources and licence. But as I did not receive your favor until the 10th July, I was sensible that from the force and progress of the Enemy, the small aid which could possibly have been lent from hence to the settlements at Kentucky, must have been much exposed and could not prevent the Dangers that threatened them.

I have the honor to be, &c.,   D. B.

MS not located. Text from *Pennsylvania Archives*, 1st ser., XII, 273 (Brodhead's Letter Book).

TJ's REQUEST OF THE 16TH OF JUNE was in a letter to Brodhead now missing.

To Horatio Gates

SIR   Richmond Septr. 23. 1780.

I have empowered Colo. Carrington to have twelve Boats, Scows or Batteaux built at Taylors Ferry and to draw on me for the cost. I recommended the constructing them so as to answer the transportation of Provisions along that river, as a change of position of the two Armies may render them unnecessary at Taylors Ferry, and I am thoroughly persuaded that unless we can find out some Channel of transportation by Water, no Supplies of Bread of any Consequence can be sent you from this State for a long time to come. The want of Waggons is a bar insuperable at least in any reasonable time. I have given orders to have Fry and Jeffersons and Henrys Maps of Virginia sought for and purchased. As soon as they can be got I will forward them. I have also written to General Washington on the subject of wintering the French Fleet in Chesapeake. Our New Levies rendezvous in large numbers. As General Washington had constituted them into 8 battalions, and allotted none to Colo. Harrison, we think to deliver him about 400 Drafts of another kind who are to serve 18 Months also. Unless Congress furnish small Arms we cannot arm more than half the Men who will go from this State. The prize you mention of Tents and Blanketts is very fortunate. It is absolutely out of our power to get these Articles to any amount in this Country, nor have we Cloathing for our new Levies. They must therefore go to you cloathed as Militia, till we can procure and send on supplies. They will be as warm in their present Cloathing at Hillsborough as at Chesterfield Court House.

We have an Agent collecting all the Beeves which can be got from the Counties round about Portsmouth to send off to you. They have there also plentiful Crops of Corn growing. We have instructed him to try whether means of conveying it down into the Sounds, and up some of the Rivers of North Carolina, or by Land to Meherrin River and thence down Chowan and up Roanoke cannot be rendered practicable.

I am with every sentiment of esteem & respect Sir Your most obedient & most humble servt., TH: JEFFERSON

P.S. I inclose a certificate acknowledging satisfaction for the money furnished Colo. Kosciuoske.

RC (DLC); endorsed: "From Governour Jefferson 23d: Septembr: 1780." Tr (DLC: PCC, No. 171, enclosed in Gates to Huntington, 13 Oct. 1780). Enclosure missing.

To the North Carolina Board of War

GENTLEMEN   Richmond September 23rd. 1780.

I am sorry that it is utterly out of our Power to furnish a single stand of Arms for the Use of your Troops. After making reasonable Deductions we have right to expect, that 5000 or 5,500 Regulars and Militia will march from this State to yours in the Course of this and the ensuing Month; for these we have but 3000 Stand of Arms. I have apprised Congress and General Washington of this and written pressingly for Supplies, and intimated what must certainly take place, a Countermand of Half the Troops, unless we can receive Arms for them. Our State Stores of Ammunition we still are as we have been making up and sending on to you with all possible Dispatch. We have received no Supplies of these Articles as yet from Congress. It is with real pain therefore that instead of assisting you with Arms for your Troops I am obliged to hold up to you a Prospect of even shortening our Reinforcements of Men to the Southern Army for want of Arms.

I am with every Sentiment of Esteem and respect Gentlemen Your most obedient & most huml Servt., TH: JEFFERSON

Tr (DLC: PCC, No. 72). At foot of text: "Mess Martin, Penn & Davis [Alexander Martin, John Penn, Orondates Davis] Hillsbo." Enclosed in N.C. Board of War to N.C. Delegates in Congress, 12 Oct. 1780 (same location; printed in *N.C. State Records*, XIV, 419-20).

The North Carolina Board of War had been very recently established and had begun its proceedings at Hillsborough on 14 Sep. 1780 (same, XV, p. vii; XIV, 376ff.). Its journal under 15 Sep. records "A Letter sent Governor Jefferson, Virginia, requesting him to furnish and forward to this place Arms, &c., thro' Hurry not copied." This letter has not been found. TJ's answer was received on 12 Oct.

To George Washington

I yesterday forwarded to you a letter from Colo. Wood informing you of his situation. That Post has been for some time past
pretty regularly supplied, and I hope will continue to be for some
time to come. A Person whose punctuality can be relied on offers
to contract for victualling it. If we can agree on terms and the Assembly will strengthen our Hands sufficiently, We think to adopt
that Method, as the only one to be relied on with certainty. I have
heard it hinted that Colo. Wood thinks of quitting that Post; I
should be exceedingly sorry indeed were he to do it. He has given
to those under his charge the most perfect satisfaction, and at the
same time used all the cautions which the nature of his charge has
required. It is principally owing to his prudence and good temper
that the late difficulties have been passed over almost without a
murmur. Any influence which your Excellency shall think proper
to use for retaining him in his present situation will promote the
public Good and have a great tendency to keep up a desirable harmony with the Officers of that Corps. Our new levies are rendezvousing very generally. Colo. Harrison was uneasy at having none
of them assigned to his Corps of Artillery, who have very much
distinguished themselves in the late unfortunate action, and are
reduced almost to nothing. We happened to have about 400
draughts raised in the last Year and never called out and sent on
duty by their County Lieutenants whom we have collected and are
collecting. We think to deliver these to Colo. Harrison. They are to
serve 18 Months from the time of rendezvous. The numbers of
Regulars and Militia ordered from this State into the Southern
service are about 7000. I trust we may count that 5500 will actually proceed; but we have arms for three thousand only. If therefore
We do not speedily receive a supply from Congress We must countermand a proper number of these Troops. Besides this supply
there should certainly be a magazine laid in here to provide against
a general loss as well as daily waste. When we deliver out those
now in our Magazine We shall have sent 7000 stand of our own
into the southern Service, in the course of this Summer: We are
still more destitute of Clothing, Tents and Waggons for our troops.
The Southern Army suff[ers] for Provision which we could plentifully supply were it possible to find means of transportation:
despairing of this we directed very considerable quantities collected
on the navigable waters to be sent Northwardly by the Quarter

Master. This he is now doing, slowly however. Unapprised of what may be proposed by our Allies to be done with their Fleet in the course of the ensuing winter, I would beg leave to intimate to you that if it should appear eligible to them that it should winter in Chesapeake they may be well supplied with Provision taking their measures in due time before hand. The Waters communicating with that Bay furnish easy (and in that case) safe Transportation, and their money will call forth what is denied to ours. I am with all possible esteem & respect Your Excellency's Most obedt. & most humble servt.,   TH: JEFFERSON

RC (DLC: Washington Papers); in a clerk's hand except for complimentary close and signature by TJ; addressed: "His Excellency Genl. Washington Head Quarters"; endorsed: "Govr Jefferson: 23 Septr. 1780. recd. 8 ansd. 11. The number of Levies that are rendezvoused. Want of Arms." Tr (DLC). Enclosure: James Wood to George Washington, Charlottesville, 21 Sep. 1780 (DLC: Washington Papers).

The LETTER FROM COLO. WOOD to Washington of 21 Sep. was obviously written in response to TJ's letter to Wood dated 14 Sep., q.v. In it Wood assured Washington that "the Convention Troops have been fully Supplied for the last three weeks . . . and that I shall have it in my Power within a few Days to begin paying up the Arrears due to the Troops"; his situation previously had been "truly Distressing; the Guards, as well as the Troops of Convention, were entirely without Meat or Bread for Several Days"; under this situation he had permitted a few men from each regiment to go into the country to purchase provisions, an indulgence that he would not otherwise have granted and one that, happily, was "not Abused in Any Instance"; during all this the Convention troops had borne their privation "with the utmost Patience, and seemed fully Convinced that it Did not Proceed from Design, but from Causes Altogether Accidental."

To James Wood

SIR   Richmond Sep. 23. 1780.

I am sorry the supplies of provision to the troops have been less plentiful than Mr. Tate represented them, and am only to ask the tender I mentioned when the condition of your stores will admit of it. There is no probability of a supply of money to your purchasing commissary till the meeting of assembly. I have forwarded your letters to Genl. Washington and inattentively sent also the packet directed to Colo. Harrison. However I think it's passage will be expedited as I know no prospect of a flag from this place to N. York. Mr. and Mrs. Maxwell have our consent to pay the visit you mention to Culpeper and Fauquier, and Mr. Hepburn to remain with his relation in Orange. The spirits lodged at the barracks are to be issued to the garrison. I inclose you the proportions allowed. The dragoon, bearer of this, informs me he deserted and was confined for it some time, and that you desired him to ask for a pardon.

As you do not mention it in your letter I inclose a pardon to be delivered him or not as you please. Mr. Marks the commissary of hides promised us a supply of shoes ready made and of leather to make up on receiving Genl. Muhlenburg's order. Our new levies rendezvousing cannot march for want of shoes. I shall be much obliged to you to have us relieved on this head with all possible dispatch. I am Sir with great esteem, your most obedt. humble servt., TH: JEFFERSON

P.S. Since writing the above a reasonable supply of shoes and leather is come from Mr. Marks with a promise of a further supply much desired.

RC (Lloyd W. Smith, Madison, N.J., 1946); endorsed. Addressee identified from internal evidence; see TJ to Washington, 23 Sep. 1780. Enclosures not found.

Wood's letter to which this is an answer has not been found, but it was obviously a reply to TJ's letter of 14 Sep., q.v., correcting the misinformation that Tate had given TJ, as stated in that letter. YOUR LETTERS TO GENL. WASHINGTON: Wood's letter of 21 Sep. to Washington had been forwarded by TJ on 22 Sep. (see TJ to Washington, 23 Sep.); in it Wood stated that "General Hamilton requests the favor of your Excellency to send the Inclosed Letter by the first Flag"—an enclosure (not found) which probably accounts for TJ's use of the plural.

From Horatio Gates

SIR   Hillsboro. 24th: Septr: 1780

The receipt of my Four last Letters to Your Excellency remains unacknowledged. I believe the Station'd Expresses purposely avoid each other. The Accounts I receive from the Westward and Southward, Vary in Nothing from that which I last sent Your Excellency, in the Examination of William Allmond: but the moment Lord Cornwallis has his Instructions from Sir Harry Clinton, I expect the Campaign to recommence. Should Col. Senf return by Richmond, I wish Your Excellency would send Him to Portsmouth, to see, and report what might be done for the Security of that post by Land. He is the best Draughtsman I know, and an Excellent Engineer: if he is Detain'd to The Northward, as I have some reason to Expect, I think some Man of Science should be immediately sent upon the Service here mention'd. Let me know if you have such a Man. I must beg your Excellency will order me some more falling Axes. Those sent forward are very badly temper'd. The maker should be directed to mend this Fault. With much respect I am Sir Your Excellencys most Obedient Humble Servant,   HORATIO GATES

Dft or FC (NHi); endorsed: "Copy to Govr. Jefferson 24th. September 80." Tr (DLC).

THE EXAMINATION OF WILLIAM ALL-MOND: See Gates to TJ, 20 Sep. 1780.

From ——— ———

Bladensburg, *Sept. 26.* [1780].

Meeting with an immediate conveyance to Richmond by the bearer, I do myself the pleasure to give you the following agreeable intelligence. This morning on my return from the northward, I was overtaken by a Gentleman who left Philadelphia so late as last Saturday (the 23d instant) and had Dunlap's Pennsylvania Gazette, in which I read extract of a letter from Bevernwick of the 18th instant, assuring that "we have it from undoubted authority that a French fleet of 16 sail of the line with some frigates was arrived at Rhode Island"; the Gentleman farther informed me that the news was generally believed at Philadelphia late on Saturday afternoon.

MS not located. Printed from an extract in *Virginia Gazette* (Dixon & Nicolson), 4 Oct. 1780.

In his letter to Gates of 4 Oct. 1780, TJ stated that this extract was from a letter addressed to himself by "a particular acquaintance of mine whose cred-

it cannot be doubted"; this acquaintance has not been identified, but it may possibly have been Joseph Jones, who left Congress on 7 Sep. 1780 and returned to Virginia (Burnett, *Letters of Members*, v, p. lxiv).

To Samuel Huntington

SIR   Richmond Sep. 26. 1780.

At the desire of Genl. Gates I transmit you the inclosed letters from Genl. Harrington and Colo. Marian and the deposition of a prisoner escaped from the enemy.

A Gentleman will set out from this place within two days for Philadelphia to receive and bring our quota of the new money, which we hope will be in readiness for him.

I have the honor to be with the greatest respect Your Excellency's Most obedient & most humble servt.,   TH: JEFFERSON

RC (DLC: PCC, No. 71, I); addressed by TJ; endorsed in the hand of Charles Thomson: "Letter from Govr Jefferson Sept 26. 1780. Read Octr. 2. Enclosing intelligence from the Southward. Referred to the commee of intelligence." Enclosures: (1) H. W. Harrington to Gates, Camp near Cross Creek, 16 Sep. 1780 (copy with letter in PCC, No. 71, I; printed in *N.C. State Records*, XIV,

623); (2) Francis Marion to Gates, without place or date (missing; printed in same, p. 621-2); (3) the prisoner's deposition (not found) was undoubtedly the examination of one William Allmond referred to in Gates' letters to TJ of 20 and 24 Sep., qq.v.

Read in Congress 2 Oct. and referred to Committee on Intelligence (JCC, XVIII, 890).

From James Madison

DEAR SIR   Philada. Sepr. 26h. 1780

I am at length able to give you some answer on the subject of the map in the hands of Dr. Smith. As the Doctor lived out of Town and it was difficult to know when he was to be found in it, and as I supposed the request would go with greater weight through Mr. Rittenhouse, I asked the favor of him to speak to the Doctor on the subject. Through forgetfulness or want of opportunity he failed to do it till lately and brought me for answer that the Doctor although anxious to oblige you was unwilling to let it go out of his hands, but would suffer any transcript to be taken from it at his house and would even assist in it himself. Yesterday evening I had an opportunity of being introduced to him and renewed the application, that he would spare it till I could get a copy taken, which he again declined by politely assuring me that he was proud of an opportunity of obliging you and that he would have a correct and authentic copy made out by his son for you.

I am Dr. Sir Yrs. respectfully,   JAMES MADISON JR.

RC (DLC: Madison Papers).
DR. SMITH: William Smith, D.D., until lately provost of the College of Philadelphia; he lived at the Falls of Schuylkill near Philadelphia (DAB). The MAP in Smith's hands has not been identified; but see TJ to Gates, 23 Sep. 1780. Smith had several sons.

From James Maxwell

[*Richmond, 26 Sep. 1780.* Minute in the Journal of the Commissioner of the Navy (Vi), under this date: "Letter written to the Governour inclosing a List of Prisoners sent to the Deputy Commissary of Prisoners at Winchester." Not located, but see George Washington to TJ, 5 Sep. 1780.]

To George Washington

SIR   Richmond September 26. 1780.

The inclosed Copy of a letter from Ld. Cornwallis to Colo. Balfour was sent me by Govr. Rutledge: lest you should not have seen it I do myself the pleasure of transmitting it, with a letter from Genl. Harrington to Genl. Gates giving information of some late movements of the Enemy.

I was honored yesterday with your favor of the 5th. inst. on the subject of prisoners and particularly Lt. Govr. Hamilton. You are not unapprised of the influence of this Officer with the Indians, his activity and embittered Zeal against us; you also perhaps know how precarious is our tenure of the Illinois country, and how critical is the situation of the new counties on the Ohio. These circumstances determined us to retain Govr. Hamilton and Majr. Hay within our Power when we delivered up the other Prisoners. On a late representation from the People of Kentuckey by a person sent here from that County, and expressions of what they had reason to apprehend from these two Prisoners in the event of their liberation; we assured them they would not be parted with, tho we were giving up our other Prisoners. Lt. Colo. Dubuysson Aid to Baron de Kalb lately came here on his parole with an offer from Ld. Rawdon to exchange him for Hamilton. Colo. Towles is now here with a like proposition as to himself from Genl. Phillips, very strongly urged by the General. These and other overtures do not lessen our Opinion of the importance of retaining him: and they have been and will be uniformly rejected. Should the settlement indeed of a Cartel become impracticable without the consent of the States to submit their seperate Prisoners to its Obligation, we will give up these two Prisoners, as we would any thing rather than be an obstacle to a general Good; but no other circumstances would I believe extract them from us. These two gentlemen with a Lt. Colo. Elligood are the only seperate prisoners we have retained, and the last only on his own request, and not because we set any store by him. There is indeed a Lt. Govr. Rocheblawe of Kaskaskie who has broken his parole and gone to N. York, whom we must shortly trouble your Excellency to demand for us as soon as we can forward to you the proper documents. Since the 40 Prisoners sent to Winchester as mentioned in my letter of the 9th. ulto. about 150 more have been sent thither, some of them taken by us at sea, others sent on by Genl. Gates.

The exposed and weak state of our western settlements and the dangers to which they are subject from the Northern Indians acting under the influence of the British Post at Detroit, render it necessary for us to keep from five to eight hundred Men on duty for their defence. This is a great and perpetual expence. Could that post be reduced and retained it would cover all the States to the South-East of it. We have long meditated the attempt under the direction of Colo. Clarke but the expence would be so great that whenever we have wished to take it up the circumstance has obliged us to decline it; two different estimates make it amount to two Million of Pounds, present Money. We could furnish the Men provisions and I believe every necessary except powder; had we the Money, or could the demands from us be so far supplyed from other quarters as to leave it in our power to apply such a Sum to that purpose and when once done it would save annual expenditures to a great amount. When I speak of furnishing the Men I mean they should be Militia: such being the popularity of Colo. Clarke and the confidence of the western people in him that he could raise the requisite number at any time. We therefore beg leave to refer this matter to yourself to determine whether such an enterprize would not be for the general good, and if you think it would, to authorize it at the general expence: this is become the more reasonable if as I am informed the ratification of the Confederation has been rested on our Cession of a part of our western Claims, a Cession which (speaking my private opinion only) I verily believe will be agreed to if the Quantity demanded be not unreasonably great. Should this proposition be approved it should be immediately made known to us as the season is now coming on at which some of the preparations must be made. The time of execution I think should be at the breaking up of the Ice in the Wabache and before the Lakes open. The interval I am told is considerable. I have the honor to be with every sentiment of esteem & respect Your Excellency's Most obedient & most humble servt., TH: JEFFERSON

RC (DLC: Washington Papers). Tr (DLC); text defective. RC in a clerk's hand except for complimentary close and signature by TJ. Endorsed: "Govr Jefferson—26 Septr 1780—recd 8—ansd 11th. [actually answered 10 Oct. 1780, q.v.]. About Lt Govr Hamilton & Majr Hay's inexchangeability. Copy of Lord Cornwallis's letter to Colo. Balfour marking out *a severe line* of conduct to be pursued. Lt. Govr. Rocheblawe." Enclosures: (1) Cornwallis to Nisbett Balfour, Aug. 1780, copy of an intercepted letter (in Washington Papers; Tr in DLC; printed in Washington, *Writings*, ed. Sparks, VII, 555-6); Washington in turn enclosed a copy of Cornwallis' letter with a protest to Sir Henry Clinton, 16 Oct. 1780, *Writings*, ed. Fitzpatrick, XX, 194-5. (2) H. W. Harrington to Gates, 16 Sep. 1780 (missing, but for another copy see TJ to Huntington, 26 Sep. 1780).

Despite the continued fears and representations of Virginians residing on the frontier, Henry HAMILTON was paroled soon afterward; see under 10 Oct. 1780. On his case generally see TJ to Theodorick Bland, 8 June 1779, and references there. Washington continued to support TJ's position on this question to the end; see Washington to Gen. Phillips, 13 Dec. 1780 (*Writings*, ed. Fitzpatrick, XX, 471). ROCHEBLAWE (i.e., Rocheblave): See Board of War to TJ and reply, 26 Mch. 1780. For TJ's further endeavors to mount an offensive against the British posts in the West, particularly Detroit, see letters to Washington, 13 Dec., and to G. R. Clark, 25 Dec. 1780.

To George Rogers Clark

SIR   Richmond Sep 27. 1780

Mr. Randolph having been prevented by sickness from setting out for the Westward, gives me an opportunity of sending you by him my last orders to Col. Crocket. I am with great respect Sir Your most obedt. Servt.,   TH: JEFFERSON

RC (WHi); in a clerk's hand, signed by TJ.
See TJ to Crockett, following, which was perhaps enclosed in the present letter.

To Joseph Crockett

SIR   Richmond, Septr. 27th. 1780

I suppose Mr. Baker must by this time be in readiness to do his part towards moving your battalion to the Westward. As soon as he is so, you will please to proceed with them. Let your pay rolls be made up to the day of your march, as so far they will be chargeable to the continent. The inclos'd advice of council pointing out your destination and that of the quotas of militia call'd from the Western counties, with Genl. Lewis's letter also inclos'd, containing his sentiments as to the best manner of executing the intention of the Executive, render it unnecessary for me to take up that part of the subject. You know that our dependance is on you to direct the march and route of those militia, and their mode of proceeding to establish themselves. I have further to add, that as soon as you have an opportunity you are to give notice to Colo. Clarke of your movements, num[ber] of regulars, success in collecting the militia, progress in making your establishments and general prospects, and afterwards from time to time whenever opportunities occur to give him like information. The purpose of this is to put it in his power to leave you to pursue the plan chalked out by the Executive, or to take up any other, or call you on any different enterprize which he shall think better, our intention being to submit the disposal of this force perfectly to the will of Colo. Clarke whose knowledge of the Country to be defended, of its weaknesses and resources, enables him to form the best plans for preserving it under its actual circumstances; and whom we do not mean to trammel in the execution of his plans by any positive instructions to you. Those therefore which have been and now are given, you are only to pursue till you receive contrary directions from him. I wish you to be speedy in your departure and subsequent movements, and health and success in your undertakings & am with great esteem Sir, Your most obedt. hum. Servt., TH: J.

RC (WHi); in a clerk's hand, signed by TJ; endorsed: "From Government [sic] to Col. Crocket." Enclosures missing.

This letter may have been sent enclosed to G. R. Clark in the preceding letter; but see TJ to James Wood, 5 Oct.

From Horatio Gates

SIR   Hillsborough 27th. September 1780

Inclosed is a Copy of a Letter I received Yesterday Afternoon by Colonel Senf, it deserves immediate Notice, and Attention, for unless the Troops, when they are assembled and Equip'd are enabled to march forward, it will cause a most injurious Delay to the Public Service. If Bills at Sixty Days sight, upon the Treasuries of Virga. and Maryland will supply the necessary and unavoidable Expences of the Q M General's Department. I will with your Approbation, engage to issue them to Mr. Elliott or Colo. Finnie, for the Engagements they are oblig'd to make, in providing the Troops to be sent to the Southward. This State are providing, and promise to equip their own Troops, which is all we can ask from them except paying their Quota of the Expence of Victualling, or by their specific Tax, supplying that Quota. I think Colonel Finnie should directly waite on Your Excellency, to know your Sentiments upon this Subject. Inclosed is my Letter directing him to do so, and then to proceed to my Quarters through Petersburgh, to take such orders and Directions, as in Consequence of his Conference with your Excellency, and the public Exigency may require. Colonel Senf has the Honor to deliver you this Letter. I send him to your Excellency to be employ'd upon the Service mentioned in my last Letter. His Abilities are great, in the Engineer's Department, and a better Draughtsman I never saw. His Integrity I am Satisfied is unquestionable, but for the Satisfaction of the Executive I think Genl. Nelson, or some person of the First Consideration in the State might be requested to go with Colonel Senf, to see, and report, His plans and Observations. Earnest that Congress should have every Information of the State of public Affairs in this Department, I request Your Excellency will please to Order Copies of all the Letters and Papers I have the Honor to Address to You to be sent by the First proper Conveyance to President Huntington. Col. Morgan acquaints me that the Bacon collected in Virginia for the Army, is, at Several of the Posts between Roan Oak and Richmond

Issued to passing Troops and Others. This I must request your Excellency will possitively Forbid, as Cattle will be good for Six Weeks to come, consequently we ought to save the Bacon for Winter and for a March. Please to Seal and Forward the Letter to Col. Finnie. With very Great respect I am Sir Your Exccy. &c.,

HG

FC (NHi); endorsed: "Copy to Governor Jefferson 27th. Sepr 1780." The missing RC must have been dated 28 Sep.; see TJ to Gates, 15 Oct. 1780. Tr (DLC). 2d Tr (DLC: Washington Papers). 3d Tr (DLC: PCC, No. 154, II).

Enclosures missing; a transcript of Gates' letter to Finnie, Hillsborough, 27 Sep. 1780, is, however, in DLC. Gates' letter and its enclosures were transmitted to Samuel Huntington in TJ's letter of 3 Oct. 1780, q.v.

Circular Letter to the Governors
of the Other States

SIR   In Council Sepr. 27. 1780

I beg leave to present to your Excellency Copies of the Acts of the Virginia Assembly from the begining of the Year 1779. and will do myself the pleasure of transmitting their future Acts regularly hereafter, not doubting but an interchange of this kind, should it take place generally among the States, will prove equally useful and agreeable.

I have the honor to be with every sentiment of esteem and respect Your Excellency's Most obedt. Servt.,   TH: JEFFERSON

RC (RPA); in a clerk's hand, signed by TJ; without indication of recipient, but William Greene was governor of Rhode Island from 1778 to 1786. A letter with identical text, with the date altered from 27 to 28 Sep. (or vice versa) and inadvertently left unsigned, is in MdAA and was therefore no doubt addressed to Gov. Thomas Sim Lee of Maryland; the answers of Gov. Meshech

Weare of New Hampshire, 6 Dec., and Gov. William Livingston of New Jersey, 27 Dec., will be found below under their dates. See also the following letter, addressed to Samuel Huntington. The publications accompanying TJ's circular must have been the Virginia "session laws" for May and Oct. 1779 and May 1780 (Swem, "Va. Bibliog.," 7128, 7166, 7223).

To Samuel Huntington

[*Richmond*, 27 Sep. 1780. JCC, XVIII, 912 (9 Oct. 1780): "A letter, of 27 September, from Governor Jefferson was read, accompanied with copies of the acts of the Virginia assembly, from the beginning of the year, 1779." Letter not located, but the Journals record two days later that, on a motion by Madison and Bland, "*Ordered*, That the letter, of 27 September, from Governor Jefferson, with the copies of the acts of the legislature of Virginia enclosed therein, be referred to the

Board of Treasury, to enable them to ascertain and insert in the bills to be emitted by the said State, pursuant to the resolutions of Congress, of the 18 of March last, the time of the passing of the act adopting the said resolutions" (same, p. 916). Concerning the enclosures see the preceding letter.]

To George Rogers Clark

SIR   Richmond Sepr. 29. 1780

I sincerely congratulate you on your late Victory over the Shawanese and am sorry a want of Provisions prevented its being improved as far as it was capable of improvement. I hope those Savages will be taught to fear, since they cannot be taught to keep faith. Crocketts reinforcement will perhaps enable you with the occasional aids of Volunteers to give them so little rest as to induce them to remove beyond our mutual interference. His delay has been hitherto occasioned by those wants of Cloathing and Money which now encrease on us daily and cramp and suppress every effort. Mr. Randolph's stay here has given him an Opportunity of becoming so fully acquainted with our situation that I need not put it on Paper. The loss of Charles Town and defeat of Genl. Gates left us a powerful enemy in the South without an Army to oppose them. We had to raise, clothe, equip and subsist an Army without a Shilling of Money. You will judge from this whether our difficulties in the Eastern quarter are far short of yours in the Western. I have written to Genl. Washington on the subject of an attempt against Detroit, and asked from him nothing more than such a releif from other continental Calls as will enable us to spare so much Money as may be necessary for that enterprise and to have this considered as a Continental Expence. I have ventured to assure him that with the Regulars you will have; you can raise Volunteers enough to reduce the place, and that we can furnish every article, except Powder, if they will only leave us at liberty to apply our Money for that purpose. While I wait for his Answer, Capt. Moore is authorised to purchase all the flour he can in the Vicinities of Fort Pitt, for which purpose we furnish him with £10,000. and an instrument of assurance to the Sellers that they shall be paid as soon as the approaching Session of Assembly shall have had time to provide supplies. We wished he would have undertaken the office of Commissary for you to have continued in the neighbourhood of Pittsburg and supplied you regularly from thence, calling on us for Money. As he is not disposed to do it I am to desire you will appoint from time to time such person as you can rely on notifying always the appointment to us. The Accounts of expences incurred in your expedition must by law be settled with the Auditors here. Capt. Moore seems to think wild Meat may be got in sufficient quantity with you if Money is furnished. If this be the case whatever sum it shall be in our power to spare you, will go much further towards your support in this way than if invested in Cattle on this side the Alleghaney and driven to you. If you will point out the mode and measure of supplies for your purposes we will endeavor to comply with them as far as we shall be able.

I am Sir with great respect & esteem Your most obedt. servt.,

TH: JEFFERSON

RC (WHi); in a clerk's hand, with complimentary close, signature, and address by TJ: "Colo. George Rogers Clarke Louisville." Endorsed: "Govr. Jefferson Sept. 29th 1780. Thanks for expedition against the Shawnees. De-troit."

CAPT. MOORE: James Francis Moore; see Gwathmey, *Hist. Reg. of Virginians in the Revolution*; also *George Rogers Clark Papers, 1771-1781, passim*.

To James Barron

SIR   In Council September   1780

The inclosed deposition will inform you of the reason we have [to] believe that the inhabitants of the Tangier islands supply the enemy's cruizers in the bay with provisions. We have therefore adopted the only legal method we have of drawing from them their surplus of provisions. We think it will be prudent to leave them no more than what is absolutely requisite for their own subsistance. You will of course be obliged to execute this business principally by deputy and as to the mode of getting their cattle which we are told are nearly wild we leave it to yourself to contrive. I suppose they must be slaughtered and salted there, for which reason I inclose you an order for salt. I really think the effecting this business immediately and fully an object of consequence. I write to the governor of Maryland on the same subject not doubting they will pay attention to their part of the same islands equally culpable with ours.

I am sir Your very hble servant,   TH: JEFFERSON

FC (Vi, photostat from Brit. Mus.: Add. MSS 38,650). Enclosures not further identified. The letter was probably written before 13 Sep. 1780, the date of the last letter in the Governor's Letter Book in the British Museum.

THE TANGIER ISLANDS: In Chesapeake Bay opposite and northward of the mouth of the Potomac, dividing Tangier Sound from the Bay; these islands lie partly in Virginia and partly in Maryland (*Lippincott's Gazetteer of* *the World*, Phila., 1882). TJ's letter to THE GOVERNOR OF MARYLAND on this subject is missing.

To James Barron

SIR   In Council Sepr.   1780.

As large quantities of provision are of necessity drawn from the western part of this state for the support of the army, and it is just that this burthen shou'd be borne equally by all, we think it necessary to extend the provision law to the islands within this state, lying between the middle of Chesapeake bay and the eastern shore, and hereby appoint you commissioner of the said law within those islands. We inclose you for your government a copy of the provision law and an extract from another act made in aid thereof. The provision you shall collect there more than sufficient for the use of our cruizers vessels you will deliver to the commissary for the time state[d?]. You are to transmit me from time to time returns of the quantities you take and lists of all certificates or receipts given by you specifying the name of the owner the price to be paid and date of the certificate.

I am sir, Your most obedient servant,   TH: JEFFERSON

FC (Vi, photostat from Brit. Mus.: Add. MSS 38,650). Enclosures: presumably copies of the Act for procuring a supply of provisions for the use of the army (Hening, x, 233-7) and of that part of the Act empowering the Governor and Council to seize livestock, &c. (same, p. 312).

Probably written before 13 Sep. 1780, the date of the last letter in the Governor's Letter Book in the British Museum.

Preliminary indexes will be issued periodically for groups of volumes. A comprehensive index of persons, places, subjects, etc., arranged in a single consolidated sequence, will be issued at the conclusion of the series.

THE PAPERS OF THOMAS JEFFERSON is composed in Monticello, a type specially designed by the Mergenthaler Linotype Company for this series. Monticello is based on a type design originally developed by Binny & Ronaldson, the first successful typefounding company in America. It is considered historically appropriate here because it was used extensively in American printing during the last thirty years of Jefferson's life, 1796 to 1826; and because Jefferson himself expressed cordial approval of Binny & Ronaldson types.

✧

Composed and printed by Princeton University Press. Illustrations are reproduced in collotype by Meriden Gravure Company, Meriden, Connecticut. Paper for the series is made by W. C. Hamilton & Sons, at Miquon, Pennsylvania; cloth for the series is made by Holliston Mills, Inc., Norwood, Massachusetts. Bound by the J. C. Valentine Company, New York.

DESIGNED BY P. J. CONKWRIGHT